# WORKING WITH THE ELDERLY

## GROUP PROCESS AND TECHNIQUES
second edition

# Irene Burnside

Department of Nursing
San Jose State University

*Jones and Bartlett Publishers, Inc.*
*Boston and Monterey*

To the memory of Morty, Sr.,
who did not have
the privilege of growing old.

And also
for my new grandchild.

Sponsoring Editor: Adrian Perenon
Production Services Coordinator: Marlene Thom
Production Supervision: Michael Bass & Associates
Manuscript Editor: Beverly DeWitt
Interior Design: Lorena Laforest Bass
Cover Design: Debbie Wunsch
Illustrations: Tony Betancur
Typesetting: Quality Tech Pubs, San Diego, California

Page 339 photograph © Karen Preuss, from *LIFE TIME, A New Image of Aging,* published by Unity Press, Santa Cruz, California, 1978.

**Library of Congress Cataloging in Publication Data**

Burnside, Irene Mortenson
    Working with the elderly.

    Reprint. Originally published: 2nd ed. Monterey, Calif. : Wadsworth Health Sciences, c1984.
    Bibliography
    Includes index.
    1. Social work with the aged.  2. Social group work.
I. Title.
HV1451.B88   1986        362.6        86-10582

ISBN 0-86720-379-X

# Preface

The second edition of *Working with the Elderly: Group Process and Techniques* has been expanded to include 19 new chapters written by contributors from more disciplines. The organization has also been changed slightly, to place the theorists' contributions at the beginning of the book.

The new chapters include two reprinted articles. One is the classic article on life review therapy by Myrna Lewis and Robert Butler; the other, an article by Jean Kiernat, an occupational therapist. Other chapters provide perspectives from the disciplines of nursing, psychiatry, social work, psychology, and music therapy, as well as the point of view of the volunteer. The scope of the book has been broadened to reflect the fact that many disciplines are now conducting group work.

In an effort to keep pace with the fast-forming new self-help groups, a chapter is devoted to this subject. The proliferation in the past few years of self-help groups begun by families of persons with Alzheimer's disease is most impressive. Also, because interest in reminiscing groups has escalated considerably since publication of the first edition, I have included an entire section on reminiscing therapy.

As with the first edition, this second edition does not attempt to teach the reader about group dynamics; its purpose is to delineate the modifications and special types of groups appropriate for work with older clients/patients. This textbook is meant to be used by beginning group leaders and/or instructors teaching group work with the elderly. Educators and students should be pleased to know that learning objectives appear at the beginning of each chapter, with key words from the chapter. As in the first edition, each chapter ends with exercises.

Part 1 of the book includes demographic data about older persons and an introduction to group work with the elderly. Chapter 2 provides an overview of the types of groups that are currently being conducted and the types of workers needed now and in the future. Ends with a section on resources available for the instructor.

Part 2, the theoretical framework section, discusses four important theorists. These theoretical concepts can be adapted for group work with the elderly.

Part 3 deals with education, contracts, group membership, leadership and maintenance, and work with the cognitively impaired.

Part 4 is the "how to" section of the book. Many of the suggestions included in the section may seem obvious, but it is well to remember that a myriad of details and complex arrangements precede the smooth running of a group.

Part 5 is the section on reminiscing therapy. Practitioners from a variety of disciplines have written about their perspectives in Part 6. An entire section is devoted to the reminiscing modality, because of its popularity and because so many disciplines conduct reminiscing groups.

Part 7 discusses curriculum changes needed to promote group work and innovative approaches to teaching. It also deals with the responsibilities of preceptors.

Controversy often erupts over who should be doing group work with old people. Professionals tend to guard their territory zealously and to feel that nonprofessionals doing group work will unleash strong feelings and emotions with which they cannot deal. This attitude sells the elderly short; they are a tough lot. Moreover, group experiences help dilute feelings in a way that one-to-one relationships do not, and peer support and feedback are valuable assets of group work. The danger is not in the practice of group work with the elderly: The real danger is in not conducting groups and thereby fostering the still-prevalent attitude of "therapeutic nihilism." It is better to take a risk than to sit by and watch apathy, fear, sensory deprivation, loneliness, and helplessness continue in the aged.

The professionals are not and will not be carrying the load in group work with the elderly. The tremendous need for leaders in reality orientation, remotivation, reminiscing, art, exercise, and discussion groups will continue. I have made a clear distinction in the book between group work and group psychotherapy. Instructors will have to do the same with their students.

The mentor who launched me in group work and in writing about it was Marian Kalkman, an outstanding teacher of psychiatric nursing. Barbara Sene was also influential in her supervision of my group methods as a "bumbling" student. I have been greatly influenced by the geropsychiatrists I have known: Robert N. Butler, Alvin I. Goldfarb, Maurice Linden, Eric Pfeiffer, and Jack Weinberg.

For me, being a group leader with older members has been a humbling experience. I learned how much they knew and how little I knew; that was also true in groups of the frail and demented.

I can be cavalier about whatever oversights or omissions there may be in this book because I am quite sure the older people in your group will teach you whatever content may be missing here.

I want to express my gratitude to three anonymous reviewers who gave me some of the most excellent and pertinent feedback I have had in a critique. Changes in the second edition can be credited to their careful reading, incisive comments, and support of this textbook in general. Thank you. Evelyn Butorac handled a myriad of editorial details with great efficiency, and Pearl Bladek managed the typing with her usual aplomb. They made my job easier, if not downright enjoyable.

*Irene Burnside*

# Contributors

**Judith A.S. Altholz**, Ph.D.
Assistant Professor and Aging Specialist
School of Social Work
Florida State University
Tallahassee, Florida

**Jean A. Baumler**, R.N., M.S., G.N.P.
Director: Day Care Center
Honolulu, Hawaii

**Heather Booth-Buehring**, S.C., B.A.
Dance/Movement Specialist Working towards a
B.F.A. degree in dance
Edmonton, Alberta
Ponoka, Alberta

**Robert N. Butler**, M.D.
Chairman, Department of Geriatrics and Adult
Development
Mount Sinai School of Medicine
New York, New York

**Linda A. Byrne**, B.S.
Elder Coordinator
Youth C.A.R.E. Force
Peninsula Volunteers and Little House
Menlo Park, California

**Helen Dennis**, M.A.
Project Director and Lecturer
Ethel Percy Andrus Gerontology Center
University of Southern California
Los Angeles, California

**Elizabeth M. Donahue**, R.N., M.S.N., G.N.P.
Senior Socialization Center of Catholic Social
Service
San Jose, California

**Sally A. Friedlob**, O.T.R.
Clinical Coordinator
Life-Skills Training Program
Sepulveda Veterans' Administration Medical Center
Sepulveda, California

**Mary Jane Hennessey**, R.N., M.S.
Violinist, Monterey County Symphony
Health Educator: Gerontology, Geriatric Patient
Care, and Music in Geriatric Groups
Instructor: Hartnell College, Project Soledad
Salinas, California

**John H. Herr**, Ph.D.
Family Interaction Center
Research Associate
Palo Alto, California

**Jean Hogan**, R.N., M.S.
Gerontological Nurse Specialist
Director of Nursing Services
Fremont, California

**James J. Kelly**, Ph.D.
Associate Professor
Department of Social Work
California State University
Long Beach, California

**Jean M. Kiernat**, O.T.R., M.S.
Professor, Occupational Therapy Program
Center for Health Sciences
School of Allied Health Professions
Madison, Wisconsin

**Kathleen S. King**, R.N., M.S.
College of Nursing
University of Utah
Salt Lake City, Utah

**Peter R. LeBray**, Ph.D.
Health Psychology Department
Good Samaritan Hospital and Medical Center
Portland, Oregon

**Myrna I. Lewis**, ACSW
Faculty, Department of Community Medicine
Mount Sinai School of Medicine
New York, New York

**Ardis Martin**, R.N.
Certified Gerontological Nurse
Coordinator of The Adult Partial Hospital
Psychiatric Pavilion, Northwest Texas Hospitals
Amarillo, Texas

**Mary Ann Matteson**, R.N., M.S.N.
Clinical Assistant Professor
University of North Carolina
School of Nursing
Chapel Hill, North Carolina

**E. Catherine Moore**
Administrator
Sunset Hall
Los Angeles, California

**Lorraine O'Dell**
Outreach Program
San Rafael Public Library
San Rafael, California

**Raymond G. Poggi**, M.D.
Associated Psychiatric Services
Boulder and Longmont, Colorado

**Mary Gwynne Schmidt**, M.S.W., Ph.D.
Associate Professor
School of Social Work
San Diego State University
San Diego, California

**Bernita M. Steffl**, R.N., M.P.H.
Acting Assistant Dean for Baccalaureate Program
College of Nursing
Arizona State University
Tempe, Arizona

**Linda M. Szafranski**, ACSW
Psychiatric Social Worker
Geropsychiatric Center
Mendota Mental Health Institute
Madison, Wisconsin

**Lucille R. Taulbee**, R.N., M.A., C.
Clinical Specialist and Consultant in Gerontological
Nursing
New Port Richey, Florida

**John H. Weakland**
Research Associate and Associate Director
Brief Therapy Center
Mental Research Institute
Palo Alto, California

**Shelly Weaverdyck**, M.A.
Ph.D. Candidate
University of Michigan
Ann Arbor, Michigan

# Contents

# PART 2   THEORETICAL FRAMEWORKS (continued)

# PART 3   BASICS OF GROUP WORK

# PART 4   PRACTICE OF GROUP WORK

# PART 4   PRACTICE OF GROUP WORK (continued)

# PART 5   REMINISCING THERAPY

# PART 6  MULTIDISCIPLINE PERSPECTIVES ON GROUP WORK WITH THE ELDERLY

# PART 6 MULTIDISCIPLINE PERSPECTIVES ON GROUP WORK WITH THE ELDERLY (continued)

# PART 7   INSTRUCTION FOR GROUP WORKERS AND EPILOGUE

# PART 1

# OVERVIEW

© DON IVERS/JEROBOAM, INC.

The second edition of this textbook begins with an overview of the elderly population in the United States and considerable demographic data about the aging population. To alert the student of group work with the elderly to some of the conditions to expect and to watch for, some information about normal and pathological aging is also included in Chapter 1.

Chapter 2 is an overview of group work; it gives a brief history of group work and group psychotherapy with the elderly population in the United States.

These two chapters are intended to set the stage for the remainder of the book, which moves from the theoretical positions presented in Part 2 into the general knowledge needed to start and maintain groups and on to the practical aspects of leading groups of all types.

# chapter 1

# Demography and Aging

*Irene Burnside*

*I do not seek to follow in the footsteps of the men of old; I seek the things they sought.*

RICHARD LEWIS (1970)

## LEARNING OBJECTIVES

- Discuss the semantics used to describe aged persons.
- Describe the demography of the aged population in the United States.
- State three changes in the demographic that could have implications for group workers.
- List ten factors in normal aging that a group leader needs to consider in planning a group.

## KEY WORDS

- Activity theory
- Ageism
- Confabulation
- Dementia, multi-infarct type
- Developmental tasks
- Disengagement theory
- Ego integrity versus despair
- Elderly
- Senescent
- Senile dementia, Alzheimer's type

## SEMANTICS

The term *aged* still seems difficult to define. To members of the health professions, the term has different connotations. Some people use chronological age as the criterion: A person is aged when he or she reaches the age of 65. The elderly are frequently lumped together as a single, homogenous group. This is especially noticeable in some early research studies, in which the life span was carefully divided into four- or five-year periods, but all persons over the age of 65 were placed in one category entitled "65 plus."

Other professionals disregard chronological age and choose to use physiological functioning or personal or social characteristics to determine that a person is aged. These professionals use the terms *aged, older,* and *elderly* interchangeably; they rarely use the word *senescent.*

Still others use *elderly* to describe those who are involved, alert, and full of energy and vitality; they apply the term *aged* to those who are withdrawn, apathetic, uninvolved, or ill. Some health professionals make a distinction between the "elderly," who live in the community, and the "aged," who reside in institutions. This writer does not consider *aged* to be a pejorative term; "elderly" and "aged" are used interchangeably in this book.

One word that carries negative connotations is *geriatrics.* The term may connote illness/ deterioration/ doddering and may even bring to mind the image of a nursing home resident in a wheelchair. Its use is appropriate in reference to illness or problems.

A desirable change in terminology—one that has been slow in coming—is the banishment of the words *senile* and *senility* from textbooks, textbook titles, and descriptions of patients. The word *senility* was used as a category in the *Cumulative Index to Nursing and Allied Health Literature* for 10 years!

### Ageism

*Ageism,* a term coined by Robert Butler, refers to a negative, sometimes hostile attitude toward old people. Although ageism and negative attitudes may seem to be declining, one wonders if they are not simply becoming less overt; that is, that people are more guarded about expressing their negative views. Levin and Levin (1980) have written a book on the concept of ageism, in which they delineate how social forces determine the status of the elderly (Table 1–1).

TABLE 1–1.  How social forces determine the status of the elderly

| Institutional factors for aged | Social-structural causes |
| --- | --- |
| Property ownership | Diffusion of ownership, separation between ownership and management, and increased opportunities for the young diminish control of aged over property. |
| Strategic knowledge | Changes and increased rate of changes in technology and automation, evade the knowledge, skills, and esteem in which the elderly are held by the rest of society, reducing their authority. |
| Productivity | Technology has eliminated labor shortages and made older workers' marginal (or outdated) skills unnecessary. |
| Mutual dependence | High productivity, economic growth and building, and some forms of government aid such as small business loans have increased personal independence and autonomy—this lessens need to get help from one's family. |
| Tradition and religion | Our emphases on the secular and material reduce our need to see the elderly as a link to a symbolic and meaningful past. We are present oriented. |
| Kinship and family | Occupational structure of society emphasizing mobility is best suited by nuclear family and so extended family with its concern for needs of aged declines. |
| Community life | Specialization of roles (as in labor), residential mobility, and impersonal urban relationships weaken communities that once helped integrate the aged into society. |

SOURCE: From *Ageism: Prejudice and Discrimination Against the Elderly*, by J. Levin and W. C. Levin. Copyright © 1980 by Wadsworth, Inc. Reprinted by permission of the publisher, Wadsworth Publishing Company, Belmont, California.

There are subtle but noticeable cues and communications indicating an underlying negativism and apathy toward the elderly and their concerns and problems. For example, in spite of a plethora of books and journals on the subject of aging, bookstores and libraries often have outdated materials on their shelves and stock very few new publications. It is important for the beginning group leader to analyze his or her personal views about the aging process, because the bias and perceptions of the leader influence the group. Does the leader view aging as a normal process that continues across the life span and consider the individuality of each person as he or she faces the aging process? Or does the leader feel that aging means decrepitude?

This introductory chapter presents data on the elderly population in the United States. The figures speak for themselves and indicate the great need for health workers in this field.

## DEMOGRAPHIC DATA

Statistics indicate that the elderly population in the United States is growing faster than that of the nation as a whole. In 1980 the median age of the population was 30.0 years (Figure 1–1). This growth is expected to continue until

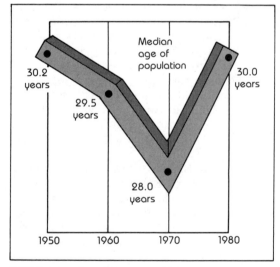

FIGURE 1–1.  *America grows older.*

SOURCE: Reprinted from *U.S. News and World Report* 93(9): 27 (August 9, 1982). Copyright 1982, U.S. News and World Report, Inc.

the first third of the twenty-first century (Fowles 1978, 1). Since 1965 the 65-plus age group has increased by 35 percent; however, the nation's population as a whole has grown by only 19 percent (Myers and Soldo 1979, 17). The U.S. Census Bureau projects that by the year 2000 there will be almost 32 million individuals age 65 and over, representing about 12 percent of the total population (Figures 1–2 and 1–3). If this group is expanded to include individuals between the ages of 60 and 65, the number of elderly increases by 10 million and represents 16.1 percent of the nation's population (Fowles 1978, 5). Figure 1–3 indicates that 17 percent of the population will be 65 and over by 2030.

Breaking the statistical data down further reveals an increase in those over age 75. These individuals are grouped by Randall (1977) into the "middle-aged old" (71–80), the "old-old" (81–90), and the "very old-old" (91–100) and are the fastest growing segment of the elderly population in the United States. Currently one-fourth of the elderly population is 75 and over; this figure is expected to grow to one-third by the year 2000. In 1974 half of the individuals over age 75 were women, and one-third of those women were living alone (Fowles 1978, 3, 8). Figure 1–4 indicates the changing marital status among women in the United States, which could mean an even greater number of single elderly women in the future.

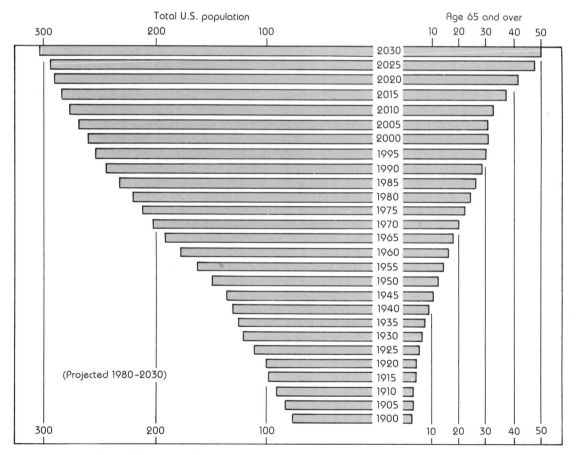

FIGURE 1-2. *U.S. population: Number (in millions) age 65 and over compared with total, 1900–2030.*

SOURCE: National Institute on Aging. 1980. *Epidemiology of aging* (Bethesda, Md.: U.S. Department of Health and Human Services), fig. 1–1. Based on data from U.S. Census Bureau.

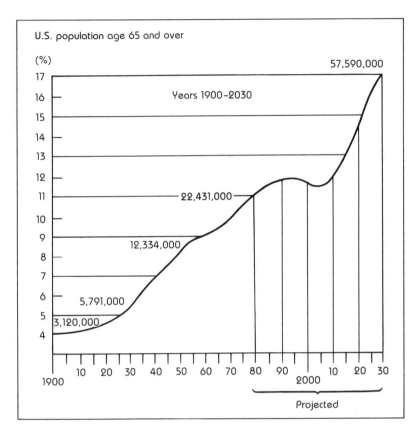

U.S. population age 65 and over

Years 1900–2030

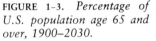

FIGURE 1-3. *Percentage of U.S. population age 65 and over, 1900–2030.*

*SOURCE:* National Institute on Aging. 1980. *Epidemiology of aging* (Bethesda, Md.: U.S. Department of Health· and Human Services), fig. 1–2. Based on data from U.S. Census Bureau.

Another factor that has impact on nursing and health care delivery is the difference between the health of individuals age 75 and over and that of those who are in the age range 65–74. The "old-old" tend to have greater incidences of depression, organic mental disorders, and chronic disabling illnesses. They average four to five times as many days in acute care hospitals as the national average, and 70 percent more than individuals aged 65–75 (Fowles 1978, 3).

If the current admission rate continues in the nursing home industry, the number of elderly persons in those residences is expected to increase from 1.3 million to 2.1 million in the twenty-first century. Moreover, if death rates continue to fall, the number of nursing home residents could reach 2.8 million (Hyatt 1979, 23).

A walk through any nursing home in any state will convince one of the frailty of the elderly who live there. Many of these residents have no family. See Figure 1–5 regarding shrinking family size. Three-fourths of all nursing home residents are over 75 and one-third are 85 or over (Fowles 1978, 3). These persons present some of the most complex and challenging demands for care, yet nursing homes are largely staffed by persons who are the least qualified to handle complexity. Robert Butler, former Director of the National Institute on Aging, states that operation of nursing homes alone costs $15.8 billion per year. He predicts that by the years 2020 to 2030 "something like 75% of health-provider time will be spent on older people" (Butler 1980, 166). Many of those health providers will need to focus on the psychosocial aspects of care of the elderly.

Although most elderly people are not confused, an estimated 10 percent of those over 65 have moderate to severe intellectual impairment

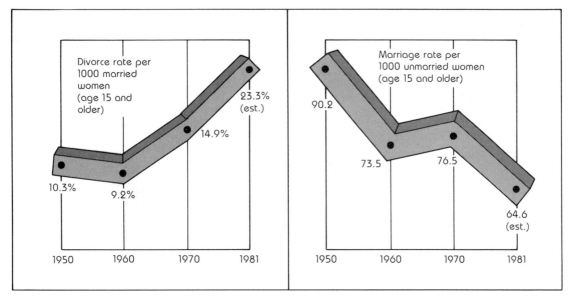

FIGURE 1-4. *A rise in divorces . . . while the marriage rate drops.*

SOURCE: Reprinted from *U.S. News and World Report* 93(9): 10 (August 9, 1982). Copyright 1982, U.S. News and World Report, Inc.

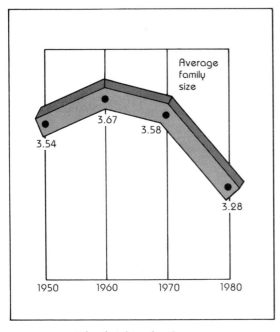

FIGURE 1-5. *The shrinking family.*

SOURCE: Reprinted from *U.S. News and World Report* 93(9): 27 (August 9, 1982). Copyright 1982, U.S. News and World Report, Inc.

(Task Force 1980). With predictions for an increasing number of persons in the over-75 category, skilled leaders will be needed for group work that focuses on alleviating confusion.

A 1973–74 survey revealed that 57 percent of residents in nursing homes were intellectually impaired (National Center for Health Statistics 1977, 14). Anselm Strauss notes that the majority of persons who are admitted to acute care facilities are admitted because of the recurrence of a chronic illness, not due to the onset of an acute illness in one who was previously well (Strauss and Glaser, 1975, 3). One study revealed that 5.5 percent of the elderly in an acute care hospital showed signs of confusion daily; the findings were the same for all three shifts (Chisholm et al. 1982, 87).

The percentage of total health care costs spent on nursing home care rose from 3.8 in 1971 to 7.8 six years later (Praiss and Gjerde 1980).

The care of younger (less than 60 years of age) and older (more than 60) individuals (and their families) suffering from Alzheimer's disease will continue to be a challenge for nurses. At this time the disease is considered to be epidemic, occurring in 15 percent of all individuals over age 65 and responsible for more than 50 percent of all nursing home admissions. It is estimated that 1.5 million American adults are affected by Alzheimer's disease, at a cost of about $20 billion annually. Alzheimer's disease is the fourth most common cause of death in the United States. One family in three will see a parent succumb to this tragic disease (ADRDA 1982).

The need for professionals has been described by Butler (1980, 166). "This increase [of elderly] will place unprecedented demands on all segments of the health-care community, including nurses, psychotherapists, administrators, technicians, physicians, teachers, and health professionals, among many others." The profound demographic revolution indicates that the need for group work (especially in institutions) will be great. The projection for 2020 to 2030 is about 2.5 to 3 million people over age 65 in nursing homes. In terms of 1980 dollars, the bill could well be $40 to $50 billion a year (Butler 1980). Butler further states that we will need to develop fundamental services and methods of cost containment and provide specific services from a variety of professionals. The rising health costs are delineated in Figure 1–6.

A population shift to rural areas will mean changes from traditional health care models in urban and suburban areas. See Figure 1–7 for data on population shifts.

## NORMAL AGING

A knowledge of some of the variables in the patterns of normal and abnormal aging is useful to the group leader. The important variables fall into the triad used by most gerontologists: social, psychological, and physical/physiological. These variables ultimately have a great influence on the type of group chosen, the knowledge needed by the leader, and the adaptations that will have to be made.

Scientists have reached no consensus on the biological theories about how and why the body ages. One difficulty, according to Finch and Severson (1981, 23), lies in distinguishing between changes that are caused by aging and those that are the result of disease.

The following list, adapted from Ware (1979) and Yurik and Spier (1980), outlines normal changes in the sensory system that accompany aging.

1. General sensory changes
   a. General decline in awareness of environmental stimuli.
   b. Concomitant decreases in ability to respond and adapt.
   c. Some sensory deficits after age 75 in three out of five persons.
   d. Sensory deprivation and sensory overload possible.

2. Hearing
   a. Progressive decrease in auditory threshold.
   b. Increased inability to hear higher frequency sounds.
   c. Decline in ability to discriminate speech (for example, when background noise is present or speech is faster than normal).
   d. Greater loss with long-time exposure to noise pollution.
   e. "Feeling of paranoia" in some people.
   f. Decline in time-related processing abilities (more time needed to process auditory input).

3. Sight
   a. Sunken appearance of eye due to loss of orbital fat.
   b. Laxity of eyelids; redundancy of skin on eyelids.
   c. Lessening of accommodation rate.
   d. Decrease in ability to accommodate (generally no further decrease after age 60).
   e. Accommodation abilities affected by glare.
   f. Decline in adaptation to darkness.
   g. Reduction in pupil size and reactivity.
   h. Decrease in acuity (progressively greater for females than for males).
   i. Diminished color perception due to loss of cones in retina.
      (i) Decrease in transmission of colors from green to violet.

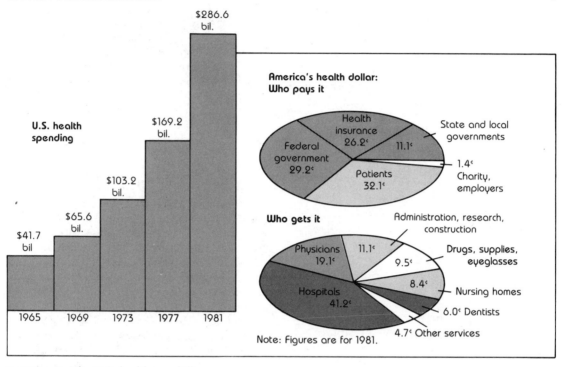

FIGURE 1-6. *The U.S. health care bill.*

*SOURCE:* Reprinted from *U.S. News and World Report* 93(9): 26 (August 9, 1982). Copyright 1982, U.S. News and World Report, Inc. Based on data from U.S. Department of Health and Human Services.

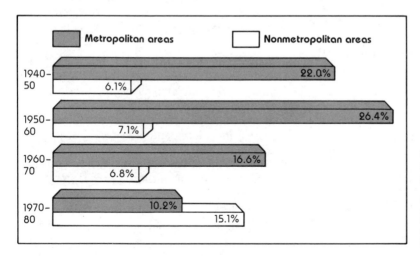

FIGURE 1-7. *U.S. growth shifts to rural areas: rates of population change by decade.*

*SOURCE:* Reprinted from *U.S. News and World Report* 93(9): 26 (August 9, 1982). Copyright 1982, U.S. News and World Report, Inc. Based on data from U.S. Department of Commerce.

(ii) Decrease in sensitivity to blue and possibly red.

(iii) Presbyopia resulting from inability of crystalline lens to adapt its shape to focus nearby objects.

(iv) Impaired night vision and decreased ability to adjust to dark/light changes resulting from decrease in permeability of lens, cornea, and vitreous humor.

    j. Reduced accuracy of depth perception.
    k. Decrease in lacrimal secretions.
4. Proprioception
    a. Impaired perception of position in and relationship to space, affecting balance and coordination.
5. Smell
    a. Some decline in sensitivity usual; research findings conflict.
6. Taste
    a. Decrease in number of taste buds and in salivary gland secretions (results of studies not uniform, however).
    b. Increased complaints about food.
7. Touch
    a. Decline in sensitivity.
    b. Reduction in reflexes and reaction time.
    c. Altered ability to adapt to environment.
    d. Increased pain threshold.
    e. Decrease in perception of vibration, temperature, and pressure.

### Psychosocial Theories of Aging

**Disengagement Theory.** One of the best known and most controversial theories in gerontology is the disengagement theory, which emerged in 1960 in a study commonly referred to as the Kansas City Study. For a fairly complete bibliography on disengagement theory, the reader is referred to Hochschild (1975). The four premises of the theory are as follows:

• Disengagement is a gradual process.
• Disengagement is inevitable.
• Disengagement is a mutually satisfying process for both the society and the individual.
• Disengagement is the norm.

The research has stimulated a great deal of response, including differing positions by theorists who do not see disengagement as an intrinsic or inevitable part of the aging process.

**Activity Theory.** Some theorists who do not agree with the disengagement theory use the activity theory to describe normal aging. This theory advances the idea that development of a high level of physical, mental, and social activities is needed by the individual. If roles in society are given up, then new roles must be found to take their place. The major criticism of activity theory is that activity may not ensure high morale. Not all older people want high activity; they are happy to reduce their activity and enjoy a more relaxed schedule. There have been relatively few empirical attempts to test activity theory.

**Erikson's Stages of Man.** Another popular theory is Erik Erikson's eight stages of man. Erikson believes that an individual must successfully complete each stage before passing into the next. The eighth stage, which Erikson (1959) calls ego integrity versus despair, is the least developed in his writings. Some authors who criticize the Eriksonian model feel that it is "idealistic and . . . seen from a middle class perspective" (Riegel 1977, 83). Riegel also states that detailed studies of the intrinsic changes and the outer, sociological conditions that affect the aging individual are needed to better explain the movement from one stage to another. In fairness to Erikson, however, one must admit that beginning students take to this model, and it seems to give them an understanding of the life span approach and the concept of developmental tasks across the life span.

**Peck's Contribution.** Erikson's work provided a basis for later work by Robert Peck (1955), who formulated psychological developments for the second half of life. Peck (1968) suggests that the eighth stage of man seems to represent in a global and nonspecific way all of the psychological crises, and also the solutions to those of the latter half of the life span. Peck divides the development into two categories:

*Middle Age*

1. Valuing wisdom versus valuing physical powers.
2. Socializing versus sexuality in human relationships.
3. Cathectic flexibility versus cathectic impoverishment.

*Old Age*

1. Ego differentiation versus work-role preoccupation.
2. Body transcendence versus body preoccupation.
3. Ego transcendence versus ego preoccupation.

Peck's interpretations are well described in a chapter in the fine book *Middle Age and Aging* by B. L. Neugarten (1968); the reader is referred to that book for an in-depth discussion.

**Clark and Anderson Framework.** One other theory should be mentioned; that of M. Clark and B. Anderson (1967), who described five adaptive tasks of the aged. These delineations may be useful in helping a new group leader better understand group dynamics among the elderly:

1. Perception of aging and definition of instrumental limitations.
2. Redefinition of the physical and social life space.
3. Identification of sources of need satisfaction and substitutes for these.
4. Reassessment of the criteria of self.
5. Reintegration of life values and goals.

**Continuity Theory.** A popular theory—and one that makes a good deal of sense to many students—is the continuity theory. It postulates that the maturing adult develops certain habits, preferences, associations, and commitments that become ingrained in the personality. As one ages, there is a continuity to that personality. The theory is reminiscent of the maxim: "In aging you are like you always were, only more so." It also allows for the various ways individuals adapt to aging. To study an individual's reaction to aging, one must study all of the complex interactions in the biological, psychological, personality, and situational experiences of the person. A group leading experience often gives the leader insight into the various patterns of individual aging, especially if the group work continues over a long period of time so that the leader gets to know the members well.

**Developmental Tasks in Later Maturity.** R. Havighurst (1975) calls later maturity the "examination stage," and his developmental tasks are well known and widely used:

1. Decide where and how to live out remaining years.
2. Continue supportive, close relationships with spouse or significant other (including sex).
3. Find a satisfactory, safe living place.
4. Adjust living standards.
5. Maintain maximum level of health.
6. Maintain contact with children, grandchildren, and other relatives.
7. Maintain interest in people, civic affairs, and so forth.
8. Pursue new interests; maintain former ones.
9. Find meaning in life after retirement.
10. Work out philosophy.
11. Adjust to death of spouse and other loved ones.

## AGING AND PHYSICAL CHANGES

The physical changes that occur during aging require that a group leader maintain a constant health orientation. The leader needs to be aware of physical changes (or mental changes that may indicate a physical problem) because such changes may require adaptations in the group structure and format. Illness that precludes a member's attendance at a meeting may be a reason for the leader to see or call the individual outside of the group.

Group leaders must be aware of the common disorders that occur in later life, both because they may cause absenteeism or loss of members through death, and also so that the leader can encourage prevention or early detection of diseases or exacerbations of chronic illness. In Chapter 18 (on dance therapy/movement) Booth describes chronic illnesses to consider. These are important because members will discuss their physical problems in the group. Often they can be helpful to and supportive of one another (for example, two people in a group who have suffered a stroke).

Common disorders of the coronary system include hypertension, congestive heart failure, and strokes. Common abnormal changes in the respiratory system may include chronic bronchitis, asthma, emphysema, pulmonary edema, and pneumonia. See Figure 1-8 for major causes of death for those over age 65. These data will give the reader an idea of common illnesses to anticipate in groups, including those conducted at senior centers, housing complexes, institutions, or day care centers.

The leader will need to work slowly and be especially patient with those suffering from disorders. A person with emphysema, for example, may have great difficulty speaking and will need extra time. The energy level of ill elderly people is low; the leader must be able to gauge when an individual (or the group) is weary. Weariness or low energy can be misin-terpreted as boredom or apathy by a new group leader.

Abnormal changes in the genitourinary system include urinary tract infections, urgency and frequency of urination, benign prostatic hypertrophy, and incontinence. It is difficult for the leader to have incontinent members in a group; attendance should be discouraged unless the member is very well protected or the group is of the reality orientation type. Urgency and frequency of urination may cause some problems, and the leader should be very tolerant about trips to the bathroom during group meetings.

Common gastrointestinal system disorders include dental problems, malnutrition, dehydration, anemia, and constipation. The two most serious are malnutrition and dehydration, which can occur in those living in institutions or in the community. Malnutrition can be related to loneliness, poverty, low energy, and so forth.

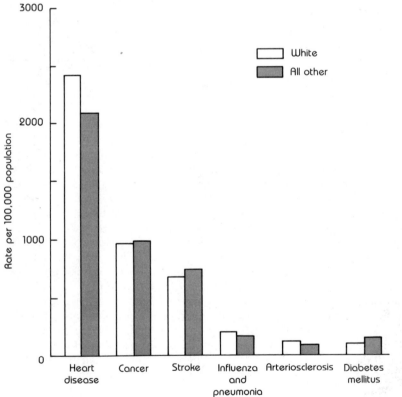

FIGURE 1-8. *Major causes of death for Americans 65 years and older, 1976.*

SOURCE: U.S. Department of Health and Human Services. 1979. *Healthy people: The Surgeon General's report on health promotion and disease prevention* (Washington, D.C.), Publication no. 79-55071, p. 73. Based on data from the National Center for Health Statistics, Division of Vital Statistics.

Dehydration may be caused by severe confusional states or limited access to drinking water. Serving fluids at group meetings can help alleviate dehydration.

Problems to anticipate in the musculoskeletal system are osteoarthritis and rheumatoid arthritis, gout, osteoporosis, and hip fractures. A member may complain of arthritic pain or extreme fatigue. Again, the leader needs to be aware of pacing in group meetings and should assist members in the use and care of adaptive devices to promote ambulation.

Disorders of the nervous system will tax and challenge the group leader. Dementia and delirium are common in institutional groups. A chronic state of dementia can be worsened by drug toxicity. In my nursing home group I have noticed patients who experienced increased confusion a few weeks before they died. Dementia secondary to alcoholism is also a common diagnosis in institutionalized populations. It has been my experience that many of these patients served in the armed forces during World War II and started their heavy drinking then.

A large percentage of older patients with Parkinson's disease develop dementia. Multi-infarct dementia is the type that occurs following a stroke. Mood fluctuations and labile moods can also be anticipated in group work with frail elderly, especially those who have suffered a stroke.

Presenile and senile dementia, Alzheimer's type, are neurological diseases of the primary type. With increasing interest in the disease and sophisticated diagnostic procedures, group leaders in day care situations or nursing homes will likely be working with these individuals. For excellent materials on this tragic disease see the resource list at the end of this chapter.

Regarding the endocrine system, diabetes mellitus is a common disease among the elderly. The main cautions for a group leader are diet, weight management, and self-care. Self-care includes careful attention to sores, not cutting corns with razor blades, and so forth.

Sensory losses will generally cause many problems for a group leader. Hearing and vision problems increase the effort the leader must make to communicate. The leader must monitor the setting to avoid glare and sudden changes in illumination. Lighting should be adequate. Blind persons will need special attention.

For the hard-of-hearing, who also may be somewhat paranoid, it is important to check that the hearing aid is functioning. Reduce distractions and noise in the meeting room. Speak slowly, face the person, and enunciate clearly in a normal tone of voice. Female group leaders should wear bright red lipstick during meetings to facilitate lip reading.

Other behaviors include confabulation (making up replies), anger, aggressiveness, hostility, and high dependency needs. The last can frustrate a new and inexperienced group leader.

A note about confabulation: Some of the finest and funniest, albeit untrue, responses a leader will receive come from persons who are confabulating. The leader needs to be wary;

WILL PATTON

*The sensitive group leader of the elderly will consider the sensory deficits of the group and realize that its meaningfulness to each member may be related to isolation or to inability to read, drive a car, or do crafts.*

one can be carried along for a good while before realizing that there is more fiction than fact in a story. Other members of the group will sometimes be helpful in such instances.

## PSYCHOLOGICAL VARIABLES

Developments in the field of aging and mental health and aging can be seen in Figure 1–9. A comprehensive handbook edited by James E. Birren and R. Bruce Sloan (1980), a psychologist and a psychiatrist, should be mentioned as a fine reference.

Four psychological variables to consider in group work with the elderly are depression; anxiety; agitation; and suspicious, paranoid behaviors. The presence of these behaviors in a potential group member can often be assessed by the group leader in the meeting to form a contract. Chapter 9 explains the contract-making process in detail, and Chapters 13, 23, and 24 discuss the manifestation of these conditions in group meetings.

Defensive responses to aging must also be considered; the two most frequently observed are denial and regression. The leader will need to be able to handle denial very well in group experiences.

Behavior that is studied or handled before the first group meeting (or early in the life of the group) may save the leader from many problems after the group is established; an ounce of prevention can avoid pounds of intervention later. Clinical concerns in working with the elderly are delineated in the following list.

1. Cognition
   a. Learning does not necessarily decline with age and is facilitated when individuals set their own pace.
   b. Short-term memory generally wanes with age.
   c. Crystallized intelligence is based on past experiences and shows a slight decline with age.
   d. Fluid intelligence is biologically mediated and declines from adolescence on.
   e. Information overload increases "neural noise."
   f. Need for activities with meaningful outcomes increases.
   g. Cognitive decline may be related to nearness to death (called terminal drop).

---

| | |
|---|---|
| 1975 | The creation of the National Institute of Aging, which includes research and training programs in the field of aging. |
| 1975 | The creation of the National Institute of Mental Health Center for Studies of the Mental Health of the Aging. |
| 1976 | The appointment of the Secretary of Health, Education, and Welfare's Committee on Mental Health and Mental Illness in the Elderly. The Committee's report was submitted in 1978. |
| 1977 | The appointment of the Task Panel on the Aging, part of the President's Commission on Mental Health. Its report was accepted in 1978. |
| 1978 | The establishment of the American Association of Geriatric Psychiatry, with a membership of more than 500 psychiatrists to date. |
| 1979 | The National Legislative Conference on Mental Health of Older Americans sponsored by the United States Congress. |
| 1979 | The establishment of a Council on Aging by the American Psychiatric Association. |
| 1980 | A Mini-Conference on the Mental Health of Older Americans. This Conference was preparatory for the White House Conference on Aging and was co-sponsored by the American Nursing Association, American Psychiatric Association, American Psychological Association, and National Association of Social Workers. |
| 1981 | The establishment of the International Psychogeriatric's Association with its first International Symposium planned for Cairo, Egypt, in November 1982. |

FIGURE 1-9. *Major developments in aging in the United States.*

SOURCE: From "The Mental Health of Aging," by S. I. Finkel and G. Cohen. 1982. Reprinted by permission of *The Gerontologist* 22(3): 227–28 (June).

2. Self-concept/self-esteem
   a. Ability to accept age-related changes becomes important.
   b. Need to find meaningful substitutes for multiple losses increases.

3. Drug therapy
   a. Most dynamic effects are frequently accomplished, not through administration of drugs, but through their withdrawal.
   b. Age-related changes may greatly affect rate of absorption, distribution, metabolism, and excretion.
   c. Vulnerability to adverse effects increases with age.
   d. Problems related to intravenous fluid therapy increase.

4. Elimination
   a. Disturbances are usually due to diet and/or fluid intake change.
   b. Constipation is usually due to decrease of bulk in diet. Decreased fluid intake also causes constipation.
   c. Diarrhea is usually due to laxative abuse. (Incidence is higher in women than in men.)
   d. Urinary changes include the following:
      (i) Sensitivity of kidneys to sudden acid/base balance changes increases.
      (ii) Nocturia increases.
      (iii) Significance of an adequate fluid intake increases.
      (iv) Lack of urinary control increases social isolation.
      (v) Prostatic enlargement increases frequency.

5. Nutritional state
   a. Low income has an adverse effect on nutrition.
   b. Loneliness may be related to nutritional problems.
   c. Degree of physical activity is a major consideration.
   d. Condition of mouth and dentures are factors.
   e. Importance of food and rituals surrounding food seem to increase in older persons.

6. Pain
   a. Sensitivity changes have been both asserted and disputed.
   b. Indications exist that threshold is dependent more upon physiological changes, and tolerance is related more to psychological factors.
   c. Tolerance to deep pain decreases; tolerance of subcutaneous pain increases.
   d. In some instances death is welcomed.

7. Skin
   a. Generally grows thin and appears dry, brittle, and fragile.
   b. Increased wrinkling is due to loss of subcutaneous fat.
   c. Ability to remain properly hydrated is lost.
   d. Shows decreased turgor.
   e. Collagen content greatly increases.
   f. Ability to maintain body temperature decreases.
   g. Sexual and cultural differences are manifested.
   h. Sweat gland support decreases.
   i. Pigmentation spots (called liver spots) increase.
   j. Number of capillary loops and other blood vessels decreases.

8. Nails
   a. Growth slows slightly.
   b. Impairment of peripheral circulation results in thickening and brittleness.

9. Hair
   a. Loss occurs but differs between the sexes.
   b. Loss of pigmentation causes graying. Decrease in oil makes appearance dull and lifeless.
   c. Axillary hair often disappears.
   d. Overall body and pubic hair decreases.

10. Mouth
    a. Need for dentures increases.
    b. Periodontal disease increases.
    c. Secretions diminish.

d. Decline in number of taste buds results in decreased capacity to taste.

11. Physical exercise and mobility
   a. Muscle size diminishes, and muscle tone and strength decrease; maximum peak is between 20 and 30 years of age.
   b. Loss may be secondary to decreased activity.
   c. Grip strength is one of the earliest indications of change.
   d. Potassium content declines.
   e. Tendency toward spinal kyphosis (dowager's hump) develops.
   f. Involuntary and painful muscle cramps result from decreased circulation to the extremities.

12. Bone mass
   a. Widespread decrease occurs.
   b. Fractures occur more frequently in weight-bearing areas.
   c. Reduction in height may occur due to intravertebral disc changes.

13. Safety
   a. Ambiguous environments increase confusion.
   b. Need for specific environmental clues increases (for example, hand rails on walls, large-size room numbers).
   c. Need for appropriately designed equipment and furnishings increases.
   d. Slick and uneven walking surfaces can cause falls.

14. Sleep
   a. General pattern frequently changes; periods of sleep become shorter.
   b. Spontaneous interruptions increase.
   c. Proportion of REM and non-REM sleep remains fairly constant until about 60 years of age.
   d. Reduction in slow wave sleep occurs.
   e. Deep sleep (Stage 4) is often absent.
   f. Concern and anxiety about pattern changes increases.

15. Time perception
   a. Tendency to underestimate time. (Satisfaction with current life situation reduces tendency to underestimate.)
   b. Need for structure and adherence to time schedules increases.

Involving elderly group members in participatory planning is often overlooked. The leader is advised to plan with them and also with agency personnel, families, health professionals — whomever is involved in the care and support of the individuals in the group.

## SUMMARY

In this introductory chapter, data were presented regarding demographic changes in the United States, and normal and abnormal aging changes were discussed. The intent was to familiarize the new leader with gerontological terms and content and to emphasize the factors that may present the greatest difficulties: physical and psychological changes that are not due to normal aging processes.

Areas of concern for the future include a shortage of persons educated and skilled in gerontology and geriatrics. It is paramount that a cadre of health care workers in a variety of disciplines be educated in these two specialties.

Economic factors have become important issues in public policy formulations in the health field: the magnitude of health expenditures, inflation in the health sector, and the cost-effectiveness of health expenditures. There has been a prolonged escalation of national health expenditures. Health spending is taking a larger and larger portion of the country's resources, as indicated by the gross national product (Aiken 1981). See Figure 1-6.

The combination of an increasing number of aged in the population and increased spending on health matters indicates the need for health innovations and health maintenance. Group work will continue to be important because the health needs of many subgroups remain unmet: among them, the inner-city and rural poor, nursing home residents, and the chronically ill.

Group leaders who work with the aged will have an important contribution to make in improving the health and well-being of the elderly.

## EXERCISE 1

Give a brief definition of ageism; then write a two-page account of an incident in which an individual displayed ageism. The expression of or behavioral cues indicating ageism can be either overt or covert. (If the cues are subtle, provide enough detail to identify them.)

## EXERCISE 2

Select as an example an older person (a member of a group you are leading or a past or present client) and choose a developmental task from one of the theorists in this chapter. State the task and explain how the person successfully (or unsuccessfully) fulfilled it. (It usually is better not to use relatives in writing assignments, for obvious reasons.)

## EXERCISE 3

Interview one elderly person to find out if he or she has incorporated negative views of aging (for example, old people cannot learn new things, or old people are not interested in sex) into the self-system. What is the belief? How does it affect the person? Has the aged person passed on the belief to others?

## REFERENCES

ADRDA. *See* Alzheimer's Disease and Related Dementias Association.

Aiken, L. 1981. The practice setting: An overview of health policy issues. In *Health policy and nursing practices,* ed. L. Aiken. New York: McGraw-Hill.

Alzheimer's Disease and Related Dementias Association (ADRDA). 1982. Brochure. Mountain View, Calif.

Birren, J., and R. B. Sloan. 1980. *Handbook of mental health and aging.* Englewood Cliffs, N.J.: Prentice-Hall.

Butler, R. N. 1980. Meeting the challenges of health care for the elderly. *Journal of Allied Health* 9:166–80.

Chisholm, S. D., O. Deniston, R. Igrisan, and A. Barbus. 1982. Prevalence of confusion in elderly hospitalized patients. *Journal of Gerontological Nursing* 8(2): 87–96 (February).

Clark, M., and B. Anderson. 1967. *Culture and aging.* Springfield, Ill.: Thomas.

Erikson, E. 1959. Identity and the life cycle. In *Psychological issues,* Monograph 1, p. 166. New York: International Universities Press.

Finch, C. E., and J. A. Severson. 1981. Biological theories of aging. In *Nursing and the aged.* 2d ed., ed. I. M. Burnside. New York: McGraw-Hill.

Fowles, D. G. 1978. *Some prospects for the future elderly population: Statistical reports on older Americans.* Washington, D.C.: U.S. Department of Health, Education, and Welfare. January.

Havighurst, R. 1975. A social-psychological perspective on aging. In *Human life cycle,* ed. W. Sze. New York: Aronson.

Hochschild, A. R. 1975. Disengagement theory: A critique and proposal. *American Sociological Review* 40 (October) 553–69.

Hyatt, J. C. 1979. Aging Americans. *Wall Street Journal,* October 23.

Levin, J., and W. C. Levin. 1980. Blaming the aged. In *Ageism: Prejudice and discrimination against the elderly.* Belmont, Calif.: Wadsworth.

Lewis, R. 1970. *The way of silence.* New York: Dial Press.

Myers, G. C., and B. J. Soldo. 1979. Older Americans: Who are they? In *The later years: Social application to gerontology,* ed. R. A. Kalish. Monterey, Calif.: Brooks/Cole.

National Center for Health Statistics. 1977. Profile of chronic illness in nursing homes, United States. In *National nursing home survey, August 1973, April 1974.* National Center for Health Statistics Series 13, no. 29, HEW Publication no. (PHS) 78 1780. Washington, D.C.: U.S. Department of Health, Education, and Welfare.

Neugarten, B. L., ed. 1968. *Middle age and aging.* Chicago: University of Chicago Press.

Pearson, D., and T. Wetle. 1981. Long-term care. In *Health care delivery in the United States.* 2d ed, ed. S. Jonas. New York: Springer.

Peck, R. C. 1955. Psychological developments in the second half of life. In *Physiological aspects of aging,* ed. J. Anderson. Washington, D.C.: American Psychological Association.

———. 1968. Psychological developments in the second half of life. In *Middle age and aging,* ed. B. L. Neugarten. Chicago: University of Chicago Press.

Praiss, I., and C. Gjerde. 1980. Cost containment through medical education. *Journal of the American Medical Association* 244:53–55.

Randall, O. 1977. Aging in America today: New aspects in aging. *The Gerontologist* 17(1): 6–11.

Riegel, K. 1977. History of psychological gerontology. In *Handbook of the psychology of aging,* ed. J. Birren and K. Warner Schaie. New York: Van Nostrand Reinhold.

Strauss, A. L., and B. G. Glaser. 1975. *Chronic illness and the quality of life.* St. Louis: Mosby.

Task Force Sponsored by the National Institute on Aging. 1980. Senility reconsidered: Treatment possibilities for mental impairment in the elderly. *Journal of the American Medical Association* 244 (July 18): 259–63.

Ware, A. 1979. Caring for ill elderly persons. In *Basic nursing: A psychophysiologic approach.* Philadelphia: Saunders.

Yurik, R., and E. Spier. 1980. Appendix. In *The aged person and the nursing process.* New York: Appleton-Century-Crofts.

## BIBLIOGRAPHY

American Academy of Nursing. 1976. *Long-term care: Issues for nursing.* Supporting Paper no. 4. Kansas City, Mo.: American Nurses Association.

Bergman, S. 1974. Nursing attitudes to psychiatry and geriatrics as preferred work areas with deviant groups. *The Israel Annals of Psychiatry and Related Disciplines.* June: 156–60.

Burnside, I. 1981. *Nursing and the aged* New York: McGraw Hill.

———. 1980. *Psychosocial nursing care of the aged.* New York: McGraw-Hill.

Butler, R. N. 1981. Meeting the challenges of health care for the elderly. *Journal of Allied Health* 9(3): 166–68 (August).

Campbell, M. E. 1981. Study of the attitudes of nursing personnel toward the geriatric patient. *Nursing Research.* March–April: 147, 151.

Crandall, R. G. 1980. *Gerontology: A behavioral science approach.* Menlo Park, Calif.: Addison-Wesley.

Decker, D. 1980. *Social gerontology.* Boston: Little, Brown.

DeLora, J. R., and D. V. Moses. 1969. Specialty preferences and characteristics of nursing students in baccalaureate programs. *Nursing Research* 18 (March–April): 137–44.

Furukawa, C., D. Shomaker, 1982. *Community Health Services for the aged,* Rockville, Md.: Aspen Systems. Chapters 6, 7, 10, 11, 13.

Gilliam M. 1973. Attitudes of nursing personnel toward the aged. *Nursing Research* 22 (November–December): 517–20.

Goldstein, S., W. Reichel, 1978. Physiological and biological aspects of aging in ed. W. Reichel, *Clinical Aspects of Aging,* Baltimore, Md. Williams & Wilkins.

Gunter, L. 1971. Students attitudes toward geriatric nursing. *Nursing Outlook* 19 (July): 466–69.

Harman, D. 1968. Free radical theory of aging. *Journal of Gerontology* 23(4): 476–582 (October).

Harris, C. 1978. *Fact book on aging: A profile of America's older population.* Washington, D.C.: National Council on Aging.

Hayter, J. 1981. Nursing care of the severely confused patient. *Nursing Homes* 30(6):30–37 (November–December).

Horn, J., G. Donaldson, R. Engstrom, 1981. Apprehension, memory and fluid intelligence decline in adulthood, *Research on aging* 3(1):33–84 (March).

Kart, C., E. Metress, and J. Metress. 1978. *Aging and health: Biologic and social perspectives.* Menlo Park, Calif.: Addison-Wesley.

Kayser, J., and F. Minnigerode. 1975. Increasing nursing students' interest in working with aged patients. *Nursing Research* 24 (January–February): 23–26.

Leininger, M. 1981. *Caring: An essential human need,* Thorofare, N.J.: CB Slack.

Mailick, M. 1982. Understanding illness and aging. *Journal of Gerontological Social Work* 5 (Nos. 1–2): 113–126, (Winter).

Makinodin, T. 1977. Immunity and aging. In *Handbook of the biology of aging,* ed. C. E. Finch and L. Hayflick, 379–408. New York: Van Nostrand Reinhold.

Mayer, M. 1983. Demographic change and the elderly population. In *Group work with the frail elderly.* New York: Haworth Press.

Miller, M. B. 1980. A burgeoning crisis in physician–nurse relationships in long-term care. *The Journal of Long-Term Care Administration,* September: 13–23.

Moschetto, C. A. 1981. Predictions about the future of LTC. *Nursing Homes* 30(5): 42–50 (September–October).

National Center for Health Statistics. 1977. *Health, U.S.* Washington, D.C.: U.S. Government Printing Office.

_____. 1978. *Health, U.S.* Washington, D.C.: U.S. Government Printing Office.

Orgel, L. 1963. The maintenance of the accuracy of protein synthesis and its relevance to aging. *Proceedings of the National Academy of Science* 49: 517–21.

_____. 1970. The maintenance of the accuracy of protein synthesis and its relevance to aging: A correction. *Proceedings of the National Academy of Science* 67:1476.

Rogers, M. E. 1972. Nursing: To be or not to be? *Nursing Outlook* 20(1): 43 (January).

Schlotfeldt, R. M. 1981. Nursing in the future. *Nursing Outlook,* May: 295.

Smith, S., V. Jepsen, and E. Perloff. 1982. Attitudes of nursing care providers toward elderly patients. *Nursing and Health Care* 3(2): 93–98 (February).

Spiegel, P. 1972. Theories of aging in P.S. Timara, ed. *Developmental physiology and aging.* New York: Macmillan.

Stagner, R. 1981. Stress, strain, coping, and defense, *Research on Aging* 3(1):3–32 (March).

Taylor, K. H., and T. L. Harned. 1978. Attitudes toward old people: A study of nurses who care for the elderly. *Journal of Gerontological Nursing* 4(5): 43–47 (September–October).

White, M. A. 1981. Successful aging in *Occasional papers in mental health and aging,* Salt Lake City, Utah: University of Utah Gerontology Program.

## RESOURCES

### Films

*The Art of Silence* (color, 8 minutes). This pantomime by Marcel Marceau reveals how mime can condense time. In four minutes Marceau symbolically presents the cycle of life. Film Library, University of Minnesota, Minneapolis, MN.

*Aging.* This film challenges the common stereotype that old people are one homogeneous group. The film emphasizes the individuality of the elderly and the breadth of their needs and desires. It focuses on the life styles of older people. James Branch Cabell Library, Virginia Commonwealth University, Richmond, VA 23284; phone (804) 257-1098.

### Audiovisuals

*And When You Grow Old* (16 mm, color, 30 minutes). In this positive and unpretentious portrayal, the elderly share their ideas about old age and their attitudes toward life. They discuss sickness, death, limited income, and housing arrangements. Department of Mental Health, James Madison Building, 109 Governor Street, 13th Floor, Richmond, VA 23219; phone (804) 786-1332.

*Growing Old: Something to Live For* (color, 15 minutes). This film is informative and optimistic in its treatment of aging, focusing on successful adaptations to growing old. There are interviews with enthusiastic older persons as well as learned advocates. CRM McGraw-Hill Films, 110 Fifteenth Street, Del Mar, CA 92014.

### Tapes/Cassettes

*Gramp—A Man Ages and Dies.* A poignant case of senile dementia; Alzheimer's type. A teacher's guide is supplied. Sunburst Communications, 39 Washington Avenue, Pleasantville, NY 10570.

### Organizations

*Alzheimer's Disease and Related Disorders Association,* 360 North Michigan Avenue, Suite 601, Chicago, IL. Check with this organization for state chapters.

chapter 2

# History and Overview of Group Work with the Elderly

*Irene Burnside*

*. . . understanding is obtained by explaining what we know.*

ROBERT L. CAUSEY (1969, 24)

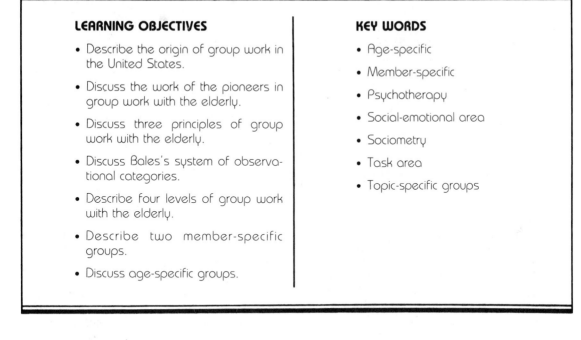

**LEARNING OBJECTIVES**

- Describe the origin of group work in the United States.

- Discuss the work of the pioneers in group work with the elderly.

- Discuss three principles of group work with the elderly.

- Discuss Bales's system of observational categories.

- Describe four levels of group work with the elderly.

- Describe two member-specific groups.

- Discuss age-specific groups.

**KEY WORDS**

- Age-specific

- Member-specific

- Psychotherapy

- Social-emotional area

- Sociometry

- Task area

- Topic-specific groups

This chapter provides a brief history of group work with the elderly and an overview of current group work. The following sections introduce students, health care workers and volunteers, and instructors to some principles of group work and to the most common types of groups and group methods used with elderly clients or patients.

The psychosocial care of the elderly in the United States needs improvement. Group work is one form of treatment that is effective with the elderly and that should be considered in prevention and maintenance aspects of the health care of older persons. In this book *group work* covers a wide range of groups of older people that could be conducted by nonprofessionals. *Group psychotherapy,* as used in this book, designates only groups that are conducted with older people who have psychiatric problems and that are led by professionals with psychology or psychiatry training.

_____

This chapter is a revised version of two papers: Burnside 1975 and Burnside 1976.

## HISTORICAL BACKGROUND

The originator of group psychotherapy was Joseph Henry Pratt, an internist. In 1905 in Boston, Dr. Pratt developed a plan for the treatment of tuberculosis in poor patients. At that time the disease was often called consumption; however, he called the group meetings "tuberculosis classes." The group consisted of 15 to 20 patients who met with him once a week. Although aimed at fostering an understanding of tuberculosis, the classes also showed positive results in the mental health of the group members; unfortunately, other physicians who tried to emulate his classes were not nearly as successful. Some writers feel that Pratt's personality had a great deal to do with the success of his group and that he tended to conduct the group work intuitively. It was the improvement of the emotional status of the tuberculosis patients in these groups that led to the use of the treatment modality for patients who suffered from mental illness.

Elwood Worchester, director of the Emmanuel Church in Boston, advanced money to Pratt to assist him in launching the tuberculosis classes. At a later date, Dr. Worchester, assisted by Isidore Coriat (one of the first members of the American Psychoanalytic Association), began seeing patients in group meetings to assist them with health problems; these groups were not restricted to tuberculosis patients.

Pratt continued to work in the group modality but switched his attention to patients who had emotional problems. At that time no theoretical basis for group psychoanalytic therapy existed for teaching the method. Also, no worthwhile research had yet appeared. Pratt then applied the ideas of Joseph Deperine, who emphasized persuasion and reeducation. Pratt continued his work as a group psychotherapist into the 1950s.

In 1909 L. Cody Marsh worked with psychotics in classes and lectures. Psychiatric patients were treated by group psychotherapy as early as 1921. Although Marsh's groups probably would not be recognized as psychotherapy, he did realize the therapeutic value of group treatment for psychotics. He also applied such techniques as formal lectures, art classes, and dance classes (Ruitenbeck 1970).

In the 1920s and 1930s, Louis Wender worked with institutionalized borderline cases. He thought of his groups as psychoanalytic rather than educational or orientational, his view of the other groups of that time. Wender saw groups of six to eight patients two or three times a week. Group members were of the same sex; each group meeting lasted for one hour. He also combined individual and group psychotherapy and suggested that the group might represent the family to its members. In 1934, Paul Schilder, who was at Bellevue, also worked with groups in the psychoanalytic framework (Pinney 1970).

J. L. Moreno came to the United States from Germany in 1930. He introduced the concept of sociometry and diagramming the interactions that occur in groups (Hardy and Conway 1978).

It is said that the term *group psychotherapy* originated with Moreno, a fact that Moreno confirms (Ruitenbeck 1970). He is the leading exponent of a treatment technique called psycho-

drama. Since Moreno's death, the teaching of psychodrama has been carried on by his widow.

Samuel Slavson, a civil engineer, practiced group psychotherapy with children for the Jewish Board of Guardians in the 1930s. In 1943 he published *An Introduction to Group Therapy.* Later he was instrumental in the formation and development of the American Group Psychotherapy Association. He became the first editor of the *International Journal of Group Psychotherapy* in 1951 and was an active force in the advancement of group psychotherapy for both social work and psychiatry.

During World War II, group psychotherapy began to be used extensively as a treatment modality in military hospitals. The army psychiatrists then returned to civilian practice and applied group therapy in their own settings.

In the early studies done in the 1960s and 1970s, mostly by psychiatrists, the goal of the therapist was insight. A table organized by K. Gunnar Götestam (1980, 787) shows these data very well. The reader is referred to that reference.

## REVIEW OF THE LITERATURE

Since World War II group work has become an increasingly popular form of treatment in the care of the aged—partly because it is economical. Moreover, according to Leonard Gottesman, Carole Quarterman, and Gordon Cohn (1973, 422), "Small-group treatment can be used in both contrived settings like psychotherapy and naturalistic ones like families or communities of aged persons. This technique is valuable because it can be more naturalistic and more long lasting than individual therapy."

The literature is beginning to include more about both the benefits and the limitations of such work, but book chapters and journal articles on the topic are still widely scattered. Irvin Yalom's (1975) excellent book on group psychotherapy, for instance, does not discuss psychotherapy with the aged at all, while Gwen Marram's (1973) book on the group approach in nursing only briefly describes some of the aspects of working with the aged.

Nevertheless, the available literature does indicate that such work with the elderly is conducted by a very diverse occupational group, including psychiatrists; recreational, occupational, and physical therapists; social workers; psychologists; nurses; and administrators of skilled nursing facilities (Burnside 1970a). For example, Maurice Linden (1953), a psychiatrist, pioneered group work with the aged when he co-led a group of 40 to 51 regressed women in a state hospital. He also wrote a chapter, entitled "Geriatrics," that offers a variety of interesting case studies (Linden 1956). In the same year Susan Kubie and Gertrude Landau published a book about their nine years of group work experience in a recreation center for the aged. Jerome Kaplan (1953) was one of the first social workers to write about group work with the elderly, and Eugenia Shere (1964), a psychologist, wrote a classic article on group work with the very old.

The trend for nurses to publish reports about their group work with the elderly came later. The first collection of papers appeared in *Psychosocial Nursing Care of the Aged* (Burnside 1973). Most were written by nurses in graduate nursing programs (Blake 1973; Burnside 1973; Gillin 1973; Holland 1973; Holtzen 1973; Morrison 1973; Stange 1973).

Unfortunately, at international meetings on gerontology, reports on group work with the aged are still scarce. After combing three thick volumes of abstracts published following the International Congress of Gerontology held in Kiev, USSR, in 1972, I could locate only four papers pertaining to group work with the elderly: Three were from the United States (Bloom 1972; Finkel and Fillmore 1971; Weinstock and Weiner 1972), and one was from the Netherlands (ter Haar 1972). During the International Congress of Gerontology held in Jerusalem three years later, two papers were given dealing specifically with group work and older adults (Burnside 1975; Kahana 1975). Other papers merely alluded to group work (Gaitz 1975; Kennedy 1975). At the 1978 International Conference, one paper on the subject was listed in the abstracts (Stevens and Wimmers 1979). Three years later at the conference in Hamburg, Germany, two papers

were presented, one about music therapy and one about group work with the confused elderly (Bright 1981; Burnside, Baumler, and Weaverdyck 1981).

## GENERAL GROUP PROCESSES

Space limitations preclude all but a few comments on interaction in groups generally. Kurt Lewin (1948) organized and developed *field theory,* which he saw as "a method of analyzing causal relations and building scientific constructs." His work at the University of Iowa in the 1930s and later at the Massachusetts Institute of Technology established the field of group dynamics. *Group dynamics* refers to the study of individuals who are interacting in small groups. *Dynamics* means "the motive and controlling forces, . . . also the study of such forces" (*Webster's* 1976). Other terms used are *group processes, group interaction, group psychology,* and *human relations.*

Robert Bales's (1951) system of observational categories is useful to study for an analysis of the interaction process. See Figure 2–1 for Bales's diagram of group tasks of members.

The reader who feels deficient in group process theory is referred to *Groups: Facilitating Individual Growth and Societal Change,* by Walter Lifton (1972); *Group Processes: An Introduction to Group Dynamics,* by Joseph Luft (1963); *The Small Group,* by Michael Olmsted (1959); *The Process of Group Communication,* by Ronald Applbaum et al. (1974); and *Groups in Social-Work,* by Margaret Hartford (1972). These works deal with groups in general but do not include group work with the elderly. For those interested or engaged in group psychotherapy, Yalom's *The Theory and Practice of Group Psychotherapy* (1975) and Chapters 5, 21, and 28 in this book are recommended.

## SOME PRINCIPLES OF GROUP WORK WITH THE ELDERLY

The differences between group work with the elderly and work with other age groups are

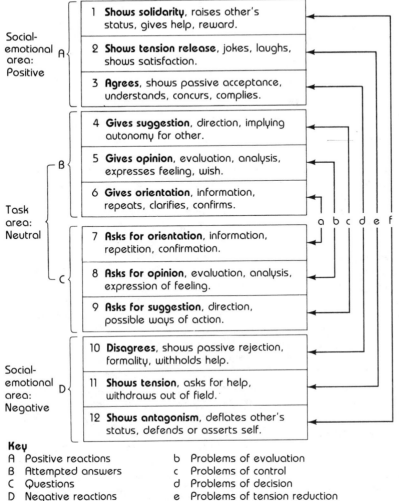

**Key**

| A | Positive reactions | b | Problems of evaluation |
| B | Attempted answers | c | Problems of control |
| C | Questions | d | Problems of decision |
| D | Negative reactions | e | Problems of tension reduction |
| a | Problems of communication | f | Problems of reintegration |

FIGURE 2–1. *Bale's system of observational categories.*

SOURCE: R. F. Bales. 1951. *Interaction process analysis* (Chicago: University of Chicago Press). Reprinted with permission of the publisher.

itemized in Chapter 6. In general, group work with the aged involves a more directive approach (Corey and Corey 1977; Rustin and Wolk 1963), and leaders must take a more active role in giving information, answering questions, and sharing themselves with the group members.

Group leaders need to provide much support, encouragement, and empathy because the elderly often have special problems that must be recognized and dealt with. On the emotional level, elderly people may be preoccupied with loss and death and may refer to these topics again and again (Burnside 1970b). A major objective in group work is to alleviate this general anxiety by helping group members solve immediate

problems. Thus, psychotherapy groups for the aged stress this aspect of mental health more than insight or personality changes (Rustin and Wolk 1963).

Group leaders must also contend with the physical problems of the elderly. Sensory defects, for example, require special techniques. Speaking slowly and clearly, sitting close to the members, and keeping the groups and circles small are all helpful. Assessing the energy level of each member is another important aspect of group work with the elderly.

Psychological support from the leader increases group members' confidence and promotes cohesiveness. For example, group members may use their advancing age and/or illness as defenses against attending group sessions (Rustin and Wolk 1963). But making meticulous *contracts* (agreements between leaders and members), attending to physical complaints, and personally visiting or telephoning members outside the group may help reduce the need for such defensive behavior. Of course, maintaining such groups is a demanding task for the leaders, especially since they must feel comfortable with the dependency on them that may develop among their group members.

Group leadership can be much easier if a leader emerges from the group itself. Even with mentally impaired elderly persons diagnosed as organic brain syndrome, I have had a member become a "helper" and try to assist me, although in institutions the frailty of members seems to have an impact on their leadership potential, and their own dependency needs preclude leadership roles for them. Nonetheless, leaders need to praise and encourage a member who demonstrates an inclination toward group leadership; this reward in itself can help raise the low self-esteem that so many of the aged experience.

All these principles of group work with the elderly presuppose carefully handled communication between leaders and members, leaders and staffs, leaders and families. Poor communication creates problems, confusion, ill feelings, and disinterest. With forgetful, confused, or disoriented elderly especially, it is crucial to communicate clearly and consistently.

## COMMON GROUPS AND GROUP METHODS

The possibilities for group work with the aged are varied, which makes it such a challenging and exciting form of treatment. Some of the current groups and group methods are described here briefly, and in detail in subsequent chapters. Although avant garde groups are increasing in popularity, they are not covered in this book.

The following list shows the possible levels of group work and of the group member. The levels will indicate the knowledge base, skill, and practice needed by the leader. The four levels are

1. Reality orientation.
2. Remotivation.

3. Reminiscing; music (creative movement), art, and poetry; bibliotherapy; scribotherapy; health teaching; current events; family therapy.
4. Group psychotherapy.

The levels of group work and some general information about each can be seen in Table 2–1.

### Reality Orientation

Reality orientation (RO) groups are currently very popular, especially for regressed elderly persons who are affected with dementia. These groups were first started at the Veterans Administration Hospital in Tuscaloosa, Alabama, by a nurse and a psychologist (Taulbee and Folsom 1966).

Reality orientation groups are designed for confused, disoriented elderly. Meetings are half an hour long, held usually Monday through Friday, and led by a nursing assistant, a volunteer, or an activities coordinator. (Although meetings are regularly scheduled, the reality-orienting process should be continued around the clock.) A group should not have more than four members because of the tremendous demands such a group places on the leader. A large reality orientation board is kept in the meeting room. Posted on it daily is such common information as the weather, the date, and the next meal.

Reality testing is an important aspect of reality orientation groups, and correct information must be constantly given to the confused, disoriented elderly person. It is sometimes important to reduce disorientation in the three spheres of time, place, and person. Misperceptions of the environment are commonplace among confused elderly, especially those with poor vision. This area is neglected in reorienting the elderly; staff members often do not clarify or reality test for visual illusions (Burnside 1977).

Reality orientation groups are often mistakenly called reality therapy groups. Reality therapy is a specific type of psychotherapy begun by William Glasser (1965) for delinquent adolescents. See also Chapter 14.

Two glaring problems are frequently seen after RO is introduced in an institution. One problem is that reality testing is not continued

TABLE 2-1.  **Levels of group work with the elderly**

| Group modality | Number of members | Type of leader | Length of meeting | Props useful | Refreshments |
|---|---|---|---|---|---|
| Reality orientation | 4 | Nurses' aide with special training | As tolerated: 15 or 30 minutes to 1 hour | Yes | Yes |
| Remotivation | 12–14 | Student, nurses' aide, or psychiatric technician with special training | 1 hour | Yes | No (according to founder of remotivation therapy) |
| Reminiscing | 6–8 | Activity director, psychologist, nurses' aide, bibliotherapist, nurse, occupational therapist, social worker, or student volunteer | 1–1½ hours | Yes | Yes |
| Art | 4–6 | Artist/art major | 1 hour | Yes | Optional |
| Music | 6–8 (or a very large group) | Musician or a person who is musically talented | 1 hour | Yes | Optional |
| Poetry | 6–8 | Poet/teacher of poetry | 1 hour | Yes | Optional |
| Bibliotherapy | 6–8 (if frail elderly); otherwise 10–12 | Librarian, volunteer | 1 hour | Yes | Optional |
| Health teaching | Variable | Health-related professional, nurse, health educator | 1 hour | Optional | Optional |
| Psychotherapy | 6–8 | Psychiatric nurse, psychiatric social worker, psychologist, psychiatrist, certified counselor | 1 hour or 2 times weekly | No | Usually no |

around the clock by all shifts, so it is not as effective as it might be. The other problem is that the instructor (or responsible shift) does not keep the all-important reality orientation board up to date. I have been in a skilled nursing facility where the board read, "The weather is sunny today," and I had just come in from a rainstorm!

Chapter 15, by Lucille Taulbee, describes how to conduct reality orientation groups. Because RO has been immensely popular and garnered its share of publications, an overview of the concept is presented in Chapter 14 by Elizabeth Donahue.

### Remotivation Therapy

Remotivation groups, the next level in group work, are also popular. The focus of remotiva-

tion therapy is on simple, objective aspects of day-to-day living. The leader arranges a very structural classroom setting, with props, and tries to get the patients to discuss their experiences in regard to a specific topic.

Generally, patients in remotivation groups are helped toward resocialization. For example, Mary Ann Miller (1975) studied different types of group therapy and selected a remotivation group to conduct in a nursing home. She reached all levels of confused individuals and described the experience as successful. Miller observed that many of the members began to converse and ask questions after not having spoken for several years. They began to ambulate and feed themselves, and they asked for bathroom assistance after long periods of incontinence. (See Chapter 16 for Helen Dennis's review of other research findings and a report on her own.)

The model of the remotivation technique and its application to the mentally ill originated with Dorothy Hoskins Smith, an English literature teacher from Claremont College, Claremont, California. She trained a large group of personnel at the Philadelphia State Hospital in 1956. Because this treatment method was developed in a state hospital for use with mental patients, adaptations are necessary if it is to be used with older persons in other settings.

Although many remotivation groups seem to have been successful, such groups do have drawbacks. Elaine Brody and Leonard Gottesman (1974, 202) feel that "this therapy has reached many patients and reinvolved them in ideas of the non-institutional world, but it fails to reach many because of its abstract character." There are several reasons that remotivation groups lack appeal and challenge for me as a leader: They do not (1) explore feelings; (2) permit the leader to touch the members; (3) focus on leisure, but rather are based on the "work world" (which is fine for young institutionalized persons but is unrealistic for very old persons who are in extended care or intermediate care facilities or even boarding homes); (4) allow for much spontaneity or originality in leadership; or (5) permit refreshments to be served. All of these characteristics violate the principles and philosophy so vital to group work with the aged. It seems especially inappropriate for an elderly group to have the work world as part of its focus. That implies being a producer. To old people who can no longer work, it is a reminder that they not only cannot produce but may also be in a quite dependent role. That remotivation groups were launched in a state hospital has influenced the model. We need new and different models for individuals in extended care facilities and perhaps for community residents as well.

## Reminiscing Groups

Because reminiscing therapy (RT) is so important as a treatment modality with the aged population, an entire section in this text (Part 5) is devoted to RT. Reminiscing groups are designed to explore memories with a group of six or eight elderly persons and can meet in either an institutional or a noninstitutional setting. Meetings are held once or twice weekly, according to the leader's and the group's wishes, for approximately one hour. The leader encourages the sharing of memories that run the gamut from happy to sad, carefree to somber, and include all stages of life. Many subjects can be discussed in a reminiscing group— holidays, birthdays, major events, families, geographical places, travel, modes of transportation.

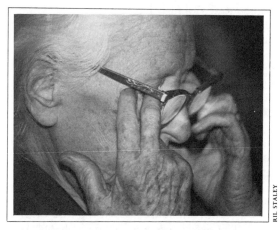

*In reminiscing groups, sad feelings often emerge. Elderly people have an amazing resiliency in group and will often bounce back after such sharing. Of course, the leader must always consider labile moods, which could be related to tears.*

## Topic-Specific Groups

**Music Groups.**   Music Groups can accommodate a large number of members and can be led by a registered music therapist or a musically talented person with leadership skills. A solid base in gerontology is needed. Some leaders also incorporate creative movement into their music groups. Groups with other foci often incorporate appropriate music into some of the group meetings.

The type of music group—whether singalong, listening group, instrumental group, and so forth—will depend on several factors: (1) available space for meetings, (2) available musical instruments, (3) talent of the leader, (4) talent of members, (5) talent of staff personnel, (6) talent of family members, and (7) budget for sheet music, rental or purchase of instruments, and so on.

It is not the goal of music groups to teach music per se. The goal can vary; common ones are (1) to improve the quality and enjoyment of daily living, (2) to increase body movement, (3) to reach withdrawn members, (4) to provide props in group work, (5) to increase or enhance reminiscing within the group through music, and (6) to increase feelings of relatedness to cohorts through familiar music.

Mary Jane Hennessey (1976a, 1976b), nurse and concert violinist, has experimented with a variety of music groups. She worked with large and small groups of elderly people and always used the central theme of music. She observed a gradual but varied effect among group members: increased socialization and sensory stimulation, increased reminiscing, enhanced self-esteem, decreased hostility and loneliness, lessened incontinence. (See Chapters 17 and 33 on methods for establishing music groups with the elderly.)

**Art Therapy and Poetry Groups.** Art therapy and poetry groups are highly recommended, but they are not commonly used in the care of the aged. This book does not include a chapter on poetry groups; the reader is referred to an excellent book by Kenneth Koch entitled *I Never Told Anybody* (1977). Space does not permit a lengthy description of that poet's warm and human approach to old people in a nursing home. His book is based on weekly meetings in a nursing home in New York City with residents in their seventies, eighties, and nineties. He offers guidelines for leaders of poetry groups.

Most art and poetry groups are therapy groups conducted with children or young adults. Simple drawings can be incorporated into group meetings at any level for discussion and exploration. The use of drawing is further described and illustrated in Chapter 13, "Group Work with the Cognitively Impaired." B. Weber (1981) describes her group work in art therapy with members ranging in age from the sixties through the nineties. Hers was a practicum placement at a nutrition site. She perceived isolation and boredom in the members. She responded to the women's interest in cloth and quilting and assisted the group in making a cloth mural, which she describes (p. 52) as "concrete evidence of the strength, vitality, and creativity of a group of largely disadvantaged old people."

**Bibliotherapy.** Bibliotherapy is a special form of therapy that can be done individually or in a group. It uses reading aloud as a therapeutic approach to problems and problem solving. See Chapter 32 for an in-depth discussion of bibliotherapy in group work with the elderly.

**Scribotherapy.** Another type of group, called scribotherapy, was the subject of a paper presented at the Twenty-Ninth Annual Scientific Meeting of the Gerontological Society (Stewart 1976). Scribotherapy, derived from the Latin *scribo,* which means to write, is "writing therapy."

For more than a year Janice Stewart, an activities therapist at Philadelphia Geriatric Center, conducted scribotherapy with 32 severely mentally impaired and behaviorally disturbed residents from a wing of the center. The group wrote material to publish in their own newspaper, which was distributed to staff, families, administrators, and other residents. The benefits of scribotherapy include a chance for self-expression, the enhancement of self-esteem, the encouragement of reminiscence, and an increase in social interaction.

**Health-Related Groups.** Health-related groups are currently often conducted at nutrition centers. Nurses seem to be the logical leaders for health-related groups, but people in a variety of disciplines could also lead them. A podiatrist might teach foot care, a dentist might teach dental care, a cardiologist might teach about heart problems; a nurse or health educator could coordinate the group. Old people do need more information about such things as glaucoma, cataracts, hearing problems, diabetes, arthritis, strokes, organic brain syndrome, and even sexuality and aging. One effort to provide family members with information was handled through a stroke club.

These groups can be organized as large, formal classes with a lecture approach, or they can be small and informal discussion groups. Few kinds of groups for the elderly lend themselves to large size; health-related groups can be larger than most other groups because of their educational nature. However, regardless of size or subject matter, it goes without saying that prevention should be a recurring theme in any health-related group.

Health-related groups can have a wide range of goals. For example, N. Johnston (1965) used group reading of a stroke victim's experiences as a therapeutic approach to treatment with elderly cerebrovascular accident (CVA) patients. L. N. Murphy (1969) and Lois Valentine (1970) conducted health-teaching groups. E. G. Anderson and A. A. Andrew (1973) describe "health conferences" for groups of elderly people. Other health-related groups described in the literature include those in which all of the members struggle with the same affliction (Conte, Brandzel, and Whitehead 1974; Heller 1970; Holland 1973).

In other research W. Schwartz and A. Papas (1968) stated that group therapy minimized the anxiety of older patients with medical problems. Group therapy techniques were adopted to improve communication. Through identification in the small group (see Yalom's "curative factors" in Chapter 5) and association with members of a small group, elderly persons with diabetes and heart problems coped with many of their symptoms.

P. C. Liederman and V. R. Liederman (1967) described a group of 11 persons, ranging in age from 62 to 86, who were referred to outpatient therapy because of maladjustment in day-to-day living situations. These people had consulted from two to seven physicians in a period of one and a half to two years before being referred to group therapy. The group helped them resolve crises and reduced feelings of isolation.

### Member-Specific Groups

**Groups for Grievers.** Some groups use grief as the common denominator for membership. Such groups can be especially beneficial for elderly widows, any of whom have little or no preparation for the widow role, by helping them adjust to widowhood and preventing subsequent problems. Statistics reveal that most older men are married; in fact, there are four widows to every widower. In 1975, 52.5 percent of older women were widowed (U.S. Bureau of the Census 1975). This neglected group of older women has not been extensively studied or adequately considered in our policies or in medical and nursing care planning. Widow groups can be conducted in either high-cost or low-cost housing units, senior citizen centers, extended care facilities, day care centers, and in the community.

Loneliness, the most pervasive complaint of widows, occurs especially during the first six months of widowhood (Silverman 1969).

*The fundamental rationale for group work with the aged is to improve the quality of the individual's life. One approach is through a current events discussion group like the one shown here, which meets regularly in an extended care facility.*

Groups of grievers can be conducted during the early stages of grief—say, the first few weeks or months—or even later.

Patience and empathy are required of a leader who chooses to conduct a group of recently widowed elderly women. The leader also must be able to listen without consoling; should discourage verbalizations of "I can top that" (that is, descriptions of the most tragic suffering or demise); and must be aware of the pacing necessary for widow groups and not attempt to accelerate the process of grief work. Decision making should be held to a minimum. Here other members as well as the leader can be helpful. Before initiating such a group, the leader should have a good understanding of the research and results of Helen Lopata (1975), C. Murray Parkes (1965), and Phyllis Silverman (1976).

**Groups for Family Members.** Group work with family members may be initiated for a variety of reasons: (1) to reduce hostility, anxiety, and guilt feelings of the family; (2) to orient the family to nursing home life; (3) to educate the family about the aging process or the pathological processes occurring; (4) to encourage family interest in the progress of the relative; and (5) to reduce family conflicts detrimental to the aged person. Such family groups can be conducted by administrators of nursing homes, chaplains, nurses, social workers, or psychologists.

The interaction of the family with their older member frequently reflects unrealistic expectations (Herr 1976), and this incongruence between "significant other" expectations and the aged individual's capabilities leads to discomfort and the possibility of behavioral disturbances (Gottesman, Quarterman, and Cohn 1973). Establishing a group experience for family members can provide an opportunity for catharsis and can help them identify incongruencies, realign their expectations with the aged member's present level of functioning, and focus on the future potential for rehabilitation and/or change. (John Herr and John Weakland discuss group work with families in Chapter 31.) Also, group work with families of newly institutionalized elderly members can be thera-

peutic in the expression of guilt feelings and anticipatory grief.

Such groups can be particularly helpful when family members are old too. Parent and child may both be elderly, but we are not accustomed to thinking of old children. I am reminded of an incident that occurred on the back ward of a state hospital. A very confused old man kept saying that he was going on pass for the weekend with his mother. Since he was so old, the staff did not believe him until Friday afternoon, when a spry old lady in her nineties drove up to take her son home.

**Age-Specific Groups.** In age-specific groups age is a criterion for membership. Although some writers believe that topics in a group of exclusively elderly people center mainly on illness, death, loneliness, and family conflict, thus increasing the sense of isolation among the members (Butler and Lewis 1982), others feel that age-specific groups can contribute to the mental health of the members. Eugenia Shere (1964), a psychologist who conducted a group of 90-year-olds, observed the following improvements in the members: (1) increased self-respect, (2) diminished feelings of loneliness and depression, (3) reactivated desires for social exchange, (4) reawakened intellectual interest, and (5) increased capabilities to resume community life. It is worth noting that Shere's colleagues made fun of her for choosing such a group.

As life experiences are shared, empathic listening increases both the cohesion and the desirability of the group. I once grouped six nonagenarians for an evening meal each week. The frailties of the group made it a difficult one to lead. However, one day a woman wheeled herself into the office and stated, "Today I'm ninety! Where is that group that I'm now eligible to join?" The eliteness of the group had not dawned on many of us until she asked to join it.

Leaders who choose to work with an intergenerational group will need to have a solid knowledge base in developmental tasks across the life span. Leaders of such groups must understand changes in puberty, young adulthood, mid-life, and later years. Always when there are older persons in a group, the leader must be sensitive to the developmental tasks of later life. Handling sensory loss, sad themes of personal loss, and increasing illness or frailty will be a few of the responsibilities inherent in the leadership role.

Leaders of intergenerational groups might be from the disciplines of nursing, psychiatry, psychology, social work, or theology. Group methodology would depend on (1) the leader's style, philosophy, training, and experience; (2) the ages of the group members; and (3) the size and disabilities of the group.

## Psychotherapy Groups

Group psychotherapy is often the preferred treatment for elderly psychotic patients because it makes the most of the therapist's time and is economical. There are benefits for the aged person too. Adrian Verwoerdt (1976, 138) states that "supportive psychotherapy with aged patients is best carried out in a group context. The experience in the group enhances a sense of belonging, also an appreciation for the value of external sources of satisfaction, and the effectiveness of reality testing." Reality testing in a group context is an important component in therapy, as was mentioned earlier in this chapter in regard to reality orientation groups.

S. Finkel (1982, 167) writes:

> In my experience, *group therapy* is the treatment of choice for the nonpsychotic elderly who are experiencing difficulty in adjusting to loss(es). Groups offer a number of advantages for the older person: they decrease the sense of isolation, facilitate the development of new roles or the reestablishment of familiar roles, provide information on a variety of topics from other group members, and afford group support for effecting change or enhancing self-esteem.

Group therapy for the elderly differs from group therapy for younger groups in the following ways:

1. Therapists share more personal information.
2. There is more physical contact—hugging, touching, kissing.
3. There is more tolerance of silent group members.

4. There is usually a predominance of female members.
5. Common themes are loss (physical, social, economic), intergenerational conflicts, and struggle to adapt.
6. There is a greater emphasis on reminiscence and life review.

My attempts to mix demented patients with patients with other diagnoses have proved unsuccessful. In general, nondemented patients become anxious, fearful, and sometimes hostile in such circumstances; especially early in therapy, these 'threatened' patients tend not to return to group sessions—it is as if dementia were an infectious illness.

There are two major obstacles to outpatient group therapy: transportation (particularly during the winter), and economics. Paradoxically, though group therapy is less costly than individual psychotherapy, its longer-term nature means additional cost as well as additional benefit. Medicare limitations act as a particular deterrent for those of modest means.

A. Verwoerdt (1976) discusses the value of psychodrama, which can be used by a group therapist. The therapist assigns a specific role for the aged person to play. Portraying the role is therapeutic because it involves the expression of specific emotions and ideas; a spin-off is the catharsis experienced without feeling guilty or unduly inhibited. I recall a psychiatrist who asked a depressed, guilt-ridden man to play the role of a judge and mete out a punishment. The man's guilt feelings subsided and his feeling of self-worth improved when he realized how self-castigating he had been.

Psychotherapy groups for the elderly should have a professional leader well educated in psychiatric theory and group dynamics. Clergy, nurses, psychiatrists, psychologists, and social workers all conduct such groups. Since there are as yet no geropsychiatric nurses, the nurses are usually psychiatric nurses. A new group therapist should be familiar with the writings of Butler and Lewis (1974, 1982), Goldfarb, Linden, and Shere. Yalom's *The Theory and Practice of Group Psychotherapy* (1975) is recommended for the basic principles in group therapy. A. I. Goldfarb's article "Group Therapy with the Old and Aged," in *Comprehensive*

*Group Psychotherapy* (1971), is suggested for all beginning group psychotherapists. Chapter 21 describes in detail a psychotherapy group co-led by a male psychiatrist and a female social worker. Raymond Poggi writes in Chapter 28 about the therapist's needs and interests in working with the elderly and discusses transference and countertransference. That chapter is recommended for psychotherapists.

## PROGRESS IN GROUP WORK

Several changes have been observed since the publication of the first edition of this book. There appears to be diminished emphasis on reality orientation and increased use of reminiscing groups by leaders from a variety of disciplines. There has been a steady increase in controlled studies regarding group therapy with the elderly. The number of articles appearing in a variety of journals is also steadily increasing. The impact of support groups for relatives of individuals with Alzheimer's disease will be felt nationwide; these groups continue to expand, and there is a large network devoted to education, research on the disease, and support to the families.

Textbooks now carry chapters about group work with the elderly (Lowy 1979; Harbert and Ginsberg 1979; Furukawa and Shomaker 1982; Janosik and Miller 1982). This trend is most encouraging.

A wide variety of resources are now available to instructors for teaching about groups or sensitizing an audience to the needs of the elderly. Many of these resources are listed at the end of the chapters in this book.

Another change is the emphasis on day care centers to maintain the elderly in the community; however, there are not nearly enough day care centers in the United States. The need for group leaders in this area will grow. One vital component of day care centers is the opportunity for group work and activities.

## SUMMARY

This chapter presents a brief history of group work with the aged and an overview of current group work. In this book *group work* covers a wide variety of groups led by nonprofessionals; *group psychotherapy* designates group work by professionals having psychology or psychiatry training with people who have psychiatric problems.

Since World War II group work with the elderly has become increasingly popular—partly because it is economical. This work is conducted by people in many occupational specialties.

Group work with the elderly is more directive than work with other age groups. Because the elderly often have special emotional and physical problems, leaders need to provide much encouragement and empathy. Groups will provide psychological support for their members and focus on ego enhancement rather than confrontation. A cardinal principle of such group work is careful communication between leaders and members, leaders and staffs, and leaders and families.

There are a variety of levels of group work: reality orientation, remotivation, reminiscing (which may include art, poetry, and music), and group psychotherapy. These levels also indicate the knowledge, skill, and experience needed by the leader. See Table 2–1 for a more detailed explanation of the levels of groups.

## EXERCISE 1

Prepare a chronological list of types of group work with the elderly, indicating the important publications pertaining to each type.

List chronologically the important articles about group work you have read. Study the list, and write one thoughtful page on each of the following:

1. A classic book or article that influenced subsequent group work with elderly clients. Your answer should include:
   a. Complete documentation of the book or article.
   b. Whether it was a pioneering effort.
   c. How you think it influenced subsequent group work.
   d. A description of the leadership style.
2. A discipline that has influenced group work (selected from your readings of the literature). Give reasons why.
3. The aspects of group work that are not covered in the literature. Select one or two readings and state the missing aspect in each. This missing aspect can be based upon your own group work with older adults, or it can be an omission you have discerned in your reading of the literature.

## EXERCISE 2

To test your understanding of the cognitive ability and the physical and emotional requirements necessary for group participation, write a one-paragraph description of a person you would place in each of the following groups. For each individual, state cognitive level, physical abilities, and emotional requirements.

- Reality orientation group
- Remotivation group
- Reminiscing group
- Music therapy group
- Art therapy or poetry group
- Health-related group
- Psychotherapy group

## REFERENCES

Anderson, E., and A. Andrew. 1973. Senior citizens health conferences. *Nursing Outlook* 21 (September): 580–82.

Applbaum, R., E. Bodaken, K. Sereno, and K. Anatol. 1974. *The process of group communication.* Chicago: Science Research Associates.

Bales, R. F. 1951. *Interaction process analysis.* Chicago: University of Chicago Press.

Blake, D. 1973. Group work with the institutionalized elderly. In *Psychosocial nursing care of the aged.* 1st ed., I. Burnside. ed. New York: McGraw-Hill.

Bloom, S. 1972. Sensitivity training with elderly. Paper presented at Ninth International Congress of Gerontology, Kiev, USSR, July 2–7.

Bright, R. 1981. Music therapy as a socializing and reorienting influence for the aged. *Programme, Twelfth International Congress of Gerontology.* Hamburg, Germany.

Brody, E., and L. Gottesman. 1974. Issues in institutional care. In *A social work guide for long-term care.* Rockville, Md.: National Institute of Mental Health.

Burnside, I. 1970a. Group work with the aged: Selected literature. Part 1. *The Gerontologist* 10(3): 241–46 (Autumn).

_____. 1970b. Loss: A constant theme in group work with the aged. *Hospital and Community Psychiatry* 21(6): 173–77 (June).

_____. 1973. Long-term group work with hospitalized aged. In *Psychosocial nursing care of the aged.* 1st ed., ed. I. Burnside. New York: McGraw-Hill.

_____. 1975. Overview of group work with the elderly. Paper presented at Nursing Symposium, Tenth International Congress of Gerontology, Jerusalem, Israel, June 24.

_____. 1977. Reality testing—An important concept. *Association of Rehabilitation Nurses Journal* 11(3): 3–9 (May–June).

Burnside, I., J. Baumler, and S. Weaverdyck. 1981. A model for group work with confused elderly in a day care center. *Programme, Twelfth International Congress of Gerontology.* Hamburg, Germany.

Butler, R., and M. Lewis. 1974. Life-review therapy: Putting memories to work in individual and group psychotherapy. *Geriatrics* 29(11): 165–73 (November).

_____. 1982. *Aging and mental health.* 3d ed. St. Louis: Mosby.

Causey, R. 1969. *Scientific Progress Texas Engineering and Science Magazine.* October: 24.

Conte, A., M. Brandzel, and S. Whitehead. 1974. Group work with hypertensive patients. *American Journal of Nursing* 74(5): 910–12 (May).

Corey, J., and M. Corey. 1977. Groups with the elderly. In *Groups: Process and practice.* Monterey, Calif.: Brooks/Cole.

Finkel, S. I. 1982. Experiences of a private practice psychiatrist working with the elderly in the community. *International Journal of Mental Health* 8(3–4): 147–72.

Finkel, S., and W. Fillmore. 1971. Experiences with an older adult in a private psychiatric hospital. *Journal of Geriatric Psychiatry* 4(2):188–99 (Spring).

Furukawa, C., and D. Shomaker. 1982. *Community health services for the aged.* Rockville, Md.: Aspen Systems Corporation.

Gaitz, C. 1975. Rehabilitation of the elderly: Mental health aspects. Paper given at the Tenth International Congress of Gerontology, Jerusalem, Israel, June 22–27.

Gillin, L. 1973. Factors affecting process and content in older adult groups. In *Psychosocial nursing care of the aged.* 1st ed., ed. I. Burnside. New York: McGraw-Hill.

Glasser, W. 1965. *Reality therapy: A new approach to psychiatry.* New York: Harper & Row.

Goldfarb, A. 1971. Group therapy with the old and aged. In *Comprehensive group psychotherapy.* ed. H. Kaplan and B. Sadock. Baltimore: Williams & Wilkins.

Götestam, K. G. 1980. Behavioral and dynamic psychotherapy with the elderly. In *Handbook of mental health and aging,* ed. J. Birren and B. Sloane, 787. Englewood Cliffs, N.J.: Prentice-Hall.

Gottesman, K., C. Quarterman, and G. Cohn. 1973. Psychosocial treatment of the aged. In *The psychology of adult development and aging,* ed. C. Eisdorfer and M. Lawton. Washington, D.C.: American Psychological Association.

Harbert, A., and L. Ginsberg. 1979. *Human services for older adults.* Belmont, Calif.: Wadsworth.

Hardy, M., and M. Conway. 1978. *Role theory.* New York: Appleton-Century-Crofts.

Hartford, M. 1972. *Groups in social-work.* New York: Columbia University Press.

Heller, V. 1970. Handicapped patients talk together. *American Journal of Nursing* 70(2):332–35 (February).

Hennessey, M. 1976a. Group work with economically independent aged. In *Nursing and the aged.* 1st ed., ed. I. Burnside. New York: McGraw-Hill.

_____. 1976b. Music and group work with the aged. In *Nursing and the aged.* 1st ed., ed. I. Burnside. New York: McGraw-Hill.

Herr, J. 1976. Psychology of aging: An overview. In *Nursing and the aged.* 1st ed., ed. I. Burnside. New York: McGraw-Hill.

Holland, D. 1973. Co-leadership with a group of stroke patients. In *Psychosocial nursing care of the aged.* 1st ed., ed. I. Burnside. New York: McGraw-Hill.

Holtzen, V. 1973. Short-term group work in a rehabilitation hospital. In *Psychosocial nursing care of the aged.* 1st ed., ed. I. Burnside. New York: McGraw-Hill.

Janosik, E., and J. Miller. 1982. Group work with the elderly. In *Life cycle group work in nursing.* ed. E. Janosik and L. Phipps. Belmont, Calif.: Wadsworth.

Johnston, N. 1965. Group reading as a treatment tool with geriatrics. *American Journal of Occupational Therapy* 19(4): 192–95 (July–August).

Kahana, B. 1975. Training the aged for 'competent coping'—A psychotherapeutic strategy. Paper presented at Tenth International Congress of Gerontology, Jerusalem, Israel, June 22–27.

Kaplan, J. 1953. *A social program for older people.* Minneapolis: University of Minnesota Press.

Kennedy, B. 1975. The rehabilitation of the elderly: The role of the therapist. Speech given at Tenth International Congress of Gerontology, Jerusalem, Israel, June 22–27.

Koch, K. 1977. *I never told anybody.* New York: Random House.

Kubie, S., and G. Landau. 1953. *Group work with the aged.* New York: International Universities Press.

Lewin, K. 1948. *Resolving social conflicts: Selected papers on group dynamics.* New York: Harper & Row.

Liederman, P., and V. Liederman. 1967. Group therapy: An approach to problems of geriatric out-patients. *Current Psychiatric Therapy* 7:179–85.

Lifton, W. 1972. *Groups: Facilitating individual growth and societal change.* New York: Wiley.

Linden, M. 1953. Group psychotherapy with institutionalized senile women: Study in gerontological human relations. *International Journal of Group Psychotherapy* 3:150–70.

_____. 1956. Geriatrics. In *The fields of group psychotherapy,* ed. S. R. Slaven. New York: Schocken.

Lopata, H. 1975. On widowhood: Grief work and identity reconstruction. *Journal of Geriatric Psychiatry.* 8(1): 41–56.

Lowy, L. 1979. *Social work with the aging.* New York: Harper & Row.

Luft, J. 1963. *Group process: An introduction to group dynamics.* Palo Alto, Calif.: National Press.

Marram, G. 1973. *The group approach in nursing practice.* St. Louis: Mosby.

Miller, M. 1975. Remotivation therapy: A way to reach the confused elderly patient. *Journal of Gerontological Nursing* 1(2): 28–31 (May–June).

Morrison, J. 1973. Group therapy for high utilizers of clinic facilities. In *Psychosocial nursing care of the aged.* 1st ed., ed. I. Burnside. New York: McGraw-Hill.

Murphy, L. 1969. A health discussion group for the elderly. In *ANA clinical conferences.* Atlanta, Ga.: Appleton-Century-Crofts.

Olmsted, M. 1959. *The small group.* New York: Random House.

Parkes, C. 1965. Bereavement and mental illness: A clinical study of the grief of bereaved psychiatric patients. *British Journal of Medical Psychology* 38(1): 1–26.

Pinney, E. 1970. *A first group psychotherapy book.* Springfield, Ill.: Thomas.

Ruitenbeck, H. 1970. *The new group therapies.* New York: Avon.

Rustin, S., and R. Wolk. 1963. The use of specialized group psychotherapy techniques in a home for the aged. *Group Psychotherapy* 16(1–2):25–29 (March –June).

Schwartz, W., and A. Papas. 1968. Verbal communication in therapy. *Psychomatics* 9 (March/ April): 71–74.

Shere, E. 1964. Group therapy with the very old. In *New thoughts on old age,* ed. R. Kastenbaum. New York: Springer.

Silverman, P. 1969. The widow-to-widow program: An experiment in preventive intervention. *Mental Hygiene* 53(3): 333–37 (July).

_____. 1976. *If you will lift the load . . . I will lift it too: A guide to the creation of a widowed to widowed service in your community.* Hakensack, N.J.: Gutterman-Musicant-Krietzman (P.O. Box 648).

Stange, A. 1973. Around the kitchen table: Group work on a back ward. In *Psychosocial nursing care of the aged.* 1st ed., ed. I. Burnside. New York: McGraw-Hill.

Stevens, N., and M. Wimmers. 1979. Encounter groups from a life cycle perspective. In *Recent advances in gerontology,* 622. Tokyo, Japan: International Congress of Gerontology.

Stewart, J. 1976. Scribo-therapy: Meaningful words from the mentally-impaired. Paper presented at the Twenty-Ninth Annual Scientific Meeting of the Gerontological Society, New York, October 13–17.

Taulbee, L., and J. Folsom. 1966. Reality orientation for geriatric patients. *Hospital and Community Psychiatry* 175:133–35.

ter Haar, H. 1972. Adaptation therapy for psycho-geriatric patients. Paper presented at Ninth International Congress of Gerontology, Kiev, USSR, July 2–7.

U.S. Bureau of the Census. 1975. *Current population reports.* Series P-20, no. 287. Washington, D.C.: U.S. Government Printing Office.

Valentine, L. 1970. Self-care through group learning. *American Journal of Nursing* 70(10): 2140–42 (October).

Verwoerdt, A. 1976. *Clinical geropsychiatry.* Baltimore: Williams & Wilkins.

Weber, B. 1981. Folk art as therapy. *American Journal of Art Therapy* 20(2): 47–52 (January).

*Webster's new twentieth century dictionary.* 1976. New York: Collins & World.

Weinstock, C., and M. Weiner. 1972. Community aged in problem-solving groups. Paper presented at Ninth International Congress of Gerontology, Kiev, USSR, July 2–7.

## BIBLIOGRAPHY

Burnside, I. 1969. Group work among the aged. *Nursing Outlook* 17(6): 68–72 (June).

_____. 1969. Sensory stimulation: An adjunct to group work with the disabled aged. *Mental Hygiene* 33(3): 381–88 (July).

_____. 1970. Communication problems in group work with the disabled aged. In *American Nurses' Association Clinical Conference.* New York: Appleton-Century-Crofts.

_____. 1971. Long-term group work with the hospitalized aged. Part 1. *The Gerontologist* 11(3): 213–18 (Autumn).

Burnside, I. 1976. Overview of group work with the aged. *Journal of Gerontological Nursing* 2(6): 14–17 (November–December).

D'Afflitti, J., and G. Weitz. 1974. Rehabilitating the stroke patient through patient-family groups. *Journal of Group Psychotherapy* 24(3): 323–32 (July).

Godbole, A., and J. Verinis. 1974. Brief psychotherapy in the treatment of emotional disorders in physically ill geriatric patients. *The Gerontologist* 14(2): 143–48 (April).

Guarino, S., and C. Knowlton. 1980. Planning and implementing a group health program on sexuality for the elderly. *Journal of Gerontological Nursing* 6(10): 600–603 (October).

Hayter, J. 1983. Modifying the environment to help older persons. *Nursing and Health Care* 4(5): 265–69 (May).

Hennessey, M. 1975. Use of music in group work with the elderly. Paper presented at workshop entitled Group Work with the Elderly, Andrus Gerontology Center, University of Southern California, Los Angeles, April 5.

Johnson, E. 1975. Health education and the elderly. *Midwife Health Visit Community Nurse* 11(3): 71–73 (March).

Levine, B., and M. Poston. 1980. A modified group treatment for elderly narcissistic patients. *International Journal of Group Psychotherapy* 30(2): 153–67 (April).

Mayadas, N., and D. Link. 1974. Group work with the aging: An issue for social work education. Part 1. *The Gerontologist* 14(5): 440–45 (October).

McKibbin, G. 1975. Social group work practice with the elderly: A conceptual perspective. Paper presented at the session entitled Social Group Work Practice with the Elderly, September 29, sponsored by the National Association of Social Workers during the annual meeting of the National Council on Aging, Washington, D.C.

McMahon, A., and P. Rhudick. 1964. Reminiscing: Adaptational significance in the aged. *Archives of General Psychiatry* 19(3): 292–98 (March).

Mummah, H. 1975. Group work with the aged blind Japanese in the nursing home and in the community. *The New Outlook for the Blind* 69(4): 160–64 (April).

_____. 1976. Fingers to see. *American Journal of Nursing* 76(10): 1608–10 (October).

Nevruz, N., and M. Hrushka. 1969. The influence of unstructured and structured group psychotherapy with geriatric patients on their decision to leave the hospital. *International Journal of Group Psychotherapy* 19:72–79.

Nolter, M. 1973. Drama for the elderly: They can do it. *The Gerontologist* 13(2): 153–56 (Summer).

Petrov, I., and L. Vlahijska. 1972. Cultural therapy in the old people's home. *The Gerontologist* 12(4): 429–34 (Winter).

Petty, B., J. Tamerra, P. Moeller, and R. Campbell. 1976. Support groups for elderly persons in the community. *The Gerontologist* 16(6): 522–28 (December).

Rosin, A. 1975. Group discussions: A therapeutic tool in a chronic disease hospital. *Geriatrics* 30 (August): 45–48.

Schmidt, M. 1982. Groups for the chronically ill. In *Life cycle group work in nursing,* ed. E. Janosik and L. Phipps. Belmont, Calif.: Wadsworth.

Wolff, K. 1962. Group psychotherapy with geriatric patients in a psychiatric hospital: Six-year study. *Journal of the American Geriatrics Society* 10: 1077–80.

_____. 1963. Individual psychotherapy with geriatric patients. *Diseases of the Nervous System* 24: 688–91.

_____. 1967. Comparison of group and individual psychotherapy with geriatric patients. *Diseases of the Nervous System* 28:384–86.

_____. 1971. Individual psychotherapy with geriatric patients. *Psychosomatics* 12:89–93.

Wolk, R. L., and A. I. Goldfarb. 1967. The response to group psychotherapy of aged recent admissions compared with long-term mental hospital patients. *American Journal of Psychiatry* 123:1251–57.

Yalom, I. 1975. 2d ed. *The theory and practice of group psychotherapy.* New York: Basic Books.

Yalom, I., and F. Terrazas. 1968. Group therapy for psychotic elderly patients. *American Journal of Nursing* 68:1690–94.

## RESOURCES

### Films

*Tell Me Where to Turn* (color, 26 minutes, 1969). The story of the information and referral service: how it assists people who need help, and find it, through their local health and social welfare agencies.

# PART 2

# THEORETICAL FRAMEWORKS

BILL MEANS / ATOZ IMAGES

The aging process is attracting considerable interest from behavioral scientists and practitioners whose caseloads are increasingly heavy with elderly clients or patients. Part 2 offers four theoretical frameworks that can provide a foundation for group work with the elderly, as well as an example of an approach that incorporates a number of methods.

Group work with the elderly can embrace a variety of approaches. Although eclecticism makes group work challenging, such an approach may pose difficulties for inexperienced group leaders. New group leaders often do better within a more structured format—they want one theory to understand and put into practice.

Robert Butler, Myrna I. Lewis, Maurice Linden, William Schutz, and Irvin Yalom are theorists in the field of group therapy. Butler and Linden are geropsychiatrists, Lewis is a social worker, Schutz is a psychologist, and Yalom is a psychiatrist. They have long been quoted, so their contributions are considered in Part 2. Butler, Lewis, and Linden have worked with the aged; however, all four of the theoretical frameworks are applicable to group work with the elderly and have been synthesized in short chapters.

Chapter 3 focuses on Linden's group psychotherapy research. Although his writings about group work with institutionalized women have become classics, they remain as fresh and applicable as when they were first published in the 1950s.

Chapter 4 reprints a classic article focusing on Lewis's and Butler's extensive experience in life review and reminiscing therapy. This chapter sets the stage for an entire section later in the book on reminiscing therapy (Part 5). Although the authors discuss the use of memories in a one-to-one relationship, the information is applicable to group work, which is often based on a one-to-one relationship prior to group attendance.

Chapter 5 is an extrapolation of theory from Yalom's excellent book, *The Theory and Practice of Group Psychotherapy*. Roles of the leader and the "curative factors" based on Yalom's research are emphasized.

Schutz's theoretical framework for group therapy is called Fundamental Interpersonal Orientation (often shortened to FIRO). Chapter 6 covers inclusion, control, and affection as they apply to older group members.

In Chapter 7 two nurses and a psychologist describe a group they initiated at an adult day care center in California. The group consisted of Alzheimer clients and multi-infarct dementias. The chapter is included in this section of the book because it describes an eclectic blend of a variety of group methods. The format could be used for groups of confused elders in other settings.

All the theorists in this section have several things in common: strong theoretical bases; an inquisitive, observing approach to behavior in groups; and a practical, humanistic attitude essential in group work. The importance of such an attitude in group work with the elderly cannot be overstressed; unfortunately, it is sometimes obscured by overemphasis on theory and/or research or by poor staffing.

## chapter 3

# Principles of
# Group Therapy
# by Linden

*Irene Burnside*

*The therapist's mode of
managing . . . is to create out of
himself, out of the treatment
situation, and out of the group
a "good" reality.*

MAURICE E. LINDEN (1955, 64)

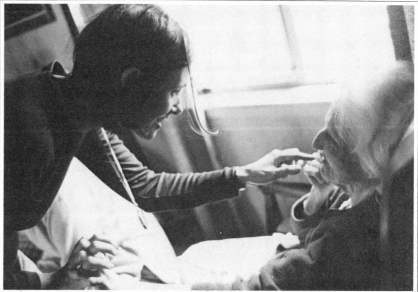

© KAREN R. PREUSS/JEROBOAM, INC.

## LEARNING OBJECTIVES

- Discuss Maurice Linden's pioneer research in group psychotherapy.
- List five outcomes of therapeutic intervention in group.
- Compare and contrast the group led by Burnside with the one led by Linden.
- Define **dual leadership**.
- Discuss five considerations in the development of a contract between co-therapists.
- List four indicators that a group leader may need supervision.
- Write six questions co-leaders might ask one another before beginning co-therapy.

## KEY WORDS

- A ''good'' reality
- Catalytic
- Contract
- Co-therapist
- Co-therapy
- Dual leadership
- Group psychotherapy
- Psychotic
- Regressed

Beginning leaders of groups of elderly people often think that they have discovered new principles of group work. However, a thorough search of the literature in different disciplines would reveal that many of the dynamics of group work have already been discovered, refined, and published. Maurice Linden's three articles (1953, 1954, 1955) on his group psychotherapy with elderly women on the back ward of a state hospital in the early 1950s are classic examples.

Although Linden wrote the articles many years ago, his words are still marvelously fresh. All that dates the articles is his frequent use of the term *senile,* which most group workers are determined to banish from their vocabularies. (Indeed, Linden himself cautioned against promiscuous use of the term in his 1955 paper.) The articles are still recommended reading for group psychotherapists working with regressed and/or psychotic aged individuals. This chapter discusses a number of principles derived from Linden's articles that are applicable to group work with the elderly in extended care facilities or day care centers.

## PRINCIPLES OF GROUP PSYCHOTHERAPY

Linden's first article, "Group Psychotherapy with Institutionalized Senile Women: Study in Gerontologic Human Relations," contains several statements that are relevant to group work with the aged.

1. Modification of behavior does occur in group work with the aged (p. 152). Because modification of behavior in the aged may be slight or slow in appearing or both, leaders may fail to realize the impact of their leadership and the catalytic quality of the group.

2. In state hospitals an interested, alert, resident staff makes therapies available to younger hospital patients; old patients receive little more than custodial care (p. 152). During my own group work in a state hospital, I learned from the staff during coffee breaks that working on the geriatric ward was used as punitive measure; if staff members—at any level—got out of line, they were immediately assigned to the geriatric unit. I have observed this managerial tactic throughout my years of nursing and have seen it occur in the acute care hospitals too. The geriatric ward is apparently considered the Siberia of the medical continent. According to Linden, the staff's attitude is "why disturb their natural decline by intervention?" (p. 153). This attitude, which is often encountered today, is a license to do nothing at all. Sometimes staff members and administrators are less than enthusiastic about reality orientation and reality-testing programs because "they [the residents] seem so happy in their confused state" (p. 153).

3. The atmosphere of state hospitals can be one of "resignation, futility, and decadence. Traditionally admission to a senile building has been a prelude to a morgue. The depressing inactivity of the typical senile ward completed the disillusionment, melancholy, and hopelessness of the aged and furnished the additional impetus toward abject regression" (p. 153). Today this statement applies particularly to extended care facilities, which abound with former state hospital patients. An additional burden for such patients is the stress of environmental change. Many U.S. state hospitals are located in pastoral settings, with trees, birds, and space. Contemporary extended care facilities are usually in the inner city or in noisy suburbs.

4. "Hospital discharges alone do not reflect the actual degree of response to therapy" (p. 153). This point is especially important to remember during group work with regressed residents because the leader may become discouraged by the seemingly insignificant changes.

5. Four important areas to evaluate in such a group are mood, alertness, memory, and orientation (p. 154). The leader who has not carefully assessed mood, alertness, memory, and orientation can describe some of the consequences. (See Chapter 10, on group membership, and also Chapter 9, on contracts.) I recall one lovely elderly woman with many social graces and much poise who never remembered who I was from one meeting to another. The fluctuation in these four areas from meeting to meeting does seem to keep the leader more alert.

6. Therapeutic intervention assists in the "resolution of depressive affects, increases alertness, diminishes confusion, improves orientation, and replenishes memory hiati, all this being reflected in bettering of the many minute factors inherent in ward socialization" (p. 154). Chapter 13 discusses in depth the change in mood I saw in a group of six regressed old people even within a couple of months after launching the group.

7. Senility "is the logical culmination of the combined social rejection of the late mature person and the senescent person's self-rejection" (p. 154). How little we have done thus far to banish the pejorative word *senility* and to raise the self-esteem of the aged.

All of these statements are as relevant for group work today in extended care facilities or day care centers as they were for Linden's state hospital residents. I compared and contrasted Linden's group of aged women and a group I led alone for 14 months in a light mental facility. (Light mental facilities are unique to the state of California. They provided locked quarters for persons who are unmanageable—for example, suicidal persons, arsonists, wanderers—in the nursing home.) My group was comprised of six persons, three men and three women, all of whom were diagnosed as chronic brain syndrome. Table 3–1 through 3–4 show the results of my analysis. Although Linden's

TABLE 3-1.  Positive and negative criteria used by Linden and Burnside for admittance to groups

| Positive criteria used by Linden (after Slavson) | Positive criteria used by Burnside (compared with Linden's) |
|---|---|
| Expressed desire to join the group | Given choice; could attend and leave later if wanted to |
| Appearance of relative alertness | No |
| A fair degree of good personal hygiene | Not considered |
| Ability to understand English | Same |
| Ability to walk or to be wheeled to the meeting | Same |
| At least a minimal range of emotions | No |
| Evidence of some degree of adult adjustment prior to entrance into senile state | Unable to secure data to assess |
| Capacity for evoking interest and affection from nursing and attendant personnel | Not considered |
| Sardonic hostility | Not considered |
| *Negative criteria used by Linden* | *Negative criteria used by Burnside* |
| Dementia | All diagnosed chronic brain syndrome or "senile" |
| Advanced physical debility | Accepted many |
| Systematized and chronic paranoia throughout life | Did not apply |
| Manic behavior | Did not apply |
| Intense chronic hositility with assaultiveness | Same |
| Unremitting bowel and bladder incontinence | Same |
| Advanced deafness | Accepted one very deaf woman |
| Monothematic hypochondriasis | Did not apply |
| Undirected restlessness with inability to sit still | Same |
| Unwillingness to participate | Same |
| Inability to understand English | Same |

group was large (40 to 51) and mine small, the similarities are obvious.

I have certainly benefited, as have many others, from Linden's writings and philosophy about the elderly. His courage in leading groups of demented women on a back ward in a state hospital inspired me to work with such individuals. I do not believe, however, that I could have led a group of 40 women (even with the best of co-leaders). For that alone, one must admire Linden.

What I learned from studying Linden's works about the groups he led was that there were things I simply could not do, so I made adaptations. I think that this is the crux of group work with the elderly: One does have to make refinements and adaptations. There is

probably no model that will perfectly fit a setting different from the one in which that group work was done.

I also found that I could not employ the deft, good-humored sarcasm that Linden used—gentle teasing, yes, but not sarcasm.

## DUAL LEADERSHIP

Linden's second article is entitled "The Significance of Dual Leadership in Gerontologic Group Psychotherapy: Studies in Gerontologic Human Relations III." In that article he uses the term *dual leadership* to describe what is currently called co-leadership or co-therapy, although his definition refers to male and female leaders.

TABLE 3–2.  Characteristics of Linden's and Burnside's group members

| Linden | Burnside |
|---|---|
| Mean age 70 (mode = 69). Three persons younger than 60; one member aged 89 at beginning of group. | Mean age 79 (mode = 79). Ages 64–82. No member younger than 60; one man aged 90 at end of group. |
| All were women. | Both men and women. |
| All were institutionalized. | All had been confined to nursing homes or light mental facilities from 2 weeks to 10 years. |
| All had needs inherent in pathological later maturity. | Severe physical disabilities plus mental problems, mostly depression. |
| All had virtually the same kind of care and daily experiences, since environmental factors could be fairly well controlled. | Same. |
| **Diagnoses** | **Diagnoses** |
| Psychosis with cerebral arteriosclerosis:  12<br>Involutional psychosis:  8     Schizophrenia:  6<br>Senile psychosis:  5     Paranoid condition:  4<br>Senile dementia:  3     Character neurosis:  2<br>Psychosis with intracranial neoplasm:  2 (operated)<br>Psychoneurosis:  1     Huntington's chorea:  1 | Male, 68: postfracture, right hip; ASCVD;[1] alcoholism with secondary OBS.[2]<br>Female, 82: ASCVD with CBS;[3] postfracture, right hip, with prosthesis; neurofibroma of scalp.<br>Male, 64: CBS associated with arteriosclerosis; secondary polyneuritis.<br>Female, 79: ASCVD with associated CBS.<br>Female, 81: ASCVD with associated CBS.<br>Male, 80: CBS due to arteriosclerosis; CNS[4] lues; blindness; anemia. |

1. Arteriosclerotic cardiovascular disease.          2. Organic brain syndrome.
3. Chronic brain syndrome.          4. Central nervous system disorder (syphilis).

The female leader in this instance was a registered nurse, and one can only wish that she, too, had written about her co-leadership experience. The nurse's role was somewhat serendipitous; she was supposed to be there when the male therapist "found it necessary to leave the therapy room occasionally to answer urgent telephone calls and attend emergencies" (p. 265). (In those days there was no outcry from the women's movement, and liberated nurses were few.)

However, we can still empathize with Linden. Of his experience during the first six months of the group work, before the nurse became his co-leader, he wrote, "The temptation to give up the group as an unsuccessful experiment was very strong" (p. 265). That strikes me as a really important sentence, especially since he ultimately wrote three articles about the experiment. New leaders, particularly young ones, are impatient and may be tempted to give up their group as an unsuccessful venture. They can learn from Linden's perseverance and leadership skill.

## Seating of Co-Leaders

Another point of interest in the 1954 article is the seating of the co-therapists during meetings. They sat side by side at a central table. (See Chapter 11, Figure 11–2a for an example of this type of seating.) Although the elderly women in the group certainly must have been impressed with the importance of the nurse because she sat so close to the authority figure on that ward, the arrangement leaves one wondering about communication between the leaders. Most group leaders find that sitting across from each other is most effective for continual group assessment, eye contact, and nonverbal messages. Also, in such a seating arrangement four group members can sit next to a leader. This advantage is important because it allows each leader to lessen the anxiety of members, to support grieving members, and to reach out and touch members. (There is no reference to the use of touch by either leader in any of the three articles by Linden.) The patients sitting next to the therapists can also be more easily

TABLE 3–3.  Type of groups led by Linden and Burnside

| Group characteristics | Linden | Burnside |
|---|---|---|
| Physical setting | Day hall | Half of dining room (folding door shut) |
| Number asked to join | 25 | 6 |
| Number later attending | 40 | 6 |
| Type of group | Open | Closed |
| Time of meetings | Twice weekly (1 hour) | Once weekly (45 minutes to 1 hour) |
| Duration of group | 2 years | 14 months |
| Group arrangement | Semicircles before table in tastefully decorated day room | Close circle; round table |
| Visitors welcomed (catalytic effect on group) | Yes | Yes |
| Staff in other disciplines visited | Yes | Never, although invited; group used as a teaching group for classes for 3 years; many disciplines represented among students |
| Group leader | Male ward psychiatrist | Psychiatric nurse (a volunteer) |
| Co-leader | In 6 months, ward nurse | None |
| Auxiliary leaders emerged | Yes | No |
| Formal approach | Yes | No |
| Rules | No violence or physical acting out; confidentiality | Basically none |

and quickly assessed for mood, group participation, anxiety, and nonverbal cues than those seated further away. Students in a group work class agreed that sitting next to the monopolizer in a group of aged people was helpful in decreasing the verbal flow of that member (Group Work with the Elderly 1976).

## Contracts Between Co-Therapists

Linden's dual leadership evolved out of necessity, not preplanning. Preplanning might be facilitated by use of a co-leader's questionnaire like this one developed by Clark (1977, 98–99).

What are your goals for this group?

What is your theoretical orientation to group leading?

How do you see yourself functioning in this group?

How do you see me functioning in this group?

What group-leader strengths do you think you have?

What group-leader weaknesses do you think you have?

What suggestions do you have for handling possible disagreements between us in the group?

Do you think we will try to compete with each other and, if so, how can we recognize and deal with this to keep it from interfering with group movement?

How do you feel about our seeking out supervision?

How could we present group data to a supervisor?

What are your thoughts about how we can deal with such group problems as monopolizing, scapegoating, silence, new members, transferences, physical aggression, nonverbal members, absences, and manipulation?

Today co-therapists generally make a contract between themselves before the group work begins. Reg Williams (1976) lists 10 considerations in the development of a contract between

TABLE 3-4.  Progress in Linden's and Burnside's groups

| Areas of progress | Linden | Burnside |
|---|---|---|
| In the beginning, group quiet | Yes | Yes |
| Gripe sessions | Yes | No |
| Deft, good-humored sarcasm | Yes | Never used; leader's role supportive; always took ego-enhancing stance (staff provided sarcasm) |
| Leaders patient and persevering | Yes | Yes |
| Welcomed any amount of complaining | Yes | Members rarely complained; often denied problems |
| Change in morale throughout building | Yes | Did not occur; interest in classes, groups began; reminiscing groups started later by licensed vocational nurse and activity directors |
| Strong affectional ties between group members | Yes | Yes |
| Group identity evolved | Yes | Yes |
| Cliques of patients formed | Yes | No |
| Saving things to tell the leader | Yes | Rarely |
| Improved personal appearances | Yes | Yes (perhaps partly due to the fierce pride the aides had in their assigned residents) |
| Both leaders complimented | Yes | Leader always responded |
| Method of group approach at one time or another "opportunistic group therapy" | Yes | Yes |
| Every opportunity for fun and laughter exploited to the fullest | Yes | Yes |
| Mutual support and protectiveness | Yes | Yes |
| Benefits through group dynamics other than verbal participation | Yes | Yes |

two therapists. The co-therapists: (1) must talk with their partners; (2) need to analyze the group process—the movement of the group members and of themselves; (3) need to know their own assets and limitations, so that they can build on the assets of the partner rather than exploit the limitations; (4) need to resist competitive temptations to be number one therapist in the group; (5) need to be accepting of their differences in therapeutic techniques and approaches; (6) need to ask for supervision or consultation; (7) need to clarify unclear messages sent by the partner; (8) must share honest feelings; (9) need to be willing to work out conflicts that arise between them; and (10) must practice what they preach.

Those 10 points seem simple, but that is deceptive. It is only after one has tried to put them into practice and has juggled the variables of the intense interpersonal relationship with a co-leader plus all the variables of group work that the complexity of the co-leader relationship becomes apparent. Preceptors of co-leaders often spend as much time working with the problems between the co-leaders as on the dynamics occurring within the group itself.

The leader probably needs supervision if she or he answers any of the following questions affirmatively (Clark 1977, 95):

Do problems arise in beginning a new group?
Are tension or anxiety levels in the group high?
Is conflict that is not useful proliferating?
Is the group apathetic?
Is decision making unilateral or fragmented?
Is leadership autocratic?
Is the group lacking in cohesiveness?

Does the group continue in the orientation phase for more than six sessions?

Do one or more members always monopolize group sessions?

Is one group member being scapegoated?

Are silences always broken by the leader?

Are new members about to enter the group?

Do group members leave the group abruptly?

Are members absent frequently?

Does physically aggressive behavior occur in the group?

Are group members primarily nonverbal?

Is the group approaching termination?

Does the group seem unable to reach its goals no matter what is tried?

The advantage of co-leadership in groups of the aged is that there is someone to take over during the times when one feels bogged down, bored, or unable to fulfill the commitments of the original contract with the group. Linden (1954, 266, 267) states:

> It is a common experience among organizers of gerontologic groups, formed for whatever purpose, that it is difficult to obtain a group *esprit* with aged people. . . . The elements characteristic of senility of vacillating amnesia, capricious disorientation, and variable confusion which may have presented an insurmountable obstacle to therapy were partially overcome by two factors: the spacing and frequency of the sessions and dual leadership. The first gave the group a predictable, routinized, serial continuity generating a rhythmic expectation in the participants. This allowed them to bind other realities as well to space-time guideposts.

Linden's second factor, dual leadership, tended to reinforce the first factor. The male therapist frequently had to miss meetings; then the nurse led the group. She was a benevolent authority on the ward, so she was a supportive and therapeutic factor in the interim between meetings.

## SUMMARY

This chapter discusses salient points made by Maurice Linden, one of the pioneers in group psychotherapy with the elderly. His writings are now classic and should be read by all those who intend to work with the regressed elderly. According to Linden, the emphasis in gerontological group psychotherapy should be on resocializing the individual and should promote tranquility, a chance for happiness, and a return to some self-sufficiency. An intelligent system of care and group management can help to decrease defenses and stimulate the return of object interest.

Co-leadership is termed *dual leadership* by Linden (1954). The nurse co-leader played an important role in his research study. The reader is referred to Figure 11–1 and 11–2 to contrast usual seating arrangements with that of Linden and his co-leader.

The contract between co-therapists is discussed in this chapter rather than in Chapter 9, which focuses on contracts between the leader and the group members. Communication, analysis of group process, self-awareness, reduction of power struggles, acceptance of each other, availability of consultation, clarification of the colleague's messages, sharing, and resolution of conflicts are all important in the contract between co-leaders.

It seems appropriate to end a chapter about Linden's work with a repetition of his excellent admonition for all group leaders working with the aged: The leader's focus should be to "create a 'good' reality" for and from the group.

## EXERCISE 1

Describe how you think Linden or the nurse co-leader went about accomplishing a "'good' reality" out of themselves and the treatment situation in the groups they led. Discuss how sarcasm might have been used by Linden.

## EXERCISE 2

Relate the points discussed by Reg Williams regarding contracts between leaders to Maurice Linden and his co-leader. Are any of those 10 considerations discussed in any of Linden's articles? Describe.

## REFERENCES

Clark, C. 1977. *The nurse as group leader.* New York: Springer.

Group work with the elderly. 1976. Class session, San Francisco State University. San Francisco, October 30.

Linden, M. E. 1953. Group psychotherapy with institutionalized senile women: Study in gerontologic human relations. *International Journal of Group Psychotherapy* 3:150–70.

_____. 1954. The significance of dual leadership in gerontologic group psychotherapy: Studies in gerontologic human relations III. *International Journal of Group Psychotherapy* 4:262–73.

_____. 1955. Transference in gerontologic group psychotherapy: Studies in gerontologic human relations IV. *International Journal of Group Psychotherapy* 5:61–79.

Williams, R. A. 1976. A contract for co-therapists in group psychotherapy. *Journal of Psychiatric Nursing and Mental Health Services* 14(6):11–14 (June).

## BIBLIOGRAPHY

Dick, B., K. Lesser, and J. Whiteside. 1980. A developmental framework in co-therapy. *International Journal of Group Psychotherapy* 30(3): 273–85 (July).

Getty, C. and A. M. Shannon. 1969. Co-therapy as an egalitarian relationship. *American Journal of Nursing* 69 (April): 1482–85.

Goldfarb, A. I. 1971. Group therapy with the old and aged. In *Comprehensive group psychotherapy,* ed. H. J. Kaplan and B. Sadock. Baltimore: Williams & Wilkins.

Linden, M. E., and D. Courtney. 1953. The human life cycle and its interruptions: Studies in gerontologic human relations I. *American Journal of Psychiatry* 109(12): 906–15 (June).

_____. 1956. Geriatrics. In *The fields of group psychotherapy,* ed. S. R. Slavson. New York: International Universities Press.

_____. 1962. The emotional problems of aging. In *Psychiatry in medicine,* ed. N. Brill. Berkeley: University of California Press.

_____. 1963. The aging and the community. *Geriatrics* 18:404–10.

Maizler, J. S., and J. R. Solomon. 1976. Therapeutic group process with the institutionalized elderly. *Journal of the American Geriatric Society* 24: 542–46.

Msyzka, M. A., and D. Josefiak. 1973. Development of the co-therapy relationship. *Journal of Psychiatric Nursing* 11 (May–June): 27–31.

Rustin, S. L., and R. L. Wolk. 1963. The use of specialized group psychotherapy techniques in a home for the aged. *Group Psychotherapy* 16(1–2): 25–29 (March–June).

chapter 4

# Life-Review Therapy: Putting Memories to Work

*Myrna I. Lewis and Robert N. Butler*

*Everyone has a story to tell—if
only someone would listen
if only someone would ask.*

SOURCE UNKNOWN

## LEARNING OBJECTIVES

- Define **life review**.

- Describe four methods for evoking memories in older persons.

- Give one reason why a therapist would **not** use life-review therapy.

- Define **catastrophic reaction**.

- Discuss reminiscence as a defense or a weapon.

- Define **social suicide**.

- Compare and contrast the behavior of young and old group members in an intergenerational group.

## KEY WORDS

- Emotions

- Group psychotherapy

- Individual psychotherapy

- Life-review therapy

- Memories

- Psychotherapeutic intervention

- Reminiscence

- Sharing

Consideration of the developmental stages of late life must be part of any psychotherapy with older persons. Yet, surprisingly little theory has been formulated and used for this purpose. What do older people experience as they age? Are there predictable feelings that reflect this last phase of the life cycle? After observing older persons clinically and in research situations, Butler postulated in 1961 the presence of the life review as a prominent developmental occurrence of late life. Since that time, we have been experimenting with the use of the life review in individual and group psychotherapy.

The life review is seen as a universal mental process brought about by the realization of approaching dissolution and death. It marks the lives of all older persons in some manner as their myths of invulnerability or immortality give way and death begins to be viewed as an imminent personal reality. The life review is characterized by the progressive return to consciousness of past experiences and, particularly, the resurgence of unresolved conflicts.

The tendency of older persons to reminisce about the past has often been dismissed derogatorily as living in the past, second childhood, or senility or, somewhat more sympathetically, as an expression of loneliness, absence of new experience, or tenacious clinging to a previous identity. It is regarded as boring, time-consuming, and meaningless. But the predilection toward reminiscence appears to have a much more positive function, a psychotherapeutic one, in which the older person reflects on his life in order to resolve, reorganize, and reintegrate what is troubling or preoccupying him.

In its natural state, the life review is spontaneous, often quite unselective, and occurs in younger persons as well (for example, in adolescence, in middle age, and in the face of death). However, it takes on a striking intensity in early old age. Older persons comment with surprise on their ability to recall previous life events with sudden and remarkable clarity: "It's as though it happened only yesterday;" "I felt as though I was there." They may have memories of smell, taste, and feel as well as sight and sound. The capacity for free association seems to be renewed, bringing up memories deeply buried in the unconscious.

This chapter was first published in 1974 as an article in *Geriatrics* 29(11): 165–73 (November). It is reprinted with the kind permission of *Geriatrics* and of Myrna I. Lewis and Robert N. Butler.

Some persons are fully aware of the process and openly state a desire to "put my life in order," while others are only dimly conscious of something compelling them to muse about the past. Still others are totally unaware, perhaps in an unconscious attempt to avoid the pain of unpleasant memories or to protect themselves against the stereotype of living in the past.

The emotions accompanying the life review vary, but an element of pain and discomfort often arises as problems surface. The intensity of the experience may range from a mild nostalgia, reminiscing, and storytelling to a feverish preoccupation, sometimes centered on a particular subject. The person may feel compelled to give his entire life story to anyone who will listen. Past happenings may be repeated over and over again. Since repetition and emphasis on the past also are seen in brain-damaged persons, it is important to observe diagnostically whether the compulsion to repeat can be abated by the resolution of underlying issues.

## INDIVIDUAL PSYCHOTHERAPY

Life-review therapy is action oriented and psychoanalytically influenced. In individual psychotherapy, the life review obviously is not a process initiated by the therapist. Rather, the therapist taps into an already ongoing self-analysis and participates in it with the older person. The outward manifestations of life review are varied. Persons may present themselves as garrulous, agitated, or depressed. They may actively reach out for others or quietly or angrily withdraw. Some appear passive, effectively masking an active life review. Any indication that the person is not viewing something for the first time can be a clue, including such statements as: "Yes, that has been going through my mind," or, "Lately I've been worrying about that."

The purpose of psychotherapeutic intervention into the life review is to enhance it, to make it more conscious, deliberate, and efficient. Therapy begins at the first contact with the gathering of information. History taking or the collecting of facts about an older person can trigger memories of conflict and concern, providing important diagnostic perceptions. The emotional impact of the memories, the emphasis or de-emphasis of crucial areas of memory, and repetitious patterns of remembering can be observed. Some parts of the older person's past may be of little interest to him simply because difficulties have been resolved and the potential benefits of remembering are not worth the effort. Other topics have been buried out of reach of conscious memory because of fear or guilt and should be reviewed and resolved.

We have devised several methods of evoking memory in older persons that are useful and often enjoyable to them.

### Written or Taped Autobiographies

We frequently ask older patients to compile an autobiography, which may be as long and as detailed as they wish. This is an interesting and relatively nonthreatening way to open up communication. Again, the therapist searches for clues in the style, detail, and emphasis that a person gives to various aspects of his life. Omissions must be examined. For instance, one man provided an intricate history of his professional and social life, with newspaper clippings, letters from important persons, and pictures of himself and his wife. There was nothing about his two children except for several news items on their graduations and weddings. Upon questioning, the patient revealed that the son, then 45 years old, had not spoken to his parents in 20 years and that the daughter had minimal contact. The focus of therapy became the parents' buried feelings toward these estrangements.

We also have used the autobiography in therapy with younger persons, suggesting that they go to their elders with tape recorder or pencil and pad to talk over family history, personalities in the family, and childhood reminiscences. Younger family members often become intrigued with such efforts and begin to look to their elders as important sources of information. We have seen profound changes in family communications as old and young take a mutual interest in their past.

In addition to aiding memory, the tape recorder is useful for playing back therapy sessions. The older person begins to pick up on his own areas of conflict, to hear what may be boring and repetitious in his manner, and to generally take an outsider's look at himself, sometimes for the first time. Self-confrontation in front of a mirror also is helpful. Many are surprised at what they project to others and, as a result, deliberately begin to alter their behavior or appearance.

## Pilgrimages (in person or through correspondence)

For those persons for whom this is possible, we encourage actual trips back to the location of their birth, childhood, youth, and young adult life. Taking photographs and notes is useful. Even for persons who make such journeys as a matter of course to visit friends and relatives, we emphasize a new use of their time to rediscover the past by recalling and talking over old times with family, neighbors, and friends.

Some people go with a specific purpose. One older woman returned to her childhood home to discover why she was forbidden to go into the attic as a youngster. She discovered that there had never been any stairs, only a hole in the ceiling, thus explaining her parents' "arbitrary" refusal. She recalled many fantasies of what might be in the attic and her anger at her parents for forbidding her to look.

Others make the journey home through correspondence or even through talking with others who have recently been there. These efforts reflect a search both for continuity and for late-life discoveries regarding preceptions of the past.

For example, after talking with persons who had known him in his childhood town, a 69-year-old man decided that he had purposefully tried to make himself into a "noble image" as a little boy. "I was orphaned at nine years of age," he recalled. "I was so scared that I decided to be the best boy there was. To avoid the orphan home secluded behind high brick walls, I vowed to go to church and Sunday school and never to swear, smoke, drink, steal, cheat, or hurt persons or animals. I would work hard to buy presents for everyone, scrub the floors, shovel snow, and split wood. The formula seemed to work, and the philosophy gained a strong hold on me. People tell me I never grieved openly or got angry. Now I'm understanding why I'm still such a damn nice guy all the time."

## Reunions

Annual reunions (high school and college classes, family, church, and so forth) offer a unique opportunity for the intensification of the life review. An individual can look at himself in the context of other meaningful people and take a measure of where he stands in the course of the life cycle as the years pass. Reunions usually are bittersweet experiences. One woman in her eighties met regularly with her college classmates, and only two of them were left when she died. She both mourned the loss of her peers and rejoiced in her own survival. Reunions that occur on a regular basis provide a gradual adjustment to change, but ones that take place irregularly can have a shock effect ("My God, I didn't realize how many years have gone by!").

## Genealogy

We encourage the interest many older persons begin to take in their own parents and grandparents, as well as distant ancestors, as they strive to find themselves in history and to take comfort in the fact that they are part of a long line of relatives. One of the ways the old seem to resolve fears of death is to gain a sense of other family members having died before them. This reflects the search for universality, a sense of the long chain of birth and death, and the basic fairness of each person having a life to live that must eventually be given up.

Some older persons have put ads in newspapers in search of relatives or family information. Others visit cemeteries to look for family names and dates. Local libraries, town and church records, and family bibles also are sources of data.

## Scrapbooks, Photo Albums, Old Letters, and Other Memorabilia

These are rich sources of information and memory. We frequently ask older persons to bring such items to therapy sessions, where we go through them together. This is an especially pleasant form of interviewing for the older person and quickly establishes positive rapport. Even persons with moderate brain damage can remember many details through pictures and keepsakes. On visits to older persons at home or in nursing homes or hospitals, the therapist can learn a good deal by commenting on pictures, momentos, or other personal items that are likely to have emotional meaning.

Some persons compile scrapbooks and albums in old age. This is helpful in summing up their own lives and handing on a family record to the next generation.

## Summation of Life Work

This is a particularly useful technique for persons whose work was important to them and for those who have no children or have had little contact with their children. Persons without familes have an especially keen need to feel they have participated meaningfully in the world. We ask people for a verbal or written summation of their work that will reflect what they regard as their contribution and also the history of their particular craft as they experienced it. Some of these summations have grown into full-scale books or published poetry and music.

## Preserving Ethnic Identity

Many older persons have an ethnic identity that has been ignored or forgotten. In many instances, first-generation Americans have been so involved in establishing themselves that they have not facilitated the transmission of the ethnic heritage of their immigrant parents to their own children. A resurrection of this identity can have positive personal and social value.

The therapeutic possibilities of the life review are complex. There is the opportunity to reexamine the whole of one's life and to make sense of it, both on its own terms and in comparison with the lives of others. Identity may be reexamined and restructured. There is the chance to resolve old problems, to make amends and restore harmony with friends and relatives. (Family members have been known to decide to talk to one another after 30 or 40 years of angry silence.)

The dreams of youth may be relived through memory. (People seem to regret what they did not do more than what they actually did.) There is the opportunity to understand and

accept personal foibles, to take full responsibility for acts that caused true harm but also to differentiate between real and neurotic guilt. The patient may demonstrate a maturing of the ability to tolerate conflict and uncertainty when these exist within himself and in his relationships to others.

Fears of death and dissolution may be mitigated as myths of invulnerability are confronted. People can become ready to die but in no hurry to do so. The future assumes less critical importance as the present is emphasized. "Elementality," the lively capacity to live in the present, may be fostered through the direct enjoyment of people, nature, colors, warmth, love, humor, and beauty in any form. There may be a greater capacity for mutuality, with a comfortable acceptance of the life cycle, the universe, and the generations. Pride in one's life and feelings of serenity often center around having done one's best. Older persons in difficult circumstances may give themselves a diagnosis of "extenuating circumstances," which credits them with surviving against terrible odds.

The elderly often become interested in teaching and in conservation of knowledge and the natural resources of the earth for future generations. They have a need to work out emotional and material legacies. They may revise their wills, give away possessions in advance, and generally simplify their lives. Creativity may be restimulated or emerge for the first time in the form of memoirs, arts, music, handicrafts, teaching, and so on. The elderly may put together family records and study their genealogies. They often talk of deciding "how I want to live the rest of my life." For those who are infirm or bedridden, the life review can have the added function of learning how to be "responsibly dependent" in the appropriate acceptance of help.

The success of the life review depends on the outcome of the struggle to resolve old issues of resentment, guilt, bitterness, mistrust, dependence, and nihilism. All the truly significant emotional options remain available until the moment of death—love, hate, reconciliation, self-assertion, and self-esteem.

A reason used for not offering life-review therapy (and psychotherapy in general) to older persons is the fear that they are psychologically fragile. This is especially true if they look physically frail. What we fail to remember is that older persons are master survivors compared with the young. They can hardly be seen as inexperienced in defending themselves from the painful forces of life. As in all good therapy, the therapist begins where the older person is and proceeds sensitively and respectfully. Inappropriate interpretations or poor timing will be met with a variety of defenses perfected over a lifetime (withdrawal, denial, open hostility) as well as new ones that capitalize on the possibilities of old age (pretended senility, pseudofrailty, or even deafness that conveniently comes and goes).

However, the life review, by its very nature, evokes a sense of regret and sadness at the brevity of life, the missed opportunities, the mistakes, the wrongs done to others, the chosen paths that turned out badly. The therapist sees anxiety, guilt, despair, and depression. In extreme cases, persons may become terror stricken, panicked, and even suicidal, particularly if they have irrevocably decided that life was a total waste. However, in our experience, this is more likely to happen when the person makes judgments on his own, without testing or sharing them. Most people have the capacity to reconcile their lives, to confront real guilt, and to find meaning, especially in the presence of acceptance and support from others.

Life-review therapy need not be ruled out because of brain damage. The Goldstein catastrophic reaction, resulting from overwhelming stimuli, can be minimized or avoided if the therapist proceeds carefully and observantly. Brain damage, of course, cannot be reversed, but overlying depression may be alleviated and adaptation may be encouraged.

Some therapists fear that encouragement of the life review will lead to egocentricity and "getting stuck" in the past, with neglect of the present. A certain self-centeredness occurs naturally during the life review. This may appear to become fixed if problems are not resolved. "Enshrinement" of certain ideas and possessions may occur as the person goes back to think about them again and again. This problem may be spontaneously resolved in time by the patient himself, or it may respond to attentive listening by others or to active psychotherapy.

Psychiatrists, psychologists, social workers, psychiatric nurses, and other professionals trained in the art of psychotherapy can be helpful to the older person. But beyond that, the life review is greatly enhanced by listeners, that is, persons who personally bear witness to the older person's struggles. We have seen high school students successfully aid the elderly in nursing homes, for example, by listening attentively by their beds as they talk. Family members and friends can partake in an older person's life review, adding their own memories and commenting with insights and support. The therapist must realize that some older persons prefer to work alone, with a tape recorder or pencil and paper. One of the interesting fringe benefits for therapists and listeners is in obtaining a rich supply of information and models for their own eventual old age.

The most introspective part of the life review seems to occur in the sixties and then begins to abate in the seventies and eighties. Gorney (1968) noted that the very old may enter a further developmental stage involving ego integration and serenity in the face of death.

## GROUP PSYCHOTHERAPY

In our opinion, the life review as it occurs in age-integrated group psychotherapy can be a rich, active reexperiencing of the past through the lives of others. All the generations participate in clarifying problems and working at solutions for the older person. There is a kind of recapitulation of the family.

We began experimenting with age-integrated group psychotherapy in 1970. Five groups of eight to ten members each were formed. Each group contained elderly persons over age 65, adults, young adults, and teenagers. The oldest member was 75 years of age; the youngest was 15. Criteria for inclusion were the absence of active psychoses and the presence of a major life crisis. Under study were reactions, ranging from essentially normative to pathologic, to the usual changes that occur in the life cycle (adolescence, marriage and divorce, parenthood, retirement, widowhood, and impending death). Groups met weekly with both of us as co-therapists.

Initially the older members tended to treat the young as mascots, not to be taken too seriously, while deferring leadership to the middle-aged. Some elderly persons assumed a rigid pedant role; others withdrew in silence. As therapy progressed, the elderly dropped some of their more rigid defenses and began to openly demonstrate their feelings about themselves, particularly with regard to aging. One woman spoke with indignation, "I don't like old age. I'm damn angry at the fact that I'm getting old and that I'm going to die."

Some displayed an unwillingness to grow up and accept their age, exhibiting a kind of Peter Pan wistfulness about youth. Certain individuals separated themselves from their peers as if to say, "I'm unique, not like the rest of those old fogies." Others overplayed aging through a pseudosenility that involved feigned forgetfulness and other pretenses aimed at fulfilling popular misconceptions about senility. In a similar ploy, of pseudofragility, persons declared themselves too emotionally fragile to deal with certain subjects in order both to avoid difficult issues and to make the younger generations feel guilty.

Closely related to this was the "old man" or "old woman" act, wherein persons in their sixties acted as though they were decrepit and about to die. They were determined that life was over, there was no hope, and group members might as well give up on them. Yet, they became resentful if ignored. Some older persons worked hard at projecting an image of sweetness and tranquility when they were in fact boiling over with rage. Others cast dire threats to the younger generation: "You'll see what it's like when *you* are old," or, "Wait until you reach my age. You won't talk so smart."

Reminiscence was occasionally used as a defense and even as a weapon to irritate others. Especially striking was the stubbornness of certain defenses that had been practiced over a lifetime but proved even more tempting to use in old age, for example, manipulation. Older persons who have been stripped of social status easily turn to manipulating others emotionally to achieve a sense of power.

Some persons will cling to old-fashioned theories and beliefs for psychologic purposes. A college-educated and thoroughly informed woman nonetheless insisted on believing in a totally hereditary basis for mental illness so that she could punish herself for her son's troubles. In doing so, she managed to avoid the guilt she felt about her own sexual activities after the death of her husband.

There is a danger that certain older men will commit "social suicide" on entering a new group. They show themselves as severely judgmental, especially of the young, and they rigidly refuse to accept anyone's point of view but their own. They will not tolerate negative reactions to themselves and usually insist that they could handle their own problems if everyone simply would listen and cooperate. These have been hard-driving, highly successful, often professional men who are used to a leadership role and have forgotten how to interact in any other manner. Therapists must intervene quickly before irreparable damage is done and the person flees the group as it becomes rejecting. Several individual sessions with the person may help.

Initially, young and middle-aged members are prone to see the old members in stereotyped terms. One young man openly stated, "My first reaction in coming to this group was to ask myself what I had in common with that old fart." The young are influenced by powerful cultural patterns of age prejudice and discrimination. The old in turn show prejudice toward the young through active dislike or more subtle avoidance. They may be embarrassed at the concept of sharing and learning with the young and have fears of losing status and self-respect. Some feel that they should arbitrarily be in a position of authority and teaching, while others feel they have nothing relevant to teach, that their knowledge is obsolete. There also is the fear of measuring their own education and intelligence against that of the young, whom they see as smarter and much better educated. The frequent envy of youth is based on a view that younger people have the prerogatives and priorities, which, of course, is partly grounded in reality. Many especially envy the young their experiences in a more open sexual climate. Others covet their educational opportunities, financial security, medical advantages (nasal plastic surgery, orthodontia), and lack of experience with catastrophe (the Great Depression).

These issues are dealt with overtly and covertly as groups progress. The elderly often assume an active learning role as well as a teaching role. They may go through a period of saying outrageous things to those who are younger and thus slowly defuse anger and envy toward youth and middle age. Members of all ages comment on becoming less conscious of age and are surprised if a new member, on entering an already long-functioning group, begins reacting to someone in a stereotyped way as "old" or "young."

Groups are especially useful in decreasing the sense of isolation and uselessness felt by many elderly persons. One man commented, "My life is so 'daily.' I love to share the adventures of others." In a well-functioning group, the generations unite against the vicissitudes of the life cycle rather than warring against each other. There is a sense of solidarity in facing grief, anger, intimacy, fear, aging, and death. (An interim step often is an alliance between the young and the old against the middle-aged.) The old also see these groups as a way to "catch up with the times." For example, sex is a favorite topic of discussion as the elderly test their views.

A common experience for the old is to "hear echoes of my own life" as they listen to those who are younger. In many instances, the old become skilled at how and when to use their accumulated life experience to instruct and serve as a model for others. Rather than forcing their views and feeling hurt when they are rejected, they learn to listen for the appropriate time when a younger person is open to this kind of learning. Their unique contributions to

younger members include a personal sense of life's flow from birth through death, personal solutions for encountering grief and loss regarding old age and death, and models for growing older and for creating meaningful lives.

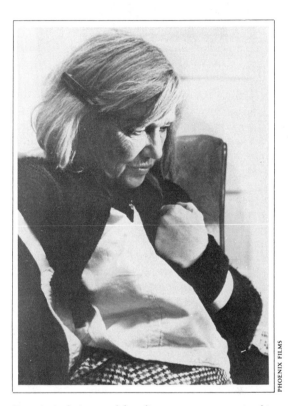

PHOENIX FILMS

*Peege's isolation and loneliness are apparent in this still from the film* **Peege.**

---

## EXERCISE 1

Select an older person in your family who is interested in helping you complete a family tree. Answer these questions:

1. What did you learn about your ancestors that you did not know?
2. How was the older person helpful?

## EXERCISE 2

1. View the film *Peege.*
2. Answer the following questions about the film: *

   a. What do you think of the kind of care that Peege seems to get in the home? What are the alternatives?

   b. What were the attitudes of the various family members toward Peege? How did they reveal these attitudes?

   c. What was your own attitude toward Peege, both in her present condition and in the flashbacks? Did your attitude toward her change at the end of the film? In what way?

   d. What was the difference between the older son's attitude and actions toward Peege and those of the rest of the family? Why do you suppose he was different?

   e. What do you suppose was going on in Peege's mind during the family visit? During the latter part when the eldest son stayed alone with her?

   f. How did you respond to the last shot of Peege, when she smiled? Why did you respond that way?

   g. While watching the film, did you think of a relative, friend, or yourself? What kinds of thoughts about these persons (or yourself) did the film prompt?

   h. Did you see Peege as being in some sort of "intolerable situation that did not *have* to exist? How could she be helped?

   i. Did you see the family as being in some sort of intolerable situation that did not *have* to exist? How could they be helped?

   j. How can the elderly be better integrated into our society today, not only so that they are not so lonely, but also so that society can benefit from their wisdom, their image, their comparative serenity in many cases? Do you know about experimental communities in which this "age-integration" has been attempted?

## REFERENCES

Butler, R. N. 1980–81. The life review; an unrecognized bonanza. *International Journal Aging Human Development* 12(1):35–8.

Gorney, J. E. 1968. Experience and age: Patterns of reminiscence among the elderly. Thesis, Committee on Human Development, University of Chicago.

\* The questions about the film *Peege* are from a guide prepared by G. William Jones, professor of film art, Southern Methodist University, Dallas, Texas. Reprinted with permission of Phoenix Films, New York. Copyright © 1976.

## BIBLIOGRAPHY

Baum, W. 1980–81. Therapeutic value of oral history. *International Journal of Aging and Human Development* 12(1): 49–53.

Beaton, S. 1980. Reminiscence in old age. *Nursing Forum* 19(3): 270–83.

Butler, R. W. 1963. The life review: An interpretation of reminiscence in the aged. *Psychiatry* 26(1): 65–76 (February).

———. 1970. Looking forward to what? The life review, legacy and excessive identity versus change. *American Behavioral Scientist* 14:121–28.

_____. 1971. Age: The life review. *Psychology Today,* December: 49–50, 89.

_____. 1974. Successful aging and the role of the life review. *Journal of the American Geriatrics Society* 22(12): 529–35 (December).

_____. 1980–81. The life review: An unrecognized bonanza. *International Journal of Aging and Human Development* 12(1): 35–38.

Butler, R. N., and M. I. Lewis. 1973. *Aging and mental health.* St. Louis, Mo.: Mosby.

Ellison, K. 1981. Working with the elderly in a life review group. *Journal of Gerontological Nursing* 7(9): 537–41 (September).

Falk, J. M. 1969. The organization of remembered life experience in old age: Its relation to subsequent adaptive capacity and to age. Thesis, Committee on Human Development, University of Chicago.

Gibson, D. 1980. Reminiscence, self-esteem; other satisfaction in adult male alcoholics. *Journal of Psychiatric Nursing* 18(3).

Harris, R., and S. Harris. 1980–81. Therapeutic uses of oral history techniques in medicine. *International Journal of Aging and Human Development* 12(1): 27–34.

Hausman, C. 1981. Life review therapy. *Journal of Gerontological Social Work* 2(3): 314 (Spring).

Havighurst, R. J., and R. Glasser. 1972. An exploratory study of reminiscence. *Journal of Gerontology* 27(2): 245–53 (March–April).

Ingersoll, B., and L. Goodman. 1980. History comes alive: Facilitating reminiscences in a group of institutionalized elderly. *Journal of Gerontological Social Work* 2(4): 305–19 (Summer).

Liton, J., and S. C. Olstein. 1969. The specific aspects of reminiscence. *Social Casework* 50:263–68.

LoGerfo, M. 1980–81. Three ways of reminiscing in theory and practice. *International Journal of Aging and Human Development* 12(1): 39–48.

McMahon, A. W., and P. J. Rhudick. 1964. Reminiscing: Adaptational significance in the aged. *Archives of General Psychiatry* 10(3): 294 (March).

Merriam S. 1980. The concept and function of reminiscence: a review of the research, *Gerontologist,* Oct. 20 (5 pt. 1); 604–9.

McMordie, W., and S. Blom. 1974. Life review therapy. *Perspectives in Psychiatric Care* 17(4).

Perrotta, P., and J. Meacham. 1981–82. Can a reminiscing intervention alter depression and self-esteem? *International Journal of Aging and Human Development* 14(1): 23–30.

Pincus, A. 1970. Reminiscence in aging and its implications for social work practice. *Social Work* 15(4): 47 (October).

Revere, V., and S. Tobin. 1980–81. Myth and reality: The older person's relationship to his past. *International Journal of Aging and Human Development* 12(1): 15–26.

Ryant, C. 1981. Comment: Oral history and gerontology. *The Gerontologist* 21(1): 104–5 (February).

Ryden, M. 1981. Nursing intervention in support of reminiscence. *Journal of Gerontological Nursing* 7(8): 461–63.

Tobin, S. S., and E. Etigson. 1968. Effect of stress on earliest memory. *Archives of General Psychiatry* 19 (October): 435–44.

## RESOURCES

### Films

*Steps Back in Time* (color, 10 minutes, 1974). In this film by Andrew Ruhl, an old woman reminisces about her youth. The scene is an old rehearsal hall, and the woman again becomes the young ballet dancer she once was. Hundreds of still photographs are arranged to create an effect of continuous movement. A study guide is included. AIMS Media Inc., 626 Justin Avenue, Glendale, CA 91201.

*The Women of Hodson* (color, 30 minutes, 1980). This Josephine Dean film is about a group of septuagenarians in the South Bronx section of New York City, who, after a life of hard work and struggle, now finally have time for themselves. The women at the Hodson Senior Citizens Center develop and perform original works based on their own life experiences. This film is useful as a pilot program. Filmakers Library Inc., 133 East 58th Street, #703A, New York, NY 10022.

*Peege* (16 mm, color, 28 minutes, 1976). This film by Peege's grandson shows the dynamics of family relationships and is an excellent example of reminiscing. Phoenix Films, 743 Alexander Road, Princeton, NJ 08540.

# chapter 5

# Principles from Yalom

*Irene Burnside*

*Aging is just a process by which one's weaknesses get stronger.*

FANNY SCARL, *Penultima*, 1979

MIMI FORSYTH/MONKMEYER

### LEARNING OBJECTIVES

- Discuss subgrouping.

- Describe crises in elderly group members.

- State an important area of expertise of the group therapist.

- Discuss culture building of a group.

- Describe two roles of the group leader.

- Discuss six of the curative factors developed by Yalom.

### KEY WORDS

- Altruism
- Catharsis
- Culture building
- Fractionalization
- Group cohesiveness
- Guidance
- Identification
- Instillation of hope
- Interpersonal learning
- Social reinforcement
- Subgrouping
- Universality

Irvin Yalom, in his excellent book *The Theory and Practice of Group Psychotherapy* (1975), does not specifically discuss group psychotherapy with the aged. However, students, health care workers and administrators, and instructors can profitably adapt his ideas for group work with older people. Although Yalom does not direct his book to group therapy with the elderly, one has to realize that "group counseling, goals of problems resolution, improved coping skills, and personal growth are not unrealistic for many older adults" (Tappen and Touhy, 1983, 44). As these writers state, "Group psychotherapy is still seldom offered to older adults in comparison to other age groups" (p. 44). This chapter discusses a number of Yalom's principles in relation to group work with the elderly, including the maintenance of stable groups, subgrouping, crises in group life, the group leader as a transitional object, roles of the group leader, social reinforcement, and curative factors in group work.

Yalom's book is extremely comprehensive. It is also technical; he uses psychiatric jargon freely. The reader will have to be very selective about reading the portions deemed most relevant to work with the aged but may ferret out appropriate sections other than those described here.

### THE MAINTENANCE OF STABLE GROUPS

According to Yalom, an important function of leaders is the maintenance of stable groups. He states, "Stability of membership seems to be a sine qua non of successful therapy" (1975, 84). If members do leave the group, they should be replaced. However, dropouts may be an advantage for students in group work with the elderly. New group leaders often select too many members when they begin a new group. Thus, if one or two members leave and are not replaced, the size of the group becomes more manageable.

In my own work I naturally have made wrong choices for group membership. Usually the person who did not tolerate the group or disrupted the meetings left before I had a chance to discuss the separation. Such dropouts do help the leader become more careful in selecting future group members. In other cases aged people may be placed in groups against their will but remain passive in the beginning. Later they may state their own views and leave. Such actions can be one way of retaining some control over their own constricted lives, for some old people are allowed to make few decisions.

Death is, of course, a much more common cause of attrition among aged groups than younger age groups. After a death occurs, leaders are immediately faced with three tasks: (1) dealing with their personal feelings of loss for that member, (2) helping the group deal with the death of the peer, and (3) finding a replacement to join the group. In institutions there is often a waiting list for entry into the group, so someone is ready to move into the group immediately. Well-established groups soon become a topic of interest and concern to nongroup patients, and if these patients do not request to be in the group, very often their relatives will request it for them.

Such interest in a group may not occur as readily with psychotherapy groups. For one thing, the present generation of elderly people are not particularly impressed by psychiatric interventions, and many of them still prefer pastoral counseling. It may also be difficult to replace a member in a noninstitutional group because of transportation problems. Finally, the group may be known to only a few employees in an agency—for example, those who work in an outpatient clinic. At this writing, I know of no psychiatrist doing group work with old people in nursing homes, although I have heard several speak on their consulting roles. Psychiatrists in nursing homes are usually counseling staff members and doing groups with them.

In spite of all these problems, stable groups do frequently occur among the aged, especially if the leader is conscientious about dealing with tardy and absent members. The effect of day-to-day crises on attendance can be minimized if the leader is alert for them (Burnside 1970a). Another reason for tardiness and absenteeism in elderly groups in institutions is staff apathy, neglect, or lack of information about group schedules. If the patients need staff help to manage the activities of daily living, they may be in the bathtub at meeting time, be in the process of being dressed, or lack the necessary help to get to the meeting.

## SUBGROUPING

Subgrouping, or "fractionalization—the splitting off of subunits" as Yalom (1975, 257) describes it, may be transient or enduring, but it is inevitable. Yalom finds that it is usually disruptive. I have found it quite the opposite in group work with the elderly. Perhaps the need for friendship, mutual support, and a confidant makes it less threatening than in other groups. It probably should even be encouraged at times.

Margaret Hartford (1972, 267) states that "as people become involved in subgroups of two, three, and four, they may acquiesce to the dominant or influential partners, or to the more aggressive initiators to the extent that the relationships between or among them have particular meaning." However, leaders strive for increased relationships and "particular meanings" in groups of old persons. Perhaps subgroups are not so deleterious to the group process.

Subgrouping does not seem to be as common among the institutionalized elderly as it is in other groups. These persons tend to avoid one another in a search for privacy. One member of a group I led always sat in a corner of the patio when the weather permitted. His reasons were "to get away from the old folks," "to read in peace and quiet," and "to be outdoors." Yet group meetings had great meaning for him, and eventually he made friends with another man in the group and asked to be transferred to his room. They got along well as roommates.

Groups can provide a much-needed mechanism for the development of friends in either an institution or an outpatient setting. One is reminded of Toffler's comments in *Future Shock* (1970) about the importance of groups in helping to increase stability in our fast-changing world; his words surely apply particularly to the elderly, who face so much duress, loss, and change in late life.

Leaders may choose to encourage subgrouping outside the group meetings. Meeting outside the group need not be detrimental to the group process. Until more research has been conducted on groups of older people and adverse effects have been delineated, it is safe to say that many friendships begin and increased socialization occurs when group members gather outside regular meetings.

I have not had group experience in settings such as senior citizen centers, nutrition sites, or residential homes for the aged. Therefore, I cannot comment on subgroupings as it occurs in these places or in larger groups in the community.

## CRISES IN GROUP LIFE

Many large and small crises plague old people and can be the reasons for absenteeism. We should redefine the term *crisis* in group work with the elderly. Crises usually mean deaths, suicides, holocausts, and other tragic happenings, but I have worked with institutionalized patients whose behavior and functioning changed during such episodes as fires, employee strikes, serious illnesses, losses of pets, high staff turnovers, and rejections by family (Burnside 1970a). The cumulative effect of "small" crises also needs to be considered. What seems to be a simple, easily solved problem may not be one in the eyes of the elderly person experiencing the problem. "Small" crises can include losing one's glasses, teeth, or hearing aid or being constipated and consequently functioning poorly. Even slight falls can rattle the elderly considerably and tip them into a state of functioning less well.

For example, a small fraternity pin was stolen from a member of a group I led in a nursing home. He had had the pin for more than 50 years, and his wife had worn it for much of that time. I thought it was the value of the small diamond in the pin that concerned him, but it was the sentimental value of the pin. As he said, "I can always buy another diamond." He never got the pin back even though he offered a $50 reward for it, and he mentioned the loss to me frequently both in and outside the group. Another man's watch was stolen while he was in the same group. These were both sharp, alert men who might misplace their canes occasionally but who always managed to find them. This man said bitterly in a group meeting, "They'd steal the eye out of a snake here!" (Burnside 1970b).

Much group time can be spent discussing the losses experienced by the members. I think it is very important to allow these expressions of grief. Younger people are so much more geared toward "let's replace it." We need to learn what

Loss—for example, of a pet— is one of the causes of grief in the elderly; caretakers frequently miss or overlook the importance of such a loss to the aged person.

losses cause the aged to grieve. Restitution may be more difficult than we realize.

## TASKS OF THE GROUP PSYCHOTHERAPIST

According to Yalom, the two basic tasks of the group psychotherapist are group maintenance and culture building. The leader has the sole responsibility for creating and carrying the group. "A considerable part of the maintenance task is performed before the first meeting . . . the leader's expertise in the selection and the preparation of members will greatly influence the group's fate" (Yalom 1975, 84). The members are strangers as the group begins, so the therapist serves as a "transitional object" and is the group's primary unifying force. This is especially true in working with the elderly. The members may ignore one another and relate to, and sometimes speak only to, the group leader in meetings. This sort of behavior seems to be particularly characteristic of depressed, withdrawn, or regressed individuals. Group maintenance also includes gatekeeping functions to prevent absenteeism and member attrition. Continued tardiness, absences, disruptive socializing, subgrouping, and scapegoating are all factors that can be harmful to a group; the leader must constantly watch for them and intervene.

Culture building is assisting the group to develop therapeutic norms. The group will turn to the leader for direction, and the leader must help the group establish norms consistent with the goals of therapy. The leader must, however, remember that norms "are created relatively early in the life of a group and once established are difficult to change" (Yalom 1975, 86).

The following anecdote from my group experience is an illustration of a norm set by a member of a group of 80-year-olds who met weekly in a nursing home. One group member was a man of 85 who attended the meetings regularly each week. He admitted that the intellectual stimulation and the camaraderie meant a great deal to him, and even when he did not feel up to par he came to the meetings. On several occasions when he was not feeling well, he arrived at the meeting in his bathrobe and pajamas. The leader hesitated to comment on his attire, since the man's energy level was low and he was making the effort to attend. After he had come to his second or third meeting in his night-clothes, one of the women in the group eyed him and said tartly that she thought he could dress up a little bit for the meetings and have enough respect not to come in a robe and pajamas. Her statement had a marked effect; thereafter the man's grooming improved, and he never again came to the meetings in his robe and pajamas.

## TWO ROLES OF THE GROUP LEADER

According to Yalom, group leaders use two roles to accomplish their basic tasks and to influence the group: the technical expert and the model-setting participant. The technical expert role involves using all the leader's technical knowledge and skill. One important task is to develop a pattern of communication that will help the group move toward a "social microcosm" and enhance subsequent learning among members. The schematic form of the communication and interaction pathways can be seen in Figure 5–1. With older persons, the leader must

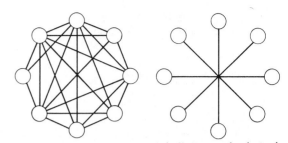

FIGURE 5–1. *The diagram at left illustrates the desired mode of communication and interaction in a group. The diagram at right shows what may actually happen for a long time in a group of elderly persons: communication primarily through or to the group leader.*

SOURCE: I. D. Yalom. 1975. *The theory and practice of group psychotherapy,* 2d ed. (New York: Basic Books), 108.

be very active to move the group toward the interactive mode shown in the left-hand diagram.

The role of model setter and participant in the group is concurrent with the role of technical expert. The leader role-models behavior to help the group members develop therapeutic norms. For a group to be maximally effective, the members should interact with one another "in a confrontive, forthright, nondefensive, nonjudgmental manner." For many elderly people who were taught to be seen and not heard, this is obviously new and unaccustomed behavior. The safety of the group can be enhanced as the members see the therapist interacting freely without adverse effects.

The leader who offers nonjudgmental acceptance and who can appreciate the strengths of the elderly as well as their frailties and problems can help to shape a group to a health orientation. Yalom, incidentally, discourages being a "detective of psychopathology."

Yalom discusses monitoring the amount of affect (mood) in neurotic and psychotic groups, but the opposite has been true in my experience as a group leader of the aged. One does not always monitor the affect; just waiting to see what happens may be more useful. Patience is an important attribute in a leader. Apathy in the institutionalized aged may be overpowering at times. New leaders must always keep in mind that such apathy may be a mask for depression (Levin 1967) and be on guard against it for the members' sakes and their own.

## SOCIAL REINFORCEMENT

Social reinforcement in group psychotherapy may be subtle or nondeliberate. More often, in group therapy with the aged, it is very deliberate, as in the use of touch in group meetings.

Touch is important in working with the aged (Burnside 1975). Its use—a quick hug, a pat on the hand or shoulder—can be a simple, positive reinforcement. Sheer enjoyment of the elderly is another positive and powerful kind of reinforcing—a hearty laugh by the leader may go a long way to convince old people that they still have a sense of humor and that they are appreciated.

Listening is important in all therapy situations with the elderly. Again, the leader must role-model for attentive listening because many old people are impatient with one another. In the effort to make someone listen to them, they may not be able to listen to others effectively. Such behavior is often due to high anxiety and diminishes after a few meetings.

## CURATIVE FACTORS IN GROUP WORK

Yalom developed 12 general categories of curative factors from the data he received from patients in group therapy:

1. Altruism.
2. Group cohesiveness.
3. Universality.
4. Interpersonal learning: "input."
5. Interpersonal learning: "output."
6. Guidance.
7. Catharsis.
8. Identification.
9. Family reenactment.
10. Insight.
11. Instillation of hope.
12. Existential factors.

Yalom does not state the ages of the patients who reported, but seven of the categories seem especially important in elderly groups: group cohesiveness, universality, interpersonal learning ("input"), interpersonal learning ("output"), catharsis, identification, and instillation of hope.

### Group Cohesiveness

One way of defining group cohesiveness is the togetherness feeling that a group develops over time. The relationships among members become very meaningful. This is terribly important for the aged, who are slowly being stripped of such relationships. Even after the group disbands, the members will remember the basic acceptance they had in the group and again feel that they belong.

Numerous writers have discussed group identity, although they have referred to it by different names. Charles Cooley (1909), the first to note this phenomenon, described it as "we-feeling." Grace Coyle (1930) also described it. It is of utmost importance for the leader to strive for the "we" feeling. This can be most difficult when working with several egocentric elders. The leader should listen carefully for the pronouns and for any changes in substance or timing during group meetings. Group cohesion, according to Leon Festinger, Stanley Schachter, and Kurt Back (1950), can be seen by how much the members want to be a part of the group. Hartford (1972) states that evidence of cohesion appears when the members refer to themselves and the group as "we" and when they begin to take hold of an idea or a problem and go to work on it. (The reader is referred to Hartford's book for a discussion of changes in cohesion and their effects.)

### Universality

Learning that others have had many of the same feelings and experiences can be very reassuring to old people. Stroke patients, for example, will often share in group meetings what it is like when they had their stroke (Holland 1973). In one of my groups with frail elders three patients with vision problems used to compare their loss of vision in group meetings and their methods of handling it. Adroit leaders can maximize the universality aspect of groups.

Groups also give elderly people the chance to discuss the problems of aging, so that the members begin to feel that they are not so different after all. Sometimes listening to how others have coped with their losses, illnesses, and tragedies can inspire a group member toward better adjustment. Moreover, a nursing background is a special advantage in work with the disabled elderly; the group leader can do health teaching during group work. Encouraging nurses to take on this task may be fruitful. One health maintenance clinic, for example, conducted weekly programs on sight conservation (Storz 1972). Problems with vision can vary in degree but tend to be pervasive among elderly clientele. Impaired hearing is another common sensory defect that would be an appropriate topic for such group work.

### Interpersonal Input and Output

Many older people suffer from what I call conversation deprivation. The need to talk and share is very important for these people, and finding persons who will listen and take them seriously is a problem. This need for human interaction occurs not only in institutions but also in private homes. Old people as a rule get very little feedback. They need to know what relatives, peers, and staff members think about them and also how they are coming across.

Group membership gives such people a chance to learn about their own habits and their ability to communicate with others. Although membership can be one means of working out difficulties with peers — or of communicating dislike — the personal closeness generated by group meetings may be one of their most important contributions. In my own group work I often have the residents hold hands as we sit in the circle to say a nonverbal goodby. Blind people still hold the hand of the person next to them long after the others have dropped one another's hands.

### Catharsis

The importance of catharsis in groups becomes apparent early in the meetings. Once aged individuals find that the leader is not going to write down their every word, they feel free to express many feelings, especially hostile ones. With no fear of retribution, elderly people are quick to use the group as a sounding board.

Catharsis is especially important for groups in nursing homes. Group meetings give members a place to rant and rave about the coffee, the food, the bathing procedures, the pills, the night nurse, and so forth — usually in that order. I recommend the book *As We Are Now* (1973), by Mae Sarton, as one example of the tremendous need for patients who feel downtrodden to have a place to air their feelings. For the aged in community settings, day-to-day living problems, discouragement about living conditions, high prices, and problems with agencies or personnel are fertile ground for group digging.

### Identification

Upon first glance, identification seems closely related to interpersonal learning, both input and output. This curative area largely involves honest feedback and improvement of skills in getting along with people, especially group members (no small feat, with feisty, cantankerous old ones in a group). Identification of self increases self-esteem in the older person because the individual can identify with others in the group or even admire and behave like the therapist. Here again, the importance of role modeling by the leader is stressed. Its effect is most noticeable when the aged emulate the leader's communication. Increased articulateness is one result of an aged member's identification with the therapist. The leader of old people must, however, also encourage expression of self — of the importance and uniqueness of each old person in the group.

Identification is commonly seen in groups of regressed elderly persons. In such instances the members may emulate the leader. Since one strives to promote individuality in the aged, this curative factor plays an important part in groups of mentally impaired elderly. Identification with other members in a group is a positive force in group work. In my own experience, I was struck with how well a group of aged persons — all of whom were over 90 years old — identified with one another. Identification may be one very important rationale for leading cohort groups. Eugenia Shere (1964) also found that to be true.

### Instillation of Hope

Many institutionalized aged have little hope left in their lives. The group meeting each week offers hope and something to look forward to.

They can be inspired by other persons in the group. The leader also can inspire them by helping them discover that they still have power over their own lives. These people can also learn that their autonomy exists outside group meetings and that they can meet on their own. Instilling hope and working on a future are important goals for group leaders.

## SUMMARY

This chapter describes various extrapolations from Irvin Yalom's *The Theory and Practice of Group Psychotherapy* (1975) and their application to group psychotherapy with the elderly. The focus is on how the leader can maintain stable groups and underlines the material in Chapter 11.

Subgrouping, or fractionalization of groups, is usually considered deleterious, but it may have benefits for long-term residents.

Crises both large and small can occur during group life. Large crises include loss of loved ones (including pets), suicide, employee strikes, staff turnover, and rejections by family. Little crises are day-to-day problems that may tip the functioning level of the elderly person.

Two tasks of group therapists are group maintenance and culture building. The leader must use considerable technical expertise to prevent absenteeism, tardiness, and attrition. The therapist serves as a "transitional object" during the time the members do not relate to one another but rather to the leader. Culture building is accomplished through development of therapeutic group norms.

Two roles of the group leader are being both a technical expert and a model-setting participant. The group has to be helped to move toward a "social microcosm," but growth and learning also need to occur in the group. Social reinforcement is a powerful shaper of behavior and may be used knowingly or unknowingly by a leader. A wise leader is generous with the use of touch as a social reinforcer with the aged group member.

Curative factors selected for discussion from Yalom's book are cohesion, universality, interpersonal learning (input and output), catharsis, identification, and hope. Each curative factor has an application and ramifications in elderly groups.

The depth and breadth of Yalom's book cannot easily be indicated in one chapter. The group therapist who is leading psychotic or neurotic persons should read the entire book.

## EXERCISE 1

Understanding shades of meaning, innuendos, and the importance of definitions and semantics is necessary in group theory. To test your own meanings and thoughts, take one of the seven curative factors described in this chapter and write an in-depth analysis of what that term means to you and of instances in your life when you felt that curative factor was operating.

## EXERCISE 2

Imagine yourself as an aged person. Select an age you think is "really old." Take the same curative factor chosen in Exercise 1 and describe an ideal group you would like to be a member of so that the quality you described could flourish.

## REFERENCES

Burnside, I. M. 1970a. Crisis intervention with geriatric hospitalized patients. *Journal of Psychiatric Nursing* 8 (March–April): 17–20.

_____. 1970b. Loss: A constant theme in group work with the aged. *Hospital and Community Psychiatry* 21 (June): 173–77.

_____. 1975. The therapeutic use of touch. Paper presented at conference entitled Sensory Processes and Aging, Dallas, December 3.

Cooley, C. H. 1909. *Social organization: A study of the larger mind.* New York: Scribner's.

Coyle, G. L. 1930. *Social process in organized groups.* New York: Smith.

Festinger, L., S. Schachter, and K. Back. 1950. *Social pressures in informal groups: A study of human factors in housing.* Stanford, Calif.: Stanford University Press.

Hartford, M. E. 1972. *Groups in social work.* New York: Columbia University Press.

Holland, D. L. 1973. Co-leadership with a group of stroke patients. In *Psychosocial nursing care of the aged.* 1st ed., ed. I. M. Burnside. New York: McGraw-Hill.

Levin, S. 1967. Depression in the aged. In *Geriatric psychiatry: Grief, loss, and emotional disorders in the aging process,* ed. M. Berezin and S. Cath. New York: International Universities Press.

Sarton, M. 1973. *As we are now.* New York: Norton.

Shere, E. 1964. Group therapy with the very old. In *New thoughts on old age,* ed. R. Kastenbaum. New York: Springer.

Storz, R. R. 1972. The role of a professional nurse in a health maintenance program. *Nursing Clinics of North America* 7 (June): 207–23.

Tappen, R., and T. Touhy. 1983. Group leader— Are you a controller? *Journal of Gerontological Nursing* 9(1):44 (January).

Toffler, A. 1970. *Future shock.* New York: Random House.

Yalom, I. D. 1975. 2d ed. *The theory and practice of group psychotherapy.* New York: Basic Books.

## BIBLIOGRAPHY

Yalom, I. D. 1966. Problems of neophyte group therapists. *International Journal of Social Psychiatry* 12:29–52.

Yalom, I. D., P. S. Houts, G. Newell, and K. H. Rand. 1967. Preparation of patients for group therapy: A controlled study. *Archives of General Psychiatry* 17:416–27.

Yalom, I. D., P. S. Houts, S. M. Zimberg, and K. H. Rand. 1967. Prediction of improvement in group therapy. *Archives of General Therapy* 17:159–68.

Yalom, I. D., and K. Rand. 1966. Compatibility and cohesiveness in therapy groups. *Archives of General Psychiatry* 13:267–76.

Yalom, I. D., and F. Terrazas. 1968. Group therapy for psychotic elderly patients. *American Journal of Nursing* 68 (August): 1690–94.

# chapter 6

# Fundamental Interpersonal Orientation

*Irene Burnside*

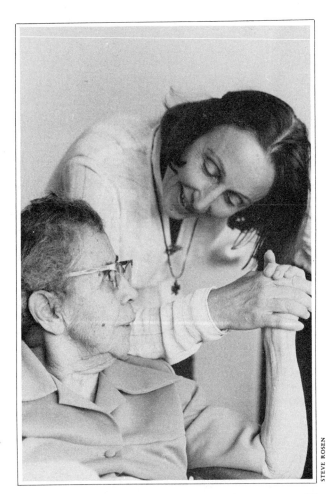

To help is to enter the existence
that is the other's.

J. H. VAN DEN BERG (1955)

## LEARNING OBJECTIVES

- List eight interpersonal problems in group work.

- Select three interpersonal problems that are particularly applicable to groups of aged members.

- Define Schutz's interpretations of **inclusion**, **control**, and **affection**.

- Analyze the leader's role in promoting inclusion in the group.

## KEY WORDS

- Affection
- Control
- Inclusion
- Underinclusion
- Underpersonal
- Undersocial

William Schutz (1958) has written about several important aspects of group leadership that can be applied to work with the elderly. This chapter briefly discusses interpersonal problems in groups and then examines three interpersonal needs—inclusion, control, and affection (intimacy)—in more detail.

## INTERPERSONAL PROBLEMS IN GROUPS

Schutz describes a variety of interpersonal problems that spell difficulties for a leader. Although he was not referring to groups of elderly persons, the following list is certainly applicable:

1. Withdrawing members.
2. Personal hostilities between members.
3. Members who are either inactive and unintegrated or overactive and destructive.
4. Power struggles between group members.
5. Members battling for attention.
6. Dissatisfaction with the leadership in the group.
7. Dissatisfaction with the amount of acknowledgment that an individual's contributions are getting.

8. Dissatisfaction with the amount of affection and warmth in the group.

Of the eight interpersonal problems, three deserve special mention: (1) the withdrawing member, (2) power struggles between group members, and (3) dissatisfaction with the amount of affection and warmth. The withdrawing member is ever a challenge to a group leader. Reasons for withdrawal by a group member need to be fully explored. Is it illness or pain? Is it grief? Is it lack of inclusion? Is it a communication problem, such as a language barrier? I encourage power struggles between members. Sometimes they are the first indication of spark in the individuals. The tremendous effect of members' constant losses may mean that the leader has to step up the amount of affection proffered in a group.

Formality has to go out the window when one is struggling with these problems. Leaders need to concentrate on their own style and, particularly, on how adroit they are in including each member in each meeting.

## INTERPERSONAL NEEDS IN GROUPS

Schutz describes inclusion, control, and affection (intimacy) as interpersonal needs of a

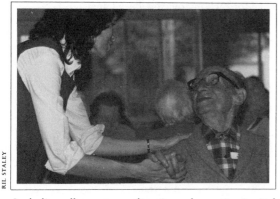

R.L. STALEY

*Including all group members in each meeting is vital in working with the elderly. Schutz (1958) has described the importance of inclusion, identifying it as one of the interpersonal needs of groups.*

group. If the group has been cohesive (that is, has maintained a high level of closeness) and if a process of control has been in effect, decisions can be made and the group has made a healthy adaptation.

## The Need for Inclusion

Inclusion of all members in each meeting is vital in working with the elderly. Inclusion can be either verbal or nonverbal. The impact of the nonverbal behavior of group leaders has not yet been studied, but it is a very important factor, as I learned after I had not been conscientious about including two very quiet women in my first group of old people. They dropped out of the group and returned only after I had seen them on a one-to-one basis for several weeks (Burnside 1969). Group members, even the less alert ones, often watch the leader intently. Such watchfulness may be one way of compensating for hearing loss.

It is easy to ignore the quiet, shy ones or those with difficulty in speaking, especially if there is a monopolizer in the group. Monopolizers increase the difficulties of the leader; hence careful selection of group membership is important. Underinclusion may also occur when the anxiety of the leader is high. When new group leaders begin a group, they have many variables to consider, and they tend to ignore one or two

members. Absenteeism should be carefully studied to rule out underinclusion as a cause.

Leaders need to maintain satisfactory relationships with the staff, family members, friends, and peers in order to assess group members' interaction or belongingness needs. Some people are very gregarious, while others want much less personal contact. They prefer to stay out of groups and to maintain their own privacy.

The FIRO theory attempts to explain interpersonal behavior in terms of orientations to others in the group. This theory holds that people behave toward others in certain characteristic patterns; these patterns are the major determinants of interpersonal behaviors. Table 6–1 presents a schema for looking at orientation toward others. But instead of focusing on the terminology (such as "abdicrat" or "underpersonal"), it is best to remember the acronym ICA in group work. ICA stands for inclusion, control, and affections. That is the important point to be remembered from the table.

Some specific methods of inclusion that work well with aged group members follow.

1. A personal hello and goodby to each member is a basic way to make everyone feel included. In the early meetings a handshake is appropriate; in later meetings, when everyone is better acquainted, more affection is often displayed by both the leader and the members.

2. Another common method of verbal inclusion is frequently calling the members by name.

3. The leader should keep track of who has not spoken and gently draw them into the discussion. An analogy is playing a game of bridge; one always keeps the number of trumps in mind as the hand is played.

4. Sometimes it is helpful for the leader to go around the circle to be sure that everyone is included. New group leaders might try using this method until they are able to balance the contributions of the members in each meeting so that all are included.

5. Eye contact is one form of nonverbal inclusion. Since members may have serious vision problems or may not be wearing their glasses, such members should be seated where they can see the leader. If the leader sits in front of a window or bright lights, for example, vision difficulties are increased. Group meetings

TABLE 6-1.  Descriptive schema and appropriate terminology for each interpersonal need area

|  |  |  | I initiate interaction with others. | |
|  |  |  | Low | High |
| --- | --- | --- | --- | --- |
| Inclusion | I want to be included. | High | Undersocial Social-compliant | Oversocial Social-compliant |
|  |  | Low | Undersocial Countersocial | Oversocial Countersocial |
|  |  |  | I try to control others. | |
|  |  |  | Low | High |
| Control | I want to be controlled. | High | Abdicrat Submissive | Autocrat Submissive |
|  |  | Low | Abdicrat Rebellious | Abdicrat Rebellious |
|  |  |  | I try to be close and personal. | |
|  |  |  | Low | High |
| Affection | I want others to be close and personal with me. | High | Underpersonal Personal-compliant | Overpersonal Personal-compliant |
|  |  | Low | Underpersonal Counterpersonal | Overpersonal Counterpersonal |

SOURCE:   From *The Interpersonal Underworld,* by W. C. Schutz. Copyright © 1966 by Science & Behavior Books, Inc., p. 60. Reprinted by permission.

should not be held in dimly lit rooms, for the same reason.

6. Sitting close to an individual may help to satisfy the need for inclusion. Physical closeness is also a way to support shy, withdrawn, or anxious individuals.

7. In group work with regressed members, nonverbal communication is very important. For example, in a demonstration of a group for teaching purposes, a 90-year-old regressed man was very anxious and kept noisily stamping his feet on the wheelchair footrests. I was talking to another member, so I reached over and placed my hand on his knee. His agitation decreased. Try to touch two members simultaneously; frequently the two members will interact with each other. Holding a member's hand can also serve as a means of inclusion.

New leaders who are trying to strengthen the inclusion aspects in their group leadership should remember a Spanish proverb, "Habits are first cobwebs, then cables." As new leaders refine their skills, the cobwebs may develop into cables.

## The Need for Control

This chapter focuses on the importance of control to the members of the group. However, there is another aspect of control, which is described so well by R. Tappen and T. Touhy (1983). They state that a purpose of group work with institutionalized older adults is to increase their feelings of satisfaction and well-being and to raise their self-esteem. However, Tappen and Touhy add that there are numerous examples of control and condescension in group approaches designed for older adults. This is an important component of group work that is not fully explored in the literature at this time.

Young students often balk at the use of the word *control* in discussing one-to-one relationships and group work (Burnside 1976). However, after observing or trying to lead a group that is out of control, students better understand the crucial balance of inclusion, control, and affection in a group.

We all need to maintain a satisfactory balance of power and influence in our relationships with other people. One reason is that we need to make our environment predictable to some degree. Keeping it predictable often amounts to controlling other people, because they are the main agents creating unpredictable and uncontrollable situations. The degree of predictability needed varies widely. Some individuals want to control their entire environment, while others do not want to control anyone in any situation, no matter how appropriate controlling them would be.

Older people who have lived alone and made their own decisions for a long while are accustomed to being in control. However, the institutionalized elderly lose so much control over their lives that a group meeting provides one area where the individual can say an adamant "no" or vie for control. New group leaders need to be helped with feelings of rejection when such occasions arise in group meetings, for students often do not realize the great need of the elderly to maintain an "inner locus of control."

Despite this need, lack of exertion to secure control is common in institutionalized groups. Some of the reasons may be lack of energy, institutional neurosis, depression, boredom, or lack of finesse in groups. I have frequently had to encourage older persons to exert more control in group meetings as well as over their own lives. Student leaders have had similar experiences (Blake 1973; Holland 1973; Holtzen 1973).

Student leaders need to be guided into encouraging aged members in institutions to take more initiative and control. In my own experience, the overcontrolling group member is usually less of a leadership problem than the passive, submissive member. The dependency and helplessness of the groups can often frustrate and/or depress a new group leader. One example of such a group is a reality orientation group.

New leaders often feel a loss of control of the group when a member leaves abruptly. Although elderly members generally do not leave their groups as abruptly as some younger persons do

because they are physically slowed down for one reason or another, older persons may leave the group before it is dismissed if their anxiety is high. Anxiety in new group members and the leader may result in especially tight control of the group by the leader. Overcontrolling may be demonstrated by the leader's making all the decisions alone, by impatience with tardiness or absenteeism, or by ignoring the needs of the members.

Old people who are not accustomed to groups may take some time to warm up to the group. Or they may try the forms of control they used in their own families. Many of the present generation of older persons came from extremely large families, and the place they had in the family constellation may influence their actions within the group—thus, "the mother" (she was the oldest girl in the family) or "the father" (he was the oldest boy) or "the baby of the family," "the clown," "the teaser," and so forth.

In general, the style of leadership and control for group work with the elderly is different from that for other age groups. In groups of elderly people the leaders are more often "completers," the ones who enable the group to accomplish any task the group is not doing for itself, either by having it done or by doing it themselves.

## The Need for Affection

We all need to maintain a balance between ourselves and others regarding love and affection. In essence, affection is a relationship between two people only. At one extreme, some people like very close, very personal relationships with each individual they meet. At the other extreme are those who like their relationships to be quite impersonal and distant, friendly perhaps, but not close and intimate. Arthur Schopenhauer (Freud 1922) once compared people to porcupines in winter. He said that the problem is to find positions close enough together for them to enjoy each other's warmth but far enough apart so that their quills will not prick.

The affectional (or intimacy) needs of the members are an important component of group work with the elderly (Table 6–2). According to Amitai Etzioni (1971), the withdrawal of

TABLE 6–2.  **Affection in groups of elderly people**

*Occasions for expression of affection to aged group members*

| | | |
|---|---|---|
| 1. During hellos | 5. Assuage guilt | 8. Spontaneous reaction of leader |
| 2. During goodbys | 6. Ease forgetful moments, | 9. Alleviate grief |
| 3. Congratulate over | memory loss | 10. Share happiness of leader |
| accomplishment | 7. Intervene in loneliness | or member |
| 4. Assuage embarrassment | | |

*Problems in giving affection*

| Leader | Group member | Staff or agency |
|---|---|---|
| 1. Professional, reserved stance | 1. Too lonely | 1. Lack of role models in agency |
| 2. Embarassed by affectionate | 2. Grieving | 2. Philosophy of agency inhibited |
| gestures | 3. Lifestyle; not used to it | 3. Hurried atmosphere; everyone |
| 3. Lifestyle; not used to it | 4. Cultural background | always "busy" |
| 4. Cultural background | 5. Depressed | 4. Task-oriented physical care takes |
| 5. Aged person dirty; has bad | 6. Embarrassed | priority over psychosocial care |
| odor, jaundiced, etc. | 7. Lack of significant others | 5. Rapid turnover of staff precludes |
| | 8. Apathy | close relationships |
| | 9. Dying | |
| | 10. In pain | |
| | 11. Angry | |
| | 12. Paranoid state | |
| | 13. Low energy level | |

*Problems in receiving affection*

| | | |
|---|---|---|
| 1. Embarrassed by affectionate | 1. Embarrassed by affection | 1. Embarrassed by affectionate |
| gestures | 2. Barricades: bed rails, | overtures: |
| | wheelchairs, walkers | (a) staff/staff, (b) staff/patient, |
| | | (c) patient/patient |
| | | 2. Need to maintain a professional |
| | | stance; discomfort in role |

affection is one of the forces that pushes an aged person into senility. Elderly people may need much more affection than younger ones because they have lost so many peers and significant others. How the leader demonstrates and uses affection may also be different. The easy flow of affection between the leader and a group of aged people would not be seen if the same leader were working with schizophrenic young people.

Lack of affection and warmth in a group is to be expected in the beginning meetings if all the members are strangers, but that should change as the group continues to meet. Expression of affection may occur soon if the group members have known one another before.

The response of aged persons in group meetings mirrors the way they are treated in the facility or in their home. If they receive affection, they tend to give affection in the group. If they live in a hostile or punitive environment, they are guarded, shy, or draw away from affectionate gestures offered them.

Groups offer student leaders a chance to understand better the sexuality needs of the aged members. The importance of body image, self-esteem, and sexual drives may all appear to some degree in group work with the elderly. As leaders display interest and affection (both verbally and nonverbally), they role-model behavior that can be emulated by the group. The leader's touching the very obese person, the jaundiced patient, the unattractive aged, for example, may make a great impression on all involved in the care of and interaction with that person (Figure 6–1).

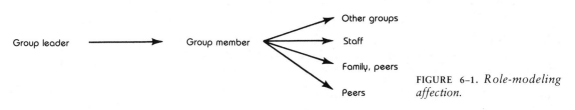

FIGURE 6-1. *Role-modeling affection.*

## SUMMARY

Several important aspects of group leadership that are applicable to the elderly can be extrapolated from William Schutz's theory of fundamental interpersonal orientation. Three of the interpersonal problems discussed by Schutz can be especially significant in group work with the aged: withdrawing members, power struggles between members, and dissatisfaction with the amount of affection and warmth in the group.

Some applicable interpersonal needs of a group are inclusion, control, and affection. Carefully balanced fulfillment of these needs helps to keep individuals in the group and helps them flourish as group members.

Inclusion can consist of either verbal or nonverbal acknowledgment of individual members. Underinclusion of a member by the leader may lead to absenteeism. Some suggestions for inclusion are (1) personal attention before and after the meeting, (2) frequent use of names, (3) allowing every member a chance to speak, (4) frequent touching, (5) sitting close to an individual, and (6) eye contact.

Encouraging older people to seize more control over their day-to-day situations and their lives in general is a difficult leadership task. Yet it is important for the institutionalized aged especially, who seem to have lost or given up the locus of control. Group members can be important in increasing control.

Affection is lacking in initial meetings, when everyone is a stranger. Affection for the leader and between members usually increases as the group continues. The intimacy should not overwhelm the group member. The group leader can be a role model for giving and receiving affection.

## EXERCISE 1

Schutz describes inclusion, control, and affection as components of a group. In the following case study of a group meeting, describe at least one example of inclusion, one example of control, and one example of affectional needs.

This is the twentieth meeting of a long-term, closed group that meets weekly in a retirement home. The group was begun by a baccalaureate student from a nearby college who was interested in reminiscing groups. After the student completed the semester, the activity director continued the group. The group had been discussing important people in their childhood and had brought photograph albums to share with one another. One rather quiet lady had no photographs with her. The leader noticed and made a special effort to draw her out and to get her to describe some of the people in her early life for the rest of the group. As she described them, she quietly explained that the family possessions had been lost when their home burned to the ground. She started to cry. The activity director said, "Oh, let's be brave now," and quickly changed the subject. A woman sitting next to the crying woman reached over and took her hand. At that point, an elderly man stated that no one had listened to him when he talked about being a fireman in the 1906 earthquake in San Francisco. The activity director ignored him and asked what the group would like to see in next month's activity programs.

## EXERCISE 2

From the list of eight interpersonal problems Schutz describes, select one problem that you think could be related to the situation depicted in Figure 6–2. Describe why, and then list several ways you would try to get each of the members back into the group.

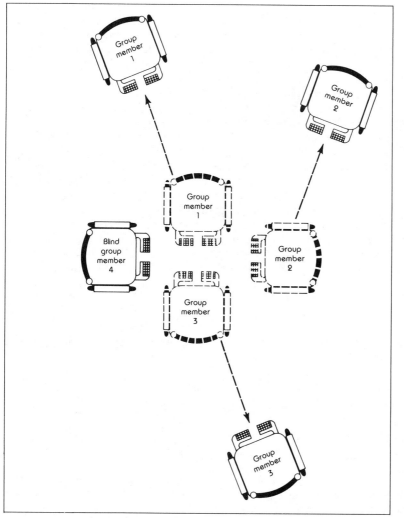

FIGURE 6–2. *An example of difficulties with inclusion and control that occurred during an initial meeting of a group of aged persons in a skilled nursing facility.*

## REFERENCES

Blake, D. 1973. Group work with the institutionalized elderly. In *Psychosocial nursing care of the aged.* 1st ed., ed. I. M. Burnside. New York: McGraw-Hill.

Burnside, I. M. 1969. Group work among the aged. *Nursing Outlook* 17(6): 68–72 (June).

————. 1976. One-to-one relationship therapy with the aged. In *Nursing and the aged.* 1st ed., ed. I. M. Burnside. New York: McGraw-Hill.

Etzioni, A. 1971. Home—A Buberian play. *Psychotherapy and Social Sciences Review* 5(10): 26–27 (September 17).

Freud, S. 1922. *Group psychology and the analysis of the ego.* Trans. J. Strachey. London: Hogarth.

Holland, D. L. 1973. Co-leadership with a group of stroke patients. In *Psychosocial nursing care of the aged.* 1st ed., ed. I. M. Burnside. New York: McGraw-Hill.

Holtzen, V. 1973. Short-term group work in a rehabilitation hospital. In *Psychosocial nursing care of the aged.* 1st ed., ed. I. M. Burnside. New York: McGraw-Hill.

Schutz, W. C. 1958. *FIRO: A three-dimensional theory of interpersonal behavior.* New York: Holt, Rinehart & Winston.

Tappen, R., and T. Touhy. 1983. Group leader—Are you a controller? *Journal of Gerontological Nursing* 9(1): 34 (January).

Van den Berg, J. H. 1955. *The phenomenological approach to psychiatry.* Springfield, Ill.: Thomas.

## BIBLIOGRAPHY

Jones, D. C. 1975. Spatial proximity, interpersonal conflict, and friendship formation in the intermediate-care facility. *The Gerontologist* 15(2): 150–54 (April).

Kuypers, J. A. 1972. Internal-external locus of control, ego functioning, and personality characteristics in old age. Part 1. *The Gerontologist* 12(2): 168–73 (Summer).

Kuypers, J. A., and V. L. Bengston. 1973. Competence and social breakdown: A social-psychological view of aging. *Human Development* 16(2): 37–49.

Lowenthal, M. F., and C. Haven. 1968. Interaction and adaptation: Intimacy as a critical variable. *American Sociological Review* 33(1): 20–30.

Reid, D. W., G. Haas, and D. Hawkings. 1977. Locus of desired control and positive self-concept of the elderly. *Journal of Gerontology* 32(4): 441–50 (July).

Schutz, W. 1961. On group composition. *Journal of Abnormal and Social Psychology* 62:275–81.

Thelen, H. A. 1954. Control: Developing the group culture. In *Dynamics of groups at work.* Chicago: University of Chicago Press.

## RESOURCES

### Films

*Joy of Communication* (color, 18 minutes, 1975). This film, produced by Albert Saparoff, attempts to show how people of all ages communicate. It has no dialogue, only music. Dana Productions, Inc., 6249 Babcock Avenue, North Hollywood, CA 91606.

chapter 7

# Group Work in a Day Care Center

*Irene Burnside, Jean A. Baumler, and Shelly Weaverdyck*

*Lost brain cells cannot be replaced, and lost capabilities may not be restored. Yet the severely impaired need not be doomed to vegetable-like existence. Most of them have resources and capabilities which they can use pleasurably, with dignity and confidence if we have the knowledge, skill, and patience to help them use their remaining skills.*

ALVIN GOLDFARB (1973, 82)

BARBARA KALT

---

### LEARNING OBJECTIVES

- List four distinctive features of the model described in this chapter.

- Define **Mental Status Questionnaire**.

- Define **Face-Hand Test**.

- List three goals of the working phase.

- Discuss termination techniques groups leaders might use.

### KEY WORDS

- Aphasia

- Catastrophic reactions

- Dehydration

- Goals

- Group modality

- Termination

- Ventilation

---

There is currently very little in the literature regarding group work with confused elderly who attend day care centers and who are being maintained in the community (Burnside 1981; Blackman 1980). The authors believe this paucity indicates the need for a model that can be easily implemented in a day care setting. This chapter describes the operationalism of such a model by the authors. The model subsequently was adapted and adopted by one author, Irene Burnside, for groups that were co-led by baccalaureate nursing students, which is described in Chapter 36.

The model presented has four distinctive features: (1) the eclectic use of these group modalities: art therapy, discussion, physical exercise, reality orientation, reminiscing therapy, remotivation therapy, and problem-solving; (2) the ability of the group agenda and process to accommodate a wide variety of chronic handicaps and diagnoses among the group members; (3) a focus on a holistic approach to health; and (4) members who lived in the community with families or had been placed in board-and-care homes.

Most papers and research reports on group work with confused elderly concern the institu-

tionalized elderly (Burnside 1981, 1978; Goldfarb 1971; Rechtschaffen 1959; Lesser et al. 1981; Linden 1953, 1954, 1955). We extrapolated what we thought were the best qualities of several different group modalities that appeared to be successful with institutionalized elderly and adapted them to the group to be described in this chapter.

This chapter is divided into three sections: Part 1 discusses the launching of the model group, Part 2 describes the group process during the 13-week period, and Part 3 presents the observations and recommendations of the leaders.

### PART 1: LAUNCHING THE GROUP

The three authors—a gerontological nursing instructor (Burnside), a gerontological nursing student in a master's program (Baumler), and a doctoral student specializing in gerontological neuropsychology (Weaverdyck)—served as group leaders. Prior to beginning the group, the leaders spent two days of intensive planning, which included: (1) interviewing and administering Mental Health Status Questionnaires (MSQ) (Kahn, Goldfarb, and Pollack 1960) (Figure 7–1) and Face-Hand (FH) tests (Kahn, Goldfarb, and Pollack 1960) (Figure 7–2) to each group member, (2) listening to staff descriptions and the medical-social history of each member, (3) determining specific goals and

This chapter is based on a paper presented to the International Congress of Gerontology, Hamburg, Germany, July 12–17, 1981. The authors are grateful to Marianne Mannia, R.N., Darcy Anderson, and Drew Bradley for their support of this group work endeavor at Rosener House, Menlo Park, California.

| Guidelines |
| --- |
| 1. Patients often say that the question is silly or that they do not want to answer, usually indicating that they do not immediately know the answer. Rephrase the question and *urge* the patient to answer. With urging, patients often do know the answer; they simply need more time to respond. |
| 2. Tell the patient when an incorrect response is given and again urge the patient to try again. |
| 3. When asking time-related questions, be sure that the patient has access to this information. *Homebound and institutionalized patients often do not have access to calendars that they can read, and their daily activities do not vary enough to help them orient themselves to time.* |

| Mental Status Questionnaire | |
| --- | --- |
| 1. Where are we now? | Place |
| 2. Where is this place located? | Place |
| 3. What are today's date and day of month? | Time |
| 4. What month is it? | Time |
| 5. What year is it? | Time |
| 6. How old are you? | Memory—recent or remote |
| 7. What is your birthday? | Memory—recent or remote |
| 8. What year were you born? | Memory—recent or remote |
| 9. Who is president of the United States? | General information—memory |
| 10. Who was president before him? | General information—memory |

| Ratings of Mental Status Questionnaire | |
| --- | --- |
| No. of errors: | Presumed mental status: |
| 0–2 | Chronic brain syndrome, absent or mild |
| 3–5 | Chronic brain syndrome, mild to moderate |
| 6–8 | Chronic brain syndrome, moderate to severe |
| 9–10 | Chronic brain syndrome, severe |
| Nontestable | Chronic brain syndrome, severe |

FIGURE 7–1. *Mental Health Status questionnaire (MSQ): ratings, and guidelines to aid the examiner in obtaining the most accurate results possible from it*

SOURCE: Modified from R. L. Kahn, A. I. Goldfarb, and M. Pollack. 1960. Brief objective measure for the determination of mental status in the aged. *American Journal of Psychiatry* 117:326. Reprinted by permission of the American Psychiatric Association.

objectives for each member, (4) deciding on pre-test and posttest group evaluation standards, (5) planning the group meeting format, (6) scheduling rotation of leader and observer roles among the three leaders, and (7) ironing out philosophical differences among the leaders.

The group members were selected by the director of a day care center, a nurse who enthusiastically supported our endeavors. The day care center averaged 25 to 30 frail elderly daily. The director selected nine participants who had serious communication and/or mental health problems as potential group members. Of that number we selected three men and three women.*

---

*The three excluded were seen on an individual basis by the leaders. They were not included in the group because their cognitive abilities and communication skills seemed greater than those of the individuals we selected.

## PART 2: GROUP PROCESS

### Beginning Phase

**Goals.** The goals of the beginning phase of the group were to increase orientation, allay anxiety, prevent "catastrophic reactions," and bolster self-esteem.

To increase orientation, we made name tags and/or helped group members to make their own. We always called members by the names they requested. Robert was always known as Bob; another man wanted to be called Bud. We established rituals and a regular schedule for the meetings. For example, we used a great deal of touch. As participants entered the meeting room, we greeted them; after the first few meetings, each leader began to hug each member.

We believed that establishing a structured agenda for each session would help minimize

---

### Instructions

The client sits facing the examiner, feet flat on the floor, hands resting on the knees. The client is touched or brushed simultaneously on one cheek and the dorsum of one hand, usually in a specified order. The face-hand test is done first with the client's eyes closed, then the series is repeated with the eyes open. Eighty percent of individuals who make errors with the eyes closed will show no improvement with the eyes open. In trials 1 through 4 the client becomes accustomed to the procedure. In trials 5 and 6 the examiner informs the client where he or she touches and reinforces a correct response by saying something such as, "That's right, both cheeks."

---

### Common Order of Stimulation in Face-Hand Test

1. Right cheek—left hand
2. Left check—right hand
3. Right cheek—right hand
4. Left check—left hand

Initial trials. Response evaluated in context of further trials.

5. Right cheek—left cheek
6. Right hand—left hand
7. Right cheek—left hand
8. Left cheek—right hand
9. Right cheek—right hand
10. Left cheek—left hand

Teaching trials. Almost always correctly reported. Examiner informs, or reinforces response that there were two touches. Incorrect response and stimulation not reported, felt but displaced, projected, or located in space are presumptive of brain damage.

---

### Results

A client who learns to correctly report where he or she is touched after the fifth and sixth trials is presumed free of brain damage. Only steps 7 through 10 (which is a repeat of 1 through 4) are considered presumptive of brain damage. The test results are highly correlated with the degree of brain syndrome as measured by the mental status questionnaire and by psychiatric evaluation. However, alert, well-educated people may score well even when some brain damage is present. If there is a discrepancy between the results of the MSQ and the face-hand test, it is possible that the cognitive functioning can be improved to the level of the better test performance.

In an acute brain syndrome all signs are not necessarily present at the same time. In chronic brain syndrome, while there may be variability in the degree of disorientation, memory, and intellectual function, all these are always simultaneously present.

FIGURE 7–2. Face-Hand (FH) Test*

SOURCE: Modified from R. L. Kahn, A. I. Goldfarb, and M. Pollack. 1960. Brief objective measures for the determination of mental status in the aged. American Journal of Psychiatry 117:326. Reprinted by permission of the American Psychiatric Association.

*This test is also called Double Simultaneous Stimulation Test (DSST).

confusion and anxiety. We hoped it would also strengthen the memory of the group experience among the members by establishing continuity from one session to the next. See Chapter 3.

By the end of the first three meetings, a schedule had emerged and was followed thereafter. The agenda of the sessions follows:

1. Leaders greet each person with a hug and by name.

2. Leader assists each person to wear a name tag.
3. Everyone sits down and drinks a glass of water.
4. Leader notes who is present and who is absent.
5. General discussion begins with (a) date, (b) review of the previous session, and (c) encouragement for each individual to share events of life since last meeting.

6. Discussion continues on topic for meeting, or group does a task (sometimes with props).

7. Refreshments are served and members socialize.

8. Members review the session: what happened and how each member feels about the meeting.

9. Group members hold hands in silence.

10. Members say goodbye to each other within the group meeting.

11. The leaders stand and go to the door.

12. The observer joins the leaders.

13. Each individual is hugged, thanked for attending, and bid goodbye.

Dehydration in some elderly clients, particularly confused individuals, has been reported in the literature (Todd 1976; Seymour et al. 1980). This is why we encouraged members to drink a glass of water at the beginning of the meeting. The leaders drank water with them and patiently waited until all were finished. Because of the disease process and poor coordination, the task often took a long time, so we offered toasts with the water!

At the conclusion of each meeting, we always shared coffee, tea, or juices and light refreshments. We carefully catered to individual preferences.

Early in the life of the group, we became aware of low self-esteem of most of the members, although we did not attempt to measure it. An ego-enhancing behavior practiced by the leaders of the group was *immediate* praise for grooming, for responses, for sharing, or for assuming any type of leadership responsibility in the group. A particular effort was made to avoid any "catastrophic reactions" (Goldstein 1959) during the meetings. A catastrophic reaction is the heightened anxiety that occurs when a brain-damaged or demented person is asked to perform tasks or answer questions and is unable to do so. This common occurrence is often overlooked by professionals. The low self-esteem of the members seemed to accompany changing body image, the ridicule and/or exasperation the member may experience in the family setting, loss of memory, and/or the knowledge of losing control of one's life. We became aware of the high degree of leader activity needed by this level of group (Table 7–1).

### Working Phase

**Goals.** The goals for the working phase were ventilation of feelings, acquisition of problem-solving skills, and improvement in the individual's ability to assess his or her own needs and skills.

In a short-term group such as this, leaders must work swiftly and have excellent timing when the group is together. We timed the introduction of topics and props in an attempt to foster expression of some of the intense feelings that we believed to exist in the members. We also used humor and encouraged laughter and enjoyment of the humorous moments in the group and the day care milieu.

From the authors' experience, we have noted that many group therapists seem reluctant to use any techniques that would make the group appear to be only a social group. Such leaders prefer a more directly penetrating insight therapy, but we find that such an approach with confused older people tends to fail. Equally unsuccessful are groups that patronize members and treat them as though they were children. We were determined to create a group atmosphere that fostered humor, spontaneity, and enjoyment, while at the same time encouraged members to address pain, feelings, and the current problems they faced. In this way, the group was truly a therapy group, yet laughter occurred frequently in group meetings.

Because our goals for this phase were specifically to encourage ventilation of feelings, self-assessment, and problem-solving skill acquisition, we paid close attention to the progress of the group members in these areas. We gradually adjusted the pace of transition from the pure socialization of the beginning phase to the more vulnerable working phase. At first, we largely reminisced about old times using props such as an old toaster and a cowbell, and the leaders encouraged acknowledgement of painful and sad memories only intermittently. Then gradually the references to, and the time spent on, psychic pain increased until we were devoting much of the session to discussing the individual's

TABLE 7-1.  **Degree of activity of worker as indicated by social health of group members**

*State of social health of the members; attitude towards responsibilities and satisfactions of group life*

| Degree of activity of the worker | Out of touch with reality | Withdrawn or very aggressive | Indifferent | Interested, but lack knowledge and experience of group life | Interested, and have knowledge and experience of group life | Eager and competent to participate |
|---|---|---|---|---|---|---|
| Controller | X | | | | | |
| Leader (very active) | | X | | | | |
| Stimulator Instigator (active) | | | X | | | |
| Adviser Teacher (less active) | | | | X | | |
| Participant-observer (occasional suggestion) | | | | | X | |
| Enabling observer (active when asked) | | | | | | X |

SOURCE:  From *Social Group Work Practice*, by G. Wilson and G. Ryland. Copyright © 1949 by Houghton Mifflin. Reprinted by permission.

particular limitations and feelings regarding them. Some of the feelings ultimately were expressed with leader encouragement. Planned intervention included gentle encouragement of members to express anger, feelings of insecurity and dependency, frustration, grief, and sorrow. Tears were not uncommon during the working phase; we encouraged both the verbal expression of the sad feelings and tears. At those times group members received much support from each other.

"Working" sessions included moving (the day care center moved to a new location during the life of the group), birthdays, and one entire session on mental/physical illnesses (discussed more fully under "Special Aspects of the Group"). In all of the sessions, the focus was consistently on the individual and past and present experiences regarding the topics being discussed. The leader made efforts first to encourage recognition of each member's limitations and emotional pain, and then immediately to discuss how the individual had successfully dealt with similar challenges and emotions in

the past. The application of past successes to the present situation was then explored.

The working sessions also included these tasks: making name tags, sorting playing cards, and constructing Easter baskets as gifts. These tasks provided opportunities for concrete observations by the leaders and further discussions of the skill strengths and limitations of each member.

### Termination

**Goals.**  The goals of the termination phase were to ease the leaders out of the group, to help the members to determine their future as a group, and to administer the MSQ and FH tests.

Termination must be carefully planned because many elderly members have suffered a series of losses, a number of them traumatic. Our last group session was about weddings, which helped the group to terminate on an upbeat note because one of the leaders was resigning to be married. That meeting blended happiness and sadness.

To reduce the trauma of termination, we continued to remind the group during the final four sessions of the date and the number of group meetings remaining. We also kept the staff informed of the group's progress so that they could help the members adjust to our leaving and, if possible, help them continue group meetings with minimal support. The leaders helped the group members to list on the blackboard their plans for future group meetings. The suggestions remained on the blackboard for future use by the group members and personnel. During the last meeting, a Polaroid camera was used to take pictures of the group for participants and leaders. The members could instantly see the photos, and they took them home to serve as reminders of that special group experience.

### Special Aspects of the Group

**Aphasia.** Aphasia was one difficulty in communication we experienced. For those with aphasia, we allowed more time for expression of thoughts. The leaders tried to interpret incorrect words and/or phrases and to assist with incomplete thoughts/sentences. One member (F. B.), who had marked aphasia from a stroke, made significant progress. She moved from reluctance to speak and miscomprehension to increased sharing and improved comprehension by others. In fact, F. B.'s verbal skills improved markedly over the 13-week period. One man (R. O.), diagnosed as having Alzheimer's disease, progressed from anxious one-word answers to speaking occasional and complete thoughts. His spontaneous humorous comments were delightful. Improved communication, we believe, was facilitated by the patience and the acceptance demonstrated by peers and leaders when an individual experienced difficulty expressing thoughts. Marianne Bartol (1979) has addressed this point in her fine article about Alzheimer's patients.

**Health Fair.** The seventh group session was atypical because it was an all-day Health Fair that involved all of the participants and staff members of the day care center. The fair was conducted by the leaders and a team of practitioners to provide a holistic health approach.

Activities included a physical examination by a family nurse practitioner, a foot examination by a gerontological clinical nurse specialist, and administration of MSQ and FH tests to each member of the day care center. (See Table 7–2 for the test results of the members of the small group described here.)

The break in the continuity of the group did not seem to affect group progress, perhaps because all leaders and group members were involved in the health fair.

**Unexpected Spin-off.** One spin-off of the group was the educational role the group provided for outside observers. After the group was stabilized, it was not uncommon to have visitors observing the meetings. Observers included gerontological nursing students, social workers, psychology students, and activity directors. We permitted only one visitor at a meeting, because we did not want the group to be too distracted. We held postmeeting conferences with the visitors to explain our interventions and philosophies.

The leaders also served as catalysts for the first meeting of the spouses of the three group members diagnosed as having Alzheimer's disease. A buffet supper was provided for the meeting, which was designed to give the wives an opportunity to discuss the coping problems they were experiencing. Shortly after this meeting, one wife got in touch on her own with another spouse. The self-help group was now expanded, and the three original members still remain in the group which formed.

### PART 3: OBSERVATIONS AND RECOMMENDATIONS

The day care center changed location after the fifth meeting. Although we had planned to take the group to the new location for a visit before the move, to reduce relocation trauma, we found it was not possible. The difficulties in arranging transportation and the unsafe environment created by the carpenters deterred us. During our sixth meeting, which was held at the new location, we were surprised to find that the participants experienced only minimal anxiety

TABLE 7–2. **Data on group members**

| Name | Age | Sex | Marital Status | Diagnosis and Medications | Physical Exam | Foot Examination | Errors/MSQ Pre | Post | Face-Hand Test Pre | Post* |
|------|-----|-----|----------------|---------------------------|---------------|------------------|-----|------|-----|-------|
| A. C. | 79 | F | W | Cardiovascular accident (no meds.) | Excellent | Excellent | 3/10 | 3/10 | 0 | 2 |
| E. B. | 62 | F | W | Closed head injury — subdural hematoma | Excellent | Excellent | 5/10 | 6/10 | 20 | 20 4 more RH E 2 more LH E |
| F. B. | 73 | F | M | Cardiovascular accident with severe aphasia and dysarthria; L. hemiparesis | Dentures / Arrhythmia present | Refused | 4/10 | 3/10 | 17 | 20 6 more RH E |
| H. N. (replaced F. P. after 4th meeting) | 67 | M | M | Alzheimer's; aphasia — severe | Excellent | Excellent | not present | 4/10 | not present | 20 3D |
| R. O. | 61 | M | M | Alzheimer's (Haldol; Cogentin; Dilantin; aphasia — severe | Normal (but elevated blood pressure) | Excellent (feet dirty) | 10/10 | 10/10 | 20 | 20 |
| F. P. (removed from group after 4th meeting) | 52 | M | M | Alzheimer's (Mellaril); aphasia — severe | not present | not present | not present | 8/10 | not present | 20 |
| E. R. (left state after 6th meeting) | 69 | F | W | Cardiovascular accident; aphasia — severe; depression | not present | not present | 10/10 | not present | 19 | not present |

*RH = Right hand; LH = Left hand; E = Extinction; D = Displacement.

from the move; the staff members fared less well as they continually searched for items and records still packed.

We received a weekly report from the personnel at the day care center and from the significant others regarding observed behavioral changes in group members. We observed the changes in affect immediately within the group itself. Changes in affect included an increase in smiling and laughter among the behaviors. The moods indicated their delight in seeing one another and the leaders again. On one occasion, an aphasic man picked up one of the leaders in a bear hug and swung her around in a circle. The leaders were so tuned in to relocation trauma that we had expected negative results. We simply underestimated the security and stability of these group members. Observed

behavioral changes also occurred outside of the group: F. B., who had been very picky and complained constantly about the lunch served, began eating more and complaining less. R. O., who had grown aloof and distant from his wife, became more affectionate toward her and began responding to her. On one vacation trip he sat holding her hand during the entire drive to a distant city.

On all behavior tabulated, improvement occurred throughout the 13-week period. This included performance on tasks, which became increasingly complex with each meeting, and facility with verbal skills on the part of those with aphasia. All of these improvements are particularly notable given the fact that the pre- and post-MSQ scores remained essentially the same and the FH scores either stayed the same or declined. (The FH scores of three members declined; they were retested at a different time of the day by another tester and received the same score.) Signs of increasing organic impairment occurred in the Alzheimer patients; R. O. began urinating in a wastebasket and another showed marked increases in distractibility and irritability.

## SUMMARY

The group approach described in this chapter to the treatment of the affective and cognitive aspects of disorders is useful and can be easily adapted to various situations and disorders.

Group leadership was enhanced by a multi-discipline approach. Group process included much use of humor and spontaneity. We highly recommend that leaders plan not only for the total group experience but for each meeting as well. Individual goals for members must be delineated at the outset of the group and must be reevaluated weekly. Careful weekly records are helpful in writing accounts and reports and for teaching interested observers.

We highly recommend this group model for implementation in other day care centers for older people who are frail.

## EXERCISE 1

Conduct a literature search in one area of group work—for example, reality orientation, music therapy, poetry, psychotherapy.

1. Select two research articles about the same modality from this search, summarize them in outline form, and critique them.
2. Compare and contrast the findings of the two studies you selected.
3. Select from the literature search the studies that have valid findings and state the rationale for their validity in your own words.

## EXERCISE 2

Select a partner from the class. One student will role-play a confused elderly person; the other will administer an MSQ to the role-player and score it.

## EXERCISE 3

Select a partner from the class. Practice performing a Face-Hand Test on one another and score it.

## REFERENCES

Bartol, M. 1979. Nonverbal communication in patients with Alzheimer's disease. *Journal of Gerontological Nursing* 5(4): 21–31.

Blackman, J. C. 1980. Group work in the commu-
nity: Experiences with reminiscence. In *Psychosocial nursing care of the aged.* 2d ed., ed. I. M. Burnside. New York: McGraw-Hill.

Burnside, I. M. 1981. Reminiscing as therapy: An overview. In *Nursing and the aged.* 2d ed., ed. I. M. Burnside. New York: McGraw-Hill.

_____. 1978. *Working with the elderly: Group process and techniques.* North Scituate, Mass.: Duxbury Press.

Goldfarb, A. I. 1971. Group therapy with the old and aged. In *Comprehensive group psychotherapy,* ed. H. J. Kaplan and B. Sadock. Baltimore: Williams & Wilkins.

_____. 1973. *Aged patients in long-term care facilities.* Department of Health, Education, and Welfare Publication no. 1724–00321, p. 82. Washington, D.C.: National Institute of Mental Health.

Goldstein, K.: 1959. Functional disturbances in brain damage. In *American handbook of psychiatry,* ed. S. Arieti, 770–94. New York: Basic Books.

Kahn, R. L., A. I. Goldfarb, and M. Pollack. 1960. Brief objective measure for the determination of mental status in the aged. *American Journal of Psychiatry* 117:326.

Lesser, J., L. W. Lazarus, R. Frankel, and S. Havasy. 1981. Reminiscence group therapy with psychotic geriatric inpatients. *The Gerontologist* 21(3): 291–96 (June).

Linden, M. E. 1953. Group psychotherapy with institutionalized senile women: Study in gerontologic human relations. *International Journal of Group Psychotherapy* 3:150–70.

_____. 1954. The significance of dual leadership in gerontologic group psychotherapy: Studies in gerontologic human relations III. *International Journal of Group Psychotherapy* 4:262–73.

_____. 1955. Transference in gerontologic group psychotherapy: Studies in gerontologic human relations IV. *International Journal of Group Psychotherapy* 5:61–79.

Rechtschaffen, A. 1959. Psychotherapy with geriatric patients: A review of the literature. *Journal of Gerontology* 14:73–84.

Seymour, D. G., P. J. Henschke, R. D. T. Cape, and A. J. Campbell. 1980. Acute confusional states in dementia in the elderly: The role of dehydration/ volume depletion, physical illness and age. *Age and Ageing* (9)3: 137–46 (August).

Todd, J. 1976. Water depletion in mentally disturbed patients. *Nursing Mirror* 142(18): 60–61 (April 29).

## BIBLIOGRAPHY

ACNHA's research brief: Survey on adult day care services. 1977. *Journal of Long Term Care Administration* 5(1): 27–34.

Birren, J. E., and R. B. Sloan. 1980. *Handbook of mental health and aging.* Englewood Cliffs, N.J.: Prentice-Hall.

Burnside, I. M. 1979. Alzheimer's disease: An overview. *Journal of Gerontological Nursing* 5(4): 14–20.

_____. ed. 1980. *Psychosocial nursing care of the aged.* 2d ed. New York: McGraw-Hill.

Dunn, T., and T. Arie. 1973. Mental disturbance in the old person. *British Medical Journal* 4:413–16.

Finkel, S. I. 1982. Experiences of a private-practice psychiatrist working with the elderly in the community. *International Journal of Mental Health* 8(3–4): 147–72.

Friedlander, H. 1983. Differential use of groups in mainstreaming the handicapped elderly. In *Group work with the frail elderly.* New York: Haworth Press.

Gilbert, J. G. 1977. The day care center—An alternative to institutionalization of the elderly. *Long Term Care and Health Services Administration Quarterly* 1(1): 71–77 (March).

Hughes, C. P. 1978. The differential diagnosis of dementia in the senium. In *Senile dementia: A biomedical approach,* K. Nandy, ed. New York: Elsevier North-Holland.

Jana, D. K., and L. Romano-Jana. 1973. Hypernatraemic psychosis in the elderly: Case reports. *Journal of the American Geriatrics Society* 21:437–77.

Katzman, R., R. Terry, and K. Bick, eds. 1978. *Alzheimer's disease: Senile dementia and related disorders.* New York: Raven Press.

Lezak, M. D. 1978. Living with the characterolically altered brain injured patient. *Journal of Clinical Psychiatry* 39(6): 592–98.

_____. 1976. *Neuropsychological assessment.* New York: Oxford University Press.

Novick, A. 1973. Day care meets geriatric needs. *Hospitals,* November 16: 47–50.

Pfeiffer, E. 1975. A short portable mental status questionnaire for the assessment of organic brain deficit in elderly patients. *Journal of the American Geriatrics Society* 23(10): 433–39.

Slaby, A. E., and R. J. Wyatt. 1974. *Dementia in the presenium.* Springfield, Ill.: Thomas.

Stabler, N. 1981. The use of groups in day centers for older adults. *Social work with groups* 4 (Nos. 3/4): 49–58 (Winter).

Verwoerdt, A. 1976. *Clinical geropsychiatry.* Baltimore: Waverly Press.

Wells, C. E. 1977. *Dementia.* Philadelphia: Davis.

Zarit, S. H. 1980. *Aging and mental disorders: Psychological approaches to assessment and treatment.* New York: Free Press.

## RESOURCES

### Program Kits and Training Slide/Tapes

Kit titles are Remembering County Fairs, Remembering Train Rides, Remembering 1924, Remembering School Days, Remembering the Depression, Remembering Farm Days, Remembering Fall, Remembering Automobiles, Remembering Birthdays, and Remembering Summertime. Training slide/tapes include Group Programs Involving the Older Adult. Catalogue available. Bi-Folkal Productions Inc., Route 1, Rainbow Farm, Blue Mounds, WI 53517; phone: (608) 241-7785 or (608) 437-8146.

# Basics of Group Work

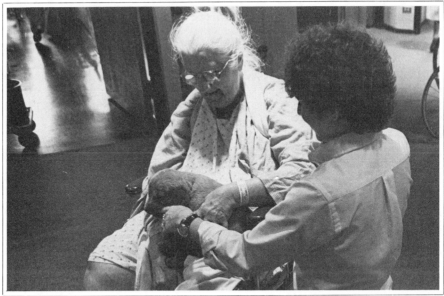

EUGENE RICHARDS/MAGNUM PHOTOS

Part 3 pulls together a variety of topics to provide some background on group work with the elderly and to help launch the new practitioner. In the past little systematic attention has been paid to the ways in which levels of group work with the aged are similar and different, or to the specific differences between group work with the aged and group work with younger persons. That is beginning to change; the literature in the field is increasing, and sophisticated studies are beginning to appear. (Chapters 7, 16, and 22 through 25 in this book bear out that fact; all are based on studies). The sheer number of old people is forcing all the disciplines to consider approaches for improving the quality of care and of life for their clients.

Chapter 8 discusses current needs and necessary training for mental health workers who deal with the aged in group settings. The projections of the number of mental health specialists needed to work with the aged population in the near future are staggering, and the need for group workers will continue to increase.

Contracts for group work, if they are initiated at all, are often poorly executed by new group leaders. Chapter 9 discusses the components of a contract and warns the reader of possible pitfalls to avoid during contract formation.

Chapter 10 focuses on group membership criteria, group settings, and group goals. Again, cautions are offered.

Chapter 11 explores a variety of problems in leadership and maintenance commonly encountered in group work with the elderly, such as high anxiety in a new leader. Common group concerns and steps that can be taken to avoid sabotage by the staff are also discussed.

Linda Szafranski, a social worker, took an interesting stance in her group leadership by using patients as co-leaders in group sessions. Others may have done something similar, but their attempts may have lacked the planning and conscious structuring described by Szafranski in Chapter 12.

The projected increase of elderly persons in the population also means an increase in persons with dementia. Chapter 13 looks at leadership struggles with a mentally regressed group of elderly people. Three groups are compared and contrasted: One group was conducted in a 287-bed, locked facility; another, in a 91-bed nursing home; and the third, in a 66-bed, all-female, locked facility.

## chapter 8

# Education for Group Work

*Irene Burnside*

*The question today is not whether "older people are no longer educable" but whether we, the mental health professionals, are.*

J. L. RONCH AND J. S. MAIZLER (1977, 283)

JIM MENDENHALL

---

### LEARNING OBJECTIVES

- State four aspects of the demographic pattern of the aging population in the United States.

- Discuss the projected need for personnel to care for the elderly.

- Describe four cautions that new group leaders should heed.

- List four goals implicit in the educational objectives for mental health workers.

### KEY WORDS

- Chronicity
- Extended care facilities
- Intermediate care facilities
- Leadership
- Motivation
- Preceptor
- Projection
- Training requirements

---

This chapter describes the current and projected mental health needs of the aged and the implications for group workers. Students, health care workers and administrators, and instructors will be interested in the projection of the number of disciplines needed, the training requirements for mental health workers, and the problems and cautions for new group leaders.

Demographic aspects of the elderly in the United States are covered in detail in Chapter 1. This chapter describes special conditions the professional group leader will encounter in elderly members. If by the year 2030 persons 65 and over will comprise 20 percent of the U.S. population, we will be in dire need of well-educated and experienced health practitioners.

## HEALTH PROBLEMS

The proportion of persons with health problems increases with age, and the elderly as a group are more likely than younger persons to have not only multiple and chronic, but often severely disabling conditions.

Health problems are far more common among the elderly than among their juniors. Chronic disabling conditions occur more frequently and are likely to persist for longer periods of time than among those who are younger. In 1980—the latest year for which this type of information is available—nearly half (45 percent) of all noninstitutionalized persons aged 65 and over were reported to have a chronic health condition that limited their activities. In contrast, less than a quarter (24 percent) of those in the age range 45–64 and only about one in sixteen (7 percent) of those younger than 45 were so limited (Metropolitan Life Foundation 1982, 3).

## Chronicity

Chronicity will be one of the stark contrasts for the group leader of the elderly. The professional working with the aged must be able to work with both chronic physical and chronic mental conditons without excessive depression, frustration, or hopelessness.

Chronic disabling conditions—defined generally as those lasting longer than three months—are usually more severe among the elderly than among younger persons. In 1980, about seven eighths of the chronically disabled population aged 65 or older were restricted in their major activity—working at a job or keeping house—and three out of every eight were so severely disabled as to be unable to pursue this activity at all. At ages 45–64, about four fifths of the chronically disabled were restricted in their major activity, with about a quarter unable to carry on that activity (Metropolitan Life Foundation 1982, 3).

See Table 8–1 for a comparison of the frequency of chronic conditions in those age 65 and older and persons under the age of 65.

These disabilities will have a great impact on group attendance, drop-out rate, and absenteeism. Conditions that the group leader will need to understand fairly well include arthritis, cancer, hypertension, visual losses, hearing losses, and diabetes; group members may have complaints related to these ailments or may be unable to attend or participate fully in meetings during exacerbations of these particular illnesses.

Arthritis and rheumatism, followed closely by heart conditions, were the most common causes of activity limitation at ages 65 and over during the survey year. Among those unable to carry on their major activity, the order was reversed. Nearly half of the elderly were restricted to some degree by these two chronic conditions. Hypertension, visual impairments,

and diabetes were also major causes of disability among those aged 65 or older (Metropolitan Life Foundation 1982, 3).

A two-year effort to establish a much needed Separate National Institute on Arthritis at the National Institute of Health failed to pass in the final days of the 97th Congress.

Depression and mental confusion are two additional problems caretakers can expect to find in elderly clients. Note that Table 8–1 lists only chronic physical conditions. This is also true of Figure 8–1, which illustrates the major chronic conditions found among the elderly. Depression and confusion may be reasons for implementing groups, and many of the chronic diseases listed earlier indicate the need for health education groups and disease-related, or self-help, groups. (See Chapter 20 for the importance of self-help groups.)

In a recent General Accounting Office (GAO) report, it was stated that the mental health needs of the elderly are not being met. It further stated that, "nursing homes are loathe to admit the mentally ill because these patients require supervision, are often covered by Medicaid,

**TABLE 8-1. Frequency of chronic conditions among U.S. population, 1980**

| Health status | All ages | Percent distribution | | |
| | | Under age 45 | Ages 45–64 | Ages 65 and over |
|---|---|---|---|---|
| **All persons** | 100.0 | 100.0 | 100.0 | 100.0 |
| Persons with no activity limitation | 85.6 | 93.2 | 76.1 | 54.8 |
| Persons with activity limitation | 14.4 | 6.8 | 23.9 | 45.2 |
| With limitation in major activity | 10.9 | 4.1 | 18.8 | 39.0 |
| Unable to carry on major activity | 3.7 | .8 | 6.4 | 17.2 |
| **Persons limited in activity\*** | | | | |
| All degrees of limitation | 100.0 | 100.0 | 100.0 | 100.0 |
| Arthritis and rheumatism | 17.0 | 5.1 | 20.1 | 25.3 |
| Heart conditions | 16.3 | 4.4 | 20.3 | 23.9 |
| Hypertension without heart involvement | 9.2 | 3.0 | 12.1 | 12.2 |
| Visual impairments | 4.5 | 3.9 | 3.2 | 6.4 |
| Diabetes | 5.2 | 2.3 | 6.9 | 6.3 |
| Unable to carry on major activity | 25.0 | 10.9 | 26.9 | 36.7 |
| Arthritis and rheumatism | 4.4 | .6 | 4.6 | 7.7 |
| Heart conditions | 6.3 | .6 | 7.8 | 10.2 |
| Hypertension without heart involvement | 2.6 | .4 | 3.4 | 3.8 |
| Visual impairments | 1.5 | .5 | 1.1 | 2.9 |
| Diabetes | 1.7 | .5 | 2.0 | 2.7 |

SOURCE: Metropolitan Life Foundation, 1982. *Statistical Bulletin* 63(1): 2 (January/March). Reprinted with permission.
NOTE: Basic data from National Center for Health Statistics.
*Survey year 1979.

All degrees of limitation

Unable to carry on major activity

Percentage of persons limited in activity

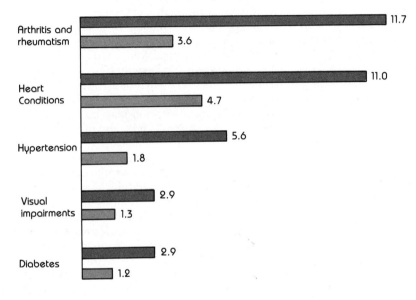

Arthritis and rheumatism — 11.7 / 3.6

Heart Conditions — 11.0 / 4.7

Hypertension — 5.6 / 1.8

Visual impairments — 2.9 / 1.3

Diabetes — 2.9 / 1.2

FIGURE 8–1. *Leading chronic conditions among the U.S. elderly (ages 65 and over), 1979.*

and may damage the reputation of the community" (Quinn 1983, p. 363). GAO advised that personnel in nursing homes should be provided with training in mental health diagnosis and treatment.

### Acute Conditions

We tend to focus on chronic conditions in the elderly. We forget that they are prone to acute conditions just as other age groups are.

Acute conditions—defined as those conditions lasting less than three months and involving medical attention or activity restriction—occurred less frequently but were responsible for more disability days among the elderly than among those under age 65. In 1980, persons 65 years of age or older averaged 1.1 episodes of disability from acute conditions, compared with 8.8 days of restricted activity and 3.6 days of bed confinement for those in the age range 45–64, and 10 days of restricted activity and 4.5 days of bed confinement among those under 45 years of age. For each episode of ill-

ness, those who were 65 years of age or older averaged 9.3 days of restricted activity . . . (Metropolitan Life Foundation 1982, 3).

Alvin Goldfarb (1970) predicted increases in mental disorders. The need for groups for Alzheimer's patients and self-help and support groups for their relatives will continue. Projections of the need for mental health specialists are staggering. According to Morton Kramer, Carl Taube, and Richard Redick (1973, 487), "Mental health manpower planners realize that it will never be possible to train the necessary number of psychiatrists, psychologists, social workers, and psychiatric nurses to handle the expected increase in demand."

The GAO study criticized community mental health centers which were federally funded because only 4 percent of the clients were 65 years old or over and there was a lack of outreach (Quinn 1983).

Even now only a third of a million professional and technical workers are employed in programs designed primarily or solely for older

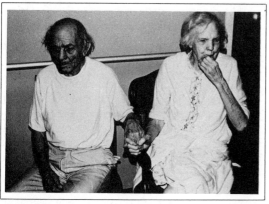

WILL PATTON

*The plight of the mentally impaired aged is a poignant one.*

persons, but fewer than 10 to 20 percent of these people have had formal training for their work (Butler 1975, 171). Moreover, to provide at least basic care for the elderly, professionals are needed to teach and supervise undergraduate, ancillary workers and volunteers. This acute shortage of qualified personnel is intensified by the rising rates of hospitalization, the growth in public and voluntary health agencies, the rapid advances in medicine, and the increasing sophistication of a television-watching public about mental health.

We need skilled professionals with various levels of expertise in geropsychiatry to spearhead a national program to provide basic health care for every elderly person who needs it. The program would include the maintenance of optimum health for those who are in good health and the prevention of illness, the treatment and care of those who are ill, and the rehabilitation and resocialization of those who are recovering from illness. Group work with the elderly can be especially valuable in rehabilitation and resocialization, in maintenance, and with relatives of the elderly.

## FUTURE HEALTH CARE OF THE ELDERLY

R. W. Besdine (1979) stated that the traditional health care systems we have were not structured with the elderly clients in mind.

C. Pegels (1981) explores a few areas that he feels will have an impact on the health care pro-

cess and the health care costs of the future. While he feels that some of these will improve the quality of health care, and the quality of life, this will be accomplished only at a cost to the taxpayers. He predicts that:

- Health care costs will keep rising.
- There will be an expansion of diagnostic procedures. (We have already seen the new PET [positive emissions transmission] scan.
- Self-evaluations by clients will continue and there will be considerable support for preventive medicine.
- There will be an increase in therapeutic procedures (for example, rehabilitation programs).
- The elderly will become health care providers. As the number of persons over age 65 increases, the younger elderly, between 65 and 70, will rejoin the work force. This could develop into a self-help movement in which groups of elderly aid each other as much as they can. Pegels suggests that not only would this group provide economic value but also the work could boost the mental outlook of those individuals who feel they are ignored by society.

R. W. Besdine (1979) stated that the number of health care professionals in the United States who are knowledgeable about the normal process of aging and who have the special skills of caring for the elderly population is grossly inadequate.

## NECESSARY DISCIPLINES IN MENTAL HEALTH CARE

Now and in the future large numbers of skilled professionals in the fields of nursing, psychiatry, psychology, and social work are needed to provide mental health care for the elderly (Kramer, Taube, and Redick 1973). Of these types of professionals, nurses are most involved in the care of the elderly, but the nursing profession has not yet fully addressed itself to the specific mental health needs of the elderly.

A promising if partial solution to this problem is the recent emergence of gerontological nursing. However, nurses specializing in gerontology are still rare in the United States (American Nurses' Association 1975). This shortage has both quantitative and qualitative implications. Quantitatively, of course, the shortage makes it impossible to supply acute care hospitals, extended care facilities, intermediate facilities, state hospitals, and other health facilities and educational programs with adequately prepared gerontological nurses. Qualitatively, the shortage decreases the effectiveness of nursing care and creates a further shortage through the lack of adequately prepared instructors.

Regarding medicine, the Regional Institutes Geriatrics in Medical Education (RIGM) convening in 1982, found the 66 percent of 127 medical schools in the United States offer geriatric electives and only 2 percent of the medical students take them. Few schools require medical students to rotate through long-term care settings. Other studies indicate 75 percent of practicing American physicians thought they had insufficient knowledge to care for older adults (Quinn, 1983).

R. L. Kane, D. Solomon, J. Beck, E. Keeler and R. A. Kane (1981) project a need for 1,500 academic geriatricians in academies, plus 47,000 additional staff for training, consultation, and primary care. About 8,000 persons specializing in geriatrics will be needed in the next decade.

The chronic shortage of nurses, psychiatrists, psychologists, and social workers underlines the continuing need for a variety of counselors, workers, and group leaders from humanities fields, such as art, music, poetry, and so on. Also, many paraprofessional-technical assistants are needed to help with direct patient care when professional care is not needed. Geriatric outreach workers (or home health aides) can also be enormously valuable. The primary purpose of these workers is "assisting older people to sustain their social, physical and emotional functioning, enabling them to remain in their own home and community and postponing or averting the need of institutionalization" (Kramer, Taube, and Redick 1973, 487). Volunteers can be used to give added assistance to the elderly and to provide input and support of the community in such organizations as Friendly Visitors and Meals on Wheels and in ombudsman programs and neighborhood health and legal services.

R. Tappen and T. Touhy (1983, 37) state that "people with little or no training often are used to lead groups of older adults. The use of untrained leaders frequently goes unnoted, as if there was no doubt about the appropriateness of this procedure." The need for professionals with psychosocial expertise, group leadership skills, and excellence in teaching will continue.

*A nurses' aide works with her peers to refine a nursing care plan. Note that the elderly resident is included in the plan so that the decisions are mutual.*

There is a trend now toward teaching classes to students from a variety of disciplines; that trend is not likely to cease. Murray Raskind (1977), for instance, describes the "blurring" that occurred when a psychiatrist–social worker–nurse team worked together on a geriatric project in the state of Washington, visiting the aged with mental health problems who were still living in their own homes.

## TRAINING REQUIREMENTS FOR MENTAL HEALTH WORKERS

The basic philosophy behind the training of mental health workers at any level is to give life more meaning and to make death less fearsome for the elderly. Thus, long-range training goals should be to keep the aged as physically, psychologically, and socially healthy as possible and to maintain them as contributing members of society for as long as possible. These goals are implicit in the educational objectives for mental health workers:

- Giving expert care.
- Learning how to work with professionals from all disciplines: chaplains, physicians, sociologists, occupational and physical therapists, psychiatrists, psychologists, nurses, and staffs of community agencies.
- Assuming primary responsibility for a group of aged people.
- Instructing ancillary workers in group principles.

The wide range of training requirements for mental health professionals and ancillary workers reflects the different ways in which various instructors try to achieve these goals. Some or all of the following principal methods must be employed:

- Traditional classroom instruction.
- Field experience.
- Supervised group instruction.
- Community teamwork experience — multidisciplinary.
- Case studies.
- Participation in research projects.

Volunteers need an initial orientation period and then a supervisor who will serve as a bridge between them and the appropriate agency or program. Paraprofessional-technical assistants should be required to complete a basic three-month program approved by the State Department of Education and/or the appropriate licensing board. At the college level, undergraduates should take some courses in group theory and practice as well as gerontology in an accredited professional school. Graduate courses should be available in teaching, administration, and/or implementation of group work or group therapy. At the postgraduate level, every student should have the opportunity to specialize in geropsychiatry. Beyond that, professionals need doctoral degrees for the highest level of expertise — that is, as authorities in the field and as administrators, professors of geropsychiatry in universities, and researchers.

WILL PATTON

*"People therapy" can be immensely important in improving the quality of life for the elderly (Pfeiffer 1973). This woman is part of a current events discussion group that meets regularly in an extended care facility.*

Appropriate sites for such training are general hospitals, extended care facilities (ECF), intermediate care facilities (ICF), family homes, retirement residences, public and private geriatric clinics, and universities. The training should be both multidisciplinary and unidisciplinary, but the emphasis should be on multidisciplines because the health care of the aged involves intervention in multiple complex physical and mental health problems. The standards of training should be set by an accrediting body of the profession.

This brief survey of training requirements does not, of course, cover the special problems that inevitably arise. However, two should be emphasized here. First, the newness of the field of knowledge requires teachers and researchers with open, inquiring minds and a willingness to try new methods, as well as the cooperation of many people from both private industry and the community. Second, training requirements must be flexible enough to meet the special needs of different groups of elderly people. Mental health workers should be able to communicate effectively with their clients and understand their customs, to empathize with the problems of the elderly, and to combine a sincere interest in their welfare with patience and tolerance.

## THE GROUP LEADER

One problem that confronts the prospective group leader is the wide variety of educational programs, which range from a two-year degree (A.D.N. or A.A. program) to a doctorate. In other words, who can do what in group work? The ability to lead groups of old people varies enormously and is based on the individual's knowledge of psychology, group theory, psychodynamics, and psychiatry and a background in gerontology and geriatrics. However, even with a satisfactory background the leader may lack the motivation needed to begin a group or the necessary supervision. Sometimes one simply cannot find knowledgeable people to supervise.

### Helping Group Leaders Flourish

The education of the leader, the type of group to be led, and the special talents of the leader are all factors to be considered in the group leadership role. We have not yet sufficiently encouraged group leaders to flourish and develop their own style. Style in group leading is important. Some leaders have a flair for psychotherapy groups, some for music or art groups; others are abundantly patient with the regressed aged; and still others do beautiful interventions with dying patients. Group leaders and their special talents are described by a variety of contributors to this book: Booth, Byrne, Hennessey, Martin, Moore, and O'Dell.

Instructors and persons in leadership positions who maintain an optimistic, warm attitude toward both students and the elderly can also assist in the development of group leaders. A variety of co-leadership pairs should be encouraged, for they have much to learn from one another. The importance of people from multiple disciplines planning together in the care of the aged is best demonstrated in coleadership, which is one way for leaders to share their multidisciplinary accomplishments.

Instructors are remiss when they do not encourage students to submit reports of their accomplishments for publication. Students in graduate programs, especially are often very articulate and sophisticated practitioners. Many caring, innovative ideas and a great deal of knowledge can come through in a student's paper.

Because instructors become role models, they do need to maintain a clinical orientation. Their own interaction with aged clients and the ability to use real-life examples when teaching, in lieu of hypothetical cases, will endear them to students. And students will begin to emulate the instructors.

### Cautions for New Leaders

Some of the secrets of successful group leadership are meticulous communication, scheduling, and attention to details. Students often create problems through lack of communication with and consideration for the families of group members and the staff. Poor scheduling and general disorganization lead to unnecessary demands on the staff and increase everyone's anxiety level.

For these and other reasons, new leaders need close supervision and an available preceptor.

For example, one potentially serious problem is that it is not always possible for the group leader to limit or control what occurs in a group meeting. Difficult situations that new leaders need to be cautioned about include agitated members; hostile, belligerent members attacking other group members physically; sad sessions where crying may prevail; and discussion of suicide by a member. Nonprofessionals should be warned not to probe or encourage strong feelings or emotions and should be reminded that they are doing group work, not group psychotherapy.

I have observed psychiatrists, psychologists, and social workers challenge instructors who place students in a facility to do group work, fearing that they may be doing psychotherapy. The territorial turf may account for the reaction, but they usually seem to feel that a student will unearth strong emotions and that the old people will go flying out of control. Although this may have been observed with younger age groups, I have never heard new leaders of aged groups discuss such results in spite of hearing many warnings — perhaps others have. Old people are far less emotionally frail than suggested by many professionals.

A related problem is both subtle and not-so-subtle sabotage by staff members in institutions or agencies. On the day of group meetings, the patients may be on pass, or they may be having an X ray, or they may still be in bed. The cook may not know that coffee is needed. It may take time to break through the wall of resistance. However, resistance is not always the reason for the problem; sometimes it is simply brouhaha in the facility and lack of organization and efficiency.

A well-run facility can take group work in stride and can encourage both the elderly members and the group leader in the endeavor. That cooperation and support has to come from the top. A supportive administrator and director of nurses will pass support down to the nurses' aides. But students usually have to prove themselves before there is much support from the staff. The doubting Thomases in facilities may not be sure what it is all about when a leader first begins a group. *Students doing group work — or any new group leader, for that matter — should have strong preceptor support.* Students may get discouraged with the group process and staff interpersonal relationships; Chapter 35, on preceptorship, deals with this aspect of group work.

## SUMMARY

This chapter discusses the mental health needs of the elderly and their implications for group workers. The proportion of the population over 65 is continuing to grow. This increase will lead to an expanding list of psychosocial problems, especially mental disorders. Projections of the need for psychiatric nurses, psychiatrists, psychologists, and social workers indicate that there will not be nearly enough to meet the demand. Even now the shortage of such personnel and of qualified ancillary workers and volunteers is acute.

Mental health workers should learn how to (1) give expert care, (2) work with members of all disciplines, (3) assume primary responsibility for a group of elderly people, and (4) instruct ancillary workers in group principles. Training methods include (1) traditional classroom instruction, (2) field experience, (3) supervised group instruction, (4) community teamwork experience, (5) case studies, and (6) participation in research projects.

The ability to lead groups of old people varies widely and is based on the individual's knowledge of psychology, group theory, psychodynamics, and psychiatry and a background in gerontology and geriatrics. Educational programs range from a two-year degree to a doctorate. Group leaders should be encouraged to flourish and develop their own style. Co-leadership can be an important part of the process, for leaders can share their multidisciplinary accomplishments.

New leaders should be warned not to probe or encourage strong feelings; they are doing group work, not psychotherapy. Meticulous communication, scheduling, and attention to details are also important. Student leaders may encounter resistance from staff members or simply disorganization and inefficiency, but a well-run facility in which support for the new leader filters down from the top administrators can take group work in its stride. In any case, however, students or any group leader should have strong preceptor support.

## EXERCISE 1

Select one special ability or talent you feel you have and consider how you might use it in a group leadership role.

## EXERCISE 2

Conduct a small survey of the group work with the elderly being done in your own community. If none is being conducted in your community, where did you have to go to find it? Give a brief analysis of the group that interested you the most.

## REFERENCES

American Nurses' Association. 1975. *Nursing and long-term care: Toward quality care for the aging — A report from the Committee on Skilled Nurs-Care.* ANA publication code GE 4 e m 4/75. Kansas City, Mo.

Besdine, R. W. 1979. Observations on Geriatric Medicine. Washington, D.C.: U.S. Government Printing Office, NIH 79-162, p. 21.

Butler, R. 1975. *Why survive? Being old in America.* New York: Harper & Row.

Goldfarb, A. I. 1970. Harmful psychosocial effects of life-expectancy. *Geriatric Focus* 9(16): 5-6 (June–July).

Kramer, M., C. A. Taube, and R. W. Redick. 1973. Patterns of use of psychiatric facilities by the aged. In *The psychology of adult development and aging,* ed. C. Eisdorfer and M. P. Lawton. Washington, D.C.: American Psychological Association.

Metropolitan Life Foundation. 1982. *Statistical Bulletin* 63(1): 2-16 (January/March).

Pegels, C. 1981. *Health care and the elderly.* Rockville, Md.: Aspen Systems.

Pfeiffer, E. 1973. Use of drugs which influence behavior in the elderly: Promises, pitfalls and perspectives. In *Drugs and the elderly,* ed. R. Davis. Los Angeles: University of Southern California Press.

Quinn, C. C. 1983. Nursing homes not meeting mental health needs, *Journal of Gerontological Nursing,* 9(6): 363, (June).

_____. 1983. American Association of Medical Colleges Issues Report on Geriatric Training, *Journal of Gerontological Nursing* 9(6) 363, (June).

Raskind, M. 1977. Recognition and assessment of mental disorders in later life. Paper presented at training program on mental health needs of the aged, Issaquah, Wash., February 23.

Ronch, J. L., and J. S. Maizler. 1977. Individual psychotherapy with the institutionalized aged. *American Journal of Orthopsychiatry* 47(2): 283 (April).

Tappen, R., and T. Touhy. 1983. Group leader— Are you a controller? *Journal of Gerontological Nursing* 9(1): 34 (January).

## BIBLIOGRAPHY

Anderson, C. J. 1970. Instituting change in psychiatric geriatric settings. *Journal of Psychiatric Nursing* 8(4): 13-18 (July–August).

Babic, A. L. 1973. The older volunteer: Expectations and satisfactions. Part 1. *The Gerontologist* 5 (13): 87-90 (Spring).

Berger, L., and M. Berger. 1973. A holistic group approach to psychogeriatric outpatients. *International Journal of Group Psychotherapy* 23(4): 432-45 (October).

Bergman, S. 1974. Nursing attitudes to psychiatry and geriatrics as preferred work areas with deviant groups. *Israel Annals of Psychiatry* 12(2): 156-60 (June).

Birren, J. 1977. Report on manpower and training for mental health and aging. Unpublished report.

Bok, M. 1971. Some problems in milieu treatment of the chronic older mental patient. *The Gerontologist* 2(1): 141–47.

Bourestom, N. C. 1970. Evaluation of mental health programs for the aged. *Aging and Human Development* 1(3): 187–98.

Brody, E. M. 1974. *A social work guide for long-term care facilities.* Rockville, Md.: National Institute of Mental Health.

Brody, E. M., M. H. Kleban, M. P. Lawton, and H. A. Silverman. 1971. Excess disabilities of mentally impaired aged: Impact of individualized treatment. *The Gerontologist* 2(2): 124–33.

Burnside, I. M. 1970. Group work with the aged: Selected literature. Part 1. *The Gerontologist* 19(3): 241–46 (Autumn).

———, ed. 1980. *Psychosocial nursing care of the aged.* 1st ed. New York: McGraw-Hill.

———, ed. 1976. *Nursing and the aged.* 1st ed. New York: McGraw-Hill.

Cohen, R. G. 1972. Reach out and advocacy: Effective strategies in the treatment of the aged. Unpublished paper, annual meeting of the Gerontological Society, San Juan, P.R.

Davis, B. 1980. The gerontological nurse's role in implementing geropsychiatric primary nursing. In *New directions for nursing in the 80's.* Kansas City, Mo.: American Nurses' Association.

Feldman, R. A., and J. S. Wodarski. 1975. *Contemporary approaches to group treatment.* San Francisco: Jossey-Bass.

Gottesman, L. E., N. Bourestom, W. Donahue, and D. Coons. 1971. The technology of milieu treatment of the aged mental patient. Institute of Gerontology Library, Ann Arbor, Mich.

Group for the Advancement of Psychiatry, Committee on Aging. 1970. *Toward a public policy on mental health care of the elderly.* Report no. 79:651–700. New York.

Kahn, K. A., W. Hines, A. S. Woodson, G. Burkham-Armstrong, and C. Holtz. 1975. *A multi-disciplinary approach to assessing the quality of life and services in long-term care facilities: Research report.* Report of HEW Grant 5-R 18-HS-01243-02. Rockville, Md.: National Center for Health Services Research. November.

Kay, D. W., K. Bergman, and E. M. Foster. 1970. Mental illness and hospital usage in the elderly: A random sample followed up. *Comprehensive Psychiatry* 11:26–35.

Murray, J. 1976. Failure of the community mental health movement. *American Journal of Nursing* 75:11, 2034–36.

National Institute of Mental Health. 1972. *Mental health: Principles and training techniques in nursing home care.* Rockville, Md.

Naylor, H. H. 1972. Administration for services of older volunteers. Part 1. *The Gerontologist* 5(13): 85–87 (Spring).

Professional workers' attitudes toward the aged. 1971. *Journal of the American Geriatrics Society* 19 (July): 7.

Sainer, J. S., and F. K. Kallen. 1972. Serve: A case illustration of older volunteers in a psychiatric setting. Part 1. *The Gerontologist* 5(13): 90 (Spring).

Visiting Nurse Service of New York. 1965. *A study of psychological needs of aged patients at home.* A. I. Goldfarb, proj. dir. New York.

Washington University School of Nursing. 1961–62. *Effects of skilled nursing care upon personalization of older patients: A research report.* St. Louis, Mo.

Williams, R. H. 1972. *Perspectives in the field of mental health.* Rockville, Md.: National Institute of Mental Health.

Wolanin, M. O., and L. Phillips. 1981. *Confusion.* St. Louis, Mo.: Mosby.

## RESOURCES

### Films

*Aging, The Extension of Life* (black-and-white, 29 minutes, 1972). A famous biologist, Bernard Strehler, discusses how life may be extended and some of the social ramifications of living longer. University of Michigan, Media Resources Center, 416 Fourth Street, Ann Arbor, MI 48109.

*Stalking Immortality* (color, 20 minutes each part, 1978). *Part I* (narrated by Jason Robards): What you can do to prolong life. *Part II:* What medical science is doing to prolong life. Produced by J. F. Janewill Production, New York. Mass Media Ministries, 2116 North Charles Street, Baltimore, MD 21218.

# chapter 9

# Group Contracts

*Irene Burnside*

*Contracting is essentially a process by which the necessary elements of the desired behavior are explicitly outlined in the form of a contract.*

SUSAN BOEHM STECKEL (STECKEL AND SWAIN 1982, 33)

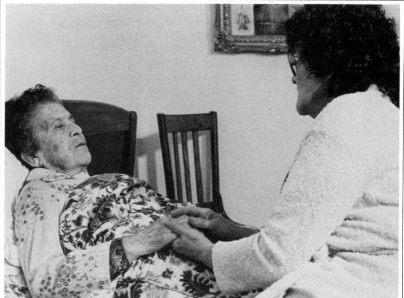

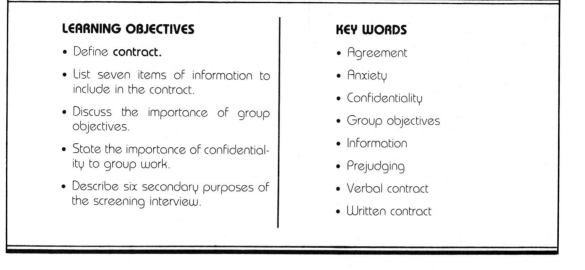

This chapter offers students, instructors, health care workers, and volunteers a discussion of verbal and written contracts and of a variety of things a group leader should consider during the contract-making stage—for example, criteria for selecting members and procedures in handling such matters as anxiety and confidentiality.

## VERBAL AND WRITTEN CONTRACTS

One important task of the group leader is the formation of a contract with each aged group member. This aspect of professional performance in group leadership is often ignored by beginners.

A *contract* is "a binding agreement between two or more persons or parties" (*Webster's* 1973). Sometimes students confuse the words *contract* and *contact*. To make contact with a person is not the same as to contract with the person. A contact can be a casual "good morning" followed by the usually meaningless "How are you?" but a contract contains very specific information given to and hopefully received by the individual.

A contract is considered to be voluntary for both parties and is agreed to by both individuals. One can never simply assume that an elderly individual is eager to be in a group, so the leader must move gently and never assertively in the initiation and completion of the contract. This is especially true of the frail elderly and the institutionalized aged, who have little control over their lives. R. Tappen and T. Touhy (1983, 37) remind us that "group members frequently are selected on the basis of their ability to participate in a group (for example, mobility, hearing, social and cognitive functioning), but their desire to attend often is not considered." However, because many elderly in institutions have little opportunity to say no, they may refuse to enter into a contract agreement. The leader needs to consider if the older person is saying no and means yes or if he or she is saying no because this is one nonthreatening opportunity to do so. In either of these cases, the leader of the group should invite the individual to attend each meeting on a meeting-by-meeting basis. A personal invitation often works well. Respect for the client's wishes is important. It should also be remembered that too much explanation can sometimes rattle the potential group member, so that is a caution.

In group work a contract is an agreement between the leader and a member regarding the group experience and should include a careful explanation of the objectives of the group. The aged person should be allowed to ask questions, especially if it is the member's first group experience. It is very important to give the potential member an opportunity to discuss the goals of the group as expressed in the original contract.

Contract information usually has to be repeated both in and out of the group for a variety of reasons. The leader cannot assume that a nod of the head means either understanding or compliance. It has been my experience that a nod of the head or even a verbal "yes" can mean "I am hard of hearing" or "Please go away and quit bothering me"—something I learned after some rather embarrassing or ludicrous situations in which the one-upmanship of the aged became very obvious. This one-upmanship of the confused elderly is difficult for the professional to acknowledge. Regardless of how confused or disoriented a potential group member may seem, however, the leader is obliged to make an effort to establish a contract with the individual. One can never be sure how much of the message gets through, but that does not mean a concerted effort should not be made to communicate. This is especially true with the aged who are diagnosed as having an organic mental disorder.

A contract may be verbal or written. If one is working with forgetful, disoriented elderly persons, it is best to make both types of contract. Written contracts can be referred to by the patients, by their families, and by the staff. M. Fatis and P. Konewko (1983) were writing about family contracts when they made this excellent point, ". . . contracting procedures make use of productive language . . . (family members) are taught to avoid vague terms and to be precise in their decision-making" (p. 161). The contract should include the following information (Burnside 1976):

1. Time.
2. Place.
3. Duration of group sessions.
4. Lifetime of the group.
5. List of other members. (This information can be important because the presence of

a peer or roommate on the list may serve as an incentive for a shy person to try the group.)
6. Purpose of the group.
7. Name of the leader.

In making the contract, the leader should keep the characteristics of the group members clearly in mind. (Group membership is discussed in detail in Chapter 10.) Essentially, the group leader should consider the following information about the prospective member: (1) age; (2) physical and psychological problems; (3) diagnosis; (4) functional capacity; (5) communication abilities; (6) sex, race, and religion; (7) amount of affect—whether depressed, sullen, giggly, and so forth; (8) mobility; (9) transportation; and (10) living arrangements. Nursing care plans may be helpful as a source of some of this information. For example, a director of nurses in a Canadian nursing home keeps a small book entitled *Openers,* which contains a list of the interests, accomplishments, and talents of each resident. The lists give nurses' aides some leads for conversation during care. Such information would also be helpful to a group leader. These "openers" can then be placed on individual plastic-coated cards which can be inserted on a metal ring. The nurses aide then gathers up the cards of her patients for care, or for a reality orientation group. The aid then has possible topics to discuss or reminisce about with the resident.

It is well known that relationships with the aged begin on a one-to-one basis; this is also true in group work with the elderly. The vis-à-vis encounter is of great importance while establishing the contract. The time spent making the contract gives the group leader a chance to assess the individual both physically and psychologically. If the group is to be co-led, Irvin Yalom (1970) states that both leaders should meet with the potential member. This principle is especially important in egalitarian leadership. If there is to be a senior-junior or teacher-student co-leadership style, the individual carrying the responsibility for the group may choose to make the contract alone. Yalom does not speak favorably of co-leadership that is not egalitarian, but I would disagree with him in regard to group work with the elderly. We desperately need to train people to replace present leaders and to train workers to take on new group leadership roles, so the apprentice approach may be a necessary means for training. Also, role modeling is viewed as an excellent mode of learning for many students.

## GROUP MEMBER SELECTION

Assessment of the potential group member during the contract-making period is of crucial importance. It is better not to negotiate a contract if one has some doubts but rather just to visit with the older person for a while and secure more information.

A group leader should not take an individual into the group solely on someone else's advice—for example, the doctor, the family, the director of nurses. The leader should make the final decision about the appropriateness of the individual for a specific group. After several inappropriate decisions, students will learn how to make the correct ones. Judy Altholz (1975) gives an example. She was co-leading a group with a psychiatrist, and they had selected an uncontrollable manic-depressive.* The member proved to be more than both the co-leaders and the group could handle and had to be removed from the group. I once accepted a woman into a group whose behavior was upsetting to all of us. She was agitated, restless, and ruined our refreshment period by drinking the cream and eating the sugar on the serving tray; it was necessary to remove her from the group.

Kathryn Gardner (1979) describes secondary purposes that may be accomplished during the screening interview:

1. Begin to develop a relationship between the therapist and the member.
2. Determine the motivation of the possible member.
3. Determine if the member's goal or goals are in agreement with those of the group.
4. Educate the member about the nature of the group.
5. Determine the kind of group experience the individual has had.

6. If appropriate, begin to review the group contract.

The size of the group should be carefully considered. Chapter 3 describes Maurice Linden's work (1953) with 40 to 51 regressed aged women on a geriatric ward; one wonders how he managed them all. Students often get carried away and feel that group work is like cooking potatoes—one more will not matter very much.

The frailties and physical status of the members should be carefully evaluated in considering a manageable group. If there are able, helpful, mobile members in the group, they will often be of great assistance to the leader. Also, if there are co-leaders, a larger group can be planned because there will be one leader available to handle the extraneous occurrences such as observing the nonincluded, the silent members, or the nonverbal cues that might otherwise be missed. It is also helpful to have someone to assist with the transportation problems that inevitably arise, in both hospital-based groups and those conducted on an outpatient basis. In outpatient or day care groups, the receptionist or a volunteer is often most helpful with some of these logistics.

The leader should select a variety of persons, keeping in mind that two hard-of-hearing or three silent, withdrawn, depressed persons can make the work of a leader extremely difficult. If all group members are in wheelchairs, extra help will be needed. In an outpatient setting, the needs of the group members must be carefully analyzed. Subsequent poor attendance may be due to transportation difficulties that were not taken care of before the group began.

The group leader needs to be prepared to work hard, plan ahead, and change plans as group needs emerge in the meetings (Burnside 1971). Staff members and other individuals often view group work as an easy intervention, but group work with the elderly requires energy, spontaneity, organization, and tenacity.

## GROUP WORK EXPENSE AND PAYMENTS

Cost must be carefully considered at the time of the contract. Costs in terms of leadership, manpower, materials, supplies, refreshments,

---

*This term is now being changed to bipolar disorder.

and staff time to assist in assembling group work can be an overhead expense for the leader — something I learned from my own experience. I once had a weekly group in a facility far from my home, which involved a fair amount of traveling. When gasoline was rationed during the "energy crunch," I had to discontinue the group because I did not have the necessary fuel. Similarly, it is unfair for students to carry the costs of all props and materials used. Costs should be shared by the agency. Volunteers may wish to contribute, but it should be their own choice. In one group I led the patients found out that I was furnishing the refreshments; they wanted to pay and would often share the expenses because they enjoyed the snacks that were served. Group psychotherapy in a private office and groups in an outpatient clinical setting would involve a cost to the aged person, but students usually work without pay.

## GROUP OBJECTIVES AND ANXIETY

Group objectives should be explicit in the beginning, even though they may change as the group evolves. Most new leaders and the group members need some structure to reduce anxiety. It is to be expected that a group of strangers meeting together for the first time will experience some anxiety.

The purposes of the group meetings may have to be restated frequently, since they are often unheard by anxious group members. Anxiety must be dealt with continually, first in the vis-à-vis encounter of the contract making and later in the group meetings. The new group leader should begin to look for cues to anxiety during the contract making; these may be cues the leader will observe in later group meetings. S. R. Slavson (1953, 386) stated:

> All groups evoke anxiety in all people. No person can be in a group without feeling anxious, even though the group may be one to which he is accustomed. The degree of anxiety is diminished with acquaintance and length of membership in it. However, no person feels as comfortable in a group as he does with one individual. An individual is seldom as threatening as a group, where anxiety is always present.

The leader may therefore see less anxiety in the initial interview for the contract than is later observed in the same individual during group meetings.

New leaders must also be prepared to deal with their own anxiety. Many of us who do group work with the elderly feel that we floundered when we began; we had no definite guidelines to follow and experienced high anxiety. Out of such floundering, however, came a sound rationale and an awareness of what to do and what not to do in group work.

## CONFIDENTIALITY

Therapists agree that maintaining confidences is an essential component of group work and provides the member with "a sense of safety in the group" (Whitaker and Lieberman 1964). However, they do not agree on the means by which standards of confidentiality should be initiated and maintained. The crucial issue is whether the therapist should structure the situation by making a ground rule about confidences or should wait for an agreement to come from the group itself. According to Dorothy Whitaker and Morton Lieberman, "To be effective, a group solution or standard must emerge in response to the felt needs of the group" (p. 209). Yalom (1970) states that the rule about confidentiality can be raised by either the group or the leader and that a valuable discussion about trust, shame, fear of disclosure, and commitment to the group may arise when confidentiality is a matter of concern. In groups of elderly who cannot verbalize well or have problems being articulate, the leader may need to provide the direction and formulate the rule of confidentiality.

For new group workers the structuring mentioned earlier in the chapter is applicable to confidentiality. Old people in insitutions suffer from lack of privacy and often are afraid of punitive treatment by family or staff. For suspicious or paranoid persons, a ground rule of confidentiality stated by the group leader may offer some reassurance. In most cases a group leader can announce in the contract that the group is to honor confidences. If problems arise later that need to be discussed with staff members or doctors (such as talk of suicide by a group member, a sudden change in mood, or a drastic change in behavior), the leader can request permission of the group member to discuss the matter with the staff or the doctor. Doing so can be seen as being an advocate for the old person in the group.

## PREJUDGING THE MEMBER

New group leaders have a tendency to underestimate the potential of the individual members of a group in an institutionalized setting. Older persons living in the community are also often coping more creatively with their problems than health care workers realize. Underestimating the potential of a group member is more common than overestimating it.

## SUMMARY

This chapter discusses contracts for group work with the elderly and suggests that the new group leader carefully consider: (1) group member selection, (2) expenses and payments, (3) anxiety, (4) confidentiality, and (5) prejudgment of members.

Initial interviews are needed to assess the potential group member and may lead to rejection of the individual for membership. The leader makes the final decision on whether a particular person is to be admitted to the group and should not be swayed by others.

A carefully made contract with each prospective group member is the first step in initiating a new group. The contract can be either verbal or written (preferably both) and should include the following information: (1) time, (2) place, (3) duration of group sessions, (4) lifetime of the group, (5) list of other members, (6) purpose of the group, and (7) name of the leader.

In making the contract, the leader should assess the prospective member both physically and psychologically and make as sure as possible that the member understands and agrees to the contract. Size of the group, availability of assistance from both staff and group members, and financial arrangements must also be considered.

The initial contract meeting may give the leader a clue to the prospective member's anxiety level and effective methods for reducing it. Giving some structure to the group by carefully explaining group objectives early in the contract stage and throughout the life of the group may help to reduce anxiety in both new leaders and the group members.

Confidentiality in the group may be announced in a ground rule in the contract, or the leader may let the group decide. Protecting the confidences of the wary institutionalized aged is extremely important.

It is well to remember that we often underestimate the potential of aged group members; they may delightfully surprise us with their ability, talent, and performance in a group.

## EXERCISE 1

1. Define *contract*.
2. List at least four important kinds of specific information that a leader should give to an elderly client while making a contract.
3. Suggest several steps a leader can take to reduce anxiety among group members.

## EXERCISE 2

You have interviewed six older persons to make a contract for group work. The answers are two "maybes," one "I will think about it," and four "yes, I'll attend." List the three steps you would take next with the persons who answered "maybe" and "I will think about it." Give your rationale for each step.

## REFERENCES

Altholz, J. 1975. Group work with the elderly. Paper presented at conference entitled Successful Treatment of Mentally Ill Elderly, Duke University, Durham, N.C., May 22–23.

Burnside, I. M. 1971. Long-term group work with the hospitalized aged. Part 1. *The Gerontologist* 11(3): 213–18 (Autumn).

_____. 1976. Formation of a group. In *Nursing and the aged.* 1st ed., ed. I. M. Burnside. New York: McGraw-Hill.

Fatis, M., P. Konewko; 1983. Written contracts as adjuncts in family therapy, *Social Work* 28 (2): 161–163 (March–April).

Gardner, K. G. 1979. Small groups and their therapeutic force. In *Principles and practice of psychiatric nursing,* ed. G. W. Stuart and S. J. Sundeen. St. Louis, Mo.: Mosby.

Linden, M. 1953. Group psychotherapy with institutionalized senile women: Study in gerontological human relations. *International Journal of Group Psychotherapy* 3:150–70.

Slavson, S. R. 1953. Sources of counter-transference and group-induced anxiety. *International Journal of Group Psychotherapy* 3:373–88.

Steckel, S. B., and M. A. Swain. 1982. *Patient contracting.* Norwalk, Conn.: Appleton-Century-Crofts.

Tappen, R., and T. Touhy. 1983. Group leader—Are you a controller? *Journal of Gerontological Nursing* 9(1): 34 (January).

*Webster's New Collegiate Dictionary.* 1973. Ed. Henry B. Woolf. Springfield, Mass.: Merriam.

Whitaker, D. S., and M. A. Lieberman. 1964. *Psychotherapy through group process.* New York: Atherton.

Yalom, I. D. 1975, 2d ed. *The theory and practice of group psychotherapy.* New York: Basic Books.

## BIBLIOGRAPHY

Bristol, M. M., and H. N. Sloane, Jr. 1974. Effects of contingency contracting on study rate and test performance. *Journal of Applied Behavior Analysis* 7:271–85.

Compton, B., and B. Galaway. 1979. *Social work processes.* Homewood, Ill.: Dorsey Press.

Croxton, T. 1974. The Therapeutic Contract in Social Treatment in P. Glaser, et. al. (eds.). *Individual Change through Small Groups,* New York: Free Press, pp. 169–185.

DeResi, W., and G. Butz. 1975. *Writing behavioral contracts.* Champaign, Ill.: Research Press.

Homme, L., M. Csanyi, J. Gonzales, and J. Rechs. 1969. *How to use contingency contracting in the classroom.* Champaign, Ill.: Research Press.

Maluccio, W., W. Marlow, 1974. The case for the contract. *Social Work* 19: 28–36, (January).

Pincus, A., A. Minahan, 1973. *Social Work Practice: Model and Method,* Itasca, Ill.: Peacock Publishers, pp. 162–193.

Seabury, B. 1976. The Contract; Uses, Abuses, and Limitations. *Social Work* 21:16–21 (January).

_____. 1979. Negotiating Sound Contracts with Clients. *Public Welfare,* Spring, pp. 33–38.

Steckel, S. B. 1976. Utilization of reinforcement contracts to increase written evidence of the nursing assessment. *Nursing Research* 25:58–61.

Steckel, S. B., and M. A. Swain. 1977. Contracting with patients to improve compliance. *Hospitals* 51:81–84.

_____. 1980. Contracting with patient-selected reinforcers. *American Journal of Nursing* 80:1596–99.

_____. 1980. Written reinforcement contracts as a nursing intervention. *American Journal of Nursing,* September.

## RESOURCES

There are no resources currently available on the topic of contracts.

# chapter 10

# Group Membership

*Irene Burnside*

*By the crowd they have been broken;
by the crowd shall they be healed.*

L. CODY MARSH (1935, 392)

DAVID S. STRICKLER/MONKMEYER

## LEARNING OBJECTIVES

- List 20 potential settings for group meetings.

- Describe four beneficial effects of intergenerational groups.

- Define **catastrophic reaction.**

- Discuss the types of persons to exclude from groups.

- State three factors to consider in regard to group size.

- Analyze the possible consequences of mixing demented and alert aged in a group.

## KEY WORDS

- Agitated

- Catastrophic reaction

- Catharsis

- Group setting

- Initial composition

- Intergenerational

- Life cycle

- Safety

Old people comprise a fascinating, unique collection of individuals wherever they are, but what are the criteria for membership in a group? A student or a new group leader may approach the assignment of elderly people to groups with dismay, reluctance, trepidation, or any combination thereof. In this chapter group settings, criteria for group membership, goals, and some cautions to consider are discussed.

## SETTINGS FOR GROUP MEETINGS

The places where group meetings can be held vary widely. They include:
- Acute care hospitals
- Board-and-care facilities
- Churches
- Community mental health centers
- Day care centers
- Domiciliary care by Veterans' Administration
- Foster homes

- Hotel-apartment residences
- Hotels in geriatric ghettos of cities
- Industrial plants (for example, preretirement groups)
- Low-cost housing units
- Mobile home units
- Nonproprietary intermediate care facilities
- Nonproprietary skilled nursing care facilities
- Nutrition sites
- Outpatient departments
- Prisons
- Private offices
- Private residences
- Proprietary intermediate care facilities
- Proprietary skilled nursing care facilities
- Recreation and park centers
- Rehabilitation hospitals
- Religious homes for retired persons
- Retirement homes
- School settings

- Senior centers
- State mental hospitals
- Veterans' Administration Hospitals
- Volunteer centers

The setting for group meetings can give some indication of the type and caliber of individual who will ultimately be available for group membership in that milieu. One can also make some assumptions about the age and physical condition of such individuals. For example, in nursing homes one can expect to find very elderly people. I once did a demonstration group for a class at Prince Edward Island University and discovered later that the mean age of the six-member group was 87.3! Residents of skilled and intermediate care facilities can also be expected to be old and frail and to have multiple diagnoses. However, at a senior center there may be participants in their fifties who retired early and are in quite stable health.

Because nurses' involvement with the aged population is so widespread, it is conceivable that nurses could be doing group work in any of the above settings. The most likely settings, of course, are acute care hospitals, rehabilitation hospitals, skilled and intermediate nursing care facilities, outpatient departments, and senior centers. It has been well documented that only 3 to 4 percent of those treated at community mental health centers are older persons, so group psychotherapy with the elderly is still in its infancy.

## GROUP MEMBER SELECTION

Irvin Yalom's (1975) and Robert Butler and Myrna Lewis's (1973) considerations for group membership are discussed here as they relate specifically to group work with older persons. Yalom, writing from the stance of a group psychotherapist, states:

> The fate of a group therapy patient and of a therapy group may, in large measure, be determined before the first group therapy session. Unless careful selection criteria are used, the majority of patients assigned to group therapy will terminate treatment discouraged and without benefit. Research on small groups . . . sug-

gests that the initial composition of the group has a powerful influence on the ultimate outcome of the entire group (p. 156).

One aspect of group work with the elderly that I learned about early is described by Yalom:

> Members are prone to terminate membership in a therapy group and are thereby poor candidates when the punishments or disadvantages of group membership outweigh the rewards or anticipated rewards. When speaking of punishments or disadvantages of group membership, I refer to the price the patient must pay for group membership. This includes an investment of time, money, energy, as well as a variety of dysphorias arising from the group experience, including anxiety, frustration, discouragement, and rejection (p. 173).

Butler and Lewis, who conduct group psychotherapy with persons of various ages, feel that beneficial effects occur when different generations relate to one another in a group setting. These benefits include: (1) the ability to understand better the various developmental phases of the life cycle, (2) the chance to act out family roles, (3) the chance for the older adult to give support and advice to younger group members, and (4) the opportunity for older members to review their values and experiences.

Butler and Lewis list the following goals in the life-cycle approach to group therapy: (1) the amelioration of suffering, (2) the overcoming of disability, (3) the chance for new experiences of self-fulfillment and intimacy, and (4) the chance to verbalize emotions. See Chapter 4 for further details on life-cycle therapy.

Many nurses are employed in settings where elderly people do not have other age groups with whom to interact; some exceptions would be acute care hospitals, recreation and park settings, outpatient departments, and community mental health centers.

A neophyte group leader should exclude younger members from the first group led. The rationale is that the leader can focus on the problems of the aged, and exclusion of younger members should also decrease the number of variables for the leader to handle. Many new group leaders do not have a basic grounding in the developmental tasks of each age group. One beginning leader* compared her first group meeting to a birthday party for preschoolers because of the brouhaha. The new leader should be quite knowledgeable about the eight stages of man (Erikson, 1982; Hall 1983). And for leaders of all women groups, I suggest an excellent review and critique by Hedva Lewittes entitled, "Women's Development and Old Age" (1982).

## Personality Dynamics of Members

It is important to assess carefully the personality of the older person while negotiating the contract (Figure 10–1). (See Chapter 9 for details on making a contract with each potential group member.) Group work requires the skillful selection of a variety of personalities. A well-balanced group should have both talkative and quiet persons, depressed and not-so-depressed persons. Mistrusting members need to be balanced with trusting persons. Hyperactive individuals can be offset by calm, serene individuals.

Members will take on various roles and tasks in a group. Making an assessment during contract negotiation is possible and important because the leader has an opportunity then to observe the patterns of behavior in each individual.

A "catastrophic reaction"† may occur when a person is overwhelmed by a task or an exercise that he or she cannot perform. It might cause the person to weep or blush or to become agitated, angry, or paranoid. The person may even strike out or get up and leave the situation. The best tactic for dealing with catastrophic reactions is, of course, prevention. When the interviewer or group leader perceives a slight increase in agitation or anxiety, the subject should be changed or the limelight removed from the group member. The leader can also avoid some catastrophic reactions by simplifying the task facing the individual and by assisting and helping the individual through the task. This is also a good role-model approach. The best information about preventing and handling catastrophic reactions is provided by Nancy Mace and Peter V. Rabins (1981) in their excellent book *The 36-Hour Day*.

The leader should be aware that the members do not have to be at the same cognitive level, but that to mix very regressed, older individuals with alert and lucid persons is to court problems. The regressed individuals may be sent into a catastrophic reaction, since they will not be able to perform as well as some of the more alert members of the group. Also, the alert members may well perceive themselves to

FIGURE 10–1. *A new group leader will be faced with a variety of personalities on the team, as indicated in this illustration. Monopolizing and silent group members cause much anxiety for new group leaders.*

Source: N. I. Brill. 1976. *Teamwork: Working together in the human services* (Philadelphia: Lippincott), 32 (fig. 1). Reprinted by permission of Harper & Row, Publishers, Inc.

---

*Hazel Mummah, personal communication, 1975.

†A reaction described by Kurt Goldstein (1942) that occurs when a brain-damaged individual cannot perform the tasks requested.

be slowed up and regressed if they are requested to attend such a group, and the experience could be harmful to their self-esteem.

Educational level alone cannot be used as an accurate tool for group selection. In one group in a skilled nursing facility, I observed a man with a third-grade education and another with a college degree. They got along famously and had the utmost respect for each other; in fact, when the group was terminated, the men asked to be roommates because the bond of friendship between them was so strong.

Mobile persons should be included with persons in wheelchairs if the group is in an institutional setting, especially if there is to be only one leader. There is also the matter of proxemics to consider. A group consisting entirely of wheelchair patients is unwieldy—that is, the leader and the members cannot get close to one another in early group meetings. The leader may often have to assist in seating arrangements, especially with the physically frail or seriously impaired elderly. Wheelchairs will also require a larger meeting room. One unusually brave student included gurney patients in her group (Holland 1973). (A gurney is a West Coast term for a cart with wheels to transport patients who cannot sit up.)

## Persons to Exclude

From a brainstorming workshop on group work with the elderly (Altholz 1975) come these recommendations on people to exclude from a group.*

1. Disturbed, active, wandering persons.
2. Incontinent persons.
3. Patients with a psychotic depression.
4. Patients recommended solely by the staff.
5. Individuals diagnosed as having bipolar disorder.
6. Deaf persons.
7. Hypochondriacal persons.

## Medical Problems

It is important that the group leader be aware of the medical problems of each person in the group. Patients with emphysema, for instance,

may need medication before group meetings to enable them to participate more fully. Arthritic patients may need aspirin before meetings so that they are not uncomfortable; patients with recent hip fractures may also need medication. It would be wise for the leader to check the medications of the members. Sometimes overmedicated patients doze off in a group meeting, and their sleepiness has nothing to do with the quality of the meeting itself or with anxiety or withdrawal. New leaders may blame themselves for such behaviors.

Leaders should also be very alert to the physical problems of group members. Edematous feet, for example, could be elevated during the group sessions to prevent severe stasis edema. Kidney problems are common in old age, and prostatitis or benign prostatic hypertrophy is a common problem in old men. Patients who have to urinate frequently may also need some special consideration in group meetings; for example, perhaps they should sit near the door, so they can easily go to the bathroom and come back into the group with a minimum of disturbance. Such individuals should also be advised to stop at the rest room enroute to the group meeting.

## Number of Group Members

The number of people in the group is also a decision of the group leader. New leaders often have trouble deciding how many persons to include in a group. The number depends on such factors as: (1) who is available for group membership, (2) the type of group (reality orientation and remotivation groups have different numbers of persons), (3) whether there is a single leader or the group is co-led, (4) available space (for example, wheelchair-bound persons require more physical space), (5) whether it is an open or a closed group (an open group may allow for greater fluctuation of the membership and therefore would be a larger group),* (6) whether any members have a sensory loss, (7) the degree of frailty of the members, and (8) the past experience of the group leader. Reality orientation groups usually have four members (Acord 1975). There can be as many as fifteen

---

*I am grateful to Judy Altholz for helping to ferret out these recommendations from the group discussion.

in a remotivation group. If the leader chooses to work with organic mental disorders and regressed, or very frail individuals, six is usually a workable number.

One of the difficulties encountered in institutions is that the elderly people who are not asked to join the group are offended. Elderly persons often become jealous of their roommates who go off to group metings (or "classes," as many older persons describe them). Sometimes they request to be put on the waiting list. I recall a 90-year-old man, Mr. H., who approached me in the hall one day when I was on my way to a group meeting. "Excuse me," he said, "but I would sure like to join that group of old people who meet with you every Friday." He entered the group after another member died. Mr. H. had taken the initiative to join, was readily accepted by the group, and seemed to get a great deal of pleasure from the meetings. In fact, he insisted his daughter attend a meeting and meet "the friends"; he told her she would have to change her visiting hours because he had to go to his meeting on the afternoon she usually visited.

There are three salient points to be drawn from this man's experience: (1) A request for membership should be honored if at all possible. If older people take responsibility for their own lives, and are observant about their own milieu, they should be rewarded for such behavior. It also says something about the importance of group work if the residents discuss it among themselves. (2) The importance of the group meetings to the member must be considered. This man even had his family change their visiting hours! (3) Families may resent the group if it interferes with their own schedule, and some work may have to be done with members of the family if they express displeasure.

## SUGGESTIONS FOR THE NEW LEADER

A few hard-learned examples may serve as suggestions for the new leader. Including two or more persons of the same minority group in the membership will facilitate the group process. Once a student of mine included in her group a full-blooded Indian and a white man who hated Indians. The Indian dropped the group within a few meetings. In the Hawaiian Islands, the melting-pot islands, I found that it is easier to include many ethnic groups because of greater tolerance for racial diversity and for different lifestyles there. In general, however, if a single minority person is included, he or she may drop out soon after the group has begun.

### Safety of Members

Another caution for the new leader concerns the unstable person who blows up frequently and is verbally or physically abusive. Just the verbal abusiveness can intimidate some group members. Even if obstreperous people behave in the meetings, their reputations have probably preceded them, and group members will have heard enough hair-raising stories to be inclined to give such people a wide berth.* Meetings can be strained if such an individual is included. New group leaders will eventually learn how to handle such a member. One of my group members, a tiny, 95-year-old lady, was knocked off her chair by another resident during a violent outburst in the dining room before the group meeting (Burnside 1978). She was badly shaken up; although not physically hurt, she was thoroughly frightened and avoided the other woman thereafter.

It is the responsibility of the leader to provide for the safety of the members and to protect the frail members of the group. Some of the aged are truly frail and can be taken advantage of by stronger group members, by other residents, and unfortunately, by the staff.

### Agitated Members

Agitation should not be confused with the initial anxiety group members experience when they first enter a group. Agitation is observable outside group meetings as well as within the group.

Initial anxiety is often seen in the resident who leaves the group. This problem is fairly common, and the leader will soon learn the most effective intervention for keeping the

---

*In open groups members may come and go as they wish. The membership from meeting to meeting varies widely. Closed groups have a stable membership, and new members are usually decided upon by leaders and group members together.

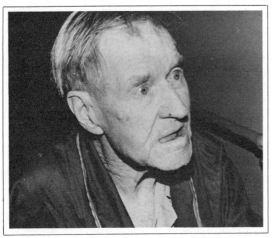

WILL PATTON

*Agitation can be difficult to handle in a group. A potential member should be observed outside of group meetings to determine the severity of the agitation and whether the leader can handle the individual in a group.*

member in the group. Initial anxiety is also seen in chain-smoking, rapid talking, monopolization of the group, and nervous mannerisms of the extremities. Others handle anxiety by staring out the window or at the floor and avoiding eye contact with others, especially the group leader.

Confinement in a small circle at the group meetings seems to increase anxiety, especially in the early meetings. Because of the sensory defects usually apparent, however, the group has to be seated close together. It may take a while for group members to adjust to such physical closeness, and they may pull back from the circle.

Agitated members can be very disruptive, so the leader should carefully investigate agitated potential group members. Is the agitation fairly constant, or is it vacillating and triggered by events or certain people? Is there medication that will decrease such behavior? Will group membership really be beneficial to this person? I once accepted a woman because the staff convinced me that group membership would help her. She disrupted the group so much that I finally had to remove her. Ideally, there would be a doctor available with whom the leader could discuss the severity of agitation evident in an individual and the medication regimen.

## State Hospital Patients

One problem a group leader may face in a skilled nursing facility concerns discharged state hospital patients. In some states, particularly California, New York, and Illinois, there was a push some years ago to get the elderly out of the state hospitals and into the community. The community for many of these less physically able turned out to be nursing homes, or to use Carl Eisdorfer's (1975) description, "semi, demi, hemi hospitals." In the nursing homes many of the state hospital discharges received different treatment from that of the average resident because they were immediately branded as state hospital refugees by both the personnel and the residents. For example, I remember that in one nursing home six state hospital women were placed in one room at the far end of the facility. It was not long until some of the mobile, lusty men in the facility discovered them, and multiple problems ensued. I have heard roommates of state hospital patients shout, "Get her out of here; she is crazy; she came from the loony bin!"

Mixing former state hospital patients and non–state hospital members in a group may create problems for a new leader. If such patients are combined in a group, the leader should be prepared to deal with the resentment, hostility, and rejection that is often shown to these poor, shuffled-about human beings.

Staff members are often afraid of ex-psychiatric patients. The anxiety of the staff may be lessened, and they may be more accepting of a person, when the leader shares with them the behavior observed in a group. Group behavior may be quite different from the usual behavior during the rest of the time in the institution. Staff members are often quite surprised at how well patients do in group settings. Labels such as *senile, violent, obstreperous,* and *suicidal* may be on a patient's chart, and the staff latches onto the label even though it is no longer accurate.

One man of 83 had spent 50 years in a state hospital; he was a "burned-out" schizophrenic, and harmless; yet the nurses' aides were terrified of him. Someone had read on his chart that he had been violent in his early years in the state hospital and had been put in a straitjacket. He had had ground privileges for years at the state hospital and had been used to being outdoors all day. He felt very confined in the nursing home, and he paced the halls with the same nervous restlessness of animals in a zoo. Then he started urinating on some expensive artificial trees in the corridors, which greatly upset the owner. Old men who have lived on farms or have been outdoors as much as this man had used trees and toilets interchangeably. Yet the staff had trouble understanding the difficult transition for this old man when he was sent to a skilled nursing facility miles from the state hospital.

### Religious and Politically Interested Members

If very religious or very politically minded persons are accepted in the group, the leader must be prepared to deal with the desires of such members to convert other members—either religiously or politically. One colleague handled this problem by making a ground rule that religion and politics could not be discussed in the group psychotherapy meetings (Altholz 1975). In that way the group meeting time could be spent on the problems of the patients.

### SUMMARY

This chapter discusses criteria for group membership, based on the writings of Yalom (1975) and Butler and Lewis (1973). Yalom urges careful selection to prevent early termina-

tion by members. Butler and Lewis list goals for intergenerational groups as (1) assuaging suffering; (2) handling disabilities; and (3) providing an opportunity for self-realization, intimacy, and catharsis.

Settings for group meetings, which can range from acute care hospitals to prisons, may well indicate the competence and caliber of a potential group member. In selecting members the group leader should strive for a balance by including a variety of personalities. The leader is cautioned not to be too cavalier in mixing alert and nonalert members, however, and to remember that educational level alone is not an accurate indicator of group potential. The leader must consider the number of minority members to be included and always provide a safe, non-threatening milieu. Former state hospital patients placed in nursing homes create anxiety in residents and staff. Finally, the leader should be skilled in handling political or religious issues if very pious or politically minded individuals are included in the group.

Persons who should probably be excluded from groups are those who are agitated, incontinent, or deaf. Persons diagnosed as psychotic, manic-depressive, or hypochondriacal also should be excluded. The new leader needs to be wary of any individual enthusiastically recommended by the staff. Medical problems need to be assessed because they may affect group participation.

The size of the group will depend on the level and type of the group and whether there are co-leaders. Open groups allow for fluctuation of membership from meeting to meeting. Closed groups have a stable membership.

---

### EXERCISE 1

The following is a list of elderly persons described by the staff as potential members for a group you are planning. Carefully screen out those you would *not* include if you were leading your first group. Give your rationale for not accepting them into your group.

1. Mrs. Loquacious is 90 years old, very stubborn and controlling, and talks incessantly. It is impossible to stop her, and she irritates both residents and staff by bawling them out for not listening to her.

2. Mr. Deaf is 78 years old and extremely hard of hearing but often pretends he hears by nodding his head or saying yes. He refuses to wear a hearing aid.

3. Mrs. Depressed is 88 years old and is now withdrawn, listless, and confused. Her husband died a month ago. She says over and over, "What's the use of living?"

4. Mr. Alone is 79 years old, a loner, and has been a heavy drinker most of his life. He never married, never had a steady job, and was a drifter. He does not mingle with any residents in the long-term care facility.

5. Mrs. Obnoxious is a 68-year-old behavior problem. She is aggressive, noisy, and scares other residents. She pushed Miss Frail off her chair in the dining room recently. Mrs. O needs help.

6. Miss Frail is 95 years old and has outlived all her friends. She is petrified of Mrs. Obnoxious and avoids her. Miss Frail is very paranoid; she thinks that the government took her house and that the nurses are having affairs with her brother.

7. Mr. Flirt is blind and 86 years old. He used to drink heavily, chased women, and was not a very good father. He is getting increasingly depressed and withdrawn and refuses to get out of bed.

8. Miss Learned is a 75-year-old former school teacher, sweet but terribly confused. She is especially confused at night. She keeps talking about her mother coming to visit. (Mother has been dead 20 years.)

9. Mrs. Old is a centenarian, physically frail but mentally alert. She loves to reminisce. She has become the "pet" because of her sweet disposition and sharp wit.

10. Mr. Sly is 86 years old and pretends to be "out of it," but he bedevils the staff by hiding wheelchairs and linens; then he pleads innocence. When things get very boring, he pulls the fire alarm, turns up the thermostat, or calls the police department at 2 A.M. to tell them that the staff is beating up the residents and they'd better come down.

## EXERCISE 2

Describe four possible settings for group meetings, and for each, indicate how the setting determines the type of elderly who will be available.

## REFERENCES

Acord, L. 1975. Reality orientation. Paper presented at conference entitled Mental Health in Nursing Homes, San Antonio, Tex., October.

Altholz, J. 1975. Group work with the elderly. Paper presented at conference entitled Successful Treatment of the Mentally Ill Elderly, Duke University, Durham, N.C., May 22–23.

Burnside, I. M. 1978. Eulogy for Ms. Hogue. *American Journal of Nursing* 78(4): 624–26 (April).

Butler, R. N., and M. I. Lewis. 1973. *Aging and mental health*. St. Louis, Mo.: Mosby.

Eisdorfer, C. 1975. Speech at conference entitled Successful Treatment of the Mentally Ill Elderly, Duke University, Durham, N.C., May 22.

Erikson, E., 1982. *The Life Cycle Completed: A Review*, New York: Norton.

Goldstein, K. 1942. *Aftereffects of brain injuries in war and their evaluation.* New York: Grune & Stratton.

Hall, E. 1983. A conversation with Erik Erikson. *Psychology Today,* 17(6):22–30, (June).

Lewittes, H. 1982. Women's Development in adulthood and old age. *International Journal of Mental Health* 11 (No. 1–2): 115–131.

Mace, N. L., and P. V. Rabins. 1981. *The 36-hour day.* Baltimore: Johns Hopkins University Press.

Puppolo D. 1980. Co-leadership with a group of stroke patients. In *Psychosocial nursing care of the aged.* 2d ed., ed. I. M. Burnside. New York: McGraw-Hill.

Yalom, I. D. 1975. *The theory and practice of group psychotherapy.* 2d ed. New York: Basic Books.

## BIBLIOGRAPHY

Francis, A., J. Clarkir, and J. Marachi. 1980. Selection criteria for outpatient group psychotherapy. *Hospital and Community Psychiatry* 31(4): 245–50 (April).

Hartford, M. E. 1972. *Groups in social work.* New York: Columbia University Press.

Klein, W. H., E. J. LeShane, and S. Furman. 1965. *Promoting mental health of older people through group methods.* New York: Mental Health Materials Center.

Lowy, L. 1979. Working with groups of older persons. Chapter 12 in *Social work with the aging.* New York: Harper & Row.

Perlman, B., A. Weinstein, and J. Compton. 1976. Group work with the elderly in a community center. *Journal of Geriatric Psychiatry* 9:89–91.

Sampson, E. 1981. *Group process for the health professions.* 2d ed. New York: Wiley.

Shaw, M. E. 1981. Group composition. Chapter 7 in *Group dynamics: The psychology of small group behavior.* New York: McGraw-Hill.

## RESOURCES

### Videocassettes

*When Did You Know You Were Old?* (3/4-inch cassette, black-and-white, 40 minutes). Available from Department of Instructional TV, Rutgers University, New Brunswick, NJ.

### Journal

*Journal of Gerontological Nursing* 1983, 9(16:320–347, June). The entire issue is devoted to the VA system and the care of veterans.

## chapter 11

# Problems in Leadership and Maintenance

*Irene Burnside*

It is the anxiety of not being
able to preserve one's own being
which underlies every fear and is
the frightening element.

PAUL TILLICH (1952)

## LEARNING OBJECTIVES

- Discuss entrée into an agency.

- List four techniques in group leadership.

- List six categories of problems that may occur in a group.

- Discuss depression in relation to the leader.

- Discuss absenteeism.

- Define **sabotage** as it relates to group leadership.

- List 10 ways a leader may be sabotaged in an agency.

- List five qualifications for a group leader.

- State 15 simple techniques to promote a stable group of elderly persons.

## KEY WORDS

- Absenteeism

- Entrée

- Hostile member

- Monopolist

- Roadblocks

- Sabotage

- Sensory deficits

- Silent member

The problems in maintaining a group of elderly are varied and unique, and they differ from those of leading a group of younger persons. In this chapter students, health care workers, instructors, and volunteers are alerted to some of the common problems a new leader may encounter. One participant in a conference on group work with the elderly wrote on the evaluation form, "Why do groups get started and fall apart when we need them, and how can we make them more lasting?" The purpose of this chapter is to answer those questions.

Leaders need to keep in mind the developmental tasks of the aged. These tasks are described by several authors (Duvall 1971; Erikson 1982, 1963; Hall 1983; Havighurst 1968; Peck 1968). An awareness of these developmental tasks will help the leader understand the group

members better. The knowledge of group theory and process needs to be underscored.

Irvin Yalom (1975) feels that the curative factors in group therapy are mediated not by the therapist but by the members, who provide the qualities of acceptance, support, and hope plus the experiencing of universality, interpersonal feedback, testing, and learning.

Maurice Linden (1956) feels that the leader can reinstate independence in the older person only when the leader steadily divests the authority and moves to an area of mutuality. If the leader does not follow this pattern, the older person becomes more blissfully dependent.

Louis Lowy (1967) discusses roadblocks in group practice with older people: the attitude of the leaders, who may have little belief in the creative potential of an older member; the difficulty of leaders in communicating their hopes and feelings; and leaders' overconcern about time—ignoring the timing and sense of time of older people.

L. Smith (1980), a nurse who began therapy groups with chronically ill patients in a state psychiatric hospital, describes in an interesting manner how she carved out her own group leadership style. Basically she went through three stages in her personal quest for a style:

1. I am the leader, and this is the law.
2. We are all equal, and whatever happens, happens.
3. The group is self-directing but there are rules and guidelines. I am here if you need me.

Some of Smith's guidelines include the following: (1) the size of the group must be ideally suited for the level of therapy intended; (2) to avoid isolating group members, use "one of a kind" membership selection; and (3) the group can be homogeneous or heterogeneous in terms of diagnostic categories.

## ENTRÉE INTO AN AGENCY

One of the first problems faced by the group leader is the need to gain entrance into an institution or agency. This may be difficult for both nursing students and volunteers. Often credentials are simply not enough. It is easier now with the tremendous pressure to upgrade the care of the aged in this country, but I had a difficult time some years ago when I wanted to begin group work in a skilled nursing facility. The director of nurses kept avoiding me; the administrator canceled appointments I made to see her. Finally, a doctor who was interested in groups being started wrote an order for six of his patients to be included in group work so that I could begin. He also spent precious time one afternoon going over his entire list of patients in the facility, letting me choose those I wanted to interview for the group. After the group began, I sent him a monthly report on all his patients. I also initially gave a short talk in an in-service class describing what I planned to do with this particular group, but the staff was

not very interested in group work. They remained disinterested for several months, until they began to notice some changes in the group members.

The staff criticized me for my short skirts, the bright colors I wore, and my jewelry. My attire was not happenstance; I selected what appealed to the aged. I was reminded that nurses do not do group work and that group work belongs in the domain of social workers and psychologists. Struggling to be the type of group leader–nurse–professional person I wanted to be in the face of opposition was difficult, and I sought preceptor support. I found a psychiatric nursing faculty colleague willing to supervise me, but as she so candidly said, "I don't know a thing about group work with the elderly, but I will certainly be your sounding board." Because group work with the elderly by nurses is still fairly new, it is important that beginning group leaders have that kind of support. (Chapter 35 deals with the responsibilities of the person who is supervising a new group leader.)

It is well to warn new group leaders that they may not be accepted by the staff until they prove themselves, especially in facilities where group work has not been part of the treatment plans. As nurses carve new roles for themselves, they will need support. These new roles include geriatric nurse practitioner, geriatric nurse clinician, geriatric researcher, teacher in gerontology classes for multidisciplines, and, of course, group leader of aged persons.

At the time I began group work, no activity programs were required in skilled nursing facilities. There were occasional bingo games and sing-alongs. The residents I met were so bored with their lives that they welcomed the chance to be involved in a group meeting. I believe that their boredom motivated them to continue in the group experience. They frequently discussed their boredom and said how much they looked forward to the next meeting.

## MULTIPLE PROBLEMS OF THE ELDERLY

The group leader must juggle multiple problems simultaneously. Although thic can be true in all group work, it is especially true in work with the aged, who may have socioeconomic, physical, and mental problems simultaneously. Eric Pfeiffer (1975) said it so well in a statement applying to nurses as well as psychiatrists: "In aging, the patient drives you back to being a generalist."

The prevalent and multiple health problems of the aged are both physical and psychological, and they will challenge the imagination of even the most creative leader. "About 85% of older persons not in institutions have one or more chronic conditions but only 20% have an interference with their mobility. Older people are twice as likely to wear glasses and 13 times as likely to use a hearing aid" (U.S. Dept. of HEW 1973). Patients in institutions are often diagnosed as having five or six different problems. The leader will have to be aware of that fact constantly. Deterioration will be observed in members if the group continues over a substantial period. There will be vacillation between good and bad days, and the group experience may be very helpful in the maintenance of such persons. Often they become ill or have a crisis situation (Burnside 1970). I have seen patients in the group become very sick, stay in bed for a while, and eventually return to the group.

The secret seems to be in always including absent members; that is, the leader sees those people at their bedside and finds out why they are absent and what is happening. Also, the leader reports to sick members what happened in the group session. Some new group leaders, however, are unaccustomed to working with elderly clients and do not seek out absent group members. It is not usually the role of a group leader of adults, but one needs to remember that the aged are actually incapacitated on some days. And, of course, forgetfulness on the part of aged group members plays havoc with any group. (Forgetfulness on the part of the group leader delights the group members no end.) Follow-up work is easy in an institution where one has a captive group; but if one is leading a group in a day care center, an outpatient clinic, or elsewhere in the community, the leader might have to make phone calls to absent members.

Once the group is rolling, the leader is in essence the glue that holds the group together. Groups fall apart when the leader is insensitive to the needs of the group members. (See Chapter

6 on the importance of inclusion in group work with senescent people.) Groups also fail if the leader is not conscientious about the group leadership role; that is, if the leader is late, absent, cancels meetings frequently, and so on. The elderly soon sense when a leader is making every effort to keep the group intact; and when concern is shown for an absent member, they are well aware that the same type of concern will be shown for them if they break a hip, have an embolus, or are so incapacitated that they cannot attend the group.

One lady in a group was bedridden due to a pulmonary embolus. When I visited her, she expressed regret about missing the meetings but could not get out of bed even though she felt much better. I rolled her bed into the meeting room, and she visited with the group for a portion of the meeting.* She felt somewhat nauseated and did not want any coffee; she had ginger ale. There is something symbolic about sharing coffee and refreshments, but this area has not been fully studied in reference to working with older persons (Burnside 1970). When I visited absent patients at their bedsides, I also brought them the refreshments we were having that day. Such continual inclusion, whether or not the member attends meetings, is an important factor in the maintenance of a group and should be remembered by new leaders.

Another important way to maintain the group is for the leader to pay meticulous attention to the levels of discomfort or pain of the group members.

The leader must also learn to handle the sensory defects of the group members and how to maximize the vision, hearing, and understanding of each member in the group. Usually sensory defects are not much of a problem in younger age groups. One way to minimize them is to pay close attention to the environment itself. Students can be sensitized to the problem of sensory deprivation with the use of experiential exercises (Hickey, Hultsch, and Fatule 1975; Hultsch, Hickey, and Rakowski 1975; Pennsylvania State University 1975).

---

I learned this from Diane Holland Puppolo who included patients on gurneys in her group.

## GROUP CONCERNS

There are several categories of problems that may arise in a group. The following list illustrates those common group concerns.*

1. Problems with co-therapist or co-therapy.
   a. Nonacceptance of co-leader by group.
   b. Leadership role of co-therapist.
2. Problems with individual patients in group—that is, managing individual problem patients.
   a. The monopolist.
   b. The silent member.
   c. The hostile member.
3. Problems with the leadership role.
   a. Leader's degree of directiveness or activity.
   b. Leader's role in maintaining group—for example, problem of attendance.
   c. Leader's role in establishing trust and confidentiality.
4. Miscellaneous concerns.
   a. Problem of inclusion.
   b. Ground rules.

The new leader should consider which problems may have to be dealt with, especially in the initial meetings. A list of problems in rank order appears in Table 11–1; in a class of 27 students, these were the problems the students requested help with on their weekly group summaries.

### Problems in Co-Leadership

Problems in co-leadership run the gamut from interpersonal squabbles to power struggles. Preceptors can be most helpful in mediating some of these problems. (See Chapter 3 for a good example of effective co-leadership in a group.)

Special attention must be paid to the location of co-leaders in a group. Both the arrangement of the room and the seating arrangements play important roles in the success of a group meeting. The seating arrangement for the members must be carefully planned. They must be close so that they can see, hear, and touch one another. I once observed co-leaders trying to conduct a group of confused elderly in a day care center. They had placed sofas around a coffee table to form a large square. The leaders sat close to one another. Needless to say, the group meeting was chaotic.

Elderly persons cannot be expected to plan how a room should be arranged; therefore, the leaders must plan *ahead* to have the chairs and tables in the best position. Figures 11–1 and 11–2 show a variety of seating arrangements. I find that the one shown in Figure 11–2c is the most successful positioning of clients and leaders.

It is wise to remember that although the leaders may be aware of the problems inherent in poor seating arrangements, an attempt should be made to include the members in planning. R. Tappen and T. Touhy (1983, 37) note, "Group members may be treated as if they were helpless or incapable of contributing meaningfully to the group process. The leader may tell the people where to sit or rearrange their wheelchairs after they have moved into the group circle." The caution here is that if it is necessary to move a member, the leader should explain the reason why. "Mrs. Jones, I am going to move your chair over beside me so that I can hear what you say better," or "Mrs. Anderson, I am going to move you over here so that the glare from that window will not be in your eyes because I know that bright sunlight makes you uncomfortable."

### Depression of the Leader

The new group leader should be warned that it is not uncommon to experience feelings of depression, and the leader should examine how this depression might be affecting the group. (The need for the preceptor to intervene in a student's depression is described in Chapter 35.) Is the leader more quiet and withdrawn? Is the leader aware of how depressing the frailties of members and all the people in wheelchairs or with canes and crutches can be? During this time, when some of the enthusiasm of the leader is waning, strong peer support or preceptor support can be very helpful. Not all students will be able immediately to pinpoint their depression and may need some help from the instructor.

---

*Reprinted from class entitled N217B Graduate Psychiatric Nursing. 1968. University of California School of Nursing, San Francisco. January.

TABLE 11–1.  Problems experienced by new group leaders, by rank order

| Rank order of problems | Type of problem |
|---|---|
| 1. | Monopolizers. |
| 2. | Members forget about meetings. |
| 3. | Absent members. |
| 4. | Adding new members to group. |
| 5. | Group members approaching leaders individually after meetings for further discussion. |
| 6. | The use of the group summary form. What is the purpose of describing mood of group? |
| 7. | Anxiety and/or depression in leaders. |
| 8. | How to handle person who refuses to join group. |
| 9. | How to handle situation when member does not wish to remember sad parts of the past. |
| 10. | Members who leave group while it is still in progress. |
| 11. | Dealing with deafness, loss of memory, poor speech, soft voices, and so on. |
| 12. | Interventions for withdrawn members. |
| 13. | The one-to-one by the leader that occurs in early meetings. |
| 14. | Touching during crying; is it helpful? |
| 15. | Leaders' worries about lessening self-confidence of members. |
| 16. | How much discussion of past changes, such as death and moves, is helpful to members? |
| 17. | Dealing with leaders' feelings about losing group members or when the group members say meetings are not useful for them. |
| 18. | What to serve for a snack. |
| 19. | Getting members to feel more relaxed with leaders. |
| 20. | Whether to pursue reality testing in group in the face of massive denial. |
| 21. | How does leader respond to flat affect in members? |
| 22. | Group members' problems hit close to leaders' own problems. |
| 23. | Lack of support from staff. |
| 24. | Topics to reminisce about. |
| 25. | How to use props. |
| 26. | Leader needs more professionalism and objectivity. |
| 27. | Seating arrangements—continue same? Change? |
| 28. | Co-leaders' attitudes and beliefs that conflict with elderly members' attitudes and beliefs. |
| 29. | Co-leader conflict about roles, styles of leadership, and so on. |
| 30. | Closure of group meeting. |
| 31. | How to include all members in topics being discussed. |
| 32. | Topics to include in groups. |
| 33. | Group members concerned about taping the meetings. |
| 34. | Inclusion of staff in meetings. Pros and cons? |
| 35. | Strategies for dialog when group member comments *after* meeting, "I want to be dead." |
| 36. | Termination: How to plan so members do not feel abandoned. Feelings of leader about termination. |
| 37. | Leader needs to be better organized. |

SOURCE: Reprinted from class entitled Group Work with the Elderly. 1976. San Francisco State University. Fall semester.

A student from Argentina studying in the United States wrote after her first group meeting:

My first experience was that of sadness and depression. I felt completely lost, strange. I thought, "This is not my place." I thought that my place should be with the older children and young people. I know that I've got to continue ahead but I don't know how to face these feelings (Kratzig 1976).

Another comment from a student was that "I was feeling *very depressed* about Mrs. B., and her expression of futility—and just *the whole* institutional setting in general! I felt depressed the whole weekend . . ." (Leudtke 1976).

## Problems in Attendance

As mentioned earlier, inpatient groups rarely have problems with attendance. Once the group is off the ground, the aged residents are usually there and waiting. A good deal of their receptivity may be prompted by the emptiness and bore-

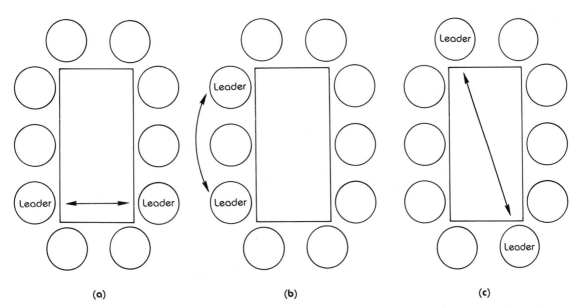

FIGURE 11-1. *Because of its length, a rectangular table can present seating problems—for example, the inability of group members to see or hear the leaders or others in the group. The leaders should position themselves with care. In diagram a the co-leaders are "weighted" at one end of the group and are unable to assist the four members at the opposite end of the table. In diagram b the co-leaders weight one side of the group; the arrangement also makes it difficult for the leaders to interact—they must look over the head of the member sitting between them. Diagram c shows the best seating arrangement for co-leaders if a long table must be used.*

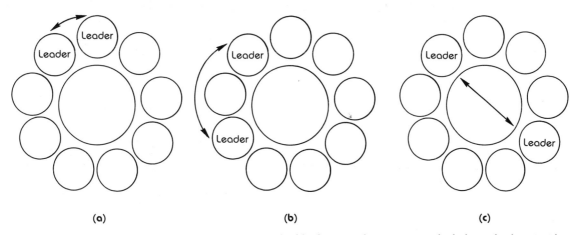

FIGURE 11-2. *In the seating arrangement using a round table shown in diagram a, in which the co-leaders sit side by side, both authority figures are on one side of the table; the arrangement does not allow eye contact between the leaders or permit each of them to be close to two members. In the arrangement in diagram b, the member seated between the co-leaders may feel overwhelmed, and eye contact between the leaders is limited. Diagram c shows the ideal seating arrangement for a round table. It offers eye contact, and each leader can assist the member on either side. This is important when the group contains frail, confused, disoriented members or aged persons with severe sensory losses. A round table is always preferable over a rectangular or square table.*

dom of institutional life. As the atheist in a group once said to me when questioned about going to mass so regularly, "Sure I go. There's nothing better to do around here on Thursday afternoon."

The real problem with group work in institutions is handling the residents who are not in groups. They may request that they be put on a waiting list. Sometimes relatives ask on behalf of their family member for a place in the group. One relative said, "I don't like to ask for special favors, but could my mother please be placed in one of the groups? I believe it would help her."* Such interest in groups may spur the administrator or the activity director to find other activities for the residents.

Most group leaders find that they have a stable membership with inpatient groups, but that is because they have concentrated on making a cohesive group. Outpatient groups are different. For example, in rainy weather many of the group members may call in with transportation problems and/or complaints of their arthritis. Older people are also afraid of falling during rainy or snowy day.

### Administrative Support for the Leader

Sometimes groups fail because of lack of interest and support by the administration. It is of paramount importance that the leader have support from two directions: (1) from the administrative staff of the agency where the group is to be held and (2) from a preceptor, supervisor, colleague, or whomever will be serving in that capacity.

The support of the administrator and the director of nurses is important because they influence both staff and residents. The director of a senior center would influence the staff and the seniors coming to the group meeting. Lip service is not enough; there must be active encouragement and support by the people in top positions. The following list includes examples observed in which the administration made group leading easier for volunteers and students.

1. One facility provided lunch for the volunteer group leader because the leader had a hectic

schedule on that particular day and was skipping lunch to be at the group meeting on time.

2. One interested administrator sat in on several group meetings so that she could observe the behavior of patients in the group setting (which may be quite different from usual behavior on the ward). However, if the administrator chooses to sit in on a meeting, the leader must realize that there may be some resentment from the members, there may be some concern about the authority figure there, and there may be real reluctance to share. Confidentiality is one important factor to consider when there are observers.

3. The same administrator always had a special "goodby cake" for the group leader when she completed a group and left the facility.

4. One director of nurses was very conscientious about having the patients ready in the room when the student arrived. She made a special effort to dress the patients neatly that day. The men came in white shirts and ties; the women had their hair done nicely. The message to both the staff and the residents of such concern for appearance was that "this is important for them; they must look their very best."

5. In one facility the nursing instructor who began a new group was provided with an assistant because of the multiple handicaps of the members.

6. Photographers took pictures of group meetings and placed them on a bulletin board in the hallway, where the residents showed them to family members and friends.

7. An in-service class or two devoted to group work or group dynamics also shows interest in the efforts of the leader.

8. Training a co-leader who can take over the group when the student or volunteer leaves is also a way of maintaining the group. (It has been my experience that when the original leader leaves, patients will demand that the group be continued because it is meaningful to them, but that there is difficulty in finding someone to replace the leader.)

### Sabotage

There are numerous ways in which a facility can sabotage the work of a leader and make it difficult to maintain the group.

---

*Florence Patton, personal communication, 1975.

1. Constant criticism of the leader may occur—a put-down type of feedback implying that the group work is incorrect, foolish, or bothersome.

2. Staff members may show no interest in the group, fail to report on the patients in the group, and ignore what is occurring in the group.

3. Patients are not ready for group meetings, they are brought in late, or the wrong patients are brought in and left.

4. Patients are sent home on pass, to X ray, or to other areas on the day of the group meeting.

5. A negative approach regarding group meetings is used to the patient—for example, "You *don't* want to go to the group meeting today, do you?" (Hennessey 1976).

6. Patients are incompletely dressed when they do arrive—shoestrings not tied, one shoe missing, no lap robe (so bare knees are showing), no sweater (and the patient says she is chilled), no hearing aid or glasses or false teeth. The last do affect the ability to communicate.

7. There may be a reluctance to help the leader provide coffee, tea, fruit juice, or refreshments to enhance the group meetings. The kitchen staff may openly balk.

8. Lack of equipment can create problems—not enough cups for coffee, no paper napkins, no table available to do a group project, no record player for music, and so on.

9. There may be insufficient room space for the group.

10. The group may be shuffled around from area to area (which is not good for elderly patients; a minor "translocation shock" often occurs).

11. Patients may be taken out of a group meeting after it has begun, to go to X ray, the dentist, and so on.

12. When no assistance with transporting patients is available, the group leader has all the responsibility. (This may happen both in the institution and in the community.)

13. Blame may be directed at the group for all that goes wrong with a patient. Such blame may stagger a new group leader; generally, the resident does not hear it because it is directed to the leader.

14. The facility may constantly assign different staff members to assist in transportation, and so forth. They do not know about the group and therefore have to be told what it is and why and where.

15. When patients become more assertive (which they often do after group experiences) and more demanding, the group may be blamed and seen as a disruptive force in the facility.

16. Staff members neglect to tell leaders important information—for example, when patients die, go AWOL, are critically ill, or have had a death in the family.

There are several steps a new leader can take to reduce sabotage by the staff.

1. Do not be defensive when criticized or given negative feedback.

2. Take care of your own feelings, such as depression, resentment, and frustration, by having a sounding board in a colleague, peer, or preceptor.

3. Gently remind the staff about the meeting in advance so that patients can be ready on time.

4. Write reminders to the patients to help them remember the meeting day, time, and place.

5. Develop a rapport with the nurses' aides who prepare patients for group meetings. Try to learn their names, praise them when patients look nice, and give them some feedback about how their patients are progressing in the group.

6. Explain what you are doing with the group to kitchen personnel so that they know the reason you need refreshments.

7. Make a contract with the director of nurses, the administrator, or the activity director, and state the type of equipment you will need from them.

8. Carefully plan the group experience so that you have adequate room space for all group members. Also, explain to management the difficulty when a group has to be moved so that they understand why the group should remain in the same location.

9. Conduct an in-service class and explain some of your expectations—for example, that patients will not be taken out of group meetings and that interruptions will be kept to a minimum.

10. Let the staff members know when you arrive and when you leave if you are not doing the group work as an employee of the facility.

## QUALIFICATIONS FOR A GROUP LEADER

The qualifications for group leadership with the aged are very similar to those for working individually with the elderly client. General qualities that are important in the care of the elderly are patience, flexibility, tenacity, compassion, gentleness, intelligence, and an astute ability to observe. Specific qualities to look for in group leaders include: (1) background in normal aging; (2) background in the pathology of aging; (3) experience in groups of any kind; (4) tolerance for groups (as opposed to one-to-one relationships); (5) ability to tolerate dependent relationships; (6) ability to handle directness and criticism (old people can criticize par excellence); (7) ability to handle one's own feelings regarding chronic illness, disabilities, depression, hostility, grief, and the various stages of dying; and (8) organization in work.

In an excellent article on aspects of group leadership with the elderly, Tappen and Touhy (1983) describe control and condescension in group work. They state, "Our particular concern here is that group work can extend and reinforce already-existing tendencies to control and be condescending toward older adults. It is important to be alert to these dangers and to conduct groups in such a way that these potentially negative effects are avoided and the most positive effects of group work can be achieved." The reader will recall that cautions against control and disrespect were raised in Chapter 9, which discusses making contracts with older persons.

Marianne Corey (Corey and Corey 1977, 214) feels that the following qualities are needed to work successfully as a counselor/leader with the elderly:

1. Genuine respect for old people.
2. A history of positive experiences with old people.
3. A deep sense of caring for the elderly.
4. The ability and desire to learn from old people.
5. An understanding of the biological aspects of aging.
6. The conviction that the last years of life can be challenging.

7. Patience, especially with repetition of stories.
8. Knowledge of the special biological, psychological, and social needs of the aged.
9. Sensitivity to the burdens and anxieties of old people.
10. The ability to get old people to challenge many of the myths about old age.
11. A healthy attitude regarding one's own eventual old age.

D. Shomaker and C. Furukawa (1982, 229) make the point that "a group does not usually convene as an ideally matched set of members, and the members are not always ideally qualified for group discussion. This is one of the growth processes that results from group work. Initially it is often necessary to ask each person's opinion on an issue in order to stimulate conversation."

## SUGGESTIONS FOR NEW GROUP LEADERS

The following suggestions should be helpful to new group leaders.

1. Explain to the staff what you are planning.
2. Include a variety of personalities to make group work easier. Try to balance the number of talkative and quiet members.
3. If there is only one leader, keep the group small—six to eight members.
4. Place members in a circle to maximize vision and hearing.
5. Ensure that the meeting place is well lighted and warm and that intercoms, glare from windows, and outside distractions are eliminated.
6. Provide a table if refreshments are to be served.
7. Always give individual attention at the beginning and end of the meeting.
8. In institutions pay brief visits to the absent members at their bedsides; this is especially helpful in serious illnesses and crises and also encourages members to return to the group again.
9. Use names profusely.
10. Keep the rules few and simple.

11. Confine the purposes of the group to sensible goals that both leader and elderly can meet.

12. Capitalize on birthdays, holidays, current events, and so on. Themes can help—for example, nature, travel, books, and reminiscing. Dealing with sad themes is part of the leader's role.

13. Do not change meeting places or times too often; this has a tendency to rattle some members. Never be late for a meeting. If you anticipate being late, notify the members. Never fail to appear without an explanation or without providing a substitute leader. Do not make promises you cannot keep.

14. Make a contract with each person in the group. (See Chapter 9 on contracts). Contracts are important; they alert the elderly person, particularly the confused, forgetful one, to the time and place of the meetings and give the leader a chance to assess that individual for confusion, disorientation, disabilities, and the like, before taking him or her into the group. Do not depend on the staff for a list of potential group members. They may list, for various reasons, people difficult to handle in a group or people who cannot benefit at all from the group experience.

15. Recognize the importance of hellos and goodbys to old people. They need to know the limits—how much time you will spend with them and where you are both physically and psychologically in the relationship. Handling this aspect of group work is an art. For example, a death may occur and a member will not be at the next group meeting. I have seen persons who felt guilty because they did not say a "neat, clean" goodby to someone. But promising to come back when you never intend to is not a neat, clean goodby.

16. Deal with all absences in the group. If a member has died, be sure to try to handle the death in the meeting. (I leave an empty chair in the meeting after the death so that if the members do not hear what I say, at least they can see what has happened.)

17. Recognize that touching and closeness—both leader-member closeness and member-member closeness—are of crucial importance.

18. Mix men and women when possible and alternate the group seating pattern.

19. Be meticulous in anticipating and meeting members' needs, since they cannot always verbalize them. Either say the words or allow the members to say what their needs are. Pain is one area to consider.

20. Use food and beverages to add surprise and a nice quality to meetings.

21. Recognize the importance of spontaneity and surprises. Do not let the surprise be, "Look, we are all moving to a new room today!" Jostling the group about is not helpful to the members. Surprise should be within the structure of the group; but members who have dementia do poorly if moved about too much. Some of the surprises could be changing the food or beverages from week to week, adding an activity, occasionally having a guest leader take over the group, or changing the usual structure of the group.

22. Use the here and now. Talk about the weather, the seasons, or whatever to get started. The superficial is OK. You will also have to share things about yourself; the elderly will not often let you out of that.

23. Work on self-image. Praise and compliment whenever possible, but be sincere. Do not have confrontation groups.

24. Arrange transportation to help members get to meetings.

25. Consider, when possible, the era and the geographical areas in which the members lived most of their lives and talk about them in the meetings.

26. Acknowledge your own feelings.

27. Do not mix individuals with dementia with alert patients; it creates problems. It is hard to keep all members interested because situations may occur in which alert patients think that maybe they are really slipping.

It takes courage, stamina, creativity, and great patience to be a group leader, but there are results and rewards. The results may seem miniscule, but they are there. The rewards are an individual matter; what is rewarding for one group leader may not be so for another. As you continue to lead groups, you will discover your own style of leadership—one that is comfortable for you, therapeutic for the members, and always uniquely yours. When you have all that in tow, you can feel assured that you have arrived as a group leader with elderly clientele.

## SUMMARY

The problems of maintaining a group of older persons are different from those encountered in other age groups. The problems of the elderly may stagger the new leader, since they are multiple, complex, and sometimes recurring. Locating a receptive facility is usually the first hurdle. Sensory loss requires exquisite handling by the leader. Meticulous attention must also be given to psychosomatic complaints.

Conducting a group may present such problems as sabotage by the staff; nonacceptance of a co-leader; and monopolizing, mute, or hostile members. Trust, confidentiality, inclusion, and ground rules are also concerns. If absenteeism is a problem, the leader should consider possible reasons. Nursing home residents are usually so bored that they welcome a group experience.

Qualifications and abilities needed for group leadership with the aged include: (1) background in normal aging, (2) background in the pathology of aging, (3) experience in groups of any kind, (4) tolerance for groups, (5) ability to tolerate dependent relationships, (6) ability to handle directness and criticism, (7) ability to handle one's own feelings, and (8) organization.

Suggestions for new leaders are given as guidelines to facilitate group movement, to decrease anxiety, and to promote learning from the elderly themselves.

## EXERCISE 1

A leader's role can be active or passive. Which is the more common stance in group leadership with the aged? State the reasons for your choice.

## EXERCISE 2

Absenteeism is a common problem in groups of older persons and may be due to a variety of factors. Below is a sample form that you might use as a model. Make your own form and list as many reasons as you can that elderly people might not attend a group meeting. In the adjacent column, list interventions by the leader that might improve group attendance. Document if you have the sources for such information. The following is an example:

| Reasons for absenteeism | Leader intervention |
| --- | --- |
| Example:<br>Ill health | Leader vists resident at bedside (or phones home on day of meeting) and states that the member was missed at the group meeting; inquires about health problem. Uses active listening and is supportive and concerned. |

## REFERENCES

Burnside, I. M. 1970. Crisis intervention among hospitalized aged. *Journal of Psychiatric Nursing* 8(2): 17–20 (March–April).

Corey, G. and M. Corey. 1977. *Groups: Process and practice.* Monterey, Calif.: Brooks/Cole.

Duvall, E. 1971. *Family development.* 4th ed. Philadelphia: Lippincott.

Erikson, E. H. 1963. *Childhood and society.* 2d ed. New York: Norton.

_____. 1982. The Life Cycle completed: A review, New York, Norton.

Hall, E. 1983. A Conversation with Erik Erickson, *Psychology Today,* 17(6):22–30, (June).

Havighurst, R. 1968. Psychological developments in the second half of life. In *Middle age and aging,* ed. B. Neugarten. Chicago: University of Chicago Press.

Hennessey, M. J. 1976. Group work with economically independent aged. In *Nursing and the aged.* 1st ed., ed. I. M. Burnside. New York: McGraw-Hill.

Hickey, T., D. L. Hultsch, and B. Fatule. 1975. Age effects in practitioner training for attitude change. Paper presented at Gerontological Society meeting, Louisville, Ky., October 28.

Hultsch, D. L., T. Hickey, and W. Rakowski. 1975. Adult learning in a meaningful context. Paper presented at Gerontological Society meeting, Louisville, Ky., October 27.

Kratzig, E. 1976. Student assignment for class entitled Group Work with the Elderly, San Francisco State University, San Francisco, Calif., October 7.

Leudtke, M. 1976. Student assignment for class entitled Group Work with the Elderly, San Francisco State University, San Francisco, Calif., October 7.

Linden, M. E. 1956. Geriatrics. In *The fields of group psychotherapy,* ed. S. R. Slavson. New York: Schocken Books.

Lowy, L. 1967. Roadblocks in group work practice with older people: A framework for analysis. Part 1. *The Gerontologist* 7(2): 109–13 (June).

Peck, R. 1968. Psychological developments in the second half of life. In *Middle age and aging,* ed. B. Neugarten. Chicago: University of Chicago Press.

Pfeiffer, E. 1975. Plenary speech given at conference entitled Successful Treatment of Mentally Ill Elderly, Duke University, Durham, N.C., May 22.

Shomaker, D., and C. Furukawa. 1982. Working with groups of elderly. In *Community health services for the aged,* ed. C. Furukawa and D. Shomaker. Rockville, Md.: Aspen Systems.

Smith, L. L. 1980. Finding your leadership style in groups. *American Journal of Nursing* 80(7): 1301–3 (July).

Tappen, R., and T. Touhy. 1983. Group leader—Are you a controller? *Journal of Gerontological Nursing* 9(1): 34 (January).

Tillich, P. 1952. *The courage to be.* New Haven, Conn.: Yale University Press.

U.S. Department of Health, Education, and Welfare. 1973. *New facts about older Americans.* Publication no. (SRS) 73–20006. (Pamphlet.) Washington, D.C.: Office of Human Development, Administration on Aging. June.

Yalom, I. D. 1975. 2d ed. *The theory and practice of group psychotherapy.* New York: Basic Books.

## BIBLIOGRAPHY

Brost, B. E. 1970. The "active leader" in group therapy for chronic schizophrenic patients. *Perspectives in Psychiatric Care* 8(6): 268–72.

Burnside, I. M. 1969. Group work among the aged. *Nursing Outlook* 17 (June): 68–71.

_____. 1970. Communication problems in group work with the disabled aged. *American Nurses' Association Clinical Conference.* New York: Appleton-Century-Crofts.

Chan, D. C. 1973. Using patients as group leaders in a VA hospital (program briefs). *Hospital and Community Psychiatry* 24(8): 531 (August).

Folsom, J. C., and G. S. Folsom. 1974. The real world. *Mental Hygiene* 58 (Summer): 29–33.

Forman, M. 1971. The alienated resident and the alienating institution: A case for peer group intervention. *Social Work* 16(2): 47–54 (April).

Goldfarb, A. 1971. Group therapy with the old and aged. In *Comprehensive group psychotherapy,* ed. H. Kaplan and B. Sadock. Baltimore: Williams & Wilkins.

McLaughlin, F. E. 1971. Personality changes through alternate group leadership. *Nursing Research* 20 (March–April): 123–30.

## RESOURCES

### Videocassettes

*If I Had My Life to Live Over* (3/4-inch cassette, black-and-white, 40 minutes). Group leader: Dr. Michael Berlin. Available from Department of Instructional TV, Rutgers University, New Brunswick, NJ.

Pennsylvania State University. 1975. *Sensory deprivation and the elderly.* (Videotape.) University Park, Pa.

# chapter 12

# Using Patients as Co-Leaders

*Linda M. Szafranski*

*Few things help an individual more than to place responsibility upon him, and to let him know that you trust him.*

BOOKER T. WASHINGTON

## LEARNING OBJECTIVES

- State the value of small groups with elderly residents.

- Compare and contrast patient co-leadership with professional co-leadership.

- List four guidelines for organizing a group.

- Describe how to organize a small group session.

- Discuss rationale for guest status.

- State the role of nursing staff involvement in small groups.

- List four guidelines for using a patient co-leader.

## KEY WORDS

- Co-leadership

- Bipolar disorder

- Group organization

- Group sessions

- Guest status

- Mutual support

- Patient co-leader

- Senile dementia

- Stereotypes

One of the questions that often plagues a group leader conducting sessions with the elderly is "How am I going to get these people to start talking to one another?" When my group was initially formed, I remember feeling anxious because I found myself doing most of the talking. I wanted the group to be "their group" rather than mine, and I wanted more interaction among group members. Using patient co-leadership in small groups does provide a means for actively involving members in the sessions.

A review of the literature uncovered only one brief article that deals directly with the use of patients as group leaders: "Using Patients as Group Leaders in a VA Hospital" (Chan 1973). The writer notes that "the members of the group perceived the patient-leader as a representative of the group" (p. 531). He concludes that the leader role is an important position in the group because it fulfills a person's need for recognition and gives a feeling of success. (See Chapter 6 which discusses aspects of control in group members.)

There may be several reasons why patient co-leadership is not widely used, particularly in group work with the aged. First, the idea of sharing the leadership role with a patient may be threatening to some professionals, particularly if they view the leader's position in the traditional way, as a role of power and control. They may also fear that the patient may not be able to handle the leadership role. I would have to agree that the leader is taking a risk in initiating patient co-leadership, but with any new procedure there is an inherent chance of failure. The outcome will never be known unless one takes the chance and tries the new idea. "Many leaders, schooled in traditional beliefs about leadership, hesitate to try newer methods lest they appear weak and inadequate in front of group members" (Bradford 1976, 15).

This chapter is a revised version of "Using Patient Co-Leaders in Group Sessions," which first appeared in *Aging*, September–October 1981 (nos. 321–322). The author wishes to acknowledge Linda Bagneski, R.N., who encouraged her to write the article.

The risk of patient co-leadership is compounded when utilizing it with the elderly, about whom numerous myths abound. N. Mayadas and D. Hink (1974, 444) discuss "the stereotypic image of the older individual as dependent, losing command of his physical facilities, and relatively inferior to the more privileged younger adult." Also, the myth that the elderly are incapable of change or growth prevails. It has been noted (Tuckman and Lorge 1953) that as people grow older, the stereotypes about them become more negative. Thus, group leaders need to examine their personal attitudes about the elderly.

The practice of group work with the elderly may be subject to these stereotypes and myths. However, groups have been shown to "provide an opportunity for mutual support and are an aid in the reorganization of behavior in old people who are under the stress of declining resources" (Goldfarb 1971, 640). Daniel Lago and Stephanie Hoffman (1977–78) conclude that groups aid in the continued development of the healthy older person by providing a means of dealing with the problems they encounter.

## PATIENT CO-LEADERSHIP

Small group sessions are part of the treatment offered at the Geropsychiatric Center (GPC) at the Mendota Mental Health Institute. The Institute, located in Madison, Wisconsin, is part of the state's mental health care delivery system. The Geropsychiatric Center is a 20-bed short-term care unit that provides specialized psychiatric services (both evaluation and treatment) to those 60 and older.

The patients reflect a variety of personalities and backgrounds, as well as varying degrees of psychiatric and medical problems. The majority of the patients are diagnosed as having organic brain syndrome (OBS), schizophrenia, or an affective disorder. As a social worker on this unit, I have conducted small half-hour group sessions over the past four years.

Traditionally, a co-leader of a group is another professional or staff person assisting the designated leader. However, I have expanded upon that idea to utilize patients in the capacity of co-leader. The ways in which co-leadership by professionals and co-leadership using group members differ are summarized in the following table.

| Co-leadership by professionals | Co-leadership using group members |
|---|---|
| 1. Leaders may have more control over group. | 1. Group members control the topics to be discussed. |
| 2. Co-leadership is stable. | 2. Co-leadership changes weekly. |
| 3. Co-leaders often are of same discipline or one is in a health field. | 3. The abilities and personalities of patient co-leaders can differ greatly. |

A newly admitted group member served as the catalyst for the idea of having a patient co-leader. About three months after I started my group, a new group member candidly said to me, "You know, you talk too much." I explained that I wanted to make this "their group" but that the members were not actively participating in the discussions. The group was unable to come up with any new suggestions, but I felt I had an opportunity to try something new with this patient, who was not afraid to speak his mind.

After the session, I asked him if he would help me plan some questions for the next group meeting. He agreed to do this and brought up the topic of school. Together we planned the questions. I encouraged him to devise his own questions for they following session. At the next meeting, I announced that my new co-leader had decided on the topic for the group and that he had four questions he wanted to ask of the members. This particular gentleman had a diagnosis of organic brain syndrome and was unable to direct his questions to others, so he answered first when each question was asked. I believe, however, that he still had the feeling of being in charge of the session from other comments he made on his own during group. For example, at one point he turned to another group member and said, "Speak up."

This first experience with patient co-leadership was so successful that the group voted to have a co-leader once a week and encouraged members to volunteer for this position. I explained that I would meet with the co-leader before the session to assist him or her with the topic and questions. The range of ability to handle co-leadership varied; some patients were able to write down their own questions and others needed assistance.

Each individual was encouraged to choose a topic that he or she found meaningful and thought would be of interest to the rest of the group. One co-leader chose to bring a letter he had received from his sister. He read it to the group, and it generated a group discussion. His sister had included stories about the fun they had in the winter as children, sledding and ice-skating, which stirred old memories for other group members to share.

Another co-leader chose ice-fishing as a topic and discussed some practical ideas on how to get set up and succeed, adding some anecdotes from his ice-fishing days. He then directed questions to others in the group about fishing and inquired about their experiences; questions were then asked about how people ice-fish today, since his experiences had taken place 20 years earlier. We decided to invite a staff member who currently ice-fishes to the group's next session; the staff member even brought some of his new fishing gear to the meeting to show to the group.

It was interesting to observe the style of co-leadership of a former schoolteacher. She called on people by name for answers to her questions even before they had a chance to volunteer. She asked members one by one if they had gone to school in the city or attended school in a rural area. She had taught in a one-room schoolhouse and talked about the great distance children had to walk to school. Other questions revolved around favorite lard-pail lunches and game-playing during recess.

One gentleman wanted to know about each member's first girlfriend or boyfriend. It was surprising how many people even remembered the person's name! One man who had a diagnosis of senile dementia was unable to recall the name of his first girlfriend but said, "It was my schoolteacher." He obviously had had a crush on the teacher and vividly described her, saying, "She was a good-looking, red-headed Irish gal." The co-leader then proceeded to ask members about their first date, where they had gone, the type of transportation they had used, and how old they were at the time.*

---

*Lard came in tin pails and these containers would subsequently become the counterpart of present day lunch boxes.

One patient who was diagnosed as having a bipolar disorder (in the depressed phase) began attending the group shortly after her admission. As her treatment progressed, she volunteered to be co-leader. It was interesting that she chose the topic of trips and vacations, since she had been unwilling even to leave her own home prior to her admission. She seemed to enjoy talking about past vacations, and it helped her to recall better days in her life.

Topics for discussion, as well as the style of handling co-leadership, varied with each individual. One co-leader made a point of including me in any questions he asked the rest of the group, saying in his German accent, "You get to ask us, so we get to ask you." I have found that groups are interested in the leader's response. They expect the leader to be more than just a facilitator and to share some information about personal life.

Some of the topics chosen by patient co-leaders included special remembered holidays, school days, favorite games played as a child, graduation day, first pets, special times with a relative, a story about an adventure with a brother or sister, birthday celebrations, musical instruments played or enjoyed, and growing up on a farm versus growing up in the city. A few residents brought in personal pictures or some special item to begin their discussion. To begin a discussion on leisure interests, one woman brought in a ceramic animal she had made.

## GUIDELINES FOR ORGANIZING A GROUP

During the planning process in organizing my group, I needed to decide on a meeting place. Ideally, such an area should be free from noise and distractions; however, many facilities lack areas that can be used specifically for meetings. One may have to make some compromises and perhaps think of ways to use the space that is available. For example, I use a patient visiting room down the corridor from the residents' rooms, but unfortunately there is still the interruption of the paging system. I am able to use this room because my group is held in the early morning before visitors arrive. It is a private room with chairs arranged in a circle. There is a table in the room that can be utilized for refreshments, materials for discussion, or to arrange the group around.

A leader should set a regular time for the group meetings. Choose the time in coordination with the rest of the staff's programming. In selecting a time for group, one should consider what time of day seems best for the residents. I held my group from 8:30 to 9:00 A.M., three days a week. Also, I would urge the leader to bear in mind the attention span of residents when deciding on the length of the session.

When a time has been decided, tell the staff what it is and give them the names of the group members who will be attending the sessions. With an aged population, one will need assistance to be sure residents are dressed and ready. I have found it helpful to use nursing staff in my group, a topic I will discuss more fully later in the chapter. This involvement in the group allows the nursing staff to become familiar on a first-hand basis with members and with what occurs in group; this can provide an incentive to have people ready for group and perhaps for members of the nursing staff eventually to try group leadership themselves.

Usually I arranged the seats in a circle to facilitate communication. My rationale for doing the placements was that I knew each member's handicaps better than the co-leaders did. Generally, my group functioned best with six to eight members, although sometimes the group was as small as three or as large as eleven. Depending on the size of the group, the leader may want to place members around a table. This type of arrangement seems to work well for people with a hearing loss or those who have a very short attention span. However, this type of seating arrangement can probably accommodate no more than six people.

It is important when choosing group members that the leader meet each person to assess the individual both physically and psychologically. Each person is also assessed regarding his or her need for socialization and potential to function in a group setting. The leader should meet with each person, rather than accepting him or her blindly on the recommendation of a staff member. The group leader has the right to decide who will best function in the group (Burnside 1978). For example, the leader is the best judge of whether the size of the group can accommodate a resident with a hearing loss.

## Guest Status

If there is uncertainty about whether a person will benefit from group, it is possible to extend an invitation to attend a session as a guest. I explain to the person that "guest status" is a special invitation to attend group for one week and that a guest should feel free to contribute to the group discussion. After this time period, the leader should meet with the person to discuss his or her feelings about the group. A decision will then be made as to whether regular group membership would be a positive arrangement for both the person and the group. I've found that this usually eases a new leader's fears of choosing the wrong person for the existing group.

## One-to-One Beginning

I've found that building a relationship with the elderly can be enhanced by meeting with them on a one-to-one basis. I meet with each new member and explain the purpose of the group, who is in the group, and some of the topics we have discussed in group; I also give each new member a general idea of what can be expected from the sessions. This pregroup, one-to-one session can also be used to provide an opportunity for a regular member to talk with the new member, perhaps generating a new friendship. The leader could ask the regular group member to walk to the meetings with the new member for the first two weeks until the new person becomes familiar with the time and location.

## Treatment Plan

One should explain to a new group member that a treatment plan will be written for him or her and ask what the new member hopes to gain from the group experience. Often people are unable to come up with ideas, and the leader will need to offer examples. *An individual treatment plan with specific goals is written for each participant in the group.* These goals vary from simple attendance or speaking loudly enough for people to hear to initiating a group discussion. Goals are intended to be realistic ones that the person can reach, so that neither the patient nor the leader is frustrated. The treatment plan also delineates the approach to meeting the goals.

The first time a new member attends group, I ask the individual to tell the others about himself or herself. I also state this in my individual contact before the first meeting so that this request does not come as a surprise. Depending on the person, the leader might need to ask some specific questions, such as "How many brothers or sisters do you have?" or "How do you like to spend your leisure time?" or "What type of employment have you had?" This is usually no more than a five-minute social introduction. I've also found that this can be a way to foster new relationships; one can point out, for example, that "Mrs. Smith also enjoys playing rummy" or "Mr. Joseph was raised on a farm, too." This also serves as a way to make new members feel more a part of the group and can lead to future interactions. Ask the new group member to sit next to you for the first few sessions to foster a sense of security.

### Role of the Nursing Staff

It has been helpful to have a member of the nursing staff assist with the group. In my particular work setting, I have involved nursing staff available on a particular shift. Usually the charge nurse will assign one nursing staff member to assist with group, or the charge nurse may attend herself. This rotation provides an opportunity for numerous members of the nursing staff, from registered nurse to nursing assistant, to interact with the patients in a group setting rather than in the typical physical-care situation. It gives them a chance to hear about the patient's early life, family, work, and other areas of personal concern or interest.

I, as a social worker, was responsible for the group, but a nurse familiar with group process could also run the sessions and have a member of another discipline serve as facilitator. There are benefits to having the same person assist in running the group, such as continuity should one staff member not be present. Also, a consis-

tent staff duo would be more attuned to picking up subtle changes that occur in an individual or the group. However, since we all seem to be facing staff shortages, you might have to decide what is feasible in your particular setting. On occasion, I have been the only staff involved in the group session; however, I have asked for assistance in getting people to the meeting as needed. There are definite advantages to having another staff member in group meetings, but I would rather see the group go on with one leader than not at all. As a group leader, I feel it is important to be flexible and develop a framework that reflects the realities of the particular work situation and the needs of the patients.

In general, it helps to have another staff person involved with the group, to personally invite and physically help people get to group. Also, it is beneficial to have someone observe the interactions among participants. There is often a great deal of nonverbal communication on the part of those elderly who have difficulty expressing themselves; this might be totally lost if there is only one staff person in the group setting. Also, some group discussion may involve emotion-laden areas such as loss, illness, and loneliness, which may be difficult for one staff person to deal with on a regular basis.

Mary Goodson (1964, 26) addresses the role of nurses in group. She writes, "The patient could observe his nurse as a model in interacting with others, and the nurse could, in turn, observe the patient's response to the group." Goodson further notes that the patient's interaction in the group may lead to areas of discussion for individual sessions.

Another benefit of having nursing staff involved in group is their level of medical expertise. Diane Puppolo (1980, 266) relays that she "functioned in an information-giving capacity when opportunities arose in the group." With this age group a number of medical concerns do come up that could be explained by a nurse. Groups are enriched by having co-leaders from two disciplines, with different areas of expertise to share with the group as questions arise.

A social worker and a nurse can share the leadership role of a group and still utilize a patient as co-leader of the group session. Two staff members can help provide group members with an increased physical sense of security. Two staff are a source of support not only to the residents but to each other as well. Staff can share observations of group process and concerns about individual participants. They can consult with each other and may be able to come up with improved approaches or techniques for dealing with problematic issues.

## Format of Session

I always begin each group session with introductions, to reacquaint members with each other and to enhance socialization. First the co-leader is introduced; then he or she chooses one of the two forms of introduction. The standard form is for members to state their names. The second form is the handshake greeting, in which each person goes around the circle and introduces himself or herself by name while shaking hands. The patients are encouraged to address each person in group by name as they shake their hand. As Dorothy Rinehart Blake (1973, 154) points out in "Group Work with the Institutionalized Elderly," encouraging group members to learn one another's names is a way of helping them to use forgotten social and communication skills. The elderly often lack physical contact, so the handshaking affords a means of social contact. Lynne Berger (1978, 65) talks about using sensory motor exercises, "such as reaching into the center of the circle to touch one another's feet with their own feet while saying 'Hello'," to initiate her group. The majority of co-leaders in my group picked the handshaking greeting. It is important to give each person this opportunity for contact. Some patients readily go around the circle, while others do not feel comfortable with this physical gesture. No one is pressed to get up and shake hands. However, it is interesting to note that even some patients who were initially reluctant later actively participated in this group greeting. One woman used her wheelchair as an excuse for not reaching out to other members. After several sessions, she, too, began to navigate her wheelchair around the circle. Patients who have organic brain syndrome may enjoy shaking hands but may need individual attention to be able to follow through on it. Often persons with this disorder will say yes

when asked if they would like to go around the group and introduce themself—but will remain sitting. At this point I get up and *physically* walk them through the handshaking procedure. I point this out because in early sessions I did not offer additional help to these people. Later I found that with a little assistance they could follow through on this social interaction.

I give assistance to the patient co-leader in hosting the group, depending upon individual limitations, and at the end of the session the other group members are encouraged to give the co-leader a round of applause.

## BENEFITS OF PATIENT CO-LEADERSHIP

Patient co-leadership helps to raise the group's feeling of self-esteem. I recall one co-leader who was asking questions about individuals' educational backgrounds. He asked another man in group if he had graduated from grade school. The man to whom he addressed the question was diagnosed as having senile dementia, and he did not always respond appropriately to questions asked of him. On this occasion, however, the man related that the had gone through college and worked as an engineer. The co-leader obviously had made some assumptions about this man and was quite surprised to hear his response. He looked to the group leader, who supported the gentleman's answer. The co-leader, in turn, was very supportive of this man and complimented him, saying, "You really did well." Then he said to the group, "You better listen to him." I viewed this interaction as having a two-fold positive effect. The self-esteem of this gentleman was enhanced by recognition of his educational accomplishments. Also, the group's feeling of self-worth was increased by knowing that this educated man was a group member. This gentleman continued to have days when he was more alert than other days, but the group seemed more accepting of him after they knew more about him.

Co-leadership gives members responsibility for their group as well as personal recognition. I remember one nurse telling me after group that she was quite surprised to see how well one resident functioned as a co-leader. Before making this group observation, the nurse had mainly interacted with this resident in a traditional nursing situation in which the resident appeared less capable. "Excess disabilities" is a term used by Brody, Kleban, Lawton, and Silverman (1971) to describe such incongruent behaviors. This resident's high level of performance made me believe that she felt some investment in and responsibility for the group.

Co-leadership fosters a feeling of independence. The group members no longer have to look to the staff to choose the area of discussion. As the weeks progressed, I found that people whom I had never expected would be interested were volunteering to be co-leaders. The fact that they volunteered to participate actively in their group discussion served as a significant reinforcer for me.

## GUIDELINES FOR UTILIZING GROUP MEMBERS AS CO-LEADERS

The following nine points should guide group leaders who wish to use group members as co-leaders.

1. Explain the role of the co-leader to the group.
2. Tell the group that you will meet with the co-leader to prepare for the group meeting.
3. Give a few examples of topics that could be used for the group session.
4. Ask for a volunteer from the group to co-lead the next session.
5. Meet with the co-leader to assist with topic selection and discussion questions.
6. Introduce the co-leader to the group at the beginning of the session.
7. Ask the co-leader to begin the introductions in group, either by having members state their names or by using the handshake greeting.
8. Assist the co-leader during the group session as needed.
9. Conclude the group session with a thank you or round of applause for the co-leader.

## SUMMARY

This chapter describes the use of group members as co-leaders. Co-leadership is a visible means of placing responsibility for the group with group members. The role of co-leader makes group members aware of the value staff place on them. I believe that a positive group experience can be attained by utilizing co-leaders who are themselves members of the group.

## REFERENCES

Berger, L. 1978. Activating a psychogeriatric group. *Psychiatric Quarterly* 50:63–66.

Blake, D. R. 1980. Group work with the institutionalized elderly. In *Psychosocial nursing care of the aged*. 2nd ed., ed. I. Burnside. New York: McGraw-Hill.

Bradford, L. F. 1976. *Making meetings work*. La Jolla, Calif.: University Associates.

Brody, E. M., M. H. Kleban, M. P. Lawton, H. Silverman. 1971. Excess disabilities of mentally impaired aged: impact of individual treatment, Part 1. *The Gerontologist* 11(2):124–33 (Summer).

Burnside, I. 1978. *Working with the elderly: Group process and techniques*. 1st ed. North Scituate, Mass.: Duxbury Press.

Chan, D. 1973. Using patients as group leaders in a VA hospital. *Hospital and Community Psychiatry* 24(8): 531 (August).

Goldfarb, A. 1971. Group therapy with the old and aged. In *Comprehensive group psychotherapy*, ed. H. Kaplan and B. Sadock. Baltimore: Williams & Wilkins.

Goodson, M. 1964. Group therapy with regressed patients. *Perspectives in Psychiatric Care* 2(4): 23–31.

Lago, D. and S. Hoffman. 1977–78. Structured group interaction: An intervention strategy for the continued development of elderly population. *International Journal of Aging and Human Development* 8(4): 311–24.

Mayadas, N., and D. Hink. 1974. Group work with the aging. *The Gerontologist* 14(4): 440–45 (October).

Puppolo, D. 1980. Co-leadership with a group of stroke patients. In *Psychosocial nursing care of the aged*. 1st ed., ed. I. Burnside. New York: McGraw-Hill.

Tuckman, J., and I. Lorge. 1953. Attitudes toward old people. *Journal of Social Psychology* 37: 249–60.

Saul, S. and S. Saul. 1974. Group psychotherapy in a proprietary nursing home. *The Gerontologist* 14(4): 446–50 (October).

## BIBLIOGRAPHY

Erickson, R. 1981. Small-group psychotherapy with patients on a short-stay ward: An opportunity for innovation. *Hospital and Community Psychiatry* 32(4): 269–72.

Kubie, S. and G. Landau. 1953. Group work with the aged. New York: International Universities Press.

Lowy, L. 1967. Roadblocks in group work practice with older peoples: A framework for analysis. Part 1. *The Gerontologist* 7(2): 109–13 (June).

## RESOURCES

### Audiocassettes

*How to Use Group Psychotherapy: Successful Treatment of the Elderly Mentally Ill* (audiocassette series). By J. Altholz and I. Burnside. Wyeth Laboratories, division of American Home Products Corporation, P.O. Box 8299, Philadelphia, PA 19101.

# chapter 13

# Group Work [with the] Cognitively Im[paired]

*Irene Burnside*

**LEARNING OBJECTIVES**

- Describe 10 ways...
  one's self dur...
  regressed d...
- Analy...

142

*Tell me; I'll forget. Show me, I may remember. But involve me, and I'll understand.*

ANCIENT CHINESE PROVERB

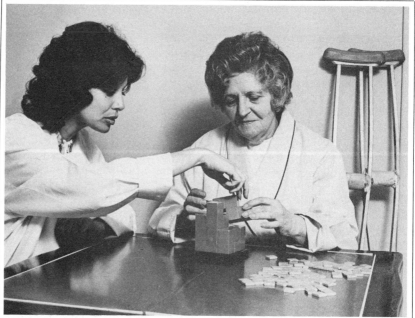

LEO CHOPLIN/BLACK STAR

to take care of
ng work with the
derly.

e four inappropriate group
mber selections.

- Discuss changes in behavior that might occur during the course of a group.

- Discuss individualization within the group setting.

- Expand on the "staying near" phenomenon frequently observed in dementia.

## KEY WORDS

- Alzheimer's disease
- Aphasia
- Delirium
- Dementia
- Flat affect
- Individualization
- Nonverbal communication
- Organic mental disorder
- Paranoia
- We-ness

Although reports on a variety of aspects of caring for the mentally impaired elderly in institutions have appeared in the literature,* the "therapeutic nihilism" prevalent among health professionals about treating the aged is especially blatant in regard to the mentally impaired elderly. The word *senile* is used with great frequency by health care professionals, both in discussions about residents and on their charts. The patient whose diagnosis is dementia is often relegated to a back room (or the back ward in a state hospital), and little effort is made by staff members to prevent further slippage. The staff's ennui and lack of hope are soon picked up by family and friends, who sometimes cease even to correspond with and/or visit the patient.

Nurses' aides, in spite of their lack of knowledge and sophistication, are still the staff people most likely to offer support and hope to this group of elderly people. The aides must patiently

struggle against formidable odds; some of them do a remarkable job of relating to the mentally impaired. But instilling hope is not an easy task, and a hopeful (but realistic) attitude toward the care of the regressed and mentally impaired aged is relatively rare. The book *Gramp* (Jury and Jury 1976) provides an outstanding example of caretaking and caring by a family. A filmstrip and cassette by the same authors is entitled *Gramp: A Man Ages and Dies.* This family's struggle with destructive behavior, incontinence, and loss of memory is a shining instance of the caring component of care.

Group work with the mentally impaired elderly can be extremely difficult, but it can also be highly rewarding. This chapter offers students, instructors, and health care workers and administrators some cautions for the new leader and three examples of groups I led in institutions. Group A illustrates behavioral problems and membership selection; group B, individualization within a group; and group C, nonverbal communication. Each group contained six or seven members. (Group leading is much easier if the group is kept to about six persons, partic-

---

*For example, Brody et al. (1971); Brody et al. (1972); Brody et al. (1975); Kleban and Brody (1972); Kleban, Brody and Lawton (1971); Kleban et al. (1975, 1976); Kobrynski (1975); and Salter and Salter (1975).

ularly if there are frail and/or disabled members in the group.) All met on a weekly basis except during the termination phase, when meetings were spaced further apart.

## CAUTIONS FOR NEW GROUP LEADERS

While doing group work with the mentally impaired elderly, I am often reminded of this passage from A. A. Milne's *Winnie-the-Pooh*:

> The Old Grey Donkey, Eeyore, stood by himself in a thistly corner of the Forest, his front feet well apart, his head on one side, and thought about things. Sometimes he thought sadly to himself, "Why?" and sometimes he thought, "Wherefore?" and sometimes he thought, "Inasmuch as which?"—and sometimes he didn't quite know what he was thinking about. So when Winnie-the-Pooh came stumping along, Eeyore was very glad to be able to stop thinking for a little, in order to say "How do you do?" in a gloomy manner to him. "And how are you?" said Winnie-the-Pooh. Eeyore shook his head from side to side. "Not very how," he said. "I didn't seem to have felt at all how for a long time."†

Group work with the mentally impaired aged pushes leaders into some "thistly corners" and sometimes even into conversations like this one.

Leading groups of regressed or mentally impaired elderly people requires intense involvement to combat low affect and lack of emotional response and to meet affectional needs of the members. The leader must grapple with superdependency, listlessness, apathy, low energy levels, and lack of information about the group members. The leader also needs to be comfortable with long silences in a group. Careful observation by the leader for any cues of increased awareness (verbal or nonverbal) helps pinpoint progress, but it is often slow, and observed changes may seem miniscule if the leader sets unrealistic goals. These problems help produce the anxiety or boredom that can overtake (and

sometimes overwhelm) a leader about midway through the life of the group. Indeed, introducing crafts, projects, music, and exercises may be necessary to sustain the leader as well as the group.

New group leaders need reminding that to be effective they must take care of themselves. Some specific suggestions follow:

1. Use a support system; have one person available on the staff to whom you can talk in confidence about your group experiences.

2. Use staff meetings to explore feelings—not as a gripe session but as constructive catharsis with problem solving.

3. Consider more frequent rest breaks (for example, go out for a brief walk and take deep breaths instead of taking the usual coffee break).

4. Practice more spontaneity. Don't get so bogged down in routine that you become bored and indifferent.

5. Assess your own reactions to the dependency and deterioration of the patients. Are the problems of the patients hitting too close to those of your own relatives, for example? Consider whether you are conducting the right group for you.

6. Continued awareness of self is important. There are often subtle clues that you may overlook or ignore: slight pains, depressed feelings, physical fatigue, loss of interest in the job, resentment, a feeling of martyrdom.

7. Plan careful, individualized programs within the group so that deteriorating patients have maximum support but continue to do as much for themselves as possible.

8. If you are a staff member, suggest a monthly morale booster meeting. At each meeting look at positive approaches to what is happening, find something to feel good about in your work, permit no negative input, and reward everyone with something different—a surprise. (Remember the psychological importance of beverages and food.)

---

†Lines from Winnie-the-Pooh by A. A. Milne, illustrated by Ernest H. Shepard. Copyright © 1926, by E. P. Dutton; renewal 1954, by A. A. Milne. Reprinted by permission of the publishers, E. P. Dutton, Inc., and The Canadian Publishers, McClelland and Stewart Limited, Toronto.

9. Discover new ways of being good to yourself, both on the job and off.

10. Examine your own patterns of coping with discouragement and depression, dependency, and deterioration. What will you do about the patterns?

11. Learn from one another. What people do you know who have unique and successful ways of taking care of themselves?

12. Practice observing your patients. How do they take care of themselves? The aged are our best teachers; borrow from their wisdom.

Leaders also have to be willing to try varied approaches. If one technique is a fiasco, they should abandon it and try another. Student leaders often get discouraged when their plans go awry, but problem solving is a learned leadership skill. I am reminded of the woman who called a local agency about a skunk under her home. They advised her to put a line of bread crumbs leading to the outside of the house. The next day she called to say that she had done so and now had two skunks under the house.

New solutions do have a way of backfiring, and the successful ones may even create new problems. If there is a change in a "problem" resident who has been a member of a group, the staff may think the group leader can perform minimiracles and then want to place obstreperous residents in the group to "straighten them out." The leader should be very cautious about staff overenthusiasm about residents or clients. Such enthusiasm may mean that they want to hand over an especially difficult patient and then sit back and watch the leader struggle with behavior that they cannot handle or tolerate.

However, group work can still create the "Hawthorne effect"—that is, heightened interest and unanticipated spin-offs. Curiosity is aroused when an "outsider" comes in and plans and prepares for the group. As a result, interest in the group members by the administrator and the staff often increases, and they begin to observe the members more closely. This curiosity and interest helps group leaders in contacting the staff while planning the group. The cook may be involved if refreshments are to be served.

Receptionists and office personnel can provide a great deal of help. Indeed, maintenance men often helped me round up missing patients for groups B and C, since the men knew where the patients "hid out."

A series of classic experimental studies called the Hawthorne studies was conducted in the late 1920s and the early 1930s at the Hawthorne Plant of the Western Electric Company in Chicago. The Hawthorne effect is a term used to describe psychological reactions that occur in subjects and that tend to alter their responses. Subjects may change their behavior in an effort to please the researcher (Demsey and Demsey 1981).

The biggest spin-off I have observed is that friendships outside the group setting often become very significant, especially when the group is completed. I have gone back to visit later and have seen such friendships continue to grow.

## GROUP A: BEHAVIORAL PROBLEMS AND MEMBERSHIP SELECTION

Group A met 30 minutes weekly for seven months. I led seven elderly women who were hospitalized in a 68-bed light mental (locked) facility situated in a quiet California neighborhood not far from a famous motion picture studio. The facility, once used to dry out overimbibing movie stars, was old and resembled a large, rambling house. No sign or name anywhere indicated that the house was an institution, as the neighbors objected strenuously.

Group A did not really get going until the seventh meeting. Staff members had suggested to me potential group members who they felt would benefit from a group experience. Selection of appropriate members for the group turned out to be a big problem. Five individuals had to be removed from the group soon after it was launched; each person was immediately replaced. Descriptions of the five individuals removed from the group follow. They were a colorful, albeit unmanageable, group and underline the danger of inadequate assessments of potential group members.

## Inappropriate Group Selections

**Mrs. A.** Mrs. A, in her mid-sixties, was born in Warsaw. She rarely spoke, even in Polish. Though she seemed to understand English, her behavior left me doubting it much of the time. She attended five meetings and displayed unusually high anxiety. She frequently jumped up and left the room; when she did remain seated, she fidgeted and mumbled constantly. In the second meeting, with the leader's constant reminding, she was able to sit still, but she continued to disrupt the group by drinking the cream from the pitcher on the coffee serving tray, snatching the sugar when the cream pitcher was empty, and grabbing the refreshments before they could be served.

Improving social graces has always been one of the goals I try to incorporate into group work with regressed aged, but there was absolutely no improvement with this woman. After the fifth meeting I decided to remove her. Her behavior unnerved me at times so much that I focused on her instead of handling the entire group. This "overindividualization" wears the leader down and leaves the rest of the group resentful. It was soon clear that her disruptive behavior impeded the group's progress.

Someone once said, "You must look into people as well as at them." This was certainly true in this selection; I had not looked into Mrs. A. *The lesson Mrs. A taught me is to obtain adequate data about behavior (and observe a while if in doubt) before selecting a group member.*

**Mrs. F.** Mrs. F, in her mid-seventies, was religious—but more temperamental than religious most of the time. Her diagnosis was chronic brain syndrome with paranoia. Although she sat still, her tongue did not. She monopolized the conversation. She was constantly supercilious. She came to group meetings only sporadically but always with aloof, condescending behavior. By the seventh meeting a close group was forming, but Mrs. F was not interested enough to attend, although she gave no specific reason. I did not encourage her to continue and finally terminated with her. *Mrs. F taught me that paranoid individuals can be very difficult*

*at times to keep in a group and may int̶̶̶̶ both leader and group with their hostile w̶̶̶̶*

**Mrs. H.** Mrs. H, age 72, attended only three meetings. She, too, felt the group was beneath her. Once after a meeting she came up to me and said, "And how did you pick that motley crew?" In the second meeting she flatly announced her dislike of men. I learned later from the staff that she was a long-time lesbian. Since I often touch aged individuals, I realized she already inhibited me in the group setting. I was disinclined to touch her; I thought she might misconstrue my touching as having sexual connotations. I had not experienced such a situation in group work before, nor did I wish to tackle such a problem when I was beginning a new group. My own anxiety has to level off in new groups; leaders have to strive continually to lower their own anxiety in group work. I felt that my own reserve and inhibitions with this woman would ultimately influence my interactions with the entire group. Much to my relief, she voluntarily dropped the group after the third meeting. *Mrs. H taught me not to let the staff sway me in my selections and to double-check for "missing" information on a potential member.*

**Mrs. M.** Mrs. M, age 78, was a retired nurse. She was very hostile; her verbal abuse was sometimes matched by physically striking out at other residents. She usually hit patients when she could not be seen by the staff, so that particular behavior was observed only if a staff member unexpectedly walked into the room. The staff thought she might benefit by joining the group. It soon became apparent that she wanted to attend meetings only at her whim. The nurse began setting strict limits with her at about the time the group was forming. Because of her quick and ill temper, her hostile remarks, and the fear she engendered in other patients, I did not encourage her to continue attending group meetings and finally terminated with her. Frail patients in groups need to be protected, and the group milieu should be safe and secure. There was a 95-year-old woman in this particular group, and I found myself frequently considering her frailty (Burnside 1978).

...th meeting Mrs. M had ...ed in the meetings was ...at sweets were served ... decided she wanted to ...irector of nurses and I ... She had had her chance; ...o at her whim. *I learned ... an abusive person can have on a group. I also learned to be more protective of the very old and very frail members.*

**Mrs. L.** Mrs. L was 74 years old. She had been hospitalized for several years and spent most of her time in a wheelchair. She would not try to walk or talk. At the first meeting she stiffened her body and nearly slid out of the wheelchair. Her eyes became rather glassy, and she frothed a little at the mouth. I was not sure what was happening. The nurse helped me return Mrs. L to her room, adding that this was not uncommon behavior for her. She died suddenly two months after the trial group experience. *Mrs. L taught me to investigate physical problems in greater detail and to interrogate several staff members about a resident's life history, behavior, and physical complaints.*

These patients were simply too much of a challenge. However, one should not lose hope in working with even difficult old people. Janet Specht* once brought that home to me, and her perseverance in new approaches to the mentally impaired is commendable. These patients might have benefited from a one-to-one relationship with a student, an interested staff member, or a volunteer, or one of them might have been absorbed into an already established, stable group.

### The Final Group Membership

The final group membership is shown in Table 13–1. The mean age of the group members was 79.7. Each individual in the group had a diagnosis of cerebral arteriosclerosis, and five of the women were diagnosed as having psychiatric problems. One resident had "delusional" for a diagnosis! It is not uncommon to find a symptom for a diagnosis in an elderly person's records.

There were several impressive things about this group. One was the lack of physical disabilities; there was a certain physical toughness about them, which I attributed to their many years of hard work. (Lack of education was also a characteristic of the group; most completed eighth grade only.) Another noticeable thing was the brevity of the diagnoses on the member's charts. There was no lists of six or seven ailments, as is usually seen in an average elderly person's record. It is possible that the admitting doctors did not write down all the diagnoses or that complete physical histories were not done. It is also possible that the most "fitting" diagnosis was emphasized—that is, the one diagnosis that would gain fastest entrée into a locked facility and also pass the medical review team.

There were no aphasics in the group, no immobile persons, and no paralyzed persons. One woman, though legally blind, said one day, "I have ten eyes," and held up her 10 fingers to show the group. One reason for the lack of such impairments may be that to be admitted to this facility most patients had to be able to care for themselves. Bedridden and wheelchair patients were not admitted.

One rather quick way a group leader can assess the sharpness of the members is to assign drawings.† Even if members follow short, simple instructions well, the leader can note problems as I did with Mrs. V as she struggled to draw, to spell, and to organize the simple assignments I gave (Figures 13–1 and 13–2).

FIGURE 13–1. *Mrs. V, a member of group A, had extreme memory loss, was very aware of it, and struggled with it constantly. Asked to draw a memory, she drew a barn in South Dakota. Then she tried to write a description of it, and one can see what happened when she tried to organize the statement.*

---

*Personal communication, 1976.

†I am grateful to Dr. Robert Katzman for his discussion about the use of clock drawings in assessment.

TABLE 13-1. **Members of group A**

| Patient | Age | Marital status | Diagnosis | Ambulation | Strengths in group | Problems in group |
|---------|-----|----------------|-----------|------------|--------------------|--------------------|
| Mrs. L. M. | 71 | Married | CAS,[1] schizophrenic, paranoid | Ambulatory | Gentleness | Dependency, crying spells, depression |
| Mrs. T | 85 | Widow (from age 63) | CAS, paranoid | Ambulatory | Warmth, loving ways, quick to praise | Forgetfulness |
| Miss H | 95 | Single (never married) | CAS, paranoid | Ambulatory | Toughness, sharpness, observation ability, articulate | Hallucinations |
| Mrs. V | 78 | Married | OMD,[2] degenerative arthritis, CAS | Ambulatory | Sense of humor, warmth, spontaneity | Forgetfulness |
| Mrs. H | 72 | Widow | Legally blind, congestive heart failure, epilepsy, CAS | Ambulatory | Sense of humor, articulate, courage, acceptance of blindness | Monopolization of group |
| Mrs. S. M. | 79 | Widow | CAS, manic-depressive appreciative | Ambulatory | Sharpness, helpfulness, appreciative | Bitterness, constant carping |
| Mrs. D. M. | 78 | Widow (at age 34) | CAS, reactive-depressive state | Ambulatory (with assistance) | Gratitude, articulate | Crying spells, depression |

[1]Cerebral arteriosclerosis.
[2]Organic mental disorder.

FIGURE 13-2. *During a session when we reminisced about first toys, Mrs. V drew a tea set that she remembered from her childhood. Note in Table 13-1 that she had a severe memory problem yet she drew the correct dishes for the tea. The strange object to the left of the creamer probably was the container for spoons, which was a common way to place spoons on a table in those days.*

## Observed Changes

Improvements in social graces and/or behavior often make staff members more receptive to a resident. Behavioral changes in members of group A often followed a rewarding group experience. For example, Mrs. D. M. entered group A at the sixth meeting and was considered by the staff to be a "problem" patient. She refused to walk and had many psychosomatic complaints. She expressed guilt about her only child's suicide; her daughter had committed suicide while the woman was in a board-and-care home. Mrs. D. M. became so depressed and agitated that she was transferred to a locked facility. The director of nurses and I discussed the nursing care plan so that I could support the staff's therapeutic regimen during group meetings. Specifically, I would (1) encourage her to walk, (2) listen to but not encourage the psychosomatic complaints, (3) offer her an opportunity to express guilt (and other feelings) in group meetings, and (4) observe her degree of depression from week to week.

The staff and I were surprised at her rather sudden improvement. The day before Mother's

Day the group had weathered a stormy session. My small, inexpensive gifts for each member caused visible sadness, especially in Mrs. D. M. She took her gift, cried openly, and said, "I don't deserve it. I am not a fit mother. Plus I don't even have ten cents to give anyone else a gift." I sat on the arm of her chair and put my arm around her. I served her tea, which she preferred to coffee. (Fixing a member's coffee or tea exactly as requested is one simple way to individualize care and is more important than the leader may realize.) We talked about the daughter's suicide and the mother's guilt. All of us acknowledged feelings we had had on Mother's Day. When the meeting was over, an aide and I helped her walk back to her room.

In the subsequent meeting Mrs. D. M. was tearless, though obviously still depressed. I noticed that a staff member had shaved off the hairs on her chin. (That had been in the nursing care plan—she hated the hair on her face.) She apologized for not having combed her hair before coming to the meeting. This time she would not let me serve her tea and said that coffee was fine (if I would "just put a little cold water in it"). She did not mention her stomach ache, as she had done many times in the previous meeting. I sat close to her but touched her arm or shoulder only occasionally.

During the sad expressions of loss during the Mother's Day session, I suggested homework. Since coping with losses was a task the members were facing, they were to recall how they coped with a particular loss in their lives and share with the group what had been helpful to them. It was during such sharing that we discovered that two members had lived very close to each other before their admission to the hospital. Such discoveries are important because they reveal information that helps members develop friendships outside the meetings. One should always capitalize on such serendipity when it occurs.

A similar incident occurred in group C; Mr. B and Mr. Z both spoke a French patois, so I encouraged them to converse in French. The talents of the aged so often go unnoticed, and group experiences do give the aged a chance to share talents, interests, and accomplishments.

## Group A: A Summary

Several women in a light mental (locked) facility met weekly for seven months. We talked about things of interest to them, such as feelings about being a woman, clothes, teas, social affairs, and the "prisoner's life" they led (their description). Although we drew occasionally, mostly we talked. I always ended the group meetings with sweets and coffee.

After the weekly meetings were terminated, I often taught group work at the same facility. Some of the women were interviewed or participated in group demonstrations, and they did miss the regular meetings. Lack of staff and volunteers was the reason the meetings were not continued. I saw Mrs. H from time to time until she died, since she was the only one in the group without any relatives (Burnside 1978).

## GROUP B: INDIVIDUALIZATION WITHIN A GROUP

Group B met weekly for six months in the small, cozy employees' dining room of a 91-bed extended care facility. (Group members are listed in Table 13–2.) This group was launched in an unusual fashion. A biologist-researcher* suggested to me that there might be a relationship between testosterone levels and institutionalized depressed men. I met with an administrator and discussed plans for a group to study. Contracts were made, a group of six men was assembled, and testosterone assays were done. The "Hawthorne effect" in this instance was that elderly men not in the group would line up, expose an arm, and say, "I want to give my blood too!" However, since the biologist found that the levels were not unusually low, there was no reason to continue the group for the research project.

Since the group was under way, I did not feel that I could terminate it, especially after the men had been so cooperative. The two least interested men were phased out of the group and replaced by two women.

---

*Caleb Finch, personal communication, 1974.

TABLE 13–2. **Members of group B**

| Patient | Former occupation | Age | Ambula-tion | Diagnosis | Visitors | Length of hospi-talization | Restorative potential (by M.D.) | Strengths in group | Problems in group |
|---|---|---|---|---|---|---|---|---|---|
| Mr. D. M. | Automobile mechanic | 75 | Ambula-tory | TBC (inactive),[1] malnutrition, dementia | None | 2 years, 6 months | Fair | Sweet, gentle air, beautiful smile | Apathy, withdrawal listlessness |
| Mr. G | Railroad clerk | 63 | Ambula-tory | Schizophrenic, simple type, marked deterioration | None | 3 years, 6 months | Zero | Tried hard | Lack of social graces, sometimes inattentive |
| Mr. P | Fisherman, Construction worker | 58 | Ambula-tory | CVA[2] | None | 3 years | Poor | Sharp, improvement in self-care | Stubborn, cross, sometimes would not talk |
| Mrs. B | Registered nurse | 79 | Ambula-tory | Dementia secondary to Parkinson's (although she was extremely paranoid, not in diagnosis) | None | 5 years, 8 months | Fair | Sharp, observ-ing, enjoyed drawing | Hallucinating, high anxiety, would leave group abruptly, quiet |
| Mrs. M | Journalist | 90 | Wheel-chair | Dementia | Yes | 2 years | Zero | Articulate | Anger at staff, monopolizing |
| Mr. D | Gardener | 88 | Ambula-tory | Dementia | Yes | 2 years | Fair | Gentleness, obvious enjoy-ment of group, smile | Aphasic, difficulties in communication |

[1] Tuberculosis.
[2] Cardiovascular accident.

The lack of affect, spontaneity, and motivation in the group forced me to try various methods: (1) topics were assigned to discuss, (2) reminiscing sessions were tried, and (3) simple art sessions were instituted, using chalk, crayons, and so forth. The last was the most successful of the three techniques tried. Members were assigned a building, toy, pet, boyfriend, or girlfriend to draw—some thing or person out of their past (Figure 13–3). Only one art exercise was not successful, and now I understand why. Because I was still in a euphoric state from a trip to Africa, I asked the group members to draw an African animal. These people were never a wildly enthusiastic group at any time, but this day their enthusiasm hit a new low. In my eagerness I had assigned something to meet my need, not theirs—a common problem (and often nontherapeutic) in leaders. Neither had I reckoned with asking them to draw the unfamiliar—after all, elephants and giraffes

FIGURE 13–3. *Mrs. M drew a picture of her first toy, a doll.*

are usually at the very back of the average old person's memory file. And I was working with mentally impaired people besides!

An informal, relaxed atmosphere is a must in work with the mentally impaired. A quiet, warm, well-lit area with plenty of space is important. Notice that the former operating room nurse at the right in the photograph still wears her watch in a position for scrubbing. A leader should observe for cues to past life-style, present life-style, and ways in which the elderly are striving to cope. For example, Mr. D placed the straw in his beer because he has such a severe tremor that it is difficult for him to hold a can.

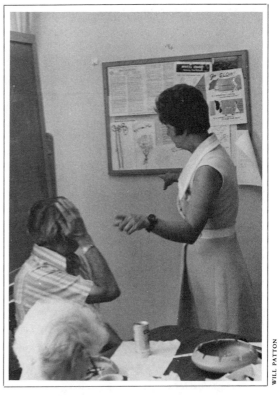

Drawings were placed on the bulletin board and praised by the leader; each member was praised for drawing. They smiled when the leader commented, but members said little about each other's drawings.

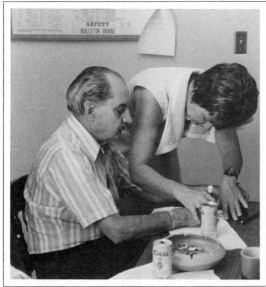

In early group meetings the leader helped bewildered members get started with the drawing assignments. That was not necessary later on as the drawings progressed. Mr. G looks rather grim about the project. The author is trying to help him "unfreeze" and get started. A group leader must be responsive and close yet not intrusive or interpretative in art projects with the elderly.

## Mr. D. M.

The drawings in Figures 13–4a through 13–4d are from a series done by Mr. D. M. over a six-month period. Severe chronic brain syndrome was his diagnosis. His ability to compose a likeness, and neatly (Figure 13–4d), especially after the scribbling of his first drawing (Figure 13–4a), seemed remarkable, especially to a nonartist leader. As Sally Koslow (1976, 140) says, "Signs of therapeutic progress can be disheartingly small—a patient whistling a tune, holding your hand, and this after months of work."

Mr. D. M. was easy to work with and was easily encouraged to draw. He was so quiet in the meetings that I wondered whether he understood. He smiled instead of answering me. (A

FIGURE 13–4a. *Mr. D. M. scribbled intensely during the first drawing session but kept the scribbling contained in one area (unlike the member diagnosed as a burned-out schizophrenic, who scribbled all over the entire page). Mr. D. M. signed his own name with ease (and pride) on his drawings.*

FIGURE 13–4b. *Houses were the theme for this group meeting. (*House *was the term used;* home *seemed a rather threatening word.) This drawing is of a house in Tucson, where Mr. D. M. lived for a short time as a young boy. Readers familiar with southwestern architecture will note that he captured the essence of his boyhood home. Often group members did successfully capture the essence in their crude sketches.*

FIGURE 13–4c. *This drawing was Mr. D. M.'s response to a request to draw an old girlfriend or boyfriend. To identify the drawing, I printed in Mr. D. M.'s description, "Mary (16)" and "Las Vegas."*

FIGURE 13–4d. *Mr. D. M. eventually drew a self-portrait. Contrast this with his drawing in Figure 13–4a, done early in the life of the group.*

way of conserving energy? A nonverbal way to handle unsure areas? A successful way to win over staff?)

Mr. D. M. attended the meetings consistently. He was also filmed by a CBS cameraman after the "Sex after Sixty" television show was filmed. One cameraman, taken by Mr. D. M.'s expression and eyes, had a cigarette with him on the patio. Shortly afterward, Mr. D. M. was transferred to another facility, and he died within two weeks.

### Mr. S

Mr. S, the youngest member of the group, had suffered a stroke in his late sixties while on a construction job. He was sullen, morose, and withdrawn before joining the group. He often wheeled himself out of the meeting, but he always returned. He smiled, almost with disdain, when drawings were introduced, but he worked carefully on them. His left hand was paralyzed, so he placed a heavy ashtray on the paper to hold it still as he drew. The drawings in Figures 13–5 and 13–6 were done by Mr. S.

After several months Mr. S began to loosen up and started combing his hair and wearing a clean shirt to meetings. After the group was completed, he went out AMA (against medical advice) and wheeled himself to the beach to live!

### Mrs. B

This 79-year-old woman suffered from Parkinson's disease and chronic brain syndrome. She also had severe paranoid ideation, which was not noted anywhere in her chart. She was very self-conscious about her crossed eye. She drew readily and with great concentration; she called the group "the drawing class." Her drawings are shown in Figures 13–7 and 13–8. Her anxiety in early meetings was manifested by jumping up suddenly and leaving. During the drawing sessions, she was able to concentrate intently on the drawings and did not leave the meetings.

The woman's decline over the span of the group can best be seen by comparing one of her first group drawings with one of her very last (Figures 13–9a and 13–9b).

### Group B: A Summary

Group B had a rather unusual beginning. Members' problems included poststroke paralysis, aphasia, flat affects, and immobility of

FIGURE 13–6. *The subject for this drawing session was a pet. Note the bone Mr. S added for the dog. Mr. S also recalled the name of the dog, but later labeled the drawing "Dog" after another member said, "Oh, that's a billy goat."*

FIGURE 13–7. *When asked to draw her first remembered important building, Mrs. B drew a picture of a church.*

FIGURE 13–5. *Mr. S drew one of his first remembered toys, a wagon or possibly it is what present children might build using a box.*

FIGURE 13–8. *One of the assignments in group B was for members to draw their first house. Mrs. B drew this house and windmill remembered from a childhood spent in foster homes in the Midwest.*

FIGURE 13–9b. *This drawing by Mrs. B, a member of group B, was done during a group demonstration for a class three years after the original drawing (Figure 13–9a). Note the differences—a coolie hat instead of a sailor's cap, for example—and the deterioration in that interim.*

FIGURE 13–9a. *This is a drawing of a sailor Mrs. B dated in Seattle during World War I. Note her attention to detail—the tie, the chevrons on the sleeve. The buttons on the fly (as an old sailor will quickly notice) should probably have been positioned in the direction of an inverted U instead of as drawn by Mrs. B. Her drawing ability seemed to improve temporarily as the meetings continued, but three years later there was a noticeable deterioration in her work as can be seen in Figure 13–9b.*

members. The most successful strategy was drawing and discussing the drawings. Perhaps the most significant aspect of this group was that it launched an entire group program in the facility, which later included current events groups, reminiscing groups by students, practice groups for students, and a group comprised only of residents over 90. That kind of ground breaking is one important aspect of the experimental groups described in this chapter.

## GROUP C: NONVERBAL COMMUNICATION IN A GROUP

The life of group C has been described in another article (Burnside 1973), in which the importance of touch as communication with the regressed elderly is discussed. A colleague described group C (Table 13–3) as experiencing "nonverbal living."

TABLE 13-3. **Members of group C**

| Patient | Age | Marital status | Length of hospitalization | Diagnosis | Ambulation | Strengths in group | Problems in group |
|---------|-----|----------------|---------------------------|-----------|------------|---------------------|--------------------|
| Mrs. K | 82 | Widowed | 1 year, 8 months | Dementia, fractured right hip with prosthesis, neurofibroma of scalp | Ambulatory and wheelchair | Affectionate ways awareness, sense of humor | Aphasia, fidgeting, withdrawing by closing eyes |
| Mr. Z | 64 | Divorced | 2 years, 10 months | Dementia, arteriosclerosis, secondary polyneuritis, old TBC[1] | Ambulatory | Gentleness, kindly air, awareness | Inarticulate, listless, anxious at times |
| Mrs. S | 81 | Single | 5 months | Dementia | Ambulatory | Assisted leader, observed others in group, change gradual: increase in affect, increase in orientation | Forgetful |
| Mrs. S. T. | 79 | Widowed | 1 year, 4 months | Dementia | Ambulatory, to wheelchair in 13th meeting | Sweetness, responsiveness, appreciative | Severe hearing loss, in wheelchair |
| Mr. B | 80 | Single | 10 months | Dementia, central nervous system lues (meningoencephalitic type), blindness, anemia | Wheelchair | Sense of humor, openness, courageous, uncomplaining gratitude, gave feedback to leader | Overweight, in wheelchair (hard to push chair), blind, heavy personal loss, speech impediment |
| Mr. K | 86 | Single | 8 months (died 2 weeks after 8th group meeting) | Dementia | Wheelchair | Independent, sense of humor, observant, slowly responded to increased interaction contacts with leader | Withdrawn, depressed, nearly mute, fiercely independent (I originally labeled it "stubbornness!") |
| Mr. J replaced Mr. K | 68 | | | Fractured right hip, CAS[2], dementia secondary to alcoholism | Ambulatory | | |

[1] Tuberculosis.
[2] Cerebral arteriosclerosis.
SOURCE: Revised from I. Burnside. 1973. Touching is talking. *American Journal of Nursing* 73(12): 2062 (December).

The group of six met weekly for 30 to 60 minutes in a light mental (locked) facility in Gardena, California. The group was closed, and the group experience lasted for fourteen months. Subsequently, every four to six months, I took my classes of students from the University of Southern California to the facility. I taught three-hour classes there and always used this same group for a class demonstration. Although the members could not recall my name, they remembered me. Mr. B called me "the doughnut lady," and Mrs. S. T. used to say as she hugged me, "God love you. I can't remember your name, but I'm sure glad you came!"

Eventually, during the demonstration classes, the group members turned into hams. Mrs. K would turn and wave to the students or blow them a kiss as she was wheeled out of the classroom by an aide. Mr. B and Mr. Z would smile as they conversed in a French patois to the class.

I still underestimate the ability of the quite regressed elderly to perform well—even in stressful situations. The reader should be cautioned not to underestimate group members. These people brought home to me their strengths. Their ability to care, to receive and give affection, also became more obvious to me during the years I knew them.

The projects tried with this group were many: (1) exercises, (2) music in the form of records, (3) sheer socializing and discussing the refreshments and what they meant, (4) slides of themselves (an absolute fiasco), (5) bringing young people to group meetings. My 20-year-old daughter once went to a meeting with me. Since she had worked in a nursing home and on a back ward of a state hospital, she could relate to the group members with great ease. They also enjoyed the day my secretary played the banjo for them. But pervasive passivity was the outstanding feature of the total group.

### Group C: A Summary

Nonverbal communication was an important component of the group leadership. Mrs. K especially had high affectional needs, which were obvious at the first group meeting (Burnside 1973). The use of touch with the mentally impaired would be a productive area for research, as well as the use of food, beverages, and music to maintain interest.

Students often describe the flat affect and/or apathy as a wall they cannot get through. That was my experience in group C. In fact, the slightly or overtly psychotic often make a far more interesting group to lead. Some of the illusions, delusions, and fantasies can be quite intriguing! *Gramp* is a fine example (Jury and Jury 1976).

It is amazing that in spite of some severe dementia, some persons retain their conversation ability, their interpersonal skills, and their fabulous sense of humor. In one day center I was going to do a spontaneous demonstration group for a group of students. Since I remembered that one lady had been a star in a previous group, I was glad when she agreed to be a member. There was also a psychiatrist suffering from senile dementia yet with many of his social graces still intact, and others suffering from either the primary disease of Alzheimer's or a dementia secondary to Parkinson's, stroke, or alcoholism. This vignette will give the reader the reason why these sparkling people facilitate a group.

Mrs. A, a spritely lady in her eighties, fooled most people during the first meeting because of her meticulous dress; her outgoing, friendly ways; and her humor. During the demonstration group, I was attempting to have members tap into the memories of long ago, which I thought would not be too threatening for them. I asked them to sit for a few minutes and think about something they remembered very clearly from their childhood. (It is so important to allow these "thinking times." Not only does it help the members very much and give them a sense of slower pace, but it can also help the leader to assess what is happening in the group, what changes need to be made, and who has not had much of a chance to participate in the group.)

Suddenly Mrs. A became very excited and announced that she remembered something from when she was a little girl. She carefully and vividly told a story about following her brothers and their friend around until they were exasperated with her. Finally they went to the barn, and she traipsed along behind them. When they got to the haymow, they wanted to get rid of her, she said, and told her in emphatic terms to leave. She acknowledged that she was a pest, but she refused to budge. Then she said, "They sure did get rid of me all right." I asked her what had happened. With a big smile she said, "They peed on me." She absolutely broke the group up, and there was no doubt that even the most confused member of the group could enjoy her special brand of humor.

### COMBINING ALERT AND REGRESSED MEMBERS IN A GROUP

It is difficult to answer the question "Should one mix alert and confused individuals in the group?" A rule of thumb perhaps is not to mix the very confused with the very alert. If one is conscientious about making contracts before the group meetings, one can get a sense of the more alert, and sometimes haughty, members who will have no part of such a group meeting. It would be cruel to expose the demented person to insults, ridicule, and interactions that further lower self-esteem. And old persons are very up-front about their reactions and thoughts. They often speak out in the group; and while more often than not it is helpful and therapeutic, at times it can exclude some member. Elderly group members do not always "draw a circle that draws him in."

It is also important not to overload the group with so many confused members that there is no "helper," no one vivacious enough to add spark to the group or to carry some of the understanding.

I have observed that confused individuals form pairs; when I have studied these pairings closely, I have found that the individuals quite often are of about the same level of confusion. In one group, a person with presenile dementia (a man who had just turned 60) and a woman with senile dementia (who was in her seventies) developed a warm and close relationship in spite of the fact that both were aphasic. Their kindness and devotion to one another was touching and also was encouraged by the staff. It is fortunate that the man's wife was quite understanding and felt that if she could no longer communicate with him, it was all to the good if there was someone else who could reach him. The group leader can also encourage such interactions by seating "paired" members next to one another in the group so that they can draw support and comfort from one another. Often they will walk to and from the group meetings together.

While a group leader may not encourage subgrouping in other types of groups, it becomes quite important in group work with the frail and demented elderly. It may be the subgrouping that keeps members in the group and gives them the courage to attend and to be a part of the larger group. I have discussed subgrouping in Chapter 5.

## CAUTIONS

It is well to caution students and new group leaders that they must assess the capabilities of prospective group members so that they do not overload the group with persons who either have the same diagnosis (for example, all depressed individuals) or are grossly impaired.

I have said elsewhere regarding sensory losses that it is easier to take no more than one blind person or one hard-of-hearing person. If the entire group is in wheelchairs, the burden on the group leader will be incredibly heavy—just transporting members back and forth to the meeting place will be an arduous and time-consuming task.

Regarding Alzheimer's persons, the leader should check potential members for apraxia (inability to distinguish and correctly use objects) because such people will have difficulty participating in any of the assigned tasks or crafts, and even during refreshment time. One man had to be helped each meeting simply to get the coffee cup to his mouth; he would wave it around in the air and yet be trying so hard to follow the leader's instructions.

It seems to be easier to draw in some of the withdrawn and quiet members than it is to curb the loquacious and noisy ones, at least for the student or the new group leader. One woman, who came to the group on her walker, sat at a separate table and refused to join the group in the early meetings. The student turned, addressed her, included her, and served her coffee as though she were participating in the group. It was difficult for the beginning student to do, but it helped the woman gain enough trust to move into the group gradually.

Arrangement in group meetings should follow some of these guidelines:

1. Put the most alert, helpful person next to the disabled or anxious member.

2. The leaders should sit between the two weakest (either physically or psychologically) members of the group.

3. A hard-of-hearing person should have someone next to him or her who is willing to explain some of the group process. The same is true of a blind person.

4. Two members who are always together and seem to have a symbiotic relationship should sit next to one another.

5. If there are two minority persons (and one should never take just one into the group), they should be placed next to one another in the seating. This strategy (and #4) is to help increase the "we-ness" of the group.

6. Crafts should be checked carefully to ensure that they are safe. (After recently watching a woman grab the souffle cup that was filled with white glue and try to drink its contents, the activity director changed the type of container used to hold the glue.)

7. A very quiet area with no distractions should be used for group meetings. This is crucial for the demented, who can easily be overloaded.

8. Push fluids in group meetings to prevent dehydration and increased confusional states. (See Chapter 7 for an elaboration of this basic concept.)

9. Be careful not to pressure group members because of the potential for a "catastrophic reaction." (See Chapters 7 and 10 for information on catastrophic reactions.)

10. Be aware of your own boredom and ennui. Group leadership with the elderly can be a very draining experience; if you do not build in rewards for yourself, you may burn out.*

11. Save the refreshments until the end of the group meeting. Confused elderly clients enjoy food and will often stay until they receive their share.

12. If the group meeting is held on a ward that houses many demented persons, it is best to close, and if fire regulations will permit, lock the doors to the meeting area; otherwise wanderers and others may disrupt the meeting—especially if they see food or drinks.

13. An easy, quick assignment to assess skills and literacy is a project that requires signing the name or reading aloud briefly. The results will give you an idea of who you should not put on the spot.

14. Men in the group may balk at drawing or at "arty" crafts. It is best to have an alternate project that they can also do.

Not all men will view the tasks as "kid's stuff," but those who do will be adamant about not participating.

15. Be prepared for strange things to happen to your supplies, props, food, and so on. One lady put the plum blossom stem in her coffee. Another woman stirred her coffee with an orange crayon. Still another rolled her bingo card and placed it in her bedroom slipper. Another one colored her banana with a green felt-tipped pen. When things such as this occur, check to see if you have overloaded the group with materials or instructions, a common problem for many of us.

16. A variety of approaches—use of exercises, music, reminiscing strategies, crafts, food—helps keep the group more interesting for both members and leaders.

17. Do not expect to conduct insight groups or groups that are geared toward psychotherapy with the very confused.

18. Analyze *all* nonverbal behavior for possible meanings. (This, of course, includes your own nonverbal behavior.)

## SUMMARY

This chapter includes descriptions of three nurse-led groups of mentally impaired aged. Cautions of such group work are discussed. Group leaders of regressed aged persons must remember to supplement and/or complement the individualized nursing care plans. The quality of life for aged people, whether in an institution or a day care center, can be greatly improved by membership in a group that meets regularly with a patient, empathic leader in a familiar, somewhat structured setting.

It was observed in all three groups that behavior does change and sometimes can improve rather suddenly and dramatically when the group process—for example, the "weness" of the group—is maximized. The leader's sensitivity, empathy, and dedication are of paramount importance. The leader should also be skillful in nonverbal communication. "Nor-

---

The following vignette occurred in one long term care facility.
* A nurses' aide became uninterested in her reality orientation group. She began to be late to work, and her absenteeism increased. It turned out that she had been assigned to five RO groups daily.

mal" behavior by a leader can be emulated by group members, and they will gain in confidence and trust with a leader who treats them with warmth and respect.

The difficulties of group work with regressed elderly include behavioral problems, passivity, short attention spans, superdependency, apathy, and minimal information on each member.* Long silences are common. Miniscule changes observed in group members can be discouraging for impatient leaders. The ability to discard techniques that do not work and try new ones proves to be one of the challenges of work with this type of group, since so many approaches to problems simply do not work.

Mark and Dan Jury, in their sensitive account *Gramp* (1976), write:

While planting the garden, Gramp took Dan aside and admitted his confusion for the first time, "Gramp asked me what was wrong with him. . . . He said that he didn't know who the people around him were. And that he was scared."

I was scared myself. Up until then, I'd looked at Gramp's antics as "senility"—I'd done some reading on the subject and thought I understood what was going on—but that day I realized I had no idea what he'd do next. I didn't know what to say to him and when he asked me to stay near and not leave him alone, I said I'd stay near him.

Perhaps the "staying near" is one aspect of intervention that a professional may provide for the confused, frightened, regressed elderly person.

---

## EXERCISE 1

When group therapy is begun, staff members often notice a decrease in problems of managing the group members, since they are stimulated to engage in more appropriate social behavior. However, the staff has to try to maintain that gain and may become very discouraged with such continued responsibility. Staff members may feel that much effort is expended for little observable gain, or they may feel burned out—tired of the job, the residents, and so on.

Consider ways that staff morale might be maintained or even improved during such discouraging times. Then list five suggestions for taking care of oneself, both as staff collectively and as staff members individually.

---

## EXERCISE 2

Select one of the case histories from group A and write a one-page description of how you would have handled that person if you had been the group leader.

---

## EXERCISE 3

Read the following poem and in your own words explain what the poet is trying to convey in the poem:

              Dementia
Mind fields
Once untilled and fertile soil,
Lie quiet.
Memories stand,
Leafless as winter trees
Bare monuments of accumulations.
Intellect decays

Thorny brambles of overgrowth,
Remnant of complexity.
Emotions spoil
Fallen like overripe fruit,
Discarded nourishment.
Spinal fluid circulates
Crystalline and unspeaking,
In purposeless motion.

                    Jane Hawes, M.D.

## REFERENCES

Brody, E. M., M. H. Kleban, M. P. Lawton, R. Levy, and A. Woldow. 1972. Predicators of mortality in the mentally-impaired institutionalized aged. *Journal of Chronic Diseases* 25(12): 611–20.

Brody, E. M., M. H. Kleban, M. P. Lawton, and H. Silverman. 1971. Excess disabilities of mentally impaired aged: Impact of individual treatment. Part 1. *The Gerontologist* 11(2): 124–33 (Summer).

Brody, E. M., M. H. Kleban, A. Woldow, and L. Freeman. 1975. Survival and death in the mentally-impaired aged. *Journal of Chronic Diseases* 28:389–99.

Burnside, I. M. 1973. Touching is talking. *American Journal of Nursing* 73(12): 2060–63 (December).

——. 1978. Eulogy for Ms. Hogue. *American Journal of Nursing* 78(4): 624–26 (April).

Demsey, P., and A. Demsey. 1981. *The research process in nursing.* New York: Van Nostrand.

Hawes, J. 1981. Dementia. *Lancet* (January).

Jury, M., and D. Jury. 1976. *Gramp.* New York: Grossman.

Kleban, M. H., and E. M. Brody. 1972. Prediction of improvement in mentally-impaired aged: Social worker ratings of personality. *Journal of Gerontology* 27(1): 69–76.

Kleban, M. H., E. M. Brody, and M. P. Lawton. 1971. Personality traits in the mentally-impaired aged and their relationship to improvements in current functioning. Part 1. *The Gerontologist* 11(2): 134–40 (Summer).

Kleban, M. H., M. P. Lawton, E. M. Brody, and M. Moss. 1975. Characteristics of mentally-impaired aged profiting from individualized treatment. *Journal of Gerontology* 30(1): 90–96 (January).

——. 1976. Behavioral observations of mentally-impaired aged: Those who decline and those who do not. *Journal of Gerontology* 31(3): 333–39 (May).

Kobrynski, B. 1975. The mentally-impaired elderly — Whose responsibility? *The Gerontologist* 15(5): 407–11.

Koslow, S. P. 1976. New, exciting direction in psychiatry: Dance/music/art therapy. *Mademoiselle* 82(1): 106ff (January).

Milne, A. A. 1926 and 1954. *Winnie-the-pooh.* © 1926 by E. P. Dutton, New York; renewal © 1954 by A. A. Milne.

Salter, C. de L., and C. A. Salter, 1975. Effects of an individualized activity program on elderly patients. Part 1. *The Gerontologist* 15(5): 404–6 (October).

## BIBLIOGRAPHY

Armstrong, S. W., and S. Rouslin. 1963. *Group psychotherapy in nursing practice.* New York: Macmillan.

Barnett, K. 1972. A theoretical construct of the concepts of touch as they relate to nursing. *Nursing Research* 21(2): 102–11. (March–April).

Bartol, M. 1979. Nonverbal communication in patients with Alzheimer's disease. *Journal of Gerontological Nursing* 5(4): 21–31 (July–August).

Burnside, I. M. 1969. Sensory stimulation: An adjunct to group work with the disabled aged. *Mental Hygiene* 33(3): 381–88 (July).

——. 1970. Clocks and calendars. *American Journal of Nursing* 70(1): 117–19 (January).

——. 1970. Loss: A constant theme in group work with the aged. *Hospital and Community Psychiatry* 21(6): 173–77 (June).

_____. 1973. Touching is talking; and poem Baroque pearls. *American Journal of Nursing* 73(12): 2060–63 (December).

_____. 1979. Alzheimer's disease—An overview. *Journal of Gerontological Nursing* 5(4): 14–20 (July–August).

Feil, N. 1983. Group work with disoriented nursing home residents. In *Group work with the frail elderly*. New York: Haworth Press.

Fowler, R. S., and W. Fordyce. 1972. Adapting care for the brain-damaged patient. *American Journal of Nursing* 72(11): 2056–59 (November).

Haycox, J. A. 1980. Late care of the demented patient. *New England Journal of Medicine* 303: 165–166.

Hirschfeld, M. 1976. The cognitively impaired older adult. *American Journal of Nursing* 76(12): 1981–84 (December).

Huss, A. J. 1977. Touch with care or a caring touch. *American Journal of Occupational Therapy* 31(1): 11–18 (January).

Katz, B. 1980. The struggle against senility. *Discover*, November.

Katzman, R. 1976. The prevalence and malignancy of Alzheimer's disease. *Archives of Neurology* 33(2): 217–18 (April).

Kent, S. 1977. Classifying and treating organic brain syndrome. *Geriatrics* 32(9): 87–89, 93–96 (September).

Lawton, M. P., M. H. Kleban, E. M. Brody, and M. Moss. 1972. Variables relevant to prediction of improvement of mentally-impaired aged. Paper presented at Twenty-fifth Annual Meeting of the Gerontological Society, San Juan, P.R., December.

Lee, J. 1983. The group: A chance at human connection for the mentally impaired older person. In *Group work with the frail elderly*. New York: Haworth Press.

Lezak, M. D. 1978. Living with the characterologically altered brain injured patient. *Journal of Clinical Psychiatry* 39:592–98.

_____. 1978. Subtle sequelae of brain damage. *American Journal of Gerontological Nursing* 57(1): 9–15.

Libow, L. S. 1977. "Senile dementia" and "pseudo-senility": Clinical diagnosis, cognitive and emotional disturbance in the Elderly. In *Clinical issues*, 75–88. Chicago: Year Book.

Manaster, A. 1972. Therapy with the senile geriatric patient. *International Journal of Group Psychiatry* 22(2): 250–57 (April).

Marshall, M. A. 1963. Hopelessness. In *Some clinical approaches to psychiatric nursing*, ed. S. Burd and M. Marshall. New York: Macmillan.

Maurin, J. T. 1970. Regressed patients in group therapy. *Perspectives in Psychiatric Care* 8(3): 131–35 (May–June).

Mueller, D. J., and L. Atlas. 1972. Resocialization of regressed elderly residents: A behavioral management approach. *Journal of Gerontology* 27(3): 390–92 (July).

National Institutes of Health. 1980. *Alzheimer's disease: A scientific guide for health practitioners*. NIH Publication no. 81–2251. Bethesda, Md.: Office of Scientific and Health Reports. November.

_____. 1981. *Progress report on senile dementia of the Alzheimer's type*. NIH Publication no. 81–2343. Bethesda, Md.: National Institute on Aging. September.

_____. 1981. *Q and A: Alzheimer's disease*. NIH Publication no. 80–1646. Bethesda, Md. June.

_____. 1981. *The dementias: Hope through research*. NIH Publication no. 81–2252. Bethesda, Md. March.

Preston, T. 1973. When words fail. *American Journal of Nursing* 73(12): 2064–66 (December).

Robinson, K. 1974. Therapeutic interaction: A means of crisis intervention with newly institutionalized elderly persons. *Nursing Clinics of North America* 9(1): 89–96 (March).

Wahl, P. 1976. Psychosocial implications of disorientation in the elderly. *Nursing Clinics of North America* 11(1): 145–55 (March).

Weisberg, J. 1983. Raising the self-esteem of mentally impaired nursing home residents. *Social Work* 28(2): 163–164 (March–April).

Yalom, I. D., and F. Terrazas: 1968. Group therapy for psychotic elderly patients. *American Journal of Nursing* 68(8): 1690–94 (August).

## RESOURCES

### Organizations

*Alzheimer's Disease and Related Disorders Association (ADRDA)*. Located at 360 North Michigan Avenue, Suite 601, Chicago, IL 60601.

### Films

*Aging and Organic Brain Syndrome*. Featuring Alvin J. Goldfarb and Shervert Frazier. McNeil Laboratories, Camp Hill Road, Fort Washington, PA 19034.

*Behavioral Manifestations in the Aging Patient* (8 mm, color, 16 minutes). Film of the residents at the Dallas Home for Jewish Aged in Dallas, Texas. The symptoms shown are typical of those that nursing home staff members might encounter in their own work. The film stresses the importance of diagnosis and care. The message is that a better understanding of elderly patients and their problems can lead to improved care and quality of life. Author is Carl Eisdorfer, Ph.D., M.D. Film Department, Sandoz Pharmaceuticals, East Hanover, N.J. 07936 (also Association Films [AF] regional offices) or Medical Services Liaison, 1560 Litina Drive, Alamo, CA 94570. Confronting Confusion. Black and white. 25 minutes. Electric Sunrise Films.

*Coping with Brain Disease: Alzheimer's Disease and Family Involvement.* These are videotape recordings of a seminar on Alzheimer's disease held at College of Medicine, University of Arizona in 1981. Biomedical Communications, University of Arizona, Health Sciences Center, Tucson, AZ 85724.

*Dementia in the Middle and Later Years.* A series of four half-hour films containing interviews with patients with dementing illness and their families. Produced by Dr. Carl Eisdorfer and Dr. Donna Cohen. Film Department, Sandoz Pharmaceuticals, East Hanover, N.J. 07936 (also Association Films [AF] regional offices) or Medical Services Liaison, 1560 Litina Drive, Alamo, CA 94570.

*Facing It* (black-and-white, 24½ minutes, 1974). This film documents experiences of staff and patients in an institution where a program of reality orientation has been in operation for two years. An organized therapeutic approach is used and staff share reactions and discuss changes noticed in the residents. Produced by Maimonides Hospital and Home for the Aged, with John Geeza. Distributed by TM Canada: Dr. G. Rosenberg, Maimonides Hospital, 5795 Caldwell Avenue, Montreal H4W 1W3.

*Gramp: A Man Ages and Dies* (black-and-white filmstrip with cassette, 30 minutes). Based on the book *Gramp,* by Don and Mark Jury. Sunburst, P.O. Box 40, Pleasantville, NY 10570.

*Medical Aspects of Alzheimer's Disease.* Michael S. Smith, M.D., and Alfred W. Kaznich, Ph.D., Biomedical Communications, University of Arizona, Health Sciences Center, Tucson, AZ 95724.

*Older Adult Assessment* (videotape). Interviewer is Peter LeBray, Ph.D. Audio-Visual-Video Department, Good Samaritan Hospital Medical Center,

1015 N.W. 22nd Avenue, Portland, OR, 97210. *One-half-hour Educational Television panel discussion* on Alzheimer's disease aired on KTCA-TV2 public affairs program (2) "People and Causes." Available on loan in ¾-inch cartridge and VHS T-30 home video-type cartridge. (3) One-half-hour "Take 30" interview type. Canadian Broadcasting Company program on Alzheimer's disease taped with the assistance of Alzheimer's Societe of Toronto, Canada. Available on loan in ¾-inch cartridge. (4) In-service presentation by Madelon Byrne, R.N., Counselor, Educator, and member of the Board of Directors of ADRDA. This is a "teaching" video available to professionals (nurses, etc.) on statistical data, pathology, theories as to cause, related diseases, symptoms of Alzheimer's disease, nursing care, and family support. Available on loan in ¾-inch cartridge.

*Organic Brain Syndrome I; Organic Brain Syndrome II; Depression I; Depression II; Paranoia* (super 8 mm in Fairchild 70-20 cartridges, color, 15 minutes each). A comprehensive series discussing labels and differentiating between delirium, dementia, and depression. Sandoz Pharmaceuticals, East Hanover, NJ 07936.

*Organic Brain Syndrome: Recognition, Diagnosis, Management* (8 mm, color, 40 minutes, 1971). The importance of early recognition and diagnosis of acute brain syndrome is emphasized; simple and practical diagnostic tests are shown in a straightforward teaching manner. Two geriatric patients and one alcoholic patient are presented. Award-winning film. Author is Leon Marder, M.D., University of Southern California, School of Medicine, Los Angeles, CA. Film Department, Sandoz Pharmaceuticals, East Hanover, NJ 07936 (also Association Films [AF] regional offices) or Medical Services Liaison, 1560 Litina Drive, Alamo, CA 94570.

*Symptoms of Senility: Recognition and management.* 8 mm. Fairchild 10-20 cartridge. Color. 18 min. Psy 22. Film Dept., Sandoz Pharmaceuticals, East Hanover, NJ 07936

*Someone I Once Knew.* ¾" VHS T-30 cartridge. J. Walter Thompson Producers. 160 Lexington Ave., New York, NY 10020.

*The Disturbed Nursing Home Patient.* Produced by Hugh James Lurie, M.D., University of Washington, Seattle. Funded by NIMH-PH grant. Bureau of Mental Health, Department of Social and Health Services, Olympia, WA 98504.

## Audiocassettes

*All Things Considered.* A short National Public Radio presentation on Alzheimer's disease featuring comments by members of the Baltimore ADRDA chapter and medical professionals from Johns Hopkins University School of Medicine. On loan or may be purchased from Association for Alzheimer's and Related Diseases, 2501 West 84th Street, Bloomington, MN 55431.

*Alzheimer's Disease Research—1980.* ADRDA program presentation by Dr. James Mortimer, Director of Research, VA Medical Center, Minneapolis, Minn. Two tapes; includes questions and answers.

*Alzheimer's Disease Research Update—1981.* Dr. William H. Frey, director of psychiatric research, St. Paul Ramsey Medical Center; Dr. James Mortimer, research director, VA Medical Center, Minneapolis, Minn.; June White, researcher, Psychiatric Research Unit, University of Minnesota. ADRDA presentation, June 9, 1981. Two cassettes. On loan or may be purchased from Association for Alzheimer's and Related Diseases, 2501 West 84th Street, Bloomington, MN 55431.

*Bobbie Glaze testimony* in Washington, D.C., July 1980 to the Senate Sub-Committee on Aging and the Sub-Committee on Labor–HEW Appropriations on the impact of Alzheimer's disease in families. On loan or may be purchased from Association for Alzheimer's and Related Diseases, 2501 West 84th Street, Bloomington, MN 55431.

*Denver, Colorado, ADRDA chapter meeting* including a presentation on Alzheimer's disease by Dr. Schneck, neurologist at the University of Denver. On loan or may be purchased from Association for Alzheimer's and Related Diseases, 2501 West 84th Street, Bloomington, MN 55431.

*Management of Confusion in the Elderly* (30 minutes, 1979). From a symposium on delirium in the elderly conducted by Dr. Fred B. Charatan at Manhattan Psychiatric Center. Roerig, a division of Pfizer Pharmaceuticals, New York, NY 10017.

## Programmed Instruction Unit

*Mental Status Assessment* (prepared by Stephen Cohen, Step-design Inc., New York, NY). A course that teaches how to assess a patient's mental status, provides a checklist for performing a mental status assessment, teaches interviewing procedures, and teaches how to increase the reliability of mental status assessments in your practice. Reprints available from American Journal of Nursing Company, Educational Services Division, 555 West 57th Street, New York, NY 10019 (refer to product code P-48 1981).

# PRACTICE OF GROUP WORK

Part 4 is the pragmatic section of the book; practitioners from a variety of disciplines explore implementing group work with the aged. This section should be of interest to readers from many disciplines, and families of regressed older persons may find it useful in their own experiences with improving orientation.

Chapter 14 by Elizabeth Donahue, a gerontological nurse specialist, opens this section

with a literature review of the widely used modality reality orientation (RO).

Lucille Taulbee, a nurse, is one of the pioneers in reality orientation methods. In Chapter 15 she elaborates on reality orientation groups designed for those sadly neglected people, the mentally impaired elderly.

Remotivation therapy groups, less frequently seen than other kinds of groups, are discussed by Helen Dennis in Chapter 16. For her master's thesis, Dennis conducted a remotivation research project in a state hospital in California; the chapter is based on that year of intensive study.

Chapter 17, on music therapy, was written by Mary Jane Hennessey, a concert violinist and nurse who conducts weekly music groups. (Chapter 33 also discusses music therapy.)

Heather Booth, a young Canadian dance therapist, describes dance and movement therapy in Chapter 18. Her experience has been with regressed state hospital patients.

Chapter 19 describes the creative endeavor of a nurse, Ardis Martin, to combine several forms of therapy into a new modality. She relates her experience in a geriatric day care center in western Texas.

Chapter 20 is about self-help groups in the United States. It is estimated that there are three-quarters of a million self-help groups in the United States with a total membership of more than 15 million.

Judith Altholz, a psychiatric social worker, describes strategies and problems in group psychotherapy with the elderly in Chapter 21.

# chapter 14

# Reality Orientation: A Review of the Literature

*Elizabeth M. Donahue*

*Every human being gains under-standing of his meaning and self-worth from his interaction with others.*

MIRIAM J. HIRSCHFELD (1977, 126)

---

## LEARNING OBJECTIVES

- Outline the historical development of reality orientation as a modality.

- Distinguish between reality orientation, reality therapy, and reality testing.

- Compare and contrast positive and negative findings of reality orientation research.

- Identify the major flaws in reality orientation research.

- Describe at least three factors that are important to keep in mind with reality orientation.

- State for whom reality orientation should be implemented and why.

- Plan how reality orientation can be incorporated into an existing therapeutic program.

## KEY WORDS

- Confusion

- Reality orientation

- Reality testing

- Reality therapy

---

Reality orientation (RO) has been credited as the first psychiatric technique to bring elderly confused people back to reality (Schwenk 1979). This chapter will explore the historical development of and research findings on RO and show how RO is used in a geropsychiatric day care center.

The reality orientation process is thought to help alleviate or in some cases stop memory deterioration through continual stimulation and repetitive orienting activities in one-to-one contacts or in groups (Letcher, Peterson, and Scarbrough 1974). The concept is viewed as preventive, remedial, or both (Taulbee 1976). RO has been stressed for elderly who experience confusion and/or disorientation in any number of care settings: acute care hospitals, convalescent homes, day care centers, foster care homes, nursing homes, psychiatric day care centers,

psychiatric hospitals, senior centers, and even in their own homes (Taulbee 1978; McDonald et al. 1971; Colthart 1974; Burnside 1970; Brockett 1981; Lee 1976; Mulcahy and Rosa 1981).

### Definitions

*Reality orientation, reality therapy,* and *reality testing* are three terms that are often used interchangeably. Sometimes these terms confuse the beginning student, who mistakenly thinks that all three are the same process. *Reality therapy* is a specific treatment modality developed by a psychiatrist, W. Glasser (1965). It is a confrontive therapy to assist individuals in assuming responsibility for themselves and in facing up to the reality of their life situations (Silverstone 1976). Glasser worked with juvenile delinquents in the early part of his career as he firmed up the concepts for reality therapy.

*Reality testing* is done by all disciplines and is a necessary part of working with demented or delirious individuals in any setting. Reality testing is the process of giving information about the environment, events, or one's perception of a situation, which may differ from that of the confused person. Confused persons may misidentify people or objects. Some of this misidentification may be related to sensory losses. The caregiver should provide steady reality testing to alleviate the skewing of reality, the environment, and events (Burnside 1978). As an example, a caregiver working with a person who is hallucinating would say to the person, "I know you hear voices, but I do not hear them."

*Reality orientation* is a specific treatment modality that usually occurs in a group setting but is also done on a one-to-one basis.

## HISTORY OF REALITY ORIENTATION

The development of RO occurred as a three-step process. In 1959, while at the Topeka, Kansas, Veterans Administration Hospital, Dr. James Folsom developed a pilot project to rehabilitate elderly geropsychiatric patients. Nursing assistants, who gave total care, were encouraged to initiate activities for the patients and to assist the patients in becoming more responsible for their own care. The approach succeeded. The elderly patients were able to assume some of their own care, began conversing with one another, and took part in different activities on and off the nursing unit. The new approach also influenced the staff's attitude; staff members were more interested in their patients as individuals and more enthusiastic about their jobs (Folsom 1968).

The initial guidelines for RO grew out of an attitude therapy program implemented by Folsom while he was at the Mental Health Institute in Mt. Pleasant, Iowa. According to Folsom, the expectation of participation in one's recovery was communicated to the new patient upon admission to the pilot research unit. The specific guidelines developed for the staff were "(1) a calm environment, (2) a set routine, (3) clear responses to patient's questions, and the same types of questions should be asked of the patient, (4) talk clearly to the patient, not necessarily loud, (5) direct patients around by clear directions, if need be guide them to and from their destinations, (6) remind them of the date, time, etc., (7) don't let them stay confused by allowing them to ramble in their speech, actions, etc., (8) be firm, if necessary, (9) be sincere, (10) make requests of patient in a calm manner, implying patient will comply, and (11) be consistent" (Folsom 1968, 299).

Patients were awakened by calling their names; the persons awakening them would introduce themselves. Calendars were given to patients who had difficulty with time orientation, and they were assisted in marking off the day. Folsom states that after one year 57 percent of the patients returned to their prehospital adjustment, and some were able to leave the hospital.

The final stage of RO development occurred in 1965 at Tuscaloosa, Alabama, Veterans Administration Hospital; the program designed at Tuscaloosa by Folsom and Lucille Taulbee is the model for all RO programs used today. By that time the process had been identified as consisting of three parts: (1) basic classroom instruction, (2) advanced classroom instruction, and (3) 24-hour follow-through (Folsom 1968; Taulbee and Folsom 1966). See Chapter 15 in this text for an update of RO by Lucille Taulbee.

The basic class met twice daily, for half an hour, and the advanced class met once a day five days a week. The class was held at the same time daily, and as much as possible the same personnel participated to give consistency. A specific attitude of "active," "passive," or "matter of fact" was employed consistently with each patient. The use of an RO board with the name of the facility; month, day, and year; and other pertinent information was part of the basic class. Simple activities and games were part of the advanced class. The process started in the classroom was carried over through the 24-hour period following the class by all personnel coming into contact with the confused person. J. Folsom (1968) states that 24-hour orientation used in conjunction with the structured classroom experience improved the orientation of the majority of the patients.

Robert A. Mitchell, nursing assistant at the Tuscaloosa Veterans Hospital, made the following comment about RO: "Keep in mind that it may not be the actual activity or project that the patient is doing, but more likely the social interaction with others that helps him return to reality as his self-confidence and dignity are restored" (Folsom 1968, 302). R. E. Lee (1976) and Taulbee (1976) stress a similar point. Folsom's premise is that if you "behave as though you expect him [the patient] to participate in his own recovery . . . and that he will be able to get his life back into shape again . . .," RO will work (Freese 1978, 152).

## REVIEW OF THE LITERATURE

A literature review of RO by M. Schwenk (1979) notes that most of the research on RO lacks scientific validity because few of the studies were conducted under experimental conditions. Schwenk states that more than half of the studies fail to spell out the study participants' degree and source of confusion and the length of time participants were confused. The research did not control the age groups studied; that is, not all subjects were over 60, and the young-old (60–70) were studied along with the old-old (over 80). Ratings by caregivers were noted to lack validity because of the increased attention given by staff to disoriented elderly in an RO project (Harris and Ivory 1976). Length of time studied is another factor that lacks reliability— RO was studied for many different time spans.

A total of 24 research studies on RO were located in the literature. Of that number, 8 demonstrate inconclusive or negative effects of RO therapy (Barnes 1974; Zepelin and Wade 1975; MacDonald and Settin, 1978; Winkler, as reported by Whitehead 1978; Voelkel 1978; Hogstel 1979; Johnson 1980; Zepelin, Wolfe, and Kleinplatz 1981). The remaining studies conclude that RO is effective (Taulbee and Folsom 1966; Folsom 1968; Stephens 1969; Trotter 1972; Browne and Ritter 1972; Lehman 1974; Letcher, Peterson, and Scarbrough 1974; Brook, Degun, and Mather 1975; Salter and Salter 1975; Settle 1975; Harris and Ivory 1976; Citrin and Dixon 1977; Merchant and Saxby 1981; Mulcahy and Rosa 1981).

All of the studies that are inconclusive or that demonstrate RO to be ineffective were controlled experimental studies (Schwenk 1979); only one of them had control validity problems (Winkler, as reported by Whitehead 1978). Eight of the studies indicating RO to be an effective method were controlled experimental studies; four of these studies had severe methodological problems (Browne and Ritter 1972; Letcher, Peterson, and Scarbrough 1974; Salter and Salter 1975; Mulcahy and Rosa 1981); the remaining studies that indicate RO to be effective are anecdotal in nature.

J. Barnes's (1974), H. Zepelin and S. Wade's (1975), and M. Hogstel's (1979) experimental data indicate no significant statistical changes in orientation for the experimental groups. Barnes notes small changes in the behavior of the experimental participants, but these changes were not tested for in the study. The anecdotal notes indicate that the participants were more cooperative and more interested in their surroundings. D. Voelkel (1978) notes that those in the experimental group who were moderately confused seemed to improve most in orientation and behavior, even though the statistical data did not bear this out.

Zepelin, S. Wolfe, and F. Kleinplatz (1981) demonstrated that after a one-year program of 24-hour RO and supplemental therapy, the experimental study participants exhibited statistically an increase in belligerent behavior and a decrease in social responsiveness. The authors write that the experimental group had slightly higher mental status scores initially (although the difference was not significant) but that these scores decreased during the final six months of the study.

M. MacDonald and J. Settin (1978), Voelkel (1978), C. Johnson (1980), and Winkler (as reported by Whitehead 1978) compared and contrasted an RO class with a sheltered workshop, a resocialization group, an activity program, and an operant approach, respectively. Those participants in treatment modalities other than an RO class improved more in sociability and alertness than those in an RO class only.

MacDonald and Settin (1978) indicate that performing a meaningful task in a sheltered workshop program is more beneficial for life satisfaction than RO. The one very large drawback to the validity of this study's findings and application in regard to the elderly is that the age range of the study participants was 34 through 74. Also, there are questions as to the level of confusion of the study participants (Schwenk 1979).

Participants in Voelkel's (1978) and MacDonald and Settin's (1978) RO groups expressed negative feelings about reading the RO board and as to the value of the class itself. Sessions were called "boring."

The main failure of Winkler's (as reported by Whitehead 1978) study is that RO classroom participants received only three hours a week of reinforcement, while those participants in the operant conditioning group received constant 24-hour positive reinforcement from the staff.

The studies that demonstrate RO therapy to be positive note less confusion and disorientation; more interest in surroundings; a decrease in resistive, combative, striking-out behavior; more pride in self-care; and an increase in socialization of the study participants (Folsom 1968; Taulbee and Folsom 1966; Browne and Ritter 1972; Mulcahy and Rosa 1981; Salter and Salter 1975).

L. Browne and J. Ritter (1972) demonstrated that an RO classroom with 24-hour follow-up assisted nine elderly chronic schizophrenic men to improve in behavior, orientation, and activities of daily living. N. Mulcahy and N. Rosa (1981) wrote a care plan for confusion and took the RO board to the bedside in an acute care hospital to use with elderly confused patients. The sample was very small, five, but the authors were positive about the progress noted in two patients they were able to study for three weeks. One patient became more interested in feeding himself, and the other showed more interest in self-care.

P. B. Letcher, L. P. Peterson, and D. Scarbrough (1974) state that the more self-sufficient the individual at the onset of RO therapy, the more likely improvement is to occur. The researchers suggest that RO should be instituted at the first sign of confusion, especially after a stroke, surgery, deaths, or other losses that affect the stress response. They advocate RO techniques as a preventive measure to assist the individual in adapting to a new institution or situation.

C. Salter and C. Salter (1975) found that a total rehabilitative program consisting of an RO class, 24-hour RO, retraining in activities-of-daily-living skills, and recreational activities were very effective in decreasing confusion and disorientation. A study by C. Loew and B. Silverstone (1971) found similar improvement in those elderly over 80 years of age in a nursing home when the staff was sensitized to the kinds of psychological and social needs the elderly have. The program consisted of changes in the environment to provide cues to assist in orientation (for example, color-coded doors) and activities such as music therapy, a sheltered workshop program, religious services, and a volunteer visiting program. Reality orientation per se is not mentioned in the study — but the study is worth noting because the technique incorporates RO concepts.

Hogstel (1979) and Salter and Salter (1977) report that if RO is discontinued and not used consistently, the participants will slip back into a confused state and become more regressed. Salter and Salter (1977) indicate that the process can be reversed if RO is reinstated. Salter and Salter suggest that patients receive individual and group therapy in a day care program after discharge.

R. Erickson et al. (1978) describe a two and a half year old RO program on the Rehabilitation Medicine Service of the Seattle Veterans Administration Hospital. Weekly records kept on 127 patients revealed that 75 percent did not show changes in level of orientation during hospitalization. Seventeen percent showed improvement in terms of confusion and disorientation. Two patients declined, four vacillated from one level to another, and four died. Three of the four who died showed a decline in mental status before their death.

## IMPACT ON STAFF ATTITUDES

U. P. Holden (1979), a clinical psychologist in the United Kingdom, describes three groups of individuals: the people in Group 1 were the most deteriorated; those in Group 2 were confused and withdrawn; those in Group 3 were mildly confused. Group 1 had a ratio of three clients to one therapist and was conducted in the traditional reality orientation format. Group 2 was apparently more of a reminiscing group. Group 3 combined cooking sessions, reminiscence therapy, theater and drama therapy, and so forth, with the therapists acting as "guides, encouraging, assisting and advising." Holden does not state what therapeutic results were obtained in the three groups.

Two articles specifically discuss the positive results RO technique has on the attitude of staff toward confused elderly (Reorientation stimulates . . . 1975; Smith and Barker 1972). The change in staff attitude is attributed to the positive changes noted in the patients' behavior or orientation. R. Citrin and D. Dixon (1977) suggest that RO may help the caregivers because the process teaches staff how to communicate better with the confused elderly. Other studies previously mentioned also state that RO is beneficial for the staff.

N. Langston (1981) writes that the lack of empirical evidence as to the effectiveness of RO may be related to the format in which RO is currently conceptualized. She does not support the abandonment of the technique but urges a reassessment of RO as it relates to learning theory with positive reinforcement of desired behaviors (behavior modification).

M. Wolanin and L. Phillips (1977, 1981), R. Hussian (1981) and B. Reisberg (1981) do not advocate RO therapy alone but favor a more total approach through environmental cues, behavior therapy, teaching of activities-of-daily-living skills, or cognitive training by mnemonic devices. These authors believe that these activities can serve the confused person in different situations and aid the elder to care for himself or herself better than RO therapy alone can do. Hussian suggests that the materials and tasks in the classroom need to be upgraded instead of allowing the participants to graduate to an advanced RO group or a remotivation, resocialization, or attitude therapy group. A. Fisk (1981, 91) writes that a "well run recreational program will be more useful to the demented patient than the most sophisticated psychiatric care."

G. Gubrium and M. Ksander (1975), R. Butler and M. Lewis (1977), F. Hellebrant (1978), and Reisberg (1981) have reservations about forcing all confused elderly to face reality. Butler and Lewis suggest that dementia is a positive defense mechanism against painful realities. Gubrium and Ksander note that "reality," as defined by the RO board, has been forced on confused group members by aides who are rigid

and not sensitive to the elderly's needs. An example given by the authors demonstrates their point: If, in response to a question about the weather, a confused person answered that it was sunny, the aid would point to the RO board, which read "raining," and direct the patient to respond that way, when indeed the patient was voicing reality based on what he had seen through a window—sunshine.

R. Tappan and T. Touhy (1983) remind us that the design of some group modalities for older adults is very highly structured and very controlling; they cite reality orientation and remotivation groups as two examples. These are certainly highly structured group modalities. The writers feel that the focus on one topic or theme may suppress the real concerns of individuals who need to discuss issues, the airing of which the leader would encourage in group work with younger adults. The danger of patronization of elderly group members by the leader is also pointed out in this article.

Another writer (Schwenk 1979) feels that the competitive aspects of orientation to time, person, and place may be quite boring, useless, and devoid of meaning to the older person who has a serious cognitive impairment.

It must be noted that all the literature cited stresses one very important point—kind, human contact that builds trust does more than all other therapies combined to relieve confusion. *The mechanical repetition of information will not reorient* (Taulbee 1976).

P. Wahl (1976) states that day care is the most effective means of maintaining orientation for those confused elderly who live in the community. Day care programs do incorporate RO theory into the daily program (Kalish et al. 1975; Ansak 1975); Chapter 7 offers the reader a model of group work in a day care center.

## RO IN AN ADULT DAY CARE CENTER: A CASE STUDY

Currently I am employed as a geriatric nurse practitioner (GNP) in a geropsychiatric adult day care center, the Senior Socialization Center of Catholic Social Service in San Jose, California. The center has been in operation for nine years. The staff includes the project director, a psychiatric social worker, the program coordinator, an occupational therapist, a part-time social worker, a driver, a secretary, and myself, a GNP.

The program employs the principles of RO; however, the overall therapeutic approach is eclectic. We utilize the concepts of remotivation, resocialization, recreational therapy, and various psychiatric therapies in planning our total rehabilitative milieu program. Our main objective is to prevent mental breakdown and deterioration through the various activities and through work with the client and the family. We want to maintain the clients in their community, in their own homes, with their family, or in a retirement complex or a residential care facility and prevent premature institutionalization.

The clients who attend the day care center are the elderly with mental and/or physical diagnoses: senile dementia (we have had a few diagnosed as having Alzheimer's disease), strokes with varying degrees of physical handicaps and/or aphasia, hypertension, diabetes, obesity, and so on. Many of the clients have long-standing histories of mental illness (that is, depression, schizophrenia, bipolar disorder, or paranoia). Not all of those with mental or physical health problems are confused, but a large number of our clients are.

### Usual Props

The center uses the usual RO props: the RO board, a calendar, and a clock. The RO board

*A reality orientation board should be easy to read and free of extraneous, distracting designs; it should be placed in a much-used area. Sometimes patients or clients help to keep the board up-to-date.*

is large and movable. One of the participants is usually responsible for changing the date daily. The calendar is on heavy-duty cardboard, and the numbers and month can be changed as necessary. The spaces for the date are large enough so that the main activity for the day can be posted. A copy of each month's calendar is given to each of the clients.

Name tags on three-by five-inch cards in large print are worn by all staff and clients. Clients and staff are called by their first names. The name of our program is above the entrance to the center. On the door are labeled photographs of all the staff and volunteers.

### Program Format

The activities change daily, but we follow a specific schedule everyday. This is a helpful way to provide orientation and a sense of continuity for the clients.

Upon arrival at the center, the clients are encouraged to socialize, have a cup of coffee, work on an individual project, listen to music, read, or discuss special problems with staff members. Those who are especially confused may be engaged in simple concentration games. The period after lunch is spent in much the same way.

At 11 A.M. the occupational therapist gathers the clients in a circle for a basic RO exercise. We do not ask each client to read the RO board; the group as a whole is queried on the date, time, weather, next holiday, and so forth. If the person responding gives an incorrect answer, he or she is referred to the RO board. We have 18 to 21 participants daily. We have limited time, space, and staff, so a true RO is impractical. The very confused but socially adept elderly are mixed with the oriented clients. The oriented clients do not seem to be "put off" by the RO exercise. We inform new clients that this is a daily exercise for those who cannot remember this information and that their intake memory is helpful in keeping those who are confused more oriented. We maintain a matter-of-fact attitude and at times a humorous one if clients poke fun at their own memory loss. After RO, the clients are led through simple chair exercises.

Upon completion of the exercises, the clients are engaged in an activity that is designed to

*A calendar of daily events should be easy to read and very visible. Often artistic designs on a calendar can be distracting to older viewers. This calendar is legible and easy to understand; it has no extraneous material around the edges or on the individual dates (See also guideline 3 in Figure 7–1).*

stimulate one of the five senses; revive old memories; instruct them in something new; or involve them in planning for an upcoming event, such as our annual vaudeville show, senior olympics, or a party. Cooking is a popular activity. Everyone gets to put a finger in the pot—stir, measure, add—and with this many cooks we still do not ruin the soup! Anagrams, crossword puzzles, current events, painting, pottery, singing, horoscopes, talks about holidays, or guest speakers (from the police, Social Security, or the telephone company) may be one of the planned activities. The OT and myself may lead a discussion on activities of daily living (ADL) or a health topic. Picnics and outings are popular events.

The Monday and Friday afternoon sessions may be music, reminiscing, or special exercises led by an instructor from adult education. Group milieu therapy is on Tuesday and Thursday mornings and afternoons. (The large group is split into two smaller groups; one group has therapy while the other group is engaged in the day's activity.) The moderately confused are included in the therapy; only the very confused, those who are disruptive to the group process, and those who refuse to be part of therapy are excluded.

Another way orientation is maintained is the process by which the client is scheduled to attend the center. All clients come at least two days a week (if their physical and emotional health does not permit, then one day); they may attend up to four days a week if they are experiencing great emotional or familial stress, confusion, paranoia, and so forth. The clients are scheduled for Monday/Thursday or Tuesday/Friday from about 10:30 A.M. to 2:15 P.M. The participant is called each day he or she is scheduled to attend, to ensure that he or she is ready when the center's van or a taxi arrives.

Depending on the client, our overall approach is active friendliness—these people receive many hugs and kisses because they themselves are this way. For the less demonstrative participants we employ passive friendliness, ensuring that they also receive positive reinforcement and touch when appropriate.

Families are provided needed respite by having the older person attend our program. Family members are encouraged to attend the family meetings held monthly, to share their frustrations but also to learn from other families how they cope with the elderly person in their lives.

## SUMMARY

The reality orientation technique incorporated with other therapeutic approaches works well in diminishing the confusional state of the moderately confused elderly. As the literature demonstrates, however, RO is not a panacea. It succeeds only if the staff working with the elderly person is committed and involved. An overall approach that includes other therapies and techniques. Provision of a cheerful, cue-filled environment; and activities that stimulate the senses, can be done successfully, and promote self-esteem are more effective than RO therapy alone. The one key to successful care of the elderly is providing caring human contact. J. Alfgren (1977, 88L) stresses an excellent point: "We must realize that not all patients will progress rapidly. Our attitude should be that patients are progressing as long as they're not regressing."

And isn't that the important point? Progress can't be measured solely by whether an elderly person is oriented in all three spheres—time, person, and place. It's the quality of the person's life that is really important. Reality orientation alone cannot improve the quality of life, but an overall eclectic approach can.

## EXERCISE 1

Visit an adult day care center. Observe how reality orientation is used (or not used) and what environmental cues are employed to promote orientation. Describe other techinques that you think the center could use to improve orientation.

## EXERCISE 2

Select a partner. Role-play three examples of reality testing with a disoriented person.

## REFERENCES

Alfgren, J. 1977. Reality orientation: Starting your own program. *Nursing* 7(4): 88C–88L (April).

Ansak, M. 1975. *On Lok senior health services manual.* San Francisco: On Lok.

Barnes, J. 1974. Effect of reality orientation classroom on memory loss, confusion, and disorientation in geriatric patients. *The Gerontologist* 14(2): 138–42 (April).

Brockett, R. 1981. The use of reality orientation in adult foster care homes: A rationale. *Journal of Gerontological Social Work* 3(3): 3–13 (Spring).

Brook, P., G. Degun, and M. Mather. 1975. Reality orientation: A therapy for psychogeriatric patients: A controlled study. *British Journal of Psychiatry* 127:42–45.

Browne, L., and J. Ritter. 1972. Reality therapy for the geriatric psychiatric patient. *Perspectives in Psychiatric Care* 10(3): 135–39 (May–June).

Burnside, I. 1970. Clocks and calendars. *American Journal of Nursing* 70(1): 117–19 (January).

_____. 1978. *Working with the Elderly: Group process and techniques.* 1st ed. North Scituate, Mass.: Duxbury Press.

Butler, R., and M. Lewis. 1977. *Aging and mental health: Positive psychosocial approaches.* 2d ed. St. Louis, Mo.: Mosby.

Citrin, R., and D. Dixon. 1977. Reality orientation: A milieu therapy used in an institution for the aged. *The Gerontologist* 17(1): 39–43 (February).

Colthart, S. 1974. A mental health unit in a skilled nursing facility. *Journal of the American Geriatrics Society* 22(10): 453–56 (October).

Erickson, R., S. English, E. Halar, and J. Hibbert. 1978. Employing reality orientation in a short term treatment setting. *ARN Journal* 3(6): 18–21 (November–December).

Fisk, A. 1981. *A new look at senility: Its causes, diagnosis, treatment, and management.* Springfield, Ill.: Thomas.

Folsom, J. 1968. Reality orientation for the elderly mental patient. *Journal of Geriatric Psychiatry* 1(2): 291–307 (Spring).

Freese, A. 1978. *The end of senility.* New York: Arbor House.

Glasser, W. 1965. *Reality therapy: A new approach to psychiatry.* New York: Harper & Row.

Gubrium, G., and M. Ksander. 1975. On multiple realities of reality orientation. *The Gerontologist* 15(2): 142–45 (April).

Harris, C., and P. Ivory. 1976. An outcome evaluation of reality orientation therapy with geriatric patients in a state mental hospital. *The Gerontologist* 16(6): 496–503.

Hellebrant, F. 1978. Comment: The senile dement in our midst, a look at the other side of the coin. *The Gerontologist* 18(1): 67–70. (January–February).

Hirschfeld. M. J. 1977. Nursing care of the cognitively impaired. In *Cognitive and emotional disturbance in the elderly,* ed. C. Eisdorfer and R. Friedel. Chicago: Year Book.

Hogstel, M. 1979. Use of reality orientation with aging confused patients. *Nursing Research* 28(3): 161–65 (May–June).

Holden, U. P. 1979. Return to reality. *Nursing Mirror* 149(21): 26–29 (November 22).

Hussian, R. 1981. Psychotherapeutic intervention. Organic mental disorders. In *Geriatric psychology: A behavioral perspective,* ed. R. Hussian. New York: Van Nostrand Reinhold.

Johnson, C. 1980. Reality orientation in the nursing home: A test of effectiveness. Abstract in *The Gerontological Society of America, Thirty-third annual scientific meeting program.* Part 11, p. 132. November.

Kalish, R., E. Lurie, R. Wexler, and R. Zawadski. 1975. *On Lok senior health services: Evaluation of a success.* San Francisco: On Lok.

Langston, N. 1981. Reality orientation and effective reinforcement. *Journal of Gerontological Nursing* 7(4): 224–27 (April).

Lee, R. E. 1976. Reality orientation: Restoring the senile to life. Parts 1 and 2. *Journal of Practical Nursing,* January: 34–35; February: 30–31.

Lehman, E. 1974. Reality orientation. *Nursing* 3(3): 61–62 (March).

Letcher, P. B., L. P. Peterson, and D. Scarbrough. 1974. Reality orientation: A historical study of patient progress. *Hospital and Community Psychiatry* 25:801–3.

Loew, C., and B. Silverstone. 1971. A program of intensified stimulation and response facilitation for the senile aged. *The Gerontologist* 1(11): 341–47 (Winter).

MacDonald, M., and J. Settin. 1978. Reality orientation versus sheltered workshops as treatment for the institutionalized aging. *Journal of Gerontology* 33(3): 416–21 (May–June).

McDonald, R., A. Neulander, O. Holod, and N. Holcomb. 1971. Description of a non-residential psychogeriatric day care facility. Part 1. *The Gerontologist* 11(4): 322–27 (Winter).

Merchant, M., and P. Saxby. 1981. Reality orientation—A way forward. *Nursing Times* 77(32): 1442–45 (August 5–12).

Mulcahy, N., and N. Rosa. 1981. Reality orientation in a general hospital. *Geriatric Nursing* 2(4): 264–68 (July–August).

Reisberg, B. 1981. *Brain failure: An introduction to current concepts of senility.* New York: Free Press.

Reorientation stimulates patients—and staff. 1975. *Modern Health Care* 3(1): 33–35 (January).

Salter, C., and C. Salter. 1975. Effects of an individualized activity program on elderly patients. *The Gerontologist* 15(4): 404–6 (October).

————. 1977. Regression among the elderly after an interruption in their therapeutic program. *Hospital and Community Psychiatry* 28(2):101–5 (February).

Schwenk, M. 1979. Reality orientation for the institutionalized aged: Does it help? *The Gerontologist* 19(4): 373–77 (July–August).

Settle, H. 1975. A pilot study in reality orientation for the confused elderly. *Journal of Gerontological Nursing* 1(5): 11–16 (November–December).

Silverstone, B. 1976. Beyond the one-to-one treatment relationship. In *Geriatric psychiatry: A handbook for psychiatrists and primary care physicians,* ed. L. Bellak and T. Karasu. New York: Grune & Stratton.

Smith, B., and H. Barker. 1972. Influence of reality orientation training program on the attitudes of trainees toward the elderly. Part 1. *The Gerontologist* 12(3): 262–64 (Autumn).

Stephens, L., ed. 1969. *Reality orientation.* Washington, D.C.: American Psychological Association, hospital and community psychiatry service.

Tappen, R., and T. Touhy. 1983. Group leader— Are you a controller? *Journal of Gerontological Nursing* 9(1): 34 (January).

Taulbee, L., and J. Folsom. 1966. Reality orientation for geriatric patients. *Hospital and Community Psychiatry* 17:133–35.

Taulbee, L. 1976. Reality orientation for the aged. In *Nursing and the aged.* 1st ed., ed. I. Burnside. New York: McGraw-Hill.

_____. 1978. Reality orientation. A therapeutic group activity for the elderly. In *Working with the elderly: Group process and techniques,* ed. I. Burnside. North Scituate, Mass.: Duxbury Press.

Trotter, R. 1972. Reality orientation. *Science News* 411 (December 23).

Voelkel, D. 1978. A study of reality orientation and resocialization groups with confused elderly. *Journal of Gerontological Nursing* 4(3): 13–18 (May–June).

Wahl, P. 1976. Psychosocial implications of disorientation in the elderly. *Nursing Clinics of North America* 11(1): 145–55 (March).

Whitehead, A. 1978. The clinical psychologist's role in assessment and management. In *Studies in geriatric psychiatry,* ed. A. Issacs and F. Post. New York: Wiley.

Wolanin, M., and L. Phillips. 1977. The Cinderella effect, an administrative challenge. *Concern Care Aging* 3(3): 8–12.

_____. 1981. *Confusion: Prevention and cure.* St. Louis, Mo.: Mosby.

Zepelin, H., and S. Wade. 1975. A study of the effectiveness of reality orientation classes. Paper presented to the Twenty-eighth Annual Meeting of the Gerontological Society, Louisville, Ky.

Zepelin, H., S. Wolfe, and F. Kleinplatz. 1981. Evaluation of a year long reality orientation program. *Journal of Gerontology* 36(1):70–77 (January–February).

## BIBLIOGRAPHY

Barns, E., A. Sack, and H. Shore. 1973. Guidelines to treatment approaches: Modalities and methods for use with the aged. *The Gerontologist* 13(4): 513–27 (Winter).

Busse, E., and D. Blazer. 1980. The future of geriatric psychiatry. In *Handbook of geriatric psychiatry,* ed. E. Busse and D. Blazer. New York: Van Nostrand Reinhold.

Charatan, F. 1980. Therapeutic supports for the patient with OBS. *Geriatrics* 35(9):100–102 (September).

Conlin, J. 1981. A hotel or hospital? Applying the principles of reality orientation. *Journal of Practical Nursing* 31(7): 25–26, 51 (July–August).

Cornbleth, T., and C. Cornbleth. 1977. *Reality orientation for the elderly.* Washington, D.C.: American Psychological Association.

Day, R. 1981. An integrative group approach to treating the dysfunctional elderly . . . reality orientation, remotivation therapy, and sensory training. *Nursing Homes* 30 (September–October): 38–40.

Drummond, L., L. Kirchhoff, and D. Scarbrough. 1978. A practical guide to reality orientation: A treatment approach for confusion and disorientation. *The Gerontologist* 18(6): 568–73 (November–December).

Ferm, L. 1974. Behavioral activities in demented geriatric patients. *Gerontologica Clinica* 16(4): 185–194.

Gillette, E. 1979. Apathy versus reality orientation. *The Journal of Nursing Care* 12(4): 24–25 (April).

Godber, C. 1976. The confused elderly. *Nursing Times* 72(28): vii–viii, x (July 15).

Greene, J. 1979. Reality orientation with geropsychiatric patients. *Behaviorial Research Therapy* 17(6): 615–18.

Hackley, J. 1973. Reality orientation brings patients back from confusion and apathy. *Modern Nursing Home* 31(3): 48–49.

Hahn, K. 1980. Using twenty-four-hour reality orientation. *Journal of Gerontological Nursing* 6(3): 132–35 (March).

Ireland, M. 1972. Starting reality orientation and remotivation. *Nursing Homes* 21(4): 10–12.

Nodhturft, V., N. Sweeney. 1982. Reality therapy for the institutionalized elderly 18(7): 396–401 (July) 1982.

Phillips, D. 1973. Reality orientation. *Nursing Digest* 22 (October–November): 6–7.

Raskind, M., and M. Storrie. 1980. The organic mental disorders. In *Handbook of geriatric psychiatry,* ed. E. Busse, and D. Blazer. New York: Van Nostrand Reinhold.

Robinson, K. 1974. Therapeutic interaction: A means of crisis intervention with newly institutionalized elderly persons. *Nursing Clinics of North America* 9(1): 89–96 (March).

Scarbrough, D. 1974. Reality orientation: A new approach to an old problem. *Nursing* 4(11): 12–13 (November).

Shaw, J. 1979. A literature review of treatment options for mentally disabled old people. *Journal of Gerontological Nursing* 5(5): 36–79 (September–October).

Sherman, E., and E. Newman. 1977–78. The meaning of cherished personal possessions for the elderly. *Journal of Aging and Human Development* 8(2): 181–91.

Stevens, C. 1974. Breaking through cobwebs of confusion in the elderly. *Nursing* 4(8): 41–48 (August).

Sylvester, K., J. Kohut, and J. Fleshma. 1979. *Reality orientation for the elderly.* Oradell, N.J.: Medical Economics, Book Division.

Taulbee, L. 1976. *The A-B-C's of reality orientation: An instructional manual for rehabilitation of confused elderly persons.* New Port Richey, Fla.

Trockman, F. 1978. Caring for the confused or delirious patient. *American Journal of Nursing* 78(9): 1495–99 (September).

Veterans Administration Hospital, Tuscaloosa, Alabama. 1974. *Guide for reality orientation.* April.

Weiler, P., and E. Rathbone-McCuan: 1978. *Adult day care: Community work with the elderly.* New York: Springer.

---

## RESOURCES

### Films

*Interacting with Older People* (black-and-white; Part I, 30 minutes; Part II, 26 minutes; 1971). Using interchange format, these films identify techniques to promote interaction with older persons in terms of meeting psychosocial needs. They examine attitudes of hospital staff in dealing with older persons. Directions for Education in Nursing Via Technology, Wayne State University, c/o College of Lifelong Learning, Detroit, MI 48202.

*Rescue from Isolation* (color, 22 minutes, 1972). This film documents the problems experienced by the elderly who are socially isolated and the effects a psychogeriatric day hospital can have on decreasing isolation. Gerontological Film Collection, Media Library, P.O. Box 12898, North Texas State University, Denton, TX 76203.

*Behavioral Manifestations in the Aging Patient* (color, 16 minutes, author: Carl Eisdorfer, Ph.D., M.D.). Selected symptoms of common behavioral manifestations seen in the elderly within the nursing home setting are shown in this film. It stresses the importance of the staff in diagnosis and care of elderly patients and leads to a better understanding of the elderly and their problems. Free loan from Film Department, Sandoz Pharmaceuticals, East Hanover, NJ 07936. Also available from Association Film, 866 Third Avenue, New York, NY 10022.

### Sources for Reality Orientation Boards

*W. H. Collins Cabinets,* Department N77, Route 1, Box 326, Cottondale, AL 35453. Board $33.00.

*Hillhaven, Inc.,* Printing Department. Department N77, P.O. Box 11222, Tacoma, WA 98411. Board $33.00; complete set of letters on cards an additional $9.00.

*Raymco Products Inc.,* 212 South Blake, P.O. Box 248, Olathe, KS 66061. Model OC-32, self-contained, with a five-year supply of cards for days, months, year.

chapter 15

# Reality Orientation and Clinical Practice

*Lucille R. Taulbee*

*I once saw an old key that bore the inscription: "If I rest, I rust." I have never forgotten it. A key that is constantly being used always keeps bright and shiny, and it is not so different with people, is it? We may have limitations imposed on us by age or infirmity, but how important it is to keep as active as we can.*

F. GAY (1981, 34)

**LEARNING OBJECTIVES**

- Define **confusion** in elderly persons.

- Differentiate between organic and functional confusion.

- Identify some of the major causes of confusion in elderly persons.

- List three reasons a reality orientation program has potential to improve care of the elderly.

- Describe five techniques for creating and maintaining a consistent 24-hour reality environment.

- List six therapeutic group activities for confused elderly individuals.

- List three guidelines for establishing a reality orientation program.

- Describe five ways to assist the family in caring for confused family members at home.

**KEY WORDS**

- Activities

- Confusion

- Consistent

- Environment

- Functional

- Organic

- Reality

- Reorientation

In recent years reality orientation (RO) has been used as the first step in treating confusion in the elderly. Such a program may also be effective in health maintenance for aged citizens.

As a therapeutic and meaningful activity, RO has many possibilities: (1) It is a simple technique and can be learned by anyone; (2) it can be conducted while giving daily care and supervision to the elderly in the home; (3) it can be modified to fit a variety of settings—therapy clinics, day care centers, convalescent centers, hospitals, private homes, senior multiservices centers, adult education centers, hobby centers, recreational clubs, and others; and (4) the cost is minimal.

The reality orientation program was developed to improve the quality of care for patients with a nursing diagnosis of confusion, defined as disorientation with respect to time, person, place, or thing. Confusion may have multiple causes in the elderly, among them an infection, a head injury, arteriosclerosis, stroke, dehydration, malnutrition, medications, stress and anxiety, depression, and social isolation. Also, confusion may be a defense mechanism for the elderly. Knowing the cause helps with preventive measures, but it does not give direct and immediate help in caring for the confused person.

First, it needs to be determined if the patient is functionally or organically confused. Functional confusion is a mental condition related to developmental and psychosocial factors; schizophrenia is such a condition. Organic confusion has physical causes, for example, infection, respiratory disturbances, electrolyte imbalance, alcohol withdrawal, medication, high fever, malnutrition (Morris and Rhodes 1972).

A severely confused person needs constant direction, supervision, and assistance with the activities of daily living. An ambulatory confused individual may require more care and surveillance than a nonambulatory one. Hospitalization is not indicated for many ambulatory confused; their families may bring them to a psychiatric hospital or nursing care center on an outpatient basis.

That was the situation that existed in 1965 when I worked as a geriatric nurse/supervisor in a Veterans Administration hospital. Once the problem was identified, the nursing staff met to develop a program to improve nursing care for the disoriented patients. The nursing assistants noted that confused patients appeared to respond somewhat when told who they were, where they were, and why they were there. We began on that basis, and our reality orientation program was launched (Taulbee and Folsom 1966).

We continued to learn as we developed the program requirements. Rapidly it became evident to us that to have a successful RO program, the emphasis should be on creating and maintaining a 24-hour reality environment and allowing the RO classroom activities to play a supplemental role in the RO program. However, we used the RO classes to train personnel as class instructors through observation and participation. Much of our knowledge came from the patients themselves. For example, we learned that 30 minutes is the maximum length of time one can hold the attention of confused patients. Residents also displayed turned-off behavior if juvenile material was introduced; it was simply inappropriate for teaching adults. We learned through trial and error that the classroom sessions were more effective if held each day at the same time and in the same place in an environment conducive to learning. It also helped to have the same instructor for at least two weeks. We also discovered that while only three or four patients could be accommodated in basic classes, eight or ten persons could attend advanced sessions.

Since there is a reason for all behavior, we were often given a clue to the reason for a patient's disoriented behavior if we asked simple questions, such as "What makes you seem anxious and restless? or "Is there some reason

you store your sandwich in your pocket instead of eating it for luncheon?" (The patient responded that he got hungry before bedtime and wanted to have food "where he could find it.") One patient, when asked why he preferred to disrobe, said, "It's ten o'clock in the morning, and I shouldn't be in pajamas." On another occasion a patient who was asked the same question informed us, "These are not my pajamas, so I have to take them off."

When we noted extreme anxiety, restlessness, and agitation in a confused patient, we sought the reason. One elderly gentleman, although secured in his wheelchair with a safety belt, insisted on propelling his chair to the back door of the unit each evening at 5 o'clock. One evening, as I assisted him to the door, I asked him about his reason for going there each evening. His answer was quick and to the point: "I have to put out the cat." Before we attempted to change the behavior, we questioned his wife. She verified that before coming to the hospital her husband had put the cat out the back door each evening and had let him in again the next morning. It took nearly a week of consistent reality orientation before the man realized that he was in the hospital and that while he was hospitalized his wife would put out the cat.

## TWENTY-FOUR-HOUR REALITY ORIENTATION

It is unfortunate that society believes 65 years of age is "old" and that when a person reaches that age, he no longer needs to know what time or what day it is. This has been brought to our attention by repeated episodes. In one hospital, an elderly gentleman, not finding a clock or calendar in his ward room, asked a nursing assistant, "What day is it?" The curt reply was, "Why do you need to know what day it is, or why do you ask what time it is, Pop? You aren't going anywhere!" Such insensitivity to the needs of elderly patients and replies such as this one constitute verbal abuse of patients.

In working out our reality orientation program, we observed that confused persons needed reorientation on a 24-hour basis and that, to be most effective, the reorienting techniques had to be applied consistently by all personnel who came in contact with confused individuals. "Personnel" includes family, visitors, neighbors, volunteers, social workers, nursing and medical personnel in hospitals and clinics, dietetic personnel, and maintenance workers.

To ensure a consistent approach, we composed guidelines for creating and maintaining a 24-hour reality environment to care for and rehabilitate confused individuals.

1. The secret of success for reality orientation is a positive, hopeful attitude on the part of all personnel. With the help of dedicated people, confused individuals will be given a chance for rehabilitation. *Your* attitude can make the difference.

2. Treat the confused individual with respect and dignity at all times. *Elderly confused persons should never be treated as children.*

3. Endeavor to inject the current date, day of the week, and the time into *all* conversations with persons who may be mildly or severely confused.

4. Encourage and reward confused persons who try to remember day-to-day realities. A smile or a compliment serves as a fitting reward.

5. Do *not* encourage or accept confused rambling, but be tactful and courteous in bringing the confused individual back to reality.

6. Encourage self-care; doing basic activities of daily living keeps people in touch with reality.

7. The 24-hour reality environment is the most important aspect of a reality orientation program. Classroom instruction is used to supplement the 24-hour techniques. All group activities (grooming classes, exercise sessions, and sing-alongs) may be made to reinforce reality.

8. It is important to teach *all* family members so that they may encourage and assist in maintaining a 24-hour reality environment in the home.

Rehabilitation in the activities of daily living should be stressed each day. These simple, insignificant daily tasks keep the elderly alert and functioning with dignity and pride. It is important that basic reality techniques be used consistently by all persons who come in contact with the confused or disoriented person.

On a 24-hour basis, the reorientation began at 6:00 A.M., when the patients were awakened. The nursing assistants called them by name and told them the time, the day, and what time breakfast would be served. The assistants serving the breakfast trays continued RO by calling the patients by name, introducing themselves to the patients, explaining the food on the trays, and perhaps introducing the schedule for the day—especially what the patients would be doing in the next several hours. The nursing assistants giving the patients their baths or taking them to a clinic continued the reorienting process. If a patient seemed confused during a conversation, the staff member would take a few extra seconds to reality-test. The process continued all day and through the evening and night shifts.

## RO CLASSROOM ACTIVITIES TO SUPPLEMENT 24-HOUR RO

The group classroom sessions were 30 minutes in length, and accommodated small groups of patients. During sessions, clocks, calendars, a reality bulletin board, and other educational materials at a first- to third-grade level were

BERNITA M. STEFFL

*Reality is talking about food.*

used, but the materials were always presented in an adult manner. As the patients became better oriented to the basic information of time, date, month, year, next meal, and so forth, the level of instruction was raised to make the classwork more stimulating. Eventually we found that we had to accommodate advanced "students." We then gave classroom instruction at approximately the sixth-grade level. Memory games that were not complicated but required concentration and those that stimulated recall ability were used to vary the group sessions (Taulbee 1976).

Some elderly people steadfastly cling to their independence and are reluctant to admit their confusion; however, such persons may accept group activity in the classroom. In our classes, reorientation was acceptable because we did not single out any one person or emphasize the severity of an individual's confusion.

After we began the 24-hour reality orientation program and the group classroom sessions, we observed dramatic changes in residents and also in the atmosphere on the unit. Not only were patients more alert and beginning to take care of themselves, but the staff attitude changed. Staff members began to report progress in individual patients and to take pride in their accomplishments. Residents were given verbal reinforcement for successes, and failures were given little consideration.

## GUIDELINES FOR ESTABLISHING RO PROGRAMS

Reality orientation as a therapeutic approach to the elderly should incorporate the following basic principles:

1. Do not hurry elderly people.
2. Explain all procedures before asking the elderly to perform them. Face the elderly when speaking; speak distinctly but not too loudly.
3. Talk to aged persons—even those who are disoriented or confused—as though you expect them to understand.
4. Treat elderly persons with dignity and respect.

5. Encourage ' selves as r
6. Use  soc succes'
7. Maintai.. first for abu..
8. Establish a climat. concern for each indi..

Health care personnel must rea.. tance of holistic care. No matter how . the service and the physical assistance or beautiful the accommodations, life can be blea.. and dreary without someone to care about and something to do. Life involves movement. Activity is necessary for some persons to achieve happiness or contentment. Inactivity discourages both curiosity and enthusiasm.

## TRAINING THE STAFF

Once the decision is made to start a reality orientation program, staff members must be selected who will be responsible for the activity. To be effective in the program, these staff members should be creative, self-directed, and enthusiastic. They must believe that no patient is hopeless. Although group work with persons suffering from dementia is different from group work with the alert and economically independent elderly, the therapeutic approach is to be maintained in all contacts.

An initial training period and some supervision of new group leaders is recommended in developing program philosophy and standards. If possible, the staff should have some formal training in the techniques of reality orientation through attending seminars and using films, training kits, and instruction manuals for resource materials. Role playing has also been found to be effective with students. Some advice from students who participated in simulated reality orientation groups follows (Burnside 1976):

1. "Groups must be small; six was too many."
2. "Selection of patients is important."

the selection process it was impor-
ant to include patients who could answer
some of the questions."

. "Props were useful."

5. "The leader must learn to cope with the group as a whole and teach individuals all at the same time, which can be frustrating."

6. "The leader felt there was a real value in having a co-leader."

7. "Co-leaders need to meet, plan, and set goals before they begin with the group of patients."

8. "It is helpful to know something about the dynamics of co-leadership when it is used."

9. "Some role players felt that reality orientation needs a definite one-to-one component to be effective."

10. "Be careful not to isolate any patient who is quiet and not responding to very much."

11. "Make everyone feel a part of the group; individual attention is important, especially for those who are quiet and not responding as well."

12. "It is difficult always to use reality orientation."

13. "Reality orientation is only one step in a process; patients need to be reality oriented to something other than just rote learning."

## THE CLASSROOM

A formal classroom area for the group sessions is most desirable, as learning depends upon environment. In selecting the room it is important to consider temperature, glare, noise, space for a blackboard to stand (if not mounted on a wall), privacy, space for wheelchairs, tables around which to seat patients, and sufficient lighting.

## SCREENING AND MONITORING THE PATIENTS

Careful screening of the groups is suggested, in order to consider the potential of each individual patient. A class for severely confused individuals should have only three or four members. As soon as class members have grasped the basic information, they are promoted to an advanced class of eight to ten members. Patients should never be retained in the basic class if they are bored and know the material.

Experience has demonstrated that if a confused member has been attending classes for two months but has been unable to retain sufficient knowledge for reorientation (such as patients with a diagnosis of Alzheimer's disease), it is better to discontinue the class sessions for the time being and emphasize 24-hour orientation. The patient may be brought into a basic group again at a later date and may do better.

The families of patients should be trained in reality orientation techniques (Lee 1976) and helped to use the material when the patients go home, so that progress can be sustained. A simple five- or ten-minute session each day while reading the morning paper or eating breakfast may be all that is necessary. With assistance, family members may set up an ongoing reality environment in the home, so that reorientation is consistently maintained (International Center for the Disabled 1981).

At the end of 30 days the program should be evaluated and necessary changes made. Meetings with staff, patients, and families provide feedback on improvement or nonimprovement. Patients should progress through the basic and advanced classes and then move to the remotivation groups (Birkett and Boltuch 1973) and other group activities.

## DAILY ACTIVITIES ARE REALITY

Group sessions may be set up to emphasize reality, including grooming classes; group exercises (using armchair calisthenics if necessary); group wheelchair instruction; sensory training; self-feeding techniques; juice bars (which serve refreshments at mid-morning and mid-afternoon); clothing-exchange sales; special TV news programs; documentaries, travelogues, and wildlife series; resident council meetings; and welcoming committees for new arrivals in the facility. Sessions on food and diets can be stimulating and educational. Publication of a newsletter for the facility, with items submitted by resident reporters, helps to create interest and to keep residents and staff in touch.

## REALITY MATERIALS

Reality devices for relearning are easy to find and need not be expensive. We used clocks, calendars, adult scrapbooks, and pictures, with identifying words and phrases in large print. We talked about food, the weather, holidays, and so forth, and posted this information, together with the year, month, and day of the week, on a reality orientation bulletin board to be read and reread by the patients.

Reality bulletin boards can be made of various materials. A cork bulletin board, pegboard, felt board, or blackboard can be used to display information on a daily basis. These types of bulletin boards make it easy to change the information daily; for effective reorienting, the informa-

tion must be current and correct. See Resources section at the end of Chapter 14 for sources.

Other reality materials include flash cards with words and pictures; U.S.-map jigsaw puzzles; county, state, and world maps; large-print books; plastic fruit and foods; magnetic alphabet boards; arithmetic boards and/or flash cards with numerals; Scrabble sets (with large letters); adult picture books (may be scrapbooks with reality pictures but nothing juvenile); large-piece jigsaw puzzles of animals, birds, or foods at the adult level; and illustrated dictionaries with large print and pictures. Many of these materials can be purchased at a flea market, garage sale, or thrift shop.

## EXPANSION OF REALITY ORIENTATION

Correcting sensory deprivation may be one of the most fundamental responsibilities of any activity program. Reality orientation counteracts deprivation through *daily* activities, not through activities in special places at special times. Sensory training encourages geriatric patients to use their senses to respond to stimuli, thus retarding deterioration (Heidell 1972).

A group activity, whether recreational, educational, or religious, should offer enough possibilities for elderly people to be able to choose what they want. Determining what is therapeutic for each resident, with or without physical or mental disabilities, is the responsibility of the treatment team, but protection of the privacy and dignity of each resident at all times should be a primary consideration. Freedom to choose to participate in an activity adds the possibility of choice to the daily lives of residents. One great loss as we age is the loss of choice. Choice supports self-respect; when denied, it promotes helplessness.

## OTHER TREATMENT PROGRAMS

As Elizabeth Donahue explains in Chapter 14, reality orientation should not be confused with reality therapy (Glasser 1965), which is conducted under the direction of a psychiatrist

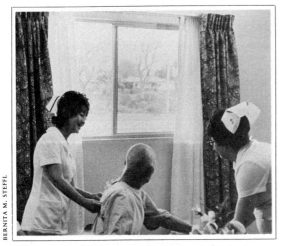

The weather is often a topic used as information on the reality orientation board and in reality orientation groups. It is helpful to look out the window and actually discuss what is seen.

or another professional specifically trained in the theory and technique of reality therapy. The purpose of reality orientation is to reorient confused people, but it can also be used as a means of preventing confusion in any elderly individual. Remotivation therapy may be recommended for individuals on completion of both levels of RO classes. A severely confused person is unable, usually, to participate in the larger group meetings of a remotivation series. RO, remotivation, and resocialization as treatment methods have a distinct purpose and are employed in a specific manner (Barns, Sack, and Shore 1973).

## SUMMARY

Reality orientation has gained popularity in recent years in the treatment of the mentally impaired elderly. For confused individuals, reorientation means independence and dignity. A reality orientation program can help many

aged persons continue to function with minimal assistance and care. The program has been widely used because it is not difficult; it can be done by a person without a formal teaching background or a knowledge of group dynamics. Another reason for its popularity is the ease with which it fits into nursing tasks and care by the family in the home. Also, the program can be adapted and implemented in a variety of other settings.

The reality orientation group sessions are used to supplement the 24-hour RO. These activities can vary from the usual orienting procedures to memory games that require concentration. Group sessions also may include grooming classes, group exercises, and sensory training. Props for reality orientation sessions are quite easy to find and are inexpensive. Basic classroom materials are a must.

Reality orientation techniques should be explained to the family. They should be asked to allow the patient to participate in family decisions to help him feel needed and self-reliant.

## EXERCISE 1

Briefly define *reality orientation* and explain in one or two pargraphs how it differs from *reality therapy*.

## EXERCISE 2

Prepare a brief report on steps you would take to create and maintain a consistent 24-hour reality environment for an elderly person living in your home.

## REFERENCES

Barns, E. K., A. Sack, and H. Shore. 1973. Guidelines to treatment approaches: Modalities and methods for use with the aged. *The Gerontologist* 13(4): 513–27 (Winter).

Birkett, D. P., and B. Boltuch. 1973. Remotivation therapy. *Journal of the American Geriatrics Society* 21 (August): 368–71.

Burnside, I. M. 1976. Student feedback from class entitled Interviewing and Group Work with the Elderly. Summer Institute, Andrus Gerontology

Center, University of Southern California, Los Angeles, July.

Gay, F. 1981. Thursday, April 8. *The Friendship Book*. London: Thomason.

Glasser, W. 1965. *Reality therapy: A new approach to psychiatry*. New York: Harper & Row.

Heidell, B. 1972. Sensory training puts patients "in touch." *Modern Nursing Home* 27 (June): 39–43.

International Center for the Disabled. 1981. *Help begins at home*. (Pamphlet.) New York.

Lee, R. E. 1976. Reality orientation: At-home training brings the senile back to life. *Practical Psychology for Physicians* 49 (March) 43–45.

Morris, M., and M. Rhodes. 1972. Guidelines for the care of confused patients. *American Journal of Nursing* 72(9): 1630–33 (September).

Taulbee, L. R. 1976. *The A-B-C's of reality orientation: An instruction manual for rehabilitation of confused elderly persons*. New Port Richey, Fl.

Taulbee, L. R., and J. C. Folsom. 1966. Reality orientation for geriatric patients. *Hospital and Community Psychiatry* 17(5): 133–35 (May).

## BIBLIOGRAPHY

Barnes, J. A. 1974. Effects of reality orientation on memory loss, confusion, and disorientation in geriatric patients. *The Gerontologist* 14(2): 138–42 (April).

Brook, P., G. Degun, and M. Mather. 1975. Reality orientation: A therapy for psychogeriatric patients — A controlled study. *British Journal of Psychiatry* 127 (July): 42–45.

Conroy, C. 1977. Reality orientation: Basic rehabilitation technique for patients suffering from memory loss and confusion. *British Journal of Occupational Therapy* 40(10): 250–51 (October).

Cornbleth, T., and C. Cornbleth. 1979. Evaluation of effectiveness of reality orientation classes in a nursing home unit. *Journal of American Geriatric Society* 27(11): 522–24 (November).

Gubrium, J. F., and M. Ksander. 1975. On multiple realities and reality orientation. *The Gerontologist* 15(2): 142–45 (April).

Hanley, I. G., R. J. McGuire, and W. D. Boyd. 1981. Reality orientation and dementia: A controlled trial of two approaches. *British Journal of Psychiatry* 138:10–14.

Harris, C. S., and P. Ivory. 1976. An outcome evaluation of reality orientation therapy with geriatric patients in a state mental hospital. *The Gerontologist* 16(6): 496–503 (December).

Holden, U. N.d. *24-hour approach to the problems of confusion in elderly people*. (Pamphlet.) Department of Psychology, Moorhaven Hospital, South Devon, England.

Phillips, D. F. 1973. Reality orientation. *Nursing Digest* 22 (October–November) 6–7.

Ponsar, W., and J. Alfano. 1973. *Policy and procedures manual: Reality orientation*. Tacoma, Wash.: Hillhaven.

Taulbee, L. 1968. Rx nursing intervention for confusion of the elderly. *Alabama Nurse* 22(1): 1–3 (March).

_____. 1973. Reorientation means independence and dignity. *Modern Nursing Home* 31(3): 50–51 (September).

_____. 1976. Reality orientation and the aged. In *Nursing and the aged*. 1st ed., ed. I. M. Burnside. New York: McGraw-Hill.

Taulbee, L., and J. C. Folsom. 1973. Attitude therapy: A behavior therapy approach. In *Direct psychotherapy*. Vol. 1, ed. R. M. Jurjevich. Coral Gables, Fl.: University of Miami Press.

Taulbee, L., and H. W. Wright. 1971. Attitude therapy: A behavior modification program in a psychiatric hospital. In *Behavioral intervention in human problems,* ed. H. D. Richard. New York: Pergamon Press.

Tuscaloosa Veterans Administration Hospital. 1975. *Reality orientation pre-training program catalog*. Tuscaloosa, Ala.: Manual Arts Therapy Clinic, VA Hospital.

Walker, M., and R. Nepom. 1980. Reality orientation: Establishing a climate of trust in geriatric care. *Canadian Nurse,* July/August.

Wershow, H. J. 1977. Comment: Reality orientation for gerontologists: Some thoughts about senility. *The Gerontologist* 17(4): 297–302 (August).

Wolff, K. 1971. Rehabilitating geriatric patients. *Hospital and Community Psychiatry* 22(1): 8–11 (January).

Woods, R. T. 1979. Reality orientation and staff attention: A controlled study. *British Journal of Psychiatry* 134:502–7.

## RESOURCES

### Films

*A Time to Learn: Reality Orientation in the Nursing Home* (16 mm, color, 28 minutes). Demonstrates some of the "how to" in implementing reality orientation, as illustrated in three different nursing homes.

*December Spring: 24-Hour Reality Orientation* (16 mm, black-and-white, 29 minutes). Illustrates the application of 24-hour reality orientation, utilizing staff members and patients at the Tuscaloosa Veterans Administration Hospital.

*Return to Reality* (16 mm, color, 35 minutes). Introduces the concepts of reality orientation as they are used in the case of an elderly stroke patient by a team at the Veterans Administration Hospital in Tuscaloosa, Alabama.

Correspondence concerning rental or purchase of preceding three films should be sent directly to National Audiovisual Center (NAC), General Services Administration, Order Section, Washington, D.C. 20409; phone (202) 763-1891.

*Confronting Confusion* (black-and-white, 24 minutes, 1977). This documentary films an elderly patient who has withdrawn into a fantasy world and is unmotivated and confused. Group leaders of an advanced reality orientation group help the patient to confront his fantasies and offer support. Improvement is shown in a variety of ways. An Electric Sunrise Film. Distributor: Electric Sunrise, P.O. Box 11122, Piedmont Station, Oakland, CA 94611; phone (415) 655-2356.

## Training Kits

*This Way to Reality.* This kit helps one understand reality orientation and how to implement it in long-term care facilities. The kit contains a guide book including sections on introduction, planning, implementing, evaluating, training the staff, and training others. It also contains five sets of slides with accompanying audiocassettes that have audi-

ble and inaudible advance signals. Purchase price: $228.00. Correspondence regarding purchase should be sent directly to National Audiovisual Center (NAC), General Services Administration, Order Section, Washington, D.C. 20409; phone (202) 763-1891.

*Trainex filmstrips (5) on "Reality Orientation."* These filmstrips present the five sections on reality orientation techniques that are developed in the *This Way to Reality* training kit. Filmstrips available from Trainex Corporation, P.O. Box 116, Garden Grove, CA 92642.

## Instruction Manuals and Pamphlets

*The A-B-C's of Reality Orientation for Rehabilitation of Confused, Elderly Persons* (Lucille R. Taulbee, 1976). Available from L. Taulbee, 1120 Stratford Drive, No. 1, New Port Richey, FL 33552. Price: $2.75 (includes postage).

*Help Begins at Home* (New York: International Center for the disabled, 1981). This pamphlet provides information to assist the family in caring for a confused member in the home.

*Leading Reality Orientation Classes: Basic and Advanced* (Linda Drummond, Lorraine Brians, and Dorothy Scarbrough, 1980). This coordinated booklet and audiocassette program explains and illustrates how to organize and conduct reality orientation classes. Available from National Audiovisual Center, Washington, D.C. 20409.

*24-Hour Approach to the Problems of the Elderly* (Una Holden, Carol Martin, and Margaret White, n.d.). St. James' University Hospital, Leeds, England.

# chapter 16

# Remotivation Therapy

*Helen Dennis*

*Growth is the only evidence of life.*

JOHN HENRY, CARDINAL NEWMAN
(PETER 1977, 235)

© RANDOLPH FALK/JEROBOAM, INC.

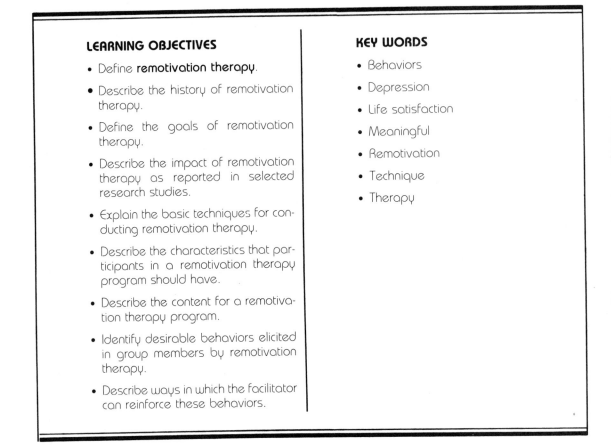

## LEARNING OBJECTIVES

- Define **remotivation therapy**.
- Describe the history of remotivation therapy.
- Define the goals of remotivation therapy.
- Describe the impact of remotivation therapy as reported in selected research studies.
- Explain the basic techniques for conducting remotivation therapy.
- Describe the characteristics that participants in a remotivation therapy program should have.
- Describe the content for a remotivation therapy program.
- Identify desirable behaviors elicited in group members by remotivation therapy.
- Describe ways in which the facilitator can reinforce these behaviors.

## KEY WORDS

- Behaviors
- Depression
- Life satisfaction
- Meaningful
- Remotivation
- Technique
- Therapy

Remotivation therapy (RT) is a group technique for stimulating and revitalizing individuals who are no longer interested and involved in either the present or the future. This technique is essentially a structured program of discussion based on reality coupled with use of objective materials to which individuals are encouraged to respond.

## HISTORY AND GOALS

Remotivation therapy was originally designed to remotivate mentally ill patients. It has been used in mental hospitals and nursing homes for patients diagnosed as having mental disorders,

physical disorders (Robinson n.d.), alcoholism, and depression (Donahue 1966).

Dorothy Smith originated the remotivation technique in her work as a hospital volunteer (Pullinger and Sholly n.d.). Subsequently, in 1956, she trained a large group at the Pennsylvania State Hospital (Long 1962). In response to increased interest from many hospitals, the American Psychiatric Association formed a Remotivation Advisory Committee. This committee, working with Smith, Kline, and French Laboratories, established remotivation therapy programs throughout the country. By the end of 1967, 15,000 nurses and aides at 250 mental hospitals had participated in remotivation training programs (Robinson n.d.).

The following comments are by R. S. Garber (1965, 220):

> Remotivation is based on reality. A goal of the mental health professional is to help mentally ill persons recognize the realities we recognize. Through trust and communication, the professional attempts to restore a patient's ability to perceive people, things, and relationships for what they really are. A patient has sick and healthy roles. . . . Remotivation tells a patient that he is accepted as an individual . . . with specific features, with many roles, with unique traits that make him distinguishable from everyone else.

Garber also says that the older person has an objective existence to other people rather than an existence depending on what the individual thinks of the self. Remotivation creates a bridge between the individual's self-perception and the perception of others. Reminiscing about one's experiences with the concrete world and identifying and asserting one's experiences through interactions often strengthen the concept of reality. To accomplish this, the information and description of experiences must be concrete and specific.

The individual is strengthened by remotivation in two ways: (1) by being encouraged to describe the self concretely as a person with roles and specific social functions and (2) by being encouraged to speak accurately about past and present experiences. The individual also learns of roles to play that do not cause anxiety or create problems. Freedom, competence, dignity, and pleasure can be shared without revising or blocking every aspect of one's life. The smell, touch, and feeling of reality are recognizable and often give the individual a sense of meaningfulness from the past.

## REVIEW OF THE RESEARCH LITERATURE

A preliminary report on remotivation therapy examined the effects of RT on chronic and acute hospitalized patients (Long 1962). Subjects were assigned randomly to one of six remotivation groups, three male and three female. A total of "nearly 1000" patients were involved in the study. The Solomon four-group design was used to control several of the variables. The experimental group was given a pretest, remotivation therapy, and a posttest. Control group 1 was given a pretest and posttest with no remotivation therapy. Control group 2 was given remotivation therapy and a posttest. Control group 3 was given only a posttest with no remotivation therapy. Attendants rated patients' behavior, which included response to meals, response to other patients, response to work, attention to dress, and speech. A two-by-two analysis of variance on the four posttests of behavior ratings indicated a significant difference between remotivation therapy and no remotivation therapy beyond a .01 level of significance. This analysis was performed only for chronic patients. Remotivation therapy patients were described as exhibiting a significantly higher level of behavior than patients who had no remotivation.

J. S. Bovey (1971), in a doctoral dissertation, investigated the effects of remotivation therapy on ward behavior, self-concept, and visual motor perceptions. The three groups were remotivation therapy with emphasis on patient-staff and patient-patient interaction; remotivation therapy with no emphasis on interaction, implemented by the staff reading to the patients; and a group that acted as a control and most likely received nothing. A pretest-posttest design with a six-week experimental period was used. Forty-five male and 45 female mental patients were selected randomly from a geriatric unit at a state hospital. Co-variant analysis, using pretreatment scores as the co-variant, suggested that remotivation therapy techniques were significantly more effective than reading in producing changes in self-concept. Remotivation and reading were significantly more effective than a no-treatment control group on all variables.

A trial of remotivation therapy versus conventional group therapy was conducted with 39 ambulatory, nondeaf geriatric patients (Birkett and Boltuch 1973). Patients were assigned randomly to remotivation therapy or group therapy. The researchers acted as co-therapists. The group therapy was intended as a placebo group, which took the form of psychoanalytically oriented therapy sessions. The subjects were treated for 12 weeks, receiving one hour of therapy per week. Personal relationships and group responses were tested before and after the therapy. Results on the two measures showed no significant group differences. However, group responses such as interest, awareness, participation, and comprehension did favor the remotivation group.

I conducted a study (1976) to evaluate the effectiveness of remotivation therapy with hospitalized geriatric patients. Twenty-three females and 14 males from two geriatric wards were assigned randomly to remotivation therapy, an extra-attention condition, and routine care. The routine care condition was dropped because of attrition. The remotivation and extra-attention condition consisted of 12 sessions, of 30 minutes to one hour, three times a week. The remotivation sessions were structured and based on a different topic for each session. The 12 topics were vacations, gardening, holidays, sports, rocks, pets, art, the sea, transportation, weather, hobbies, and animals and their by-products. In the less structured extra-attention condition, discussion topics included hospital activities, reasons for hospitalization, families, and past experiences. The routine care group received routine care and was not seen by the leader. Measurement of depression, life satisfaction, and behavioral ratings were completed after the treatment. Contrary to the hypothesis, $t$ test results indicated that subjects receiving remotivation therapy were significantly ($p > .02$) more depressed and less satisfied with life than the extra-attention group. No significant difference between the groups appeared in the behavioral ratings. One possible reason for the unexpected results is that remotivation therapy aroused feelings of conflict. Relating to meaningful and stimulating material could have stimulated the RT group to realize more fully their hospital situation. After completion of therapy, patients' control over their lives, day-to-day ritual, and prospects of release remained unchanged. Remotivation therapy may have caused the subjects to gain better contact with reality by realizing previous independence, interests, opportunities, and pleasures and by recognizing their absence during confinement. The realization of these differences could have been partially responsible for the increased depression and dissatisfaction in the remotivation group compared with the extra-attention

group. If the conflict or dissonance analysis is correct, then the subjects were in a drive or motivational state. Remotivation therapy may be the first important step in motivating individuals to gain maximum benefit from subsequent therapeutic programs.

Linda Moody, Virginia Baron, and Grace Monk (1970) found patients alert and interested in life again as a result of remotivation therapy. The patients were involved in group interaction consisting of discussion topics geared to the group's past history and interests. An effort was made to involve the senses of touch, taste, and smell. Measures of life satisfaction revealed higher posttreatment scores. No tests of significance were performed, nor was a control group used. The authors advocated varied sensory stimuli and social interaction for maintenance of contact with reality.

## HOW TO CONDUCT REMOTIVATION THERAPY

### Initial Steps for Remotivation Therapy

Starting a new program in a facility with traditional and ongoing treatment techniques may be difficult for many reasons. Some of them are

1. Changing methods or adapting to new ones may be threatening to some staff members.
2. Not understanding a new program may arouse suspicion and nonconstructive criticism.
3. Added responsibilities may be too much for an overworked and underpaid staff.

Some of these difficulties can be avoided by effectively communicating the nature and intent of the new program to all interested staff members. First, approval should be obtained in writing from the facility's director or chief administrator. Next, the nursing director should fully understand and support the remotivation therapy program. The staff may be involved in conducting remotivation therapy, selecting individuals for the program, escorting individuals to the sessions, or keeping individuals available for remotivation. Staff members should be invited to attend a session to understand more fully the remotivation process. Information, experience, and understanding of the new program will increase the chances for acceptance and support.

Leading remotivation therapy does not require extensive training or degrees. Anyone sensitive to human needs could conduct remotivation therapy with training in the objective, technique, and process.

After the completion of the remotivation program, the leader may offer observations of individuals' responses to the therapeutic team. This new information will encourage a broader view of individual potentials.

## Selection of Group Members

Ideally, group members should have some ability to interact with others and not be totally regressed. For the regressed person, therapy should start with reality orientation, followed by remotivation therapy and reminiscing therapy (Barnes, Sack, and Shore 1973). However, few facilities for the elderly offer a series of therapies tailored to specific levels of a "mental health" continuum. If remotivation therapy is the only program available for the unmotivated person, criteria for selection include willingness to join the group, ability to hear and speak, and lack of preoccupation with hallucinations (Pullinger and Sholly n.d.; Dennis 1976). The group should consist of a maximum of 15 members (Robinson n.d.).

The remotivation leader has little need for information on diagnoses, prognoses, or histories. In fact, this type of information may influence the leader's expectation of individual participation and potential for change. As a remotivation leader, I found that not knowing about patient histories permitted me to strengthen my attitude of optimism. The group member in remotivation therapy has the chance to start anew and assume a different label from the one given by society or an institution. For example, a "mental patient" or "sick person" can become an "individual," "group member," or even a "student." Consequently, the remotivation leader must approach a group with the intention of offering new opportunities, change, and optimism with little or no reference to institutional or societal labels.

The ward staff is influenced in persuading an individual to attend the first remotivation meeting. In some cases the individual will attend if told to—rather than asked to—by the charge nurse. Invitations to join the group can range from "Please join us" to "I think it's important that you attend" to "Please attend." The same approach may not be effective for each person.

## Content of Remotivation Therapy

According to the *Remotivation Technique's* manual (Robinson n.d.), remotivation therapy sessions are usually held once or twice a week for 12 sessions. I found a more intensive schedule preferable—three times a week for four weeks. Sessions last from 30 minutes to one hour, depending on the attentiveness of the group (Robinson n.d.). Each remotivation session includes five basic steps (Robinson n.d.):

1. "Climate of acceptance" consists of introductions and getting acquainted (p. 7).
2. "Bridge to reality" encourages individuals to participate in reading an article aloud (p. 7).
3. "Sharing the world we live in" is topic development by means of questions, visual aids, and props (p. 8).
4. "An appreciation of the work of the world" prompts individuals to think about work in relation to themselves (p. 9).
5. "Climate of appreciation" is a time to express pleasure that the group has met and to plan the next meeting (p. 10).

From experience with geriatric patients in a state psychiatric facility, I found that steps 2 and 4 created little interest. For example, many subjects had poor vision or were unable to read. Consequently, I omitted the second step, "bridge to reality." Also, topics that were not applicable to work in relation to the group were discussed in terms other than work. For example, the topics of rocks, holidays, hobbies, and vacations arouse interest in related visual aids and individual experiences, but work-related discussions did not. Consequently, step 4 was frequently omitted.

Each remotivation therapy session is based on a different topic. The topics are geared to appeal to diverse backgrounds, experiences, and interests and to appeal to as many senses as possible. Visual aids and appropriate objects are used to maintain a high level of attention, interest, and reaction.

The first few minutes of each session are devoted to greeting and establishing rapport. Comments on dress, hairstyle, or the leader's family are all part of establishing this beginning relationship. Reminiscing is encouraged as part of sharing experiences. Visual aids are passed from one person to another to encourage communication among group members.

The leader structures each therapy session to focus on nonpathological interests and behaviors. Discussion centers on those things that constitute the real world for the members, to which they can relate. Topics dealing with individuals' problems and family relationships are avoided.

The group is told how many times they will meet. Halfway through the program the leader prepares the group for termination. For example, the leader may state, "The seventh session has been completed, and the group will meet five more times." After the last meeting, the leader may arrange to visit with the group, although the formal therapy has ended.

## AN EXAMPLE OF REMOTIVATION THERAPY

I became interested in remotivation therapy as a graduate student searching for a thesis topic. From personal involvement with several nursing homes, I was keenly aware of the desolate existence of most nursing home residents. Claims in a news magazine that reality orientation could deter or reverse the aging process aroused my curiosity. Subsequently, while reviewing the literature on reality orientation, I read about remotivation therapy.

The following description of group responses is a partial summary of the remotivation procedure I used at Metropolitan State Hospital in Norwalk, California. The remotivation group consisted of 12 geriatric patients hospitalized for an average of five years. The mean age of the group was 73.1. The group met three times a week for one month.

### Session 1: Vacations

For the first session I wrote each member's name on a card and placed it by the member's chair. I introduced myself and told the members something about my family and residence. The group was told that different topics of interest would be presented. To start the vacation topic, I took a heavy bucket of sand from person to person for each individual to feel. Then I asked the members where they would like to take a vacation. Previous vacation experiences were shared.

**Group response.** The members were interested in my background and family. All except two appeared to enjoy feeling the sand. The group seemed cautious and reserved. One individual screamed throughout the session. Others shared some vacation experiences.

### Session 2: Gardening

Gardening experiences and plant growth needs were discussed. The members each planted bean seeds in a cup with their name on it. Different green plants were passed around to look at, touch, and smell. A box of strawberries were distributed among the group for smelling and tasting. The meeting ended with reminiscences of preparing strawberries for pies and jams.

**Group Response.** The group seemed to enjoy planting seeds. All the members smelled and touched the different plants. Experiences in growing flowers and vegetables and preparing fertilizer were shared. All except two members tasted the strawberries.

### Session 3: Sports

I showed large, colorful posters of different sports, such as basketball, football, and baseball. Various sporting balls passed around included a basketball, golf ball, tennis ball, and softball, as well as a mitt. I bounced some of the balls to different persons, who bounced them back. Different sporting experiences were shared, as well as various sports individuals had tried. I also displayed pictures of sky-diving, ice hockey, and croquet. Several pieces of sporting equipment were passed around, such as a bat, tennis racket, and golf clubs.

**Group Response.** All the members held a piece of sporting equipment, and many told of experiences in that particular sport. Comments such as "when I used to caddy" or "when I played baseball" were made to the group.

### Session 4: Rocks

Many different kinds, shapes, and sizes of natural rock of geodes, quartz, and granite were passed around and discussed in terms of shape, texture, temperature, and weight. Polished rock stimulated a discussion on the rock-polishing technique.

**Group Response.** A group member led a discussion on rock polishing. Everyone stated that the meeting devoted to rocks was their favorite one so far. Several said that certain rocks would make attractive jewelry.

### Session 5: Pets

I displayed a covered cage housing a live rabbit, a procedure used by Hahn (1973). The group was asked to guess what was in the cage, given a few hints from me. The members were then asked to volunteer to feed the rabbit. After I showed different pictures of pets, I asked the members which pets they had owned or would like to own. Large paintings of rabbits and other animals were shown.

**Group Response.** Prior to session 5 one woman in the group had been very quiet. I subsequently discovered that she was considered mute. This "mute" lady spoke and guessed that the animal in the cage was a dog!

### Session 6: Art

The group was shown examples of many art forms, such as sewing, painting, and sculpture. I displayed eight large tempera paintings completed by kindergarten children and asked each member to act as a judge for a children's art show. Clay was used by the group for tactile stimulation and pleasure. Each one chose the color of clay he or she preferred. Puppets were shared as an art form.

**Group Response.** One individual responded by performing a puppet show for the group. All the members stated opinions on which picture should win first and second prizes and gave reasons for their choice.

### Session 7: The Sea

The group compiled a list of sea-related items, which were listed on the blackboard. I displayed large, colored pictures of different fish and asked the members which ones they had eaten or caught. A variety of seashells were passed around the group.

**Group Response.** Several group members shared sea-related experiences, such as visiting a marine museum and netting oysters in Louisiana.

### Session 8: Transportation

I asked the members to name different forms of transportation, which I then wrote on the blackboard, to ascertain the most popular form of transportation from the group's experience. Models of a bus, a missile, a train, a submarine, and several types of planes were passed around the group. I then read a poem about transportation.

**Group Response.** All the members volunteered information about different forms of transportation. Many reminisced about experiences with riding a ferry, bicycle, bus, or train.

### Session 9: Holidays

The group was asked to name holidays and the month of their occurrence and to associate colors with the different holidays. Holiday objects were shown, and the group matched the appropriate holiday with the objects.

**Group Response.** Several members talked about their ethnic backgrounds. One individual sang an Italian song; another described her Irish background. In general, however, the group was not very responsive to this topic.

### Session 10: Weather

The members were asked to describe the weather on that meeting day. The composition and origin of rain and clouds were discussed. A blackboard demonstration of evaporation followed the discussion, as suggested by W. F. Pullinger and E. N. Sholly (n.d.). The session closed with a poem about rain and a newspaper weather report.

**Group Response.** Only a few members appeared interested and were responsive to the topic. Several members contributed information about evaporation.

### Session 11: Hobbies

The group was asked to define the term *hobby*. Knitting, needlepoint, a matchbook collection, coins, stamps, Christmas balls, baseball cards, and newspaper headlines were passed around the group as examples of hobbies. Everyone talked about their hobbies. In discussing the collection of newspaper headlines, members were asked to recall what they were doing when President Kennedy was shot.

**Group Response.** All members recalled what they were doing when Kennedy was shot. The group accurately defined the term *hobby* and talked about their different hobbies. One member said that his hobby was shooting pool for money and that he would "love to play again." Two group members who had used wheelchairs to come to the sessions were no longer using them.

### Session 12: Animals and Their By-Products

Two types of items were presented to the group: miniature models of animals and a variety of items made from animals. A lamb's-wool hat, perfume, glue, rabbit fur, milk, and salami were some of the by-products. The group's task was to guess the animals from which the by-products originated. The session ended with a snack of cheese, salami, crackers, and sweets.

**Group Response.** The group was successful in accurately relating the by-product to the animal. The snack was enjoyed and vigorously consumed. Several individuals stated how much they enjoyed attending the meetings.

## EVALUATION AND REFERRAL

Little evaluative research on remotivation therapy has been published. Consequently, models of evaluation, areas for improvement, and personality characteristics most likely to change need investigation. To refine this therapeutic approach, the leader should specify desired behaviors and know how to reinforce them (Toepfer, Bicknell, and Shaw 1974).

In retrospect, the behaviors I considered desirable during remotivation therapy were

1. Attentiveness to leader and others.
2. Participation in discussion.
3. Responsiveness to the material presented.
4. Appearance of enjoying the experience.
5. Realism in discussion.
6. Communication with others.

These behaviors were reinforced by attention and acceptance from me as well as from the group. In addition, the new role of "group member," "individual," or "student" may have been reinforcing for some individuals.

Remotivation therapy could function as the first important step in motivating individuals to gain maximum benefit from other therapeutic programs. For example, nursing home residents might benefit more from physical therapy if they were motivated to change. F. J. O'Neil (1966) believes that even a minimal response to remotivation therapy could indicate the need for other types of therapy.

It is very difficult to attribute progress or change exclusively to remotivation therapy. Many variables contribute to changes in mood, behavior, and attitude. The institutionalized individual is part of a complex physical and psychological environment, and remotivation therapy is a small part of the total milieu.

However, remotivation therapy does offer an opportunity to increase one's sense of reality, to practice healthy roles, and to realize a more objective self-image. A new awareness of one's potential for growth and the motivation to change are two significant achievements for the RT member. These goals are not an end but a beginning. Active physical and psychological rehabilitative programs, geared to individual needs, must follow. A life of dignity and fulfillment for the institutionalized elderly is a realistic goal that must be met. Remotivation is just a beginning.

## SUMMARY

Remotivation therapy is a step beyond the reality orientation group method described in Chapter 15. Like reality orientation, it is a very structured type of group meeting; the focus is on discussion of specific objects, and the individuals are encouraged to respond to the topic or prop of the meeting.

Aged people can be helped through remotivation therapy by sharing about themselves and their former roles and functions and by describing past and present experiences so that the past can become more meaningful.

Results of studies done on behavioral changes due to remotivation therapy were published as early as 1962. Later, Bovey (1971) demonstrated that remotivation groups produce changes in self-concept. Birkett and Boltuch (1973) found no significant group differences between a control group and a remotivation group. Dennis (1976) came up with a surprising result: The subjects who received remotivation therapy were significantly more depressed than the control group. One explanation is that interesting and stimulating material and increased interactions may have been a stark contrast to the patients' bleak existence and that they had become painfully aware of their present hospital existence.

Difficulties a remotivation leader may face in beginning such a program include (1) staff concern about and reaction to change, (2) suspicion and harmful criticism from staff members due to lack of understanding of the program, and (3) staff inability to cope with the additional tasks to expedite such a therapy.

There should be no more than 15 in a group. Potential members should not be too mentally impaired and should be willing to join the group, able to hear and speak, and not be prone to hallucinations. The five basic steps of each meeting are (1) introductions, (2) reading aloud, (3) sharing time, (4) considering the work world, and (5) expressing appreciation and pleasure. Dennis (1976), in her work in a state hospital, found that patients did not eagerly participate in steps 2 and 4 and describes a variety of reasons in this chapter.

A diverse selection of topics is needed to appeal to and interest a wide range of patients. Possibilities are vacations, gardens, sports, rocks, pets, art, the sea, transportation, holidays, weather, hobbies, and animals and their by-products.

Behaviors to encourage are (1) increased attention, (2) participation in discussion, (3) response to props, (4) expression of pleasure, (5) discussion of reality, and (6) communication.

Remotivation therapy, although it does have drawbacks (for example, the structure is quite rigid), is a therapeutic technique that offers the opportunity to increase one's sense of reality, practice healthy roles, and realize a more objective self-image.

## EXERCISE 1

Take a favorite theme that you would enjoy using with a group of elderly people and answer the following:

1. Why you chose this theme.
2. Number in your proposed group.

3. Average age of members.
4. Place where group will be conducted.
5. Theme of group meeting for that day.
6. What you will do as a leader to create interest.
7. Five other themes you would find it fun to try in a remotivation group.

## EXERCISE 2

You are a nursing home administrator and are considering remotivation groups in your facility. What are pros and cons?

## REFERENCES

Barnes, E. K., A. Sack, and H. Shore. 1973. Guidelines to treatment approaches. *The Gerontologist* 13(4): 517–19.

Birkett, D., and B. Boltuch. 1973. Remotivation therapy. *Journal of the American Geriatrics Society* 21(8): 368–71 (August).

Bovey, J. S. 1971. The effect of intensive remotivation techniques on institutionalized geriatric mental patients. Doctoral dissertation, University of Texas. (*Dissertation Abstracts International* 32:4201B–02B, 1971; University Microfilms no. 72-4064).

Dennis, H. 1976. Remotivation therapy for the elderly: A surprising outcome. Unpublished manuscript. Los Angeles, Calif.

Donahue, H. H. 1966. Expanding the program. *Hospital and Community Psychiatry* 17(4): 117–18 (April).

Garber, R. S. 1965. A psychiatrist's view of remotivation. *Mental Hospitals* 16:219–21 (August).

Hahn, J. 1973. Mrs. Richards, a rabbit, and remotivation. *American Journal of Nursing* 73(2): 302–5 (February).

Long, R. S. 1962. Remotivation—Fact or artifact. *Mental Hospital Service* 151:1–8.

Moody, L., V. Baron, and G. Monk. 1970. Moving the past into the present. *American Journal of Nursing* 70(11): 2353–56 (November).

O'Neil, F. J. 1966. Involving the medical staff. *Hospital and Community Psychiatry* 17(4): 116–17 (April).

Peter, L. J. 1977. *Peter's quotations: Ideas for our times.* New York: Morrow.

Pullinger, W. F., and E. N. Sholly. n.d. *Outline of a remotivation training course.* Philadelphia: American Psychiatric Association and Smith, Kline & French Laboratories Remotivation Project.

Robinson, A. M. N.d. *Remotivation techniques: A manual for use in nursing homes.* Philadelphia: American Psychiatric Association and Smith, Kline & French Laboratories Remotivation Project.

Toepfer, C. T., A. T. Bicknell, and D. O. Shaw. 1974. Remotivation as behavior therapy. *The Gerontologist* 14(5): 451–53 (October).

## BIBLIOGRAPHY

Adams, G. 1961. I didn't know the person in the next room, but. . . . 1961. *Mental Hospitals* 12 (July): 28.

Bechenstein, N. 1966. Enhancing the gains: Remotivation, a first step to restoration. *Hospital and Community Psychiatry* 7 (April): 115–16.

Botwinick, J. 1973. *Aging and behavior.* New York: Springer.

Brudno, J., and J. Seltzer. 1968. Resocialization therapy through group process with senile patients in a geriatric hospital. *The Gerontologist* 8(3): 211–14 (Autumn).

Fields, G. J. 1976. Senility and remotivation: Hope for the senile. *Journal of Long-Term Care Administration* 4:1.

Frazier, A. 1966. Developing a remotivation program. *Staff* 3 (January–February): 5.

Garber, R. S. 1965. Why does remotivation work? *Staff* 2 (Summer): 8.

Gershowitz, S. Z. 1982. Adding life to years: Remotivating elderly people in institutions. *Nursing and Health Care* 3(3): 141–45 (March).

Greenfield, D. S. 1977. Remotivation therapy: A test of a major assumption of the treatment with domiciled geriatric veterans. *Dissertation Abstracts International* 36(6-B): 2861–62 (December).

Huey, K. 1977. A remotivation institute at Philadelphia State Hospital. *Hospital and Community Psychiatry* 28(2): 133–35 (February).

Ireland, M. 1972. Starting reality orientation and remotivation. *Nursing Homes* 21(4): 10–11 (April).

Kunkel, S. 1970. Resocialization: A technique that combats loneliness. *Nursing Homes* 19(8): 12–13 (August).

Lyon, G. G. 1971. Stimulation through remotivation. *American Journal of Nursing* 71(5): 982–86 (May).

Mandel, H. 1968. Renewed interest through remotivation. *Nursing Homes* (17)2: 21ff (February).

Martin, C. H. 1967. Place of motivation techniques in cottage and ward life programs. *Mental Retardation 5* (October): 17–18.

McCormick, E. 1962. New hope for darkened minds. *Today's Health* 40 (March): 44–45.

McFerrin, Z. H. 1967. Remotivation for family living. *Staff* 4 (November–December): 2.

Pullinger, W. F. 1958. Remotivation. *Mental Hospitals* 9 (January): 14–17.

_____. 1960. Remotivation. *American Journal of Nursing* 60 (May): 682ff.

Sink, S. M. 1966. Remotivation: Toward reality for the aged. *Nursing Outlook* 14(8): 27–28 (August).

Stephens, L. 1968. How to start a remotivation program. *Staff* 5 (January–February): 6.

_____. 1968. Remotivation. *Staff* 5 (May–June): 20.

_____. 1968. Remotivation literature. *Staff* 5 (September–October): 11.

Stotsky, B. 1972. Social and clinical issues in geriatric psychiatry. *American Journal of Psychiatry* 129(2): 32–40.

Tabler, M. 1965. Nature's therapy. *Staff* 2 (Spring): 9.

Tate, P. A. 1977. Rehabilitation and aging: The effect of remotivation therapy on activity level and life satisfaction with institutionalized elderly populations. *Dissertation Abstracts International* 36(6-B): 2890 (December).

Thralow, J. U., and C. G. Watson. 1974. Remotivation for geriatric patients using elementary school students. *American Journal of Occupational Therapy* 28(8): 469–73 (September).

Tilghman, C. 1965. A remotivator considers the "five steps." *Staff* 2 (Winter): 4.

Traul, H. 1964. Pipeline to remotivation. *Staff* 1 (Spring): 7.

Wallen, V. 1970. Motivation therapy with the aging geriatric veteran patient. *Military Medicine* 135 (11): 1007–10 (November).

Ward, E., C. Jackson, and T. Camp. 1973. Remotivation: A growing family of therapeutic techniques. *Hospital and Community Psychiatry* 24(19): 629–30 (September).

Whalen, L. 1960. Remotivation remodified. *Mental Hospital* 11 (April): 46–48.

Young, L. S. 1967. Remotivation helps community education. *Staff* 4 (January–February): 13.

Zorn, K. R. 1977. Therapeutic techniques in keeping our aged active. *Psychiatric Nursing* 18(3): 6–8.

## RESOURCES

### Organizations

*National Remotivation Therapy Technique Organization.* This organization distributes information lists and offers training at Philadelphia State Hospital and other centers throughout the country. Address is Philadelphia State Hospital, 14000 Roosevelt Boulevard, Philadelphia, PA 19114; phone (215) 671-4939.

### Training Aids

*Basic Remotivation Training Course Outline* (W. F. Pullinger and E. N. Sholly, Philadelphia: Philadelphia State Hospital, n.d.).

*Advanced Remotivation Training Course Outline* (W. F. Pullinger and C. Young, Philadelphia: Philadelphia State Hospital, rev. ed., 1976).

*Poems for Remotivation* (W. F. Pullinger, Philadelphia: Philadelphia State Hospital, 1981).

### Remotivation Kits

*Remotivation Kit No. 240-1.* For use in mental hospitals, this kit includes publications, instructional materials, and additional information. Cost: $1.50.

*Remotivation Kit No. 240.* For use in nursing homes, this kit includes publications, instructional materials, and additional information. Cost: $1.50.

For information regarding remotivation kits, write to American Psychiatric Association, Publications Services Division, 1700 18th Street, N.W., Washington, D.C. 20009.

# chapter 17

# Music Therapy

*Mary Jane Hennessey*

*It was her voice that made*
*The sky acutest at its vanishing.*
*She measured to the hour its*
*solitude.*
*She was the single artificer of*
*the world*
*In which she sang. And when*
*she sang,*
*the song*
*Whatever self it had, became the*
*self*

*That was her song, for she was*
*maker.*
*Then we,*
*As we beheld her striding there*
*alone,*
*Knew that there never was a*
*world for her*
*Except that one she sang, and*
*singing, made.**

WALLACE STEVENS (1936, 1964)

**LEARNING OBJECTIVES**

- Define **music therapy**.

- List three ways music can be used in group work with the elderly.

- State an example of a type of music that it would be inappropriate to play for a depressed person.

- Explain the style of music that would be acceptable to begin work with a depressed person.

- List seven types of group activity where music could be used effectively.

- Describe how to choose music to enhance the reminiscing process.

- Describe the style of music preferred by a regressed elderly group.

**KEY WORDS**

- Flexibility

- Group cohesiveness

- Listening

- Relaxation

- Responsiveness

- Stimulation

- Therapeutic

- Vibrations

The use of music in healing the body and mind dates back to antiquity (Carapetyan 1948; Licht 1946; Meinecke 1948). In modern times music was used in hospitals as a soporific before World War II and was considered a morale builder. Musicians who played there were called music specialists and were often music teachers, school band leaders, or choral directors who believed that music is good for people (Gaston 1968). In 1944 Michigan State University established the first curriculum for training music therapists. The first academic course was taught in 1946 at the University of Kansas. Although courses are now taught in several universities, it will be many years before there will be enough registered music therapists to staff the smaller hospitals, nursing homes,

and day care centers where music can be used as a therapeutic agent.

**THERAPEUTIC USES OF MUSIC**

Music therapy is defined as the controlled use of music in the treatment, rehabilitation, education, and training of adults and children suffering from physical, mental, and emotional disorders. (Alvin 1966). Use of music in groups of elderly people is considered therapeutic and can enhance the day-to-day existence of the institutionalized aged. Three ways of using music in groups are listening to music, having music in the environment, and making music.

Listening is one of the important areas of concern in group work. The more disturbed individuals become, the less they listen to others. Through playing music in a group, such isolated individuals can be encouraged to listen and, in so doing, communicate in a nonverbal way that

*Playing music in group meetings can encourage isolated individuals to listen.*

can be the beginning of responsiveness to their surroundings. (Catherine Moore also discusses listening in Chapter 33.)

Old age in our culture, with the many losses incurred, seems to contain much sadness and disappointment. Depression, paranoia, and disorientation are found in most institutions, and music helps provide an atmosphere for catharsis or simply getting things out in the open that are bothering a client. Old people are also often afraid of the world around them. The group experience can help reduce their fears, and music can encourage people to be aware of their feelings and then express them in the safety of the group.

Physically, music can help people move with more freedom, and with physical improvement, confidence in oneself grows. The connection between physical and mental health has been demonstrated and is the basis for the concept of holistic medicine.

Music can be used to change moods, or it has strong powers of association. Although musicians tend to view music as a way to bring joy to people, there is a large repertoire of music filled with pathos that can help work out grief through tears. In treating cases of depression, for example, it is advisable not to expose the client to an onslaught of cheerful music, but to begin with slow, familiar, sad music such as Handel's Largo. If the goal of a group is to

encourage people to be in touch with their feelings, the leader can without comment simply play some meaningful music before the group meeting starts, such as the plaintive Negro spiritual "Sometimes I Feel Like a Motherless Child." The music will help the members focus on their feelings.

Another method for getting people in touch with their feelings involves relaxing deeply and letting the mind wander on the sounds of music. Deep relaxation and specific musical selections as a method used in therapy are described in detail by Helen Bonny and Louis Savary (1973). A modification of this method is included later in this chapter.

Finally, music can be used as a way to develop group cohesiveness.

> The aim of the music session during which live music is played, or if not live music, recorded music, is to integrate each member of the group and to build up a collective memory of feelings and facts which bind the members together, thus creating interpersonal relationships based on a common experience to focus general attention on a number of combined and auditory perceptions (Alvin 1966, 132).

One advantage of group cohesiveness is that the members feel they all share the same problems or at least attempt to understand them. Troubles seem easier to bear when people feel they are not alone. Ways in which music is useful for encouraging discussion and sharing in the group experience include: (1) identification with the feelings expressed in the music; (2) associations that help relate past experiences; and (3) improvement in the perception of reality (by relaxing the individual and by stimulating free association of ideas, music tends to reveal hidden attitudes through the phenomenon of projection).

One way to begin working with music is to pay attention to your own music listening and draw up a list of selections that represent moods. Emil Guntheil and his colleagues (1952) describe music as fitting into six categories: (1) happy, gay, joyous, stimulating, triumphant; (2) agitated, restless, irritating, (3) nostalgic, sentimental, soothing, meditative, relaxing; (4) sad, melancholic, grieving, depressing, lonely; (5) prayerful, reverent; and (6) eerie, weird, grotesque. A second list could be of selections tried in groups, with a description of the groups' reactions. If enough people worked in this way and a central clearinghouse was set up to receive these impressions and recheck them with other groups, gradually excellent guidelines could be published for health professionals to use in their work.

## PHYSICAL EFFECTS OF MUSIC

The music therapist needs to be aware that music produces physical sensations in our bodies and can cause subtle physiological changes.

> . . . everyone to whom the succession of tones means anything responds by exhibiting very slight but characteristic changes of muscular tonicity. It is the listener and not the performer alone who creates the melody. In the act of response to the successive tones that strike upon the ear, he binds them together (Bingham 1968, 6).

Music also affects respiration, pulse, blood pressure, and galvanic skin response (Diserens and Fine 1939; Hyde 1968). For example, the Tchaikovsky *Symphonie Pathétique* depresses the cardiovascular system and it is not recommended for individuals who are fatigued, depressed, or ill. However, the same symphony could be employed to subdue hilarity in individuals or crowds (Hyde 1968).

Music is sensation not only because it activates our hearing but also because it stimulates the entire body. Scientific studies have demonstrated that we are an assortment of constantly moving atomic and subatomic particles (Andrews 1966). The vibrations of sound hitting against the body, which is a loose collection of its own vibrating material, are rearranged in either a good or a harmful way. This accounts for the Iso principle in using music in therapy, which is defined as "like acting on like" and is a physical reality observed by orchestra players.

Imagine the feeling in the body of a musician sitting on the stage during a performance of the Verdi *Requiem,* who is caught between trumpets and the echo trumpets. The vibrations caused by trumpets are very strong; brass instruments create clear-cut sounds that shake up our atoms. When I experience this sound's changing my own energy system at performances, I am so energized that sleep is out of the question for many hours. Monotonous, soft, repetitive music has the opposite effect. Our bodies are lulled, soothed, and comforted; many people can fall asleep to it while sitting in a concert hall. On a different level, industrial noise or hard rock at a high volume can cause deafness by damaging the delicate structures of the ear. No part of the body escapes the effects of sound (Diserens and Fine 1939).

## THE USE OF MUSIC IN GROUP WORK WITH INDEPENDENTLY FUNCTIONING OLDER PERSONS

Between 1977 and 1982 research on the effect of emotions on physical health has proliferated. One example is *Music and the Brain* (Critchley and Henson 1977), which is concerned with the neurological effects of music due to the sensory nature of stimulation on the auditory system, somatic motor system, sensory system (including the skin), and memory. Elmer and Alyce Green, working at the Menninger Foundation in Kansas, have demonstrated through the use of sophisticated biofeedback equipment a psychophysiological principle that states: "Every change in the physiological state is accompanied by an appropriate change in the mental-emotional state, conscious or unconscious, and conversely, every change in the mental-emotional state, conscious or unconscious, is accompanied by an appropriate change in the physiological state" (Green and Green 1977).

From this theoretical base has developed the use of music to slow down physiological responses to induce a deeply relaxed state and to improve physical and mental health, as well as to motivate people to make better choices in life-style.

Working with groups of independently functioning older persons, we have documented physical and behavioral changes that include decreased problems with insomnia, increased energy, and increased ability to walk farther and to perform flexibility exercises specifically designed for this age group. Combining stress management techniques that include discussions on the various stresses due to aging (Burnside 1971), nutritional information, flexibility exercises, and deep relaxation techniques has produced measurable health changes. Use of music to deepen the relaxation process has been an integral part of this program. S. Ostrander (Ostrander and Schroeder 1979) states that "the psycho-physical effects of different rhythms, time signatures and harmonic structures determine the usefulness of a composition for relaxed concentration." She recommends string music from the Baroque era with a metronome beat of 60 as being the most effective, and we have found this to be true.

If the discussion period has focused on sad material and the group morale is low, we have successfully used the concept of the Iso principle —that is, the concept of altering the mood with the music—by beginning with slow, sad music and gradually changing the rhythm and tone until a lighter, happier music is played. The use of music in groups for relaxing has increased during the past four years, and we have included some resources for this reason. They are listed at the end of this chapter.

## GROUPS FOR WHICH MUSIC IS APPROPRIATE

Music can be used in many different kinds of groups, including reality orientation groups, remotivation groups, reminiscing groups, socializing groups, sensory stimulation groups, preventive medicine groups, occupational therapy, physical therapy, recreational therapy, art therapy, and movement, exercise, and dance groups. The use of music in some of these is discussed in this section.

### Reminiscing Groups

The most useful music selections for older adults are those that were popular between 1900 and 1920. The music we listen to and sing during our formative years becomes "our music." The World War I years produced a wealth of music that is very poignant for many people in their eighties. Patriotic selections, especially those traditionally played and sung on July 4, can also be very effective. Because they are sung with gusto and enthusiasm, such songs as "God Bless America," "The Battle

Hymn of the Republic," and "Johnny Comes Marching Home" stimulate spontaneous and joyful reminiscing. One unusual approach is being employed by the staff of a senior citizens' center in Carmel, California; they are encouraging very old clients to tape their life histories using music to stimulate memories.

### Socializing Groups

Music is an easy way to encourage social interaction, especially for an isolated person. It creates a nonthreatening environment. When new patients are admitted to geriatric institutions, they frequently react with feelings of hostility and/or depression, which can quickly show up in symptoms of advancing short-term memory loss. At this time music can be used as a way to entice the patient to join a group designed for entertainment or for singing. Music that increases socializing includes dance rhythms, singable light music, and melodies familiar to the culture of the group.

### Groups for Treating Short-Term Memory Loss

One of the most disturbing aspects of aging is the deterioration of mental acuity, with progressive short-term memory loss. Ira Altschuler (1959) writes, "The percentage of senile dements in our mental hospitals is high. A certain number of persons admitted to hospitals as senile dements are *not* demented. They are rejected persons whose families got tired of them and sent them to mental hospitals." Elias Cohen (1976) says, "The mentally impaired elderly are our most ubiquitous problem and we don't like to talk about them."

Although short-term memory loss may be due to organic brain disease, it often appears when an older adult is institutionalized. All too often elderly people are admitted to institutions because it is difficult for them to manage on their own and they have no other place to go. Robert Butler (1975) calls senility a myth. He states that "the notion that old people are senile . . . is widely accepted. . . . But anxiety and depression are also frequently lumped within the same category of senility, even though they are treatable and often reversible. Old people, like young people, experience a full range of emotions, including anxiety, grief, depression and paranoid states" (p. 9). Butler lists other causes of so-called senility as drug tranquilization, malnutrition, unrecognized physical illness, and alcoholism.

My observation has been that if clients feel deserted and have not made the decision to enter the institution but have had the choice made for them, by either their families or social workers, they are apt quickly to show signs of diminishing mental functioning. The medical world has looked upon this trend as irreversible; only recently has it been shown that with consistent and daily stimulation and therapy patients can be helped back toward reality (Hennessey 1976). Although specific techniques are now being used in the area of reality orientation, these can be supplemented by the use of music in groups.

For a year and a half I worked with a small group of elderly women who were suffering from severe short-term memory loss. All came from good socioeconomic backgrounds; some had done graduate university work. Several of the women displayed acute anxiety when they experienced forgetfulness.

The group met in a central lounge with comfortable chairs and privacy. Assembling the group required two people, one to escort them and one to stay and hold their attention until all were present; otherwise they wandered about. The chairs were arranged in a circle, and I sat on the floor inside the circle looking up at them. For comfort, the group members were encouraged to take off their shoes if desired.

The first meeting began with a discussion of the difficulty in remembering things and people. I expressed my own difficulty in that area. We sometimes began group sessions with the exercise of recalling one another's names. Then I would talk about listening to music in a relaxed position, about how doing so would help us remember beautiful times and places and might even take us to new and exciting imaginary places if we let our minds go with the music. Bonny and Savary (1973) used this approach as an aid in psychotherapy and personal insight groups, and it seemed appropriate to try this

method. (See the Resources at the end of the chapter for tapes by Bonny and Savary.)

Before beginning the music, we used a method that is described by Leslie LeCron (1964) to help relax our bodies; it consists of paying attention to each part of the body in order from foot to head, tightening and then relaxing the muscles. I tried to keep the deaf women close to me to maximize their hearing during the group experience. The first time I experimented with this relaxation method, I was very apprehensive, feeling sure they would not cooperate, but I need not have worried.

I played quiet but interesting music (for example, the andantes from the Brahms symphonies), and each person was given an opportunity to talk about the experience. They all remembered where they had been and what they had seen in their imaginations; they enjoyed sharing this. A former Chicago school teacher who was never reconciled to life in a rural California community said, "I was going from floor to floor on an escalator in Marshall Fields looking at beautiful clothes." Another member said, "I was walking around in my grandmother's house looking at all the beautiful objects collected there. I haven't thought of this house for fifty years." And one woman recalled the gardens in which she had played as a child, saying she could smell the lilacs in bloom.

When the music concluded, the members expressed their approval or disapproval of the selection. They preferred symphonic or string music that was not too loud or percussive, although piano music such as Chopin's nocturnes was approved. No sudden sounds, but music building in emotional intensity was also preferred. Because of time limitations, I usually played only one movement; but if a longer selection was used, the members would be attentive throughout. This in itself was a positive change because several of the members were pacers who had great difficulty sitting still and often moved from room to room. When music was played, they remained still and content and seemed reluctant to discontinue the session.

One important example of retention occurred. Although I was generally a regular group leader, one week I was absent. Upon my return six of the eight women remarked on my absence somewhat indignantly!

## Movement and Music Groups

I have been working with a dancer and a musician to integrate singing and movement as one vehicle for giving group members a chance to express their feelings. Old people in institutions become very silent, and we have found that by adding sound to movement they are able to become much more lively and verbal.

We try to lessen the demarcation between moving and singing; when moving, members are encouraged to express the movement in a sound, and when singing, to accentuate the sound with movement. For example, when raising our arms, we take a deep breath and exhale without any sound. Then we exhale using any sound while focusing on very deep breathing. The leaders work as a team, moving back and forth from one dimension to the other, switching roles and reinforcing each other's suggestions for the deaf group members.

From these unstructured sounds, we gradually lead the group into singing simple songs unaccompanied except for clapping or using rhythm instruments played by the group, such as tambourines, drums, and wood blocks. At this point some people spontaneously start to dance. We have found that this progression helps the group to lose feelings of self-consciousness and start moving more freely.

A group leader can easily add singing to the many ways of working with a group. Singing and dancing, if encouraged on a twice-weekly or daily basis, will raise the energy level of the group for other experiences. (See Chapter 18 regarding dance/movement therapy.) Chanting is another possibility. An ancient practice used through the ages to put people in touch with themselves and sometimes with another level of consciousness, chanting has become popular again in nonmusical groups. It is a good way to raise group energy and is a useful method for beginning a group. Laurel Keyes, in a book entitled *Toning: The Creative Power of the Voice* (1973), describes in detail ways in which the voice can be used.

**Ambulatory Groups.** We work separately with ambulatory people and wheelchair people. We begin our ambulatory group the same way each time. Structure is important because it increases cohesiveness if the same things are done together. We start with formal leadership and then encourage more spontaneous movement. Forming a circle large enough so that the members have room to swing their arms, we do a range of motion exercises in the sitting position.* These include gentle, circular movement of all parts of the body but the hips. Having the member stand behind a sturdy chair and

STEVE ROSEN

*Elderly people lose their self-consciousness during group exercise.*

---

*These exercises were developed by Els Grelinger, my co-leader.

hold onto the back for support facilitates the hip motion. Care should be taken with members in this standing position because the sense of balance is very poor in many elderly people and falls can occur. Head movements should be done in a sitting position with great care to prevent strain and/or dizziness.

After warm-up exercises we work into sounds and music as already described. We dance with group members and encourage them to dance with one another. Hawaiian music, slow Beatles records, and excerpts from the classics that are dance tunes are all good. It is best to have music with a good beat but at a moderate pace.

One of the group members was a 90-year-old man who walked on crutches. Before joining the exercise program, which continued for six months, he often snoozed in his room. He did come to any music group, but he remained withdrawn. After he became involved in the music and movement group, his daughter told me one day that he was sharing his reminiscences with her as he had not done for many years. He also began to be more careful about his appearance. In the group sessions he left his crutches in a corner and danced with me.

**Wheelchair Groups.** One of the deprivations of the institutionalized elderly—especially those in wheelchairs—is a lack of touch (Burnside 1973). The movement group is a natural opportunity to incorporate it. I hold members' hands and move with the music. Similarly, their feet can be helped to move to the music. I also hold the head and rotate it very gently, ending with some massage of the shoulders, which provides more physical contact and also increases circulation.

I also work with music as a form of nonverbal communication with very regressed wheelchair people, with good results. For example, Mrs. H. was a wheelchair patient for many years. She often became very agitated, tore out her hair, and pulled at her clothes, but she was instantly calmed by the simplest musical performance, such as playing a tune on a recorder. Her son taped many favorite classical selections on cassettes, and the staff was asked to play these for her when she was upset. As long as the music was on, she was calm. The combination of personal contact (amateur musician playing or staff member starting her tape recorder) and the

music helped her to sit more quietly through the long days.

Music can also help in cases of aphasia. A woman in her early sixties suffered a severe stroke, which resulted in hemiplegia and aphasia. Her husband, a professional musician, cared for her at home but could communicate only on a nonverbal level. One day he discovered that his wife could sing along with well-known tunes. He demonstrated this; it was startling to hear her enunciating clearly the words to "My Bonnie Lies over the Ocean." It was only one step away then to teach her to sing her requests to the familiar tunes; for example, "I want a drink of water" fits nicely to "It's a Long Way to Tipperary." Ruth Bright (1972) describes this phenomenon and suggests it as a means of communication for the aphasic. Staff members who are working with the patient on an hour-by-hour basis can use this method easily. Apparently the speech center in the brain is in a slightly different place from the center for singing.

## MUSICAL INSTRUMENTS

Handbells are a beautiful way for people who have never played an instrument to make music. They are excellent for encouraging concentration, but unfortunately, they are very expensive. A church loaned me a set of handbells for six months, which I used as an adjunct to group work with people suffering from

*Handbells are beautiful instruments that do not require any special musical ability to play. Assisted by a musician, both alert and regressed individuals can play tunes on them.*

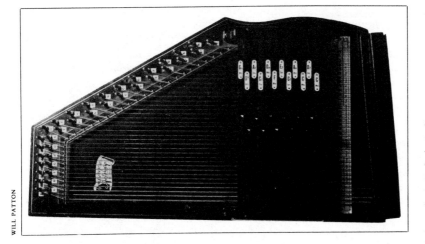

WILL PATTON

*The autoharp, a simple instrument to learn, is played by pressing buttons and strumming; it can be used to accompany any song with no more than three different chords in it. With a guitar strap attached to the back, the autoharp can be carried about just like a guitar.*

severe short-term memory loss. The activity was designed to help members concentrate in order to respond and ring the bells on cue. Although handbells require no special skills to ring, a musician is needed to give direction. (Figure 17–1 gives instructions for a handbell tune.) Very regressed or forgetful people are satisfied with working with the melody line. For alert people, chords can be introduced. The members should choose the music, but a word of caution is needed here. Leaders should begin with simple melodies and supply the rhythm themselves.

## SUMMARY

The healing properties of music have long been known, and music is an effective tool in group work with the elderly. This chapter offers

WILL PATTON

*Some extremely simple rhythm instruments, such as this kazoo, can be used in music groups. Careful and continued instructions must be given to the elderly, even for simple instruments. If played properly and in moderation, the kazoo can be fun with simple melodies like "Show Me the Way to go Home."*

suggestions that can be used by a leader with a musical background or one who simply has an interest in music.

Music can help aged members increase their movements, but it is also important in setting or changing moods because of its strong powers of association. Music need not always be joyful and can even be successfully integrated into group meetings to facilitate tears and the expression of sad feelings. Another way to help elderly people in groups to get in touch with their feelings is by the use of relaxation exercises.

New group leaders might find it helpful to draw up a list of music that represents various moods of their own. The list could then be compared to the list of moods of music compiled by Guntheil et al. (1952): (1) happy, joyous; (2) agitated, restless; (3) nostalgic, sentimental; (4) sad, melancholic; (5) prayerful, reverent; and (6) eerie, grotesque. Another suggestion is to make a list of selections used in group work and collect data on the reaction of the group members.

One important use of music is to further group cohesion. See Chapter 5 for further details on the importance of cohesion in group work.

Music helps encourage discussion and sharing among members. They can identify with the feelings expressed and relate to past experiences. Music may also improve the perception of reality.

Music is appropriate to include in many of the groups described in this book: reality orientation, remotivation, reminiscing, socializing,

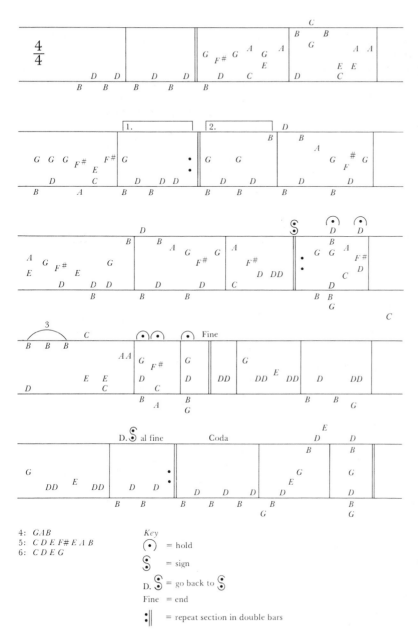

FIGURE 17–1. *This chart is an arrangement of a tune for handbells. The music encompasses three octaves of bells. The staff lines indicate octaves. the spatial arrangement of the notes indicates the pitch of the notes in relation to one another; that is, A appears and is higher than G. Bars contain four beats. The rhythmical arrangements of these beats is supplied by the conductor's pointing to each note when it is to be played. Low octave notes appear below the line, medium octave notes appear between the lines, and high octave notes appear above the line—for example, high #6, medium #5, low #4.*

SOURCE: Chart courtesy of Peggy Farlineer.

sensory stimulation, health-oriented groups, occupational therapy, physical therapy, recreational therapy, art therapy, and exercise groups. It is important to select the appropriate rhythm and mood for each of these groups.

Music encourages socializing and does help create a nonthreatening milieu. This is especially true for residents who have suffered short-term memory loss.

Music groups with regressed elderly people can be informal—for example, members can remove their shoes or the leader can sit on the floor. Learning names is an important aspect of this group work. And relaxation exercises are helpful to reduce anxiety. The mentally regressed elderly prefer symphonic or string music. It should not be too loud or percussive with sudden sounds. Pacers in a group can be helped to control their agitation and pacing with proper selection of music.

Dancers can help in such a group. Aged members may lose feelings of self-consciousness through carefully planned creative movement exercises. The reader is referred to Chapter 18 on dance/movement therapy. In music groups, unlike other groups, ambulatory and wheelchair patients need to be separated. Wheelchairs are cumbersome, for one thing, and dancing may be part of the exercise. Movement groups are often therapeutic because they maximize the use of touch during group meetings.

Singing and chanting can be important musical exercises. Musical instruments, such as drums or handbells, can be used by a trained musical leader.

## EXERCISE 1

This exercise is an introduction to how music helps people move their bodies.

1. Sit in a circle. Appoint a leader to begin simple exercises as described in the chapter. Try working for three minutes without music. Then add recorded rhythmical music—anything with a firm jazz beat. Note any difference in the body's response to these exercises with music. Examples of appropriate music are Scott Joplin's piano rags and Hawaiian music.

2. To become more aware of the physiological changes due to music, first conduct a seminar discussion on the physical changes in the body due to music. Then listen to music that gets slower. Measure your pulse rate before and after. (An example of such music is the first movement of Beethoven's *Moonlight Sonata*.) Finally, listen to music that gets faster. Measure your pulse rate before and after. (A good selection to try is Ravel's *Bolero*.)

## EXERCISE 2

This exercise focuses on unstructured use of the voice to raise group members' energy and increase nonverbal communication. The exercise requires that someone lead the group.

1. Begin with deep breathing, moving the air up slowly into the chest and holding it, and then release the air as slowly as possible.

2. Repeat, exhaling to the sound of "ahhhhh." Mouths should be open wide, and members should be encouraged to make as much noise as possible.

3. Repeat, this time humming. Ask the group to feel where the hum is in the body—they may find it in the face, the throat, or the chest. When they find it, break the group into pairs and ask them to find each other's hum. Does it change with the note? (It will be in the face when the note is high on the scale and lower as the sound lowers.)

4. Discuss student reactions to the exercise.

## REFERENCES

Altschuler, I. M. 1959. The value of music in geriatrics. In *Music therapy,* ed. E. H. Schneider. Lawrence, Kan.: Allen Press.

Alvin, J. 1966. *Music therapy.* New York: Humanities Press.

Andrews, D. H. 1966. *The symphony of life.* Lee's Summit, Mo.: Unity Books.

Bingham, W. V. 1968. Introduction to the effects of music. In *The effects of music,* ed. M. Schoen. Freeport, N.Y.: Books for Libraries Press.

Bonny, H. L., and L. Savary. 1973. *Music and your mind: Listening with a new consciousness.* New York: Harper & Row.

Bright, R. 1972. *Music in geriatric care.* New York: St. Martin's Press.

Burnside, I. M. 1971. Loneliness in old age. *Mental Hygiene* 55(3): 391–97 (July).

_____. 1973. Touching is talking. *American Journal of Nursing* 73 (December): 2060–63.

Butler, R. N. 1975. *Why survive? Being old in America.* New York: Harper & Row.

Carapetyan, A. 1948. Music and medicine in the Renaissance and in the 17th and 18th centuries. In *Music and medicine,* ed. D. Schullian. New York: Schuman.

Cohen, E. 1976. Implications for health and social services. Paper presented at Public Policy Forum, Western Gerontological Society meeting, San Diego, Calif., March.

Critchley, M., and R. A. Henson. 1977. *Music and the brain.* Springfield, Ill.: Thomas.

Diserens, C. M., and H. A. Fine. 1939. *A psychology of music: The influence of music on behaviour.* Cincinnati, Oh.: H. A. Fine.

Gaston, E. T. 1968. *Music in therapy.* New York: Macmillan.

Green, E., and A. Green. 1977. *Beyond biofeedback.* New York: Dell.

Guntheil, E. A., J. T. Wright, U. R. Fisichelli, F. Paperte, and A. Capurso. 1952. *Music and your emotions.* New York: Liveright.

Hennessey, M. J. 1976. Music and group work with the aged. In *Nursing and the aged,* 1st ed. I. M. Burnside. New York: McGraw-Hill.

Hyde, I. M. 1968. Effects of music upon electrocardiograms and blood pressure. In *The effects of music,* ed. M. Schoen. Freeport, N.Y.: Books for Libraries Press.

Keyes, L. 1973. *Toning: The creative power of the voice.* Santa Monica, Calif.: DeVorss.

LeCron, L. M. 1964. *Self-hypnotism.* Englewood Cliffs, N.J.: Prentice-Hall.

Licht, S. 1946. *Music in medicine.* Boston: New England Conservatory of Music.

Meinecke, B. 1948. *Music and medicine in classical antiquity.* In *Music and medicine,* ed. D. Schullian. New York: Schuman.

Ostrander, S., and L. Schroeder, with N. Ostrander. 1979. *Superlearning.* New York: Delacorte Press.

Stevens, W. 1936, 1964. The idea of order at Key West. In *The collected poems of Wallace Stevens.* New York: Knopf.

## BIBLIOGRAPHY

Armstrong, M. 1974. *Music therapy and physical exercises for frail elderly residents of a therapeutic community.* Ann Arbor, Mich.: University of Michigan–Wayne State University.

Bigelow, N., and P. Reuben. 1970. Music in milieu. *Psychiatric Quarterly* 44:502–15.

Bonny, H. L. 1975. Music and consciousness. *Journal of Music Therapy,* Fall.

_____. 1978. *The role of taped music in the G.I.M. process, Theory and product.* Baltimore: I.C.M. Books.

Bright, R. 1981. Music and the management of grief reactions. In *Nursing and the aged.* 2d ed., ed. I. M. Burnside. New York: McGraw-Hill.

Douglass, D. 1978. *Happiness is music, music, music! Music activities for the aged.* Salem, Ore.: La Roux Enterprises.

Eagle, C. 1976. *Music therapy index.* Lawrence, Kan.: National Association of Music Therapy.

Kartman, L. L. 1977. The use of music as a program tool with regressed geriatric patients. *Journal of Gerontological Nursing* 3(4): 38–42 (July–August).

Masters, C., and C. Masters. 1970. *Experimental research in music.* Englewood Cliffs, N.J.: Prentice-Hall.

*Music the healer, A bibliography.* 1970. Institutional Library Services, Olympia, Ore.

Plach, T. 1981. *The creative use of music in group therapy.* Springfield, Ill.: Thomas.

Pullman, L. 1982. Reaching the confused and withdrawn through music. *Aging:* (Nos. 333–334): 7–11 (November–December).

Rubin, B. 1976. Handbells in therapy. *Journal of Music Therapy,* Spring: 49–53.

Rudhyar, D. 1982. *The magic of tone and the art of music.* Boulder, Colo.: Shambhala.

Sackett, J., and J. Fitzgerald. 1980. Music in hospitals. *Nursing Times* 76:1845–48.

## RESOURCES

### Lists of Suggested Musical Selections for Special Moods

*Music and Your Mind: Listening with a New Consciousness.* By H. L. Bonny and L. Savary. New York: Harper & Row, 1973.

### Taped Music to Enhance the Relaxation Response

*Emmett E. Miller,* 945 Evelyn Street, Menlo Park, CA 94025.

*Halpern Sounds,* 1775 Old County Road, #9, Belmont, CA 94002.

*Institute for Consciousness and Music,* 31 Allegheny Avenue, Room 104, Towson, MD 21204 or (West Coast outlet) *Third Life Center,* 385 Bellevue Avenue, Oakland, CA 94610.

### Tapes Developed by Mary Jane Hennessey

*For deep relaxation:* A string quartet playing Baroque music with a metronome beat of 60, that is, one beat per second.

*For mood change:* From very sad or depressed to a happier state. Developed using the Iso principle, that is, like acting on like. Tape moves from the slow, repetitive rhythm of Handel's *Largo,* slowly changing in rhythm and tone to a bright Mozart selection.

*A sing-along tape:* Two, 30 minutes each, using very familiar music from the turn of the century through 1940. Piano, Bob Phillips; voice and violin, Mary Jane Hennessey.

Tapes available from: M. J. Hennessey, Box 1592, Carmel, Ca 93921.

### Songs in Large Print

*Sing Along Senior Citizens.* By Roy Grant. Springfield, Ill: Thomas, 1973. One hundred songs.

### Chanting and Toning Guides

*Gentle Living Publications,* 2168 South Lafayette, Denver, CO 80210. Cassette available.

*Toning: The Creative Use of the Voice.* By L. Keyes. Santa Monica, Calif.: De Vorss, 1973. Paperback to complement tape.

### Price Lists and Descriptions of Glockenspiels, Drums, Cymbals, Castanets, and So On

*Children's Music Center,* 5373 West Pico Boulevard, Los Angeles, CA 90019.

*Magnamusic-Baton,* 6390 Delmar Boulevard, St. Louis, MO 63130.

*Music Education Group,* Box 1501, Union, NM 07083.

*Rhythm Band,* P.O. Box 126, Fort Worth, TX 76101.

### Guide for Handbell Ringing

*Handbell Ringing: A Musical Introduction.* By Scott Parry. Available from Fisher, 62 Cooper Square, New York, NY 10003.

### Catalog for Handbell Music

*C. F. Peters Corporation,* 373 Park Avenue South, New York, NY 10016.

### Information on Orff Schulwerk Instruments

*Francis Goldberg,* Langley Porter Psychiatric Institute, San Francisco, CA.

*Joe Fioretti,* 415½ Livermore Avenue, Livermore, CA 94550.

### Information on the Fields of Music Therapy and Dance Therapy and Lists of Accredited College Programs

*American Dance Therapy Association,* Suite 216–E, 100 Century Plaza, Columbia, MD 21044.

*National Association for Music Therapy,* P.O. Box 610, Lawrence, KS 66044.

# chapter 18

# Dance/Movement Therapy

*Heather Booth*

*Those who think they have no time for bodily exercise will sooner or later have to find time for illness.*

EDWARD STANLEY, EARL OF DERBY (1873)

DIANE GENTRY/BLACK STAR

## LEARNING OBJECTIVES

- Create one musical exercise and one dance movement activity to use with elders.

- Describe the history of dance/movement therapy.

- Coordinate dance/movement therapy with other disciplines.

- Acquire an increased movement repertoire to use with elders.

- Describe ill effects that may occur in dance/movement therapy.

- Educate staff about dance/movement therapy and its usefulness as a therapeutic approach in the mental health field.

- Instruct group members about efficient postural habits.

## KEY WORDS

- Dance/movement

- Dance therapy

- Expressive movement

- Flower exercise

- Hyperextend

- Korsakoff's syndrome

- Tardive dyskinesia

- Warm-up exercises

Who was Marion Chase? She was a dancer who was able to recognize the need for people who were not dancers to express their emotional feelings through movement. She developed dance therapy as it is known today. How and when did dance therapy develop? During the 1930s, Chase returned to Washington, D.C., her hometown, and opened a dance school. She taught students who were outpatients from St. Elizabeth's Psychiatric Hospital in Washington, D.C. These residents were referred to Chase because the medical staff felt that dancing could help them with their physical and emotional problems. The hospital staff observed that the patients benefited a great deal from Chase's classes. Chase (1953) is recommended.

In 1940 Chase started to work as a Red Cross volunteer at St. Elizabeth's Hospital; she created the first dance therapy program in an American psychiatric hospital. Chase's dedication and determination helped her students to establish the American Dance Therapy Association in 1964. Since that time, dance therapy has played an important role in nonverbal communication and has aided people with emotional, physical, language, and learning disorders.

The American Dance Therapy Association believes that dance therapy can be defined as "the nonverbal psychotherapeutic use of expressive movement as a process which attempts to further the emotional and physical well-being, integration and functioning of people" (American Dance Therapy Association 1973).

The author would like to acknowledge Don Buehring, Malcolm McKenzie, Brian Elder, Mary Abt, Doreen Scott, Barb Dux, and Judy Weismiller, who helped with this chapter.

Note: There is not a clear distinction between dance therapy and movement therapy. However, movement therapy, which is also practiced by persons knowledgeable in dance therapy, is the broader term.

To become a dance therapist in the United States, the association requires 400 hours of field work followed by a thesis, and then 700 hours of internship in a clinical setting. The internship is followed by two years of full-time paid employment as a dance therapist, preferably in a psychiatric setting. On top of all the academic preparation, a dance therapist is also expected to have at least five years of dance training in ballet or modern technique. Dance therapists are advised to have some experience in the performing arts. The rationale is to ensure that the person is interested in becoming a dance therapist and is not a frustrated performer.

This does not imply that dance therapists cannot perform while working with disturbed or normal people, but therapists must feel comfortable with their profession.

## PURPOSE OF DANCE THERAPY FOR BRAIN-DAMAGED ADULTS

Margit Asselstine is a dance/movement therapist in Toronto. She has worked in various nursing homes and maintains that "dance therapy groups allow participants the opportunity to work effectively around any such real disabilities, and to better understand and utilize capacities they do possess" (Asselstine 1980, 1).

The older person is often reminded of what he or she cannot do. In a dance therapy session an individual is encouraged to try to do the best he or she can without criticism or judgment. The main focus of dance therapy is to encourage people to communicate at a nonverbal level, which will lead to verbal discussion—for example, asking how they felt about the session. During the verbal discussion, social awareness is increased by helping people to express their feelings and to share them with other members in the group.

Some professionals ask, "Why is dance therapy beneficial for the elderly?" Much attention is focused on the physical care of the elderly. Although proper medical care is necessary, so is attention to the emotional aspects of caring for the elderly. Many older people suffer from loneliness, loss of self-esteem, and lack of independence. Dance therapy cannot promise a cure for all these problems; however, it can aid in making people feel better about themselves through exercising, moving to music, and physical contact. "Regular body exercise," according to Hans and Sulomach Krietler, "can provide emotional satisfaction. It can break the vicious cycle in which body image distortion caused by inactivity leads to more inactivity and further distortions" (Caplow-Lindner, Harpaz, and Samberg 1979, 80).

Dance therapy also deals with the "here and now." Many mentally impaired people also suffer from aphasia or other language difficulties; dance therapy can help these people at the nonverbal level.

A summary of some of the characteristics of dance/movement therapy with the elderly, as well as patient responses to it, follows. The material is adapted from Margit Asselstine (1980).

- Primary goal in a dance therapy session is to stimulate communication through the body.
- Size of group is restricted to 10 or 12 persons.
- Group members must be positioned so that everyone is able to see and hear one another.
- Feeling of intimacy is cultivated as members become familiar with the group and the activities.
- Emphasis is on having fun during the sessions.
- Participants gain a greater range of movement.
- Participants' cardiovascular functioning improves.
- Senses are stimulated.
- Participants learn to relax and breathe effectively.
- Dance therapy helps participants effectively to work around their disabilities.
- Dance therapy increases self-awareness and social-sharing skills.
- Participants' attention to specific problems —for example, arthritis—may decrease.
- Self-worth and importance evolves.

- A change of attitude and improvements in grooming, posture, and expression may result.
- Dance therapy is a pleasurable, meaningful activity that stimulates both physical and psychosocial functioning.

## HOW TO WORK WITH OTHER PROFESSIONALS IN THE FIELD

The dance therapist will need to work with doctors and nurses and other team members to develop a better understanding in handling confused residents. Malcolm McKenzie,* a head nurse on one of the geriatric units at the Alberta Hospital, Ponoka, makes the point that sometimes the staff can be confused. The confused patient may realize what he or she is saying; however, due to a brain disorder the patient's communication process is affected, making it difficult for the staff to understand what the patient is trying to say. To establish understandable communication with confused elderly residents, there are a few basic rules to follow. Don Buehring,† a psychiatric nurse on a geriatric unit, suggests that *"listening is the most single important tool."* Because of the brain disorder, much of what is said is disjointed or garbled. The more you allow your client to speak, the clearer his or her intent will become. You have to recognize that what is being said may not always be sequential. Once the resident's meaning has been clearly established, it is the therapist's turn to communicate in a manner that can be understood. Old people who are confused often lose the capacity to communicate on an abstract level. Directions, instructions, or conversation must be carried on in simple, easy-to-understand language. Abstract communication, metaphors, similes, and such, should be avoided because they may increase the confusion.

Brian Elder, head nurse, has worked with confused older adults for many years. He feels that one should never give up on them. Like Buehring, he claims that if you give a confused person enough time to comprehend an instruc-tion, the resident will eventually do the task. Elder‡ states that it helps the resident to focus on an idea if he or she can repeat the commands, especially if the patient seems preoccupied with other thoughts. Elder also believes that exercising is extremely important for this type of resident, especially if the person has arthritis or contracture or stiffness of the joints.

If the dance therapist's approach in dealing with confused clients is consistent with that of the nursing staff, there is a good chance that the residents will feel more comfortable during the dance session.

## GUIDELINES FOR THE DANCE THERAPIST WORKING WITH CONFUSED OLDER ADULTS

A dance therapist must have a basic understanding of the medical problems older people have so that the therapist will not make unrealistic physical demands upon the participants. There are many medical factors that a movement therapist should take into consideration during the session: arthritis, diabetes, congestive heart failure, tardive dyskinesia, and Korsakoff's syndrome.

Arthritis affects a great many old people. The dance therapist has to recognize the severity of the disease and how much range of movement remains so that the exercises that are introduced (usually gentle stretching and opening of the arms) do not evoke too much pain. Diabetes entails poor circulation to the extremities; in severe cases, the feet may be prone to injury (for example, cuts, bruises, and so forth). If the person has severe diabetes, strenuous exercise may cause a reaction.

The dance therapist must also note the type of heart problem an individual has because patients who have heart conditions such as angina, congestive heart failure, pacemakers, and arrhythmias should not participate in overly strenuous sessions. They should do stretching and swinging exercises with the arms and some exercises involving bending forward and to the side. Any energetic locomotor movements, such as running, jumping, or polka dance steps, should be avoided. Be sure to check with a

---

*Personal communication, 1981.
†Personal communication, 1981.

---

‡Personal communication, 1981.

nurse or doctor before administering these movements.

Tardive dyskinesia is a condition caused by the use of antipsychotic medications. This condition causes rigidity of movement, a shuffling gait, and poor circulation. Many residents who have been institutionalized for extended periods take antipsychotic drugs and may manifest some or all of these Parkinson-like symptoms. When working with these individuals in body movement exercises, all these symptoms must be taken into account and dealt with according to severity.

Korsakoff's syndrome is a disease that affects the intellectual processes of the brain; it is caused by chronic alcoholism. This type of patient needs a lot of attention from the therapist or nurse. The resident suffers from disorientation and memory defect and is susceptible to both auditory and visual hallucinations. The dance therapist's instructions must be clear when working with a Korsakoff's person or the patient may become confused and frustrated.

These are a few examples of many possible medical complications that one should be aware of while conducting a dance therapy session.

It is strongly recommended that the dance therapist attend patient team-conferences to get to know the patients better. These meetings also offer the movement therapist an opportunity to discuss with professionals problems that have occurred during the dance sessions.

If there are other activities on the unit, such as remotivation groups, it may be helpful to participate in these sessions when possible. Participation allows the dance therapist to observe what other staff members are doing with the residents and to see how they respond to various activities. For example, Mrs. Brown is not responding to movement sessions very well, but she really does enjoy the remotivation groups. The dance therapist can learn what techniques used by the remotivation therapist work best and incorporate them into the next dance therapy session. Also, the dance and remotivation therapists can support each other when needed because working with brain-damaged adults can be very difficult at times.

It is vital to have staff participation during a dance/movement therapy session, especially with low-functioning residents. It is unrealistic

for one person to conduct these sessions alone, because the therapist will become frustrated and may give up. These residents need one-to-one attention during the session. The therapist cannot merely give instructions; he or she must become involved. In other words, the therapist should make direct physical contact, such as helping a person move her arms until she can manage to do it alone.

The dance therapist must be very well organized during the session, because most patients who have organic mental disorders have short attention spans. The therapist must not waste precious time searching for music on the tape recorder or looking for rhythm instruments that were left at home. If a session is unorganized, it is difficult to regain the group's attention. It would be beneficial if the therapist had all instruments laid out, so that the residents could see them and choose what instrument they would like to play. (This also applies to other materials used during the session.)

## DANCE THERAPY SESSION FORMAT

A dance therapy session begins with a small circle of people, no more than 10. The circle helps everyone feel closer to each other, and it also offers good visibility and reduces anxiety. The circle encourages socialization with other members in the group, for there is an opportunity to make eye contact with each other. Eye contact may be extremely difficult for older adults who have spent many years in psychiatric hospitals and have not socialized with people for years. They may have a low level of trust.

Dance therapy may be a new concept for some of the residents; therefore, it is important to create an atmosphere in which they feel secure and unthreatened. An eager dance therapist may start introducing too many ideas at once, and the patients may feel that they cannot comprehend everything that is happening. This does not mean that one should condescend to the group, but that it is important to recognize when the group is ready to learn something new.

It helps to encourage the residents to suggest some things to do in the session, such as singing and thinking of various ways of moving their arms or other body parts. Such decisions give the clients an opportunity to feel that they play an important role in contributing their own ideas.

The first thing to do in a dance therapy session is for the therapist to introduce herself or himself, and to explain briefly why they are there—for example, the therapist may inform the group that this is an opportunity to have some fun while doing gentle stretching, relaxation, and dancing exercises. The therapist should stress that one does not have to be an excellent dancer to participate and might suggest that members be willing to try new ideas and to enjoy themselves while working with others in the group.

It is also suggested that the dance therapist shake everyone's hand; most old people are familiar with this social interaction. Such an introduction is nonthreatening, and it gives the therapist an opportunity to make physical contact. This method is also used in other group modalities.

If a resident is very confused, it will take longer to make eye contact; therefore, it is important not to rush through introductions. Although this form of introduction may not be received the first time, the therapist must continue the approach until a response is received.

Next, it is time for the residents to introduce themselves. Although they may live together on the units, the chances are great that they do not know one another's names or that they may have forgotten them. A good exercise is to have each resident say his or her name and shake hands with the person on both sides. Hearing the name reinforces it in the mind of the neighbor, and shaking the neighbor's hand is an opportunity for social contact.

Another way in which people can introduce themselves is through the use of rhythm. Each member of the group claps, stamps, or pounds out his or her name. The therapist demonstrates first so that everyone will understand. For example, the name "Margaret" has three syllables in it. Therefore, the name can be broken down into three sections, "Mar-gar-et." The therapist claps out the name and everyone repeats it. The group can work with many names with various numbers of syllables—for example, Har-vey, Don-ald, Geor-ge. When the group has adjusted to this new idea, the

therapist can play various names on a tambourine, and the residents can guess which name is being played.

To make this particular exercise more interesting, the resident is free to use a rhythm instrument to beat out his or her name. The patient can also combine his name with someone else's to make different rhythm combinations. This rhythm exercise can become fairly complicated, so it should be introduced slowly to the group. This exercise should not be presented to the group during the first session; members would become frustrated. The best time to use it is after the therapist has been working with the group twice weekly for a month.

## WARMING-UP EXERCISES

A warm-up is essential for the elderly because some of them have not exercised for years and have many medical problems. It is important for the warm-up to start as simply as possible and gradually lead into other exercises. Since warm-up exercises are simple to follow, this will allow the group to feel more comfortable during the session and to develop self-confidence. D. Benjamin (1980, p. 4), an expert in musculoskeletal injuries, maintains that a good warm-up accomplishes the following goals:

1. The blood flow to the muscles increases, raising their temperature, and making them more resilient and pliable.

2. The breathing rate gradually increases as the diaphragm muscles warm-up enabling the respiratory system to meet the increased demand for oxygen.

3. The heart rate increases, allowing more oxygen-filled blood to be carried to the muscles.

4. The joints, throughout the body, are lubricated to reduce the stress of rapid or sudden movements.

5. Nerve impulses travel more quickly through the warmed tissues, enabling the body to respond more rapidly and effectively to commands.

Before starting any warm-up exercises, it is important for the therapist to observe how people are sitting or standing. If someone is slumped over to one side of the chair, instruction and guidance will be needed for relearning proper posture.

The term *misuse* was developed by Matthias Alexander (Barlow 1979), who believed people could overcome many physical discomforts, such as headaches, postural difficulties, hypertension, and various muscular disorders. Alexander felt that people developed poor postural habits through slouching, sitting to one side of the chair, or standing with shoulders rounded and neck protruding. These postural habits create a great deal of muscular tension in the neck, shoulders, and muscles along the spinal cord. Incorrect posture also reinforces poor breathing habits. This develops rigid movement of the diaphragm and promotes shallow breathing, meaning that breathing is taking place only in the upper chest rather than flowing easily throughout the abdomen and the lower back. Barlow (1979, 196) asks the question, "Are you moving your chest and abdomen in front when you start to breath in? Breathing in is a back activity. If you start breathing in by raising your upper chest in front, it is like trying to open an umbrella by pulling on the cover from the outside at the top. It can be done, but it is inefficient."

Alexander's goal was to help people achieve a balanced physical use of the body in movement or at rest, with the minimum amount of stress and tension. Integrating Alexander's philosophy of movement into a geriatric dance therapy session would be most beneficial, because this technique allows the older person to move without developing muscular strain. Ideally, most relaxation exercises take place lying down on a thin mat; however, in some nursing homes and hospitals this is not possible because of lack of mats or space. Some older people prefer not to lie down because they cannot see what is going on or feel uncomfortable in this position. If the people in the group are confused, it is better to have everyone sitting in a small circle.

## Breathing Exercise

The breathing exercise should start with everyone sitting as straight as possible in the chair. Don't tell them to throw their shoulders back and stick out their chest; this only causes discomfort and tightening of the shoulder mus-

cles. It also hyperextends the lower back. Show them a comfortable way to sit. For example, if a resident is sitting too far over to the right side, suggest that he or she move over to the center. Ask members to uncross their legs for a few minutes, at least until the relaxation part is over. Uncrossing the legs will aid relaxation and decrease tension in the muscles. This is also good for persons who have varicose veins or phlebitis.

When everyone looks alert and ready, introduce a simple-to-follow breathing technique like this one. Ask participants to place their hands on their rib cages so that they can feel the movement in the diaphragm. Instruct them to breathe deeply and feel the diaphragm expand as they inhale. Now as they slowly release the breath, tell them to be aware of the diaphragm narrowing. Make sure that they release the breath slowly while exhaling. Most breathing exercises have you inhale on four counts; then you are given eight counts to exhale. *This is fine for alert older adults; however, it is not recommended for brain-damaged residents because they will become frustrated in trying to concentrate on too many demands.* An alternative is to have members try the breathing exercise twice; then have them place their hands on top of their stomachs so that they can feel the breath circulate throughout the abdomen. They can also place their hands on the lower back and feel the breathing flow through that area as well. If some of the clients are having problems locating these areas, a helper can assist them with the exercise by placing their hands on their diaphragm, stomach, and lower back.

Do not spend too much time on breathing exercises; usually five minutes is long enough.

There are regular warm-up exercises for the head, shoulders, torso, arms, hands, legs, and feet. None of the stretching or swinging exercises should be done quickly; the muscles need to have time to adjust to exercising again and to relax. If you want to move a little faster later on in the session, that is all right so long as the group has had an adequate warm-up.

## Head and Neck Exercises

Many elderly people have problems turning their necks. There is so much tension stored in the muscles that spread upward into the head and downward over the shoulders. That is why it is necessary for them to turn the head slowly without jerking any muscles. You may discover that some have little movement range in their necks. If their movements are badly affected, then it would be advisable to have the physiotherapist assess the individual. Some of these ailments, such as rheumatoid arthritis or osteoarthritis, need more treatment than just exercising. Often massage or heat treatment is more beneficial and less painful for these people. After the resident has received physiotherapy and feels better, then a dance therapy session can be a follow-up program.

Neck, shoulder, and arm exercises help release tension and loosen up. For the following exercise, the neck should be centered, the arms and shoulders relaxed, and the spine centered in the chair. Slowly draw the head back as far as possible; then drop the head slowly forward, chin toward the chest; then bring the head back to center. Next, slowly turn the head to the right side, back to the center, and turn to the left. The exercise is done to a count of four.

No  1. Extend the head backward; then center.

2. Bring the head toward the chin; then center.

3. Turn the head to the right; then center.

4. Turn the head to the left; then center.

**Do not perform this exercise standing up, because it can create dizziness.**

### Shoulder Exercises

If there is stiffness in the neck, most likely this tension will travel down the shoulder muscles. Here is an exercise for the shoulders. As in the neck exercise just described, the shoulders must move up, down, and around *slowly* so that the exercise does not place a lot of strain on the neck and shoulder muscles. The arms must be by the person's side before starting.

1. Raise the shoulders slowly toward the ears; then slowly lower them. (Do this twice.)

2. Circle the shoulders slowly forward, making two or three complete rotations.

3. Reverse the exercise so that the shoulders are rotated backward; make two or three complete rotations.

Suzy Prudden's "back of my hand" exercise is another excellent relief for neck and shoulder tension. Prudden and Suzzman (1975, 146) suggest that this exercise should be done standing up. However, with older people who have medical problems, it is best if participants sit down.

Start off with arms at your sides. Bend your right arm at the elbow; now raising it, placing the back of your hand against your right cheek. Now swing your hand away from your face, straighten your arm, swing arm backwards, as if you were doing the backstroke. Repeat the same movement with your left hand and arm. Do this four times.

### Arm Exercises

Arm exercises help loosen up tight muscles along the shoulders, upper back, and neck. While introducing the arm exercises, play music with a ¾ time signature.

1. Allow the arms to hang loosely by the sides; then raise them up in front of the body and move the arms from side to side. The therapist can encourage everyone to move their arms at various levels: close to the knees, at the waist, and above the head. This gives members an opportunity to move at their own pace and discover different ways of moving their arms.

2. Arm swings are fun to do, and this exercise is also good for following directions. Start off with arms hanging by the sides. Swing the arms forward and back. This is a creative exercise, for it can be done at any speed and can also incorporate different levels of movement as well.

3. The next arm exercise can be done like the crawl stroke. Swing the right arm forward and the left arm back; then reverse the arms.

### Hand and Finger Exercises

This exercise, which was created by Karen Zebroff (1971, 53), a Yoga specialist, is called the flower. It focuses on easing the pain of arthritis and helps loosen stiff fingers. It also assists in improving circulation in the hands and fingers.

1. Sit in a comfortable position.
2. Squeeze the fingers of each hand together, making a fist.
3. Open the hands slowly, as though they were tight buds slowly expanding into bloom.
4. Relax the fingers by moving or shaking them.

You can have the group circle (rotate) their wrists; this promotes wrist mobility. Then extend the movement to the arms by having the group rotate their arms, first in one direction and then in the other, as if drawing a circle.

## Torso Exercises

This exercise is for developing more flexibility in the torso, shoulders, and spine. These movements should be done slowly so that the muscles have a chance to warm up without too much strain.

1. Have each person sit comfortably in a chair. If some of the participants would like to stand, they may do so. The hands should be at the sides.
2. Turn the hips, chest, and shoulders toward the right side, keeping the feet and knees facing front; only the upper part of the body should rotate. Do this exercise twice to each side.
3. To make the torso exercise more enjoyable, one can use scarves or 2-inch-wide strips of cloth about 24 to 30 inches long. Have the hands resting in the lap; hold one end of the cloth in each hand. (If the material is too long, wrap the cloth around the hands to shorten it.)
4. Raise the arms to waist height, keeping the hands together. Stretch the arms to the sides, making the cloth taut; then raise the cloth over the head. Once it is over the head, lean to the right and back to the center; then lean to the left and back to the center.

5. If the group is fairly flexible, have them try to rotate the torso. Keeping their arms apart above their heads and holding onto the cloth, have them bend the upper part of the body forward at the waist. Then rotate the torso in a circle. *Do not instruct participants to bend backward, especially if they have back problems.*

It is important to know whether the group you are working with is able to do the torso exercises.

## Leg, Ankle and Foot Exercises

Leg, ankle, and foot exercises can be done either standing or sitting down. If a participant has problems balancing on one foot, the person should sit down.

1. *Leg lifts:* Bring the right knee toward the chest; then slowly extend the leg and bring it down. Repeat the same movement on the left side. Do the exercise twice for each leg.
2. *Ankle rotations:* Sit in the chair, extend the right foot, and make a complete circle with the ankle. Do not force the ankle around. People who have swelling or arthritis in the ankle joints may have problems with this exercise. If so, have them turn their feet slowly to the right and then to the left.
3. *Point-and-flex:* This exercise is good for the lower calf muscles, ankles, and feet. It is important to work with the whole foot.
   a. Place both feet on the floor; now slowly raise the heel of the right foot so that only the ball of the foot is on the floor; make sure the toes are lengthened and not tense. Bring the heel back down slowly, allowing time to stretch the muscles in the foot. Repeat with the left foot.
   b. Keeping the heel of the right foot on the floor, flex the ankle to raise the foot off the floor; then gradually bring the foot down. Next, repeat the process keeping the ball of the foot on the floor and lifting the heel. Make sure that all the muscles are working. Repeat with the left foot.

Feet exercises are boring to do. It helps a great deal to make a rhythmic pattern to go with these exercises. For example, point/flex the foot two times; then circle the foot inward four times. Repeat the same exercise again, except circle the foot outward.

A good-sounding rhythm instrument—such as a tambourine, drum, wooden maracas, or xylophone—could be used during these exercises.

## MUSIC AND MOVEMENT

Using different types of music can promote various types of movement. For example, use very soft, delicate music for relaxation and flowing movements. Fast, staccato music can make the session more interesting and fun.

Ask the residents what kind of music they enjoy; then see whether you can find the albums to record on to cassette tapes, which are easy to carry. Bluegrass music is excellent for energetic movements, especially for hand clapping and foot stomping. It takes time to learn what music works the best for your movement groups.

It is also wise to assess the abilities of the group members. An example of an assessment form (prepared by H. Krietler and S. Krietler) can be found in Caplow-Lindner, Harpaz, and Samberg (1979, 246–47).

## DANCE THERAPY GUIDELINES

Some guidelines for dance therapy for hospitalized geriatric patients are presented here. They are adapted from Arlynne Samuels (1974, 29).

1. Start with small and familiar movements that can then be developed into larger ones using other areas of the body.

2. Do not aim to change the patient's personality, but rather work toward adjustment to the present reality.

3. Try to get staff members' understanding and support of the program.

4. If the staff is resistant or poorly educated, give inservice training or workshops on dance therapy.

5. Work with small groups of patients (groups of two to four) rather than one large group.

6. Integrate those who are mobile or can stand with those who must be in chairs.

7. Share a movement interaction, a past experience, or present feelings.

8. Discover commonalities to help members relate better.

9. Consider how to overcome resistance to movement because of pain.

10. As the therapist, be prepared to handle the death or severe illness of one of the group members.

## SOCIAL DANCING

The dance therapist can go to each member of the group and dance. This gives the therapist an opportunity to work with the residents on an individual basis. This approach is important for confused elderly people.

*This 90-year-old gentleman walks with crutches but dances with help from the group leader.*

It is an opportune time to give as much eye contact as possible. It is not important to teach steps to this population; in fact, it can be confusing and frustrating to the participants. Just let them move to the music on their own time. The residents may remember some old steps that they learned during their lifetime.

"Creative movement promotes health and integration of the self through rhythmic breathing, relaxation techniques and principles of body movement in conjunction with music, imagery, and nonverbal self-expression. Creative use of the physical modality along with these other activities in turn strengthens the emotional, psychological, and social aspects of the self; thus a positive feedback loop is begun" (Boots and Hogan 1981, 30).

## SUMMARY

This chapter described dance/movement therapy from its origins and development to the present. It is intended to give some examples of what might be done with our elderly population in institutions. The main point to be stressed is a multidisciplinary approach utilizing all available resource people. Suggestions and cautions were spelled out in detail.

It seems appropriate to end this chapter with a quote from Boots and Hogan (1981, 30).

> The elderly find re-creation of normal activities of daily living both entertaining and stimulating—motions such as those involved in kneading bread or hoeing in a garden. Movements associated with favorite social dances are also conducive to a relaxed atmosphere for creative movement. Rhythmic swaying to music that was popular during the client's younger days can be done sitting in a wheelchair or standing. American culture stresses youthfulness and thus makes it difficult for elderly persons to focus on physical beauty; appropriate music provides the needed impetus to move away from long-established negative feelings toward the physical self."

## EXERCISE 1

Explore sounds reminiscent of childhood, picture those sounds, and talk to and about those sounds. This is a valuable exercise because it encourages identification of feelings, opens up communication, and produces interesting information and because reminiscing is effective in increasing self-esteem.

1. To promote relaxation and awareness of breathing, leader says, "Feel air enter chest and then leave chest" for three complete breaths.

2. Let mind wander to sounds of past experiences and choose one that is pleasant.

3. Listen to selected sound and notice what feelings emerge. Some time and encouragement is given to the participant when necessary to stay with the feelings evoked.

4. Imagine how that sound would look if it were put into a picture with color and shape. Leader brings patients' awareness back to the present, and asks patients to draw their sound.

## EXERCISE 2

This exercise is good for those patients with short-term memory loss.

1. Assembling the group requires two people: One is the escort; the other remains to hold the patients' attention until the group is assembled.

2. Chairs are arranged in a circle. Group members are encouraged to remove shoes for comfort. If possible, have patients sit on the floor in the middle of the circle.

3. The leader initiates a discussion on the difficulty of remembering things and/or people. The leader also expresses his or her difficulty in this area. (See Hennessy's comments in Chapter 17.)

4. Begin each group session with the simple exercise of remembering and saying each other's names.

5. Talk about listening to music in a relaxed position—about how it might help each of us to remember beautiful or important times and places and might even take us to exciting, imaginary places if we let our imaginations go with the music.

6. Before beginning the music, ask the members to relax the entire body by tightening and releasing all their muscles. Play quiet but interesting music, for example, the andantes from Brahms symphonies or Chopin. Avoid sudden noises. Avoid music that is too loud or percussive. Choose music that builds in emotional intensity.

## REFERENCES

American Dance Therapy Association. 1974. Introduction. In *Dance therapist in dimension: Depth and diversity.* Proceedings of the Eighth Annual Conference, October 18–21, 1973. Columbia, Md.

Asselstine, M. 1980. The relevance of dance therapy with the elderly. Unpublished paper.

Barlow, W. 1979. *The Alexander technique.* New York: Knopf.

Benjamin, D. 1980. Creating your own warm-up. *Dance Magazine.*

Boots, S., and C. Hogan. 1981. Creative movement and health. *Topics in Clinical Nursing* 3(2): 23–31 (July).

Caplow-Lindner, E., L. Harpaz, and S. Samberg, eds. 1979. *Therapeutic dance movement: Expressive activities for older adults.* New York: Human Sciences Press.

Chase, M. 1953. Dance as an adjunctive therapy with hospitalized children. *Bulletin of the Menninger Clinic* 17:219–55.

Prudden, S., and J. Suzzman. 1975. *Suzy Prudden's family fitness book.* New York: Simon & Schuster.

Samuels, A. S. 1974. Dance therapy for geriatric patients. In *Dance therapist in dimension: Depth and diversity*, 27–30. Columbia, Md.: American Dance Therapy Association.

Stanley, E., Earl of Derby. 1873. *The conduct of life.* Liverpool College, England. December 20.

Zebroff, K. 1971. *The ABC of yoga.* Vancouver, B.C.: Fforbez Enterprises.

## BIBLIOGRAPHY

Anshel, M., and D. Q. Marisi. 1978. Effect of music and rhythm on physical performance. *Research Quarterly* 49(2): 109–113 (May).

Cohen, I., and J. Segall. 1974. Using dance therapy in the extended care facility. *Nursing Homes* 23 (1): 28–30 (December–January).

Goldberg, W., and J. Fitzpatrick. 1980. Movement therapy with the aged. *Nursing Research* 29(6): 339–46 (November–December).

Hecox, B., E. Levine, and D. Scott. 1976. Dance in physical rehabilitation. *Physical Therapy* 56(8): 919–24 (August).

Koslow, S. 1976. New, exciting direction in psychiatry: Dance/music/art therapy. *Mademoiselle,* no. 361 (January).

Owaki, S. 1976. An assessment of dance therapy to improve retarded adults' body image. *Perceptual Motor Skills* 43(2): 21, 1122 (December).

Rudestam, K. 1982. Dance therapy. In *Experiential groups in theory and practice,* ed. K. Rudestam. Monterey, Calif.: Brooks/Cole.

Sandel, S. 1978. Movement therapy with geriatric patients in a convalescent hospital. *Hospital and Community Psychiatry* 29(11): 738–41 (November).

Schoop, T. 1974. *Won't you join the dance?* Palo Alto, Calif.: National Press Books.

Wiswell, R. 1980. Exercise can help at any age. *Generations* 5(2): 25, 36 (November).

## RESOURCES

### Organizations Concerned with Dance

*Adult Education Association of the United States.* 810 18 Street N.W., Washington, DC 20006.

*American Association of Occupational Therapy.* 6000 Executive Boulevard, Rockville, MD 20852.

*American Dance Guild Inc.* 1619 Broadway, Suite 603, New York, NY 10019.

*American Dance Therapy Association Inc.* 2000 Century Plaza, Suite 230, Columbia, MD 21044.

*Committee on Research in Dance.* c/o New York University School of Education, Washington Square, New York, NY 10003.

*Laban Art of Movement Center.* Woburn Hill, Addlestone, Surrey KT15 2QD, England.

*National Therapeutic Recreation Society.* 1601 North Kent Street, Arlington, VA 22209.

*National Dance Association of America.* Alliance for Health, Physical Education and Recreation, 1201 16 Street. N.W., Washington, DC 20036.

*New England Council of Creative Therapies.* 20 Rip Road, Hanover, NH 03755.

### Films, Records, and Cassettes

*Health, Fitness and Leisure for a Quality Life* (16 mm, color, sound, 20 minutes). This film shows various settings in which physical education, dance, and recreation personnel serve in programs for older adults. Order from AAHPERD, c/o The Film Center, 938 K Street N.W., Washington, DC 20001.

*Special Music for Special People* (record or cassette). Consists of 12 musical selections that can be used by those who wish to teach geriatric dance/movement to older persons. Written guide, included, describes activities suitable for ambulatory and/or nonambulatory participants. Lindner-Harpaz, P.O. Box 993, Woodside, NY 11377.

### Exercise Manuals

*Chair Exercise Manual* (Manual and 4 cassettes). An audio-assisted manual for body dynamics, with 120 photographs for both instructors and students. Contains transcriptions of four cassette tapes, to allow the instructor or student to read the transcript and look at the accompanying photographs as he or she listens to each cassette. Beneficial for people with impaired mobility. The manual-cassette combination permits self-instruction and includes lesson plans designed for patients in convalescent hospitals. Princeton Book Company, P.O. Box 109, Princeton, NJ 08540.

*Movement is Life: A Holistic Approach to Exercise for Older Adults* (1981). This three-part exercise program textbook by Eva Garnet presents a therapeutic approach to movement for older persons who are influenced by physical limitations and mental attitudes that reduce activity. Princeton Book Company, P.O. Box 109, Princeton, NJ 08540.

### Books and Pamphlets

*Fifty Positive Vigor Exercises for Senior Citizens.* A guide encouraging the continued use of each portion of the body to improve balance and maintain good health. Specialized exercises designed for key muscles. 1979 publication no. 245-26690, vol. 3, no. 6. Available from American Alliance Publications, P.O. Box 704, Waldorf, MD 20601.

*Service-Learning: Programs for the Aging.* A guide to practicum and field work experiences in health, fitness, dance, and leisure services. Information on how to establish programs. An appendix includes sample forms for contracts, applications, interviews, and evaluations. Invaluable for persons responsible for the development and coordination of practicum or field work placements. 1980 publication no. 245-26770. Available from American Alliance Publications, P.O. Box 704, Waldorf, MD 20601.

### Modules

*Health, Physical Education, Recreation and Dance for the Older Adult: A Modular Approach.* Eight learning/teaching modules integrate gerontology and the fields of health, physical education, recreation, and dance. Includes general information, suggested learning activities, and a list of resource references. Recommended for those involved in health and activity programs for older adults and for students and teachers of gerontology courses in professional preparation. 1980 publication no. 245-26766; 264 pp. Available from American Alliance Publications, P.O. Box 704, Waldorf, MD 20601.

## Periodicals

*American Journal of Dance Therapy* (semiannual). American Dance Therapy Association, Suite 230, 2000 Century Plaza, Columbia, MD 21044.

*American Journal of Occupational Therapy* (monthly). American Occupational Therapy Association, 6000 Executive Boulevard, Rockville, MD 20852.

*Journal of Leisurability.* Leisurability Publications, Box 281, Ottawa, Ontario, Canada KIN 8V2.

*Rehabilitation Literature*—abstracts and index (monthly). National Easter Seal Society, 2023 West Ogden Avenue, Chicago, IL 60612.

*S.A.G.E. Project News.* National Association for Humanistic Gerontology, Claremont Office Park, 41 Tunnel Road, Berkeley, CA 94705.

*Social Work Journal* (bimonthly). National Association of Social Workers, Suite 600, 1425 H Street N.W., Washington, DC 20005.

*Therapeutic Recreation Journal* (quarterly). National Therapeutic Recreation Society, 1601 North Kent Street, Arlington, VA 22209.

## chapter 19

# Family Sculpting: A Combination of Modalities

*Ardis Martin*

*There are moments in our lives, there are moments in a day, when we seem to see beyond the usual. Such are the moments of our greatest happiness. Such are the moments of our greatest wisdom.*

ROBERT HENRI (1939, 43)

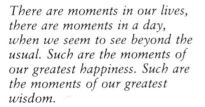

## LEARNING OBJECTIVES

- Describe the treatment modalities that were combined to create family sculpting.

- Define a **sociometric star**.

- Define a **sociometric isolate**.

- Describe the method used to identify the generations during the family sculpting process.

- Define the essential components of the psychodramatic approach.

- Delineate the expected results of family sculpting.

- Describe how the group members participate in family sculpting.

- Explain the purpose of the author's experiment.

## KEY WORDS

- Action sociogram

- Auxiliary actors

- Family sculpture

- Geropsychiatric

- Gestalt

- Protagonist/Star

- Psychodrama

- Work of art

---

I have experimentally combined the psychodrama approach of J. L. Moreno (1959), the family sculpture approach of Albert Serrano,* and the life review approach of Robert Butler (1963) to produce another possibility for integrating one's life by perceiving oneself, not only as one was in the past, but in a new way. I call this approach family sculpting.

I believe that by combining action and a form of visual perception with a structured recall of the past, the older person may be able to bring a newly created form to his or her life. Group therapy, in the words of Rollo May (1975, 140), may be a living-out of a new form. He calls this process "the struggle against disintegration,

the struggle to bring into existence new kinds of being that give harmony and integration."

The purpose of my experimentation with family sculpting was to see if it is possible to create and present for each client a living form that might give harmony and integration to his or her life.

## THEORETICAL FRAMEWORKS

### Life Review Techniques

For several years in my group work I have employed the life review therapy approach developed by Butler (Butler 1963; Lewis and Butler 1974). I have used numerous approaches to encourage clients to recall the past, with the intent of helping them come to terms with their mental illness, and gain an understanding of their mental and emotional faculties. I do agree with Robert Havighurst and R. Glasser (1972)

---

This chapter was originally a paper presented in a class entitled Collette-Meyers Lectures, Texas Tech School of Nursing, Lubbock, Texas, Summer 1982.

*Personal communication at a family therapy workshop, June 4, 1982.

that good morale and adjustment often result from this form of psychotherapy.

Life review therapy is much more effective than unstructured reminiscence. Clients do tend to perform more creatively in a structured situation (Botwinick 1973). During the past eight years, I have done group work with older persons, and I have used many techniques to evoke reminiscence.

## Psychodrama

Moreno (1951, 1953) describes interesting features of a group based on "liking," or attraction, and has used the term *sociometric star*. An unchosen person, or one who does not receive a central position in the group, is a *sociometric isolate*.

Moreno (1959) developed the psychodramatic approach and the sociometric approach. The psychodramatic approach has five essential components: (1) the group, (2) the subject or protagonist (which I call, for clarity, the star), (3) the group leader as director, (4) other group members as auxiliary actors, and (5) a system of methods and techniques adaptable to the requirements of the situation.

## Sociometry and Psychodrama Combined with Family Sculpture

B. Seabourne (1963) reports the psychodramatic approach combined with the well-known sociometric drawing, the sociogram. My experiment is a variation of Seabourne's technique, which she calls an action sociogram. This technique combines Moreno's psychodrama with the family sculpture teachings of Serrano, who uses all the members of a group to achieve a family sculpture. This living sociogram portrays visually an individual among several generations, not only in "near" and "far" dimensions, but also in high and low positions to clarify for the person who is creating the sculpture his or her actual role in his or her own complex family group.

Combining these well-known forms of group therapy produces an active and, I believe, a creative form of life review, because it provides a visual example of the position of the older client among at least four, and sometimes five or six, generations!

## Family Sculpting

The family sculpting approach is a means of obtaining a family history with a wealth of information about family members and the client's relationship to them. The client who becomes the Star also becomes the director of the family sculpture. The Star chooses other group members to play the parts of family members either living or dead; the Star then instructs the group member about the character he or she plays. The group leader acts as director in the following manner: Before the psychodrama begins, the director must inform the Star and auxiliaries about what the task is. Then, as the action proceeds, the leader helps to move the actors where the Star wants them and at the same time develops the living script. The group leader keeps the verbal action moving in the psychodrama and at the same time builds the family sculpture. One side of a room can be used, and in the beginning only one chair is used for the Star. If the Star leaves the chair, the Star's identification tag is placed on this chair, to indicate that the Star is the focal point of the family sculpture at all times.

## TECHNIQUES

### Expected Results of Family Sculpting

The technique presented here will show how a variety of combined techniques can be used to foster a nonthreatening, spontaneous sharing of one's family system, one's place in that system, and one's feelings and conflicts within that system. Older persons are often reluctant to reveal negative information about their families, and in most reminiscence activities I find that they will put their family's best foot forward.

My experience has been that the acting out with other group members of a four-generation family reveals negative family relationships as readily as positive ones.

### Philosophy

The philosophy of the Adult Partial Hospital, a day care institution, is a belief that the suffering of mental illness can be relieved and acute mental illness and institutional care can be prevented by supportive treatment intervention in a day treatment program. It is also the philosophy of the Adult Partial Hospital that this treatment be provided by an interdisciplinary team of highly qualified health professionals who believe that the client must also participate in his or her treatment. This team endeavors to help, comfort, and support the client until he or she can explore alternate ways to handle problems. By experimenting with new ways to approach and manage life, the client can learn to help, comfort, and support himself or herself.

We further believe that we learn from the clients' experience of mental illness and their feelings of hopelessness, fear, and despair. We constantly remind ourselves that change for clients is slow, subtle, and often accompanied by great anguish and pain. We truly believe in and affirm the integration of treatment with empathy.

## Description of Group and Setting

The 12-member group involved in this experiment meets twice each week, on Tuesday and Thursday, and is only one group activity of a structured Adult Partial Hospital treatment program.

Clients are transported to the Adult Partial Hospital by vans between eight and nine o'clock in the morning. Upon arrival, they drink coffee and socialize for about 20 minutes and then go to occupational therapy for 50 minutes. Then after a 10-minute break, they come to group therapy at 10:30 and are dismissed to go to lunch at 11:20. At 12:30, they rest during a relaxation and guided-imagery group on Tuesday and cards or dominoes at the same time on Thursday. At 1:00 the group has music therapy until 1:50, and then members are transported back to their homes in the community.

The meeting place is a cheerful room with a large window looking out on a patio. This room has a bright rug, paintings on the walls, and comfortable chairs arranged in a circle. For our experimental group, one wall was used as a stage. (A platform would be helpful, but as of now we pretend we have a stage.)

Three members of this group have been in our geropsychiatric program for six years, one

member for five years, two members for three years, one for two years, and the other five members from eighteen months to three months. One member is a chronic schizophrenic, two are bipolar disorders, and the other nine have depressions of various diagnoses. All have had acute psychotic episodes and are now considered to be in need of supportive therapy to prevent further psychotic breaks and to help them to live and function in their homes in the community. Table 19–1 lists information about the members of the group.

## Set-Up and Explanation to Group

The use of this particular technique is quite simplified. An explanation of the method and of the goal of the group is given to members as simply as possible. The person who volunteers to become the Star is instructed that he or she is going to create a living sculpture of his or her family using other group members. The member is to start with his or her mother and father.

The group therapist takes a very active role in helping the older client place the family members as he or she describes them. As a member of the group (auxiliary) is chosen to play a family member, the auxiliary is instructed by the Star, who tells the person his or her name and physical description (color of eyes, hair, height, and so forth). The group leader also asks the Star to instruct the auxiliary about the family member's behaviors, habits, and personality. The group therapist then pins identification tags on the auxiliaries. These tags are color coded to identify the generations. Circles are used for females and squares for males. (Figure 19–1 details the identification tag scheme used in this group.) The identification tags are very important because they enable the Star and the group to remember who each family member is. Names are written with a large black felt-tipped pen on paper and are pinned, with the appropriate colored shape, to each participant. The Star is then asked to place each family member in the group with him or her as close or as distant as indicated, depending on the client's perceptions of that family member. A fascinating result of this technique was the enthusiasm with which the auxiliary players assumed and played their characters from the information given to them by the protagonist.

TABLE 19–1. **Members of the group**

| Patient | Age* | Marital Status | Length of hospitalization | Psychiatric diagnosis |
|---------|------|----------------|---------------------------|-----------------------|
| Mrs. M. C. | 66 | Divorced | 7 months | Depression |
| Mrs. E. B. | 64 | Married | 9 months | Depression |
| Mrs. R. G. | 60 | Widowed | 9 months | Bi-polar depression |
| Mrs. F. O. | 64 | Widowed | 1 year | Depression |
| Mr. B. A. | 68 | Married | 2 years | Depression |
| Mrs. A. B. | 72 | Widowed | 3 years | Depression |
| Mr. K. T. | 58 | Married | 3 years | Depression |
| Mrs. L. A. | 72 | Married | 3 years | Depression |
| Mrs. E. M. | 79 | Divorced | 4 years | Bi-polar depression |
| Mrs. M. Q. | 90 | Widowed | 5 years | Depression |
| Mrs. P. P. | 71 | Widowed | 5 years | Schizophrenia |
| Mrs. L. M. | 77 | Divorced | 6 years | Depression |

*Mean age of members = 70.

## WORK OF A STAR

### Description of the First Star

The first group member who volunteered to become the Star was a female who had been attending the group for six years. Of course, the group members and I had learned a great deal about her. However, her psychodramatic family sculpture somehow put the bits and pieces of her life together in a form that was indeed "life as a work of art." An account of her work follows:

This client is a very small woman, a 77-year-old former teacher with a master's degree, who has suffered recurring psychotic depression for the past 20 years. She has been treated with psychotropic medications and with electroconvulsive therapy often. Her obsessive-compulsive personality has made her life miserable because she never felt that she did anything right. However, she writes beautiful poetry and has had a collection of her poetry published. The dialogue that follows describes her family and sculpture.

*Group leader:*
Which parent do you want to start with?
*Star:*
I'll start with my father.
*Group leader:*
Can you choose a group member who can play the role of your father?

*Star:*
Yes. I'll choose K—because he is so sweet looking.
*Group leader:*
Okay, now tell K what he is like: what he looks like, what he did for a living, how you and he got along, and what his personality was like.
*Star:*
Oh, my father was just wonderful. I could wrap him around my little finger, and I told him everything. He was a small man who owned a grocery store, and he always let me help him. He never said a cross word, but he worked day and night.
*Group leader:*
Would you say that you were sort of close to him, close to him, or very close to him?
*Star:*
I was very, very close to him.
*Group leader:*
Place your father in the sculpture we are creating. Would you place him above you, behind you, in front of you, or sitting at your feet?
*Star:*
Oh, I would put him right beside me, even with his arm around me. [The group member playing the part of the father was then seated very close to her with his arm around her.]

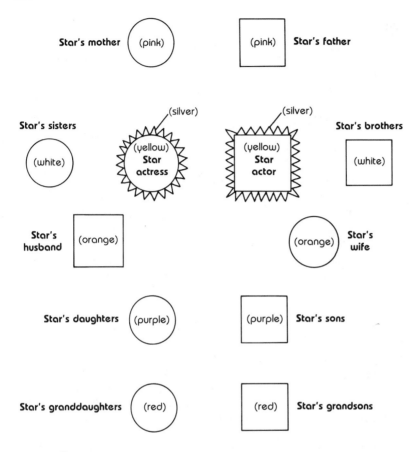

Notes:

1. Squares indicate males; circles indicate females.
2. Pink indicates Star's parents (first generation).
3. Yellow and silver indicate Star (second generation).
4. White indicates Star's brothers and sisters (second generation).
5. Orange indicates Star's spouse (second generation).
6. Purple indicates Star's children (third generation).
7. Red indicates Star's grandchildren (fourth generation).

FIGURE 19–1. *Identification tags used in family sculpting because older people do not see blues and greens as well as other colors. It is best to use vibrant colors for the tags.*

*Group leader:*

Which family member do you want to choose next?

*Star:*

Oh, my mother, I guess.

*Group leader:*

Choose a group member to be your mother and instruct her; tell her what she is like. [She chooses a small, colorless group member.]

*Star:*

My mother was pretty, but kind of an invalid. We didn't get along very well. She wanted me to be perfect, and I just couldn't be. She walked with a cane, and sometimes she hit me with it. She would make me promise not to tell Dad, but I always did and then she would whip me again.

*Group leader:*

How close would you place your mother to you?

*Star:*

Over there lying down, I guess. She stayed in bed so much, and my grandmother took care of her and of me. [She places her mother on two sectional chairs, reclining, about six feet from her and her father.]

*Group leader:*

You mentioned your grandmother. Would you like to put her in your sculpture? If you want to, choose someone to be your grand-mother. [Star chooses a plump client who is the only schizophrenic in the group. This client looks flat but rarely depressed and smiles when spoken to. She is also the most generous of the group.]

*Star:*

My grandmother did most of our work. She sewed for me and cooked most of our meals. She lived near us but not with us.

*Group leader:*

Choose a group member to play your oldest son, and tell him how you experienced him. [Star chooses the other male group member, who is quite handsome, to take the part of her son.]

*Star:*

You became the man of the house when your Dad left us. You were 14 years old, but I could depend on you for everything. You made excellent grades and you excelled in track. You won a scholarship for four years to Texas University.

*Group Leader:*

Were you close to this son?

*Star:*

Yes, very close. He was such a comfort to me, and I was so proud of him.

*Group leader:*

Would you say that he was closer to you than your father or your husband? [Star had described and placed her husband close at first and then several feet away from her.]

*Star:*

He was as close to me as my father—very, very close. [She then placed her son on her other side with his arm around her.]

## Outcome

As her psychodrama unfolded and she built her family sculpture, this client revealed more about herself than she had with other kinds of reminiscence during the past six years. She revealed much about her husband's leaving her for another woman; about keeping her parents in her home until they died (her father at the age of 97 years); her struggle to get her master's degree; her pride in her older son, who became the "man of the house"; and her grief about not getting along well with her younger son, who would not go to college. So much of her life emerged as she built her sculpture—so much more than she had previously shared.

This client was very pleased with her sculpture, and as she and the group discussed her work after the drama, she said, "You know, when I look back at my life, I see that I did a good job considering everything." She smiled and looked very proud when she said this. The group member who played her older son said, "And, boy, did you work hard."

This client died one month after she did her family sculpture. When I visited her sons, one of them said he remembered how hard she worked. She always graded her papers after the boys were in bed, in order to spend more time with them. He remembered going into her room in the middle of the night to remove her glasses and turn off the light.

This woman left the group and me a legacy of her particular sculpture.

## GOALS

### Personal

As a professional, my personal goal for group therapy with my clients has been to use life review, not just as a technique to help them to cope with their mental illnesses and the failures, losses, and disappointments of their lives, but to create more life in the here-and-now and to experience the past in a more present-centered way. In a Gestalt therapy sense (Perls, Heferline, and Goodman 1951), I am encouraging them to trust their own capacities to cope with the "now," using the two basic assumptions of Gestalt therapy: Things at this moment are the only way they can be; and, behold, the world is very good!

Perhaps the goal can be stated in another way. I am experimenting with three combined approaches to group therapy to achieve a new Gestalt, a new form of life review experienced as a creative possibility in the here-and-now. This can provide each member of the group a way to know a unique, authentic experience.

## SUMMARY

The clients who starred in this combined form of group therapy were not only eager to create their individual family sculptures but also excited about participating as auxiliaries in the family sculptures of other group members. The entire experiment had an air of excitement and pleasure. All of the clients expressed a heightened awareness of themselves and others as individuals and as members of a family. As the therapist, I experienced a sense of joy that this unique and creative approach to understanding the individual's experience in his family had helped each client to live out a new form that achieved harmony and integration. Perhaps my feelings can best be expressed by saying that as a therapist and as a nurse I hope that, by helping clients to integrate their lives, I am integrating my practice into my own "life as a work of art."

## EXERCISE 1

Make a set of identification tags of your own family (or an imaginary one) to use to conduct a family sculpture with a group of classmates. (See Figure 19-1 for instructions.)

## EXERCISE 2

Become the "Star" and appoint a class member to act as the therapist. Create your own family sculpture with your class members as auxiliaries.

## EXERCISE 3

Conduct a family sculpture with a group of older persons you know quite well at a senior citizen center, day care center, or nursing home.

## REFERENCES

Botwinick, J. 1973. *Aging and behavior.* New York: Springer.

Butler, R. N. 1963. The life review: An interpretation of reminiscence in the aged. *Psychiatry* 26 (February): 65–76.

Havighurst, R., and R. Glasser. 1972. An exploratory study of reminiscence. *Journal of Gerontology* 27(2): 245–53 (April).

Henri, R. 1939. *The art spirit.* Philadelphia: Lippincott.

Lewis, M. I., and R. N. Butler. 1974. Life review therapy: Putting memories to work in individual and group psychotherapy. *Geriatrics* 29(11): 165–73 (November).

May, R. 1975. *The courage to create,* 135–40. New York: Norton.

Moreno, J. L. 1951. *Sociometry, experimental method and the science of society.* Beacon, N.Y.: Beacon House.

_____. 1953. *Who shall survive?* Beacon, N.Y.: Beacon House.

_____. 1959. A survey of psychodramatic techniques. *Psychotherapy* 12:5–14.

Perls, F., R. Heferline, and P. Goodman. 1951. *Gestalt Therapy.* New York: Crown.

Seabourne, B. 1963. An action sociogram. *Group Psychotherapy* 16(3), September. Guest ed. J. L. Moreno, M.D. Beacon, N.Y.: Beacon House.

---

## BIBLIOGRAPHY

Altholz, J. A. 1978. Group psychotherapy with the elderly. In *Working with the elderly: Group process and techniques,* ed. I. M. Burnside. North Scituate, Mass.: Duxbury Press.

Birkett, D., and B. Boltuch. 1973. Remotivation therapy. *Journal of the American Geriatrics Society* 21(8): 368–371 (August).

Blackman, J. C. 1980. Group work in the community: Experiences with reminiscence. In *Psychosocial nursing care of the aged.* 2d ed., ed. I. M. Burnside, 134–40. New York: McGraw-Hill.

Boylin, W., S. K. Gordon, and M. F. Nehrke. 1976. Reminiscing and ego integrity in institutionalized elderly males. *The Gerontologist* 16(2): 118–24 (April).

Burnside, I. M. 1980. Loss: A constant theme in group work with the aged. *Hospital and Community Psychiatry* 21 (June): 173–77.

Butler, R. N. 1971. Age: The life review. *Psychology Today* 89 (December): 49–50.

Butler, R. N., and M. Lewis. 1973. *Aging and mental Health: Positive psychosocial approaches.* 1st ed., 43–44, 180. St. Louis, Mo.: Mosby.

Cameron, P. 1972. The generation gap: Time orientation. *The Gerontologist* 12(2): 117–19 (Summer).

Donahue, E. M. 1982. Preserving history through oral history reflections. *Journal of Gerontological Nursing* 8(5): 272–78 (May).

Fallico, A. B. 1962. *Art and existentialism.* Englewood Cliffs, N.J.: Prentice-Hall.

Frankl, V. E. 1957. *The doctor and the soul.* 211–14. New York: Knopf.

————. Man's search for meanings: An introduction to logotherapy. New York: Washington Square Press.

Gibson, D. E. 1980. Reminiscence, self-esteem and self-other satisfaction in adult male alcoholics. *Journal of Psychiatric Nursing* 18(3): 7–11 (March).

Goldfarb, A. I. 1971. Group therapy with the old and aged. In *Comprehensive group psychotherapy,* ed. H. J. Kaplan and B. Sadock. Baltimore: Williams & Wilkins.

Guerin, P. 1972. Study your own family. In *The book of family therapy,* ed. A. Ferber, M. Mendelsohn, and A. Napier. Boston: Houghton Mifflin.

Guldner, C. A. 1983. Structuring and staging. *Journal of Group Psychotherapy, Psychodrama and Sociometry,* 35(4): 141–154 (Winter).

Jourard, S. M. 1971. *The transparent self,* 211–38. New York: Van Nostrand.

Kellerman, P. 1983. Resistance in psychodrama. *Journal of Group Psychotherapy, Psychodrama and Sociometry* 36(1): 30–43 (Spring).

Lewis, C. N. 1971. Reminiscing and self-concept in old age. *Journal of Gerontology* 26:240–43.

Linn, N. W. 1973. Perceptions of childhood. Present functioning and past events. *Journal of Gerontology* 28:202–6.

Lyon, G. G. 1971. Stimulation through remotivation. *American Journal of Nursing* 71(5): 982–86 (May).

McMordie, W. R., and S. Blom. 1979. Life review therapy: Psychotherapy for the elderly. *Perspectives in Psychiatric Care* 17(4): 162–66 (July-August).

Merriam, S. 1980. The concept and function of reminiscence: A review of the research. *The Gerontologist* 20(5): 604–8 (October).

Minuchin, S. 1974. *Families and Family Therapy.* Cambridge, Mass. Harvard University Press.

Moreno, J. L. 1977. *Psychodrama* Vol. 1 (ed). Beacon, New York: Beacon House, Inc.

Ryden, M. B. 1981. Nursing intervention in support of reminiscence. *Journal of Gerontological Nursing* 7(8): 461–63 (August).

Starkey, P. J. 1981. Genograms, a guide to understanding one's own family system. *Perspectives in Psychiatric Care* 19(5–6): 164–72.

---

## RESOURCES

### Films

*The Art of Age* (16 mm, color, 27 minutes, 1972). Produced by S. Berman and J. T. Mathiew. Four people in this film have a lesson for all—that every year of life brings with it increased wisdom and knowledge to be applied to new endeavors and that a vital, healthy person never stops growing or learning. It emphasizes that one is obligated to live as long as one is living. Distributed by Ace Films, P.O. Box 1898, 12 Jules Lane, New Brunswick, NJ 08902.

# chapter 20

# Self-Help Groups

*Irene Burnside*

*Our England is a garden,*
*and such gardens are not made*
*By singing: — "Oh, how beautiful!"*
*and sitting in the shade.**

RUDYARD KIPLING

### LEARNING OBJECTIVES

- Define **self-care**.
- Define **self-help group**.
- Discuss the role of professionals in self-help groups.
- Compare and contrast self-help groups with those led by professionals.
- List Caplan's three elements of support.
- Discuss the conceptual framework of group process according to Bradford.
- List five help-giving activities that occur in self-help groups.
- Describe one successful self-help group.

### KEY WORDS

- Common goal
- Depersonalization
- Empathy
- Explanation
- Morale building
- Mutual affirmation
- Positive reinforcement
- Psychological group
- Self-care
- Self-disclosure
- Self-help
- Sharing
- Support group
- Support network

This chapter is about a special type of group, the self-help group (SHG). Self-help groups have been in existence for a long time and have been particularly effective in the areas of mental health and alcoholism.

Self-care is gaining in importance, especially with the rising cost of medical and hospital care. In nursing, an entire conceptual framework called self-care has been developed by Dorothy Orem (1971, 13–19). She defines self-care as "the practice of activities that individuals personally initiate and perform on their own behalf in maintaining life, health, and well being . . . [it] is an adult's personal, continuous contribution to his [or her] own health and well-being"

---

*Kipling, R.: Lines from poem, The Glory of the Garden, in *Rudyard Kipling's Verse*, Definitive edition, p. 736. Garden City, New York: Doubleday, 1954. Copyright 1940 by Elsie Kipling Bambridge.

(p. 13). Since self-help groups are special activities practiced by the members to promote their health and well-being, they are worth studying.

The continuing growth of self-help groups may be considered by some to indicate a failure of the helping professionals and/or social agencies to provide assistance with the problems of physical and mental health. Table 20–1 lists early self-help groups and the professionals who worked with those particular groups. Professionals have been active in the founding and the support of most groups. The members often seek professional assistance or counseling for their groups.

Professionals recognize that their help is supportive to such groups; they strengthen the self-help movement by:

- Creating new groups as needed. (For example, the widow-to-widow program, Recov-

TABLE 20-1. Characteristics of founders and supporters of self-help groups

| Group | Year formed | Founders | | Supporters |
|---|---|---|---|---|
| | | Laymen | Professionals | |
| Alcoholics Anonymous | 1935 | Bill Wilson | Robert Smith, M.D. | William Silkworth, M.D. Harry Tiebout, M.D. (psychiatry) Carl Jung, M.D. (psychiatry) |
| Recovery, Inc. | 1937 | | Abraham Low, M.D. (psychiatry) | |
| Integrity groups | 1945 | | O. Hobart Mowrer, Ph.D. (psychology) Anthony Vattano, Ph.D. (social work) | |
| Mended Hearts | 1951 | Doris Silliman | Dwight Harken, M.D. (cardiology) | |
| NAIM* | 1956 | William & Jean Delaney | | Msgr. John Egan (clergy) Father Timothy Sullivan (clergy) |
| GROW* | 1957 | | Father Con Keogh (clergy) Albert Lacey, Ph.D. (law) | |
| Synanon | 1958 | Chuck Dederich | | Daniel Casriel, M.D. (psychiatry) Lewis Yablonsky, Ph.D. (sociology) |
| Compassionate Friends | 1969 | Arnold & Paula Shamres (U.S., 1972) | The Rev. Simon Stephens (clergy) | Elizabeth Kubler-Ross, M.D. (psychiatry) |
| Parents Anonymous | 1971 | Jolly K. | Leonard Lieber (social work) | |
| Epilepsy Self-Help | 1975 | | Lawrence Schlesinger, Ph.D. (social psychology) | Doris Haar (nursing) |

SOURCE: From "Characteristics of Development and Growth," by L. D. Borman. In M. L. Lieberman and L. D. Dorman (eds.), *Self-Help Groups for Coping with Crisis*, pp. 22–23. Copyright 1979 by Jossey-Bass publishers. Reprinted by permission.

*Author's notes: Naim Conference is a Catholic organization for widowed Catholics or spouses of deceased Catholics. The name was taken from that of a village where Jesus performed a miracle for the sake of a widow (Lieberman and Borman 1979, 68–69). Lieberman and Borman do not give a specific description of what GROW stands for; the group originated in Australia.

ery Inc., and Compassionate Friends were started by professionals.)

- Referring people who can benefit from self-help groups to them.
- Providing space, equipment, and financial resources to groups.
- Acting as consultants to groups and working within the self-help framework (Gartner 1981, 2).

M. Lieberman and C. Borman (1979) have edited a book that focuses on two types of groups: those designed to modify group members' behaviors or attitudes (for example, groups for alcoholics, gamblers, drug abusers) and groups formed to help members cope with particular life crises: major illness, aging, loss of spouse or child, for example.

## DEFINITIONS

A group may be defined in a variety of ways. A definition given by D. Cartwright and A. Zander (1960, 46) stresses two aspects of the group: goals and interrelationships. "A group is a collection of individuals sharing a common goal who have relationships to one another that make them interdependent to some significant degree."

One definition of a self-help group is "clusters of persons who share a common condition, and who come together to offer one another the mutual benefit of mutual experiences, support, and counsel" (U.S. Department of HEW 1980, 16).

Self-help is defined by A. Katz and E. Bender (1976, 36) as "voluntary small group structures for mutual aid in the accomplishment of a specific purpose. They are usually formed by peers who have come together for mutual assistance in satisfying a common need, overcoming a common handicap or life disrupting problem, and bringing about desired social and/or personal change." Katz and L. Levin (1980, 333) state that "participation in self-care and self-help groups becomes a specific antidote to passivity, apathy, and dependency in the health care area, and has potential extension to other areas of living as well, including the political sphere."

Sometimes the term *support group* will be used in lieu of self-help group. G. Caplan, a psychiatrist, defines *support* based on the work he has done in the field of preventive psychiatry. Caplan (1974) considers three elements to be important:

1. Helping to mobilize psychological resources and to overcome emotional problems.
2. Sharing the tasks.
3. Providing tools, skills, and cognitive guidance that will help improve coping with the situation.

## EDUCATIONAL GROUPS

B. Kaplan and D. Fleisher (1981) recommend that information be provided in educational groups about the aging process and role losses. These authors also recommend that support groups would be helpful for middle-generation adults who are worried about the increasing demands of caretaking responsibilities. Many of them must make rather constant adjustments to handle everything on their schedules. A chance to discuss and share concerns with cohorts would help them by giving them ideas for coping and suggesting alternatives regarding their caretaking roles.

Kaplan and Fleisher (1981) also discuss "coping groups." In these groups older persons can discuss their feelings about the changes they have experienced in aging. Some of the topics that the authors suggest for selection by the members include feelings about widowhood, loss of work role, loss of social network provided by work role, loneliness, shifting patterns of friendships, and disappointments (if, for example, their children have been unable to substitute for some of the losses they have experienced). Such a group provides support for its members as they hear how their cohorts have coped and what survival strategies they have used.

## WHAT IS A SELF-HELP GROUP

L. Borman (1976, 17) explains self-help groups as a "membership of those who share a common condition, situation, heritage, symptom, or experience. They are largely self-governing and self-regulating, emphasizing peer solidarity rather than hierarchical governance. As such, they prefer control emanating from consensus rather than coercion—including majority rule. They tend to disregard in their own organization the usual institutional distinctions between consumer, professionals, and boards of directors, combining and exchanging such functions among each other." He further states that such groups advocate self-reliance and require an intense commitment and responsibility to other members. Self-help groups generally have an identifiable code of precepts, beliefs, and practices. That code could include rules for conducting group meetings, requirements for entry into the group, and also techniques for dealing with "backsliders."

Self-help groups, by their very existence, do minimize referrals to professionals or agencies. This is because, in most cases, there is no help to be had. If appropriate help is available, the groups do cooperate with professionals.

One feature of these groups is the fellowship network—face-to-face or telephone—that is usually available and accessible without charge. The groups operate on their own, are self-supporting, and manage financially with donations from members and friends. They are not funded

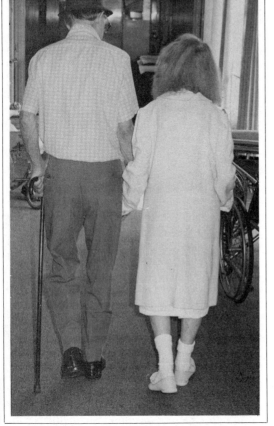

WILL PATTON

*Because of the extreme frailty and debilitation of most nursing home patients, there are few options for self-help groups. The residents are dependent on friends, relatives, and ombudsmen instead. But the elderly in the community and their families can find much support in these groups.*

by grants from the government or foundations or with any public monies.

There is a wide array of self-help groups to fulfill a variety of needs. The groups can consist of members of any age. There is a myriad of such groups in the United States; experts estimate the number to be half a million, and more appear each month.

Self-help groups provide lay help to those who need it. In some cases a self-help group may be all that is required; such groups can complement rather than compete with professional care.

## PURPOSES OF SELF-HELP GROUPS

Leon H. Levy (1976) studied 20 self-help groups and identified the following four categories, by purpose.

1. *Behavioral control*: Weight Watchers, Alcoholics Anonymous, TOPS.
2. *Stress, coping, and support:* widow and widower groups, Ostomy Association, Stroke Clubs.
3. *Survival oriented:* National Organization for Women.
4. *Personal growth or self-actualization:* One excellent example for the aged would be the Senior Actualization and Growth Exploration (SAGE) group.

Lieberman and Borman (1979) found that self-help groups have some common characteristics:

- The members share a common condition, problem, heritage, or life experience.
- The groups are both self-regulating and self-governing and tend to emphasize peer cohesiveness rather than a formal structure of governance.
- The groups advocate self-reliance, and there is an emphasis on commitment and responsibility.
- The groups maintain a code of beliefs and practices.
- The members have a support network, usually a face-to-face or phone-to-phone network. (Many groups publish a regular newsletter or bulletin.)
- The members with the most experience provide guidance for the others.
- Group members provide empathy for one another.
- The groups provide specific help in handling the problems or conditions that exist for the members.
- The members have practical ways to handle the day-to-day difficulties they experience.

## TYPES OF SELF-HELP GROUPS

Orville Kelly founded the group called Make Today Count for individuals who were faced with life-threatening illnesses. Simon Stephens, in England, established the Society of Compassionate Friends to aid bereaved parents. The first U.S. chapter began in the Miami area in 1972, and there are now more than 200 chapters in this country. These would be classified as "stress, coping, and support" groups. They are only two of the many self-help organizations. The fact that they have spread rapidly and widely attests that they do respond to some need.

Some groups, such as Alcoholics Anonymous (AA), focus on behavior modification. AA was the original self-help group. It was begun in 1935 in the United States and currently has 28,000 chapters. It is impressive to watch self-help groups organize and grow; the members' understanding, empathy, and concern for one another cannot be underscored enough. Any helping professional who has called an AA member out of bed at 3:00 A.M. to come and listen to a patient can speak to the loyalty and true "helping" of such individuals.

Self-help groups usually arise spontaneously, and some are associated with already existing, structured organizations—for example, Stroke Clubs are under the aegis of the American Heart Association, and the Arthritis Foundation sponsors Arthritis Clubs.

J. Fuller and others (1979) briefly describe a supportive group for families of demented relatives. These groups were begun in a psychogeriatric unit in London. One group met for one hour every two weeks at lunchtime; another group was begun in the evening for relatives who had to work during the day. The latter group was attended mainly by the patients' children or grandchildren. The common themes from the group described by Fuller and others included:

1. Validation of behavior of family member by other group members who experience it.

2. The cause of the dementia.

3. Disorientation.

4. Lack of recognition of spouse.

5. Anger and resentment.

6. Incontinence (not a major topic).

7. Sexual problems

Doris Weaver has begun support groups for teenagers and grandchildren of the demented in the Seattle/Tacoma area and reports the need for such groups (Weaver 1982).

Occasionally one observes the development of dissension that is not resolved in the group and the formation of factions. The splinter group sometimes takes off in what is described by Kirschenbaum and Glaser (1978) as the "let's-form-a-new-organization" syndrome. The pitfall here, they say, is that when support groups "go off exploring in this direction, the majority never do it" (p. 54). In support groups of the self-help type, anger, smoldering resentments, or unacceptable rules and codes may be reasons for groups splintering—not unlike the divisions one sees in religious groups.

The literature reveals that one group theorist (Bradford 1978) believes that a group essentially re-forms every time it meets because intervening events for each of the members, new expectations, pressures from sources outside the group, and subgroup cliques all help to provide a changed group from meeting to meeting. This phenomenon would seem to be applicable to Alzheimer's disease (AD) support groups, because of the many ups and downs that are experienced by members as their loved one moves through various stages of the disease and/or shows behavioral changes.

Bradford (1978) feels that a "psychological group" forms when:

1. Patterns of interaction are proven effective.

2. Differences in perceptions about tasks, communication, and procedures are clarified.

3. Relationships to other persons and groups are delineated.

4. Standards for participation are set.

5. Methods of work that elicit rather than inhibit contributions are established.

6. A respected "plan" for each person is secured.

7. Trust is established among members.

## Groups for Widowed Persons

Another type of self-help group that has gained in importance is the widowhood groups. Like the AD groups mentioned above, they have responded to a need felt by a particular group of people. They were begun by Phyllis Silverman in the 1960s (Silverman 1965, 1969, 1974; Silverman and Cooperband 1975).

The National Retired Teachers Association and the American Association of Retired Persons (NRTA-AARP) also have chapters of support groups for widowed people. The Widowed Persons Service (WPS) staff and volunteers organize, train, and offer consultation and materials to develop these programs. WPS goals in the community include:

- Volunteer outreach to the newly bereaved.
- Telephone referral and information assistance.
- Group meetings (allow widowed persons to share both experience and concerns).
- Public education (problems of grief adjustment and services available for widowed persons).
- A resource directory (helps the widowed to locate available local services).

For further information on how to develop a WPS program in a community, contact the national office of NRTA-AARP. (See Resources section at the end of this chapter).

These groups provide support, education, and social life for their members. A problem I observed in one group was that membership was open to those who were recently widowed as well as to those who had been widowed for 10 or more years. The needs and expectations of the group members were vastly different and conflict arose because of the difference in length of bereavement. The newly widowed needed to grieve, to ventilate, and to share their hurts in a safe milieu. Many were not ready for social activities or reaching out. The other members appeared to be well-adjusted to their loss (or losses), through the acute grief phase, and ready to socialize and/or change their life-styles. It requires unusually sensitive and skillful leaders to meet the needs of both of these types of widowed persons.

Groups that combine widows and the divorced (for example, Parents Without Partners) often face divisiveness. The newly widowed often cannot understand the bitterness or hate that some of the divorced members express about the rotten deal they feel they received in the divorce. Their ventilation is often offensive to the widowed members. A leader will need to consider these two examples carefully; situations of this sort can flare up into major conflicts once the group is off the ground and meeting regularly.

Lieberman and Borman (1981) report on the findings of a study of widows done by Elizabeth A. Bankhoff (1981) for a doctoral dissertation. Some of the findings are highlighted here:

- Informal social resources provided by one's social network do make a difference in the adjustment of a widow.
- Both the helping professions and researchers have been preoccupied with the early crisis phase of widowhood and not with long-term problems of transition. It appears that the nature of a widow's needs are both complex and changing.
- The problem of the widow's social isolation has been exaggerated. In Bankhoff's study, most widows had one or more significant individuals in their network that they could turn to for emotional and instrumental support.
- As a widow moves from the early crisis and bereavement stage to the transition stage, she grows to rely more on persons similar to herself, namely, other widows and single friends.
- A key finding is the importance of *who* provides the support, rather than *what* is provided. In the crisis phase, it is the widow's mother; through the transition phase, it is the widow's single or widowed friends.
- In the early bereavement stage, how a widow sees the situation and who she thinks she can depend upon appear more important to her than real interactions and support. Her perceptions are more important than actuality.

## HELP-GIVING ACTIVITIES

Some of the important help-giving activities that occur in self-help groups are described by Levy (1979, 260–63). Empathy is one of the most important aspects of these help-giving activities. Mutual affirmation—that is, assuring one another that one is worthwhile and valuable—is another important aspect. Explanation—a better understanding of one's self or one's reactions to a situation—is a third. Morale-building rates high; group members often are able to reassure other members that the problems will eventually be worked out positively. Sharing past and present experiences and thoughts and feelings with other members is helpful. Positive reinforcement, or applauding of behavior, by the group is highly rated among the help-giving activities. Self-disclosure—that is, the ability to relate personal thoughts or emotions that members would not normally tell other persons—is also an important part of the helpful group process. The ability to make goals and to check the progress made with the group is also helpful, according to the data provided by Levy.

N. Pender (1982) offers a list of general suggestions for enhancing support systems. Since support systems are so crucial to the maintenance and improvement of health, the list is included here.

- Increase frequency of contact with individuals with whom the client desires stronger personal ties.
- Build ties with individuals who share common life values.
- Participate in mutual goal-setting with significant others to achieve common directions in actions and efforts.
- Provide additional encouragement, personal warmth, and love to significant others.
- Support coping efforts of significant others in dealing with life experiences.
- Enhance personal identity and self-esteem of persons within support network.
- Provide increased intimacy to promote self-expression.

- Deal constructively with conflict between oneself and support-group members.
- Increase reciprocity and mutality of interpersonal relationships.
- Offer assistance more frequently to individuals within personal social network, to show concern and promote trust.
- Increase personal capacity to accept emotional support and love.
- Seek counseling as needed to enhance marital adjustment.
- Make use of self-help groups or the extended family as a source of support.
- Make use of the nurse and other health professionals as community support resources.
- Make use of the church or religious affiliation as a source of emotional and spiritual support.
- Capitalize on ties to a number of social groups to expand horizons for new growth opportunities.

## A SELF-HELP GROUP: A MODEL

A group that is gaining in chapters, attendance, and interest is the Alzheimer's Disease and Related Disorders Association (ADRDA). With increasingly more persons being diagnosed as having Alzheimer's disease, these chapters will undoubtedly continue to expand. Alzheimer's disease is the fourth leading cause of deaths in the United States (Katzman 1976, 217). Butler (1980, 167) states that AD probably accounts for about 100,000 to 110,000 deaths per year. Some writers state that AD may be responsible for two-thirds of all dementia among older people (Dreyfus 1979). Those staggering figures speak to the need to support the relatives, because "the economic, social, and human costs of dementias, which already are staggering, will increase." (Hutton 1980, 149).

The ADRDA grew into a national health organization from support groups; chapters began across the country in response to the needs of Alzheimer patients and their families. Families decided that local programs should be strengthened and supplemented by a national effort. A joint approach was needed, and in December 1979 the chapters united to form a national association. In mid-1981 there were 18 chapters; now there are close to 100 chapters.

Fundamental purposes are education, patient care, research, and advocacy. ADRDA's mission is to combat the disease by (1) research to aid in diagnosis, improve treatment, identify the cause(s), and prevent the disease; (2) education for medical professionals, to share information about the diagnosis, treatment, and management of patients; (3) education and support systems for laymen, to provide information and to cope with the practical details of daily living; and (4) functioning as an advocate to inform government and social service agencies about the long-term custodial needs of the affected population.

In 1983 the ADRDA board of directors had as its chairman Jerome Stone, of the Chicago-based Stone Container Corporation; Robert Katzman, Chairman of Neurology at Albert Einstein College of Medicine in New York City, and Carl Eisdorfer, Chairman of Psychiatry at the University of Washington in Seattle, serve as co-chairmen of the Medical and Scientific Advisory Board.

The association began a public education and awareness campaign, first to destroy the myth that "senility" is a natural part of the aging process and also to ensure that people know that the organization exists and that help is available. The group was successful in having a week in November 1982 declared as "Alzheimer's Disease Public Awareness Week." At this writing the House of Representatives will be considering a bill which places special emphasis on the disease, especially in coordinating government-sponsored research on A.D. and improving programs for care and treatment of A.D. patients.

## ASPECTS OF THE SELF-HELP HEALTH MOVEMENT

Katz and Levin (1980) offer some reasons for the growth of the self-help movement in the United States.

1. Medicine's depersonalization, overspecialization, and concentration on technology (leading to a general loss of confidence in it).

2. The health care system's embodiment of fragmented and episodic care rather than comprehensive and continuous care.

3. The changing nature of morbidity (chronic illness is now the most prevalent form of health problem).

4. The drive toward greater control of one's own life and destiny, represented in the United States by populist and anti-establishment movements. In the health field these have led to an empowering of "consumers," in the belief that they can more positively discover and control the forces that affect their own health and risks of illness.

5. The greater understanding of the relationship between environment and illness and of stress-related disorders, physical and mental.

6. The emergence and popular appeal of "alternative therapies" ranging from diet, exercise, meditation, and other practices to modes of self-observation and self-treatment via such methods as biofeedback, imaging, and other techniques derived from clinical and scientific studies.

7. The vast expansion of self-help groups in the health field; these groups offer health information and specific instruction, provide social care and mutual aid to sufferers from a wide variety of illnesses and disorders, and give material and emotional support to their families. Katz and Bender (1976) estimate that self-help groups engage several millions of participants in the United States.

8. The development, in addition to all of the above, of a public consciousness about general health practice, that is, the importance of diet to avoid obesity, coronary artery disease, and other health problems; the hazards of cigarette smoking; the importance of physical activity, and so forth. There are some 15 million

American joggers; a 25 percent replacement of animal fat by unsaturated fats has occurred in the U.S. diet in the past decade, and millions of copies of thousands of separate self-help books, pamphlets, and training programs have been sold to the public.

The reader is referred to a fascinating book by John Naisbitt, *Megatrends* (1982). A chapter, "From Institutional Help to Self-Help" is germane to this discussion.

C. King (1980, 34) asks some questions about the self-help group concept. For example:

1. What is the constraint vs. the freedom in the group?

2. What are the goals and how are individual values and differences tolerated?

3. Does the self-help group have to formally organize to survive?

4. Structural effects of "inner" vs. "outer" orientation—does the group become so homogeneous that it does not thrive and continue to grow?

## SUMMARY

This chapter provides a brief overview of self-help groups; a few of the successful groups are described and one conceptual framework of a group process is discussed. A model of one of the newer self-help groups (ADRDA) is presented. The effectiveness of such groups in meeting the needs of their members surely indicates some of the shortcomings of groups convened and run by professionals. The voluntary aspects of such groups and the motivation, ingenuity, caring, the drive of their members are qualities to impress any of us.

## EXERCISE 1

Attend a meeting of some type of self-help group. List five reasons why you think it is a successful group, and defend those reasons.*

## EXERCISE 2

Attend a support group for families. List and explain four themes that you heard expressed by family members in the group meeting.*

## EXERCISE 3

Select one self-help group that was started or aided by a professional. Study the history of the group, and write a two-page paper on the role the professional had in the formation of the group.

---

*As a cautionary note, the student should be advised that it is important to check with group leader(s) of self-help groups before going unannounced to observe the meetings.

## REFERENCES

Bankhoff, E. 1981. Doctoral dissertation. Department of Behavioral Sciences, University of Chicago.

Borman, L. D. 1976. *The Center report*, 17. Chicago, Ill.: The Center for the Study of Democratic Institutions. June.

Bradford, L. 1978. Group formation and development. In *Group development*. 2d ed., ed. L. P. Bradford. La Jolla, Calif.: University Associates.

Butler, R. N. 1980. Meeting the challenges of health care for the elderly. *Journal of Allied Health* 9(3): 6 (August).

Caplan, G. 1974. *Support systems and community mental health*. New York: Behavioral Publications.

Cartwright, D., and A. Zander, eds. 1960. *Group dynamics: Research and theory,* 2d ed. Evanston, Ill.: Row, Peterson.

Dreyfus, P. 1979. Understanding dementia: A closer look at Alzheimer's disease. *Consultant* 19 (January) 31–39.

Fuller, J., E. Ward, A. Evans, K. Massam, and A. Gardner. 1979. Dementia: Supportive groups for relatives. *British Medical Journal* 1(6179): 1684–85 (June 23).

Gartner, H. 1981. Forging a new partnership. *Self-Help Reporter* 5(3): 6 (May/June).

Hutton, J. T. 1980. In *The aging nervous system.,* ed. G. J. Maletta and J. Pirozzolo. New York: Praeger.

Kaplan, B., and D. Fleisher. 1981. Loneliness and role loss. In *Occasional Papers in Mental Health and Aging*. Proceedings of the Focus on Mental Health and Aging Conference, University of Utah Gerontology program, Salt Lake City, Utah.

Katz, A. H., and E. I. Bender. 1976. *The strength in us: Self-help groups in the modern world,* 36. New York: Franklin-Watts.

Katz, A. H., and L. S. Levin. 1980. Self-care is not a solipsistic trap: A reply to critics. *International Journal of Health Services* 10(2): 329–36.

Katzman, R. 1976. The prevalence and malignancy of Alzheimer's disease. *Archives of Neurology* 33(4): 217–18 (April).

King, C. 1980. The self-help/self-care concept. *The Nurse Practitioner* 5(3): 34–35, 46 (May–June).

Kirschenbaum, H., and B. Glaser. 1978. *Developing support groups*. La Jolla, Calif.: University Associates.

Levy, L. H. 1976. Self-help groups: Types and psychological process. *Journal of Applied Behavioral Sciences,* Vol. 12.

———. 1979. Process and activities in groups, or self-help. In *Groups for coping with crisis,* ed. M. Lieberman and L. Borman. San Francisco: Jossey-Bass.

Lieberman, M., and L. Borman. 1979. *Self-help groups for coping with crisis: Origins, members, processes and impact*. San Francisco: Jossey-Bass.

———. 1981. Who helps widows: The role of kith and kin. *National Reporter* 4(8): 2.

Naisbitt, J. 1982. *Megatrends*. New York: Warner Books. pp. 131–157.

Orem, D. 1971. *Nursing: Concepts of practice,* 13–19. New York: McGraw-Hill.

Pender, N. 1982. *Health promotion in nursing practice*. Norwalk, Conn.: Appleton-Century-Crofts.

Silverman, P. 1965. Services for the widowed during the period of bereavement. In *Social work practice*. New York: Columbia University Press.

———. 1969. The widow-to-widow program: An experiment in preventive intervention. *Mental Hygiene* 53(3): 333–37.

———. 1974. *Helping each other in Widowhood*. New York: Health Science.

Silverman, P., and A. Cooperband. 1975. On widowhood: Mutual help and the elderly widow. *Journal of Geriatric Psychiatry* 8(1): 9–27.

U.S. Department of Health, Education, and Welfare. 1980. *A guide to medical self-care and self-help groups for the elderly*. NIH Publication no. 80-1687. Washington, D.C. November.

Weaver, D. 1982. Tapping strength: A support group for children and grandchildren. *Generations* 8(1): 45 (Fall).

## BIBLIOGRAPHY

Barnes, R. F., M. A. Raskin, and M. Scott. 1981. Problems of families caring for Alzheimer patients: Use of a support group. *Journal of the American Geriatrics Society* 29(2): 80–85.

Borkman, T. 1976. Experiential knowledge: A new concept for the analysis of self-help groups. *Social Service Review* 50:30.

Cross, L., C. London, and C. Barry. 1981. Older women caring for disabled spouses: A model for supportive services. *The Gerontologist* 21(5): 464–70.

D'Afflitti, J., and G. Weitz. 1974. Rehabilitating the stroke patient through patient-family groups. *International Journal of Group Psychotherapy* 25(3): 323–32.

Donnelly, G. F. 1980. Remember . . . you're not in this alone! *RN*, July: 30–33.

Fengler, A., and N. Goodrich. 1979. Wives of elderly disabled men: The hidden patients. *The Gerontologist* 19(2): 175–83.

Foster, Z., and S. Mendel. 1979. Mutual-help group for patients: Taking steps toward change. *Health and Social Work* 4(3): 83–97 (August).

Gallo, F. 1982. The effects of social support networks on the health of the elderly. *Social Work in health care.* 8(2): 65–74, (Winter).

Getzel, G. 1983. Group work with kin and friends caring for the elderly. In *Group work with the frail elderly.* New York: Haworth Press.

Gordon, T. 1977. *Leader effectiveness training.* New York: Petery Wyden.

Harris, Z. 1981. Ten steps towards establishing a self-help group: A report from Montreal. *Canada's Mental Health* 29(1): 16.

Hartford, M. and R. Parsons. 1983. Uses of groups with relatives of dependent older adults. In *Group work with the frail elderly.* New York: Haworth Press.

Hayter, J. 1982. Helping families of patients with Alzheimer's disease. *Journal of Gerontological Nursing* 8(2): 81–86 (February).

Haywood, L., and E. Taylor. 1981. Strikes and support systems: What happened in Sudbury. *Canada's Mental Health* 29(1): 18–19.

Johnson, D. W. 1972. *Reaching out.* Englewood Cliffs, N.J.: Prentice-Hall.

Johnson, D. W. and F. D. Johnson. 1975. *Joining together: Group therapy and group skills.* Englewood Cliffs, N.J.: Prentice-Hall.

Katz, A. 1970. Self-help organization and volunteer participation in social welfare. *Social Work* 15(1), January.

———. 1979. Self-help health groups: Some clarification. *Social Science Medicine* 13 (June): 491–94.

Kilen, E. 1979. Family discussion group meetings. *American Health Care Association Journal*, Special report, January.

Knight, B., R. W. Wollert, and L. H. Levy. 1980. Self-help groups: The members' perspectives. *American Journal of Community Psychology* 8(1): 53–65.

Lacoursiere, R. 1980. *The life cycle of groups.* New York: Human Science Press.

LaVorgna, D. 1979. Group treatment for wives of patients with Alzheimer's disease. *Social work in health care* 5(2): 219–21 (Winter).

Levin, L. 1976. Self-care; An international perspective *Social Policy,* September–October.

Levin, L., A. H. Katz, and E. Holst. 1976. *Self-care: Lay initiatives in health.* New York: Prodist.

Lieberman, M., and G. Bond. 1978. Self-help groups: Problems of measuring outcomes. *Small Group Behaviors* 9:221–42.

Lieberman, M., and L. Borman. 1981. The impact of self-help groups in widows' mental health. *National Reporter* 4(7): 64 (July).

McCormack, N. 1981. *Plain talk about mutual help groups.* Rockville, Md.: National Institute of Mental Health.

Mann, J. 1983. Behind the explosion in self-help groups. *U.S. News and World Report* 94(17): 33–35 (May 2).

Petty, B., T. Moeller, and R. Cambell. 1976. Support groups for elderly persons in the community. *The Gerontologist* 16:522–28.

Politser, P. P., and E. M. Pattison. 1980. Social climates in community groups: Toward a taxonomy. *Community Mental Health Journal* 16(3): 187–200.

Powell, T. 1975. The use of self-help groups as supportive reference communities. *American Journal of Orthopsychiatry* 45(5), October.

Raths, L. E., M. Harmin, and S. B. Simon. 1966. The clarifying response. Chapter 5 in *Values and teaching.* Columbus, Ohio: C. Merrill.

Rogers, J., M. Vachen, W. Lyall, A. Sheldon, and S. Freeman. 1980. A self-help program for widows as an independent community service. *Hospital and Community Psychiatry* 31(12): 844–47 (December).

Sanford, J. 1975. Tolerance of debility in elderly dependents by supporters at home; Its significance for hospital practice. *British Medical Journal* 3(5981): 471–73.

Schwartz, M. 1975. Situation/transition groups: A conceptualization and review. *American Journal of Orthopsychiatry* 45(5), October.

Stephens, S. 1973. *Death comes home.* New York: Morehouse, Barlow.

Vachon, M. L. S., W. Lyall, J. Rogers, K. Freedman-Letofsky, and S. Freeman. 1980. A controlled study of self-help intervention for widows. *American Journal of Psychiatry* 137(11): 1380–84 (November).

Vattano, A. 1972. Power to the people: Self-help groups. *Social Work* 17(4), July.

Zola, I. 1979. Helping one another: A speculative history of the self-help movement. *Archives of Physical Medicine and Rehabilitation* 60(1): 452–56 (October).

## RESOURCES

### Film

*Beginning again: Widowers.* 30 min. color.

Pre-view rates available WHA Television Marketing Department, 821 University Avenue, Madison, WI 53706.

Describes widowers aged 39–66 who show how they coped. Program could be used for support staff training workshops or inservice.

### Organizations

*National Association of Retired Persons—National Retired Teachers Association (AARP-NRTA).* 1909 K Street N.W., Washington, DC 20049.

*The Self Help Center.* 1600 Dodge Avenue, Suite S-122, Evanston, IL 60201; phone (312) 328-0470.

### Publications

*Citizen Participation* (newsmagazine). Civic Education Foundation, Lincoln Filene Center for Citizenship and Public Affairs, Tufts University, Medford, MA 02155.

*Self-Help Reporter.* c/o National Self-Help Clearinghouse, Graduate School and University Center/CUNY, 33 West 42nd Street, Room 1206A, New York, NY 10036.

### Self-Help Groups

*Alcoholism*
Al-Anon Group Headquarters, P.O. Box 182, Madison Square Station, New York, NY 10010.
Alcoholics Anonymous, 468 Park Avenue South, New York, NY 10017.

*Alzheimer's Disease*
Alzheimer's Disease and Related Disorders Association (ADRDA), 360 North Michigan Avenue, Chicago, IL 60601.

*Arthritis*
The Arthritis Foundation, 1212 Avenue of the Americas, New York, NY 10036.

*Cancer*
American Cancer Society, 777 Third Avenue, New York, NY 10017.

Cancer Care Inc. (CCI), of the National Cancer Foundation, One Park Avenue, New York, NY 10016; phone (212) 679-5700.

Cancer Patients Anonymous (CANPATANON), 1722 Ralph Avenue, Brooklyn, NY 11236; phone (212) 649-3481.

Make Today Count Inc., P.O. Box 303, Burlington, Iowa 52601; phone (319) 754-7266 or 754-8977.

National Cancer Foundation, One Park Avenue, New York, NY 10016; phone (212) 679-5700.
Reach to Recovery, c/o American Cancer Society, 777 Third Avenue, New York, NY 10017; phone (212) 371-2900.

*Cardiac Disorders*
American Heart Association, 7320 Greenville Avenue, Dallas, TX 75231.

Cardio-Vascular Disease, The American Heart Association, 44 East 23rd Street, New York, NY 10010; phone (617) 732-5609.

The Mended Hearts Inc., 721 Huntington Avenue, Boston, MA 02115; phone (617) 732-5609.

*Diabetes*
American Diabetes Association Inc., 18 East 48th Street, New York, NY 10017.

*Hearing*
Alexander Graham Bell Association for the Deaf, 1537 35th Street, N.W., Washington, DC 20007.

American Humane Society, P.O. Box 1266, Denver, CO 80201 (trains seeing eye dogs).

American Organization for the Education of the Hearing Impaired, 1537 35th Street, N.W., Washington, DC 20007.

American Speech and Hearing Association, 9030 Old Gerogetown Road, Washington, DC 20014.

The Better Hearing Institute, 1430 K Street N, Suite 600, Washington, DC 20005; toll-free phone (800) 424-8576.

Junior National Association for the Deaf, Gallaudet College, Washington, DC 20002.

National Association of the Deaf, 814 Thayer Avenue, Silver Spring, MD 20910.

National Association of Hearing and Speech Agencies, 919 18th Street, N.W., Washington, DC 20006.

The National Hearing Aid Society, 20361 Middlebelt Road, Livonia, MI 48152; phone (313) 478-2610.

*Life Crisis*
Widow to Widow, 25 Huntington Avenue, Boston, MA 02115; phone (617) 661-6180.

*Lung/Breathing Disorders*
American Lung Association, 1720 Broadway, New York, NY 10019.

Emphysema Anonymous Inc., P.O. Box 66, Fort Meyers, FL 33902; phone (813) 344-4266.

*Mental Health*
National Association for Mental Health, 1800 North Kent Street, Rosslyn, VA 22208; phone (703) 528-6405.

Recovery Inc., 116 South Michigan Avenue, Chicago, IL 60603; phone (312) 263-2292.

*Ostomy*

United Ostomy Association Inc., 1111 Wilshire Boulevard, Los Angeles, Ca 90017; phone (213) 481-2811.

*Paraplegia*

National Paraplegia Foundation, 33 North Michigan Avenue, Chicago, IL 60601.

Paralyzed Veterans of America, 7315 Wisconsin Avenue, N.W., Washington, DC 20014.

*Parkinson's Disease*

American Parkinson's Disease Association, 147 East 50th Street, New York, NY 10022.

National Parkinson Foundation, 1501 Northwest Ninth Avenue, Miami, FL 33136.

Parkinson's Disease Foundation, William Black Medical Research Building, Columbia Presbyterian Medical Center, 640 West 168th Street, New York, NY 10032.

United Parkinson's Foundation, 220 South State Street, Chicago, IL 60604.

*Senior Advocates*

Gray Panthers, 3700 Chestnut Street, Philadelphia, PA 19104.

Senior Actualization and Growth Explorations (SAGE), 2455 Hilgard Avenue, Berkeley, CA 94709.

*Speech*

American Speech and Hearing Association, 9030 Old Georgetown Road, Washington, DC 20014.

*Stroke*

Stroke Clubs of America, 805 12th Street, Galveston, TX 77550.

*Vision*

American Council of the Blind, 1211 Connecticut Avenue, N.W., Washington, DC 20036.

American Foundation for the Blind, 15 West 16th Street, New York, NY 10011.

Blinded Veterans Association, 1735 DeSales Street, N.W., Washington, DC 20036; phone (202) 347-4010.

Blind Outdoor Leisure Development (BOLD Inc.), 533 East Main Street, Aspen, CO 81611.

Guide Dogs Users Inc., Box 174, Central Station, Baldwin, NY 11510.

Guiding Eyes for the Blind, Yorktown Heights, NY 10599.

The Library of Congress, Division for the Blind and Physically Handicapped, Washington, DC 20542.

National Association for Visually Handicapped (partially seeing), 3201 Balboa Street, San Jose, CA 94121.

National Foundation for the Blind, 218 Randolph Hotel Building, Des Moines, IA 50309; phone (800) 424-9770.

National Society for the Prevention of Blindness Inc., 79 Madison Avenue, New York, NY 10801.

# chapter 21

# Group Psychotherapy with the Elderly

*Judith A. S. Altholz*

*for life's not a paragraph
And death i think is no
parenthesis\**

E. E. CUMMINGS (1972, 67)

## LEARNING OBJECTIVES

- Define **group psychotherapy**.

- Identify three purposes of group psychotherapy with the elderly.

- Discuss six criteria for group member selection.

- Discuss the role of leadership in group psychotherapy with the elderly, identify three roles the leader(s) may choose to take, and give reasons for each choice.

- Discuss six benefits group psychotherapy may have for the elderly.

- Identify five practical considerations that must be taken into account when leading group psychotherapy with the aged.

## KEY WORDS

- Anger

- Countertransference

- Elderly

- Group composition

- Group psychotherapy

- Transference

Many older people share the same fears, questions, and concerns, and too often they suffer these feelings silently in isolation. One hears the elderly refer to themselves as "odd" or "crazy" for experiencing what professionals consider reasonable problems of old age. Group psychotherapy offers elderly people an opportunity to see that they are not "crazy," that many of their problems are not unique to them but are common problems of the aged. The realization by group members of the universality of their problems reduces their feelings of incompetence and inadequacy. This chapter is about group psychotherapy and assumes the reader has a background in psychodynamics.

According to Milton Berger (1968), *group psychotherapy* refers to all regularly scheduled, voluntarily attended meetings of acknowledged clients (patients) with an acknowledged trained leader (therapist) for the purpose of expressing, eliciting, accepting, and working through various aspects of the client's functioning and developing the client's healthier and more satisfying potentials. The group provides a "beneficial, controlled life experience within a group setting by the establishment of relationships with the leader, or interaction with group members, or both, together with some clarification of one's motives and those of others in the interaction" (Goldfarb 1972, 114).

### REVIEW OF THE LITERATURE

The first report of group psychotherapy with the aged was published by A. Silver in 1950. Three years later Susan Kubie and Gertrude

---

*The lines from "since feeling is first" from IS 5 by E. E. Cummings are reprinted by permission of Liveright Publishing Corporation. Copyright 1926 by Horace Liveright. Copyright renewed 1953 by E. E. Cummings.

Landau (1953) published a book that, although it describes experiences in group work in a recreation center for the aged, did much to bring the potential of group therapy to the attention of professionals. Maurice Linden's work (1953, 1954, 1955) with elderly women in a state hospital resulted in articles that have become classic readings, particularly on the significance of transference and dual leadership in group work with the elderly. An article by J. A. M. Meerloo (1955) began to describe the adaptation of psychotherapeutic techniques necessary in working with the elderly in groups.

In the 1960s, reports on group work with the aged became more common. Wilma Klein, Eda LeShan, and Sylvia Furman published a book entitled *Promoting Mental Health of Older People through Group Methods* (1965). *Social Group Work with Older People* (National Association of Social Workers 1963) contains examples of the group work done in the early sixties and includes not only clinical reports of groups but also some theoretical analysis of group therapy as a method of treating the aged. The works of Louis Lowy (1962, 1967) and of S. Tine, K. Hastings, and P. Deutschberger (1960) provided excellent frameworks for analysis of group therapy. Clinical reports of groups became available, including those of M. G. Barton (1962); Naomi Feil (1967): Paul Liederman and Richard Green (1965); Liederman, Green, and V. R. Liederman (1967); Betty Schwarzmann (1965, 1966); Eugenia Shere (1964); and Sheldon Zimberg (1969).

Since 1970 the amount of literature on group work with the aged has increased markedly. The works of Irene Burnside (1970), Robert Butler (1974), Alvin Goldfarb (1972), and Myrna Lewis (1974) have contributed significantly to the understanding and use of group therapy. The literature shows that group therapy is an effective technique with most problems of the aged in almost any setting (Altholz 1973; Burnside 1970; Butler 1974; Cohen 1973; Conrad 1974; Goldfarb 1972; Lewis 1974; Rosin 1975). An area not fully explored in the literature concerns the techniques of evaluating group therapy with the aged, some work has been reported (Kaplan 1959; Liederman, Green, and Liederman 1967; Lowy 1967; Tine, Hastings, and Deutschberger 1960).

## COMMON PROBLEMS WITH GROUP PSYCHOTHERAPY

Group psychotherapy with the aged is a difficult therapeutic technique to employ because expressing personal problems in a group and trying to solve them through the group is alien to most older people. They are often slow to develop into a "group," and group continuity is threatened by such practical considerations as lack of transportation for members, high absentee rate, and unwillingness of members to discuss issues appropriate to a psychotherapy group, resulting in discouragement for the leader. Careful planning, however, can avoid many common problems in group psychotherapy with the aged.

Five areas to consider before a group is begun are (1) purposes for group therapy, (2) group composition, (3) group goals, (4) leadership, and (5) practical considerations.

### Purposes of Group Therapy

It is not enough to wish to begin group psychotherapy simply because it seems to be a technique that may relieve the burden of seemingly endless and fruitless individual therapy. It is acceptable, however, to use this mode of therapy to save time and use professional personnel more appropriately. Therapeutically sound reasons for using group therapy can be determined by examining the elderly client population. Is there a significant number of clients, for example, who have difficulty relating to friends and family and who would benefit from the responses of group interaction? If a number of clients are suffering crises of aging and it is believed that their sense of isolation would decrease through the universalization of problems, group therapy is indicated.

### Group Composition

It is extremely important to remember that simply because people are old does not mean they can be put together with the expectation that old age alone will provide a sufficient binding force to enable a therapeutically sound group to develop. Each member of a group must be selected for reasons besides old age. Some groups are limited to new retirees (Wolfe and

Wolfe 1975), others to people of extreme old age (Shere 1964).

Some therapists, notably Robert Butler and Myrna Lewis (1977), favor making a group as heterogeneous as possible in terms of age, mixing persons from age 15 to age 80 and older. These therapists feel that age integration reduces the sense of isolation of the older members of the group, enabling them to "review and renew their own experiences and values" (p. 271). Such unqualified age integration, however, is not necessarily the most desirable group format. Older people have few peer-group opportunities, and a group composed solely of persons over 60 fosters a feeling of the worth of being old, exposing members to alternative solutions developed by other elderly to commonly shared problems.

Sex is a criterion for group selection. Mixed male and female groups are preferable because they foster appropriate sex role interactions and provide reality-oriented occasions for (re)learning more satisfying techniques of socialization. One should have particular reasons for assembling a group of all one sex—for example, a group of males all with problems in sexual functioning. The sex of members will be determined by and will help determine group goals.

The physical problems of potential members are also a criterion for selection. Certain physical problems bear on the practical considerations of group work with the elderly. The room in which the group is held, for example, must be equipped with doors wide enough to admit wheelchairs if any member is not ambulatory. If members must walk upstairs, all must be capable of doing so. Physical problems of some members may interfere with their participation in a group or may be upsetting to other members. For example, a woman who had had cancer, necessitating the removal of part of her jawbone, met the criteria for admission to a group, but her inability to pronounce words plainly interfered with communication with other members, many of whom were hard of hearing. Also, her drastically altered appearance upset many of the others.* This woman left

the group due to relocation, but if she had not, her inability to participate and her effect on the group would have made it necessary to ask her to leave.

The use of a psychiatric diagnosis as a criterion for member selection has important implications for group development. If all members chosen have a diagnosis of withdrawn depression, for example, a danger exists that the group will not develop, since the members may not have the energy or ability to verbalize. However, we have found it effective to make a group homogeneous regarding a diagnosis of depression, but heterogeneous in the amount of affect shown by each member—that is, the coping mechanisms used to deal with the depression and the individual differences in background, education, income, current living situation, and social resources (Yalom 1975).

If group members are chosen on the basis of a mixture of diagnoses or if diagnosis is not a criterion for selection, the leader must exercise care in mixing those with no evidence of brain impairment and those with obvious impairment. Such a combination is often very threatening to those with no impairment, whose fears of becoming "senile" or "losing their minds" are represented by the impaired members of the group. Anxiety of the nonimpaired members often reaches a level that can only be dealt with by their leaving the group.

The most obvious criterion in selecting members for group psychotherapy is their ability to communicate, which means not only the ability to talk but also the ability to verbalize thoughts and feelings. Although some members may benefit simply by attending sessions, the therapeutic worth of a group rests on the interactions of the members. A leader's goals for the group must reflect the members' ability to communicate.

Certain persons should be excluded from a group—for example, those with severe hearing impairments and those with speech difficulties. In one group an 82-year-old man who was almost totally deaf but who met most of the other criteria for selection wished very much to attend and was admitted. His hearing impairment prevented him from interacting with other members of the group. Not only did he feel isolated but the other members felt tense and anxious when he attended because their

*Editor's note. For a thought-provoking study of professionals' reaction to deformity and the aged, the reader is referred to *The Dilemmas of Care: Social and Nursing Adaptions to the Deformed, the Disabled, and the Aged,* 1979. R. P. Preston, Elsevier, New York.

attempts to include him in the normal flow of conversation were rarely successful.

Uncontrolled psychotics should be excluded. Not only are they often difficult to handle in groups, but their presence disturbs other members, most of whom are uncomfortable with and afraid of mental illness. Some leaders feel that people who are hypochondriacal should also be excluded (Yalom 1975). However, such persons do not necessarily interfere with a group of elderly people. Other members often listen sympathetically to the recitation of symptoms, viewing them as part of the "normal" illnesses and discomforts they all experience. Such uncritical acceptance of the hypochondriac's "medical" problems tends to reduce that member's need to rely upon illness, allowing the hypochondriac to move into discussion of other issues.

### Group Goals

Having defined the reasons for starting a group and the composition of the group, the therapeutic goals of the group must be defined. Goals must be determined for individual members of the group and for the group as a whole. These goals must be made clear to the members, since many will have trouble understanding even the general goals for group therapy, let alone the specific ones for this group. If the leader is unsure of the group's goals, it is certain that the members will also be unclear and may see no need to participate.

### Leadership

The number of leaders needed is dependent upon the size of the group and the goals for the group. Two leaders are usually preferable. Given the features common to many elderly — mild hearing and memory impairment, the importance of touch, and the topics of death, loneliness, and chronic illness often discussed in the group — it is very difficult for one person to sustain the enthusiasm and the energy, both physical and mental, necessary to lead a group. It is not possible, I believe, for one person to lead a psychotherapy group of more than ten elderly persons effectively, and it is preferable

to have two leaders whenever there are more than six persons (Altholz and Burnside 1976).

The profession of each leader is also important. If it is decided, for example, that group therapy will replace individual therapy and many group members are on medications, at least one leader must be familiar with the purposes, side effects, and dosages of the drugs. These questions will be raised frequently, and often the leader can turn to someone else for help in this area.

The leaders must determine between themselves what role (or roles) they will fulfill in the group. Although these may change later, distinct roles should be chosen before the group begins. The leaders can be passive, functioning as listeners and targets for the ventilation of members' feelings, or they may be active, assuming the roles of teacher, facilitator, questioner, comforter, and moderator (Goldfarb 1972). Most often the leader will fill a combination of roles, active at some times, passive at others.

The manner in which the group leaders are perceived by the members can become an important therapeutic tool. In addition to possessing the general qualities appropriate for a group leader, such as intrapsychic awareness (particularly of countertransference), flexibility, and tolerance for ambiguity. (MacLennan 1975), leaders of psychotherapy groups for the elderly should be selected for the qualities and roles they may represent to the group members (Linden 1954). I found, for example, that although an older leader represented both the wisdom and experience of age, a young co-leader symbolized the idealism and energy of youth. Butler and Lewis (1977, 272) believe that male and female therapists have the advantage of providing "both a psychodynamic and sociological orientation for a group, as well as opportunities for transference." In addition, they may represent the social reality of sex roles, serving as models for behavior outside the group. Thus, although often ignored, using the potential of dual leadership fully can enhance the benefits of group therapy.

### Practical Considerations

Practical considerations include providing transportation to and from the group as well as facilities that accommodate any physical impairments members have. Similarly, a decision must be made on the length of the session based on the energy levels of members. Group members may have frequent absences, which must be dealt with to preserve group continuity, yet allowances must be made for legitimate illness. An assistant to the group leader, someone who is able to coordinate absences, transportation, and so forth, is invaluable because the amount of time required to coordinate arrangements may negate any time saved by employing group therapy.

## GROUP PSYCHOTHERAPY: A PERSONAL STUDY

### Major Goals

Describing a psychotherapy group I led that lasted more than two years will illustrate some of the unique qualities of group psychotherapy with the elderly. This group functioned while I was affiliated with the Older American Resources and Services Program (OARS), sponsored by the Duke University Center for the Study of Aging and Human Development. The group began as part of the OARS outpatient clinic program of mental health care for elderly patients in the community. The group had three major purposes: (1) a socialization experience providing the opportunity to belong to a group at a time when group and other contacts are diminished, (2) exposure to alternative problem solutions developed by other elderly people, and (3) treatment of larger groups of people with limited personnel and time.

### Size of the Group

The group membership varied from four to nine, although fifteen persons were members for different periods. The average attendance was five persons, both male and female. The mean age of the men was 68.9 years and of the women 66.9 years. All the members had been in individual treatment with the staff of the clinic, two remained in individual treatment while in the group, and members could be seen individually in certain crises. All members

chosen shared a diagnosis of depression, but the group was heterogeneous in background, current living arrangement, and defense mechanisms used in coping with current problems. The three foci of the therapy were (1) the resolution of individual problems in adapting to growing older, (2) improvement of reality testing, and (3) social interaction.

### Dual Leadership

Two leaders were chosen for the group—a psychiatrist and a social worker. This dual leadership functioned according to Linden's (1954) concept of "social precept" wherein the therapists represent a marriage of complementary interests, the shared authority of an ideal parental team, and the social reality of the roles of the sexes. Many of the members had difficulty in social relationships and used the therapists as models for interaction outside the group. Experience showed that the members' relationships with the older male therapist "peer" and the younger female therapist "daughter" encouraged learning and experimenting with different and more satisfying ways of relating to friends and family.

### Contracts

I noted earlier that the concept of group therapy is alien to many older people. Consequently, in the beginning, members were often confused about the arrangements and purposes of the group. Much of this confusion can be dissipated at the beginning of the group by establishing a verbal and/or written contract. The leaders had met individually with each potential member before the first group session to explain the purposes of the group, to obtain a commitment for attendance, and to set individual goals. The general contract was designed by the group within the first three sessions, which were held weekly for one hour. Although regular attendance was stressed, if the leaders were apprised of absences due to illness or bad weather, the member was not charged for the session. Transportation was supplied when needed. The members decided to have an open-ended group and accept new members of the leaders' choice. The group was long term, with no stated termination date. See Chapter 9 for further discussion of contracts.

### Group Participation

We found ten minutes at least were needed for the members to warm up and begin to talk to one another. To encourage interaction, the members were asked to enter the group room as soon as they arrived at the clinic. Here they carried on general discussion and were ready to begin focusing by the time the therapists arrived.

The sessions usually began with a member's raising a topic for discussion spontaneously or by a leader's asking the members individually what had happened to them in the past week. The leaders took an active part in the group by serving as sympathetic authorities, providing information on community resources, and stimulating discussion, particularly in sensitive areas in which the members usually did not volunteer to relate their experiences. As Irvin Yalom (1975, 103) notes, "At times it is very helpful for the therapist to share some past and current real-life problem to afford a model for identification through his capacity to come through such a problem period constructively." The group encouraged all members to contribute to the discussion. However, no group pressure was exerted on members who benefited simply by attending weekly sessions even without regular verbal participation. The leaders summarized each session in the last five minutes, reemphasizing important points that had been discussed.

### Mutual Support of Members

All members saw themselves as important parts of the group, and a high degree of cohesiveness was evident (Yalom 1975). Cohesiveness displayed itself early in the life of the group; by the third session concern was expressed for those absent. By the eighth session those present asked for an accounting of the missing members before the meeting could begin! This attitude of concern was not surprising. Since all older people have suffered many losses, the members present feared an absent member might be seriously ill or even dead.

With a single exception, no members had been in group therapy before, and such a group was indeed frightening. Consequently, during the first four or five sessions members sought the protection of the therapists, whom they saw as authorities who defined group limits, behavior, and goals. Within eight months, however, long-time members took responsibility for defining group behavior to new members. The members themselves reinforced acceptance of the patient role and self-disclosure. They also reinforced group goals whenever a member attempted to ignore these goals to avoid discussing a sensitive area.

Members encouraged one another to discuss problems by conveying group understanding and by assurances that no problem would be seen as an embarrassment. Indeed, members were quick to note, "We're all here because we're going through it too." The members also supported one another in reinforcing individual strengths and assets. Sometimes they brought some of their handiwork, for example, and all samples were accepted in this positive, encouraging manner, no matter what the quality. Similarly, statements made by members were accepted in a positive, encouraging way. The concerns of each member were understood by all to be important, no matter how trivial they seemed. All aches and pains, symptoms that might be ridiculed by a professional, were taken seriously and dealt with sympathetically (Hulicka 1963).

Members of this group showed much less intermember hostility than the leaders had anticipated. Although members did indeed confront one another, they did so in indirect, nonhostile, and supportive language. It appeared that the common burden of aging increased the sense of vulnerability and created sufficient empathy among members to minimize antagonism. Possibly many hostile feelings that may have been present were ventilated on topics external to member relationships, such as inflation and poor medical care for the elderly. In her article on group therapy in a home for the aged, Feil (1967) noted the same phenomenon. Criticism and hostility in the group were often couched in humorous and subtle terms, which actually were more effective than direct attack. As Yalom (1975, 264) states, "Members can

. . . profit from conflict providing its intensity does not exceed their tolerance. . . ." The members of this group determined their own tolerance and never exceeded it, even when urged to do so by the therapists.

Several common themes emerged in group discussion. The discovery of shared problems boosted self-esteem and fostered group identification. Common problems and concerns expressed frequently by members included: (1) depression and its manifestations (including suicide), (2) development of new roles as aging persons, and (3) difficulties in social relationships. The most common concern was loss: of the work role, of dignity, of physical and intellectual capacity, of family and friends, and eventually of one's own life.

The members dealt with a number of losses within the group, including the death of one member and the severe stroke of another. These events occurred within two months of each other. The leaders feared the group ego could not cope with a second loss so soon after the first, but this was not true. The ability of older people to adapt to stresses in their lives, as Butler (1974) notes, is remarkable. The ego strength of the elderly to cope with crises is often overlooked by those who wish to place them in a fragile and dependent role and to emphasize mental illness rather than mental health. However, as one group member commented, with agreement by all, he was glad to belong to a group like this one because it was easier to face sad events with people he felt close to and with whom he could talk openly about his own fears of illness and death.

## LIMITATIONS OF GROUP PSYCHOTHERAPY

Group psychotherapy cannot be a remedy for all the problems of the aged. A large group of elderly need attention that group therapy cannot provide. Group psychotherapy cannot help individuals use community resources, nor can it coordinate those resources. Many older people need environmental manipulation, including home services or placement, which can be effected only on an individual basis. However, group psychotherapy can be an effective mode of treatment with the elderly. Simply knowing

that a group exists exclusively for them increases the sense of self-worth among older persons. Through interaction with peers, group therapy helps specifically to develop a realistic self-image and provides social opportunities.

Our society provides few peer group opportunities for the elderly. They can no longer relate to their work group, friends may have moved away or died, and those activities in which they may have participated as younger and middle-aged persons—such as civic and service activities—may no longer be relevant because of a loss of interest, "age-appropriateness," or difficulties in remaining an active member of the group (Lowy 1962). Only rarely can older people meet together in a group to discuss their feelings, concerns, and difficulties. Group psychotherapy offers the chance to discuss common problems and the alternative solutions discovered by other older people. It can also offer an answer to the question many older people ask themselves. "Now that I am old, what kind of a person am I supposed to be?"

Looking at life in terms of developmental stages, it is clear that for every age group except old age there exists a societally accepted set of expectations for behavior and achievement. However, these expectations cease with retirement, and then it becomes difficult to identify role expectations for older persons. There are some limited role definitions, such as grandparent, but that role is hardly adequate for the 24 hours a day of the 20-odd years many people live after they retire. What contributions, if any, are the elderly to make to society? How are old people supposed to act and what are they to talk about? How are they to relate to those persons around them, both younger and older? And perhaps most important, how are they to feel about themselves? The persons who can most appropriately help define a role for the aged are the aged themselves.

## SUMMARY

This chapter discusses common problems in group psychotherapy with the elderly. The foremost difficulty in such a therapeutic strategy is that group sharing and group solutions are alien to most older people. Areas that must be thought through before the group begins are (1) purpose of group therapy, (2) group composition, (3) group goals, (4) leadership, and (5) practical considerations.

Group therapy saves time and uses professional personnel more appropriately than individual therapy. The group composition is important because it is not enough to put people in a group just because they are old; there must be other reasons. Criteria for group selection might include sex, physical problems, psychiatric problems, and communication ability. The group goals must be therapeutic. Also, the leader must not be unsure of the goals, for the uncertainty will be reflected in the members' participation. Leadership will depend on the size and goals of the group. Co-leaders must decide between them what role (or roles) they intend to fulfill in the group. Practical considerations include transportation problems, the length of the sessions, and absenteeism.

A personal study was used to describe group psychotherapy co-led by a female social worker and a male psychiatrist. Common themes that emerged from the group included discovery of shared problems and increased self-esteem. Common problems were depression and its symptoms, suicidal ideation, and taking on new roles as aging persons. The most common concern was loss—of the work role, dignity, physical and intellectual capacity, family friends, and one's own life. Illness and death occurring within the group experience were handled well by the group members.

The self-worth of older persons can be increased considerably by their merely knowing that a group exists just for them. They develop a more realistic self-image and increase their social opportunities through group membership. Group psychotherapy also offers the older person an opportunity to discuss, define, experiment with, and adopt a satisfying and appropriate role in society.

## EXERCISE 1

Behavioral problems in groups run the gamut from monopolization to muteness, from paranoia to easy permissiveness. Select one behavior of an aged member in a group you have led or observed and analyze it in a page or two. Include the following points and discuss theory whenever appropriate:

1. Patient's age, diagnosis (or diagnoses), and behavioral problem.
2. Rationale for selecting this patient's behavior to analyze.
3. Behavioral change to be achieved.
4. Reasons the change is desirable.
5. Therapeutic technique to be used.
6. Criteria for evaluating the degree to which change is achieved.

## EXERCISE 2

Review other chapters in this book about group work and delineate how group psychotherapy is different from reality orientation groups, remotivation groups, reminiscing groups, and art therapy groups. Consider these components in your answer: types of leaders, group composition, group goals, and leadership goals.

## REFERENCES

Altholz, J. 1973. Group therapy with elderly patients. In *Alternatives to institutional care for older Americans: Practice and planning*. Durham, N.C.: Duke University.

Barton, M. G. 1962. Group counseling with older patients. *The Gerontologist* 2(1): 51–56 (March).

Berger, M. 1968. Similarities and differences between group psychotherapy and short-term group process experiences—Clinical impressions. *Journal of Group Psychoanalysis and Process* 1(1): 11–29 (Spring).

Burnside, I. M. 1970. Loss: A constant theme in group work with the aged. *Hospital and Community Psychiatry* 21(6): 173–77 (June).

Butler, R. 1974. Successful aging and the role of the life review. *Journal of the American Geriatrics Society* 22(12): 529–35 (December).

Butler, R., and M. Lewis. 1977. *Aging and mental health: Positive psychosocial approaches*. 2d ed. St. Louis, Mo.: Mosby.

Cohen, M. G. 1973. Alternatives to institutional care of the aged. *Social Casework* 54(8): 447–52 (October).

Conrad, W. 1974. A group therapy program with older adults in a high-risk neighborhood setting. *International Journal of Group Psychotherapy* 24(3): 358–60 (July).

cummings, e. e. 1972. Lines from: since feeling is first, is 5 collection. In *Complete poems 1913–1962*. New York: Harcourt Brace Jovanovich.

Feil, N. 1967. Group therapy in a home for the aged. *The Gerontologist* 7(3): 192–95 (September).

Goldfarb, A. 1972. Group therapy with the old and aged. In *Group treatment of mental illness*, ed. H. Kaplan and B. Sadock. New York: Aronson.

Hulicka, I. 1963. Participation in group conferences by geriatric patients. *The Gerontologist* 3(1): 10–13 (March).

Kaplan, J. 1959. Evaluation techniques for older groups. *American Journal of Occupational Therapy* 13(5): 222–25.

Klein, W., E. LeShan, and S. Furman. 1965. *Promoting mental health of older people through group methods*. New York: Mental Health Materials Center.

Kubie, S., and G. Landau. 1953. *Group work with the aged*. New York: International Universities Press.

Lewis, M. 1974. Life-review therapy: Putting memories to work in individual and group psychotherapy. *Geriatrics* 29(11): 165–73 (November).

Liederman, P. C., and R. Green. 1965. Geriatric outpatient group therapy. *Comprehensive Psychiatry* 6(1): 51–60 (February).

Liederman, P. C., R. Green, and V. Liederman. 1967. Outpatient group therapy with geriatric patients. *Geriatrics* 22(1): 148–53 (January).

Linden, M. 1953. Group psychotherapy with institutionalized senile women: Studies in gerontologic human relations. *International Journal of Group Psychotherapy* 3:150–70.

———. 1954. Significance of dual leadership in gerontological group psychotherapy: Studies in gerontological human relations III. *International Journal of Group Psychotherapy* 4:262–73.

———. 1955. Transference in gerontological group psychotherapy: Studies in gerontological human relations IV. *International Journal of Group Psychotherapy* 5:61–79.

Lowy, L. 1962. The group in social work with the aged. *Social Work* 7(4): 43–50 (October).

———. 1967. Roadblocks in group work practice with older people—Framework for analysis. *The Gerontologist* 7(2): 109–13 (June).

MacLennan, B. 1975. The personalities of group leaders: Implications for selection and training. *International Journal of Group Psychotherapy* 25(2): 177–83 (April).

Meerloo, J. A. M. 1955. Transference and resistance in geriatric psychotherapy. *Psychoanalytic Review* 42 (January): 72–82.

National Association of Social Workers. 1963. *Social group work with older people*. New York.

Rosin, A. 1975. Group discussions: A therapeutic tool in a chronic diseases hospital. *Geriatrics* 30 (August): 45–49.

Schwarzmann, B. 1965. Observations of the dynamic at play in a group of older people. Reprint of paper given at Project on Aging, Family Service Association of America.

———. 1966. Use of the geriatric group. Reprint of paper given at Conference on Community Care for the Aged, Montreal, December 5.

Shere, E. 1964. Group therapy with the very old. In *New thoughts on old age*, ed. R. Kastenbaum. New York: Springer.

Silver, A. 1950. Group psychotherapy with senile psychiatric patients. *Geriatrics* 5 (May–June): 147–50.

Tine, S., K. Hastings, and P. Deutschberger. 1960. Generic and specific in social group work practice with the aging. In *Social work with groups*. New York: National Association of Social Workers.

Wolfe, B., and G. Wolfe. 1975. Exploring retirement in a small group. *Social Work* 29(6):
481–84 (November).

Yalom, I. 1975. *The theory and practice of group
psychotherapy.* 2d ed. New York: Basic Books.

Zimberg, S. 1969. Outpatient geriatric psychiatry in
an urban ghetto with nonprofessional workers.
*American Journal of Psychiatry* 125(12): 1697–
1702 (June).

## BIBLIOGRAPHY

Berger, L., and M. Berger. 1973. A holistic group
approach to psychogeriatric outpatients. *International Journal of Group Psychotherapy* 23(4):
432–45 (October).

Berger, M., and L. Berger. 1972. Psychogeriatric
group approaches. In *Progress in group and family
therapy,* ed. C. Sager and H. Kaplan. New York:
Brunner/Mazel.

Blank, M. L. 1974. Raising the age barrier to psychotherapy. *Geriatrics* 29(11): 141–48 (November).

Butler, R. 1960. Intensive psychotherapy for the hospitalized aged. *Geriatrics* 15(9): 644–53
(September).

Finkel, S., and W. Fillmore. 1971. Experiences with
an older adult group at a private psychiatric hospital. *Journal of Geriatric Psychiatry* 4(2): 188–99
(Spring).

Goldfarb, A. I. 1964. Patient-doctor relationship in
the treatment of aged persons. *Geriatrics* 19(1):
18–23 (January).

————. 1971. Group therapy with the old and aged.
In *Comprehensive group psychotherapy,* ed. H. I.
Kaplan and B. Sadock. Baltimore: Williams &
Wilkins.

Harper, R. A. 1975. *The new psychotherapies.* Englewood Cliffs, N.J.: Prentice-Hall.

Harris, P. B. 1979. Being old: A confrontation group
with nursing home residents. *Health Social Work*
(1):152–166 (February).

Ingersoll, B., and A. Silverman. 1978. Comparative
group psychotherapy for the aged. *The Gerontologist* 18(2): 201–6 (April).

Larson, M. K. 1970. A descriptive account of group
treatment of older people by a caseworker. *Journal of Geriatric Psychiatry* 3(2): 231–40 (Spring).

Lazarus, L. W. 1976. A program for the elderly at a
private psychiatric hospital. *The Gerontologist*
16(2): 125–31 (April).

Lesser, J., L. Lazarus, R. Frankel, and S. Havasy.
1981. Reminiscence group therapy with psychotic
geriatric inpatients. *The Gerontologist* 21(3):
291–96 (June).

Liederman, P. C., R. Green, and V. R. Liederman.
1967. An approach to problems of geriatric outpatients. *Current Psychiatric Therapy* 7:179.

Manaster, A. 1972. Therapy with the senile geriatric
patient. *International Journal of Group Psychotherapy* 22 (April): 250–57.

Maxwell, J. 1960. Group services—Well-being for
older people. In *Social work with groups.* New
York: National Association of Social Workers.

Saul, S., and S. Saul. 1974. Group psychotherapy in a
proprietary nursing home. Part 1. *The Gerontologist* 14(5): 446–50 (October).

Scheidlinger, S. 1968. Group psychotherapy in the
sixties. *American Journal of Psychotherapy* 22(2):
170–84 (April).

Schoenberg, B., and R. Senescu. 1966. Group psychotherapy for patients with chronic multiple somatic
complaints. *Journal of Chronic Diseases* 19(6):
649–57 (June).

Weinberg, J. 1974. What do I say to my mother when
I have nothing to say? *Geriatrics* 29(11): 155–59
(November).

Wolk, R. L., and A. I. Goldfarb. 1967. The response
to group psychotherapy of aged recent admissions
compared with long-term mental hospital patients.
*American Journal of Psychiatry* 123(10): 1251–56
(April).

## RESOURCES

Altholz, J., and I. Burnside. 1976. How to use group
psychotherapy. In audiocassette series *Successful
treatment of the elderly mentally ill.* New York:
Wyeth Laboratories.

# PART 5

# Reminiscing Therapy

FREDA LEINWAND/MONKMEYER

Because reminiscing therapy has gained in popularity, an entire section of this book is devoted to this modality. Part 5 elaborates on the theoretical framework, which was presented in Chapter 4. Once when I was trying to say "reminiscing and memory groups" the words combined and I said "memoriscing groups"; as I think about the coined word, it seems appropriate to call this part the "memoriscing" section.

In Chapter 22 Jean Hogan reports on a research project teaching volunteers to do reminiscing groups.

Another research study is reported in Chapter 23 by Kathleen King, who considers dying and counseling and reminiscing as a group approach.

In Chapter 24 Mary Ann Matteson reports on designing reminiscing groups for depressed institutionalized aged persons.

Jean Kiernat has added to the literature by her use of a life review in groups. Chapter 25 was originally published in the journal *Aging*.

Reminiscing as a group modality for those in board-and-care homes is examined and described in Chapter 26 in great depth by Sally Friedlob and James Kelly who experimented over a long period of time with various approaches in group.

Robert Havighurst has long been a pioneer in reminiscing research. In 1952 he wrote, "A good rule to follow is to tell stories of the past only to people under eight years old or to people one's own age. Another good rule is to listen to other people's reminiscences two hours for every one hour one asks them to listen."*

---

*Havighurst, R. 1952. Social and psychological needs of the aging. *The Annals of the American Academy of Political and Social Sciences.*

# chapter 22

# Use of Volunteers as Group Leaders

*Jean Hogan*

*The cup of life held in this heart has known bright singing moments and cherished hours, and still makes music to be shared!**

SISTER PATRICIA MURPHY (1981, 69)

MIMI FORSYTH / MONKMEYER

## LEARNING OBJECTIVES

- Define **reminiscing**.

- Identify the important effects of reminiscing in the elderly.

- Define **informative, evaluative** and **obsessive** reminiscing.

- Identify three benefits of reminiscing groups for the institutionalized elderly.

- Identify the qualities of an effective group leader.

## KEY WORDS

- Ego-integrity

- Evaluation

- Life review

- Psychosocial

- Reminiscing

- Screening

- Volunteer

## INTRODUCTION

Can nonprofessional personnel be used effectively as facilitators of reminiscing groups? This subject has not been researched; however, there is empirical support for the use of volunteers in this specific area of psychosocial care. This chapter describes utilizing volunteers as reminiscing group leaders for the institutionalized elderly. Before outlining this proposal, it is necessary to discuss the great need for improved mental health care for the institutionalized elderly, the importance of reminiscing for the elderly, and the use of volunteers in other types of psychosocial interactions.

### Mental Health Care

The mental health needs of the elderly in the United States are not being met. The current trend is to bypass mental facilities and to place the mentally ill elderly in nursing homes, which were not designed to meet the special needs of these elderly patients. According to the American Psychological Association, more than half of the one million patients in nursing homes across the country are suffering from functional psychiatric illness, and most receive little or no

therapy (Maisler and Solomon 1976). Although in some instances care in mental health facilities may be preferable, it is also possible to provide psychosocial treatment modalities in nursing homes.

W. R. McMordie and S. Blom (1979); P. Ebersole (1976); and W. Boylin, S. Gordon, and M. Nehrke (1976) have demonstrated that group therapy can be successfully conducted in skilled nursing facilities (SNF); and according to J. Maisler and K. Solomon (1976), such therapy can improve the quality of life of these institutionalized elderly patients. Of the many group approaches that can be used with these patients, the life review therapy developed by R. Butler (1963) is especially effective and beneficial (McMordie and Blom 1979). Reminiscing groups are an outgrowth of this therapeutic approach and are defined as groups in which the members engage in the act of thinking about or relating past experiences (McMahon and Rhudick 1964).

### The Life Review As a Conceptual Framework

Life review as a form of therapy was first described by Butler (1963). Based upon his experience in geropsychiatry, he concluded that a life review is essential for adjustment to old age and the acceptance of the inevitability of death. This conclusion supports Erikson's the-

*Lines from "Front and Back," by Sister Patricia Murphy. In Evelyn Mandel (Ed.), *The Art of Aging.* Copyright © 1981 by Winston Press, Inc. Reprinted by permission.

ory of the eight stages of man, in which he also sees reminiscing or life review as essential for the maintenance of ego-integrity in old age (Erikson 1950). M. Lewis and Butler (1974, 168) conclude from their experience with life review therapy that it gives the elderly an opportunity to reexamine their "whole life"; to accept personal foibles, differentiating between real and neurotic guilt; to reexamine and restructure their identity; to accept the inevitability of death; and to develop a "lively capacity" to live in the present. In addition, they conclude that reminiscing therapy need not be conducted by a professional leader, but that it can be carried out by an untrained "listener."

In other studies concerned with reminiscing and stress, M. Lieberman and J. Falk (1971) found that subjects under stress engaged in the greatest amount of reminiscing, while Lewis (1971) found that subjects who reminisced were better able to maintain their self-esteem under stress than were subjects who did not reminisce.

In studies relating life review and adjustment to old age, P. Coleman (1974) found no relationship between reminiscing and present adjustment. However, he was able to support his major hypothesis that life review is related to adjustment in subjects who evidence dissatisfaction in their past lives. A. McMahon and P. Rhudick (1964), in a classic study of elderly veterans, found that those who reminisced were less likely to suffer from depression, were better adjusted, and lived longer than those who did not reminisce. R. Fallott's (1979) study on the impact of mood on reminiscing in the older adult supports these findings. He concluded that reminiscing decreased negative effects in the older person and concurred with McMahon and Rhudick (1964) that reminiscing served as an adaptive function in later life.

Reminiscing is especially important for the institutionalized elderly since institutionalization has been shown to have a deleterious effect on both their psychological and physical well-being (Lindel 1976; Goldfarb 1961). Work with institutionalized elderly done by Boylin, Gordon, and Nehrke (1976); I. Burnside (1969); A. R. Lindel (1976); and J. Kiernat (1979) demonstrated increased ego-integrity, decreased withdrawal, and improved physical appearance among participants in therapy groups.

Some studies show little or no correlation between adaptation and reminiscence. M. LoGerfo (1980) suggests that the discordance results from researchers studying very different people in very different ways: some employed, some retired, some in institutions, some not. She also cites the lack of a standard operational definition of reminiscence. She suggests that there are three categories of reminiscing:

1. Informative reminiscing, in which the focus is on factual material, providing pleasure and improved self-esteem through reliving and retelling past experiences

2. Evaluative reminiscing, in which an individual actually engages in life review, coming to grips with old guilts, defeats, and conflicts and examining accomplishments

3. Obsessive reminiscing, in which an individual becomes preoccupied with a particular past situation.

And that, with few exceptions, researchers paid no attention to the vast differences in reminiscing behavior among persons. Although there are discrepancies in the research findings, "several studies, taken together suggest that reminiscing does serve as an adaptive mechanism or facilitates personality reorganization in the older adult" (Merriam 1980, 608).

## Volunteers in Other Psychosocial Settings

A search of the literature reveals a paucity of material concerning the use of volunteers as facilitators of reminiscing groups. However, the search does reveal discussion and studies concerning the use of volunteers in a variety of settings. Volunteers are caregivers in nursing homes; in home meal programs, which include nutritional counseling as well as recreational activities; in hospital-based programs, which provide many types of services; and in a variety of psychosocial settings (Silverstone 1978; Duval and Coulter 1976; Warren and Clark 1979; Neitge and McCarney 1976).

The psychosocial settings in which volunteers are used vary greatly. M. Dixon and J. Burns (1975) describe a training program for volunteers in telephone crisis intervention and/or suicide prevention and report positive results. J. Harris (1980) describes the use of volunteers in suicide prevention and cites the correlation between the reduced suicide rate and the growth of the "Samaritans," a group of nonprofessional volunteers.

G. Grubb (1978) discusses the use of volunteers in the psychosocial setting and sees them serving as liaison between staff and patients in hospitals for the mentally handicapped and in the community at large. Also, in the mental health setting, T. Lear and J. Lewington (1978) utilized, successfully, volunteer "case aids" in the treatment of the hospitalized mentally ill. In the acute care hospital setting, the Dominican Santa Cruz Hospital in California utilizes volunteers in pastoral services, to provide support and comfort to patients and their families during times of stress, and reports positive response from both clients and staff (Ellmer 1980). Nyak Hospital, New York, used volunteers in a similar way in its "family waiting room" project and reported positive results (Moran and Sutter 1979).

Patients and families of patients are also used in a variety of ways. J. Morley (1976) describes the successful use of both the mentally and the physically handicapped as volunteers. M. Schmidt (1979) discusses the use of former mental patients in the regular volunteer program of a state hospital in Australia. M. Kleiman, J. Mantell, and E. Alexander (1977) outline a program using cancer patients as counselors for other cancer patients, an activity that includes reminiscing. Also, in the oncology setting, mothers of children who have died of cancer are used to provide emotional support and practical assistance to other children with cancer and to their families (Stuetzer, Fochtman, and Schulman 1976); and the St. Barnabas Hospice Committee, a voluntary group, focuses on the quality of life of dying persons (Noll and Sampsell 1978).

In the community setting, volunteers are used as psychoeducational agents in a remedial program for learning and psychosocially disabled children (Matefy 1978). Community volunteers are also used successfully in the rehabilitation of stroke patients with language disorders (Lesser and Watt 1978; Meikle et al. 1979) and

in hospice work with dying patients and their families and friends. See Byrne's Chapter 34 for a description of one volunteer's work with music in groups.

Although it reveals nothing concerning the use of volunteers in reminiscing groups, a search of the literature does give empirical support to the effective use of volunteers in a variety of psychosocial settings. It therefore seems plausible that volunteers can be used effectively as facilitators in reminiscing groups.

## THE USE OF VOLUNTEERS: A PROPOSAL

As described above, reminiscing therapy groups are beneficial to the elderly and require a minimum of preparation; however, few skilled nursing facilities have sufficient numbers of staff to provide leadership for these groups. If, as Butler (1974) contends, reminiscing therapy can be carried out effectively by untrained persons, either on a one-to-one or a group basis, it should be possible to instruct volunteers in the basic concepts of reminiscing therapy and to utilize them in skilled nursing facilities as leaders in ongoing reminiscing groups. These groups would facilitate the adaptation processes of the elderly patients, improve their self-concept and communication skills, and thus improve the quality of their lives.

### Recruitment

Although some extended care facilities may have formal volunteer programs, it has been my experience during visits to these facilities and in discussions with activity directors that many of these nursing homes have no organized volunteer programs but that they "welcome" volunteers and utilize them in a variety of ways. The agencies make no active effort to recruit volunteers, yet they express frustration about not having more volunteers available. Some use "volunteers" who have been sentenced by the courts to work in the agencies. What is the quality of a volunteer whose punishment is working with the institutionalized elderly?

According to S. Beer (1977), volunteers can be successfully recruited in a variety of ways. She advocates recruiting from various civic and service organizations, from local churches, and from the community at large. She claims success using the following techniques for recruitment: speaking engagements, letter-writing campaigns, mailings, and newspaper ads. In addition to the resources suggested by Beer, this author suggests recruiting from local colleges, with units of credit given for a quarter's or a semester's work; local high schools (these youngsters have demonstrated their abilities as volunteers through their success in "foster grandparent" programs and in "candy-striper" programs in acute hospitals); and from senior citizens groups.

### Screening

Not all persons who volunteer to work with the elderly will be suitable to lead groups. A screening process will be necessary to determine the applicant's qualifications. The process suggested for this program is a modification of the screening process used by Companions of Alameda County (California) Inc., a nonprofit organization that uses volunteers as companions to disadvantaged children. The process comprises three parts: letters of reference, interview, and evaluation.

During the initial contact with the prospective volunteer, the person is asked to supply the names and addresses of two references who are not relatives. A questionnaire (Figure 22–1) and a cover letter explaining the project is then sent to each of the references. The responses to the questionnaires remain confidential and are not shared with the prospective volunteers.

When the letters of reference are returned, a screening interview is held. Although there is no "list" of questions to be answered, several specific areas are explored with the prospective volunteer:

1. Motivations
   a. Why did you decide to become a volunteer?
   b. How much thought did you give to the decision?
   c. What are your expectations?
2. Limitations
   a. Is there anything that might place limits on your performance as a volunteer?

   b. Are you willing to work with residents who are culturally or ethnically different from you? With confused residents?
   c. What is your past experience with the elderly?
3. Understanding
   a. How do you understand the project?
   b. What is your understanding of the role of group leader?
4. Commitment
   a. Are you willing to make a 10-week commitment?
   b. Are you willing to attend training sessions and peer group discussions?

Following the interview, a written evaluation of the prospective volunteer is prepared. It should include a list of strengths and weaknesses and any other pertinent information. The final recommendation for reminiscing group leader is based upon this evaluation.

A large number of the volunteers recruited would not be needed as reminiscing group leaders. These volunteers could be used to establish a formal volunteer organization to provide a pool of workers who could be drawn upon for numerous purposes: recreational programs, educational programs, community service programs (Beer 1977), or other types of group work—for example, exercise, art, discussion, current events, poetry writing.

### Suggestions for Training

Training for reminiscing group leaders should include: (1) reading assignments and films, (2) an experiential exercise in a reminiscing group, (3) peer group discussion, and (4) evaluation.

The reading material and films selected should provide the trainee with the basic concepts of reminiscing therapy as well as the qualifications mentioned above. These materials should be accompanied by an evaluation form. Having the trainee evaluate the material will ensure compliance with the reading assignments and will provide the instructor with feedback on the usefulness of all the material presented.

Articles or chapters by Burnside (1969, 1971), Kiernat (1979), K. Ellison (1981), Ebersole (1976), and C. Rogers (1970) are recommended

---

**REFERENCE LETTER**

**CONFIDENTIAL**

1. I have known _____ for _____ years/months.
   (Circle one).

2. During this time he/she has been my: neighbor, pupil, classmate, friend, employee, other _____
   (Circle one).

3. In this group project, this person will be working closely with a group of elderly residents of a nursing home. Do you think he/she is flexible enough to work with these special people?

4. Dependability is one of the most important traits of a successful volunteer. A volunteer must be able to keep appointments on time, must be able to make a ten week commitment to a nursing home and must possess a level of maturity that enables him/her to cope with the special needs of the elderly residents. Do you feel that this person is capable of making such a commitment? Please Explain.

5. Please comment on other characteristics that this person has which you feel would qualify him/her as a volunteer in this project.

6. Do you have any reservations about recommending this person for this project? If so, please explain.

7. I recommend this person:   Very Strongly          Strongly

                             Noncommittally        Do Not Recommend

   Your Signature:

   _____

   Date:

   _____

FIGURE 22–1. *Questionnaire sent to references of potential volunteer group leaders.*

---

readings for the volunteers. The film *Peege* is also highly recommended. (See Chapter 4, Exercise 2 and Resources.) In addition to the previous material, I would suggest including a reading on the internal and external changes that occur in aging (for example, Rossman [1981]), to provide the volunteers with an understanding of the aging process and to correct any misconceptions they may have regarding aging.

By participating in a reminiscing group, the trainee will experience what it might "feel like" to be a member of such a group. Also, she or he will have an opportunity to observe the facilitator as a role model.

Peer group discussion should be carried out not only during the training period but at regular intervals throughout the volunteers' length of service. These discussions will provide the volunteers with an opportunity to share their concerns, problems, feelings, and experiences as reminiscing group leaders. The instructor (or another professional person) should be readily available to the volunteer leaders. Occasionally problems may arise within the groups that the volunteers are not prepared to handle. Volunteers should be apprised of this possibility during the training period and should be assured that although this is a rare occurrence, professional help is always available should it be required.

In addition to participating in the training sessions, each volunteer should be asked for a firm time commitment for a period of at least 10 weeks, to provide continuity for the reminiscing group. A contract with each volunteer will help assure this commitment. After working with the group for the 10-week period, the volunteer may wish to extend the time commitment and should be allowed to do so. Reminiscing can have as profound an effect on the leader as it has on the group members, for it allows the listener" . . . an opportunity to experience living history . . . to project himself/herself into the past and thereby into unexperienced manifestations of existence" (Erlich 1979, 64).

### Selection of Group Participants

Selection of the group participants should be done in collaboration with the professional staff. Those who work with the residents on a daily basis will be aware of any physical or emotional problems that would interfere in their participation in a group. For a group led by an inexperienced volunteer, the members selected should be oriented to person and place and should be strong enough to be out of bed for long periods of time. Working with confused, frail residents may be discouraging or frightening to new volunteers, causing them to withdraw from the program before they have had an opportunity to share in the rich experience of a "successful" reminiscing group. The more experienced volunteers may welcome the challenge of conducting a group of confused elderly residents. According to Kiernat (1979), these residents may have the greatest need to reminisce, since they do not verbalize readily and they do not actively participate in other activities. In her study of the confused elderly she found that they did benefit from participation in reminiscing groups. Residents who initially responded only to the group leader—and then only to direct questions—later responded to other residents and voluntarily shared their memories and experiences with the group without prodding. For the purposes of her study, Kiernat excluded the severely hearing or visually impaired from the group. It is my belief, however, that both types of impaired residents could benefit from participation in volunteer-led groups. The hearing-impaired, who have conversational speech, may "miss" part of the group interaction but will still be able to share their memories and experiences, although they need the assistance of the leader. The same holds true for the visually impaired.

In her work with the institutionalized elderly in a life review group, Ellison (1981) excluded residents who were labeled depressed by the staff of the nursing home or who were obviously unhappy in the nursing home. Her concern was, as several sources caution, that life review can lead to depression and suicidal panic. It should be emphasized, however, that life review groups differ from reminiscing groups in their goals. The purpose of life review is to provide psychotherapy. A reminiscing group, on the other hand, provides the members with an opportunity to socialize and to communicate. It gives them "permission" to share their memories without being labeled "senile" or "living in the past." Perhaps a reminiscing group would be appropriate for those who are unhappy with their living conditions or who are mildly depressed. (See Chapter 24 by Matteson for a discussion of depressed individuals.) Discretion should certainly be used in selecting participants for the groups; however, whole groups of residents should not be eliminated from participation based solely upon their physical or emotional limitations.

### Evaluation

The program should be evaluated by: (1) response by the volunteer group leaders to a questionnaire; (2) interviews with the nursing staff of the institution (including nursing assistants); and (3) interviews with the group participants, in which they are asked to evaluate the experience.

At the end of the 10-week period each volunteer group leader should be asked to evaluate the program by responding to a questionnaire. Based upon the results of that questionnaire, the training program can be adjusted to meet the needs of future volunteers. A sample questionnaire follows:

*Volunteer Leader Evaluation Questionnaire*

1. Overall, was the experience satisfactory?
2. Did the preliminary training prepare you adequately for this experience?
3. If no, in what way(s) was it deficient?
4. Was all of the material presented applicable to your group experience?
5. If no, what material could be deleted?
6. What part of the training program was most beneficial to you?
7. What part of the training program was least beneficial to you?

8. Were the peer group discussions helpful?
9. If not, how can they be improved?
10. Comments:

The nursing staff should be interviewed to determine if they observed changes in the group participants' appetite, appearance, ability to communicate, social interactions with other residents, or willingness to participate in other activities offered in the facility.

Finally, the participants themselves should be interviewed to determine if they found the group enjoyable, if they would be willing to participate in future groups, and if they have any comments or suggestions concerning the group.

## SUMMARY

The importance of reminiscing in adjustment to old age is especially important to the institutionalized elderly and is well documented in the literature. Lewis and Butler (1974) maintain that reminiscing by the elderly can be carried out either on an individual or a group basis and that any good "listener" can assist in this activity. It should therefore be possible to utilize nonprofessional volunteers as reminiscing group leaders. A review of the literature shows that volunteers have been used effectively in many other types of psychosocial settings. This lends empirical support to their use with reminiscing groups for the institutionalized elderly.

## EXERCISE 1

Develop a four-hour training program for volunteer reminiscing group leaders in a setting of your choice.

## EXERCISE 2

Develop a 20-item criteria list to screen prospective volunteer group leaders in a day care center.

## EXERCISE 3

Begin a volunteer-led reminiscing group in an extended care facility and evaluate its effectiveness after a one-month period. Describe your evaluation tool or tools.

## REFERENCES

Beer, S. 1977. Community outreach in a nursing home setting—A two-way road. *Journal of Nursing Administration* 9: 16–20 (September).

Boylin, W., S. Gordon, and M. F. Nehrke. 1976. Reminiscing and ego-integrity in institutonalized elderly males. *The Gerontologist* 16(2): 118–24 (April).

Burnside, I. 1969. Group work among the aged. *Nursing Outlook* 17(6): 68–71 (June).

_____. 1971. Long-term group work with the aged. *The Gerontologist* 2(3): 213–18 (Fall).

Butler, R. N. 1963. The life review: An interpretation of reminiscence in the aged. *Psychiatry* 26(1): 65–76.

_____. 1974. Successful aging and the role of the life review. *Journal of the American Geriatrics Society* 22(12): 529–35 (December).

Coleman, P. 1974. Measuring reminiscence characteristics from conversation as adaptive features of old age. *International Journal of Aging and Human Development* 5(3): 281–95 (Summer).

Dixon, M., and J. Burns. 1975. The training of telephone crisis intervention volunteers. *American Journal of Community Psychology* 3(2): 145–50.

Duval, M., and B. Coulter. 1976. Commitment leads to steadily growing home meals program. *Hospitals* 50(8): 169–72.

Ebersole, P. 1976. Reminiscing and group psychotherapy with the aged. In *Nursing and the aged.* 1st ed., ed. I. Burnside. New York: McGraw-Hill.

Ellison, K. 1981. Working with the elderly in a life review group. *Journal of Gerontological Nursing* 7(9): 537–41 (September).

Ellmer, R. 1980. Lay volunteers enlarge pastoral care department's scope. *Hospital Progress* 61(5): 78–80.

Erikson, E. 1950. *Childhood and society.* New York: Norton.

Erlich, A. 1979. The life review and elderly: A study in self-concept, recognition and re-cognition. Doctoral dissertation, California School of Professional Psychology. (*Dissertation Abstracts International,* 1979; University Microfilms no. 80-03242.)

Fallott, R. 1979–80. The impact of mood of verbal reminiscing in later adulthood. *International Journal of Aging and Human Development* 10(4): 385–400.

Goldfarb, A. 1961. Mental health in the institution. *The Gerontologist* 1(4): 178–84 (Winter).

Grubb, G. 1978. The castle concept. *Nursing Mirror* 1(12): 38–39.

Harris, J. 1980. The contribution of non-professionals in psychiatric care. *Nursing Times* 4(3): 602–3.

Kiernat, J. 1979. The use of life review activity with confused nursing home residents. *American Journal of Occupational Therapy* 33(5): 306–10 (September–October).

Kleiman, M., J. Mantell, and E. Alexander. 1977. Rx for social death: The cancer patient as counselor. *Community Mental Health Journal* 13(2): 115–24.

Lear, T., and J. Lewington. 1978. A first volunteer case aid programme in a mental hospital. *British Journal of Medical Psychology* 51:77–86.

Lesser, R., and M. Watt. 1978. Untrained community help in the rehabilitation of stroke sufferers with language disorder. *British Medical Journal* 2:1045–48.

Lewis, C. N. 1971. Reminiscing and self-concept in old age. *Journal of Gerontology* 26(2): 240–43 (April).

Lewis, M., and R. N. Butler. 1974. Life review therapy: Putting memories to work in individual and group psychotherapy. *Geriatrics* 29(11): 165–73 (November).

Lieberman, M., and J. Falk. 1971. The remembered past as a source of data for research in the life cycle. *Human Development* 14(2): 132–41.

Lindel, A. R. 1976. Nurse therapist congruence during group therapy as a factor in changing the self-concept of the institutionalized aged. Doctoral dissertation, Catholic University of America.

(*Dissertation Abstracts International,* 1976; University Microfilms no. 76–9215.)

LoGerfo, M. 1980–81. Three ways of reminiscence in theory and practice. *International Journal of Aging and Human Development* 21(1): 39–48.

Maisler, J., and K. Solomon. 1976. Therapeutic group process with the institutionalized elderly. *Journal of the American Geriatrics Society* 24(12): 542-46 (December).

Matefy, R. 1978. Evaluation of a remediation program using senior citizens as psychoeducational agents. *Community Mental Health Journal* 14(4): 327–36.

McMahon, A., and P. Rhudick. 1964. Reminiscing: Adaptational significance in the aged. *Archives of General Psychiatry* 10(3): 292–98 (March).

McMordie, W. R., and S. Blom. 1979. Life review therapy: Psychotherapy for the elderly. *Perspectives in Psychiatric Care* 17(4): 162–66 (July–August).

Meikle, M., E. Wechsler, A. Tupper, M. Benenson, J. Butler, D. Mulhall, and G. Stern. 1979. Comparative trial of volunteer and professional treatments of dysphasia after stroke. *British Medical Journal* 2:87–89.

Merriam, S. 1980. The concept and function of reminiscence: A review of the research. *The Gerontologist* 20(5): 604–8 (October).

Moran, M., and J. Sutter. 1979. Comfort, care for families who must wait. *Hospitals* 53(22): 112.

Morley, J. 1976. The handicapped (mental and physical) as voluntary social workers: A form of therapy. *International Journal of Social Psychiatry* 22(1): 61–63.

Murphy, P. 1981. Vision: Front and back. In *The art of aging,* ed. E. Mandel, 69. Minneapolis, Minn.: Winston Press.

Neitge, J., and T. McCarney. 1976. Junior volunteer program spurs interest in health care. *Hospitals* 50(6–1): 69–72.

Noll, G., and M. Sampsell. 1978. The community and the dying. *Journal of Community Psychology* 6:275–79.

Rossman, I. 1981. Human aging changes. In *Nursing and the aged.* 2d ed., ed. I. Burnside. New York: McGraw-Hill.

Rogers, C. 1970. *Carl Rogers on encounter groups.* New York: Harper & Row.

Schmidt, M. 1979. Patient as volunteer: An assault on chronicity. *Hospital and Community Psychiatry* 30(6): 404–6 (June).

Silverstone, B. 1978. The family is here to stay. *Journal of Nursing Administration* 8(5): 47–50.

Stuetzer, C., D. Fochtman, and J. Schulman. 1976. Mothers as volunteers in an oncology clinic. *The Journal of Pediatrics* 89(5): 847–48.

Warren, J., and M. Clark. 1979. Workshops enhance the role of the volunteer. *Hospitals* 53(24): 91–92.

## BIBLIOGRAPHY

Adler, L., and J. Graubert. 1975. Projected social distances from mental patient related items by male and female volunteers and nonvolunteers. *Psychological Reports* 37:515–21.

Blackman, J. 1980. Group work in the community: Experiences with reminiscence. In *Psychosocial nursing care of the aged.* 2d ed., ed. I. M. Burnside, 134–40. New York: McGraw-Hill.

Boyd, R., and R. Kaskela. 1970. A test of Erikson's theory of ego-state development by means of a self-report instrument. *Journal of Experimental Education* 38:1–14.

Bunker, B., and D. Singer. 1978. Independent nonprofessionals in the community: A case history analysis of a human relations program. *Psychiatry* 41:377–89.

Burnside, I. 1981. Reminiscing as therapy: An overview. In *Nursing and the aged.* 2d ed., ed. I. M. Burnside, 98–113. New York: McGraw-Hill.

Cameron, P. 1972. The generation gap: Time orientation. *The Gerontologist* 12(2): 117–19 (Summer).

Clemente, F., R. Rexroad, and C. Hirsch. 1975. The participation of the black aged in voluntary associations. *Journal of Gerontology* 30(4): 469–72 (July–August).

Costa, P., and R. Kastenbaum. 1967. Some aspects of memories and ambitions in centenarians. *Journal of Genetic Psychology* 110: 3–16 (March).

Garcia, S., C. Clark, and S. Walfish. 1979. Student voluntarism in transition. *Journal of Community Psychology* 7:74–77.

Gibson, D. E. 1980. Reminiscence, self-esteem and self-other satisfaction in adult male alcoholics. *Journal of Psychiatric Nursing* 18(3): 7–11 (March).

Hala, M. 1975. Reminiscence group therapy project. *Journal of Gerontological Nursing* 1(3): 34–41 (July–August).

Havighurst, R., and R. Glasser. 1972. An exploratory study of reminiscence. *Journal of Gerontology* 27(2): 245–53 (March–April).

Hogan, J. 1982. The use of volunteers to conduct Reminiscing groups. Unpublished master's thesis. San Jose State University. San Jose, CA.

Hunter, K., and M. Linn. 1980–81. Psychosocial differences between elderly volunteers and non-volunteers. *International Journal of Aging and Human Development* 12(3): 205–13.

Kastenbaum, R. 1974. . . . Gone tomorrow. *Geriatrics* 29(11): 127–34 (November).

Langs, R. 1965. Earliest memories and personality. *Archives of General Psychiatry* 12: 379–90 (April).

Langs, R., M. Rothenberg, J. Fishman, and M. Reiser. 1960. A method for clinical and theoretical study of the earliest memory. *Archives of General Psychiatry* 3(11): 523–34 (November).

Linn, N. W. 1973. Perceptions of childhood: Present functioning and past events. *Journal of Gerontology* 28:202–6.

Liton, J., and S. C. Olstein. 1969. Specific aspects of reminiscence. *Journal of Gerontology* 50:262–68.

Payne, B. 1977. The older volunteer: Social role continuity and development. *The Gerontologist* 17(4): 355–61 (Winter).

Perlmutter, M., R. Metzger, K. Miller, and T. Nezworski. 1980. Memory of historical events. *Experimental Aging Research* 6(1): 47–60.

Pincus, A. 1970. Reminiscence in aging and its implications for social work practice. *Social Work* 15(4): 42–51 (October).

Sherman, S., and R. J. Havighurst. 1970. An exploratory study of reminiscence. Abstract in *The Gerontologist* 10(3): 42 (Autumn).

Taynor, J., J. Perry, and P. Frederick. 1976. A brief program to upgrade the skills of community caregivers. *Community Mental Health Journal* 12(1): 13–18.

Tobin, S., and E. Etigson. 1968. Effects of stress on the earliest memory. *Archives of General Psychiatry* 19:435–44.

Weisman, S., and R. Shusterman. 1977. Remembering, reminiscing and life reviewing in an activity program for the elderly. *Concern,* December/January: 22–26.

Zeiger, B. L. 1976. Life review in art therapy with the aged. *American Journal of Art Therapy* 15(1): 47–50 (January).

## RESOURCES

### Films

*A Private Life* (director: Mikhail Bogin). This film is about a lively, beautiful 70-year-old who refuses to lose her grip on life. Her friend, Karl, a retired engineer, is writing his memoirs. As he reads his memoirs to her, he slips into reminiscence. Both are Jews who fled Nazi Germany and have painful memories. Their handling of the memories is of interest. Contact: Museum of Modern Art, Department of Film (Attn.: William Sloan), 11 West 53rd Street, New York, NY 10020.

### Media Kits

*Remembering Automobiles*
*Remembering Birthdays*
*Remembering County Fairs*
*Remembering the Depression*
*Remembering Fall*
*Remembering Farm Days*
*Remembering 1924*
*Remembering School Days*
*Remembering Summertime*
*Remembering Train Rides*
Available from Bi-Folkal Productions Inc., Route 1, Rainbow Farm, Blue Mounds, WI 53517; phone (608) 241-7785 or 437-8146.

chapter 23

# Reminiscing, Dying, and Counseling: A Contextual Approach

*Kathleen S. King*

*My past defines me, together
with my present and the future
that the past leads me to expect.
What would I be without it?*

V. NEISSER (1978, 15)

## LEARNING OBJECTIVES

- Define **reminiscing** according to R. N. Butler.

- Describe four ways older people use memory for enhanced sense of personal identity and adjustment during aging.

- Discuss six ways reminiscing is beneficial for old people.

- Discuss relationships among dying, reminiscing, and life review processes for elderly persons, their families, and caregivers.

- Explain two ways to include reminiscing activities in group work with elderly individuals.

- Analyze leader characteristics essential to effective group functioning with an aged population.

- Discuss the methodological issues involved in developing a clinical research project to demonstrate the usefulness of group reminiscing in preparation for death.

## KEY WORDS

- Contextual

- Dialectics

- Dying

- Group process

- Memory

- Metamemory

- Reminiscence

## INTRODUCTION

Gerontologists began to focus on research and theory about the value of reminiscence because older people exhibited the behavior whether it was encouraged or not. R. N. Butler (1963) initiated exploration of the therapeutic value of reminiscence for elderly psychiatric patients and identified life review as a type of remembering that involves analysis of the past. Most studies about the potential adaptive and therapeutic value of reminiscence have been conducted over the past decade (Merriam 1980), but these studies have not led to con-ceptual clarity or consistent results. The fact that investigators have not used compatible definitions of reminiscence contributes to the lack of congruent findings. Regardless, J. A. Meacham (1977) and S. Merriam (1980) suggest that the sum of the investigators' results emphasizes the adaptive functions of reminiscence in later adulthood and its potential to assist personality reorganization.

Although theoreticians have not agreed on a single conceptual or operational definition, I prefer to use Butler's (1963, 66) view that reminiscence is "the act or process of recalling the past." No distinction is made between internal and external recounting of the remembered past. People seem to begin reminiscing as early as age 10 (Havighurst and Glasser 1972), but this type of memory phenomenon is believed to be more commonly associated with aged individuals. As noted earlier, older adults' use of reminiscence seems to assist effective personality reorganization.

This positive view of reminiscing was not always emphasized. In fact, others often looked negatively upon the aged reminiscer: The person was seen as senile; excessively attached to the past; or, more benevolently, escapist (Butler 1963). But the researchers who have examined reminiscence over the past 20 years have emphasized not only its benefits for the older person but also its potential for unlocking mysteries of memory development and function and developmental aspects of later years. Butler (1963) and A. W. McMahon and P. J. Rhudick (1967) noted the relationship between onset of reminiscing behavior and dying. McMahon and Rhudick went further, noting that reminiscing, especially analytical life review, related in many ways to mourning and the dying process. "An essential part of normal grief consists of repetitive recollections of the lost object" (McMahon and Rhudick 1967, 77). This preoccupation with the past as it relates to a lost object is similar to persistent reminiscing in old age. Perhaps as aged individuals anticipate death, they dwell upon significant aspects of their lives as a way to say goodbye.

Reflecting on the remembered past, the older individual has the opportunity to resolve old conflicts and achieve a sense of peace about the past. In addition, the reminiscer has the chance to review and affirm past experiences that reinforce positive self-esteem. If the older individual wishes, the content of the memories can be placed in a permanent record as a legacy to the family.* In a way similar to the oral historians of more primitive societies, aged family members can help to preserve tradition and values and contribute to a sense of continuity with past generations.

---

*The illustrations in this chapter are examples of such a legacy. They are excerpts from the journal of Millie King, the author's paternal grandmother. Millie King lived in the Chicago, Illinois, area from 1897 until 1975; she died about six months after completing her journal.

## MEMORY DEVELOPMENT

An examination of the developmental aspects of memory provides a better appreciation of the functions and adaptive value of reminiscence in aging, in part because memory activities can only be understood in their genesis. Developmental psychologists have recently turned to dialectical theory to promote more effective research and theory progress. L. S. Vygotsky (1978) attempted to describe and explain development of cognitive functions from a dialectical perspective during the 1920s in the USSR. A central tenet of dialectical theory is that phenomena can be understood and studied only in the process of motion and change. An appreciation of the older person's memory activities, then, would require viewing those activities in the light of their history and development. Therefore, to place this examination of reminiscence and life review in context, I will briefly summarize a theory of memory development.

Preparing a model of memory development, A. L. Brown (1975) described three components to remembering: knowing, knowing about knowing, and knowing how to know. *Knowing* refers to "the dynamic knowledge system" (Brown 1975, 105), which is central to all cognitive behavior. Because much of the research done in the United States on memory is about intentional or deliberate remembering, the kinds of learning and memory that result spontaneously or involuntarily are not as well understood; yet the most meaningful memories result unintentionally from our interactions with the environment, and these are retained and reconstructed over the lifetime.

*Knowing about knowing* is metamemory. Brown (1975, 105) defines this as "our introspective knowledge of the functioning of our own memory." Effective memory activities cannot occur without this executive function guiding selection of skills and strategies for remembering and forgetting. In addition, the organization of knowledge is a controller function of metamemory. Memory traces undergo revision continuously. What is stored is not an exact replication of the event, but rather something that has been constructed and reconstructed over time. Our own awareness of the organization of personal knowledge is essential so that we may call into play relevant past experiences and effective strategies for intelligent function to assist present coping and problem solving. Interestingly, J. Yesavage (1980) suggests that one way to differentiate depression and dementia in aged people is to note the individual's awareness of his or her own memory function. Depressed persons are more likely to complain of memory loss and resulting feelings of helplessness and inadequacy. People experiencing dementing illness are less likely to be aware of memory impairment.

*Knowing how to know* refers to the strategies and skills one develops for the purpose of managing information. These strategies are used deliberately, to acquire new information or to retrieve knowledge stored in memory.

All three aspects of memory described by Brown must function effectively for an individual to behave in intelligent ways. Loss or decay of knowledge stored over long periods of time can interfere with use of meaningful past experience during present adaptation. If memory strategies are ineffective, then the individual will be unable to obtain new, useful information or recall already integrated knowledge. Interference with metamemory processes can have severe consequences for intelligent behavior. The person may not know what is not known, or the person retains intelligence but is unable to perform competently. Simple tasks of remembering become impossible (for example, the stove does not get turned off).

A. I. Goldfarb (1975, 150–51) delineates the severe consequences for the older individual of memory dysfunction. "The importance of memory is obvious; it is that aspect of adaptation that makes us sentient, responsive, interactional. Consciousness itself is most likely simply an awareness of being aware and therefore a memory, a recognition that one has responded; it is a response to a response . . . Loss of memory constitutes a loss in consciousness and of psychological and social self; if large enough, it leads to loss of life." Because remembering is central to judgment, learning, and problem-solving, impairment of memory means that the most mundane acts can be impossible to perform. Reminiscence, however, depends on material stored and reviewed over the lifetime. Clinicians once believed that a curious aspect of aging was

the phenomenon that relatively simple information gleaned in the present was lost so quickly when complex material from the past could be recalled with precise detail.

F. M. Craik (1977) offers one explanation for this apparent discrepancy. Rather than a difference in recent and remote memory, what distinguishes the amount of information retained about a given event is the depth to which that information was processed at the time it was recorded into memory. When an individual encounters information that is meaningful, he or she is likely to register that material carefully and in detail and to rehearse and reprocess that information at later times. On the other hand, the individual is not likely to attend as carefully to simple, everyday tasks, such as making sure the milk is put away after use. Not only do these kinds of tasks not receive the same depth of processing as more meaningful events, but they are so much a part of everyday life that memory traces usually exist that validate that the door is locked, the stove is turned off, and the ice cream is safely tucked away in the freezer even though none of these things were done today.

As mentioned earlier, one feature of an older person's account of the remembered past that impresses clinicians is the apparent accuracy of detail. More than remote memory and depth of processing, however, can help us to appreciate the reason why such detail and accuracy can exist. The definition of reminiscence—"the act or process of recalling the past" (Butler 1963, 66)—contains the explanation. It is that people rehearse the remembered past. Over the years, memories from childhood are recalled, relived, and mingled with current experience. Obviously, material that has been reviewed many times throughout the lifetime takes on a clarity that is not possible with material encountered only once in the present. And the aged person's ability to remember with accuracy of detail may only be an illusion. When the individual recalls information and events many times, that material is modified or constructed and reconstructed. F. C. Bartlett (1932) demonstrated through his work with adults' memory for meaningful events that information is not recalled exactly as it occurred. Memory is not a precise copy. Rather, people perform a variety of constructive alterations on information, including omissions, elaborations, and condensations. Or as Pear (quoted by Havighurst and Glasser 1972, 246) notes poetically, "The mind never photographs. It paints pictures." Figure 23-1, an excerpt from the journal of Millie King, illustrates the memory for detail that often impresses clinicians.

## MEMORY IN SERVICE OF THE SELF

Recognizing that memory development and function influence the process of reminiscing at any age, I want to examine the ways in which memory is useful to the individual. V. Neisser (1978) notes that a significant deficit in research on memory processes is the area of everyday application of memory. Most researchers have focused on well-controlled, laboratory experiments to investigate deliberate memorization. Some of the tasks involved remembering nonsense words or geometric shapes and relationships, tasks that bear little resemblance to the uses of memory in everyday life. Neisser (1978) adds that much of the work has centered on short-term memory phenomena, which are fleeting. Rather, he suggests: "What we want to know, I think, is how people use their own past experiences in meeting the present and future. We would like to understand how this happens

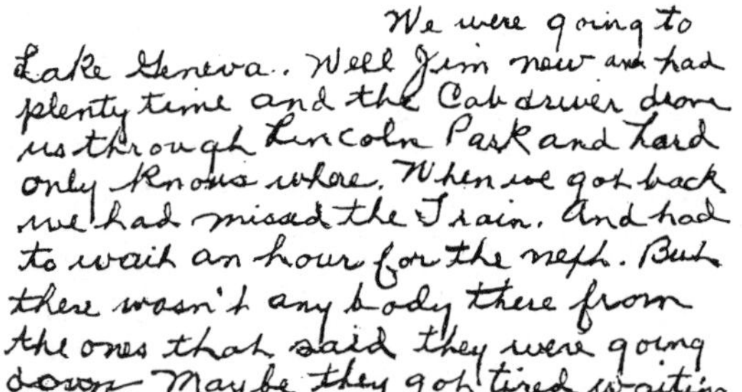
We were going to Lake Geneva. Well Jim new and had plenty time and the Cab driver drove us through Lincoln Park and Lord only knows where. When we got back we had missed the Train. And had to wait an hour for the next. But there wasn't any body there from the ones that said they were going down Maybe they got tired waiting for us we were so late. Well it was a long day and getting an hr late start it was gloomy when we got to Lake Geneva. Well that's the way it started. And he was a good husband & father & a very good friend to all and loved all you grand-children

FIGURE 23-1. *Memory for detail.*

*SOURCE:* Millie King's journal, 1975.

under natural conditions: the circumstances in which it occurs, the form it takes, the variables on which it depends, the differences between individuals in their uses of the past. 'Natural conditions' . . . means in school and at home, on the job and in the course of thought, as carefree children and as reflective old men" (pp. 13–14). The study of naturally occurring memory such as reminiscence thus may facilitate a better understanding of memory development and function.

J. A. Meacham (1977) presents a transactional view of memory and remembering that is grounded in a dialectical and contextual orientation. He sees "both the memories and the individual rememberer as changeable events, derived from a basic process of *transaction,* communication, or exchange" (p. 277). This communication occurs within a context that "is interpreted through the individual's memories, and the memories are always constructed within a current social context" (p. 278).

S. S. Tobin (1972) reports similar findings in his research, which examined older subjects' earliest memories. These subjects' feelings associated with their reports of earliest memory were more consistent with current concerns (for example, loss and institutionalization). Because the person, his or her memories, and the environment are viewed as in constant motion and change, as an interdependent system, reminiscence then becomes more important to the needs of self in the present. *The veracity of the remembered past is not the issue.* Memories are not produced as an end in themselves, but rather for the purpose of present goals. Meachem (1977, 275 states: "The subordination of reminiscing to current personality functioning is paradoxical in view of many traditional conceptions of memories as stable and permanent; memories presumably have greater value as they are thought to be more complete, accurate, and easily remembered. However, our principle means of judging the accuracy of memories is not through an assessment of their correspondence with the past but rather through a determination of whether or not they provide information that is appropriate or useful in the context or current personality and social conditions." The most important consideration, then, is whether the individual's use of the remembered past assists current adjustment. An example of the role of memories in reflection upon significant losses can be seen in Figure 23–2.

Although the relationship between reminiscence and memory remains unclear (Merriam 1980), a contextual, interactional view of reminiscence leads to a functional approach in research and clinical application. The study of natural uses of memory in everyday contexts should proceed from a theory-building, inductive point of view. In this way, memory phenomena that are meaningful to individuals in their day-to-day lives would be revealed more effectively. Brown (1975) suggests that spontaneous memory usually consists of reconstruction of the gist of past experiences. This, in turn, influences the depth to which the information is processed and retained. The act of reminiscing may also enhance the meaning of a past event for the person (Merriam 1980), thereby making that information more accessible for present and future adaptation.

Goldfarb (1975) and M. O. Wolanin and L. R. F. Phillips (1981) suggest that memory dysfunction, regardless of causality, is central to development of confusion among aged individuals. The remembered past offers benefits of personality reorganization and enhanced self-esteem because it draws upon those aspects of memory that have been rehearsed and may contain meaningful material. Neisser (1978, 16) adds: "Both private and shared recollection can have profound consequences for that sense of self which is so dependent on what one remembers." Clearly, the older person's reminiscence reflects that sense of self, both positive and negative; clinicians would be well advised to tap this rich source of information about their clients.

## REMINISCENCE AND ADAPTATION

Butler (1963) laid the foundation for later speculations and investigations on reminiscence. Based on his clinical observations of elderly psychiatric patients, he determined that reminiscing is beneficial. He also noted that many patients engaged in what he termed the life review, through which they assessed the impact and value of their lives. Believing the life review to be universal, he defined it as a "mental process characterized by the progressive return to consciousness of past experience, and, particularly, the resurgence of unresolved conflicts; simultaneously, and normally, these revived experiences and conflicts can be surveyed and reintegrated. Presumably this process is prompted by the realization of approaching dissolution and death, and the inability to maintain one's sense of personal invulnerability" (Butler 1963, 66). The foregoing characterizations of reminiscence and life review have stood the test of time well;

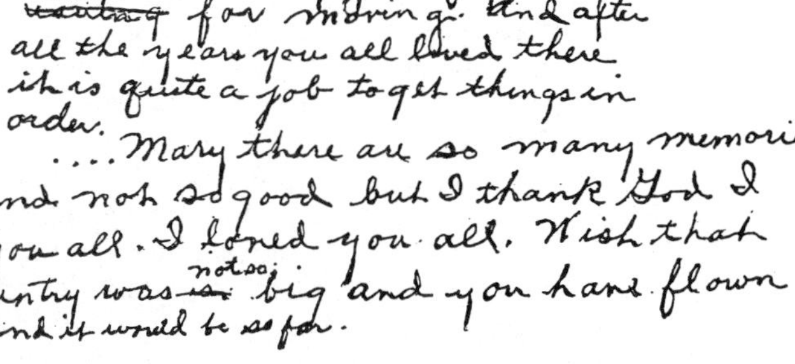
She said Charles either had to go to San. Fran. or be without a job. Well she had to go home and I was alone with my lonesome thoughts. Grandpa had died in 1965.

So of course our house was put up for sale and was sold and then the big job of getting ready for moving. And after all the years you all lived there it is quite a job to get things in order.

...Mary there are so many memories good and not so good but I thank God I had you all. I loved you all. Wish that the country was not so big and you have flown away and it would be so far.

FIGURE 23–2. *Reflection upon significant losses and the role of memories.*

*SOURCE:* Millie King's journal, 1975.

although the exact role of reminiscence is still not completely understood, gerontologists believe this memory process facilitates mourning and positive self-esteem.

Other investigators have attempted to prove and enlarge upon Butler's initial observations and speculations. McMahon and Rhudick (1967), on the basis of descriptive research and clinical evaluations, identified three types of reminiscing used by the aged veterans who participated in the study. One type of account of the remembered past glorified the past and berated the present. The second type, storytelling, neither glorified nor berated the past or the present. The third type was the more analytical life review noted by Butler. The subjects who reminisced very little or not at all were judged to exhibit more depression. Many of them died within the year following the study. McMahon and Rhudick (1967) conclude that reminiscing is correlated positively with effective adaptation in aging. They also believe that recounting of the past bears some similarity to the normal mourning process. An example of a storytelling reminiscence, from Millie King's journal, appears in Figure 23–3. This example neither glorifies nor berates the past or the present.

Believing that reminiscence could promote self-esteem under conditions of social threat, C. N. Lewis (1971) first determined the amount of time individual elderly subjects spent in recounting past experiences. He then presented these subjects with opinions that conflicted with their own. Those people who spent more time reminiscing maintained consistent past and present self-concepts more effectively during this stress.

M. A. Lieberman and J. M. Falk (1971) attempted to delineate the psychological significance of reminiscence for elderly people. Using the notion that reminiscence is a reflection of the historical self, they examined the adaptational, contextual, and developmental implications of the remembered past. The adaptational value of reflecting on the past was not demonstrated. The individual's life context, however, did influence the amount of reminiscing done. The authors also examined developmental indices, chronological age, and distance from death. The subjects closer to death did show more cognitive restructuring behavior (which may have resulted from life review) but less

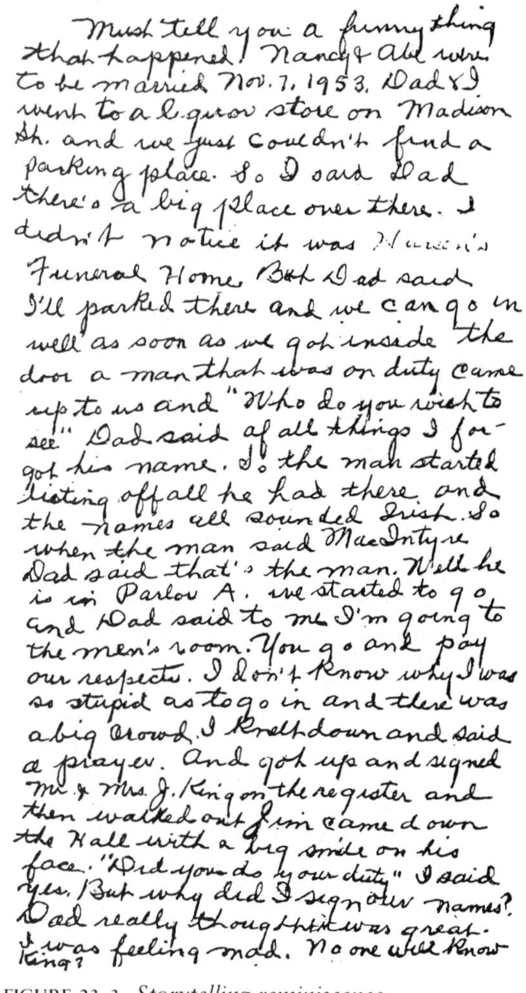

FIGURE 23–3. *Storytelling reminiscence.*

*SOURCE:* Millie King's journal, 1975.

reflecting on the past. Comparing middle-aged and aged subjects, Lieberman and Falk (1971) ascertained that elderly people derived more personal satisfaction and cognitive restructuring from reminiscence: middle-aged people used the past more for problem solving. The authors conclude that "the findings are clearest in speaking about the influences of life context on reminiscence and are strongly suggestive that some aspects of reminiscence are associated with timelines measured both by chronological age and by distances from death" (p. 140).

Tobin (1972) also studied the effect of the elderly person's current life situation on the feelings associated with reports of earliest memory. Studying three groups of aged people, he categorized the verbal reports of his subjects according to the content and affect of the memory. The institutionalized group of subjects reported the greatest number of severe loss themes, which Tobin used as support of his hypothesis that report of earliest memory is influenced by the current life context. As noted earlier, this context-dependent view of reminiscing relates to a transactional theory of memory (Meacham 1977).

R. J. Havighurst and R. Glasser (1972) conducted a descriptive study of aged persons' reminiscing behavior, in terms of both frequency and affective quality. They demonstrate "that high frequency of reminiscence is positively associated with pleasant affect of reminiscence" (p. 250). As a point of departure to interpret reminiscing behavior, this finding is significant. They caution, however, that this relationship may indicate that these two variables are "overdetermined" and that no single other variable —in particular, measures of adaptation—can strongly correlate with either aspect of reminiscence. Because reminiscing behavior seems to be a complex phenomenon influenced by many personal and situational factors, clear implications from data analysis are difficult to draw.

W. Boylin, S. Gordon, and M. F. Nehrke (1976) report on a study in which they used Erikson's developmental theory as their unifying framework and ego adjustment as their measure of impact of reminiscence on the elderly person's life. They found correlations between reminiscing behavior and positive adjustment in old age through their sample of 41 older veterans. The excerpt from Millie King's journal in Figure 23-4 is an example of a reminiscence that is positively associated with pleasant affect.

Although the relationship between successful adaptation in old age and reminiscing behavior is ambiguous, I agree with Merriam (1980) that the activity does seem to serve several purposes that could improve personality reorganization.

1. The feelings associated with current struggles may be reflected in the affect attached to reminiscences.
2. The remembered past may be pleasurable (Lieberman and Falk 1971).

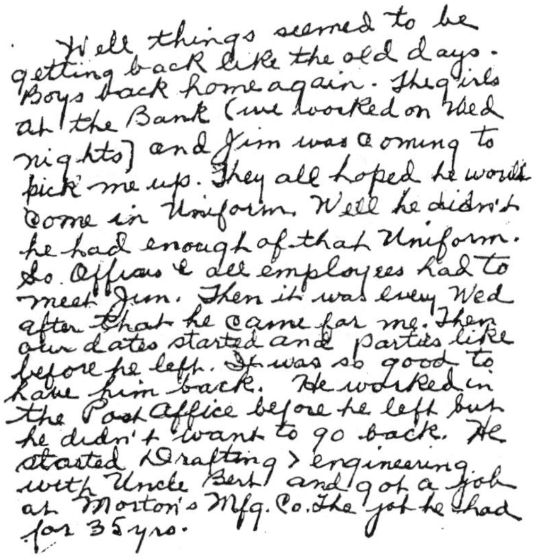
Well things seemed to be getting back like the old days. Boys back home again. The girls at the Bank (we worked on Wed nights) and Jim was a coming to pick me up. They all hoped he would come in Uniform. Well he didn't he had enough of that Uniform. So Officers & all employees had to meet Jim. Then it was every Wed after that he came for me. Then our dates started and parties like before he left. It was so good to have him back. He worked in the Post Office before he left but he didn't want to go back. He started Drafting & engineering with Uncle Bert and got a job at Morton's Mfg. Co. The job he had for 35 yrs.

FIGURE 23-4. *Reflection upon significant events.*

*SOURCE:* Millie King's journal, 1975.

3. Memories may provide the basis for problem-solving.
4. The older person can reminisce socially (Meacham 1977) and thereby receive validation or support when needed.
5. The reminiscer has the opportunity to analyze past events of which he is not proud and, through the life review, resolve these old conflicts.
6. The natural mourning process, including taking time to reflect upon shared past history, can be accomplished through reminiscing.

Many clinicians have recognized the implicit and explicit benefits of individual, group, and family reminiscing for old people. Group modalities have been tried many times in institutional and community settings with success.

## CLINICAL APPLICATIONS OF REMINISCENCE

Clinicians have noted the various benefits of attending to the remembered past for their elderly clients. Use of the individual's reminiscences can assist the counselor during the phases of assessment, relationship development, and treatment. As an adjunct to assessment, the clinician can ask for the client's earliest memories (Tobin 1972) and observe important diagnostic indications of the individual's lifelong patterns of adjustment through the quantity, content, and feeling quality of the responses. The client may exhibit depression if he or she avoids reminiscence (McMahon and Rhudick 1967), lives only in the past, and is highly critical of his or her past (Butler 1963). Important indices of current and past unresolved conflicts may be detected in the content of and affect associated with remembrances.

## Vignette

An older woman I helped care for in an adult psychiatric unit was admitted for problems with memory function. She frequently and persistently described her memories of undergraduate and graduate school. She even requested that her master's thesis be brought to the unit for the staff to read. Mourning the loss of her mind, she reviewed her education process with bittersweet recollections of all the effort she went through to train her intellect. Although little could be done to restore brain function, by listening to her reminisce, the staff provided support and validation and obtained the information necessary to diagnose her depression. Eventually, after her depression was effectively managed, she did experience some improvement in memory.

The above example illustrates not only ways in which reminiscence can provide diagnostic information but also ways it can enhance development of the relationship between the helper and the elderly client. The counselor can demonstrate acceptance of and caring for older persons by listening to their remembrances. Early in the establishment of rapport, the helper can listen without offering interpretations or probing for details, thereby creating a bond through acceptance of the client.

A. Pincus (1970) offers ideas about the adaptational benefits of reminiscence on both intrapersonal and interpersonal levels. For the individual, reminiscing can help maintain self-esteem, supply material for life review, and provide the opportunity to mourn both people and objects. In social contexts, remembrances supply material for conversation. In addition, the remembered past may also help establish a sense of congruence between older and younger individuals. Recalling his or her past, the elderly person shows how he or she was once similar to the younger person. Perceived differences due to age may decrease as a result.

M. Lewis and Butler (1974) delineate potential therapeutic benefits of reminiscence. For the older person who dwells on negative self-labels, the life review may offer the opportunity to reexamine one's life and identity and to reintegrate more positive self-statements. The older person also has the occasion to reflect upon unresolved past experiences and achieve peace with those issues. Discussing the regrets of youth, the elderly client can clear up feelings about missed opportunities and accept his or her own life. Family history can be preserved through reminiscing; this can provide a powerful legacy for subsequent generations. Fears of dying may also be examined through reminiscing. Accepting one's life as one's own and recognizing the continuance of the family, the aged person will be able to live in and enjoy the present. An example of this process of reflection is shown in the journal excerpt in Figure 23–5.

In addition to the benefits for the older individual, the family as a whole may also experience improved function from reminiscing. Because old age is a time of numerous losses, elderly members provide models of mourning for younger members. "The management of the dying process and the reactions and adaptations of the family have implications for the psychological development of the younger generations and, in turn, for their handling of the deaths, losses, and separations that are part of the human condition" (Brody 1974, 24). A child's first experience with death is likely to be the loss of a grandparent (Brody 1974), and the family's attitude toward that person and the history he represents will have a profound impact on the child's grief process and sense of continuity of human life. The older person's remembrances provide material for personal and family history and may promote acceptance of the past. When unresolved family issues emerge, the opportunity to analyze and solve these difficulties exists. Effective management of past and

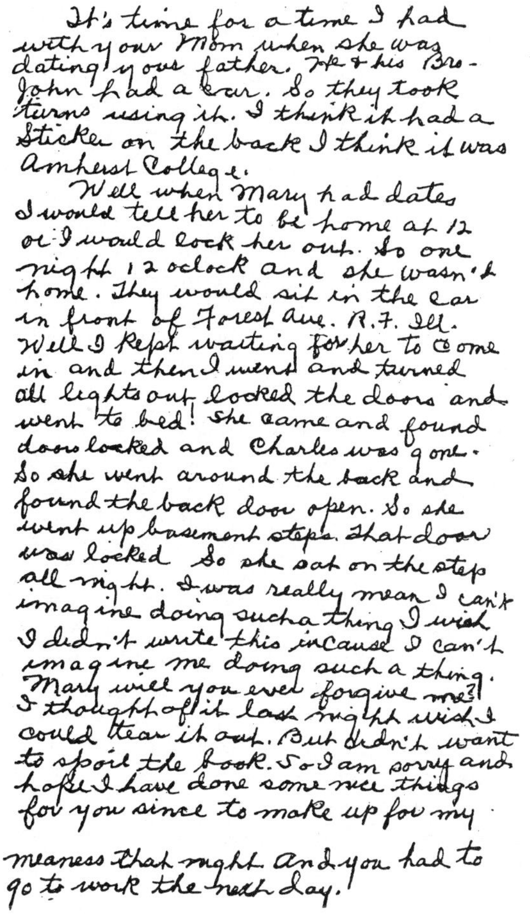

It's time for a time I had with your Mom when she was dating your father. Joe & his Bro- John had a car. So they took turns using it. I think it had a sticker on the back I think it was Amherst College.

Well when Mary had dates I would tell her to be home at 12 or I would lock her out. So one night 12 oclock and she wasn't home. They would sit in the car in front of Forest Ave. R.F. Ill. Well I kept waiting for her to come in and then I went and turned all lights out locked the doors and went to bed! She came and found doors locked and Charles was gone. So she went around the back and found the back door open. So she went up basement steps. That door was locked So she sat on the steps all night. I was really mean I can't imagine doing such a thing I wish I didn't write this incause I can't imagine me doing such a thing. Mary will you ever forgive me? I thought of it last night wish I could tear it out. But didn't want to spoil the book. So I am sorry and hope I have done some nice things for you since to make up for my

meaness that night. And you had to go to work the next day!

FIGURE 23-5. *Life review with analytical self-reflection.*

SOURCE: Millie King's journal, 1975.

present difficulties can reinforce positive aspects of growth and family interdependence.

Gerontology clinicians have most often applied the remembered past therapeutically through group modality. Whether the groups are age integrated (Butler 1974; Lewis and Butler 1974) or limited to people over 65 (Hala 1975; King 1982), the group leaders view the approach as very beneficial for both participants and leaders. Goldfarb (1971) notes that group psychotherapy, both within and outside of institutions, can foster a sense of purpose and identity for the elderly member. In addition, this approach can have positive effects on the individual's sociability, grooming, and attention to hygiene. Personal strengths may be

discovered and enhanced, and group therapy provides interpersonal support for examination of the effects of behavior on self and others and reorganization of ineffective patterns.

The leader of groups designed for elderly people carries a great deal of responsibility for the process and structure. The leader needs to generate enthusiasm and remain comfortable with slower formation of cohesive group function. Often, the participants are experiencing cognitive and sensory impairments, so more individual work within the group context may be necessary to promote comprehension and participation (Burnside 1970). The leader needs to be able to show a great amount of empathy for the group members. Because groups of elderly people, especially those who are experiencing mental and sensory complications, require an active, patient leader, most authors recommend that group size be kept small, from four to twelve participants (Burnside 1976; McMordie and Blom 1979).

Several authors have reported on the formation and process of reminiscing and life review groups, and most agree that the benefits for the members can occur on many levels. M. P. Hala (1975) noticed that the personal hygiene and sociability of elderly residents of a long-term care facility who participated in a reminiscing group improved. In addition, the staff began to view the residents in a more positive light. Goldfarb (1971) suggests that often it is staff members' attitudes toward their patients that improve after group therapy is started.

K. King (1982) organized structured reminiscing groups and used music to evoke memories and stimulate the members to share their remembered experiences. Hour-long, biweekly meetings were planned to promote interest and participation. As has been noted by other authors, I found that it took the members several meetings to begin to trust me and each other enough to raise conflictual material. After we discussed the losses they had experienced during World War II, however, the participants talked more openly of their current fears and struggles. Loss of personal health and dependence on adult children became recurrent topics. The inclusion of music seemed to help those members with diminished hearing to know which era was under discussion, because the songs were familiar and linked to a time in history. But hearing-impaired participants understood contemporary music better than speech because it is patterned evenly. So people with hearing impairment could count on ways to join in the process through listening and singing.

W. R. McMordie and S. Blom (1979) based their life review groups on Havighurst and Glasser's (1975) study, which documented that well-adjusted elderly people reflected little on conflictual material from the past. As a result, McMordie and Blom encouraged reminiscence of positive events, although they did not inhibit discussion of unresolved issues. I do not agree totally with this approach, as the bias toward sharing of positive events may constrain the older participants from discussing experiences of which they are not proud. The authors, however, did find that the participants reported improved morale and paid more attention to personal grooming.

Butler and Lewis (Butler 1974; Lewis and Butler 1974) developed life review groups that were age integrated. Believing that segregation of age groups precluded learning from individuals in different developmental stages and promoted ageism, they organized their life review groups around a crisis model to deal with normal and dysfunctional adjustment to life cycle issues. The advantages of this approach include positive models for aging, effective grief work, shared histories, and life cycle view of personal growth. Butler (1974, 535) adds, "age integration helps to recapitulate the family, something woefully missing for many older people."

The therapeutic benefits of group reminiscing include opportunities for socialization and social reintegration, resolution of old conflicts all through the life review, identification of current concerns and struggles, recognition of self as a survivor, and appreciation of one's own achievements and those of others (King 1982). Several authors (Butler 1963; King 1982; Lewis and Butler 1974) touch upon their belief that reminiscing is related to and may facilitate the process of dying, but they have not suggested clearly ways to make this a group goal.

As Brody (1974) notes, talk about dying has been "x-rated" in the past, but the growth potential of open discussion of death for older persons

and their families would be vast. F. C. Jeffers and A. Verwoerdt (1977, 142) suggest that "awareness and acceptance of death are characteristics of emotional maturity of elderly persons," although the level of awareness may vary with one's life circumstances. For example, thoughts about death may be more common for people who are experiencing poor health. They add that "concerns about death tend to occur in persons with neurotic conflicts rather than those who are either normal or psychotic" (p. 145). Many personal patterns of adjustment to awareness of impending death exist, and what is effective for one person can be ineffective for another. Methods used to adjust to past losses, however, are probably the most important factor defining acceptance of one's own death. By recounting past crises and their resolutions, the aged gain access to their most effective coping skills.

Studying an educational model for nursing home activities, J. J. Lawrence (1981) had the staff collect oral histories from 13 residents. Those who benefited most from having their life histories recorded were individuals who were intellectually active but socially withdrawn. One of the subjects died after the study was completed, and the staff member who collected his oral history "shared in the patient's preparation for death and was with him when he died" (Lawrence 1981, 142). Because the personal history information helped the nurses to see their patients as individuals, they were more available in times of crisis, including death. Although death may still be a taboo subject, open discussion of dying may lead to more effective practical, social, and spiritual preparation for the event.

The normal developmental process includes recognition and acceptance of one's impending death during the latter stages of the life cycle. Both family and friends can benefit from participating with older persons in their preparation for death. Logically, group work with aged people could focus on the recounting of one's life in anticipation of inevitable personal dissolution. Jeffers and Verwoerdt (1977, 155) write: "At the time of crisis when a person comes to full realization of the foreshortening of his life span and the approach of death, the self seeks to renew and establish itself before it may be lost. Robert

Fuller puts it succinctly: 'Death asks us for identity.' It is as if Charon, the boatman from Greek mythology, or St. Peter at the gate of heaven, were asking for the mortal to present his passport." Through the process of a supportive, structured group, the older person could carefully review the positive and negative aspects of life. Old conflicts could be worked through and put to rest. A creative, personal legacy that the family could share with generations to come could be the end product. Most important, the aging individual could find a purpose for the rich and colorful memories that intrude, invited or not, upon the present. The group leader using a contextual approach to group reminiscing would be able to help the individual make satisfactory sense out of his past, to serve the present needs of identity and integration of the self. A creative personal legacy was left by Millie King in her poignant journal, and especially in the powerful statement in Figure 23–6.

### Further Study

Further study and use of reminiscence would be valuable for several reasons. First, it would permit a better understanding of the function of memory and memory development in later adulthood. Second, it would help delineate the ways in which reminiscing is different from other cognitive functions. Third, the application of reminiscence would assist clinicians to develop rapport with and to understand their clients better. Fourth, it would identify the potential benefits to older people of having their memories elicited and valued.

### SUMMARY

Although relationships between memory and reminiscence and adaptation and reminiscence are not clear, some gerontological researchers and clinicians believe these to be valuable areas for future investigation. To better understand the functional changes in and uses of memory during old age, reminiscence may provide important data for inductive, hypothesis-generating studies. The contextual significance of the past would be delineated through descriptive research on reminiscing behavior. As Meacham (1977) notes, the personal, social, and environmental meanings of the remembered past would give important information about the ways memory for past events relates to present needs and wants.

Clinicians need to continue their application of reminiscence therapeutically, even though its exact developmental and adaptational significance has not been demonstrated. Listening to the older person's remembrances may help the clinician to establish rapport, assess current concerns, and appreciate the person's individuality. Individual and group reminiscing can result in a record of the aged person's life, an invaluable legacy to his or her family. Group reminiscing can help the participants in many ways, including socialization, identification of current concerns, and resolution of conflicts. Reflecting upon the past is a way for a person to reestablish a link to the self and to renew identity. This is especially important as people face death. Jeffers and Verwoerdt (1977, 155) state, "The constructive and therapeutic aspects of the life review . . . are apparent when the person can develop a satisfying pattern and meaning out of the conglomerate of events in his past life." Satisfactory mourning of the approaching end of one's own life or the life of a loved one can be accomplished through review of the past. If one is able to accept the past life for what it was, then a peaceful acceptance of death is possible.

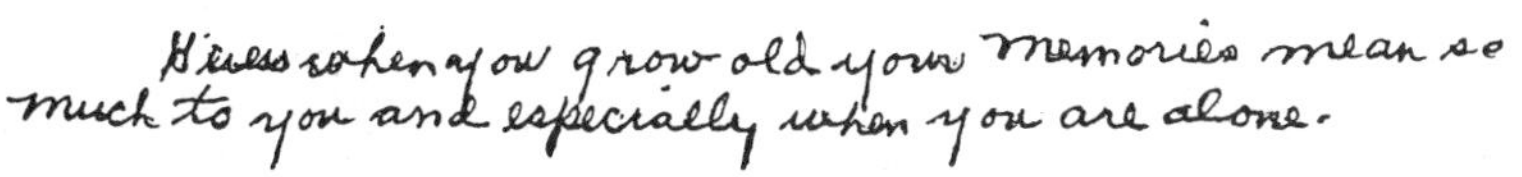

*H was when you grow old your memories mean so much to you and especially when you are alone.*

FIGURE 23–6. *Reflection on own reminiscing.*

Source: Millie King's journal, 1975.

## EXERCISE 1

*Situation:* Eleanor Smith is a 73-year-old widow who was brought to the geriatric clinic by her daughter because she has been "forgetting" things lately. Eleanor lives alone, and her daughter is concerned because if she doesn't visit every day, her mother forgets to eat, leaves food to spoil, or doesn't turn off the stove. The daughter is especially concerned because she will be moving out of the state soon and wonders who will look after her mother.

1. During the health history interview, Eleanor complains about her memory loss and sighs as she says she knows she is a burden on her daughter. Which of the following diagnoses would the clinician investigate further based on the history and her statements?
   a. Organic brain syndrome
   b. Depression, possibly mixed with dementing illness
   c. Acute grieving
   d. Personality disorder

2. The clinician asks Eleanor to tell an interesting anecdote about herself and her past. Eleanor talks about the care she gave her husband at home during the months before he died. She becomes tearful and says, "I don't know why I'm talking about that!" Which of the following concepts would explain why Eleanor brought up a memory with a loss theme?
   a. Memories are reconstructed over the lifetime.
   b. Depth of processing influences what past experiences are remembered.
   c. Dementia does not involve remote memory.
   d. Feelings associated with reminiscences reflect current concerns.

3. Eleanor and her daughter are referred to an age-integrated life review therapy group. The primary goal of this referral is to:
   a. Help both to grieve about the daughter's moving, drawing upon ways in which they coped in the past.
   b. Provide a transitional setting to prepare Eleanor for institutionalization.
   c. Help both—but especially Eleanor—to socialize and become more involved with others.
   d. Provide an environment in which mother and daughter can share pleasurable memories.

Answers: (1) B; (2) D; (3) A

## EXERCISE 2

Write a brief proposal outlining how to start a formal reminiscing group in a nursing home. Include the purpose of the group, type of leadership, frequency of meetings, and ways to initiate reminiscing.

## EXERCISE 3

Invite an elderly relative or friend to record his or her memories in an "empty book." For a period of four weeks, make regular contact with the person to review what he or she has written and to discuss the person's thoughts about reminiscing. Write a brief description of each of the following:

1. How does the theme of loss and dying emerge in the person's remembrances?

2. What could the older individual's family learn about his or her personal history, strengths, and values from the book?

3. What parts of the reminiscing seem to be life review? How did the person analyze his or her past? If conflicts emerged, how were they resolved?

## EXERCISE 4

Based on a review of the research on reminiscence, what difficulties could one expect in investigating its effectiveness in group therapy?

## EXERCISE 5

Compare your professional skills to the characteristics needed by group leaders for elderly patients. What are your strengths and vulnerabilities as a potential group leader for this population? What could you do to minimize your weaknesses? How could co-leaders help and hinder your work?

## REFERENCES

Bartlett, F. C. 1932. *Remembering.* Cambridge, England: University Press.

Boylin, W., S. Gordon, and M. F. Nehrke. 1976. Reminiscing and ego integrity in institutionalized elderly males. *The Gerontologist* 16(2): 118–24 (April).

Brody, E. 1974. Aging and family personality: A developmental view. *Family Process* 13:23–37.

Brown, A. L. 1975. The development of memory: Knowing, knowing about knowing, and knowing how to know. In *Advances in child development and behavior,* vol. 10, ed. H. W. Reese. New York: Academic Press.

Burnside, I. M. 1970. Group work with the aged: Selected literature. *The Gerontologist* 10(3): 241–46 (Autumn).

————. 1976. Group therapy with regressed aged people. In *Nursing and the aged.* 1st ed., ed. I. M. Burnside. New York: McGraw-Hill.

Butler, R. N. 1963. The life review: An interpretation of reminiscence in the aged. *Psychiatry* 26(1): 65–76.

————. 1974. Successful aging and the role of life review. *Journal of American Geriatrics Society* 22(12): 525–35 (December).

Craik, F. M. 1977. Age differences in human memory. In *Handbook of the psychology of aging,* ed. J. E. Birren and K. W. Schaie. New York: Van Nostrand Reinhold.

Goldfarb, A. I. 1971. Group therapy with the old and aged. In *Comprehensive group psychotherapy,* ed. H. E. Kaplan and B. J. Sadock. Baltimore: Williams & Wilkins.

————. 1975. Memory and aging. In *The physiology and pathology of aging,* ed. R. Goldman and M. Rockstein. New York: Academic Press.

Hala, M. P. 1975. Reminiscing group therapy project. *Journal of Gerontological Nursing* 1(3): 35–41 (August).

Havighurst, R. J., and R. Glasser. 1972. An exploratory study of reminiscence. *Journal of Gerontology* 27(2): 245–53 (March–April).

Jeffers, F. C., and A. Verwoerdt. 1977. How the old face death. In *Behavior and adaptation in late life.* 2d ed., ed. E. W. Busse and E. Pfeiffer. Boston: Little, Brown.

King, K. 1982. Reminiscing psychotherapy with aging people. *Journal of Psychosocial Nursing and Mental Health Services* 20(2): 21–25 (February).

Lawrence, J. J. 1981. Oral history and the motivation to learn: An exploratory study. *Education Gerontology Quarterly* 7:135–49.

Lewis, C. N. 1971. Reminiscing and self-concept in old age. *Journal of Gerontology* 26(2): 240–43 (February).

Lewis, M. I., and R. N. Butler. 1974. Life review therapy: Putting memories to work in individual and group psychotherapy. *Geriatrics* 29(11): 165–73 (November).

Lieberman, M. A., and J. M. Falk. 1971. The remembered past as a source of data for research on the life cycle. *Human Development* 14(2): 132–41.

McMahon, A. W., and P. J. Rhudick. 1967. Reminiscing in the aged: An adaptational response. In *Psychodynamic studies on aging: Creativity, reminiscing, and dying,* ed. S. Levin and R. J. Kahana. New York: International University Press.

McMordie, W. R., and S. Blom. 1979. Life review therapy: Psychotherapy for the elderly. *Perspective in Psychiatric Care* 17(4): 162–66 (July–August).

Meacham, J. A. 1977. A transactional model of remembering. In *Life-span developmental psychology; Dialectical perspectives on experimental research,* ed. N. Dantan and H. W. Reese. New York: Academic Press.

Merriam, S. 1980. The concept and function of reminiscence: A review of the research. *The Gerontologist* 20(5): 604–9 (October).

Neisser, V. 1978. Memory: What are the important questions? In *Practical aspects of memory,* ed. M. M. Gruenberg, P. E. Morris, and R. N. Sykes. New York: Academic Press.

Pincus, A. 1970. Reminiscence in aging and its implications for social work practice. *Social Work* 15(4): 47–53 (October).

Tobin, S. S. 1972. The earliest memory as data for research in aging. In *Research, planning, and action for the elderly: The power and potential of social science,* ed. D. P. Kent, R. Kastenbaum, and S. Sherwood. New York: Behavioral Publications.

Vygotsky, L. S. 1978. *Mind in society: The development of higher psychological processes.* Cambridge, Mass.: Harvard University Press.

Wolanin, M. O., and L. R. F. Phillips. 1981. *Confusion: Prevention and care.* St. Louis, Mo.: Mosby.

Yesavage, J. 1980. Memory, lost and found. *The Stanford Magazine,* 36–40: (Spring–Summer).

## BIBLIOGRAPHY

Blythe, R. 1979. *The View in Winter: Reflections on old age.* New York: Harcourt Brace Jovanovich.

Burnside, I. M. 1981. Reminiscing as therapy: An overview. In *Nursing and the aged.* 2d ed., ed. I. M. Burnside. New York: McGraw-Hill.

Herr, J. J., and J. H. Weakland. 1979. *Counseling elders and their families. Practical techniques for applied gerontology.* New York: Springer.

Kastenbaum, R. 1974. . . . Gone tomorrow. *Geriatrics* 29 (November): 127–34.

Maizler, J. A., and J. R. Solomon. 1976. Therapeutic group process with the institutional elderly. *Journal of American Geriatrics Society* 24(12): 542–46 (December).

Ryden, M. B. 1981. Nursing intervention in support of reminiscence. *Journal of Gerontological Nursing* 7(12): 461–63 (December).

Terkel, S. 1974. *Working.* New York: Random House, Pantheon Books.

Weisman, S., and R. Shusterman. 1977. Remembering, reminiscing and life reviewing in an activity program for the elderly. *Concern,* 22–26: (December– January).

## RESOURCES

### Films

*Bloomers* (filmmaker: Hildy Brooks). Contact University of Illinois Film Center; phone (217) 333-1360.

*Peege* (Phoenix, 1974). Contact Instructional Media Services, 205 Milton Bennion Hall, University of Utah, Salt Lake City, UT 84112; phone (801) 581-6112.

### Training Materials

*Group Programs Involving the Older Adult* (slide/tape)

*Libraries in the Afternoon* (slide/tape)

*Resource List of Program Ideas*

Available from Bi-Folkal Productions Inc., Route 1, Rainbow Farm, Blue Mounds, WI 53517; phone (608) 241-7785 or 437-8146.

chapter 24

# Group Reminiscing for the Depressed Institutionalized Elderly

*Mary Ann Matteson*

HARVEY FINKLE PHOTOGRAPHY

*The one thing in the world that could madden us all, if we allowed ourselves to think about it, is—the thought of what might have been.*

HENRIK IBSEN (DRSVP 1981, 76)

## LEARNING OBJECTIVES

- Identify the major developmental tasks of older age that may affect levels of depression.

- Discuss depressive reactions in older age and their relationship to reminiscing.

- List procedures essential in forming a reminiscing group.

- Describe the Zung depression scale and its value for measuring levels of depression in the elderly.

- Discuss the various constraints, special considerations, and problems associated with conducting a reminiscing group for older persons.

## KEY WORDS

- Endogenous depression

- Exogenous depression

- Interiority

- Reminiscing

- Self-concept

- Zung Depression Scale

Depression in the elderly is a phenomenon that has been increasingly recognized during the past several years (Burnside 1976). E. W. Busse and E. Pfeiffer (1973) recommend several forms of treatment for the depressed aged person: psychotherapy, counseling, drug therapy, and electroshock therapy. They also point to group counseling or group therapy as a mode of treatment that has gained recognition as an important technique for treating depression in older people. This chapter is based on the use of group reminiscing as a therapeutic modality for depressive reactions in the elderly. There has been no evidence of its use specifically to treat depression.

According to B. Neugarten (1978, 20–25), ego functions are turned increasingly inward with older age. This "interiority" may occur because of declining physiological and social role functioning; and there is greater self-

The author wishes to thank Ada Most and Virginia Stone for their critique and support in writing this chapter.

preoccupation, with an increased interest in satisfaction of personal needs. The introspection and self-examination leads to a mature life perspective, permitting the older person to make constructive use of past experiences without becoming enslaved by them. He or she can then face the future and the prospect of death (Kastenbaum 1978, 36–43).

## DEPRESSIVE REACTIONS IN OLD AGE

In old age, depressive reactions are exceedingly common. Depression is characterized as an affective disorder in which the feelings and moods of a person are disturbed to varying degrees. The person may feel hopeless and full of despair or may become anxious without good reason. Depressions are commonly divided into two categories: (1) psychotic, or endogenous (formed from within) and (2) reactive, or exogenous. There is usually a history of depressive episodes in the former; the depressive reactions of older age are often associated with the latter (Bromley 1966).

D. B. Bromley concluded that depression is so ubiquitous in the elderly because (1) there are social, psychological, and physiological changes of old age; (2) there are a greater number of people surviving into later life; and (3) the degenerative processes and organic disturbances of the brain may intensify and sustain depression. Elderly widows and widowers are particularly vulnerable. M. Kaminsky (1978) describes the use of old photographs in his casework with a chronically depressed woman who had never worked through her grief about her husband's death.

Busse and Pfeiffer (1973) stress, in addition to Bromley's findings, that losses concomitant with growing old are equally important in contributing to depressive reactions. "Old age has been aptly described as a season of loss and depressive reactions are, depending on their degree, either appropriate or excessive responses to losses" (p. 117). Busse and Pfeiffer cite the reason for this phenomenon of response to loss in the elderly as lack of preparation for the changes that occur in the latter part of the life cycle. Many of the elderly have not planned substitute ways of utilizing their energies or developed alternative ways of maintaining security and self-esteem.

## SUCCESSFUL ADJUSTMENT TO OLD AGE

Successful adjustment to old age, then, can be defined as "the result of having coped successfully with problems specific to this phase of life, namely the maintenance of self-esteem in the face of declining physical and intellectual capacities; coping with grief and depression resulting from personal losses; finding means to contribute significantly to a society of which they are still members; and retaining a sense of identity in an increasingly estranged environment (McMahon and Rhudick 1964, 291).

## DEFINITION

Reminiscence, the act or process of recalling the past (*American Heritage Dictionary* 1970),

may be used as a means of reflecting on previous events, making some judgments about those events, and working toward the construction of a new and final identity.

## OVERVIEW OF REMINISCING

A. W. McMahon and P. J. Rhudick (1964) hypothesize that reminiscing is characteristic of the later stage of life and that its prevalence suggests that it has adaptational significance. Their study also shows that reminiscing enhances self-esteem, increases enjoyment of social relations, promotes intergenerational understanding, and helps individuals maintain a consistent self-concept. Memory helps to establish a sense of continuity of life and to create and preserve a feeling of personal significance. Aging persons attach their personal significance mainly to events in the past, which therefore increasingly become the subjects of their conscious awareness.

R. Butler and M. Lewis (1977) postulate that reminiscence in the elderly is part of the normal "life review" process that takes place with approaching death, and that it can be used as a tool to resolve past conflicts, reintegrate them, and give new significance to one's life. It can also serve to give the aged person a feeling of accomplishment, of having done his or her best, and the opportunity to decide what to do with the time left. The process of reorganization and reintegration provides a means by which the aged person can achieve a new sense of identity and a more positive self-concept. Butler (1963) was able to document a positive correlation between reminiscence and successful adaptation to old age through maintenance of self-esteem, reaffirming a sense of identity, working through and mastery of personal losses, and as a means of contributing positively to society.

See previous chapter for further discussion of work of R. N. Butler and M. Lewis.

Group work with the elderly has become an appropriate nursing intervention out of necessity. Successful group work has recently been initiated and reported by nurses in long-term care facilities (Starks 1977; Guarino and Knowlton 1980; Sivesind 1980). In a group an older person may also benefit by sharing his or her problems with older persons who have (or have had) similar problems. The group also offers its members the opportunity to be helpful to the others in the group, regaining for them a sense of usefulness and of being wanted and needed. Finally, the older person who enters group therapy becomes a member of at least one social group with which to identify at a time in life when the person has been robbed of membership in so-called natural groups, such as the work group, the family group, or the peer group.

## GOALS FOR GROUP MEMBERS

Goals for clients involved in reminiscent group therapy include increasing self-esteem, increasing socialization and the ability to share meaningful memories with others, and increasing the awareness of the uniqueness of each participant.

Because depression is so widespread among the aging, depressive states become a problem for intervention. The group setting has been cited as a valuable mode of therapy for depressed older persons. Assuming that reminiscing and life review are useful frameworks for treatment of depression, it would follow that a structured form of reminiscing group therapy would be a therapeutic intervention for depressed elderly members.

I would like to share my experiences as a group leader in a research project I conducted to study the impact of reminiscing therapy on a group of depressed institutionalized elders.

## EXPERIMENTAL REMINISCING GROUP

### Procedure

Initial screening of potential group members took place in two intermediate care facilities (ICF) using data from patients' charts to rule out subjects with the following conditions: (1) a history of depressive illness, to rule out persons with endogenous depressions; (2) a history of physical illness—for example, severe deafness; and (3) a mental condition—for example, organic mental disorder—that would interfere with effective group participation.

All eligible subjects were to complete the Zung depression scale without help. The scale

was administered individually in the privacy of the patient's room. Written, informed consent was obtained from each subject before administration of the test. All of the people who scored over 55 on the Zung scale were invited to participate in the group. Of the 20 depressed people, 14 consented to join the group—6 lived in one nursing home and 8 lived in another in the same area. It appeared that the main reasons for not choosing to participate in the groups were (1) severe levels of depression as measured by the Zung scale, (2) "not feeling well," and (3) no prior experience with group work.

On the day that the groups were to begin in each nursing home, several subjects who had agreed to participate were unable to attend the meeting. Of the 14 people selected in both nursing homes, 1 resident had been transferred to the hospital and 3 were not feeling well enough to participate due to colds, flu, and effects of chronic illness. Another problem that contributed to the inability to attend the group was the fact that the sessions were scheduled in the morning. First, depressed persons often have difficulty "getting going" in the morning and are more active in the afternoon as the depression lifts. Second, the staff was unable to complete morning care on the group members in time to have them ready for the meeting, a common obstacle for any group leader to remember who works in an institutional setting.

When I discovered that more members were needed to fill the groups, nondepressed people were also asked to join. This was a fortuitous event for the new group leader, because it is most difficult, if not impossible, to lead a group composed completely of depressed people. Depressed people tend to be quiet and withdrawn and are reluctant to enter into group discussions. Because they are so preoccupied with self, they do not readily form a group identity, nor are they able to support others in the group. Finally, nondepressed members add vitality to a group that might otherwise assume a negative and mournful character.

### The Zung Scale

The Zung Self-Rating Depression Scale (SDS) (Zung 1973) was used for pretest and posttest measurements and the Raw-Score Conversion

Table (Merrell-National Laboratories, Division of Richardson-Merrill Inc., Cincinnati, Ohio, 1974). The test comprises 20 items, each relating to a specific characteristic of depression, such as sadness, hopelessness, sleeplessness, and loss of appetite. The subject was given the list of items and asked to place a check mark in the box that best described how the item related to him or her and to the person's feelings during the past week: None or a Little of the Time, Some of the Time, Good Part of the Time, and Most or All of the Time.

To obtain the subject's depression rating, the completed scale was placed under a transparent key for scoring. The indicated values for all items were totaled, and the raw score was then converted to the SDS Index based on 100. The index served chiefly as a quantitative measure of the intensity of depression.

The Zung scale was given to all potential participants by the group leader to be self-administered with the use of a pencil or pen. Most people were unable to read due to failing vision or lack of adequate education, so the questions on the scale were read to them and they responded verbally. Some people did not understand words such as *hopeful* or *irritable*, so accurate translations into local colloquialisms had to be made. The average educational level in this group was below eighth grade, which may not be true of other groups of depressed elderly. The ratings were raised by 5 points to allow for the special circumstances of the participants, that is, age, institutionalization, dependency.

The Zung scale is a useful measure of depression in the elderly, both clinically and for research purposes. It is important to have a sound data base to measure the effect of interventions on client outcomes. While it does have some drawbacks in terms of administration and content, the Zung scale is one of the few depression measures that can be used for older clients.

## Meetings

The two reminiscing groups met for one-half hour per week for eight consecutive weeks. The author was group leader in one group and co-leader with a clinical specialist in psych-mental health nursing in the other group. Discussion was structured around specified topics; they included: (1) birth and childhood, (2) courtship and marriage, (3) childbearing and childrearing, (4) the Great Depression (5) World War II, (6) jobs, (7) the advent of television, and (8) holidays. This order was chosen so that participants would begin with earlier life stages and then work up to the present. I had hoped that by looking at life events chronologically, participants would be able to achieve ego-integration by, in effect, "putting their life in order." An informal atmosphere was encouraged in the meetings so that participants would feel free to share their memories.

It is interesting to note that all participants remembered events of early childhood better than relatively recent events. The 1950s, 1960s, and 1970s contained world and local events that appeared to have little significant impact on the older folks. Childhood events were remembered with great joy and fondness, and even those who had to work hard on the farm looked back with pride. Conversation frequently focused on food, such as sights and smells of mother's kitchen, holiday goodies, and favorite snacks. Almost all memories were associated with food in some way, which indicates the significance of food in a social context. Most social events either include food or feature food as the main event.

Two group members (Nos. 8 and 9) attended fewer than four sessions; one dropped out after the first meeting because he was "too nervous," and the other threatened to commit suicide during the time between the first and second sessions, causing a great uproar from the administrator and the staff. It was decided, because of pressure from the administrator, that the member be dropped from the group. There was concern that the reminiscing therapy was the precipitator of his behavior. This was not validated, however, and it should be noted that he attended the sixth meeting at his own request! No further references to suicide were made. This man had bilateral above-knee amputations; he had threatened suicide prior to the group session on "courtship and marriage." He talked a great deal about how the group was going to be talking about sex, and he "didn't want any part of it." It could be that his own sexuality was threatened because of his physical disabilities and limitations and that he had never come to terms with that aspect of his life.

The average attendance of those taking the posttest was six meetings. Attendance of all individual subjects in the experimental groups is listed in Table 24–1. In one nursing home there was a flu epidemic, which lasted for several weeks; this epidemic greatly reduced attendance. Illness can often be a problem when working with the elderly in a group situation. One subject in the experimental group (No. 10) refused to take the posttest but did not state the reason. She was very hostile toward everyone in the nursing home and was angry about being there. This may have been one way in which she was able to exercise control over just a small part of her life.

Two subjects in the control group died, including a woman who had been hospitalized and had been unable to participate in the therapy. It could be that her increased level of depression was related to her increasingly poor health and impending death. One person refused to answer all of the questions in the posttest, and another did not take the test because she had been hospitalized and was subsequently transferred to the skilled care unit.

TABLE 24–1. **Attendance of experimental group members at reminiscing therapy session**

| Subject | Group meeting | | | | | | | | |
| | 1 | 2 | 3 | 4 | 5 | 6 | 7 | 8 | Total |
|---|---|---|---|---|---|---|---|---|---|
| 1 | + | + | + | + | – | + | – | + | 6 |
| 2 | + | + | + | – | + | – | + | + | 6 |
| 3 | + | + | – | + | – | + | + | + | 6 |
| 4 | + | + | + | + | + | + | + | + | 8 |
| 5 | + | – | – | – | + | + | – | + | 4 |
| 6 | + | + | + | + | + | + | + | + | 8 |
| 7 | + | – | + | – | – | + | – | + | 4 |
| 8 | + | – | – | – | – | + | – | – | 2 |
| 9 | + | – | – | – | – | – | – | – | 1 |
| 10 | + | – | – | + | – | + | – | + | 4 |

SOURCE: Mary Ann Matteson. 1978. Group reminiscence: Treatment for the depressed institutionalized elderly client. Unpublished thesis.

+ = attended meeting.

– = did not attend meeting.

The results of the study were reported by the author in 1978 (Matteson 1978).

## Interpretation and Discussion

Reactive depressions are characterized by loss of self-esteem and withdrawal. The acutely depressed person may not have sufficient role identity or motivation to become a part of a group where social interaction is expected. On the other hand, a moderately depressed person may be at the place where he or she can benefit not only from membership in a group but also from the life review that may occur in reminiscing therapy.

Empirical observations of individuals and group interactions tended to support the fact that there was a significant improvement in the experimental group. As participants reminisced about past achievements and accomplishments, they expressed pride in what they had done. One subject reflected on the years of hard work he had put into his farm; another expressed gratification about always having had a job and never being out of work. One subject began to take new pride in her appearance and wore lipstick and a brightly colored dress on the day of the group meeting. *There was a noticeable improvement in affect among the group participants. Many who appeared sullen and withdrawn at the beginning of the eight therapy sessions were more outgoing and showed more social interaction at the end of the group experience.* (See Chapter 13 for similar changes observed in the cognitively impaired.) Finally, everyone in the group expressed enjoyment of the group participation and the chance to talk about past experiences. Several said how much the therapy sessions had "helped" them and how much "better" they felt. The reminiscing seemed to help to establish a sense of continuity with the past and a new pride in past accomplishments. The group experience also provided a structure for greater social interaction and a building of new relationships.

## Comments

Group work with the elderly can be difficult, especially when one attempts to implement research. Many residents in long-term care settings have physical disabilities that greatly interfere with group participation. The very act of assembling the group can be extremely time-consuming for the leader, since most participants need assistance in getting to and from the meeting. There is usually little support from the nursing staff, so that all transportation must be provided by the leader. Since a physical disability may be an underlying reason for depression, it is unfortuante that persons who would qualify for group intervention may be ruled out due to transportation difficulties.

Hearing loss is another problem in group work with the elderly. Several subjects in this study who did not appear to have excessive hearing loss in a one-to-one interaction during the Zung scale administration demonstrated a high degree of hearing loss in the group. It was difficult to elicit spontaneous group interaction and meaningful reminiscences among these subjects, so there was much clarifying and repetition on the part of the therapist for those who could not hear; however, this did not seem to affect Zung scores.

Administration of the Zung depression scale imposed some limitations on the research study. Educational levels were low in many of the subjects, and they could not read the scale or understand the wording. The most common difficulties in understanding words or phrases were with the meanings of "full life," "irritable," and "hopeful." I had to translate by using local colloquialisms, and I wondered whether the true meanings were always conveyed. The appropriateness of the Zung test for nursing home residents is another limitation. Statements such as, "I find it easy to do the things I used to" when a subject is separated from all the things he or she used to do, or "I find it easy to make decisions" when all decisions have been taken away may not elicit a true rating of depression.

In terms of selection of the sample, there were also several limitations. The time factor (due to graduate school semester constraints) limited sample size and prevented random selection. The small sample size greatly limited the validity of the statistical data. It was not determined whether refusal to participate in a group was due to levels of depressions or to individual personality type—for example, a person who would not ordinarily enjoy a group activity.

## Recommendations for Further Research and Practice

Further research is needed in the area of group reminiscing with larger sample sizes and random selections. It is also desirable to have not only a nonintervention control group but an additional one using group therapy without reminiscing to determine whether it is group process alone or the reminiscing as a modality or a combination or both that helps to relieve depression.

Research using reminiscing groups in other settings—for example, senior centers, skilled care facilities, day care centers or outpatient clinics—would be useful. Many people on the nursing home staff suggested that several residents in the skilled care section be included in the reminiscing group and felt that they would benefit from the experience.

Because the more severely depressed subjects refused to take part in the group therapy, it would be interesting to investigate whether using reminiscing therapy in one-to-one relationships would benefit them. If it were beneficial and depression levels decreased sufficiently, then perhaps these people would be more amenable later to the group experience. It would also be desirable to assess whether certain potential members are actually of a personality type that would enjoy group participation, regardless of their levels of depression.

The Zung depression scale presented some limitations when it was used for nursing home residents; further research using and testing other tools for determining depression is indicated.

Hearing-impaired elderly are especially prone to isolation and depression. In this study, an attempt was made to eliminate people with hearing problems, but some were inadvertently included in the reminiscing group. By ruling out the hearing-impaired, those who may be most likely to benefit from the socialization of a group are arbitrarily kept from the group experience. Although leading a group of hearing-impaired persons requires a great deal of patience and stamina, it would be worthwhile to explore further the inclusion of the deaf and hard-of-hearing in reminiscing therapy groups.

Because observation of the group did show that the experience meant a great deal to the participants, not only for the socialization it provided but for the opportunity to reminisce, it is recommended that group reminiscing be used as an intervention in long-term care facilities for both depressed and nondepressed clients. Group reminiscing provides a social network for many people who would otherwise remain isolated in their rooms and an opportunity to share the joy of past experiences and accomplishments.

## GUIDELINES FOR GROUP LEADERS

The following guidelines should be kept in mind by leaders of reminiscing groups for the depressed elderly.

- Know what successful aging is, according to McMahon and Rhudick (1964).
- Know the losses in each person's life and understand the modalities of life review and reminiscing.
- Understand developmental tasks in later life.
- Recognize the phenomenon of "interiority."
- Understand the dynamics of endogenous versus reactive depression.
- Expect that some residents will not attend meetings, so plan for a slightly larger group than actually desired.
- Do not plan morning groups for depressed individuals.
- Carefully check morning care routines of the agency so that members will be dressed and coiffed in time for the group meeting.

- Recognize that it is very difficult to lead a group composed completely of depressed persons.
- Be aware in the administration of a test— for example, the Zung scale—that many elderly may not be able to see or read the questions. A special method may need to be devised for administering the test.
- Anticipate illness and epidemics in nursing homes; these will affect group attendance.
- Anticipate that a member may die and decide how to handle the death for yourself and for the group.

## SUMMARY

In this chapter I shared my experience as a researcher with depressed elderly in an intermediate care facility. I presented cautions to heed in formation of such a group of depressed elders.

Depression in older adults has become increasingly recognized as a phenomenon associated with losses in later life. While withstanding these losses, the older person must struggle to maintain identity and self-esteem; at the same time, he or she must accomplish the major developmental tasks of ego-integration and a mature life perspective. Reminiscing or life review is one method that can help older persons to accomplish the developmental tasks of older age and to achieve a new sense of identity and a more positive self-concept. Since group work has been used successfully as a therapeutic modality for older clients, group reminiscing can provide an effective framework for therapeutic intervention for depressed older persons who are unable successfully to withstand late-life losses or to accomplish developmental tasks.

## EXERCISE 1

Select a depressed client. Using the Zung rating scale, give a pretest. Reminisce regularly with the chosen client, preferably several weeks. Then administer the Zung rating scale again. Compare the results of the pretest and the posttest.

## EXERCISE 2

The animal/human bond is becoming an important area in therapy. Select a depressed client and introduce a pet similar to one the client had in the past. Develop reminiscing themes around the pet.

## EXERCISE 3

Use pets to facilitate a reminiscing group for withdrawn, depressed elders. Conduct two or three meetings to determine which pets would appeal to the group. Then introduce one of the pets at each meeting. (A note of warning: Some elders think of gerbils as rats.)

## REFERENCES

*American Heritage Dictionary of the English Language.* 1970. Paperback ed. New York: Dell.

Bromley, D. B. 1966. *The psychology of human aging.* Harmondsworth, Middlesex, England: Penguin Books.

Burnside, I. M. 1976. Depression and suicide in the aged. In *Nursing and the aged.* 1st ed., ed. I. M. Burnside, 165–81. New York: McGraw-Hill.

Busse, E. W., and E. Pfeiffer. 1973. *Mental illness in later life.* Washington, D.C.: American Psychiatric Association.

Butler, R. 1963. The life review: An interpretation of reminiscence in the aged. *Psychiatry* 26(1): 65–76.

Butler, R., and M. Lewis. 1977. *Aging and mental health.* St. Louis, Mo.: Mosby.

Durham Retired Senior Volunteer Program (DRSVP). 1981. *Wit n wisdom.* Durham, N.C.: Durham Technical Institute.

Guarino, S., and C. N. Knowlton. 1980. Planning and implementing a group health program on sexuality for the elderly. *Journal of Gerontological Nursing* 6(10): 600–603 (October).

Kaminsky, M. 1978. Pictures from the past: The use of reminiscence in casework with the elderly. *Journal of Gerontological Social Work* 1(1): 19–32 (Fall).

Kastenbaum, R. 1978. The foreshortened life perspective. In *Readings in gerontology,* ed. M. Brown. St. Louis, Mo.: Mosby.

Matteson, M. A. 1978. Group reminiscence: Treatment for the depressed institutionalized elderly client. Unpublished research paper. Duke University, Durham, N.C.

McMahon, A. W., and P. J. Rhudick. 1964. Reminiscing: Adaptational significance in the aged. *Archives of General Psychiatry* 10(3): 292–98 (March).

Neugarten, B. 1978. Developmental perspectives. In *Readings in gerontology,* ed. M. Brown. St. Louis, Mo.: Mosby.

Sivesind, D. M. 1980. A teaching program for the elderly on developmental tasks. *Journal of Gerontological Nursing* 6(11): 659–62 (November).

Starks, F. B. 1977. Group work with the aged: A successful student project *Journal of Gerontological Nursing* 3(6): 30–34 (November–December).

Zung, W. W. K. 1973. From art to science: The diagnosis and treatment of depression. *Archives of General Psychiatry* 29(3): 328–37 (September).

## BIBLIOGRAPHY

Aiken, L. R. 1982. *Later life.* 2d ed. New York: Rinehart & Winston.

Blackman, J. C. 1980. Group work in the community: Experiences with reminiscence. In *Psychosocial nursing care of the aged.* 2d ed., ed. I. M. Burnside. New York: McGraw-Hill.

Brink, T. L. 1979. *Geriatric psychotherapy.* New York: Human Sciences Press.

Burnside, I. M. 1981. Reminiscing as therapy: An overview. In *Nursing and the aged.* 2d ed., ed. I. M. Burnside. New York: McGraw-Hill.

Busse, E., and D. Blazer. 1980. *Handbook of geriatric psychiatry*. New York: Van Nostrand Reinhold.

Busse, E. W., and Pfeiffer, E. 1969. *Behavior and adaptation in late life*. Boston: Little, Brown.

Butler, R. N., and M. I. Lewis. 1982. *Aging and mental health*. 3d ed. St. Louis, Mo.: Mosby.

Cameron, P. 1972. The generation gap: Time orientation. Part 1. *The Gerontologist* 12(2): 117–19 (Summer).

Coleman, P. G. 1974. Measuring reminiscence characteristics from conversation as adaptive features of old age. *International Journal of Aging and Human Development* 5(3): 281–94.

Combs, A. W., D. H. Alvila, and W. W. Parkey. 1974. *Helping relationships—Basic concepts for the helping professions*. Boston: Allyn & Bacon.

Dietsche, L. M. 1979. Know your community resources: Facilitating the life review through group reminiscence. *Journal of Gerontological Nursing* 5(4): 43–46 (July–August).

Ebersole, P. P. 1975. From despair to integrity through reminiscing in the aged. In *American Nurses' Association clinical sessions, 1974*. New York: Appleton-Century-Crofts.

Ellison, K. B. 1981. Working with the elderly in a life review group. *Journal of Gerontological Nursing* 7(9): 537–41 (September).

Erikson, E. H. 1950. *Childhood and society*. New York: Norton.

Gibson, D. E. 1980. Reminiscence, self-esteem and self-other satisfaction in adult male alcoholics. *Journal of Psychiatric Nursing* 18(3): 7–11 (March).

Hala, M. 1975. Reminiscence group therapy project. *Journal of Gerontological Nursing* 1(4): 34–41 (July–August).

Kastenbaum, R. 1974. . . . Gone tomorrow. *Geriatrics* 29(11): 127–34 (November).

Lewis, M. I., and R. N. Butler. 1974. Life review therapy: Putting memories to work in individual and group psychotherapy. *Geriatrics* 29(11): 165–73 (November).

Lieberman, M. A., and J. M. Falk. 1971. The remembered past as a source of data for research on the life cycle. *Human Development* 14:132–41.

Perrotta, P., and J. A. Meacham. 1981–82. Can a reminiscing intervention alter depression and self-esteem? *International Journal of Aging and Human Development* 14(1): 23–30.

Revere, V., and S. S. Tobin. 1980–81. Myth and reality: The older person's relationship to his past. *International Journal of Aging and Human Development* 12(1): 15–26.

Sherman, S., and R. J. Havighurst. 1970. An exploratory study of reminiscence. *The Gerontologist* 10(3): 42 (Autumn).

Verwoerdt, A. 1981. *Clinical geropsychiatry*. 2d ed. Baltimore: Williams & Wilkins.

Weisman, S., and R. Shusterman. 1977. Remembering, reminiscing and life reviewing in an activity program for the elderly. *Concern*, December–January: 22–26.

Zarit, S. 1980. *Aging and mental disorders*. New York: Free Press.

## RESOURCES

### Bibliographies

*Assessment and therapy in aging: A Selected Bibliography*. Arthur Schwartz, ed., 1975. Available from Andrus Gerontology Center, University of Southern California, University Park, Los Angeles, CA 90007.

*Communications and the Elderly: Bibliography*. 1978. Available from University of Colorado Medical Center–School of Nursing, 4200 East Ninth Avenue, Denver, CO 80262.

*Depression, Grief and Suicide*. Edith Sutherland, 1976. Available from KWIC/ASTRA, Duke University Medical Center, Box 3003, Durham, NC 27710.

*Mental Health and Aging: Bibliography*. 1977. Available from Center for Gerontology, University of Oregon, 1627 Agate Street, Eugene, OR 97403.

### Films

*Steps of Age*. 25 min. b&w. 1954. A film which contrasts the depression of Jimmy Porter with the strength of his wife who adapts to changing conditions. University of Michigan, Audiovisual education center, 416 Fourth St., Ann Arbor, MI 48109.

### Training Manuals

*Counseling the Older Adult: A Training Manual*. P. Alpaugh and M. Haney, 1978. Available from Andrus Gerontology Center, University of Southern California, University Park, Los Angeles, CA 90007.

*Gerontology Practitioner Training Manual: Communication Skills for the Gerontological Practitioner*. H. Greenberg et al., 1976. Available from Gerontology Center, Amy Gardner House, Pennsylvania State University, University Park, PA 16802.

*Manual for Counseling Older Adults.* Sonia Pallos, 1978. Available from Human Services Program, Community College of Allegheny County, South Campus Community Services, 1750 Clairton Road, Route 885, West Mifflin, PA 15122.

*Mental Health and Aging.* 1975. Available from Duke Center for the Study of Aging, Duke University Medical Center, Box 3003, Durham, NC 27710.

## Audiocassettes

*Successful Treatment of the Elderly Mentally Ill* (3 tapes). Available from Duke Center for the Study of Aging, Duke University Medical Center, Box 3003, Durham, NC 27710.

# chapter 25

# The Use of Life Review Activity

*Jean M. Kiernat*

*You need only claim the events of your life to make yourself yours. When you truly possess all you have been and done, which may take some time, you are fierce with reality.*

FLORIDA SCOTT-MAXWELL (1968, 42)

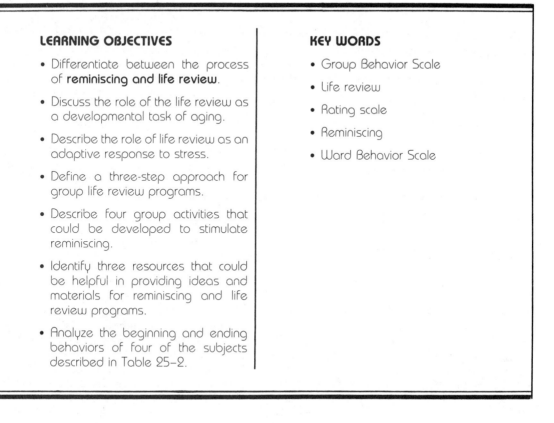

**LEARNING OBJECTIVES**

- Differentiate between the process of reminiscing and life review.

- Discuss the role of the life review as a developmental task of aging.

- Describe the role of life review as an adaptive response to stress.

- Define a three-step approach for group life review programs.

- Describe four group activities that could be developed to stimulate reminiscing.

- Identify three resources that could be helpful in providing ideas and materials for reminiscing and life review programs.

- Analyze the beginning and ending behaviors of four of the subjects described in Table 25-2.

**KEY WORDS**

- Group Behavior Scale

- Life review

- Rating scale

- Reminiscing

- Ward Behavior Scale

Until R. Butler posed the concept of life review in 1961, reminiscing by the elderly was looked upon as a negative sign of old age. The older individual who spent considerable time reminiscing was thought to be living in the past. Implied in this view of reminiscing was the belief that aged individuals were living in the past because they were losing touch with the present. Butler, (1963), however, made reminiscing respectable when he described reviewing one's past as a normal and necessary task of old age.

Earlier references to the importance of achieving a sense of satisfaction from reviewing one's past are found in the work of E. Erikson. Erikson (1950) describes the last stage of human

development, the eighth age of man, as that stage when one achieves integrity or experiences despair. Integrity, according to Erikson, is reached by looking back on one's life and determining that it has been worthwhile; that one has occupied a unique place in time; and, feeling satisfied with life as it has been lived, that one is ready to take a special place in history among those who have gone before.

The life review concept proposed by Butler appears to be the mechanism by which integrity is achieved. Butler described the life review as a universally occurring mental process of old age characterized by a progressive return to consciousness of past experiences, and particularly the resurgence of unresolved conflicts that can be looked at again and reintegrated. This review process is activated by the awareness of approaching death and involves an active, purposeful form of reminiscing or recall of past experiences.

In old age one looks back over past life experiences and attempts to reconcile what is seen with the values that have been adopted over a lifetime. There must be congruence between the concept of self and what has actually occurred. As experiences are recalled and reconciled, they are put into proper perspective and one's house is put in order. The life review is a process of taking stock of oneself.

Successful outcome of the review process leads to satisfaction with life and a sense of pride and accomplishment—a sense of personal integrity. Inability to resolve past conflicts or remorse for deeds not done can result in regret, depression, and even despair.

## REVIEW OF THE LITERATURE

The beneficial effects of reminiscing have been documented in a number of studies. Early investigation by A. W. McMahon and P. J. Rhudick (1964) led to the conclusion that old men who reminisce were less depressed than those who do not reminisce. In an exploratory study of reminiscence by R. J. Havighurst and R. Glasser (1972), a number of factors were frequently found together in upper and middle class elderly in the community. These included good personal social adjustment, positive affect of reminiscing, and a high frequence of reminiscing. W. Boylin, S. K. Gordon, and M. F. Nehrke (1976) administered a questionnaire on reminiscing to elderly institutionalized veterans together with scales to assess ego adjustment. Findings showed that men who reminisced most frequently achieved high scores on the measure of ego integrity. L. W. Lazarus (1976) noted that, when groups of geriatric patients in a private psychiatric hospital were encouraged to talk about the "good old days," there was a resurgence of happy memories, which appeared to alleviate depression concerning present problems and promoted pride in past accomplishments. The treatment team conducting the programs was frequently surprised to discover that what they had thought was memory loss based upon organicity was often forgetfulness of painful life experiences.

Other researchers feel that there is no evidence that life reviewing in general is related to present adjustment. The work of P. G. Coleman (1974) leads to the conclusion that life review is related to adjustment only in the presence of dissatisfaction with the past. Those who felt dissatisfied with something in their past but who would not or could not review this unresolved conflict appeared to be particularly unhappy and depressed. Life review, according to Coleman, is an adaptive response to dissatisfaction with the past, and refusal to review is a maladaptive response. Dissatisfaction with the past becomes associated with dissatisfaction with life in general.

The losses of old age may pose a threat to the self-esteem of some older individuals. Previously active and engaged persons may experience a discrepancy in self-concept as they experience losses in competency. Reminiscing and life review may provide ego support to these individuals by enabling them to identify with past accomplishments, thereby avoiding the full impact of these ego stresses. C. N. Lewis (1971) found that there was no difference in the correlation between past and present self-concept for elderly male reminiscers and nonreminiscers on an initial assessment. However, after the introduction of experimental social threat, a significant increase in past-present self-concept correlation was found for those classified as reminiscers. Lewis concludes that reminiscing and identifying with the past may be a defense mechanism for certain old people.

Studies by M. A. Lieberman and J. M. Falk (1971) support the concept of reminiscing and reviewing as an adaptive response to stress. They compared the amount of reminiscing engaged in by elderly in a nursing home, elderly on the waiting list of a nursing home, and elderly living in the community. It was found that those in the most unstable life situation (the waiting list) reported the greatest amount of reminiscing.

The importance of maintaining self-consistency has also been stressed by S. S. Tobin (1971), who feels that, as older persons become more psychologically disengaged, they strive to reaffirm who they are. It is in this way that the self is defined as unique, special, and worthy.

## NURSING HOME RESIDENTS

The institutionalized elderly, as a group, experience considerable personal and environmental stress. Their concepts of themselves as competent individuals are challenged by decreasing physical or mental skills, or both, and the loss of meaningful personal relationships. It may be very difficult to remember that they have ever been loved or that they have ever done anything worthwhile. The value of their entire lives may be questioned or minimized. This group of residents would appear to have a special need to reminisce in order to identify with past accomplishments.

Group reminiscing can be used effectively to encourage elderly nursing home residents to recall past experiences and to review their lives. Memories can be shared with others who have experienced the same historical events and shared the same space in time. I. Burnside (1971) and P. Ebersole (1976) have contributed extensive information on the use of reminiscing with the institutionalized elderly. The residents who have been included in their groups, however, have usually been those who could verbalize readily, thus excluding the very confused resident. It is this group that is generally unable to participate actively in most activities and that may have the greatest need to reminisce and identify with past competencies. The purpose of the following program was to facilitate reminiscing and encourage the life review process for a group of confused nursing home residents and to determine whether or not participation in such a group would result in observable changes in behavior.

### Method

**Subjects.** Subjects included in the study were 23 residents from three Madison, Wisconsin, nursing homes. The group included 2 men and 21 women. A staff therapist in each home selected residents who met specific criteria. Residents who were described as confused in the charted notes of at least two disciplines and whose confusion had been present for at least three months were selected for the study. Severe hearing or visual impairments precluded participation in the program. Only those subjects for whom written consent of their physician and legal guardian had been obtained were included.

**Procedure.** Three groups, consisting of ten, seven, and six subjects, met twice a week in the participating nursing homes. The program continued for 10 weeks or a total of 20 sessions. Each session lasted 45 minutes to 1 hour and was designed to promote reminiscing about a specific time of the resident's life and to identify the positive features of recalled experiences. Events were presented in chronological sequence beginning with childhood experiences and ending with the present time. Each group program was conducted by two leaders, one of whom was the same project staff member for all three groups. The co-leader was a staff therapist from the nursing home or an occupational therapy student participating in the project. The following format was used for the sessions:

1. Group leaders presented a prepared unit designed to stimulate reminiscing about a particular person, event, or era.

2. Group members were encouraged to discuss the materials presented and to relate events in their own lives to the material presented. Leaders asked questions such as "Was this like the school you went to as a child? How did your family celebrate Thanksgiving? What were you doing when the First World War began?" Leaders tried to have the members personalize the recalled events.

3. Group leaders helped the resident identify positive elements in the recalled experiences. "Did having so little as a child make you appreciate what you have more? That was quite an accomplishment to raise five children by yourself!" Leaders concentrated on the identification and reinforcement of accomplishments. Neither psychic probing nor interpretation of behavior was attempted.

Events such as going to a circus, attending a one-room school, recalling the Golden Twenties, or experiencing the depression were selected. Multisensory materials were used to provide auditory, visual, tactile, and sometimes olfactory stimulation. Printed pictures, slides, posters, tape recordings, historical objects, period clothing, and old catalogues were used. Corn popping added sound and smell to a circus discussion, whereas pumpkin pie and perking coffee strengthened the Thanksgiving discussion.

**The Rating Procedure.** Subjects were rated on their behavior in the life review group and on the ward. Behaviors were measured at the start of the program, midway, and upon completion of the 10-week program. The specific behaviors rated in the group consisted of items therapists employed in nursing homes had agreed were observable behaviors of confused residents and would be indicators of improvement if positive changes occurred. Items rated included facial expression, extent of conversation, attentiveness to group activity, presence of nonpurposeful behavor, and attendance. The ward ratings measured these same behaviors and also considered whether restraints were necessary or whether the resident participated in any other group activity. Ward behaviors were assessed by the charge nurse on the resident's ward, whereas group behaviors were rated by one project staff member.

The Ward Behavior Scale (WBS) and the Life Review Group Behavior Scale (GBS) used a 9-point rating scale. Raters determined whether the subject fell within the group norm or above or below the norm for behaviors of his or her reference group. The reference group for the ward ratings was the total resident group in the subject's living unit. Group ratings compared the individual participant's behavior with the life review group as a whole.

- Low or less than group:   1   2   3
- Norm:   4   5   6
- High or greater than group:   7   8   9

After deciding in which of the three groups a specific behavior belonged, the rater further determined whether this behavior was high, low, or within the middle for that group.

Both rating instruments were tested prior to the study. A charge nurse in five nursing homes was asked to rate a resident using the WBS, whereas an occupational therapist in each of the same homes administered the GBS to the same resident. After a two-week interval each evaluator was asked to retest the same resident. No significant differences were noted in the test-retest ratings of either the ward or group rating scales.

In addition to the rating scales, anecdotal records were kept for each session. Group leaders noted attendance and described the behavior of each participant for every session.

## Results

Attendance at group meetings ranged from 2 sessions for one individual to 20 sessions for two participants. Absences were due to illness, other appointments, or inability of ward staff to complete their care of a participant in time for the group. The average number of sessions attended was 12.4. Seventy-four percent of the group attended half of the sessions or more, whereas 48 percent attended at least three-fourths of the program.

A comparison of attendance records with scores from the Ward Behavior Scale (Table 25–1) indicated that those who attended most frequently showed the greatest improvement in their behavior.

The GBS presented difficulties for the rater because the group norm changed over the 10-week period. The scores of the GBS were not considered a meaningful measure of performance.

Anecdotal records of each session provided the clearest picture of resident change over the total project period. A summary of the beginning and ending behaviors of each participant in Table 25–2 shows that, of 23 subjects involved in the study, 11, or 48 percent, showed definite improvement in their behavior during the life review group. Seven, or 30 percent, showed no change, whereas two paticipants showed minimal behavioral changes. Three participants died during the 10-week program. For the members who completed the program, there were no ending behaviors that were more negative than their respective beginning behaviors.

TABLE 25-1. Comparison of attendance at group sessions and ward ratings of residents

| Resident code | Attendance (at group sessions) | Ratings 1 | 3 |
|---|---|---|---|
| A | 4 | 2.61 | 2.94 |
| B | 4 | 4.29 | 3.59 |
| C | 9 | 3.00 | 2.94 |
| D | 10 | 2.88 | 3.33 |
| E | 11 | 4.56 | 5.44 |
| F | 12 | 4.82 | 4.24 |
| G | 12 | 7.79 | 8.21 |
| H | 14 | 3.65 | 2.94 |
| I | 15 | 3.29 | 4.06 |
| J | 15 | 4.53 | 3.24 |
| K | 15 | 4.53 | 3.71 |
| L | 16 | 3.06 | 3.35 |
| M | 17 | 4.53 | 4.88 |
| N | 18 | 3.50 | 3.72 |
| O | 18 | 6.12 | 6.18 |
| P | 19 | 4.53 | 5.06 |
| Q | 20 | 4.00 | 3.94 |
| R | 20 | 4.12 | 4.71 |
| S | 20 | 5.94 | 4.40 |

Tetrachoric correlation (13):
Attendance & Rating 1 = $r_t$ = .43
Attendance & Rating 3 = $r_5$ = .69

## Discussion

Group members came to enjoy the meetings. Even the most confused participants were able to respond to familiar objects and events. Although initially most members responded only to the group leader and only to direct questions, participants later responded to other residents and offered personal memories without prodding. One member who initially resisted the group, saying the past was over and done, later shared many memories and expressed gratitude for the group, saying, "It is good for us." Some members began to anticipate the meetings, and three months after the conclusion of the project, one continued to ask about going to the group.

Recall was generally greatest for childhood experiences, and many members were able to respond to items in the present. Nearly all members had the most difficulty with recalling events that occurred during their adult years. The group leader frequently had to remind them, when the program dealt with the adult years, that they were now married or had grown children or were already grandparents.

Participants did not describe memories of personally sad events. They recalled happy times or the difficult years for society generally. No painful personal experiences were shared. There were no tears or other evidence that members were privately recalling such memories during the group session. It is not known whether private reminiscing followed the group meetings. The groups in the three nursing homes responded very differently toward the same materials. Farm folk responded heartily to animals brought into one session, but they reacted less to the difficulties of the depression years than the city dwellers, who did not have the assurance that adequate food would always be available.

Participating in life review groups is both fun and educational for the group leaders. Much is learned about the past through the experiences of those who have lived it. This mutually gratifying aspect of life review is a significant factor in the effectiveness of such a group. The leader becomes the learner and the group members provide the learning material. The positive response to the life review group is evidenced by the fact that two of the three nursing homes in the study have chosen to continue to offer life review groups with their own staff.

Illness was frequent among residents during the fall and winter months. Members would begin to respond more actively only to be sent back when "flu" or other illnesses interrupted attendance. Ten weeks is not thought to be a long enough period to see change when attendance is so often interrupted. However, to maintain an individual who has experienced the additional stress of physical illness may itself be a very positive outcome.

Preparing materials for life review groups can be quite time consuming. Locating books, pictures, and old objects requires many trips to the library and museum. It seems that volunteers could contribute very significantly in this area. A close working relationship with the local librarian would be an asset to any therapist conducting a life review program.

Difficulties with the measurement tools indicate that more sensitive instruments are needed to document the very small degrees of change seen in this severely disabled population.

Reviewing one's life is a developmental task of old age. Occupational therapists who work

TABLE 25–2.   **Summary of each subject's attendance and beginning and ending behaviors**

| Attendance | Beginning behavior | Ending behavior |
|---|---|---|
| 20 | Variable behaviors ranging from talks frequently but incoherently to pushing away from group and sleeping. | Appears alert. Facial expression consistently shows considerable recognition, interest. Tries to respond to questions but quickly loses thoughts. |
| 20 | Very talkative. Initiates conversation. Doesn't listen to discussion. Interrupts with other subjects. Doesn't attend to materials presents. Superficial chatter. | Shares personal memories. Attentive. Less interruptive. |
| 19 | Very restless. Fidgets constantly. Inattentive to group and materials. Incoherent. | Attends willingly. Sits quietly entire session. Recognizes materials. Shows pleasure in group. Makes some appropriate comments about present time. Becomes incoherent when recalling the past. |
| 19 | Responsive to questions. Attentive. Speech initially coherent, but rambles as she continues. | Attentive entire session. Able to relate some personal memories but becomes incoherent. |
| 18 | Responds only to questions. Much confusion in conversation. Much repetition of remarks. | Recalls numerous past incidents. Joins in group willingly. |
| 18 | Not responsive to questions. Admitted no memories. Did not talk. | Primarily interested in food. Interrupts group in search of treats. Views objects with apparent interest. Generally no verbal response to questions regarding the past, but some subtle jokes about the present. |
| 16 | Refused to attend. Difficult to understand her speech. | Regular and willing in attendance. Participates in group. Shared personal memories of her life. Alert and talkative. |
| 15 | Talked frequently but no complete thoughts. Tried to leave group early. | Shares understandable past experiences. Expresses appreciation for the group. Painful hip. |
| 15 | Quiet but appeared to be listening for part of session. Responds to questions but doesn't participate. | Alert entire session. Recalls many personal experiences. |
| 15 | Refused to attend. | Attends regularly. Very talkative. Relates personal memories and repeatedly tells of current family problems. Responds very positively to all materials presented. Talks with other group members. |
| 15 | Related detailed memories of past. Appeared deep in thought, much repetition in speech. | Tries to converse, some understandable recall but loses thought quickly. |
| 14 | Very talkative, Incoherent conversation. Appropriate social gestures and facial expression. | Attendance irregular. Exhibits some confusion as to place. Shares recalled events from her past life. |
| 12 | Refuses to attend. | Died. |
| 12 | Constant talking, very incoherent, shows interest in objects. | Very attentive. Shares memories of past. Responsive to others in group. |
| 12 | Attentive, sociable. Recalls past events. Responses are frequent and appropriate. | Alert and more animated. Relates some personal memories voluntarily. Showed concern for another group member. Attendance variable. |
| 10 | Attendance infrequent, appeared interested when present but didn't contribute except to give short response to direct questions. | Shows interest in group. Recalls personal events of past. Initiates some discussion. Attendance variable. |
| 10 | Refuses to attend. | Refuses to attend. |
| 8 | Slept through session. Frequently refused to attend. Speech is incoherent. | Died. |
| 8 | Sleeps through session in bent-forward posture. Could be aroused with questions. | Died. |
| 6 | Attentive and responsive. Responses are slow, generally appropriate conversation but loses thought at times and appears puzzled. | Ill for last sessions. |
| 5 | Sleeps through sessions. No response or change in facial expression. | Rarely attends. Shows little interest. Tries to leave after 25 to 30 minutes. |
| 4 | Generally refuses to attend. During rare attendance, appears very agitated, pained expression, near tears, tries to leave group several times during 45-minute session. | |
| 2 | Refuses to attend. | Refuses to attend group. On a rare attendance, she saw self apart from the group. Thought it was good for "them." |

with the elderly should encourage reminiscing as a method of stimulating the life review process and assisting the aged individual to achieve integrity.

## SUMMARY

This pilot project demonstrated that life review activity is a valuable intervention technique for use with confused residents of nursing homes. Conversation can be stimulated, interest can be sparked, and attention span can be increased through the recall and review of past life experiences.

## ACKNOWLEDGMENTS

Sincere appreciation is extended to Jane Cordero, OTR, who acted as project assistant, and to Karen Barney, OTR, Barbara Kopp, OTR, and Iris Walker, OTR, whose occupational therapy departments participated in the project. Gratitude is also expressed to Debora Olin, occupational therapy student, who prepared the materials for group presentation.

This project was carried out with partial support from the Hilldale Trust Funds, School of Allied Health Professions, University of Wisconsin–Madison.

## EXERCISE 1

Particular objects and events convey a special significance for selected age groups or cohorts and may thus serve as powerful stimuli to promote reminiscing and reviewing. For example, anyone who was a young adult in 1963 can tell you exactly what he or she was doing at the time of the Kennedy assassination. For the student of today, a backpack is a universally common item, yet the student of the 1940s or 1950s may have never used one.

Make a list of objects or events that might serve as strong stimuli to facilitate reminiscing for the following groups:

1. College students of the 1960s
2. Veterans of World War II
3. Black elementary school children during the late 1960s
4. Young adult women of the 1975–1980 period

## EXERCISE 2

Objects or events will have different meanings for individual members of the same age group.

Discuss the significance of the following items with two or three friends your own age. Focus on what memories are recalled by each object or event. Then consider the special significance this recalled event or object has for each of you. Consider how the event or object has affected your life. Did you learn something from it that has been a part of your life since then?

1. Your first date
2. A high school class ring
3. A picture of President Nixon
4. A driver's license

## EXERCISE 3

Interview an older person. Ask him or her to consider the following:

1. Describe your elementary school. How did your school differ from schools today? In what way did your school prepare you for life?

2. How did your family celebrate Thanksgiving? Do you think families today are stronger or not as strong as when you were a child?

3. Did you ever have a nickname? Why were you given that name? If you didn't have a nickname, did someone else in your family have a specal name?

## REFERENCES

Boylin, W., S. K. Gordon, and M. F. Nehrke. 1976. Reminiscing and ego integrity in institutionalized elderly males. *The Gerontologist* 16(2): 118–24 (April).

Burnside, I. M. 1971. Long-term group work with hospitalized aged. *The Gerontologist* 11(3): 213–18 (Autumn).

Butler, R. N. 1963. The life review: An interpretation of reminiscence in the aged. *Psychiatry* 26(1): 65–76.

Coleman, P. G. 1974. Measuring reminiscence characteristics from conversations as adaptive features of old age. *International Journal of Aging and Human Development* 5(3): 281–94 (Summer).

Ebersole, P. 1976. Reminiscing and group psychotherapy with the aged. In *Nursing and the aged.* 1st ed., ed. I. M. Burnside. New York: McGraw-Hill.

Erikson, E. 1950. *Childhood and society.* New York: Norton.

Havighurst, R. J., and R. Glasser. 1972. An exploratory study of reminiscence. *Journal of Gerontology* 27(2): 245–53 (March–April).

Lazarus, L. W. 1976. A program for the elderly at a private psychiatric hospital. *The Gerontologist* 16(2): 125–31 (April).

Lewis, C. N. 1971. Reminiscing and self-concept in old age. *Journal of Gerontology* 26(2): 240–43 (February).

Lieberman, M. A., and J. M. Falk. 1971. The remembered past as a source of data for research on the life cycle. *Human Development* 14(2): 132–41.

McMahon, A. W., and P. J. Rhudick. 1964. Reminiscing. *Archives of General Psychiatry* 19(3): 292–98.

Scott-Maxwell, F. 1968. *The measure of my days.* New York: Knopf.

Tobin, S. S. 1971. Psychological factors that influence safety of the elderly. *Occupational Health Nursing,* February: 11–25.

## BIBLIOGRAPHY

Burnside, I. M. 1981. Reminiscing as therapy: An overview. In *Nursing and the aged.* 2d ed., ed. I. M. Burnside, 98–113. New York: McGraw-Hill.

Lewis, M. I., and R. N. Butler. 1974. Life review therapy: Putting memories to work in individual and group psychotherapy. *Geriatrics* 22(11): 166–73 (November).

Lindell, A. R. 1976. Nurse therapist congruence during group therapy as a factor in changing the self-concept of the institutionalized aged. Doctoral dissertation, Catholic University of America, 1976. (*Dissertation Abstracts International,* 1976; University Microfilms no. 76–9215.)

Linn, N. W. 1973. Perceptions of childhood: Present functioning and past events. *Journal of Gerontology* 28:202–6.

McMordie, W. R., and S. Blom. 1979. Life review therapy: Psychotherapy for the elderly. *Perspectives in Psychiatric Care* 17(4): 162–66.

Maizler, J. A., and J. R. Solomon. 1976. Therapeutic group process with the institutional elderly. *Journal of American Geriatrics Society* 24(12): 542–46.

Merriam, S. 1980. The concept and function of reminiscence: A review of the research. *The Gerontologist* 20(5): 604–8 (October).

Pincus, A. 1970. Reminiscing in aging and its implications for social work practice. *Social Work* 15(3): 47–53 (October).

Sherman, S., and R. J. Havighurst. 1970. An exploratory study of reminiscence. Abstract in *The Gerontologist* 10(3): 42 (Autumn).

Weisman, S., and R. Shusterman. 1977. Remembering, reminiscing and life reviewing in an activity program for the elderly. *Concern*, December–January: 22–26.

## RESOURCES

### Films

*Minnie Remembers* (16 mm, color, 5 minutes, 1976; producer: Henderson/Arnold/Smith). Originally a poem by Donna Swanson from the book *Images: Women in Transition* (1976), the film is a monologue about the memories of an elderly widow. Available from Mass Media Associates, P.O. Box 427, Stewartstown, PA 17363.

*Let's Rejoice* (color, 10 minutes, 1973; producer: Centar frz films, Belgrade/N. Majdak and D. Albahari). A group of elderly Jewish men and women are in choir practice; the flashbacks reveal that they survived wartime concentration camps. Singing and music; no dialogue. Available from North Texas State University, Gerontological Film Collection, Main Library, Denton, TX 76203.

# chapter 26

# Reminiscing Groups in Board-and-Care Homes

*Sally A. Friedlob and James J. Kelly*

*We can complain because rose bushes have thorns or rejoice because thorn bushes have roses.*

ANONYMOUS

MICHAEL HAYMAN / BLACK STAR

## LEARNING OBJECTIVES

- Describe a comprehensive model program for treating the elderly at a board-and-care facility.

- Explain the individual professional roles and their relationship to standard roles in a multidisciplinary team approach to treating elderly clients in a care home.

- Explain the advantages and disadvantages of utilizing a large group in a board-and-care home.

- Define five agents of **reminiscing**.

- List five relevant activities utilized to facilitate reminiscence in a care home and the rationale for their use.

- Explain three of the possible obstacles, problems, or management issues that could arise in undertaking a reminiscence program.

## KEY WORDS

- Confidentiality
- Life skills
- Relationships
- Reminiscing agents
- Scanning
- Team

Maturity for every individual depends upon previous sequential developmental phenomena (Erikson, 1950) because during each period of human development there are unique presenting issues and opportunities. Willard and Spackman (Hopkins and Smith 1980) have stated that through the process of adaptation, the individual explores these issues and opportunities, solves problems, learns, and grows. When stress interrupts development, however, the individual may adapt by regressing or stagnat-

ing. For example, for an individual who has lived independently for the majority of his or her life, a move to a board-and-care facility can be a highly stressful life event. To cope with this stress, an individual may adapt by blending into the surroundings, thereby inhibiting growth and/or failing to maintain his or her current level of functioning.

Therefore, when working with individuals in a board-and-care setting, one needs a thorough understanding of the developmental processes and related phenomena. The worker can then assist clients in adaptation that encourages growth by providing experiences that foster more successful coping skills.

Individuals also undergo many physiological changes during the natural maturation process of aging. Among these is possible loss of cogni-

The authors would like to thank Jane Manning, registered dance therapist, for her clinical contributions to this project. George Saslow, M.D., served as an educator, role model, and group work consultant. Murray Brown, M.D., Richard Chung, M.D., Fran Kelly, O.T.R., Norma Donigan, M.S.W., Betsy Alkire, and Judith Coleman Munrello provided the necessary support to survive the system.

tive functioning. Clients sometimes display diminution of recent recall and reduced speed in learning; they show difficulty in integrating sensory input and output, and at times they are confused.

*Another major cognitive characteristic of the geriatric life stage is the ability to retrieve past memories with clarity and detail. Herein lies a major asset that can be the foundation for building structure and function in successful adaptation.* The phenomenon of reminiscence is an essential element in the continuing development of the elderly and can be utilized as an effective means of intervention in board-and-care homes because it is the one element that cuts across all special problems of individuals in these homes. (Butler 1963).

Although there has been recent debate about the homogeneity or heterogeneity of the elderly in board and care, generally the placement includes individuals undergoing the "normal" aging processes and three categories of individuals with an additional variety of special problems. The first of these three categories is former mental patients, carrying a diagnosis of chronic schizophrenia, who have been confined in hospitals for a major part of their lives. These individuals have coped with stress by regressing to earlier developmental stages. They have deficits in their social/emotional development, cognitive functioning, and perceptual motor development. They are typically withdrawn, shy, and egocentric and have poor posture and poor "fine" coordination. They have difficulty learning new tasks by trial and error, abstracting a sequence of ideas, and visualizing covert imagery. Long after the schizophrenic symptoms have been in remission, they have retained regressed behaviors that were acquired during their years of institutionalization. The term *burned out schizophrenic* has been used to describe members of this group.

Individuals with other mental disorders in remission are a second type of client. These clients cannot manage in an independent setting and need the support and structure a board and care offers. They, too, have social/emotional deficits, and often cognitive functioning is involved. Typically, they have difficulty in forming interpersonal relationships and demonstrate poor problem-solving abilities.

Clients with neurological and medical conditions constitute a third category of individual. These clients are found less frequently because board-and-care settings require independence in ambulation, continence, and self-care. Since those with neurological conditions must meet these requirements, the neurological involvement is minimal. Generally, the neurological condition involves upper motor neurons. The lesion may be located in the brain due to cerebrovascular accident (stroke) or head injury; or lesions may be located in the extrapyramidal system due to Parkinson's disease. In either case, deficits in perception, problem solving, personality, behavior, proprioception, sensation, stereognosis, hearing, sight, coordination, and voluntary or involuntary motion may be present.

After reviewing the heterogeneous issues of clients residing in board-and-care facilities, we are struck by the need for appropriate intervention that facilitates growth and effective adaptation for each client at his or her respective functional level and for group treatment by the need of "universality" stressed by I. Yalom (1975). (See Yalom [1975] for a detailed discussion of this category of curative factors; also see Chapter 5 of this text.) Despite the individual problems and deficits, there is one homogeneous factor shared by all clients—that is, all are aging and therefore share the ability to reminisce with clarity and detail. Thus, reminiscence is the one element that cuts across all special issues. Regardless of their impairment, all individuals respond to activities that are familiar and that draw upon previously learned tasks and experiences. Familiar activities employ well-known motor schemes and facilitate abstract imagery and conception of end results. Activities utilizing established learning skills increase self-confidence and self-esteem. Therefore, they promote pleasurable experiences that encourage trust. A major benefit in employing reminiscence for all clients is marked growth in social/emotional development. This aspect of human growth encompasses all 12 general categories of curative factors developed by Yalom (1975).

Reminiscence also has an impact on the naturally occurring process of life review, important for putting into perspective one's successes as well as one's unresolved conflicts during the geriatric life stage (Lewis and Butler 1974). Life review is especially important for the individual in a board-and-care home, who often feels cast aside by society.

In discussing the utilization of reminiscence in group intervention, the literature defines specific group therapy procedures, but the groups described are verbal only; group members individually explore and then share their memories. *However, the authors contend that the therapeutic technique of reminiscence can take many forms.* Some involve movement, visualization, cooking, art, music, task planning, and activities of daily living. These activities provide opportunities not only for life review but also for growth and adaptation in all areas of human development—physical, sensory, perceptual, cognitive, social, and emotional. These phenomena, according to Willard and Spackman (Hopkins and Smith 1980), are intricately interwoven; and issues, stresses, or gains that take place in one area will bring changes in another.

## THE ADVANTAGE OF THE MULTIDISCIPLINARY TEAM

The multidisciplinary team approach to rehabilitation-program planning and implementation has a distinct advantage in the board-and-care setting. As previously discussed, agents of reminiscing can take many forms. During a two- to four-hour session, a team can employ several reminiscing agents so that growth in one area will influence growth in another area. As L. J. King (1970) states, often there is little the staff can do to decrease external stress; however, the staff can help clients enhance their adjusting resources. Furthermore, a variety of modalities facilitates the clients' motivation, attention span, and tolerance to sitting and group interaction.

Each team member can provide experience in his or her area of expertise. Ideally, the team members complement each other so that the blending of resources facilitates effective, methodical treatment planning. For example, the movement therapist can initiate the session by providing a group experience that stimulates pleasure centers in the body. This pleasure

stimulation is critical because clients who have been sedentary and have had little sensory stimulation often fail to experience pleasurable body sensations, a lack that decreases risk-taking behaviors in perception, cognition, and social/emotional growth. Thus, movement facilitates experiences that increase trust, decrease anxiety, and encourage growth in integrating sensory and motor abilities. The occupational therapist can then introduce an activity that requires increased attention span, orientation, concentration, and tolerance to sitting. The occupational therapist can also promote maintenance of cognition stimulated during movement and can facilitate an increase in functional level by utilizing familiar, simple problem-solving tasks that can be readily recalled and mastered. The social worker and the nurse can expand upon the treatment process by assisting clients in integrating their group experience through verbalization.

A major advantage to a multidisciplinary team approach is that a large number of clients can be treated in a group setting. Although the current literature emphasizes small-group treatment, a large group can be treated effectively with a team approach. Such an approach can ensure the inclusion of all clients in each session, which is vital in working with this type of client. Thus, team members can serve as cotherapists, who provide mutual support and assistance in facilitating and processing a session.

Furthermore, each team member can provide training for students in his or her respective field, and the participation of students provides several advantages. They bring enthusiasm, youth, and stimulation to board-and-care clients. They offer an opportunity to encourage clients to impart advice drawn from past experiences and assist in student training, which closes the generation gap and promotes mutual growth, especially in self-confidence and self-esteem. In addition, during group activities students can be paired with clients requiring individual attention outside of the group process. Thus, in a large group, one-on-one treatment can be provided. Another benefit in utilizing students is that students learn early in their training about resources offered by other disciplines, as well as about ways to work with other disciplines to provide more effective client treatment. See Chapters 35, 36, and 37, which elaborate on teaching students.

Still another advantage of the team approach is that other services can be provided during group activities. For example, doctors and nurses can assess patients individually for medical and psychosocial needs during a session. Medical students can also be included in the group process, along with social work and occupational therapy students. In addition, young doctors must be oriented early in their training to be sensitive to these clients' total needs. This training is still often excluded from the medical model as well as the nursing model.

Volunteers can be an additional, effective resource for the team. They can include individuals who would benefit equally from group process to meet their emotional and social needs. For example, community members such as senior citizens or young psychiatric clients who have been isolated can be extremely helpful. In addition to being sensitive and empathetic to clients, these individuals can meet their own needs to be altruistic and to give and receive nurturance. However, since volunteers need guidance and structure, the team must take care to plan for sufficient volunteer guidance. See Chapters 22 and 34, which discuss volunteers.

## DEVELOPMENT OF INTERPERSONAL RELATIONSHIPS

To initiate a program at a board-and-care facility, three essential interpersonal relationships must be carefully developed. These are the relationships between (1) members of the multidisciplinary team, (2) team members and the board-and-care personnel, and (3) team members and the clients.

### Relationships Within the Team

M. Linden (1953) found that working with the aged in a process group is exhausting, because clients require constant stimulation and individual attention. He concluded that co-leadership in group work is essential. Furthermore, believing that productive intervention is dependent upon cohesion between the leaders,

he outlined 10 essential components contributing to effective communication (see Chapter 3). The authors confirm Linden's findings and believe that management of a large group particularly requires co-therapy. In addition, we found that a large group presents special leadership issues.

*Staff must be experienced professionals with a strong background in group leadership and co-therapy.* Co-leaders must communicate on multiple levels. Concurrent with dual communications and client group processing, they must guide and supervise students, volunteers, and board-and-care personnel. The demands of the position include sharp attention to detail, including constant scanning of each individual; sensitivity to the environment at all times; and continual dynamic processing of the various interactions. Judgments about setting up interactions, intervening, facilitating, and integrating material as it develops are a minute-by-minute process. These qualifications are absolutely necessary if leaders are to undertake a large group of 20 to 30 clients in a board and care without disaster. See Chapter 3 for aspects of co-leadership.

Team members need to be flexible, open to new ideas, and willing to explore their own feelings and defenses. Although each person contributes knowledge unique to his or her profession, each must be open to sharing responsibilities. Often skills overlap professional boundaries. Territoriality, which can be destructive to group cohesion, can have a negative impact upon clients, who are generally sensitive to staff process issues, by producing anxiety and conflicting attitudes toward supportive figures. On the other hand, conflicts cannot be overlooked; denial does not preclude conflict, and the feelings emerge covertly or overtly. Either way, denial will be deleterious to the prime work of the team—namely, client adaptation.

Conflicts can be discussed during regularly scheduled staff meetings. However, differences in opinion can also be dealt with during a treatment session. V. M. Satir, J. Staehowiak, and H. A. Taschmann (1975) have found that this method sets an effective model for clients in their work with families in therapy. The staff pull their chairs into the middle of the group with the clients around them and discuss issues face-to-face until there is closure. Staff then return their chairs to the outer circle with the clients and continue with treatment. The authors have found this approach to be effective in group work with the elderly. It affords an opportunity to: (1) build trust toward staff because they are open; (2) recognize that staff are human, with human flaws and feelings (rather than condescending, inexperienced young people who think they are in control); (3) avoid staff resentment, which might build through a session where feelings were not discussed and which would affect client treatment; (4) prevent splits between staff and clients; and (5) model methods for clients to express feelings.

The final opportunity is worth expanding. Many clients are resentful and angry toward family members, board-and-care personnel, and other clients. They may resent team members, who they feel are controlling their lives by requiring group participation. Many have been taught that anger is not a polite feeling to express; since they fear rejection if anger is expressed, they repress their feelings. Unexpressed anger perpetuates depression and physiological illness and can lead to decompensation. By dealing with conflict openly, staff model communication skills and demonstrate that they have neither died nor become ill, nor have they been offended by another's anger. They also demonstrate the possibility of growth and increased warmth in a relationship where taboo subjects can be discussed. Again, this method can be utilized only in an atmosphere where a close working relationship has been established by highly skilled leaders.

Satir (1972) has likened effective teamwork to a dance in which the co-therapists move gracefully and rhythmically in step together. Therefore, they must seat themselves so that they can watch each other and pick up cues from facial expression, body gestures, and eye contact. Body language will help them to employ the skills and confirming judgments previously discussed.

## Team Relationship with Board-and-Care Personnel

The relationship between the multidisciplinary team and the board-and-care personnel needs to be carefully cultivated. While board-and-care operators are receptive to increasing the quality of their programs and thereby maintaining their certification status, they may be threatened by the overwhelming power they have assigned to a professional team. Often, they fear that they will be under scrutiny by the team, who will recommend that their certification be suspended. This apprehension can be advantageous in assisting clients. Mere team presence encourages board-and-care operators to maintain and upgrade services provided for clients, utilize client monies earnestly, and interact with clients respectfully. On the other hand, the presence of team members can invoke resentment and resistance. Personnel may experience disruption in their regular routines and may displace their frustrations onto clients, thereby hindering the team's primary purpose.

Therefore, before initiating a client-centered group, the co-leaders must establish rapport with the board-and-care operators and personnel. Purposeful inclusion of personnel in treatment sessions, with verbal and/or written credit for their participation, is essential. Courtesies, such as assisting personnel with cleanup, are also important. In general, the team needs to be sensitive to the needs of the personnel. Existing creative programs and positive client involvement must be acknowledged. Nevertheless, personnel may view the team as condescending in usurping leadership roles. Some of the personnel may have been highly involved with clients over many years and may feel their efforts are being negated by the so-called experts. In addition, personnel must deal with what they view as the unsurmountable and draining issues of the elderly on a 24-hour basis. Therefore, they may feel resentful toward team members entering the home one session per week with a full entourage of staff offering "ideal" advice. Of course, the personnel may feel gratitude, relief, hope, and stimulation by having additional support and assistance. However, the team must be aware of the total perspective. Everyone needs the esteem derived from receiving credit for a job well done. The results of recognition are reflected in client attitudes and care, as previously discussed. Mutual exchange of ideas should be given mutual professional respect. Finally, the therapeutic relevance of maintaining this special relationship must be imparted to students, who can hinder the process if this training is omitted.

## Relationship Between Team and Clients

The importance of the relationship between the team members and the clients should be underscored. A well-functioning team with respect for one another does not pass unnoticed by clients.

## A MODEL PROGRAM

### Initiating the Program

**Entering the Board-and-Care Home.** Although in many cases one of the first problems faced by the group leader is the need to gain entrance into an institution (Burnside 1978), such was not the case in the following model, which includes a detailed description of the program and the way entry was facilitated.

In January 1975, the psychiatry service in a large medical center reorganized the service from a medical model to a community psychiatry model. Each inpatient ward became a mental health center serving clients living in a particular geographical catchment area in the community. Each center was to provide inpatient crisis treatment, establish a multipurpose satellite center for outpatient treatment, establish working relationships with and provide education about mental health from community members, and assist clients in utilizing the community's resources. One philosophical belief in initiating such a program was that the rapport established between the medical center, the community, and the clients on a more personal level would ultimately have a greater benefit for clients with mental health disabilities than traditional medical models. Staff could better assist clients in making a transition from the hospital into the community by providing services that helped clients to remain in the community for longer periods of time with shorter rehospitalization periods and could encourage clients to seek help before hospitalization became a necessity.

In the spring of 1977, the authors were actively involved in program development with the research team at the community satellite center. The satellite was housed in a progressive community church, which allowed use of its facilities as part of the church's commitment to community action programs. The postdoctorate social worker (Jim Kelly) was involved not only in expanding his clinical skills but also in serving as a consulting expert in the field of gerontology. The occupational therapist (Sally Friedlob) was co-developer and clinical coordinator for a life-skills training and research program designed to assist clients having psychosocial disabilities in reintegrating into the community and in developing evening resource programs at the satellite center. The elderly comprised a target population that the mental health center had not reached. In order to meet the needs of the elderly, the authors decided to initiate an evening program one time per week at the satellite center.

Because extensive groundwork had been laid by the authors and the Community Social Work Service, the board-and-care operators were receptive to the idea. The satellite center was chosen for the group work for specific reasons: (1) to involve the elderly in a community experience, to decrease feelings of isolation and feelings that they were society's castoffs; (2) to utilize the satellite center for a variety of community programs, to obtain community acceptance and participation; (3) to connect the elderly with the existing state geriatric program housed within the church; (4) to involve some of the clients in a possible grandparent program with the preschool children; (5) to increase motivation and functional capacity to each individual's fullest potential by providing the stimulation of a new environment; (6) to increase reality orientation by holding the group in a special room at the same time each week; and (7) to provide stimulation by enabling clients to experience a weekly ride in an automotive vehicle.

In the first two attempts to initiate the program at the satellite center, the clients failed to attend. Therefore, for the third session the authors decided to take the program to the facility. They found that failure to attend was due to (1) poor communication between day and evening personnel, (2) lack of personnel coverage, (3) low personnel interest, (4) transportation problems, and (5) financial problems. The physical needs of many of the clients dictated that working within the board-and-care setting would be logistically preferable. In addition, a large number of clients could receive desperately needed services. Although half of the clients were not qualified for direct services at the medical center, the authors believed that they were justified in treating the entire population because the community psychiatry model encourages exchange in services and programs between a variety of agencies.

The population was mixed and included outpatients with chronic psychosocial disabilities, former state mental hospital residents, and older adults from the community needing the structure provided by a facility. Upon seeing familiar clients who had actively participated in a resocialization program one and a half years earlier, the occupational therapist was appalled by their appearances. They had regressed in social skills, they displayed retarded motor activity, they were emaciated and showed little affect, and their grooming and clothing were poorly kept. More of the board-and-care population were withdrawn and appeared depressed. Upon interviewing clients, the authors found that few knew the names of people with whom they were living. During mealtimes, clients rarely spoke with each other. Most sat isolated all day; some drank coffee and smoked cigarettes, watching television occasionally. Most slept much of the day and evening. Three full meals were served daily, and clients were given an evening snack. Although the rooms were bare, the facility was kept clean and neat. The authors concluded that a major contributing factor to the apparent depression of the clients was the lack of nurturance, interpersonal connections, and stimulation. Furthermore, the authors concluded that a reminiscing program would be the total intervention for reasons discussed earlier in this chapter.

**Creative Staffing and Administrative Issues.** The authors decided to implement the program one evening per week for a three-hour period (6 to 9 P.M.) after the dinner hour, because this time frame avoided interference with the responsibilities of the board-and-care personnel. The authors functioned as co-therapists and included in their team a highly experienced registered movement therapist, occupational therapy students, social work students, nursing students, and medical students. The students rotated through the program; the number of weeks of participation were dependent upon their rotation schedule. Older adults from the community volunteered to assist in programming.

A unique part of the program was that a group of young outpatients with psychosocial disabilities participated as volunteers. These young adults, who had completed an intensive inpatient Life Skills Training Program (Friedlob 1982), had been discharged to their own apartments or to cooperative housing. They had increased their social skills during the training, but they required community follow-up in order to maintain treatment gains. Most were overly concerned with their own well-being, an egocentrism that inhibited their awareness of others and affected their social skills.

The young adults met with the multidisciplinary team for dinner before the board-and-care evening program, going out for dinner or rotating dinners at the outpatient's apartments. Everyone contributed money toward groceries, did the shopping, and assisted in cooking the meal. The group used the dinner hour to plan the board-and-care session and to purchase ingredients for the session's cooking activities.

Another unusual aspect was that some of the young adults living in the board-and-care home formed relationships with their peers and participated in the volunteer program. These outpatients formed friendships that they continued throughout the week. Some of the young adults formed relationships with older adults at the board-and-care home and worked individually with them during a session. These social interactions and the young people's sense of altruism decreased their self-conscious behaviors and their psychiatric symptoms by allowing them to be less concerned about their own psychological well-being and social adequacy.

The co-therapists served as role models, providing leadership in program development, clinical expertise, client and student education and supervision, liaison with the medical center's research team and administrative personnel, and liaison with university faculty. The co-therapists were also responsible for coordinating programmatic needs with the board-and-care administration. Arrangements for space, refreshments, and equipment (such as pianos) were made. The team continually strove for a combined effort in setting goals, planning implementation, and communicating about health care and staffing issues. The team was able to manage the varying needs of 20 to 30 board-and-care clients for the reasons previously discussed (see "Advantage of the Multidisciplinary Team").

Implementing this program was beneficial to the medical center, the taxpayers, and to the board-and-care facility. The board-and-care home received free services from skilled professionals, who would have been far too expensive for it to employ. Furthermore, the activity program contributed to the status of the home in maintaining its certification. The taxpayers saved monies in that the cost per day of hospitalizing a client is more than that of maintaining a client in the community. The medical center paid only small stipends to students and no salary to volunteers. The occupational therapist was able to treat a large number of outpatients during the weekly sessions. The postdoctoral social worker and the movement therapist were paid a flat consultant fee by the psychiatry service, which saved tax monies. In additon, since the Occupational Therapy Department budget included monies for supplies—such as cooking ingredients, equipment, and other materials, which qualified as treatment requisites in training patients in living skills essential in maintaining a particular living environment—the board-and-care residents received additional benefits.

### Reminiscing Program Goals

The ultimate goal of the program was to enhance clients' adjustive resources and therein facilitate growth and adaptation. To fulfill this goal, nine objectives were identified. Reminiscing experiences were aimed at providing opportunities for

1. Reality orientation.
2. Sensory stimulation.
3. Socialization.

4. Friendship networks.
5. Capitalizing on retained strengths (physical, sensory, perceptual, cognitive, social, emotional).
6. Retraining in lost skill areas.
7. Building confidence in retained skill areas.
8. Supporting independence (by allowing decision making and encouraging autonomy in carrying out tasks when feasible).
9. Increasing self-esteem (through opportunities listed above).

### Program Structure

A routine program structure is important in assisting the elderly with retention of recent memories and reality orientation. When these individuals know exactly what to expect, their sense of physical security and their self-confidence to risk participation are increased. Furthermore, motivation can be encouraged if the routine provides a pleasurable experience. For the elderly, pleasure can be derived simply by purposeful activity that has been mastered by repeated familiar rehearsals and/or experiences. Routine need not lead to boredom. *Creativity can be explored within a structured program.* The following is an outline of the basic plan used in this program, the rationale for the sequencing of events, and examples of related creative activities that were incorporated into the familiar routines. The information is summarized in Table 26–1.

**Large-Group Involvement.** I. Burnside (1976) states that students often get carried away and feel that group work is like cooking potatoes—one more will not matter very much.

Yalom (1975) states that unless clients are carefully selected, the majority of patients assigned to group therapy will terminate treatment discouraged and without benefits; the authors, in managing a large, unselected group, found quite the contrary.

However, the leaders of this group were highly skilled and experienced, and they had the advantage of adequate support systems. A number of guidelines for managing a large group have already been discussed, but a few addi-

**TABLE 26-1.** Outline of basic program plan, rationale for sequence, and associated activities

| Regularly structured program | Rationale for programmatic sequencing | Example of creative activities |
|---|---|---|
| 1. Opening greetings | Orientation to a purposeful beginning. <br><br> Orient to new individuals. <br><br> Reinforce memory of familiar persons. <br><br> Convey feelings of individual importance by remembering client's name. A name or nickname is extremely important for self-identification. Names have many meanings and implications. "This is who I am." | *Through movement:* Say your name and everyone will say your name and copy your movement. <br><br> *Game:* New staff and students will go around the room and try to remember everyone's name and movement (with creative cueing when students stumble; it is important to remember everyone). Clients sometimes feel good if they can stump a student briefly. |
| 2. Getting clients who have not attended because they are isolated in their rooms, outside, or sleeping | Everyone needs to feel that he or she is important enough to be remembered. <br><br> Everyone likes to feel included in the group process rather than left on the fringes. <br><br> Clients need to be included early in the session to reinforce participation and orientation to date, time, and place. | Other clients assisted in getting each other once relationship had been formed. <br><br> Younger clients who played guitars serenaded older client to group. <br><br> Familiar jokes and story-telling before joining the group can be instituted to motivate clients. |
| 3. Movement therapy | Developmentally, movement emerges from other abilities. <br><br> Movement is the plane on which primal learning must take place, and it is the cognitive level that must be integrated before higher thought processes can evolve (Levy 1974). <br><br> Creates a warm atmosphere and pleasurable physical experiences. <br><br> Decreases anxiety, to prepare the group for forthcoming activities. <br><br> Increases interaction and trust among individuals through shared experiences without having to verbalize cognitively integrated experiences (at the early stage). | Movement geared to expressing aspects of a particular holiday. <br><br> Movement that grows out of a client's spontaneous action or reaction. |
| 4. Music therapy period: music (harmonica, percussion, brass) and movement | Music was often used in conjunction with movement. Music stimulates affect, mood, and expression of feelings. <br><br> Music was generally a natural outgrowth of movement. Clients frequently broke out in song after moving or wanted to perform for others; for example, one man brought his harmonica to play; another a guitar. <br><br> Singing familiar songs from a book printed in large type simulated vision, hearing, and following a familiar sequence and helped task conceptualization. <br><br> Promoted increased trust and camaraderie among individuals. | Individuals in movement spontaneously pantomining piano playing from time to time sat at the piano and played familiar songs while the group moved. <br><br> Percussion instruments were included in a sing-along. <br><br> Instruments were spontaneously created from familiar objects, such as wax paper and combs. |
| 5. Task planning group | Clients are now ready to sit for a longer period, with increased attention span and receptivity to ideas. | Planning next week's treat or special program. |

TABLE 26–1.    Outline of basic program plan, rationale for sequence, and associated activities (continued)

| Regularly structured program | Rationale for programmatic sequencing | Example of creative activities |
| --- | --- | --- |
| | Familiar tasks involving decision making increase self-esteem and the feeling of autonomy. <br> Tasks require negotiation, compromise, expression of feelings, and sharing of ideas. <br> High-level thought processes are now ready to evolve. | Planning a group project and carrying it out; for example, making simple learning toys for the children at Head Start (using familiar pictures from magazines for flash card words). <br> Planning homework activities, such as taking a walk with a friend. <br> Planning utilization of the community's resources. |
| 6. Life skills activity: cooking | By this time clients need a break that reinforces participation. Response is positive to oral gratification. Cooking, which involves familiar, simple problem-solving task follow-through, reinforces higher level thought processes and can be an extremely pleasurable and beneficial venture (see appendix to chapter). | See appendix to Chapter. |
| 7. Verbal psychodynamic group | Part of closure requires integration of evening's experience through verbalization. <br> Clients need to convey unexpressed thoughts and feelings. <br> Clients have been stimulated and need to calm down before retiring. | Formal reminiscing group initiated by social worker. |
| 8. Formal goodbye | Orient clients to time. <br> A formal goodnight hug or handshake for each person reinforces personal worth and friendship. <br> Provides reassurance of closure for those worried that they will not see the staff again. Provides hope that "we will meet again" (during the early stage). | Goodbye songs—such as "Goodnight Irene" and "Goodbye Farewell" song from *The Sound of Music*—can be sung at the door. |

tional comments are necessary. First, clients are never to be treated like "another potato." In undertaking the program, the leaders carefully considered the physical and emotional needs of each client. Furthermore, the co-leaders were responsible for ensuring that each client was actively acknowledged and included in each session.

The primary technique found to be relevant for this size group was "scanning." The co-leaders observed each individual successively clockwise and then counterclockwise throughout the session. At any given moment, co-therapists were aware of the physical location, facial expressions, verbalizations, and so on, of a par-

ticular client. Periodically, while one co-leader or allied staff member directed an activity, the other co-leader(s) scanned the group, picking up behaviors that required intervention. For example, one client's left leg began quivering while he was standing with the group in group exercise. A co-therapist used eye contact and subtle hand signals to direct a student to assist the client, who was able to complete the activity from his chair.

To help with scanning and other activities, higher functioning clients and team members can be seated next to those who need assistance. Staff can be redirected as necessary. Thus, staff members should be positioned so that they can clearly see each other. Following are three other strategies for large-group management.

**Small Groups.** With adequate staffing the large group can be broken into smaller groups. One method utilized in the program was to assemble the entire group for a given activity, to explain the activity, and then to break into smaller groups. Upon task completion, group members rejoined to share their small-group experiences briefly.

Leadership for each small group was carefully assessed given the assets and limitations of team members. The small-group leaders had to be able to give directions clearly and to handle group issues. For example, an occupational therapy student was able to manage an art group that stimulated remote recall and then discussed content and process issues. A volunteer did not have the skills to lead such a group, but was included as an assistant. A volunteer outpatient was able to lead a small group successfully in a cooking activity, such as baking a Stir-and-Frost cake, while a student served as an assistant. This strategy increased the level of participation and the self-esteem for the volunteer.

**Dyads.** Dyads, or pairs, proved to be another constructive means of working with a large group. Clients who worked in pairs created new friendships that carried over to daily routines. One pair, for example, began to take the bus to the satellite center two times per week, where they interacted in a therapeutic social club and participated in the Senior Citizens Lunch Program. Dyads were utilized in task activities, such as making a Christmas decoration. They were used to personalize a group activity. For example, the leader directed the group to turn to a neighbor and discuss what he or she thought about the current topic. In addition, dyads were used in training clients to ask for help, and sometimes a buddy system was instituted for the forthcoming week.

**Individual Treatment.** Clients were treated individually while the group was concurrently convening, because clients frequently had individual problems and needs. As they formed trusting relationships with team members, they expressed pent-up feelings that they had repressed due to fear and/or isolation. For example, one aged woman had been placed in the facility by the county after she had been hospitalized for a broken hip, because she needed supervised aftercare. She was worried about her house, belongings, and garden. She was so concerned that she rarely left her room and rarely attempted to exercise her hip as directed, to increase strength. She needed someone to listen and to empathize with her. A medical student was assigned to work with her for 30 to 45 minutes a week. The session was not only of benefit to the woman, but benefited the student in expanding his medical training; he learned that the needs of an elderly patient may far exceed the physical medicine required to heal a broken hip. He found that healing was also facilitated by attitude and motivation. These needs might not be apparent to a medical team without a holistic approach to treatment.

Frequently, clients relied on team members to divulge negative feelings toward the board-and-care personnel. This is a delicate subject and will be discussed in more detail (see "Problems, Obstacles, and Management").

## AGENTS OF REMINISCING

### Movement Therapy

Movement sessions were purposefully developed with a routine structure to increase reality orientation. Predictable activities served to reassure clients who felt unsteady and unsure of their movement abilities. These sessions were developed with designated times for large-group activities, dyads, and individual expression. The large group offered skills in coping with interactions similar to those needed to cope with a large group of people on a day-to-day basis. At times interactions were facilitated to require less intimacy. For example, clients were directed to find a familiar way to move their arms. Beginning with a large group was comforting for clients who had difficulty tolerating intimacy. At other times, the large group became more personal. For example, clients were directed to form a circle, turn, and give the person in front of them a back rub.

Small-group activities, such as finding a familiar way to balance together, encouraged trust and warmth. Dyads promoted an increased opportunity for intimacy and interpersonal skills. An activity such as mirroring with another individual (one person pretends to be looking into a mirror; the other is the mirror image and copies the looker) promoted an exchange of eye contact, facial gestures, postures, and feelings and led to one-to-one discussions following the activity.

Individual activities encouraged autonomy and confidence. Some individual movement was integrated with the large-group activity. For example, during movement charades, a client showed off his or her expertise and abilities by pantomiming an activity he or she enjoyed while everyone guessed what she or he was doing. Each performance ended with group applause.

The movement sessions began and ended with a large-group activity. The final activity was to stand in a circle holding hands, find balance together, and finally let go in order to find one's own balance. This promoted trust and reinforced a sense of relatedness to others and to self. The basic group structure served to orient group members to time and also to life review—that is, there was a definite beginning, middle, and ending during each session.

Movement directives stimulated familiar body motions and encouraged discussion of accompanying memories. For example, when directed to "find a way you like to move your arms and we'll follow you," one woman began to do the crawl stroke. She then related to the group that she had been an avid swimmer when she was a young girl growing up in Sweden. Her memories stimulated and encouraged a very shy Mexican man, who rarely initiated conversation, to act out the crawl stroke and share that he too had enjoyed swimming in his youth.

Familiar movements that were coupled with similar music encouraged individuals to discuss spontaneously instruments they had liked to play. These instruments were provided during succeeding sessions and incorporated into the weekly routine. One man played the harmonica; three played the piano; one, the organ; and two, the guitar. These individuals were encouraged to take turns in providing the background music during the movement sessions. The instruments contributed to reminiscence. For example, the organ music stirred up memories about music accompanying ice skaters. The "Skaters Waltz" was played while people pretended to ice skate. The activity further stimulated a variety of related memories, which the group discussed.

Movement also promoted sensory input through tactile, visual, and auditory stimulation.

### Music Therapy

M. J. Hennessey (1978) states that the healing properties of music have long been known, and music is an effective tool in group work with the elderly. Clients were extremely responsive to music. A regularly scheduled group developed as an outgrowth of the movement group. Music increased motivation, pleasure, mental alertness, and animation. Furthermore, music proved to be an excellent agent of reminiscing.

Music from time periods such as the Big Band Era evoked activity and discussion. For example, one man who was delusional stopped his grandiose talk and began to tell a story about an experience he had had at a USO dance and demonstrated several fancy steps he knew, including the fox trot and the rhumba. For an individual to break out in solo spontaneously and for the group to listen and then applaud loudly was not unusual during a music session. In following sessions, people might spontaneously call for a favorite singer or piano player, clapping and demanding an encore performance.

Folk songs encouraged group interaction and stirred up childhood memories. One man recalled chopping wood with his father on his farm in Missouri. His memories encouraged others to share stories and stimulated sharing traditions and folk songs from various cultures.

Music encouraged closure of the generation gap. Folk songs, for example, were universally appreciated. One regressed young man, who was gifted at playing the piano, favored rock music. However, he was pleased by the opportunity to play standard tunes, such as "Sweet Georgia Brown," and slower contemporary songs, like the Beatles' "Do You Want to Know a Secret?" for the group. He was encouraged by the gratitude shown toward him by elder clients, which was expressed through applause and sing-a-longs. Clients who had been angry at him because of his "noisy music" began to accept him and to relate to him. In addition, they were willing to give special time for him to play rock music on the guitar, and he was willing to adapt some of his favorite pieces to meet their needs.

Music brought out a variety of moods and often stimulated moods correlated with past events, encouraging clients to share feelings verbally with the group. Music was also spontaneously used during other activities to assist in integrating the experience. For example, at the end of an evening's session, the group convened at the door while the staff serenaded the clients with a goodby song, and the clients responded through song and perhaps a farewell tune.

## Art Therapy

Art was not regularly scheduled as part of the program. However, it was periodically employed as a highly effective agent of reminiscing. Initially, group members would declare, "I can't draw." However, staff emphasized that artistic ability was not the purpose of the activity. Art was a means to an end; namely, it was used to facilitate large-group and/or small-group discussion. For example, one directive was to "choose a color that creates a feeling you had about a historical event that happened during your lifetime." Sometimes the colors were not included in the discussion but were used solely to facilitate memories. Other times, the use of color was tied into the discussion. Directing clients to draw symbolic figures or markings was incorporated in a similar way. The co-therapists facilitated the discussions and encouraged young staff members to learn from clients. For example, one could learn a great deal about historical events firsthand. During art sessions, clients often discovered that they had many things in common with each other. Three clients were surprised to learn that they had all grown up in the same town in Ohio. These discoveries encouraged alliances and interaction outside of the sessions.

## Occupational Therapy: The Developmental Task Group

The advantage of employing the developmental task group was that it not only promoted autonomy in performing simple problem-solving and decision-making skills but it also encouraged using these skills with others. Typically, in this type of group the end result is secondary to the developmental process. Fidler and Fiedler (1969) write that task accomplishment is not the purpose of the therapy group but, it is hoped, the means by which the purpose is accomplished. In working with the elderly, however, the authors found that the end result was equally important. Clients needed to be able to conceptualize an end result and experience mastery in task completion.

To meet these needs, familiar tasks that drew upon past memories, abilities, motor activities, and assets were presented. For example, one task was to plan, set up, and participate in an old-fashioned barbecue. The role of the co-therapists during this group activity was that of resource persons. Without assuming responsibility for the group, they also facilitated group process and made learning possible. The development task group provided a means for:

1. Increasing independence by encouraging clients to contribute ideas drawn from past experiences.
2. Providing gratification and success.
3. Fulfilling narcissistic needs for self-actualization while providing an opportunity for sharing in a cooperative venture.
4. Promoting social interaction and generalizing experiences to the community.
5. Providing repeated opportunities to perceive cause-and-effect relationships.
6. Providing parallel play-work situations that encourage modeling and limitation.
7. Providing opportunities for problem solving, carry through, and observable results.
8. Increasing sitting tolerance and attention span.

9. Increasing risk-taking behavior by increasing physical and psychological security.

10. Increasing self-confidence and self-esteem.

### Life Skills Training

**Cooking Activities.** M. A. Brown (1982) found that training in life skills should closely correlate with skills required in a particular living environment. This correlation reinforces retention of skills learned and encourages utilization and autonomy in skill application. Although board-and-care facilities do not allow clients in the kitchen (county health laws prohibit clients from handling foods in the kitchen), simple cooking activities using developed task group methods were planned and carried out in the dining area. In addition to the rationale previously outlined, a detailed summary of cooking activities, qualities, and positive aspects of the tasks, possible precautions, and preventive measures can be found in the appendix to this chapter. The authors found that issues relating to foods were extremely meaningful. Food invokes a variety of very personal feelings and memories.

To enhance the many therapeutic aspects incurred by a cooking activity, an art therapy approach was utilized after one cooking session. The art paper was divided into thirds. In the first section, clients were directed to remember a particular meal shared with their families by diagramming where each person sat. Foods served at that meal were drawn in the second section. Colors, markings, and/or drawings depicting feelings during that particular meal were placed in the last section, encouraging life review. Clients talked about their own values, habits, and feelings and then compared these. For example, many found that their parents did not allow discussions during mealtime. For others, mealtime was the only time family members gathered to share stories, jokes, and daily happenings and to plan family events. The discussion assisted clients in integrating feelings about current mealtimes. Clients also compared food preferences, mourned current losses involving consumption of favorite foods, and

*One supermarket offered old-fashioned recipes as a free presentation to shoppers. A booklet such as this would make an excellent prop in a reminiscing group.*

planned the preparation of foods, such as old-fashioned ice cream sundaes.

Activities such as the above, coupled with pleasurable cooking experiences, promoted social interaction during eating and the generalization of socialization during daily meals. Upon arriving during one dinner hour, the authors were gratified to find clients chatting, sharing, and calling each other by name. In addition, the authors found a way around the county health laws in order to assist one middle-aged client. The client was able to assist kitchen staff for minimal pay after the doctor wrote in the chart that assisting in the kitchen was essential in the client's rehabilitation. Thereafter, this client's role, image, self-esteem, and ability to take on responsibility and social skills improved.

**Other Life Skills Activities.** The evaluation of a number of clients showed individual living skills needs. Training in communication, health care, hygiene, budgeting, community resources, and time management skills were initiated when necessary. For example, one man with a progressive neurological condition was beginning to have difficulty dressing himself. His motor activity was retarded, and he displayed tremors upon voluntary motion. Inability to care for himself would lead to either rehospitalization or transfer to a nursing home facility. The OT student was assigned to work individually with him for part of each session. The patient's goal was to maintain his level of independent functioning for as long as possible.

Life skills training was sometimes employed in the group setting. For example, during one developmental task group, the members filled out a weekly schedule balancing each day with work, rest, and play. They chose homework assignments, such as taking a walk to the market for a snack with a buddy. The group members reviewed task accomplishments, difficulties, and areas for growth during the following week's session.

## Other Therapeutic Modalities

**Children.** Occasionally team members and board-and-care personnel brought children to participate with clients. Clients became animated, laughing and smiling with the children. Children facilitated the loosening of defenses and encouraged displays of warmth. For example, one client's cultural background had customs about appropriate touching; thus, he rarely touched others and never hugged them. The client was able to respond positively to a child's touch. Another 89-year-old man had difficulty communicating with others because of his poor vision and hearing. He actively engaged a small child throughout a movement session. He cooed and waved at her and played peek-a-boo. Children also stimulated clients'

childhood memories, which were reviewed and processed during verbal sessions.

**Pet-Facilitated Group Therapy.** Pets also provide meaningful experiences for the aging and chronically ill (Brickel and Brickel 1980). There is a large body of literature on the positive effects on health of elders who have pets. One older woman confined to a wheelchair was able to hide a cat in her room. (Some health laws prohibit live-in pets.) Although she was depressed about living in the care home, the maneuvering and secrecy involved in feeding and maintaining the cat were thrilling. She had difficulty relating with the other clients, so the cat became her one reliable living contact. She held it on her lap and petted and hugged it. When she began to trust team members who worked with her individually, she shared her "mischievous" undertaking with them. As other clients found out about the cat, they became cohorts and helped her with management, leading to her increased socialization and ultimately to her group participation. Pets, like children, stimulated childhood memories and other stories related to animals.

## PROBLEMS, OBSTACLES, AND MANAGEMENT

Although the program described in this chapter was well planned, well coordinated, and adequately staffed, problems were encountered. Obstacles and discerning issues were expected because the authors were well aware that any program has its drawbacks. Problems were managed with team planning and strategies.

One major problem in maintaining the program was surviving the changing conditions. Since the home had three owners within a three-year period, relationships had to be established with each new administration; furthermore, the staff changed monthly and sometimes weekly. Often, the new evening personnel had not been oriented to the program and were overwhelmed when the team appeared with a full crew and program plan. Some of the new personnel were offended when team members requested that they maintain routines, such as serving coffee after the task group. Some served the coffee before the authors could explain the rationale and disrupted the program. At first, the authors attempted to remedy this situation by calling the staff on the afternoon of the group. However, communication between the day and evening personnel was poor. Therefore, the team decided that one of them would orient the personnel upon arrival while the other would initiate the program. Then, personnel were included in the refreshment period and other festive events, such as holiday parties. Personnel were encouraged to join the group at will. The team was conscientious about postgroup clean-up, especially in the dining room where uniformed personnel had already completed their evening work by setting up the dining room for the following morning. Sometimes the team judiciously decided to reset the tables.

Providing alcoholic beverages on special occasions is another concern. In our society alcohol is a significant object; the ability to consume alcohol is the mark of maturity. General rules and restrictions imposed on the aged living in an institution, especially rules and restrictions about alcohol, promote low self-esteem and self-confidence about their ability to maintain their autonomy. At the Michael Reese Institute in Chicago, the geriatric program encourages the inpatients and staff to dress formally for dinner one night a week, and wine is served with dinner. As a result, self-image and hope for the future were observed to increase during the session. The authors also found a similar outcome when one beer was provided during barbecues and special holiday events. However, there are several precautions that need to be taken to prevent deleterious effects. Some board-and-care clients may be alcoholics, some may be on medications that cannot be ingested with alcohol, or some may have a low tolerance for alcoholic beverages. *Therefore, knowing the medical history of each client is important.* (See Chapter 2 for health problems in the elderly.) Alcohol can be regulated by type, alcoholic content, and amount. Even for the client with alcohol problems, providing one beer or a glass of wine at a special social gathering can be beneficial. For example, one man who was having a problem with alcohol spent most of his free time drinking in a nearby tavern and returned to the board-and-care home inebriated. This activity alleviated his isolation and was his primary outlet for socialization. At a structured activity he could enjoy one to two beers and socialize with others. As his peer relationships increased, the time he spent at local taverns decreased.

Clients frequently wanted to place the authors in an omnipotent role. This was both a blessing and a curse and often invoked conflicting feelings. Clients experiencing a loss in dignity improved their future outlook because of the power they invested in the team to help them with their plight. Although the team was instrumental in alleviating some of the problems, the team had to be tactful in order to prevent possible punitive actions to clients by the board-and-care staff and possible termination of the program. Clients confided in the team, and sometimes team members felt torn about their alliances. For example, when the woman who was hiding a cat in her room confided in the team, the team had to decide whether the cat might create a health problem and had to determine other possible consequences of failing to report the animal to the owner. In the end, the authors decided that the benefits derived from having the cat outweighed the possible problems and decided to overlook the situation.

Other issues were not as easy to overlook. For example, several clients accused personnel of misappropriating their funds. The team decided that the best way to deal with the situation was to report the issue to the medical center's Community Social Work Service, which was responsible for quality assurance in board-and-care settings. When the community social worker probed the situation, the operator called for a team conference and demonstrated that the two clients were confused and had fabricated stories.

### Confidentiality

The issue of confidentiality with clients is an important one. Whether clients were correct in their perception about a situation was not always as important as the thoughts and feelings they were able to express confidentially. Common themes were: (1) loss of dignity, (2) low self-esteem, (3) helplessness, and (4) lack of control. Some of their attitudes and behaviors were found to be defenses against their anger and underlying hurt. The single most important quality in helping clients cope is empathy. Empathy skills include listening, helping the client to express his or her feelings, and conveying feedback that the client has been understood.

## SUMMARY

The therapeutic technique of reminiscence is an excellent treatment in the board-and-care setting because reminiscence is a major cognitive characteristic of the geriatric life stage. Individuals with a wide range of problems and deficits can be included in such a treatment program. According to the authors, a major advantage of the therapeutic technique of reminiscence is that it can take many forms, such as movement, cooking, art, music, and activities of daily living. These activities provide opportunities for life review and for growth and adaptation in all areas of human development. In undertaking a program at a board-and-care facility, employing a multidisciplinary team is preferable. This approach can be beneficial in that a large number of clients can be treated in a group setting by utilizing skilled co-leaders directing a variety of assistant leaders. The large group can be divided into small groups, dyads, and individual group treatment.

A team member can provide experiences in his or her area of expertise to complement and enhance experiences provided by other team members. Ideally, team members need to be flexible in sharing responsibilities because territoriality can be destructive to group cohesion. There are three interpersonal relationships that must be carefully cultivated. These are the relationships between (1) the multidisciplinary team members, (2) the team members and the board-and-care personnel, and (3) the team members and the clients. In addition, a multidisciplinary team is cost-effective in that a variety of services can be provided to a large outpatient group. Creative staffing can assist in this process. There is a substantial cost-benefit in maintaining clients in the community in comparison with the cost of hospitalization. We as clinicians are focused on quality-of-life issues; however, to be able to *ensure support* in improving quality of life, we must be accountable to administration.

The quality of life for the patients in the program described in this chapter was enhanced primarily in terms of social-skills gains. Clients who had initially appeared withdrawn, emaciated, and unkempt showed improved grooming, became animated and involved in activities, and formed relationships with others. Clients acknowledged each other by first name or last name for endearment. Conversations at mealtimes became spontaneous, one-on-one friendships formed, clients independently initiated trips to the satellite center by bus, and drinking in local taverns decreased. Two major changes were noticeable: (1) clients developed interpersonal relationships that continued without staff facilitation and (2) when the physical environment began to deteriorate in terms of upkeep, food, and finances, the interpersonal relationships and morale remained high.

## EXERCISE 1

Work with one other classmate or a small group of your classmates. Lay out a box of crayons and papers. Each person is to recall an historical event in his or her lifetime. Each is to imagine where he or she was at the time, people with whom he or she was involved, and related objects and events. Each person is to imagine how he or she felt at the time, to choose a color to represent his or her feelings at the time, and to express the events and feelings on paper. Artistic ability is not required. Participants may wish simply to put a color or two or a symbolic figure on paper.

1. Allow time for each person to share his or her events.

2. After each person shares, other group members are to imagine how that person felt in one or two feeling words. The members each have a turn to tell the speaker their two words. The speaker responds by validating or invalidating the words.

3. Allow time for spontaneous interaction by members—for example, two members may have common themes.

## EXERCISE 2

Recall events in your life from childhood to the present. Associate pertinent songs that each event brings to mind.

## EXERCISE 3

Work with a group of classmates. Make a circle. Each person is to think of an activity he or she has enjoyed performing. One person is to pantomine the activity while the rest of the group guesses what the person is doing.

## REFERENCES

Brickel, C. M., and G. K. Brickel. 1980. A review of the roles of pet animals in psychotherapy and with the elderly. *International Journal of Aging and Human Development* 12(2): 119–28.

Brown, M. A. 1982. Maintenance and generalization issues in skills training with chronic schizophrenics. In *Social skills training*, ed. J. P. Curran and P. M. Monti. New York: Guilford Press.

Burnside, I. M. 1976. Overview of group work with the aged. *Journal of Gerontological Nursing* 2(6): 14–17 (November–December).

———. 1978. *Working with the elderly: Group process and techniques.* North Scituate, Mass.: Duxbury Press.

Butler, R. 1963. The life review: An interpretation of reminiscence in the aged. *Psychiatry* 26(1): 65–76.

Erikson, E. 1950. *Childhood and society.* New York: Norton.

Fidler, G. S., and J. W. Fiedler. 1969. *Occupational therapy.* 2d ed. New York: Macmillan.

Friedlob, S. A. 1982. The development of a life skills training program for chronic schizophrenic patients: Three case studies. Unpublished paper.

Hennessey, M. J. 1978. Music and music therapy groups. In *Working with the elderly: Group pro-cess and techniques,* ed. I. M. Burnside. North Scituate, Mass.: Duxbury Press.

Hopkins, H. L., and H. O. Smith. 1980. *Willard and Spackman's occupational therapy.* 5th ed. Philadelphia: Lippincott.

King, L. J. 1970. Perceptual motor training of the adult psychiatric patient. Paper presented to the Arizona Occupational Therapy Association, January 26.

Levy, L. 1974. Movement therapy for psychiatric patients. *American Journal of Occupational Therapy* 28(6): 354–57.

Lewis, M. I., and R. N. Butler. 1974. Life review: Putting memories to work in individual and group psychotherapy. *Geriatrics* 29(11): 165–73 (November).

Linden, M. 1953. Group psychotherapy with institutionalized senile women: Study in gerontological human relations. *International Journal of Group Psychotherapy* 3:150–70.

Satir, V. M. 1972. *Peoplemaking.* Palo Alto, Calif.: Science & Behavioral Books.

Satir, V., J. Staehowiak, and H. A. Taschmann. 1975. *Helping families to change.* New York: Aronson.

Yalom, Irvin D. 1975. *The theory and practice of group psychotherapy.* 2d ed. New York: Basic Books.

## BIBLIOGRAPHY

Blank, M. L. 1971. Recent research findings on practice with aging. *Social Casework,* June: 382–87.

Burnside, I. M. 1969. Sensory stimulation: An adjunct to group work with the disabled aged. *Mental Hygiene* 33(3): 381–88 (July).

_____. 1970. Loss: A constant theme in group work with the aged. *Hospital and Community Psychiatry* 21(6): 173–77 (June).

Farrar, M., and N. Ferrar. 1960. Casework and group work in a home for the aged. *Social Work* 5(2): 58–63 (April).

Harris, P. B. 1979. Being old: A confrontation group with nursing home residents. *Health Social Work* 4(1): 152–66 (February).

Ingersoll, B., and L. Goodman, 1980. History come alive: Facilitating reminiscence in a group of institutionalized elderly. *Journal of Gerontological Social Work* 2(4): 305–19 (Summer).

Lowy, L. 1962. The group in social work with the aged. *Social Work* 7(4): 43–50 (October).

_____. 1983. Social group work with vulnerable older persons: A theoretical perspective. In *Group work with the frail elderly.* New York: Haworth Press.

Mayadas, N. S., and D. L. Hink. 1974. Group work with the aging: An issue for social work education. *The Gerontologist* 14(5): 440–45 (October).

Oliveria, O. H. 1977. Understanding old people: Patterns of reminiscing in elderly people and their relationship to life satisfaction. Unpublished Ph.D. dissertation, University of Tennessee, Knoxville.

Stange, A. 1973. Around the kitchen table: Group work on a back ward. In *Psychosocial nursing care of the aged,* ed. I. M. Burnside. New York: McGraw-Hill.

## RESOURCES

### Films

*How to Save a Choking Victim: The Heimlich Maneuver* (color, 11 minutes, 1975). Presents Dr. J. Heimlich, a leading specialist in esophagus surgery, teaching a simple first-aid procedure he devised that has proven successful in saving the lives of choking victims.

APPENDIX:  **Food- and Holiday-Related Activities to Stimulate Senses and Reminiscing**

| Activity | Sensory stimulation | Memory facilitation | Positive aspects | Possible precautions | Preventive measures |
|---|---|---|---|---|---|
| **Food-Related Activities** | | | | | |
| 1. Decorating Cookies (large store-bought sugar cookies can be frosted and decorated with candies, etc.) | Colors stimulate visual senses. | Recall holidays past. | Easy to make with little preparation. | Choking on silver balls used as decorations. | Know which patients do not have teeth. |
| | Various textures provide tactile stimulation. | Recall past creative experiences. | Fun. | | Simplify decorations. |
| | | | Creative. | | Know how to perform Heimlich maneuver. |
| | Limited parts where end result is easily conceived. | Recall types of old-fashioned cookies or experiences like taffy pulls; facilitate story-telling and elaborating on stories, thereby assisting clients in becoming *raconteurs*. | Can break into dyads: (1) higher functioning clients; can assist lower functioning clients; (b) staff can pair off one-to-one and share experience with clients and listen to discussion stimulated. | Diabetes. | Make some dietetic cookies. |
| | | | Can make into small-group activity in which members each contribute to a joint venture by "round robin"; can then discuss memories stimulated. | Small candies may require too fine motor coordination and perception. | Decorate with larger foods, such as candied fruits. |
| | | | Can see immediate end result; promotes autonomy. | | |
| | | | Simple decision making. | | |
| | | | Increases control and mastery. | | |
| 2. Fresh Fruit Salad | Utilizes familiar movements and functional activities that are universal. | Seasons; past. | Nutritious. | May have poor judgment in using a knife. | Use plastic knives. |
| | | Previous experiences at home in gardening, farming. | Promotes group task sharing, cooperation, parallel activity, socialization, trust. | | Have staff supervise unreliable clients. |
| | Stimulates visual | | | | Use soft fruits that |

| Activity | Sensory/Cognitive | Memories | Therapeutic Value | Precautions | Nursing Considerations |
|---|---|---|---|---|---|
| | input through bright natural colors. | Songs about fruit ("Yes, We Have No Bananas") and corresponding time periods and life events. | Provides natural roughage, especially for patients on medications. Often board-and-care settings order canned foods to cut costs; fresh fruits provide a delightful experience and increase hopeful feelings and motivation. | May cause digestive problems if eaten close to dinner, when vegetables and/or salads are served. May cause diarrhea. | require little cutting or fruits that can be peeled and separated. Know dinner schedule and menu. Have list of clients with bowel problems and supervise intake by giving same number of servings given to other clients but smaller portions and watch types of fruits. |
| 3. Giant Group Pizza | Familiar smells. Uses a variety of familiar, universal motions: chopping, stirring, kneading, patting, shredding, smearing, cutting. Simple cognitive functioning following simple directions. | Brings back childhood memories of baking activities, family gatherings, parties, holiday cultural experiences (every culture has foods similar to pizza). Memories of travel and foreign foods, places, events. | Fun. Requires communication; sharing of preparation; breaking bread together, which symbolizes friendship in many cultures. Instills feeling of accomplishment, especially when everyone applauds finished product. Various activities can be broken into small-group activities (e.g., grating–sauce group, dough group, vegetable-chopping group); then gather in large group and each small group contributes to shared task. | Special diets. Cigarette smoking – ashes can fall into the dough and be lost with the trimmings. | Know special diet restrictions, such as allergies to milk products (client will need pizza without cheese). Reinforce smoking at a break period only. |

APPENDIX: Food- and Holiday-Related Activities to Stimulate Senses and Reminiscing (Continued)

| Activity | Sensory stimulation | Memory facilitation | Positive aspects | Possible precautions | Preventive measures |
|---|---|---|---|---|---|
| **Food-Related Activities (Continued)** | | | | | |
| 4. Homemade Ice Cream | Gross motor movements. | Some remember a season, such as summer or making ice cream from snow in winter. | Gross motor movement—affects mood by decreasing depression. | Some clients may have diabetes. | Can make a sugar-free or sugar-substitute batch. |
| | Pleasurable taste (elderly lose some taste sensations but seem to retain taste for cold, sweet ice cream). | Financial memories—when ice cream cost 5¢ (and other related areas). | Shared experience—taking turns cranking. Simple directions. | Taste stimulated, and many overeat. | Allow fourths and fifths only after everyone has had thirds; use small dishes and serve small portions. |
| | | Remembering daily events like milk deliveries and licking the cream at the top of the bottle. | | | |
| 5. Ice Cream Sundaes and/or Banana Splits (preferable to use unusual flavors that stir up memories, like praline-and-creme or pistachio or rocky road [called heavenly hash in the Midwest]) | Variety of familiar tastes that are pleasurable. | Neighborhood ice cream parlors and experiences with friends. | Introduces pleasurable foods rarely served at board and care. | Diabetes. | Can use fresh fruit toppings; unsweetened whipped cream. |
| | Ice cream is extremely pleasing to the elderly. | Life-styles in different parts of the country (example: praline popular in the South; heavenly hash, in the Midwest). | Can be nutritious depending on toppings. | Choking on nuts. | Be aware of clients who should not have nuts due to chewing difficulties. |
| | Hot fudge has a distinctly pleasurable smell. | | Promotes independence and autonomy, which increase self-esteem (i.e., person creates his or her sundae). | Overeating. | Use small dishes and supply small spoons to serve foods. |
| | Easily conceptualized end result. | | Increases creativity. | Some people are compulsive about neatness and are reluctant to get messy. | Provide lots of napkins, aprons, and equipment with long handles. Persons with dentures may dislike eating nuts. |
| | Exploration of familiar objects. | | | | |
| | Utilizes familiar sequence of learning. | | | | |

| | | | | | |
|---|---|---|---|---|---|
| 6. Old-Fashioned Cookout | Crackling sound of fire and paper. Smell from charcoal and hickory. Taste for old foods like "some-mores" (graham crackers-chocolate bar-toasted marshmallow sandwich). Visual stimulation of barbecued hot dogs and changing colors. Cognition of end result. Familiar movements. | Family gatherings. Camping trips. Organizations such as the Girl Scouts or leading a Scout troop. Friendships. Games played. Funny experiences. | Fun. Inexpensive. Can plan ahead and be scheduled into budget for one evening or noon meal. Encourages independence. | Fire. Beer may be contraindicated with medication. Some clients may be alcoholics. | Pay close attention to who is cooking. *Never* use lighter fluid; use an electric charcoal starter. Keep flammable clothing and loose apparel away from fire. Know clients' medications and conditions. |
| 7. Popcorn | Familiar popping, crackling sounds. Familiar pleasing smell. Crunching taste, which clients may not get to experience on current diet. Fun to watch pop. Multitextured and prickly to touch. | Holidays past. Life review of shared family experiences. Time parity—old movies. | Easy to make. Can be made quickly. | Choking. Care in using salt: increase can cause high blood pressure. | Have fluids available. Know Heimlich maneuver. Use salt substitute. Serve popcorn plain. Use air popper. |
| 8. Simple Dips and Chips (examples: onion soup and sour cream; avocado and plain yogurt) | Taste—usually not offered as part of regular meals. Variety of textures to taste. Variety of textures to feel. Crunching sound. | Sports events. Historical sports events. Sports figures. Sports arenas and architecture. Historical events | Simple; quick to make. Parallel work. Small-group shared tasks. Independence in making one dip. | Salty chips or dip can endanger blood pressure. Can choke on chips. | Buy unsalted chips; use salt substitute in dips. Have fluids available. Know Heimlich maneuver. |

APPENDIX: Food- and Holiday-Related Activities to Stimulate Senses and Reminiscing (Continued)

| Activity | Sensory stimulation | Memory facilitation | Positive aspects | Possible precautions | Preventive measures |
|---|---|---|---|---|---|
| **Food-Related Activities (Continued)** | | | | | |
| | Gross motor activity. | concurrent with a sports event. | Can try a variety of flavors and types of chips. | | |
| | Shape discrimination of familiar objects. | Related food memories and smells – such as boiled hot dogs at the ball park with lots of mustard and relish. | | | |
| | | Parties. | | | |
| | | Family gatherings. | | | |
| 9. Stir-and-Frost Cakes | Uses gross motor activities. | Childhood experiences, such as licking dough from mother's spoon, and associated memories. | Higher functioning client can help others, therein instilling feeling of usefulness. | Diabetes. | Make some cakes with a sugar substitute or buy a few dietetic cake mixes. |
| | Stimulates pleasurable smells. | TV commercials and characters. | Few utensils necessary (spoon, measuring cup); baking tin provided in package. | Difficulty measuring water can lead to runny batter. | Use measuring cup that exactly measures one cup. |
| | Stimulates pleasurable taste and different textures (licking raw dough from a spoon is a different feeling than tasting a baked cake). | Birthdays past. | Allows for independence and autonomy, which increases self-esteem (each person can make his or her own small cake). | | |
| | | | Facilitates parallel work. | | |
| | | | Can buy squeeze frosting and write special notes on cakes. | | |
| | | | Can make variety of flavors and have a taste of each. | | |

| Activity | | | | | |
|---|---|---|---|---|---|
| 10. Yogurt Pie<br><br>(a) Pre-made pie shell<br><br>(b) Mix two 8-oz. fruit yogurts with one 8-oz. Cool Whip<br><br>(c) Chopped fresh fruit to match yogurt flavor (optional) | Uses gross motor activities, such as stirring.<br><br>Stimulates taste (similar to ice cream). | Childhood cooking experiences, like eating the crust or canning fruit for pies.<br><br>Movies, early life TV, and vaudeville (throwing pies at people). | Simple activity—requires no baking and few steps.<br><br>Nutritious.<br><br>Sense of accomplishment—immediate success.<br><br>Can use miniature pie shells and each person can make an individual pie; this increases autonomy and promotes self-esteem.<br><br>Increases control and mastery. | Clients with allergies to dairy products.<br><br>Overeating.<br><br>Some individuals will say they do not like yogurt. | Know clients' dietary restrictions and allergies.<br><br>Same as for ice cream (item 4).<br><br>Have nontraditional flavors, such as double fudge or pina colada. |

## Holiday-Related Activities

### 1. Valentine's Day

| Activity | | | | | |
|---|---|---|---|---|---|
| Make and send each other valentines.<br><br>In movement group each person gives an imaginary valentine to another and receives one.<br><br>Valentine hugs.<br><br>In movement group stand in a circle and give person in front a back rub: turn and give person in back a rub.<br><br>Decorate cookies for Valentine's Day (see Food-Related Activities, item 1).<br><br>Dance ballroom. | Encourages touch.<br><br>Increase input to pleasure centers. | Past romances.<br><br>Family experiences.<br><br>School experiences.<br><br>Lovable pets, such as the family dog.<br><br>Best friends.<br><br>Fantasies about past crushes.<br><br>Exchanging valentines.<br><br>Teachers one has loved and been influenced by.<br><br>Candy.<br><br>Sweetheart dances.<br><br>Sexual experiences. | Encourages warm exchanges, such as shaking, hugging, stroking.<br><br>Encourages group cohesiveness. | Some people have phobia or cultural taboos about touching. | Start by holding hands and observing tolerance to touch. |

APPENDIX: Food- and Holiday-Related Activities to Stimulate Senses and Reminiscing (Continued)

| Activity | Sensory stimulation | Memory facilitation | Positive aspects | Possible precautions | Preventive measures |
|---|---|---|---|---|---|
| **Holiday-Related Activities (Continued)** | | | | | |
| 2. St. Patrick's Day | | | | | |
| Green beer and dips and chips or pretzels (whole wheat—no salt). | Stimulates taste. | Ethnic related activities. | Cultural preservation. | Some clients are alcoholics. | Use near beer. |
| | Stimulates olfactory senses. | Special interests. | Promotes group spirit and cohesiveness. | Beer may be contraindicated with some medications. | Know clients' medications. |
| Shamrocks. | Stimulates pleasure center. | Historical events and experiences, such as being in a London pub during a WW II blitz. | | Some patients may be on a restricted caloric intake. | Use light beer. |
| Irish folk songs. | Fun to watch beer —especially green beer—being poured. | Vacations. | | | |
| Irish dances. | | Musical instruments. | | | |
| 3. Easter and Passover | | | | | |
| Egg dying. | Colors stimulate visualization. | Past Easter egg hunts. | Fills emptiness experienced at holiday time. | Dye can be messy and soak into skin. | Use food coloring and nontoxic paints. |
| Easter songs. | End results easily conceptualized. | Season: spring; April showers. | Decreases isolation. | Wine can cause dizziness and may be contraindicated with some medications. | Use grape juice. |
| Decorating Easter bonnets and showing them off (in movement each person makes a bonnet and models it). | Tactile stimulation increased by variety of textures in materials utilized. | Church stories; funny experiences in church. | Opportunity to express feelings. | | |
| | | Getting new hats. | Universality of experience. | Holidays can stir up sad memories. | Process and facilitate expression of feelings. |
| Traditional Seder table or, if not possible, use symbol tray and share a few foods like matzo, one glass of wine or chorosis (wine with chopped apple and almonds); read from the Haggadah. | Stimulates cognition of familiar passages and meaningful songs. | Easter parade. | Cultural exchange. | | |
| | | Making candy. | Life review. | | |
| | | Family gatherings. | | | |
| | | Past Seders. | | | |
| | | Historical events that occurred concurrently. | | | |
| Passover songs. | | Other countries where holidays were celebrated. | | | |

| Activity | Sensory stimulation | Ideas/Topics | Therapeutic benefits | Hazards | Precautions |
|---|---|---|---|---|---|
| **4. Independence Day (4th of July)** | | | | | |
| Old-fashioned cookout (see Food-Related Activities, item 6). | Stimulates smell. | Fireworks displays. | Life review. | Sparklers can lead to burns. | Staff should do the sparklers and/or supervise a high-functioning client one on one. |
| Sparkler show. | Stimulates taste. | State fairs and related activities and hobbies. | | Fire. | See precautions under Food-Related Activities, item 6. |
| Sing-along. | Visual stimulation watching sparklers and colors. | Town picnic and parades. | | | |
| | | Flags. | | | |
| | | Historical events such as the Bicentennial. | | | |
| | | Family get-togethers. | | | |
| | | Boating experiences. | | | |
| | | Leisure activities. | | | |
| | | Other related freedoms, like 19th of June—slaves freed. | | | |
| | | Liberation from prisoner-of-war camps or concentration camps. | | | |
| **5. Halloween** | | | | | |
| Make masks. | Variety of activities increases attention span and sitting tolerance. | Changing seasons, such as fall. | Stimulates group cohesiveness. | Tripping on costume. | Avoid long, dragging costumes that can catch easily. |
| Bring in costumes that stimulate memories (for example: train coachman). | Exploration of familiar objects. | Hobbies. | Stimulates socialization. | Inability to see entire scope through mask. | Make sure eye holes are large and nostrils and mouth large if using paper bags. |
| Old-fashioned party game like bobbing for apples. | | Favorite movies or stage plays. | Decreases depression. | | |
| Talent show (trick or treats). | | Interesting people one has met or famous people. | Increases self-actualization. | | |
| In movement group, | | Dressing up when a child and going out to trick or treat— | Encourage activities like musical instruments or comb and wax paper. | | |

APPENDIX: Food- and Holiday-Related Activities to Stimulate Senses and Reminiscing (Continued)

| Activity | Sensory stimulation | Memory facilitation | Positive aspects | Possible precautions | Preventive measures |
|---|---|---|---|---|---|
| **Holiday-Related Activities (Continued)** | | | | | |
| movement charades: do a familiar activity or something you like to do and everyone will guess what you're doing. | | | funny or scary experiences. | | |
| Orange-frosted chocolate Stir-and-Frost cakes. | | | Masks can be simple and made in a few steps. | | |
| Orange sherbet punch. | | | Allows identification. | | |
| Cookies decorated with orange and chocolate frosting and candles. | | | | | |
| 6. Veteran's Day | | | | | |
| Sing-along (for time periods such as WW II songs). | Auditory stimulation. | Historical periods and events. | Permits time pariety in closing generation gap. | May stimulate sad memories, such as death and disappointment. | Allow for expression of feelings. |
| Flag ceremony. | Visual stimulation (flags). | Personal issues related to major wars. | Facilities life review and continuity. | | Facilitate positive integration. |
| Picnic, dinner, or cookout (see Food-Related Activities). | Familiar tasks easily conceptualized. | Travel to foreign lands. | Increases communication by finding and sharing common experiences. | | Build on coping resources. |
| | | Personal triumphs and strength (coping resources). | Encourages role identity. | | |
| | | Organizations like American Legion and related activities. | Offers reassurance in the face of loss (depression). | | |
| | | Food in the service. | Opportunity to vent late anger about loss (e.g., one man who had been a ranked officer was now with | | |
| | | Funny stories that happened in the service. | | | |

7. Christmas and Chanukah

| Activity | | | men who were privates in service but he was now treated with no more or with less respect than they). | |
|---|---|---|---|---|
| Decorate cookies (see Food-Related Activities, item 1). | Familiar movements that are universal. | USO shows. | | Christmas and Chanukah can stir up depression in relation to separation from families. |
| String popcorn (can eat while stringing). | Familiar tasks that are easily conceptualized. | Family gatherings. | Communication with peers can fill emptiness experienced at holiday time. | Suicide prevention. |
| String cranberries. | Abstract sequencing of familiar activity can be performed. | Religious stories. | Increases social skills and opportunity to combat isolation. | Allow expression of feelings and integration. |
| Christmas carols and Chanukah songs. | Familiar objects can be explored. | House decorations and costumes. | | |
| Sherbet punch (lime and strawberry) or eggnog. | | Christmas gifts given and received, change in prices, styles. | Opportunity to ventilate anger about loss, therein increasing sense of perspective and continuity. | |
| Send Christmas cards to each other. | | Customs of various cultures. | Encourages group cohesiveness. | |
| Movement therapy: one experience wherein each client gives an imaginary present to another individual and accepts an imaginary present. | | | Preservation of heritage. | |
| Play dreidel game for popcorn or pennies. | | | | |
| Light a menorah. | | | | |

# MULTIDISCIPLINE PERSPECTIVES

KAREN R. PREUSS/BLACK STAR

Because group work with the elderly is now being conducted by people from many disciplines, it is important that the perspectives of these disciplines be explored. Part 6 is a section I am proud to introduce, for several reasons: the integrity of the group therapists who wrote the chapters, their humanistic approaches to the elders in their groups, and the fact that all of the writers are pioneers in their own disciplines. They, too, should be proud.

This section is not inclusive. For example, it does not contain a chapter by a member of the clergy, many of whom are leading such groups, nor is there material by a director or an employee of a senior center (or a day care center), some of whom are also involved in group work with the elderly. And no poet leader could be found to write a chapter. The use of groups is still the most efficient and cheapest way to involve a large number of people, pool resources, and mobilize the drives and interests of the elderly.

I lead off in Chapter 27 with perspectives on nurses doing group work.

Raymond Poggi, in Chapter 28, gives the sensitive viewpoint of a psychiatrist with considerable experience in group leading.

In Chapter 29 Mary Gwynne Schmidt explains the perspective of a social worker, and one who has spent a good many years supervising students in a variety of clinical agencies.

There is little written by psychologists about group therapy to be found in the literature, so Peter LeBray's Chapter 30 is a welcome addition to this section.

John Herr and John Weakland discuss counseling families with aged members in Chapter 31. The authors deal squarely with the problems a new counselor may experience. The chapter also has a case history exercise that should enhance the reader's understanding of family counseling.

I know of no other work with the elderly done by a bibliotherapist, so Lorraine O'Dell's work should be fresh and helpful to those interested in that particular modality. Chapter 32 adds another dimension, another discipline, to the book.

Ellen Moore, who has a background in gerontology as well as in music, describes music therapy from the perspective of the music therapist in Chapter 33.

This section ends with the perspective of a volunteer, Linda Byrne, who also writes about music and groups in Chapter 34.

# chapter 27

# A Nurse's Perspective

*Irene Burnside*

*I shall be telling this with a sigh*
*Somewhere ages and ages hence:*
*Two roads diverged in a wood, and I—*
*I took the one less traveled by,*
*And that has made all the difference.* *

ROBERT FROST (1942, 131)

JIM HARRISON/STOCK, BOSTON

**LEARNING OBJECTIVES**

- Describe the historical growth of group work by nurses with elderly clients.

- List seven group modalities for the aged in which nurses have excelled.

- List six other terms used for reminiscing.

- Describe four therapeutic values of reminiscing.

- Analyze specific adaptations made by nurses in group therapy with the aged.

- Synthesize nurses' unique contributions to group work with the elderly.

**KEY WORDS**

- Confabulation

- Conversation deprivation

- Reality orientation

- Reminiscing

- Remotivation

- Sensoristasis

- Sensory retraining

- Somatic preoccupation

- Verbosity

Nurses deal with individuals who are experiencing or anticipating transition or who may be completing the act of transition (Meleis 1975).

Nurses leading groups also deal with their own transitions. Nurses have begun groups in a practical way, often out of their own curiosity and desire for knowledge and expertise. Sometimes when they too are in transition—for example, in school—nurses also observe in the elderly needs that they feel could be met by a group experience. Still others are enrolled in master's programs and organize and study group process and modalities. There are now excellent master's theses by nurses that focus on group work with the elderly.

My own introduction to group work in the 1960s was a difficult beginning, and I still am surprised to see the results that ensued. The

experience reminds me of the poem "The Road Not Taken," from which I quote the lines that begin this chapter. The road I took led to a variety of group work experiences with older persons. I had been offered a chance to do group work with older, affluent residents in a retirement center called Leisure World. The staff physician needed someone to work with depressed elders. However, I decided not to work as a volunteer with elderly who could afford to pay. What helped me decide to do group work was a visit to an elderly neighbor who had been placed in a nursing home after his leg had been amputated (Burnside 1969a). But when I decided to do groups in a nursing home, I was not prepared for the road ahead.

When I made the decision to conduct group work with elderly nursing home residents, I found that I was not welcome there. I could not get an entrée. I was told that nurses did not do group work—that only social workers and psychologists did. A local physician, who was interested in my conducting groups, wrote

*"The Road Not Taken," from *The Poetry of Robert Frost* edited by Edward Connery Lathem. Copyright 1916, © 1969 by Holt, Rinehart and Winston. Copyright 1944 by Robert Frost. Reprinted by permission of Holt, Rinehart and Winston, Publishers.

orders for group work on the charts of his patients I had chosen as potentials for group work! Fortunately, as group leaders of the elderly, nurses have come a long way since my own entrée!

I felt a great need for supervision in that initial group experience because my group work had been with young adult schizophrenics. However, I faced problems in finding a preceptor knowledgeable about the elderly. I was advised to seek out a psychiatrist at a large urban medical center whom I knew had published about the aged and had given frequent speeches. I told him I had been referred to him by the director of the hospital. When I stated my request, he snorted, "You've got to be kidding." The learning process that I subsequently used is best known as "flying by the seat of one's pants." I do not highly recommend that process, hence this book.

The first group moved me so much that I tried to capture that two-year experience by writing descriptive articles (Burnside, 1969a, 1970a, 1970b, 1971). What I learned in that pragmatic experience has held me in good stead and aided me greatly in teaching students. However, it was not theoretical, I learned that later.

## OVERVIEW

The following information is presented chronologically, to show the growth of group work done by nurses with older clients.

See Chapter 5 for concepts from Yalom. The first indication that nurses were doing group work appeared in the 1950s, and the name of one of the first group-leader nurses remains unknown to us. Truly a pioneer and an effective leader, she is the nurse co-leader described in the classic work by M. Linden (1953). See Chapter 3 for an elaboration of the co-leadership they provided geriatric women in a state hospital.

The first article I wrote about groups appeared in 1969, but in 1968 F. Terrazas co-authored an article with I. D. Yalom on group therapy for psychotic elders in a state hospital in California.

The first nurse-authored book to contain substantive material on group work with elders by nurses appeared in 1973 (Burnside 1973). L. Gillin (1973) described factors that affected process and content in older adult groups. J. Morrison (1973) described her master's level work in group therapy for older women who were high utilizers of clinic facilities. D. Blake (1973) had led a group in a large public institution for the aged. She based her work with demented individuals on ego psychology. V. Holtzen (1973) also worked with a group in a similar setting and recorded themes of depersonalization, lack of trust, isolation, and hopelessness in her observations. A. Stange (1973) creatively explored use of props, sensory stimulation, and social graces with elderly women on the back ward of a state hospital. D. Holland (1973) co-led a group of stroke patients in a chronic disease rehabilitation hospital. Her co-leader was a social worker. Their styles of group leadership varied, and the author describes her approach as activity-centered in contrast to the verbal style used by the social worker.

S. J. Everson and A. R. Mealey (1978) have written perhaps the most complete and best article for nurse instructors who are teaching nursing students to be group leaders with the elderly. It is highly recommended for nurses supervising students doing group work.

M. E. Loomis (1979, 136) developed a paradigm for a model of small-group variables—objectives, structure, process, and outcomes (Figure 27–1). Some alteration in that paradigm would be necessary to make it more applicable to the aged. For example, for work with the elderly, "curative factors" would be better labeled "maintenance." Also, in the circle labeled "learning," "insight" might be deleted; it usually is not one of the objectives in group therapy with the elderly (Gøtestam 1980). "Maximizing sensory input" should be added under "role of leader" because this is a role unique to leading this age group.

L. L. Smith (1980) described her struggles in leadership with chronically ill, institutionalized psychiatric patients. Although this nurse-author did not focus specifically on aged persons, her points are applicable for other nurses planning to begin groups. Smith points out that "on first making a decision that a therapy group should

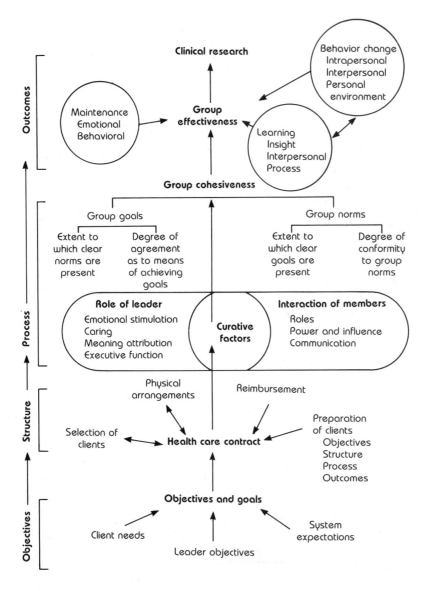

FIGURE 27-1. *Model of small-group variables—objectives, structure, process, and outcomes.*

SOURCE: From *Group Process for Nurses*, by M. E. Loomis. Copyright © 1979 by C. V. Mosby Company. Reprinted by permission. (Adapted from a model by M. Loomis & J. Dodenhoff, 1970.)

be established, one automatically sets up a chain reaction of decision making. Initial decision involves choosing group members" (p. 1301). These statements sound deceptively easy, but new nurse group leaders should be warned of difficulties; if cooperation from the agency personnel where the group is being held is not forthcoming, it can be a stormy start. Another important part of beginning group therapy, Smith points out, is that one needs the experts: the supervisors, instructors, and theorists on

group therapy. See Chapter 35 for an elaboration of the important role of the preceptor.

The other essential point for a nurse group leader is that she or he must strive to achieve balance because "a group leader must give the direction where necessary, but must remember that a certain freedom gives the group its potential to grow" (Smith 1980, 1303). I would add that the leader must give herself or himself freedom so that she or he, as well as the group members, may grow in the experience. I tell my students to allow themselves "floundering time" in the beginning. See Chapter 11, on leadership, for further discussion of Smith's initial experiences as a group leader.

The importance of literature reviews is often unappreciated. A fine review by S. Nickoley-Colquitt (1981) has examined the effectiveness of preventive group interventions for elderly clients. She notes that during the past decade group approaches emphasizing health promotion have emerged and points out that this is a shifting emphasis that parallels the preventive trend occurring in the health care system.

A review of 18 group interventions involving the family members of an elderly population was made by Nickoley-Colquitt. In spite of the great variety in the groups examined, all groups had one focus in common—that was, to provide group interventions for the elderly or their family members who were experiencing common developmental or situational changes or stresses.

Nurses, because of their orientation to wellness (rather than illness) and prevention (rather than disease processes and diagnosis), are well qualified to conduct group work with the frail or cognitively impaired elderly. Such groups often begin slowly, with exceedingly high anxiety in the members. Reducing anxiety, pain, and discomfort so that the members will remain in the group is the first task of the leader in the initial meetings. Prevention of "catastrophic reactions" is, of course, the hallmark of the leader of confused elderly. Catastrophic reactions are discussed in Chapter 13.

Nurse-authors E. Janosik and L. Phipps (1982, 252) point out that "there is an erroneous impression among some health workers that group work is inappropriate for the elderly because they have little capacity for change or because the quality of life cannot be sustained during the sunset years." The slow beginning of nurses in conducting group work with older clients is probably related to our professional and personal problems with ageism and/or the aging process, rather than with the recently acquired role as group leader. (See page 369 for Poggi's discussion of ageism). In the beginning psychiatric nurses also had to prove their ability to conduct therapy groups. So it has been with elders. At times I felt we were not taken very seriously, and this was probably because we've been locked into a traditional role for so long—that is carrier of bedpans, pills, and charts.

Janosik and Phipps (1982, 258) write about problematic behaviors to anticipate in group work in the elderly. The negative nature of the listed behaviors could discourage the neophyte leader, particularly since there is not a balancing list of behaviors that might enhance the group experience. The long list of problematic behaviors—callousness, compartmentalization, somatic preoccupation, verbosity, denial, confabulation, regression, selfishness, and repetitiousness—presents a negative view but should be a challenge to any leader! The leader needs to understand the behaviors of staff, leader, or members that may encourage or cause such problematic behaviors to continue. It is difficult to accept that the behaviors we see in elders may be influenced by our approaches and interactions.

It has been my experience that confabulation (making up answers) is related to the disease process; the leader must be very sensitive to that fact. In some groups regression and selfishness are the coping strategies for imposed institutionalization. Verbosity is often due to a lack of intervention skills on the part of the leader, and I believe it is related to "conversation deprivation." So many elderly have no one to listen to them; a group experience certainly provides multiple sounding boards. Somatic preoccupations, as pointed out so beautifully by B. Poston and M. Levine (1980), may well be attributable to the leader's neglecting to provide nurturance and care to the members. In my early work with groups, I found that somatic preoccupation was directly related to the initial anxiety of the group members. When the leader listened and empathized, the complaints decreased considerably during the life of the group. Also, because group leaders are nurses, elderly people feel that they should discuss physical complaints with them. It is difficult for some elderly to view nurses in the role of group leader and realize that we can listen to feelings and emotions as well as to physical complaints.

Nurses also are beginning to include chapters about group work with the elderly in their textbooks (Furukawa and Shomaker 1982; Janosik and Phipps 1982; Murray, Huelskoetter, and O'Driscoll 1980), which is a giant step forward.

## GROUP MODALITIES

This section of the chapter treats group modalities in which nurses have excelled: (1) reality orientation, (2) remotivation, (3) reminiscing, (4) health-related groups, (5) sensory retraining, (6) music groups, and (7) support groups.

### Reality Orientation

A nurse helped to pioneer reality orientation (RO) groups when they began in Tuscaloosa, Alabama, in the 1960s (Taulbee and Folsom 1966). See Chapters 13 and 14, both written by nurses, for in-depth discussions of reality orientation groups. D. R. Scarbrough, also a nurse, has continued to further and refine the area of reality orientation classes (Scarbrough 1974; Drummond, Kirkoff, and Scarbrough 1978, 1979).

I have been impressed as I observe nurses' work with very withdrawn patients in a group. Lois Acord once demonstrated to my class how gentle persistence and genuine expectation could produce results. Nursing home personnel had never known one withdrawn man in the demonstration group to speak. They were sure he would simply sit in the group and stare at the floor as he always did; yet he spoke for the nurse leader in that group, as she gently and tenaciously persisted, expecting a response.

M. Hogstel (1979) studied the use of reality orientation with aging confused patients. Pretests and posttesting showed no significant difference in degree of confusion in the control or the RO group. Hogstel's study is one of the few experimental studies about RO groups done by a nurse.

### Remotivation Groups

Remotivation articles date back to 1960 (Pullinger 1960). The remotivation technique manual that has consistently been used by group workers was written by a nurse-editor (Robinson 1976). J. Hahn (1973), M. Miller (1975), and G. Lyon (1971) have also described their work with remotivation groups. P. Gray and J. Stevenson (1980) designed a study to compare a remotivation and a resocialization

group in a research study. They noted that group therapy with confused aged nursing home residents resulted in positive behavioral changes. Interestingly, the staff of the facility was surprised at the ability of the subjects to socialize and enjoy one another. An orientation by the leaders helped facilitate *transition* of the groups to the routines of the ward.

Remotivation is a technique of simple group interaction that is very structured and follows five steps. See Chapter 16 by Dennis for an explanation of this group modality. L. Moody, V. Baron, and G. Monk (1970) conducted a study of remotivation therapy while in a master's program. They point out that it requires much planning to prepare the sessions and the refreshments. The most difficult task for these nurses was assembling the group quickly to reduce weariness. Nurses usually are quite sensitive to the energy levels, and the need for elders to conserve energy. The authors discuss "reactivating life-styles" which is an important and frequently overlooked aspect of group work with elders.

### Reminiscing Groups

The conceptual framework of reminiscing has been thoroughly discussed in previous chapters, so it will not be repeated here. But reminiscing may also be referred to by other terms; these include *oral history, life review, memories, life story, biography,* and *journals.* Or, as I once said when I was in a hurry and combined memories and reminiscing, "memoriscing."

Nurses have taken to this particular modality of group work with the elderly: Baker 1983; Blackman 1973; Ebersole 1976; Hala 1975; Hogan 1982; King 1982; Matteson 1978; Wichita 1974. K. King (1982), also writing in this text, presents an overview of reminiscing therapy and then describes her own group, held in an adult day care center. Because the group had a limited number of sessions, she designed the content to follow a sequence that took the members through the life cycle.

We need to consider the therapeutic value of reminiscing. It can

1. Increase body image and self-esteem.
2. Increase ability to communicate and express self.

3. Emphasize the individuality of each reminiscer.

4. Permit the aged to assume a teaching role.

5. Promote and retain cultural beliefs, pride, family tradition, and meaningful moments in life.

6. Be positive; it need not be negative.

7. Serve as a means to cope with failing memory.

8. Help adaptation to later years.

9. Be a developmental task.

10. Cause resurgence of dormant interests and/or hobbies.

11. Be an excellent learning experience about history for the leader.

Nickoley-Colquitt (1981, 82) says about reminiscing: "Reminiscing as a technique also fits into the element of helping to mobilize psychological resources and master emotional burdens. This may be helpful in meeting the need for a positive self-esteem and might be used in assisting indivduals to identify previously used coping skills."

Seven common modes of group work nurses often incorporate into a reminiscing group can be seen in Figure 27–2; they are reality orientation, remotivation, music, resocialization, sensory stimulation, art, and poetry. Figure 27–3 shows how a variety of modalities can be incorporated into a group.

### Health-Related Groups

Besides the above three categories of groups, nurses also pioneered health-related groups (Heller 1970; Holland 1973; Holtzen 1973; Murphy 1969). These groups are perhaps "a natural" for a nurse to lead because of the nurse's interest in holistic health, prevention and alleviation of distress and pain, and the transitions that fall within the domain of nursing.

Because nurses must work with the accoutrements for the visually impaired and hearing-impaired, they are sensitive to the assessment of sensory changes. Generally, nurses show exquisite sensitivity in handling sensory losses in the group setting. Nurses are accustomed to difficult patient situations, to complicated problems with a variety of people, and to juggling many variables simultaneously in a situation. H. Mummah* once said, "Group work at times can be like a birthday party for a three year old."

Besides sensory changes, the group leader must also assess sensory overload or deprivation in members. Such conditions may occur in meetings and are most obvious in nursing home residents. The field of sensory alterations and sensoristasis (sensory balance) has long been of interest to nurses.

Sexuality, nutrition, disease processes (for example, cancer, arthritis, Alzheimer's disease) losses, depressive states, stress reduction, relaxation are but a few of the topics of health to discuss. Much health teaching can be done within any of the modalities, however.

### Sensory Retraining Groups

D. Scott and J. Crowhurst (1975), two Canadian nurses, conducted sensory retraining programs to put patients in touch with one another. B. Heidell (1972) also wrote about this group modality. The program combines activities that are designed to reawaken or maintain all of the senses: sight, sound, taste, smell, and touch.

One of my early articles (Burnside 1969b) was about the use of sensory stimulation with elderly in a nursing home. That group experience taught me the value of props, the importance of food and beverages, and also the use of touch within a group.

### Music Therapy Groups

Music therapy groups have also been implemented and refined by a nurse, M. J. Hennessey (1976a, 1976b, 1978). See Chapter 17 for her contributions to this specialized group modality. Reminiscing therapy groups, as operationalized by nurses, often include the modalities seen in Figures 27–2 and 27–3, and one modality is music. K. King (1982, 24–25) writes, "Those with impaired hearing may be able to hear

---

*Personal communication 1975.

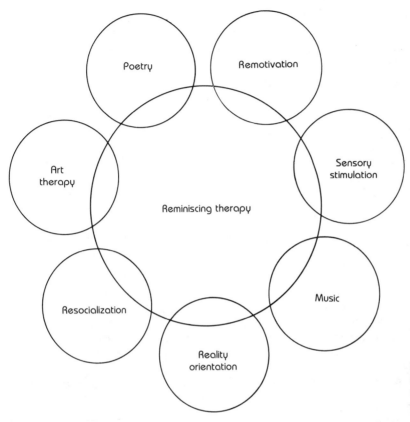

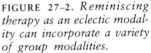

FIGURE 27–2. *Reminiscing therapy as an eclectic modality can incorporate a variety of group modalities.*

music better than speech, because music is rhythmically patterned and potentially familiar. Therefore, music offers the added benefit of sensory stimulation."

Nurses can and do combine their professional and personal talents and abilities in a unique fashion. M. J. Hennessey is one such role model; she is both a nurse group leader and a concert violinist. She describes the meld of her music and nursing beautifully.

In the past my life was split in two parts; I kept them carefully separated. I wore different clothes, worked with different people, and used different skills. Few of my musician friends were aware that I was a nurse, and my hospital associates did not know that my violin was a major part of my existence. When I discovered a way to combine work as a health professional and as a musician, it was as though I became a professionally whole person. The dichotomy that had been defined by the medical world began to disappear, and with the feelings of wholeness, the effectiveness of my work with groups increased.

This leads to the concept that many nurses could improve their skills if they were encouraged to be innovative and use all their talents. If love of music is one of these talents, a musician on the staff of nursing schools, whose work could be to introduce music into the healing environment, could be a help in further humanizing health care (Hennessey 1978, 37–38).

## Support Groups

S. Nickoley (1978) studied the effects of supportive group intervention on the functional level of health and perception of control in elderly women in the community. D. Leavitt (1978) studied the effects of a support group on adjustment to the changes of aging in elderly women living in the community. The support groups

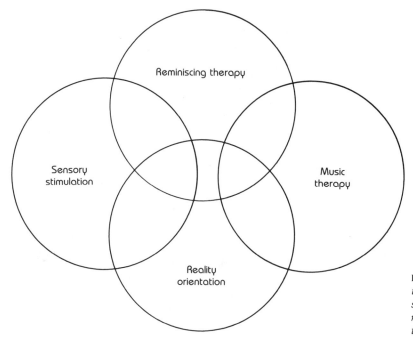

FIGURE 27–3. *A reminiscing therapy group might include several modalities in one meeting or during the life of the group.*

consisted of females, age range 65 to 83, whose mental functioning was intact but who were experiencing or had recently experienced some life change events. Support group members lived in a senior citizen high-rise apartment house. The members met for one hour twice a week, and each session was followed by a half-hour socialization and refreshment period. Goals were to provide information, assist each other in getting greater control over self and environment, strengthen problem-solving skills, and improve interpersonal skills. Evaluation was done by pretest and posttest measures. Reported outcomes were observed but were not measurable.

As the incidence of Alzheimer's disease increases, so does the need for support groups. Jean Baumler, Emily Polk, Marianne Bartol,

*Mary Jane Hennessey has said, "When I discovered a way to combine work as a health professional and as a musician, it was as though I became a professionally whole person."*

STEVE ROSEN

and other nurses have been involved in such groups both as the professional consultant and in health-teaching at the support group meetings.

## SPECIAL ASPECTS TO CONSIDER

### Group Modality Selection

The selection of the appropriate group modality is crucial. Adaptations will have to be made in any modality the leader chooses. Since nursing deals with persons in transition, it might be well to assess group members using that dimension.

The common adaptations needed in group work with the elderly should be based on the following:

1. Mutual determination of group goals and objectives by leader and members.
2. Assessment of and adaptation to losses, including:
   a. Physical (most especially hearing, vision, and mobility).
   b. Social (especially spouse and peers).
   c. Economic (home, income, personal belongings).
   d. Status (job, respect), which may result in lowered self-esteem.
3. Attention to nutritional needs and fluid intake.
4. Attention to sensoristasis.
5. Skill and expertise of the leader. See Chapter 35 on preceptorship and Chapter 36 for an elaboration of a teaching strategy.
6. Psychosocial needs of the elderly; including:
   a. Confusional states. See Chapter 13 by Burnside.
   b. Dying. See Chapter 23 by King.
   c. Depression. See Chapter 24 by Matteson.
7. Time and energy of the group leader.
8. Resources available:
   a. Financial.
   b. Support system.
   c. Locations/space for group meetings.

The nurse will need to be skilled in assessment to select the right combination of members. See Chapter 10 for an in-depth discussion.

### Refreshments

Poston and Levine (1980) have written a provocative article about their group therapy. The members came to a community-oriented psychiatric clinic for help with a depressive condition. The leader's first attempt at "a conventional group treatment with these patients was unsuccessful." That group never developed a sense of cohesion, splinter groups formed, and the patients said that they felt worse than before the group experience "because they got upset listening to other patients' problems" (p. 159).

Based on what they had learned from the failure of the first group, Post and Levine tried a second method of group treatment. A "coffee lounge" was prepared to "provide more direct gratification for these patients' needs" (p. 159), and refreshments were part of the group meeting. This is one of the rare instances in the literature in which leaders from a discipline other than nursing have approved of refreshments in group meetings. The willingness of nurses to be nurturing (even with nonnarcissistic patients) is one way that group work by nurses often differs from that of other disciplines.

Because most nurses are nurturing persons, they tend to use nurturing techniques in their group work with the elderly. Rarely does the literature note group leaders of other disciplines doing this. Poston and Levine (1980) are an exception, as are S. Friedlob and J. Kelly, who in Chapter 26 give an in-depth description of the use of fluids and food in groups. See also p. 376 for a psychiatrist's comments about serving refreshments.

The forms of refreshments served in groups vary from fluids to special types of snacks, pastries or cookies—and even popcorn! At first it might seem that these are "party-only" groups. Upon closer observation, a variety of rationale emerge why nurses can successfully incorporate refreshments into their group work:

1. Refreshments provide nurturing for those most in need—narcissistic patients, poorly nourished and/or dehydrated

individuals, lonely or alienated members, sensorily deprived individuals.

2. Food and drink also provide an easy method for improving social graces.

3. The nurturing role allows the leader to assess appetite, coordination during eating, likes and dislikes in food, former lifestyles, and eating and drinking habits.

4. The refreshments can create an element of surprise for those who complain of ennui.

5. The nourishment itself (for example, popcorn) can be the theme for reality orientation, remotivation, and reminiscing groups.

6. The nourishment can provide an educational theme for a meeting (for example, examining, discussing, and then eating papayas, mangos, or pineapples).

7. If the nourishment is prepared by the leader, it can provide a poignant moment (for example, a group member cried when I baked an angel food cake for her birthday and our meeting. "It's been eighteen years since I have tasted angel food cake. It was at my granddaughter's birthday party").

8. The nourishment can serve as an instructional aid to a student leader. Questions to be asked include:

   a. What do you serve diabetic members of the group?

   b. How full do you fill the cups/glasses?

   c. When and why do you use finger foods?

   d. How do you intervene when a member colors the peeled banana green with the felt-tipped pen used to write the name tags?

   e. Who will finance the cost of the nourishments?

   f. What is the best type of glass or cup to use for your group?

   g. Specifically how will you use the nourishment to improve activities-of-daily-living (ADL) skills or social graces?

   h. Will you serve the refreshments?

   i. Will you share the nourishment with the members?

   j. When in the meeting will you offer the nourishment—before, midway, or after?

   k. Who will clean up the mess that might occur?

One student in Lubbock, Texas, conducted a reminiscing group at a local nursing home and wrote, "To avoid the institutional look, I used table cloths, ceramic coffee mugs, brightly colored napkins, and patterned paper plates for all of our meetings. At each session at least one member of our group, man or woman, would comment on how attractive the table looked" (Slater 1982, 2).

### Transferences

A new nurse may be accustomed to group dynamic class experiential groups or confrontation groups; the average oldster will not have such group experiences. They will often reenact the family group in the group life; transference may occur—for example, one member to the other, "You sound just like my brother used to," or older member to young leader, "You remind me of my granddaughter; she talks like that." A nurse with psychiatric background will be quick to recognize transferences within the group. (See Chapter 28 by Poggi for an in-depth discussion of transference and countertransference). However, it always startled me when the transferences occurred in group; they tended to catch me off guard. One needs to be sensitive to the occurrence and also to analyze if we are treating group members like our grandparents or great-aunts and great-uncles.

Students should have an experiential group experience to learn the basics of group process. Reminiscing groups of students should be a requirement before they themselves lead a reminiscing group.

Beginning students should be familiar with the early accounts of group work written by nurses.

### EDUCATION

Everson and Mealey (1978) have written a fine article on baccalaureate student nurses as leaders of geriatric groups. That is one goal we need to work on in group work with the elderly. The benefits for all are many when baccalaureate nurses' programs introduce such practicums. See Chapter 36 for an elaboration of a successful method devised to teach baccalaureate nurses and Chapter 37 for curriculum strategies.

I believe that the current master's and doctoral students graduating from nursing programs will be important health personnel who will improve the group techniques and methods favored by nurses. Three chapters in this book (Chapters 23, 24, and 25) are based on research for master's theses by nurses: Hogan 1982, King 1982, and Matteson 1978. Nurses who conduct group work as the focus of their master's theses may be disappointed that their hypotheses do not reach significant levels, but the "Hawthorne effect" can be important in the real world. The Hawthorne effect takes the form of increased interest by the staff and sometimes relatives. It is a desired spin-off both for research and practicum.

Doctoral dissertations by nurses about group work with the elderly are needed. As stated above, the doctoral programs offer us another rich source of nurses who can improve and refine group research methods and increase our understanding of people in transition. As nurses conceptualize preventive health behavior, they will also realize that group experiences could be important health behaviors.

## SUMMARY

R. N. Butler (1979, 543) states that "nurses probably conduct more group work with older persons than do other professions." Still, it seems we do very little in that area of the curriculum; for example, how many student nurses ever receive a group experience with elders?

This chapter has delineated seven common nurse-led groups: reality orientation, remotivation, reminiscing, health-related, sensory retraining, music, and support groups. The increase in publications, theses, and chapters written by nurses in the past 10 years denotes the interest of nurses in group work with this specific age group. Evaluations of the group work are still highly subjective; nurses need to change that and move to a research posture. Evaluation of group work must be done by responsible clinicians who are able to judge the effectiveness of the group experience and the leaders objectively.

The overall goal for group work is to make the later years of life the very best that they can be instead of the very worst, as they now are for some elderly, especially the frail elderly.

King (1982, 25) reminds us that "no therapeutic modality can fulfill the wants, hopes and needs of all clients." Yet, there is no doubt that groups can change the quality of lives, including those of the leaders!

Regardless of what we write or expound, the true teachers are the aged group members. Sometimes I believe that they join our groups out of their great generosity and kindness, to please and help us nurses! I find that a humbling experience.

## EXERCISE 1

Read five nurse-written articles about group work with the elderly. Are there commonalities in the techniques described by each of the authors? List two commonalities and discuss each.

## EXERCISE 2

Choose one other chapter in Part 6. Compare and contrast the perspective of that writer with the nurse's perspective presented in this chapter.

## EXERCISE 3

Interview a nurse who has conducted group work with the elderly. What was her or his motivation to lead such a group? Then read Raymond Poggi's Chapter 28. Is there anything in the data from your interview similar to the stance presented by the geropsychiatrist? Explain.

## EXERCISE 4

Select from the reference list and/or bibliography of this chapter two nurse-written articles that discuss the theory and practice of group work.

1.  Critically read the selected articles.
2.  List three concepts regarding groups that appear in the articles.
3.  Write one intervention that a group leader might use for each of the three common concepts (problem areas) you identify. Defend your intervention.

## REFERENCES

Baker, J. 1983. Combining touch and reminiscing in institutionalized elderly. Unpublished master's thesis. San Jose State University, San Jose, Calif.

Blackman, J. 1973. Group work in the community: Experiences with reminiscence. In *Psychosocial nursing care of the aged.* 1st ed., ed. I. M. Burnside. New York: McGraw-Hill.

Blake, D. 1973. Group work with the institutionalized elderly. "In *Psychosocial nursing care of the aged.* 1st ed., ed. I. M. Burnside. New York: McGraw-Hill.

Burnside, I. M. 1969a. Group work among the aged. *Nursing Outlook* 17(6): 68–72 (June).

_____. 1969b. Sensory stimulation: An adjunct to group work with the disabled aged. *Mental Hygiene* 53(3): 381–88 (July).

_____. 1970a. Group work with the aged: Selected literature. *The Gerontologist* 10(3): 241–46 (Autumn).

_____. 1970b. Loss: A constant theme in group work with the aged. *Hospital and Community Psychiatry* 21(6): 173–77 (June).

_____. 1971. Long-term group work with hospitalized aged. *The Gerontologist* 2(3): 213–18 (Autumn).

_____. 1973. *Psychosocial nursing care of the aged.* New York: McGraw-Hill.

Butler, R. N. 1979. Psychiatry. In *Clinical geriatrics.* 2d ed., ed. I. Rossman. Philadelphia: Lippincott.

Drummond, L., L. Kirkoff, and P. Scarbrough. 1978. A practical guide to reality orientation: A treatment approach for confusion and disorientation. *The Gerontologist* 18(6): 568–73 (December).

_____. 1979. *Leading reality orientation classes: Basic and advanced.* Arlington Heights, Ill.: Intercraft Associates.

Ebersole, P. 1976. Reminiscing and group psychotherapy with the aged. In *Nursing and the aged.* 1st ed., ed. I. M. Burnside. New York: McGraw-Hill.

Everson, S. J., and A. R. Mealey. 1978. Baccalaureate nursing students as leaders in geriatric groups. *Journal of Nursing Education* 17(7): 17–26 (September).

Frost, R. 1942. The road not taken. In *The collected poems of Robert Frost.* Garden City, N.Y.: Halcyon House. Copyright 1942 by Henry Holt & Co. Inc.

Furukawa, C., and D. Shomaker. 1982. *Community health nursing and the aged.* Rockville, Md.: Aspens Systems.

Gillin, L. 1973. Factors affecting process and content in older adult groups. In *Psychosocial nursing care of the aged,* ed. I. Burnside. New York: McGraw-Hill.

Gøtestam, K. G. 1980. Behavioral and dynamic psychotherapy with the elderly. In *Handbook on mental health and aging,* ed. J. E. Birren and B. Sloan. Englewood Cliffs, N.J.: Prentice-Hall.

Gray, P., and J. Stevenson. 1980. Changes in verbal interaction among members of resocialization groups. *Journal of Gerontological Nursing* 6(2): 86–89 (February).

Hahn, J. 1973. Mrs. Richards, a rabbit, and remotivation. *American Journal of Nursing* 73(2): 302–5 (February).

Hala, M. 1975. Reminiscence group therapy project. *Journal of Gerontological Nursing* 1(3): 34–41 (July–August).

Heidell, B. 1972. Sensory training puts patients "in touch." *Modern Nursing Home* 28 (June): 40.

Heller, V. 1970. Handicapped patients talk together. *American Journal of Nursing* 70(2): 332–35 (February).

Hennessey, M. 1976a. Group work with economically independent aged. In *Nursing and the aged.* 1st ed., ed. I. M. Burnside. New York: McGraw-Hill.

———. 1976b. Music and group work with the aged. In *Nursing and the aged.* 1st ed., ed. I. M. Burnside. New York: McGraw-Hill.

———. 1978. In *Working with the elderly: Group process and techniques.* 1st ed., ed. I. M. Burnside. North Scituate, Mass.: Duxbury Press.

Hogan, J. 1982. The use of volunteers as reminiscing group leaders. Unpublished master's thesis, San Jose State University, San Jose, Calif.

Hogstel, M. 1979. Use of reality orientation with aging confused patients. *Nursing Research* 28 161–65: (May–June).

Holland, D. L. 1973. Co-leadership with a group of stroke patients. In *Psychosocial nursing care of the aged.* 1st ed., ed. I. M. Burnside. New York: McGraw-Hill.

Holtzen, V. 1973. Short-term group work in a rehabilitation hospital. In *Psychosocial nursing care of the aged.* 1st ed., ed. I. M. Burnside. New York: McGraw-Hill.

Janosik, E., and L. Phipps. 1982. *Life cycle group work in nursing.* Monterey, Calif.: Wadsworth.

King, K. 1982. Reminiscing psychotherapy with aging people. *Journal of Psychiatric Nursing and Mental Health Services* 20(2): 21–25 (February).

Leavitt, D. 1978. The effects of a support group on adjustment to the changes of aging in elderly women living in the community, Master's thesis, University of Rochester, Rochester, N.Y.

Linden, M. 1953. Group psychotherapy with institutionalized senile women: Study in gerontologic human relations. *International Journal of Group Psychotherapy* 3:150–70.

Loomis, M. E. 1979. *Group process for nurses.* St. Louis, Mo.: Mosby.

Lyon, G. 1971. Stimulation through remotivation. *American Journal of Nursing* 71(5): 982–86 (May).

Matteson, M. 1978. Group reminiscence: Treatment for the depressed institutionalized elderly client. Master's thesis, Duke University, Durham, N.C.

Meleis, A. 1975. Role insufficiency and role supplementation. *Nursing Research* 24: 264–71 (July/August).

Miller, M. 1975. Remotivation therapy: A way to reach the confused elderly patient. *Journal of Gerontological Nursing* 1(2): 28–31 (May–June).

Moody, L., V. Baron, and G. Monk. 1970. Moving the past into the present. American Journal of Nursing 70(11): 2353–56 (November).

Morrison, J. M. 1973. Group therapy for high utilizers of clinic facilities. In *Psychosocial nursing care of the aged,* ed. I. Burnside. New York: McGraw-Hill.

Murphy, L. N. 1969. A health discussion group for the elderly. In *ANA clinical conferences.* Atlanta, Ga.: Appleton-Century-Crofts.

Murray, M. R., M. Huelskoetter, and D. O'Driscoll. 1980. Group work with the person in later maturity. In *The nursing process in later maturity.* ed. M. R. Murray, M. Huelskoetter, and D. O'Driscoll. Englewood Cliffs, N.J.: Prentice-Hall.

Nickoley, S. 1978. Promoting functional level of health and perception of control in elderly women in the community through supportive group intervention. Master's thesis, University of Rochester, Rochester, N.Y.

Nickoley-Colquitt, S. 1981. Preventive group interventions for elderly clients: Are they effective? *Family and Community Health: The Journal of Health Promotion and Maintenance* 3(4): 66–85 (February).

Poston, B., and M. Levine. 1980. A modified group treatment for elderly narcissistic patients. *International Journal of Group Psychotherapy* 30(2): 153–67.

Pullinger, W. 1960. Remotivation. *American Journal of Nursing* 60(5): 682 ff (May).

Robinson, A. 1976. *Remotivation techniques: A manual for use in nursing homes.* Philadelphia: American Psychiatric Association and Smith, Kline Laboratories.

Scarbrough, D. 1974. Reality orientation: A new approach to an old problem. *Nursing* 74 11: 12–13 (November).

Scott, D., and J. Crowhurst. 1975. Reawakening senses in the elderly. *The Canadian Nurse* 71(10): 21–22 (October).

Slater, P. 1982. Group report. Unpublished paper, Texas Tech University, Lubbock, Tex.

Smith, L. L. 1980. Find your leadership style in groups. *American Journal of Nursing* 80(7): 1301–3 (July).

Stange, A. 1973. Around the kitchen table: Group work on a back ward. In *Psychosocial nursing care of the aged.* 1st ed., ed. I. M. Burnside. New York: McGraw-Hill.

Taulbee, L., and J. Folsom. 1966. Reality orientation for geriatric patients. *Hospital and Community Psychiatry* 17(5): 133–35 (May).

Wichita, C. 1974. Reminiscing as therapy for apathetic and confused residents of nursing homes. Unpublished master's thesis, University of Arizona, Tucson, Ariz.

Yalom, I. D., and F. Terrazas. 1968. Group therapy for psychotic elderly patients. *American Journal of Nursing* 68(8): 1691–94 (August).

## BIBLIOGRAPHY

Armstrong, S. W., and S. Rouslin. 1963. *Group psychotherapy in nursing practice.* New York: Macmillan.

Beck, C. 1979. Mental health and the aged: A values analysis. *Advances in Nursing Science* 1: 79–87 (April).

Donahue, E. M. 1982. Preserving history through oral history reflections. *Journal of Gerontological Nursing* 8(5): 272–78 (May).

Gillette, E. 1979. Apathy vs. reality orientation. *Journal of Nursing Care* 12: 24–25 (April).

Maney, J., and M. Edinberg. 1976. Social competency groups: A training modality for the gerontological nurse practitioner. *Journal of Gerontological Nursing* 2(6): 31–33 (November–December).

Mims, F. H. 1971. The need to evaluate group therapy. *Nursing Outlook* 19(12): 776–78 (December).

Sandel, S. L. 1978. Movement therapy with geriatric patients in a convalescent home. *Hospital and Community Psychiatry* 29: 738–41 (November).

Shaw, J. 1979. A literature review of treatment options for mentally disabled old people. *Journal of Gerontological Nursing* 5:36–42 (September-October).

Tappen, R., and T. Touhy. 1983. Group leader— Are you a controller? *Journal of Gerontological Nursing* 9(1): 34 (January).

## RESOURCES

### Films

*Interacting with older people* 56 min. black-and-white, 16 min. A two part training film primarily for nurses. Discusses psychosocial needs of the elderly and suggests techniques to use in interacting with elders. Wayne State University A-V Center, 680 Putnam, Detroit, Michigan 48202.

### Videotapes

*Gerontological Nursing Series* (eight 30-minute classes, black-and-white, 1970). The series is composed of:

*About the aged.* Defines aging; illustrated demographic statistics. Four elderly people discuss the changes that have occurred in their lifetimes.

*Health of the Aged.* Discusses normal health status of older people and how they cope with their health problems.

*Planning Care for the Aged.* Describes use of a nursing history in a nursing home.

*The Homebound Aged.* Discusses special problems of the old person who is homebound.

*The Institutionalized Aged.* Discusses the pathophysiological and psychosocial needs of the institutionalized aged and implications for nursing practice.

*Nursing Care of the Aged.* A nursing care conference; discusses information to be shared with all nursing staff members.

*Psychiatric Problems of the Aged.* Focuses on organic mental disorder, with emphasis on hypoxia and the impairment of utilization of oxygen in old age. Also, a follow-up illustration of nursing measures to cope with this type of disability.

*The Health Team and the Aged.* Explores the relationship between the nursing staff and other members of the health team.

Study guide available. Producer and distributor: American Journal of Nursing, 10 Columbus Circle, New York, NY 10020.

# chapter 28

# A Psychiatrist's Perspective

*Raymond G. Poggi*

*Soto! Explore Thyself!*
*Therein Thyself shalt find*
*The "Undiscovered Continent"—*
*No settler had the Mind.* *

EMILY DICKINSON (BIANCHI 1960)

As a psychiatrist I have concerned myself with the response of the elderly to life events. Generally this interest developed because I was ignorant about life as experienced by the elderly and because, at the time I began my work with older clients, very little literature existed that dealt in depth with the psychological experience of older citizens. A good deal had been written about the elderly in quite abstract terms—older Americans had been surveyed, grouped, and statistically measured—but it was the unusual article that aided the practitioner in applying this normative data to the hurt and ailing individual client who sought his or her help. My interest in the individual and his or her relationship to others starts with my client. Whether I see the client individually or in a group, my focus of attention is on the thoughts, feelings, fantasies, and dreams aroused by the events and people that my client encounters.

My background as a professional indicates my longstanding preference for this approach to psychiatry. I am a psychoanalyst as well as a psychiatrist. I do intensive (four or five times per week) therapy with individual clients. Together we explore the concerns of the client as revealed through dreams, fantasies, wishes, and feelings. As a psychoanalyst, I have a certain value system in addition to the preferred focus for my work that I have just mentioned. My professional values are many (an emphasis on the individual and unconscious mental life, for example), but the one I wish to single out for the purpose of this chapter is my valuing of healthy independence for my clients. In fact, a good deal of my effort as an analyst is in helping my clients to experience their feeling of dependence in order to help them examine such feelings with the goal in mind of diminishing the need for childlike dependence. My hope is that in this way my patients will discover the enjoyment of interdependence with other adults without suffering feelings of being controlled or exploited. My professional activities are primarily clinical. I provide direct services to patients. My approach is a useful adjunct to the statistical and theoretical approaches utilized by other mental health professionals. My interest in statistics and theory is pragmatic. How do the statistics about the elderly and the theories about them help me provide useful services to them?

## AVOIDING INTRUSION

Actually, the information that numbers and theories provide has not made it easier for me to help my clients. I have found it difficult at times to use that information because of my orientation to the individual and my valuing of independence. In particular, although I am trained in the use of psychopharmacologic agents, group therapy, family therapy, and agency consultation, I used to struggle to apply them to the treatment of my elderly clients. My wish was to avoid intruding in their lives as much as possible—a principle of treatment I still advocate. However, my wish sometimes led to counterproductive delays in responding to the needs of my clients. For example, at times I have felt forced to work with spouses, families, nursing staff, other physicians, and other agencies in order to treat my patient, and I consequently delayed contacting these other people. Feelings of being forced were not at all consistent with my knowledge that all these elements in the elderly patient's life need to be addressed if the best diagnostic evaluation and most helpful interventions are to be made. As my clinical experience increased and I successfully struggled to apply what I knew to the treatment of my clients, I developed an increasing respect for the role the practitioner's feelings play in the decision to work with older patients and in the quality of the work he or she does with them.

## AGEISM

Robert Butler (1975) has labeled the negative aspect of these feelings "ageism" and in so doing caused a good many Americans to question their attitudes toward the elderly. I don't think, how-

ever, that the practitioner can be content with knowing that he or she may have prejudiced attitudes toward the elderly—particularly when attempting to help these clients find solutions to difficult psychological problems. My experiences and the experiences of others indicate that our particular early experiences with the elderly not only may bias us against them but may also attract us to them (GAP 1971). Furthermore, our work with them will be subtly, but importantly, influenced by the fantasies and feelings developed from the role the elderly played in our lives during emotionally and developmentally important times (Butler 1960; Kastenbaum 1964). The problems and the benefits of countertransference (the whole of the analyst's attitudes—conscious and unconscious—and behaviors toward the client) have consumed a great deal of space in the psychotherapy and psychoanalytic literature over the years (Racker 1975). *I have noticed, however, a relative lack of interest in countertransference in the geriatric literature.* What has been said about countertransference has tended to be issue-oriented and theoretical, rather than phenomenological and practical. I think it would be most useful for more clinicians to discuss their actual response to the elderly client and describe how their response hindered or helped the work they were trying to do with them (Rubin 1977). The practitioner needs a much more detailed understanding of his or her own response biases than does the average person in order to avoid errors in treatment caused by the intensity of emotion aroused by the work (Rechtschaffen 1959). This is true for all types of clinical interventions. As a result of these aroused emotions and a lack of awareness about our own response biases, *treatment all too often becomes management of clients, with the unconscious purpose of lessening our discomfort rather than increasing the comfort or adaptability of the elderly patient.* Articles of the caliber I would like to see in print would help clinicians in all disciplines obtain that more detailed degree of personal awareness. Our reluctance to share these responses in print with our colleagues further handicaps us in developing techniques to prevent such errors (Calder 1980).

Eventually, the considerations I just raised made me examine my own motivation to work with this particular clientele. This is not a high-status area; and yet, my motivation to be a geropsychiatrist has kept me at it for more than eight years. Why do I find work with the elderly so interesting? What are the potentially helpful aspects of my desire to work with them? And, of course, what are the problems I might encounter if not alert to the reasons behind my interest? These are questions I will answer during the next part of this chapter. I think this will be a useful search not only for myself but for you, the reader, as well. By exploring with me my incentives to be a geropsychiatrist, I hope that you will gain insight into your own motives in choosing the field of aging and become aware of the power inherent in discovering the reason: power to be a far more effective helper.

Perhaps, too, the areas I explore and the way I explore them will alert you to a way of proceeding in your search for a personal answer to these quite personal questions.

## BACKGROUND

What at first seems coincidental often turns out on closer inspection to make good emotional sense. The beginning of my work with the elderly was one of these sensible coincidences.

In order to graduate from my psychiatric training program, I was required to write a graduation paper under the supervision of one of my teachers. The requirement had been tacked on the end of the three-year training program; there was no support provided in the program in the form of special training in research or writing, or time to do either. It was an afterthought that had been made a vital aspect of the last year of training: no paper, no graduation. My classmates and I were anxious and very angry about what we saw as the sense-lessness of trying to transform us into writers and researchers when all along we had been trained solely as clinicians. A colleague and friend, David Berland, and I approached the task with an ardor fueled by our unrelenting feelings of antiauthoritarian rage. We determined that this paper would be ours and not theirs. We would not submit our topic for approval (although expected to) nor work with

an advisor of the school's choosing. Instead, we would work alone, selecting help of our choosing when we thought we needed help. Our personal goal was for the paper to be published in a respectable journal. After publication of the paper, we would submit it to the school as our graduation paper.

We decided to combine our writing with our wish to do group psychotherapy. We selected a clinical supervisor, but we had no group. Our advisor knew of a social worker who was searching for psychiatrists to work in a local nursing home. Residents were having trouble adjusting to their new living arrangement. Other ideas for group therapy had been suggested, but they either hadn't appealed to us or had seemed too difficult to develop. This idea struck us as uniquely interesting and exciting. We developed a group in the nursing home and discovered a topic for our first paper: "Expressive Group Psychotherapy with the Elderly." The paper was published (Berland and Poggi 1979), and we both graduated.

Of all the possibilities available, what made work with the elderly seem so right and so possible a means of my achieving independence from what felt like an unfair imposition of authority? I was excited by the prospect of working with elderly clients and able to sustain that interest because of the association between independence and the older person imbedded in my psychological makeup. It is that association, inextricably bound to my relationship with my paternal grandmother (Nanna), that I want to explore next. First, some vignettes that will serve as the basis for my subsequent analysis and eventually as the basis for the answers to the questions I posed earlier.

## MEMORIES

My first extended trip away from home without my parents was at age 17, in the company of my grandmother. This short, stout lady in her seventies with iron-gray hair overcame my parents' initial anxiety and took me off to Europe to visit relatives. I was given a long leash and an opportunity to make my own way in the company of a variety of relatives and new acquaintances. I forgot all about home until reminded by an angry telegram to write or return immediately! With the freedom one has in a foreign land, I dated, overcame a great deal of discomfort with women, deepened my ability to be close to men, and got used to running my own life. This dramatic time during my adolescence was not the only help my grandmother gave me in my efforts to separate finally from my folks.

Throughout my life I had been regaled by stories about our relatives. Of all these stories, one has remained most vivid. As a child my father would often anger his mother (my grandmother). He was too fast for her to catch, and she was too busy to spend a lot of time in the effort; instead, she would promise him punishment. Inevitably, late at night, she would arouse him from a sound sleep and deliver her punishment accompanied by the words "I promised you your reward, and here it is!" This scene was played over and over again in my imagination as if it had happened every night of my father's young life. The vision of this little woman (smaller even than I) punishing my powerful father was called up to encourage me in my struggles with him as a means of doling out punishment for the injustices I felt were heaped on me by this big guy.

One other fact . . . I never in my life while Grandmother was alive thought a sexual thought about her. She was another kind of being separate from such influences and considerations . . . a strong and valued friend.

*Nanna.*

## ANALYSIS

What was the conflict that Nanna ("grandmother" in Italian) helped me resolve? Separation from my parents in the context of a struggle for independence from my father. In psychoanalytic terms, I was enthralled by the story of my grandmother punishing my father because as a child I was struggling intensely with the wish to defeat him and occupy a position of power in my family. However, I didn't want anyone to be hurt, especially my father and me. Quite important to the usefulness of this memory was the loving way in which it was recounted. For me, the story itself and the tone with which my father told it led me to realize that I could have power without losing the affectionate relationship I had with him. If Nanna could be angry with Dad and he could still love her, then perhaps I needn't be so afraid of my own rage. Equally important was that I imagined myself with my grandmother when she completed her promise to her son. His defeat did not leave me alone with my mother, an aspect of the Oedipal fantasy that invokes considerable guilt and often feelings of inadequacy. Instead, I was alone with a much older woman who resided outside the triangulated family relationships and who was untouched by my sexual fantasies. She was a companion who in fantasy led me to a safe and less troubling means of declaring my individuality and strength. The companionship was made wonderfully concrete by our trip together to Italy during my adolescence.

Peter Blos (1967) has referred to adolescence as the second phase of separation and individuation. All the struggles of past years are reawakened with the onset of puberty and the impending end of high school, and with it the diminishing of dependence on the family. In a few short years, all the anxieties about the opposite sex, identity, and competence must be resolved enough to enable the teenager to leave home and live his or her own life. One year before graduation from high school, my companion, Nanna, took me far from home. I was certainly safe. I was with people who could be trusted. Important, too, was that I was with people who had never known me as a child. The success of the trip for me depended on these facts. To my surprise, I had a personality that made a positive impression on these people. This success and others experienced during the trip were accomplished by me as I was. The fact that my new companions never referred to me as a child and accepted me as a man helped me to separate from the internal image of myself as a child and, in doing so, to begin to consolidate a firm impression of myself as an adult. Again, contrary to the heroic and violent fantasies that often accompany breaking

away from home, all this was accomplished in a setting of affection. My childhood could be put to rest without losing all past relationships.

## APPLICATION

In retrospect, the strong alliance I felt between my grandmother and me in a struggle for my independence made group work with the elderly the right choice of topic for my first paper and for further work. I think, too, that the contemporary prejudice toward the elderly so graphically summed up by the term *ageism* did violence to my image of Nanna and, thus, to my image of all old people. I was indignant that my "friends" could be so badly treated. I had a debt of gratitude that made me fighting mad and ready to do battle with their enemies. Perhaps, too, I was fighting to preserve Nanna's place in my personal heroic epic. More than I realized, the sense of security I felt about myself, especially at times when my wishes were severely challenged (as at the time of graduation), rested on the continued presence of my powerful companion. If she were threatened, as she was when old people in general were threatened by ageism, then I, too, felt a threat close to the source of my sense of power and well-being. These personal facts have helped me understand my initial attraction to geropsychiatry and helped me understand the source of the strong motivation that has maintained my attraction to the field for many years.

During my work, my personal need to have the elderly be a certain way has run up against reality. Bringing these two experiences, my fantasies and my perceptions, in line with one another or removing those fantasies that could not be supported by experience has been an ongoing struggle. For instance, originally I chose to work only with the physically well older person. I supported this work by concluding that most older people fall in this category but are largely neglected by mental health professionals. To a great extent this has been true. To the extent that it was true, my past experience with my grandmother helped me to do some work that aided in correcting a needlessly negativistic view of older Americans. However, I realized that my motivation for working with

RAYMOND POGGI

*Nanna and the author.*

this group of citizens was not just to correct these attitudes but to save a model necessary for the preservation of my own sense of well-being. Consequently, I tended to avoid dealing with physically ill older people, and in the groups I led I often felt pressure to get people well quickly or a temptation to eject those who were uncomfortably (for me) physically ill. I have been successful in modifying these biases by virtue, I think, of my tendency to engage in the kind of personal analysis briefly described in this chapter. As a result, I have become more able to help the frail elderly and to be more reasonable in my expectations with the strong elderly. The pressure to get them to conform to my needs has diminished. I am better now at helping them to discover their needs and ways of satisfying them.

## APPLICATION TO GROUP PSYCHOTHERAPY

I would like now to turn my attention to the effect of my reactions to the elderly on the group work I have done with them. First, I will talk briefly about the pressure placed on a therapist working in groups. Second, I will review some of the countertransference reactions described by other workers in the field. And, finally, I will describe some of the reactions I have had that are related to the experiences recounted earlier and illustrate those reactions with two clinical vignettes.

### Demands on Group Therapist

I have found group work to be especially interesting and exciting. I have also found it to be more tiring than individual psychotherapy or psychoanalysis. When I was less experienced than I am now, I was puzzled by my fatigue. According to the description of group work I received from books and classes on the subject, it should have been easier, not harder, to do. Most of these descriptions emphasized the dilution of the transference that occurs in groups and the decreased activity that occurs between therapist and patient in favor of increased activity between the clients in the group. Supposedly these differences between group therapy and individual therapy took

some pressure off the therapist. I do think that it is true that the transference (the tendency to feel and react toward contemporaries as if they were important people from your past, including the re-creation of unconscions conflicts) is different in groups. Transference takes place between the clients and not always between the client and therapist (the dilution I mentioned). When it does take place between client and therapist, other members of the group may spot it, which certainly makes life easier for the therapist. There also seems to be a tendency for those transference reactions that do occur to be less irrational—more mature, if you will. Being in front of other people tends to inhibit how far back in our lives we go in search of unfinished emotional business. Putting it somewhat differently, the presence of other adults makes us less willing to behave in more childlike ways. However, there are facets of group work that place greater demands on the therapist.

The simplest of these is the greater number of events that go on in groups compared with individual therapy. The number of people is increased, which automatically increases the number of problems the therapist is trying to understand. Then, too, these problems affect the ways in which each person in the group reacts to the others in the group. The number of interactions between people is, of course, dramatically increased. The therapist is faced with the task of understanding the individual as well as attending to the many ways in which the participants interact with one another. But that's not all. Each member of the group will have toward the leader a particular set of responses that is more or less distinctive of that person's relationship to people in authority. The therapist needs to be alert to the development of these interactions in this area of life. This is a particular facet of transference reactions in groups that is experienced quite intensely. These individual responses to the leader become organized at times into a group response to the leader. The term *group process* has been coined largely to identify this aspect of group life. The phenomenon of group process is another feature of group work that places great demands on the leader.

*To me, group process is an effort on the part of group members to work together to satisfy leadership needs common to all people.* The effort is not always a conscious one (one we are completely aware of attempting) and not always rational (sometimes we expect the impossible of leaders). Sometimes the wish is to be well cared for by the leader and, at other times, to be left alone to do our own thing. In effect, it represents a displacement to the group of desires left unfulfilled in the family.

The effort of coping with these problems led to the fatigue that I mentioned earlier following group sessions. The question occurring to the reader now may be, "Why would anyone want to do group work at all?" The very problems I have mentioned are what attract me over and over again to group work. There is no other forum that gives me the opportunity to see and feel the richness and complexity of people's interactions with one another. No other form of therapy, with the exception of family therapy, allows the client and therapist to understand the person's problems with other people, see those problems *immediately,* and, together, achieve a solution. The opportunity to interact with others with the purpose of understanding those interactions represents a chance for the client to go beyond the parent-child interaction to an interaction with fellow adults. The gain in camaraderie is, in my experience, one of the greatest therapies for loneliness and depression yet discovered. For this reason, I believe it to be an especially appropriate treatment intervention for problems confronting the elderly. And, although the stress on the therapist is great, there are certain steps the therapist contemplating doing group therapy can take to alleviate some of the potential problems I mentioned.

I am, of course, advocating one such step in this chapter; namely, understanding your own motives and biases well enough to prevent your countertransference responses from being a problem. At the end of this chapter there is an exercise designed to help you accomplish this task. However, there are other steps you can take. Education and supervised work are obviously important ways of gaining a sense of control as a group therapist. In addition, I strongly advocate being involved as a participant in a group process experience. Having once experienced the most irrational of group phenomena firsthand, you'll be less surprised and more pre-

pared for it when it occurs in one of your groups. Finally, perhaps the single most helpful step I have taken involves working with a co-therapist.

## Co-Therapy

Working with a co-therapist permits me to sit back and relax and turn things over when I'm puzzled about events in the group or about my feelings or when I'm just plain tired. I can rely upon my "friend" to spot my unusual behavior and, in so doing, to help me spot my countertransference responses sooner than I might do on my own. Together we can sort out particularly difficult situations and support one another's efforts. Practically speaking, the group continues to meet even if one or the other of us must be absent.

There are difficulties in co-therapy. In the previous paragraph, I used the word *friend* intentionally. A clinician must go into a co-therapy relationship with eyes wide open. You cannot have a superficial relationship with your partner. Each of you must invite uninhibited comments on the other's actions and words toward the clients and toward one another. As long as you embed these remarks to one another in the shared purpose of furthering your work in the group, the experience will be useful and intensely rewarding. If you forget that the demands of therapy require you to be open with one another, your lack of interaction will eventually limit the effectiveness of your work. I have always found it necessary to meet with my co-therapist at least once a week to discuss the group and the state of our working relationship. We do not discuss our relationship during the group sessions. We are in the group for another purpose—to discuss the concerns of our clients. However, our private discussions of our responses in the group provide invaluable information about the individual people and the group process that enables us to set priorities for our work in the group and to plan our interventions if a particular situation presents itself again during the next group session. Developing such a relationship with another person takes a long time and can't be rushed. In addition, both therapists need to be aware of the particular problems presented by the elderly for each of them. The countertransference reactions that the elderly inspire are unique to them and to our personal experiences with older people.

## Countertransference Reactions

Some of the possible countertransference reactions that may occur in work with the elderly are summarized in the Group for the Advancement of Psychiatry report on the elderly (GAP 1971). The report cites six attitudes in therapists elicited in work with the elderly:

1. The work stirs feelings in the therapist about his own age.

2. Working with elderly people may touch upon the therapist's conflicts about relations with parents and parental figures.

3. Some therapists may believe that treating the elderly is useless because they cannot change.

4. Other therapists may believe that their skills are wasted on the elderly because their clients are old and want to die anyway.

5. Elderly patients could die during treatment, which might be an extreme blow to the narcissism of some therapists.

6. The therapist's colleagues may not support his or her work with the elderly for any or all of the above reasons.

Many authors have elaborated on these themes. A. Rechtschaffen (1959), in his literature review of psychotherapy with geriatric patients, emphasizes Grotjahn's concept of the reversed Oedipal complex, in which the patient views the therapist as his or her child. G. Abraham, P. Cocher, and G. Goda (1980) note that the therapist may have fantasies that his words will destroy his frail, elderly patients. E. Sobel (1980) augments A. I. Goldfarb's work (Goldfarb 1955) by noting two major countertransference problems that can inhibit work with the elderly: (1) prejudice against the elderly (ageism) and (2) self-deprecating feelings that arise when the therapist indulges his clients' transference wishes (serving refreshments in a group, for example) rather than interprets

them, even though indulging the wishes may be indicated at times in work with the elderly.

S. H. Cath (1972) notes that the therapist may have an unconscious wish for devotion from parents. He or she may wish to obtain as an adult what was not available in childhood; or, the therapist may wish to establish a new symbiotic (extremely dependent) relationship with the parent and displace that wish onto the elderly client.

P. H. M. King (1974) describes a particularly important problem for those younger therapists who work with older patients. The therapist has to look into a personally unknown future. He or she cannot take comfort in having personally negotiated the developmental problem facing the patient. This lack of comfort may give rise to a host of countertransference responses that represent attempts of the therapist to minimize the anxiety that the unknown stirs up in him or her.

My particular countertransference reactions were discovered during the course of co-leading a newcomers' group (Poggi and Berland 1978) in a retirement home—some four to five years *after* my entry into the field and the incidences at the beginning of this chapter. Perhaps this will give you an idea of how long it can take to discover our own prejudicial attitudes. Dr. Berland and I are both male psychiatrists in our middle thirties. Our group focused on the move into the retirement home and the issues that develop as a result of the move. The new residents, whose average age is 84, join our ongoing group for 12 one-hour weekly sessions after they complete a two-week, staff-led orientation to the home. Members continue to live in the home after termination from the group. Residents, as they come in or go out of the newcomers' group, have an experience similar to that of moving into the home. In both experiences, the resident confronts a set of strangers, becomes acquainted with them, and then forms new friendships. I will refer to this group to illustrate some of the difficulties arising from countertransference reactions that I have encountered doing group work with older clients.

As you will recall, earlier I made a point of noting the absence of sexual feelings and fantasies toward my grandmother. At one time in my personal development, it was important that she occupy an erotically neutral place in my life. However, this personal need led to a static mental representation of all older people as sexually neutral. In the group, my co-therapist and I shared resistance to noticing the sexuality of our older clients.

*Vignette 1*

A woman in her mid-seventies was actively participating during a group session. Dr. Berland and I both quite suddenly noticed how attractive she was—a fact we shared with one another during our once-weekly rehash session. In the six years that we had been doing group work with the elderly, neither of us had had such a reaction. We realized that only a powerful resistance operating in us could have inhibited the conscious occurrence of sexual thoughts and feelings for such a long time.

There were many factors contributing to our reluctance to notice sexuality in our clients. Part of that resistance was no doubt culturally inculcated. The women in the group do not have what are thought to be the traditional attributes of sexual attractiveness. I became aware of the personal, but unconscious, motives for my naiveté as a result of this incident in the group and the subsequent discussion of it with my co-therapist. After reflecting on this experience, I began to notice as attractive some of the features involved in aging: the whiteness of a client's hair, lines and wrinkles revealing character and experience, and sparsity and economy of movement. In other words, the signs of age tended to take on an interesting quality that I had not fully recognized at a sensual level before this time. As a result of our work at overcoming this inhibition, we both found the subject of sexuality easier for our clients to discuss in the group. For the first time they talked about the lack of available men in the home. They had been alluding to it before, but because of our shared biases, we simply had not noticed their interest in the subject.

My tendency to be impatient with frailty in my elderly clients is another of my response biases. The corresponding wish is to make all my clients into strong, healthy, and independent people like Nanna. This countertransference tendency came up in another group session.

*Vignette 2*

One member of the group was suffering from chronic weakness in her upper extremities and was about to finish her participation in the group. I became concerned that she seek medical attention for her problem and began to interpret her passivity in the face of her condition, which made her feel guilty and inadequate. Soon all members of the group began to offer her advice for the problem. Finally, the other leader said, "Everybody would like to send her off . . . without any problems. We find it hard to accept the limitations she has." The fact was that she had received and was receiving competent medical help. As a result of this intervention, a more realistic discussion of her ongoing problems resulted. She was free to acknowledge the deep feelings she had about the group and about leaving it and the new friends she had made among its members. She was free to enjoy the new interdependent (mature) relationships she had formed with other, older adults.

In both of these examples, the limitations of the therapists are clearly related to limitations on what is permitted to be discussed in the group. Once these personal biases are removed, material of importance to individual members of the group can emerge. Also, the co-therapy relationship played an important part in facilitating the discovery of these limitations and, in the latter instance, facilitated a mid-course correction during the group session.

## SUMMARY

The importance of the therapist's response biases toward elderly clients are of critical importance in the decision to work with them and in deciding how to work with them. The potential for harmful reactions toward the elderly is greatly enhanced for the geroclinician by virtue of the powerful emotional situations confronting him or her in work with older people. An important tool for the clinician in enhancing the capacity to do good work is a method of self-analysis (Horney 1942) that addresses the following questions:

- Why am I interested (or not interested) in working with the elderly?

- With which of the elderly (active, frail, and so on) do I feel most comfortable?
- How do I work with them (drugs, individually, in groups, and so on)?

The answering of these questions has as its goal the discovery of our particular biases toward the elderly and of the way in which these biases influence our work. All too often, we do "to" others rather than do "with" them. As a consequence, they are manipulated rather than assisted. Our own response biases or countertransference reactions are usually at the bottom of these harmful interactions. Time spent in careful introspection can prevent us from inflicting our past growing pains on our present clients.

I hope I have convinced you that a little self-analysis is worth trying. In my self-analysis, I started with the most recent example of my involvement with the elderly and moved back in time guided by my spontaneous memories. This will not be an easy process, but it is one I believe to be vitally important for all those working with the elderly, no matter their preferred mode of therapeutic intervention. The particular results I achieved can be attained by applying the following exercises.

## EXERCISE 1

Recall your first professional involvement with the elderly.

1. Pay careful attention to the circumstances that led to it.
2. Recall other events that occurred at the same time.
3. What was the major concern in your life at that time?
4. How did you feel?

## EXERCISE 2

Who is the grandparent (or oldest person) to whom you have been closest or with whom you've had the strongest emotional attachment (loving or hostile)?

1. What is your first memory of that person?
2. Recall other events that occurred at that same time.
3. What were your major concerns in life at that time?
4. Who else plays a part in that spontaneous memory?
5. What are your feelings as you recall and elaborate on that memory?
6. What is everyone doing in the memory you have recalled?
7. Describe in detail the significant old person who is the basis of the memory.

## EXERCISE 3

Are there any similarities between the memory of your first involvement in the field of aging and your first memory of the significant old person? If so, what are they?

1. Are the feelings similar or opposite?
2. Do you think about old people then and now in much the same way?

## EXERCISE 4

Try to determine the answers to the questions I posed regarding your interest in doing group work with the elderly.

---

## REFERENCES

Abraham, G., P. Cocher, and G. Goda. 1980. Psychoanalysis and aging. *International Review of Psychoanalysis* 7:147–55.

Berland, D. I., and R. G. Poggi. 1979. Expressive group psychotherapy with the elderly. *International Journal of Group Psychotherapy* 29(1): 87–108.

Bianchi, M. D., ed. 1960. *Emily Dickinson face to face.* Boston: Houghton Mifflin.

Blos, P. 1967. The second individuation: Process of adolescence. *Psychoanalytic Study of the Child* 22:162–86.

Butler, R. N. 1960. Intensive psychotherapy for the hospitalized aged. *Geriatrics* 15(9): 644–53 (September).

———. 1975. *Why survive? Being old in America.* New York: Harper & Row.

Calder, K. P. 1980. An analyst's self-analysis. *Journal of the American Psychoanalytic Association* 28(1): 5–20.

Cath, S. H. 1972. The institutionalization of a parent —A nadir of life. *Journal of Geriatric Psychiatry* 5(1): 25–46.

Goldfarb, A. I. 1955. Psychotherapy of aged persons —IV. *Psychoanalytic Review* 43:180–87.

Group for the Advancement of Psychiatry (GAP). 1971. *Staff Attitudes and Education,* 35–38. November.

Horney, K. 1942. *Self-analysis.* New York: Norton.

Kastenbaum, R. 1964. Clinical explorations. In *New thoughts in old age,* ed. R. Kastenbaum, 139. New York: Springer.

King, P. H. M. 1974. Notes on the psychoanalysis of older patients. *Journal of Analytic Psychology* 19(1): 22–37.

Poggi, R. G., and D. I. Berland. 1978. Newcomers' group: A preliminary report. *Journal of the National Association of Private Psychiatric Hospitals* 10(1): 47–51.

Racker, H. 1975. The meanings and uses of countertransference. *Psychoanalytic Quarterly* 26(3): 303–57.

Rechtschaffen, A. 1959. Psychotherapy with geriatric patients: A review of the literature. *Journal of Gerontology* 14(1): 73–84 (January–February).

Rubin, R. 1977. Learning to overcome reluctance for psychotherapy with the elderly. *Journal of Geriatric Psychiatry* 10(2): 215–27.

Sobel, E. 1980. Countertransference issues with the later life patient. *Contemporary Psychoanalysis* 16(2): 211–22.

---

## BIBLIOGRAPHY

Aronson, J. J. 1968. Psychotherapy in a home for the aged. *Archives of Neurology and Psychiatry* 71(1): 671–74.

Bennett, A. E. 1973. The psychiatric management of geriatric depressive disorders. *Diseases of the Nervous System* 34:222–25.

Berger, L. F., and M. M. Berger. 1973. A holistic group approach to psychogeriatric outpatients. *International Journal of Group Psychotherapy* 23(4): 432–44.

Burnside, I. M. 1970. Group work with the aged: Selected literature. *The Gerontologist* 10(3): 241–46 (Autumn).

———. 1970. Loss: A constant theme in group work with the aged. *Hospital and Community Psychiatry* 21(6): 173–77 (June).

Butler, R. N. 1974. Successful aging and the role of the life review. *Journal of American Geriatrics Society* 22(12): 529–35 (December).

———. 1975. Psychiatry and the elderly: An overview. *American Journal of Psychiatry* 132(9): 893–900.

———. 1980. Research on aging: Its future in the United States. *American Journal of Psychoanalysis* 40(1): 3–11.

Cohler, B. J. 1977. The life cycle, aging and death: Dialectical perspectives. *Human Development,* vol. 20.

Erikson, E. H. 1963. *Childhood and Society.* 2d ed. New York: Norton.

Finker, S., and W. Fillmore. 1971. Experiences with an older adult group at a private psychiatric hospital. *Journal of Geriatric Psychiatry* 4(2): 188–99.

Ford, C. V., and R. J. Shordone. 1980. Attitudes of psychiatrics toward elderly patients. *American Journal of Psychiatry* 173(5): 571–77.

Gunn, J. C. 1968. An objective evaluation of geriatric ward meetings. *Journal of Neurology, Neurosurgery and Psychiatry* 31:403–7.

Heilfron, M. 1969. Co-therapy: The relationship between therapists. *International Journal of Group Psychotherapy* 19:366–81.

Klein, W. H., E. J. LeShan, and S. S. Furman. 1965. *Promoting mental health of older people through group methods: A practical guide.* New York: Mental Health Material Center.

Levin, S. 1977. Normal psychology of the aging process, revisited—II. *Journal of Geriatric Psychiatry* 10(1): 3–7.

Lonch, J. L., and J. S. Maizler. 1977. Individual psychotherapy with the institutionalized aged. *American Journal of Orthopsychiatry* 47(2): 275–83.

Mananaster, A. 1972. Therapy with the 'senile' geriatric patient. *International Journal of Group Psychotherapy* 22(2): 250–57.

Nevruz, N., and M. Hrushka. 1969. The influence of unstructured and structured group psychotherapy with geriatric patients on their decision to leave the hospital. *International Journal of Group Psychotherapy* 19(1): 72–78.

Oberleder, M. 1966. Psychotherapy with the aging: An art of the possible? *Psychotherapy: Theory, Research and Practice* 3:139–42.

Poggi, R. G., and D. I. Berland. 1981. Self-esteem and doubt in the very old. *Journal of Psychiatric Treatment and Evaluation* 3:39–43.

Portnoi, V. A. 1979. Sounding board: A health care system for the elderly. New England Journal of Medicine 300(24): 1387–90.

Pruyser, P. W. 1975. Aging: Downward, upward, or forward. *Pastoral Psychology* 24(299): 101–18 (Winter).

Rossman, I. 1976. Why we shy away from geriatrics. *Geriatrics* 31:26–27.

Saul, S. R., and S. Saul. 1974. Group psychotherapy in a proprietary nursing home. *The Gerontologist* 14(5): 446–50.

Shere, E. S. 1964. Group therapy with the very old. In *New thoughts on old age,* ed. R. Kastenbaum. New York: Springer.

Sparacino, J. 1978–79. Individual psychotherapy with the aged: A selective review. *International Journal of Aging and Human Development* 9(3): 197–220.

Wolff, K. 1963. *Geriatric psychiatry.* Springfield, Ill.: Thomas.

Zimberg, S. 1969. Outpatient geriatric psychiatry in an urban ghetto with non-professional workers. *American Journal of Psychiatry* 125(12): 1697–1702.

## RESOURCES

These specific resources are useful regarding countertransference:

Racker, H. 1953. A contribution to the problem of countertransference. *International Journal Psychoanalysis* 34(4): 313–24.

———. 1957. The meanings and uses of countertransference. *Psychoanalysis Quarterly* 26(3): 303–57.

Sandler, J. 1976. Countertransference and role-responsiveness. *International Review Psychoanalysis* 3(1): 33–37.

# chapter 29

# A Social Worker's Perspective

*Mary Gwynne Schmidt*

*Transactions between individuals and others in their environment should enhance the dignity, individuality, and self-determination of everyone.*

WORKING STATEMENT ON THE PURPOSE OF SOCIAL WORK (SGCF 1981)

## LEARNING OBJECTIVES

- Delineate the differences between social group work and related approaches.

- Describe how the history of social group work has led to differences in aim and values.

- Discuss how the values and purposes of social work have contributed to an approach especially suited for work with the aged and their families.

- Describe how the generalist practice in social work led to the demand that each graduate social worker be prepared to work with groups.

- Discuss the importance of collaboration with members of other professions also serving the elderly and appreciate the responsibilities and assumptions that influence their viewpoint.

- List beginning solutions to some of the issues raised by social work values and particular needs of the elderly client.

## KEY WORDS

- Advocacy

- Collaboration

- Confidentiality

- Dignity

- Host agency

- Self-determination

- Socialization

- Values and purpose

Social group work differs from other group work not in its knowledge base, which is shared, but in the values and purposes of social work that guide it. Sometimes these alienate social workers from their natural allies, and group services to the elderly suffer.

After reviewing the circumstances that have given social work its character, this chapter will discuss misunderstandings that sometimes occur between professionals in host agencies and steps the social worker can take to avoid them. The chapter will close with some of the practical concerns that arise from the juxtaposi-

tion of social work values and the functioning of the aged.

## THE SHAPING PAST

The social work approach to small groups acquired its character in three phases: first, as part of an undifferentiated group work movement; next, as a method within social work; and finally, as a cluster of skills and learnings disseminated throughout the profession. The range of persons it dealt with and the nature of its interventions broadened as it developed from a specialty in the second phase to part of the general repertoire in the third.

In the first phase, group work began as classes and clubs in the settlement houses and youth-serving organizations. This matrix led to optimism about man's press to health and the growth-generating power of the group. It also caused the group to be viewed as a medium for socialization.

Engaged in teaching new ways to new Americans, the settlement houses dealt with "normal" people and therefore looked to growth and learning rather than remediation. This created some reluctance later to move into group therapy, which was seen as undemocratic (Wilson 1976).

Many of the persons coming to the settlement houses worked in factories, lived in tenements, and were deprived of many of the protections and advantages automatically extended to the middle classes. Settlement-house workers advocated for the poor and encouraged them to campaign for themselves. This past is evident in social work's continuing strain of reformism. Social workers are taught the duty of advocacy and the strength of the group to help its members act on their own behalf.

The settlement house offered young people opportunities to make new friends, but beneath this was a more serious purpose—socialization. The intent was to teach these people how things were done in America so that they might succeed in their new land. The youth organizations and church groups also had an educative, character-building thrust.

In the second phase, social group work moved into the mainstream of social work proper and became one of its three major methods, along with casework and community organization.

The first phase took place in the last quarter of the nineteenth century and the early years of the twentieth. The second phase was officially complete when the American Association of Group Workers joined other social work organizations to form the National Association of Social Workers in 1955. Group work was professionalized and then moved into social work as a methodological specialization.

When Gertrude Wilson (1976, 31–32), one of the leaders of the second phase, looked back over half a century of social group work, she recalled that the leadership of the American Association of Group Workers had consisted chiefly of social workers, although only a few years earlier the group work section of the National Conference of Social Work had drawn members from adult education, physical education, the agricultural extension program, and the Children's Bureau as well. Thus a narrowing had occurred as social group work became not a profession in its own right but a method. Ten years after its introduction at Case Western Reserve in 1927, group work was being taught in ten schools of social work. Students had to choose between casework, group work, and community organization; specialization reigned.

In the meantime, two things had happened to group work. First, under the influence of persons like Fritz Redl, who worked with severely disturbed boys, it had moved beyond the original growth and task groups to include remediation (Douglas 1979). Second, social work purposes had come to determine its direction.

The third phase has seen the end of group work as a separate specialty and the merging of its skills and theory into generalist practice.

In 1961, four organizations concerned with the elderly convened a seminar on "Social Group Work with Older People." In the foreword to the proceedings, Ollie Randall states that it was appropriate that social casework comes first in the series of seminars but right also that group work should follow because group workers had been the first to make some of the adaptations in method required by older people (NASW 1980a, 3–4).

In the same year, William Schwartz (1961, 8), a group worker, had pointed out that social work's new roles in institutional and therapeutic settings indicated that the unit of service should be determined by client need, not by agency or practitioner specialization.

Today Schwartz's vision is largely realized. The generalist is taught to work with individuals, families, groups, or communities as the occasion demands. Group interventions have become part of the training of every social worker.

Social group work has emerged from its 100-year history with values like those of the other helping professions—essentially a belief in the uniqueness and worth of the individual and in each person's right to self-determination. In the case of social work, these values are undergirded by a set of assumptions growing out of the profession's past in the youth organization and settlement house, with its optimistic view of human nature and its commitment to fight injustice. These assumptions sometimes make the social worker a critical guest in host agencies.

## SOCIAL WORK VALUES AND THE ELDERLY

Social work's values and its range fit it for work with the elderly. The range is that of both clientele and intervention. Social workers' education equips them to serve this heterogeneous population: they can facilitate groups for the well elderly, provide support for organizations of older persons engaged on their own behalf, and lead patient and family groups for the institutionalized and those in day care.

Older persons experiencing losses tend to have multiple needs. The generalist is prepared to work with the individual, family, group, institution, or community and therefore can move—as the earlier group worker could not—from leading a relatives' group to following up the members' concerns about establishing eligibility or securing special resources. This capacity is useful when a nurse or physician wants to organize a group around an illness and needs a co-leader who will share responsibility for other kinds of follow-up.

Although members of all helping professions operate with an awareness of the client's social systems, it is safe to say that no other profession is so explicitly required by its mission to relate to them. This perspective is helpful when dealing with a population that includes persons who are disabled, dependent, or institutionalized.

Older persons often present with situational depressions or troubled role transitions. Emphasis on self-determination and client strengths combats learned helplessness—the apathetic, passive, depressed kinds of behavior that often ensue when aging persons discover that they have lost control over many aspects of their lives. Social workers are taught to engage

the health residue in the personalities of even the severely disabled. They emphasize coping.

This approach is illustrated in one of the early accounts of group work with the aged. In their book about the Hodson Center in New York during World War II, S. H. Kubie and G. Landau (1953) tell how the professional social worker arrived at this prototypical old people's center and quickly developed modes of leadership among these seemingly passive persons, who previously had been bossed by two or three aggressive members.

The focus on socialization is serviceable both for persons moving into a life stage for which there are few guidelines and also for individuals going into group living.

Irving Rosow (1974) has written movingly about the poor schooling society gives people for old age: The young are told clearly what is expected of them but the old are left to stumble into old-age roles, learning only through criticism and rejection.

Rosow points out that younger authority figures engender a sense of role reversal that stimulates geriatric "difficultness" as a "desperate rearguard action to retain vestiges of dignity, control, and independence that are steadily slipping away" (p. 140). Certainly this is true in long-term care settings, where administrators and nurses tend to be middle-aged or younger. Many institutions for the aged offer few inspiring role models from whom members might learn how to be self-respecting older persons.

Rosow says that the support of the peer group ordinarily maintains the morale of persons moving as cohorts into new situations, but it is hard for the elderly to identify with occupants of a devalued status (pp. 141–43). He proposes apartheid of the old—insulated enclaves of their own where they might make their own rules and find status and comfort (pp. 155–70).

What this formulation contributes to everyday life is an awareness of the strong need for older persons, especially those moving into sheltered care, to participate in small groups, particularly small groups that would provide induction into the system for newcomers and also opportunities for peer leadership. The social work group offers this kind of help because it fosters membership initiative and action.

## THE GUEST CONNECTION

If social work values and principles equip the practitioner for service to the aged, they contribute also to misunderstandings and conflict with the other professions. The more needful the client, the more likely the social worker is to be serving that person in a host agency—that is, in a hospital, a mental health facility, or a nursing home, settings where social work is not the dominant profession. The more vulnerable the client, the more likely he or she and his or her family are to be harmed if they sense disharmony among members of the treatment team.

Interprofessional collaboration is needed in the community also, but the prototypical situation, illustrating the full potential for value clash, is found in the nursing home. In all special settings for the aged, there are different degrees of disability and different responding levels of care and control. The higher these are, the more important it is to communicate.

The social worker may find that it is relatively simple to organize a poetry, music, or reminiscence group for the residents of a home for the aged. It may be necessary only to check the monthly schedule, get clearance from the administrator, and pay attention to member interests and competing events. In the same home's nursing unit, arrangements will be more complex.

The social worker who attempts to organize a patient group without consulting the director of nursing is likely to arrive to find that group members have been sent to the beauty parlor or packed off for naps. Equipment may have been tidied away, a troop of Brownie Scouts scheduled for a sing-along, and a competing activity slated for the meeting room.

Before viewing this as sabotage, the social worker would be well advised to look at the logistics of the setting and the condition of the patients. The work schedules of nursing personnel swing around a five-day week and there may be absences and substitutions: The charge nurse on duty when the group held its first meeting may not be there on the date of the second. Nurses' assistants may function on a tight schedule around a predictable patient routine. Other events are likely to be overlooked or forgotten, especially if they do not occur on a daily basis (see Chapter 11 by Burnside).

Patients tend to be very old, very frail, or both. Therefore, a group member may be in bed with the side rails up not because someone wanted to keep her out of the meeting but because she manifested mild confusion and seemed unwell.

Before beginning a group, have the fullest consultation with staff. Not only the director of nursing and the administrator but others, including the nurses' assistants, should have an opportunity to share views, suggest patients, and when feasible, participate in leadership itself. Some group members will go out with relatives just when your meeting is scheduled and others will remain in bed or be shunted off to the podiatrist, but these things will be less likely to happen if staff is included in group planning.

The moral is threefold: In these settings, every other activity is secondary to nursing care, the staff is often stretched thin, and nursing personnel must cope with accountabilities of their own. These factors lead to conflicts, even when the values held by the two professions are either the same or very similar.

## INTERACTION WITH OTHER DISCIPLINES

Other disciplines also believe in the uniqueness and inherent dignity of the individual and in client self-determination; others also respect confidentiality and view themselves as patient advocates. In addition, the physician thinks he or she could be sued for practically anything and the nurse has been taught that she or he is responsible for the physical safety of every patient. At the same time, they will sense the social worker's view that he or she is the only one in the setting who really cares. This sets the stage for some tense encounters. Unfortunately, each party assumes that the brash member of his or her own profession is deviant to its values but that the heedless member of another profession reflects its standards.

The Social Work Code of Ethics contains six sections with 16 items, but two underlying values are universally recognized; related to them are two duties that may be problematic for interprofessional collaboration (NASW 1980b). The two values are (1) respect for the inherent dignity and worth of the individual and (2) respect for client self-determination. Related duties are confidentiality and advocacy.

## Respect for Dignity and Worth of Individual

The need to respect individual dignity and worth is spelled out for nurses also (Ness 1980). Because they deal with persons in situations conducive to regression—around the provision of physical care, such as feeding, toileting, putting to bed—nurses are likely to respond to the patient's need for a comforting parental figure. The same patient may present a more coping self to the social worker because much of the business they do together involves decision making and negotiation by the patient and therefore elicits a more mature level of behavior. Nurse and social worker are reacting to different patient expectations arising out of the different circumstances of service. If nurses responded like social workers do, the patient might perceive their behavior as distancing and cold.

The social worker is likely to be jarred by the nurses' assistant who addresses an elderly patient as she might a small child ("Still dry, Rosie?"). Excellent nursing practice frowns on this, too.

## Respect for Client Self-Determination

The nurse is also aware of the patient's need for autonomy (Conti 1980), but the social worker is likely to view the nurse as needlessly restrictive and the nurse, to see the social worker as heedless of patient safety. The experienced social worker does not loosen soft ties, help a patient out of a wheelchair, or promise an outing without consulting a nurse. The patient who requests a cookie may be diabetic.

The nurse's education emphasizes responsibility for patient safety. This awareness rises whenever an insurance salesperson addresses the local nurses about malpractice—and not without cause. The very family that protests soft ties to restrain an unsteady patient may be the first to complain if that patient falls. Moreover, family members will address their complaints to the nurse even though it may have been the social worker who loosened the

ties when the patient in the group requested it. As long as the physician and laity are ready to blame the nurse, they must let the nurse set the limits.

The social worker can deal with some of these tensions by helping families to come to terms with their own feelings about placement so that they can act responsibly and determining how much risk-taking they are willing to support for their mentally frail patient. This is an appropriate issue for relatives' group.

## Confidentiality

Today's nurse is well aware of the right to privacy, both through professional education and through patients' bills of rights (Peitchinis 1976). Confidentiality falters when accountability comes in. The nurse is not supposed to withhold information from the physician, and in the case of the confused elderly patient, she or he may accept a paying relative's right to know. When the social worker has an obligation to report (as in court-related or guardianship cases), the worker usually deals with confidentiality by indicating its limits to the client, but there are persons who are unlikely to grasp such explanations.

Within the group, confidentiality is the rule and its violation checks another norm, openness. One advantage of co-leadership with a member of the nursing staff is that it makes visible the fact of sharing. In the same way, if a patient group wishes to discuss some aspect of service with administration, supporting them rather than taking over this task permits group members to decide for themselves how far they are willing to go.

## Advocacy

Social workers are taught that they have a duty to advocate for the helpless and oppressed. As born-again activists, they often campaign for patients' councils, less medication, and more freedom even when it entails an element of risk. This elicits some unpopularity, especially when the young reformer approaches the task with overtones of moral elitism. What needs to be remembered is that every person working with the aged has an obligation to prevent abuse. If the social worker is not bent on going it alone, this ethical obligation of the others will secure allies in the effort.

Three issues should be considered: the definitions of the protagonists, the principle of "least contest," and the interdependence of the individual and his social system.

First, definitions differ. For example, the social worker whose patients are dozing through group sessions may view medication as a chemical straitjacket employed by physicians for the convenience of nurses, especially if the worker was born too late to see the state of psychotic patients before psychotropic medications. The physician may counter the criticism by viewing the social worker as a trouble-making upstart. In addition, what the social worker defines as advocacy may be seen by the administrator as disloyalty to the home. Definitions influence interaction.

Second, the principle of "least contest" suggests beginning with inquiries and quiet negotiation before making negative assumptions about motivation. The physician may be unaware that he or she is medicating the patient into drowsiness and may be willing to reassess the medication in light of a changing situation. The principle of "least contest" is built on the premise that it is easier to escalate protest than to temper it after defensiveness has been aroused.

Finally, it is rarely in the client's interest to denigrate his or her social system. In attempting to make institutions and persons responsive to client needs, social workers must take care not to harm the client in the process of "rescue." Old persons cannot leave certain systems, such as the family, even if technically they are extruded by their placement and by the family's withdrawal. The individuals continue to see themselves in the context of the family and quite often are seen in that relationship by others. This is why most efforts to serve one at the cost of the other fail: The separation and alienation remain a running sore.

In the same way, the client and the long-term care setting need each other. Therefore, it is not an act of disloyalty to make a setting aware that it is failing its residents. Even the for-profit facility receives its legitimation because it delivers a service to the sick and the very old. If the setting provides good service to patients and

their families, it will fulfill its social mission and be confirmed in its profit-earning one. If it falls far below standards, it will jeopardize both. To attack the home without first attempting to change it through ordinary channels is to misserve the elderly clients: The oldest, frailest, and most vulnerable suffer transplantation with difficulty and generally are better served by improvement of conditions where they are.

This fulfills the purpose of social work, which is to "promote or restore a mutually beneficial interaction between individuals and society in order to improve the quality of life for everyone" (SGCF 1981).

## VALUES AND GROUP INTERVENTIONS WITH THE ELDERLY: PRAGMATIC ISSUES

The elderly include individuals as diverse as retired executives and working men, mental patients grown old, the organically impaired and the newly depressed, elderly priests and nuns, women and men, poor and middle-class Blacks, the rural elderly and downtown skid-row residents. Together they present age and cohort differences that test social work and invite thoughtful attention.

### Self-Determination and Reluctance to Participate

In the psychiatric facility and the rehabilitation hospital, the patient often has little choice about participating. Most persons would accept this as justified by the patient's condition, just as they would accept the necessity of liquid medication when the patient "cheeks" his pills. Social workers are likely to criticize these settings because of the therapeutic pessimism and ageism implicit in their failure to make a serious commitment to group and other talking therapies for older patients and their reliance on physical therapies instead. The community elderly cannot be compelled to take part in groups. Between the community and the rehabilitation setting there is the long-term care facility. Social workers' discomfort and uncertainty grows over how much they should press the resident to participate. There is a power differential that most would be reluctant to invoke.

The problem is that those perceived by the professional to be most in need of group services are often the least willing to try them. This dilemma is illustrated by Alice C.

Among the 25 patients in the nursing wing of the home for the aged, there were alert patients who had cocooned themselves away from the disoriented persons around them. Some had special friends who came from the boarding unit or sustaining contacts outside, but a few seemed both lonely and self-isolated and in need of something more. Miss C's transfer from the boarding unit to the nursing wing via the hospital brought this into focus.

When Miss C, 92, returned from the hospital with a broken hip, she was restless and unhappy, caught between a desire to go back to the independence of her room in the boarding home and the fears that made her reluctant to give up the safety of the nursing unit. She accused the nurses of wanting to keep her a patient and at the same time always found a reason for not walking when they came to help her. I could not deal with this in a casework relationship because she had displaced on me much of her anger at the administrator, a woman my own age, although ordinarily she got along well with both of us. I felt she might get support from her peers.

I approached Miss C and four other patients who had good minds and poor health. They agreed to try a meeting. One man had multiple sclerosis and another, Parkinson's disease. An 85-year-old woman who had adjusted well to transfer was added for balance. A fifth candidate agreed to join us and then "discovered" a plan to go off-grounds with a relative.

On the day of the meeting, the patient with Parkinson's disease "forgot" and was moving rapidly toward his room when I persuaded him to give it a try. The others gathered with less protest. I again repeated that the purpose of the meeting was to give them, as persons with keen intellects, an opportunity to lend one another some company and support. I repeated my hope that they would decide to meet on a weekly basis. They were polite but cautiously noncommittal, except for the gentle 85-year-old, the one least in need of the program. She remarked that this might be nice.

I waited, occasionally bowling in items to an essentially silent group. Finally I commented

that Dr. M, the patient with the multiple sclerosis, had recently tried acupuncture. The group's interest quickened. All eyes upon him, Dr. M smilingly described his experience while the others plied him with questions. For a little while they were truly a group, but they never agreed to meet again.

The following week, Dr. M was "too tired"; the patient with the Parkinson's disease stumped resolutely to his room with a "not today"; and Miss C was not speaking to me. Only the outgoing 85-year-old was willing—and she could hardly constitute a group by herself. Miss C could not tolerate any contact at all that might threaten her brittle defenses. Later, when she had resolved her ambivalence about staying, she readmitted me to her good graces, quite amazed that I could ever have imagined that she might have been angry. For the two men, isolation seemed a means of conserving their failing energies.

In this instance, I had had several indispensable ingredients: the separate goodwill of all the members except Miss C, who was temporarily at odds with me; the support of the administrator and the nursing staff, who shared my concern; and, as potential members, a small group of persons who had much in common. These persons had had little energy to invest in a relationship, and yet for a moment Dr. M had scintillated and his smiling peers had urged him on. The unanswered question was how much pressure to exert. During the remainder of my association with the home, I continued to look in vain for a group solution to this problem of the isolated alert patient.

In the same home, two other groups fared somewhat better. I continued an ongoing music group because it was an activity that the alert and less alert could enjoy together. After several years, it collapsed under my unwillingness to go on when the nurses' assistants plucked out the more passive, confused members and put them to bed. The earlier morning hour had had to be shifted, and the new time chosen by the nurses was unwelcome to their assistants because it interfered with their opportunity to "finish up."

A reality orientation group was designed to provide stimulation for the most disoriented members and education for a social work student. It ended with her field placement. Attendance at the music group had required only encouragement and a reminder. The reality orientation group had the support of the para-professional staff and the passive willingness of the participants. Rather than reviewing the days of the week, an early exercise for this group was teaching the members the names of the nurses' assistants, an activity both viewed as relevant.

Two factors are important in securing initial participation: a good relationship with the social worker and a low level of threat. Even when the social worker is brought in only to lead groups, he or she would be well advised to spend time first getting acquainted with the clients, the setting, and the staff.

At a downtown nutrition site, an extremely anomic group of seniors attended a current events group, a humanities group, and a men's group designed for heavy drinkers. In each instance, the group was led by students who were well known to the members and well liked by them. The humanities group provided stimulus for reminiscence of a very structured sort. The men's group was run by a male student who quickly saw that the Alcoholics Anonymous formula was not appropriate for these clients. He chose instead to support the flicker of companionship and limited here-and-now sharing. It is worth noting that attendees at these three groups represented a fraction of all the persons who used the center: It was a small pool fed by a big sea. At no time was the need for group activities, as it might be judged by the professional, a determinant of participation.

When attendance is compulsory, nonparticipation takes special forms. Lesser and his associates (1981) describe the restless, disjunctive behavior of elderly psychotics in traditional group therapy. Most members were silent; some displayed pseudoconfusion; others addressed irrelevant questions to the physician co-leader. *When reminiscence therapy was substituted, the same patients became alert and receptive, making it apparent that the disturbed behavior was a method of dealing with the threat.*

## Respect for the Individual and the Too-Bland Group

M. Forman (1967) has called attention to the rejection implicit in offering the elderly only recreational and leisure-time groups and in sup-porting the suppression of conflict. On the other hand, the elderly themselves tend to mute differences even when they are sorely tried (see Chapter 21 by Altholz). While supporting openness, one has to respect and accept this lower key. A student social worker attempted to support some expression of divergent viewpoints, especially as she became aware of the many undercurrents among the residents in the home for the aged. The 87-year-old peer leader took her aside finally and explained that they lived too close together to tolerate open conflict in the group.

While it is better for a group to police itself, the social worker may question whether extreme tolerance for the monopolist does not communicate the worker's low expectations and even a sort of disrespect for the group as a whole.

## Confidentiality and Responsible Others

Elderly participants are not likely to present material that they would be unwilling to share, and the limits of confidentiality can be discussed. When information must be passed on, it is helpful to discuss with the client how it should be presented. This solution has less meaning when the client is limited or forgetful.

In sharing with the confused person's adult children, the group worker may need to act as a surrogate ego, telling what the client would be willing to have told if he or she were aware of the circumstances. By not gossiping about the elderly individual, as adults sometimes do when discussing a small child, the social worker is modeling respect for the still-adult status of the failing parent, an important consideration when the adult children may be struggling with concerns about their own aging.

In long-term care settings, students are sometimes reluctant to include members of the patient care staff when they are leading a group. Their rationale is that the presence of these persons may be inhibiting for the patients; whereas, in fact, it may be inhibiting for the novice group leader. Exclusion seems to show a lack of trust, both of the staff members themselves and of the group members' ability to deal with them. If there is a troubled relationship, generally it is better to have it where you can observe it.

One reason for including other staff members

is to encourage their constructive interest in group activity. If time is taken to discuss the group with them before and after meetings, a major reason for their exclusion—the tendency of some to suppress the expression of negative feelings—can be checked.

The student's reorientation group described earlier had its ups and downs. One morning the student telephoned that she would be arriving too late to start the group and asked the field instructor to take over. When the student came, she found the members rehearsing the names of their favorite nurses' assistants and of the licensed vocational nurse (LVN) who was present. The student commented that the aides and the nurse had never come when she led the group. Further inquiry showed that she had never asked them. In this group, the traditional material of reorientation groups was abandoned in favor of information likely to secure the members better lives within the home. Learning the names of the nurses' assistants was a single example.

The reward came when the social worker arrived one afternoon and found the LVN, surrounded by a circle of the more regressed patients, talking with them and encouraging them to address one another.

### Advocacy and the Vulnerable Client

When dealing with dependent populations, there are three questions the practitioner must consider before embarking on advocacy.

First, will your intervention leave the client vulnerable to reprisals? This is no reason for not acting, but it does dictate a carefully thought-out strategy.

Second, what kind of changes does the client want? When I administered the Philadelphia Geriatric Morale Scale to residents in two settings, one woman with a very low morale score nevertheless replied to the item that asked, "Where would you live if you could live where you wanted?" "Right here!" (Schmidt, 1975). She saw the setting as the best arrangement available to her and would not have welcomed vigorous intervention. What she wanted was more respect from some of the nurses' assistants.

Third, what is the function of the complaint? Just as there are adult children who complain about the inconsiderate behavior of a parent but continue to reinforce it, there are elderly persons whose laments have a conversational quality. This does not mean that the complaints should not be taken seriously but only that they should be examined. Specificity is a clue, and so is willingness to act when fully supported. Either diffuseness or inaction indicates the need for deeper listening: you may not have heard what the client really said.

## SUMMARY

From its early development in settlement houses and youth organizations, social group work gained its optimistic view of human nature, its duty to fight injustice, and its use of the group to help people learn new ways. Social group work was once a separate method within the profession; but today most social workers are prepared to intervene as needed with individuals, families, groups, or communities, a flexibility that fits them well for work with the older client.

If they are to serve the most vulnerable elderly well, social workers leading groups in host settings must communicate with members of other professions and must be sensitive to the situational factors that lead them to translate similar values somewhat differently.

The social worker in the group must deal with issues raised by the interface of social work values and the special characteristics and needs of the very old: self-determination and the reluctant participant, confidentiality and the need of family and caregivers to know, advocacy without damage to a dependent client's supporting systems, and the rights of the individual and the group.

## EXERCISE 1

Interprofessional collaboration demands the ability to understand the feelings of the other. This exercise asks you to look at a situation in a nursing home from two points of view, that of the charge nurse and that of the social worker who comes once a week to lead a patient group.

1. You are the nurse. Other members of the class will read aloud:

   *Physician:* Nurse, I have to examine Mrs. Smith right now. I don't have all day. Please get her ready.

   *Administrator:* Nurse, don't let that group stay in the room too long. We have to get it ready for the board meeting tonight.

   *Patient:* Help me, help me, help me, help me . . . (continues monotonously)

   *Beautician:* Mrs. Brown's daughter wants her shampooed today so that she can take her out tomorrow. I can't do it unless you get her out of that group now.

   *Podiatrist:* Nurse, surely you don't expect me to wait until Mrs. Green gets out of that group. You should have her feet soaking now so that she'll be ready when I get to her.

   *Daugher:* After all, I drove down to see Mother. Surely she doesn't have to be in that group today.

   *Social worker:* Nurse, Mrs. Jones seems to have had an accident. Could you get the aide to do something about it?

   Explain to the group how the nurse feels.

2. You are the social worker. You have arrived to find that only two group members are ready. Mrs. Ellis has gone off with her daugher. Mrs. Green is soaking her feet, waiting for the podiatrist, who has several other patients lined up and won't get to her for another half hour. The nurse has asked you to cut your group short today because someone else wants to use the room. Mrs. Smith is with the doctor, who chose this hour for his monthly visit. One of the two group members who appeared to be ready just had an "accident." You don't know why the aides couldn't have taken her to the bathroom first.

   Explain to the group how the social worker feels.

## EXERCISE 2

After attending one session, Mrs. Black announces that she does not belong in the group: "Those people are crazy." Mr. Ellis says he is too tired today; he'll let you know next time. Mrs. Rogers, who is always an active participant when she comes but is forgetful, has already begun a nap. Miss Marion, whom you persuaded to "try it once," has—and says she doesn't want to come again.

You respect the client's right to self-determination, but you feel that each of these persons needs the group activity, especially Mr. Ellis, who seems to be depressed and withdrawing. How strongly would you act to persuade each of them to attend? What would be the determining factor in each case?

# REFERENCES

Conti, M. L. 1980. Continuity of care for elderly discharged patients. In *Psychosocial nursing care of the aged.* 2d ed. I. Burnside. New York: McGraw-Hill.

Douglas, T. 1979. *Group processes in social work.* New York: Wiley.

Forman, M. 1967. Conflict, controversy, and confrontation in group work with older adults. *Social Work* 12(1): 80–85 (January).

Kubie, S. H., and G. Landau. 1953. *Group work with the aged.* New York: International Universities Press.

Lesser, J., L. W. Lazarus, R. Frankel, and S. Havasy. 1981. Reminiscence group therapy with psychotic geriatric inpatients. *The Gerontologist* 21(3): 291–96 (June).

National Association of Social Workers (NASW). 1980a. *Social group work with older people.* Proceedings of seminar, Mohonk Lake, N.Y., 1961. New York: Arno Press.

_____. 1980b. The N.A.S.W. code of ethics. *Social Work* 25(3): 184–88 (May).

Ness, K. M. 1980. The sick roles of the elderly. In *Psychosocial nursing care of the aged.* 2d ed. I. Burnside. New York: McGraw-Hill.

Peitchinis, J. A. 1976. *Staff-patient communication in the health services.* New York: Springer.

Rosow, I. 1974. *Socialization to old age.* Berkeley, Calif.: University of California Press.

Schmidt, M. G. 1975. Patterns of norm conformity, social resources, and morale in residential settings for the aged. Unpublished doctoral dissertation, Rutgers University, New Brunswick, N.J.

Schwartz, W. 1961. The social worker in the group. In *Social welfare forum, 1961.* New York: Columbia University Press.

Special Group on Conceptual Frameworks (SGCF), Publications Committee, National Association of Social Workers. 1981. Working statement on the purpose of social work. *Social Work* 26(1): 6 (January).

Wilson, G. 1976. From practice to theory: A personalized history. In *Theories of social work with groups,* ed. R. W. Roberts and H. Northern. Columbia University Press.

# RESOURCES: AN ANNOTATED BIBLIOGRAPHY

## Group Services for the Elderly: General

Lowy, L. 1979. *Social work with the aging: The challenge and promise of the later years, 299–359.* New York: Harper & Row.
Comprehensive treatment.

Miller, I., and R. Solomon. 1980. The development of group services for the elderly. *Journal of Gerontological Social Work* 2(3): 241–57 (Spring).
If the student can read only one short chapter, this should be it.

## Group Services for the Community Elderly

Petty, B. J., T. P. Moeller, and R. Z. Campbell. 1979. Support groups for elderly persons in the community. In *Working with and for the aged,* ed. J. I. Kosberg. Washington, D.C.: National Association of Social Workers. Also in *The Gerontologist* 16(6): 522–28 (December 1976).

Waters, E., S. Fink, and B. White. 1974. Peer group counseling for older people. In *Human services for older adults: Concepts and skills,* ed. A. S. Harbert and L. H. Ginsberg, 140–48. Belmont, Calif.: Wadsworth.
Detailed account of training program. See other materials in chapter by Harbert and Ginsberg, "Serving Groups of Older Adults," pp. 120–39. This covers a great deal of material very succinctly.

## Special Approaches: Poetry and Reminiscence

Brandler, S. 1979. Poetry: Group work and the aged. *Journal of Geronotological Social Work* 1(4): 295–310 (Summer).
A poetry-reading group.

Getzel, G. S. 1980. Old people, poetry and groups. *Journal of Gerontological Social Work* 3(1): 77–85 (Fall).
A poetry-writing group.

Ingersoll, G. S., and L. Goodman. 1980. History comes alive: Facilitating reminiscence in a group of institutionalized elderly. *Journal of Gerontological Social Work* 2(4): 305–19 (Summer).
An affirming experience for elderly patients, with the development of a timeline. Acceptable to those who might have been threatened by the therapeutic model.

## Groups for Patients and Families

Allen, K. S. 1976. A group experience for elderly patients with organic brain syndrome. *Health and Social Work* 1(4): 61–69 (November).
A program of music, exercise, and psychodrama for outpatients and their relatives.

Fox, M., and M. Lithwick. 1978. Group work with adult children of confused institutionalized patients. *Long Term Care and Health Services Administration* 2(2): 121–31 (Summer).

Roozman-Weigensberg, C., and M. Fox. 1980. A group work approach with adult children of the institutionalized elderly: An investment in the future. *Journal of Gerontological Social Work* 2(4): 355–62 (Summer).
A mixed group of children of the newly admitted and those whose parents have been in care for some time.

Silverman, A. G., B. H. Kahn, and G. Anderson. 1977. A model for working with multigenerational families. *Social Casework* 58(3): 131–35 (March).
A structured educational-therapeutic approach in a community agency.

Silverman, A. G., and C. I. Brahce. 1979. As parents grow older: An intervention model. *Journal of Gerontological Social Work* 2(1): 77–85 (Fall).
This version spells out content and process for the six weekly sessions for a community-based relatives' support model.

## Groups in Long-Term Care

Cohen, S. Z., and J. Hammerman. 1975. Social work with groups. In *A social work guide for long-term care facilities,* ed. E. M. Brody. Washington, D.C.: National Institute of Mental Health.

Harris, P. B. 1979. Being old: A confrontation group with nursing home residents. *Health and Social Work* 4(1): 152–66 (February).
A group for higher functioning patients, dealing with their feelings about being old.

Kartman, L. L. 1979. Therapeutic group activities in nursing homes. *Health and Social Work* 4(2): 135–44 (May).

## Groups for Patients Receiving Electroconvulsive Therapy, Stroke Patients, High Utilizers of Clinic Facilities

Cohen, R. G., and G. E. Lipkin. 1979. *Therapeutic group work for health professionals,* 153–63. New York: Springer.
The older patient is more likely to receive electroconvulsive treatment, and patients getting electroconvulsive therapy are less likely to be involved in psychotherapy. This book deals with these vulnerable patients. The reader's attention is directed specifically to the pages cited, which appear to this writer to fill a gap in the literature.

McWhorter, J. M. 1980. 2d ed. Group therapy for high utilizers of clinic facilities. In *Psychosocial nursing care of the aged,* ed. I. Burnside, 114–25. New York: McGraw-Hill.

Singer, J. K. 1977. The use of groups with stroke patients. In *Group counseling and group psychotherapy,* ed. M. Seligman, 132–48. Springfield, Ill.: Thomas.
Detailed. Discusses implications of open-ended group versus closed group; stroke group versus postcoronary group.

# chapter 30

# A Psychologist's Perspective

*Peter R. LeBray*

> *No man is an island unto himself.*
>
> HENRY DAVID THOREAU, WALDEN

---

## LEARNING OBJECTIVES

- Define three **psychosocial theories** of later life.

- Discuss the psychological importance of elder groups.

- List four types of elder groups.

- Discuss the influence of attitude in elder group work.

- List six settings in which elder group work is useful.

- Define three elder **group process variables**.

- Describe important aspects of elder group psychotherapy.

## KEY WORDS

- Aging

- Elder

- Geriatric

- Gerontology

- Group

- Intervention

- Pre-group abilities

- Psychology

- Psychotherapy

---

## PSYCHOLOGICAL IMPORTANCE OF GROUPS

Psychologically, groups are significant in the lives of everyone. As infants and children, we are members of *primary* groups such as the family. Further, we live in an age-stratified society (Riley 1971; Decker 1980). Developmentally, we are toddlers, preschoolers, members of school classes, and members of *voluntary* organizations (for example, Boy Scouts, Y-Teens, Bluebirds) at relatively early ages.

Groups begin to define that aspect of ourselves referred to as *social self,* or self interacting with others. As we proceed toward adolescence and early adulthood, group membership becomes increasingly complex. Over the life course, we become more like ourselves, simultaneously different than everyone else (Birren 1968; Baltes and Schaie 1973). Individual differences increase over the life course and, with reference to chronological age, group variability increases (Baltes 1968). The implica-

tion is that there cannot be a *single* approach applicable to the aged.

Later life involves significant alterations in social roles, rules, and relationships (Bengston, Kasschaw, and Ragan 1977; Kalish 1975; Atchley 1980). B. L. Neugarten (1974) has categorized the period of later life as including the *young-old, middle-old,* and *old-old.* It is conceivable that important cohort differences obtain between these age groups. Psychologically, group membership and participation meet certain needs of older adults for identification, affiliation, and achievement, as well as other specific needs (such as leisure activity, socialization, or problem-solving).

## PSYCHOSOCIAL THEORIES INFLUENCING ELDER GROUPS

Society may be thought of as a series of interconnected or interrelated groups. Thus, major psychosocial theories are important in defining the policies and programs pertaining to elders in our society. Group membership forged in the "social forces" of later life (Atchley 1980) has resulted in the following major psychosocial theories of aging. (See Chapter 2 for more information on psychosocial theories).

**Disengagement Theory.** The disengagement theory postulates that in later life, it is inevitable, irrevocable, and mutually agreeable that we begin to have less interaction with others and engage less frequently in social roles. This is mutually agreeable to society and to the elderly and results in the eventual disengagement of the individuals and the social system (Cumming and Henry 1961; Atchley 1980).

**Activity Theory.** The activity theory postulates that it is important to continue the roles and activities of the middle years well into later life. Thus, opportunities for being active and engaging in leisure and other pursuits remain paramount, as exemplified in senior centers (Havighurst 1963).

**Pathology Theory.** The pathological viewpoint looks at social deviancy among elders and at departure from usual social norms and values. Behavior and social activities are considered on a normal-abnormal continuum. This theory is often applied in medical and health settings (Decker 1980; Posner 1974).

**Continuity Theory.** The continuity theory suggests that personality in earlier years has a strong influence on one's adjustment during later life. In fact, we become more like ourselves in later life (Atchley 1971; Neugarten 1968).

**Heterogeneity Theory.** The theory of heterogeneity results from recognition of individual differences and increased variability in the period of later life based on life-span developmental psychology (Goulet and Baltes 1970; Nesselroade and Reese 1973). This theory holds that there is increased variability during late life and increased *within-group* differences with respect to chronological age (Bengston, Kasschaw, and Ragan 1977).

In a sense, it is a sad commentary that in later life, older adults become bereft of group

opportunities and group membership. Reinstituting these opportunities has been deemed therapeutic. There appears to be an assumption that groups make good sense for older people, primarily since they address common problems of elders, such as isolation, loneliness, and diminished self-esteem (correlates of depression), and also because group work is both time and staff efficient (Brink 1979; Burnside 1976; Zarit 1980).

Groups may be defined as (1) task performance systems and (2) systems for structuring social interaction (McGrath and Kravitz 1982). Although difficult to define precisely, *group* can be identified when "two or more peoples be in dynamic interaction with one another. This implies that the persons are mutually aware of one another and take one another into account, and that the relationship has some temporal (past and/or anticipated future) continuity to it" (p. 199). Groups of interest to gerontologists include natural groups and therapeutic groups.

## PRINCIPLES OF ELDER GROUPS

Elementary journalism requires the reporter to define who, what, when, where, why, and how. These principles apply equally to group work with elders. The type of group will depend on: (1) defining types of elder groups, (2) identifying group attitudes, (3) recognizing aspects of process and purpose, and (4) being aware of member characteristics and needs. In addition, major dimensions for conceptualizing groups include content, process, membership, and leadership characteristics.

Vitually all elders *are* members of groups, and there are a wide variety, from adult education classes to groups for family members of the terminally ill. There are groups available for elders of all types, perhaps with the exception of those with behavioral or health problems (for example, delirium) that prohibit group participation. Attitudes such as nihilism (the belief that elders are untreatable) result in pessimistic views and seriously question and undermine the value of group work. Some of the groups that were important to older adults in early life can become the positive focus for membership in later life and can greatly influence one's personal adjustment in maturity—for example, continuing to be a student or involvement in business activities.

## Types of Groups

**Voluntary Groups.** Voluntary organizations include clubs, lodges, churches, or senior centers that provide opportunities for leisure and social participation, often essential to maintenance of social skills, positive mental health, and opportunities for activity (Cutler 1977; Ward 1979).

**Therapeutic Groups.** Groups of this sort include support and intervention along with the general goal of enhancing adjustment. Widowhood, disability, or transition groups related to institutional settings are examples of this type.

**Self-Help Groups.** Increasingly, self-help groups are being recognized as an important social fabric for elders in a variety of settings. Particularly in congregate living settings, resident groups or councils are important in giving elder residents a sense of power, importance, and access to policy and decision making. Peer counseling becomes very important as well, for the positive feelings assisting one's age peers provides. In additional, nationally organized groups and their local chapters (such as the Alzheimer's Foundation and Stroke Clubs) offer potential for positive social adjustment. See Chapter 20.

**Educational Groups.** Groups providing opportunities for continued education can serve many purposes. These groups are exemplified by lifetime learning opportunities and chapters of the American Association of Retired Persons (AARP) in many local communities. Senior emeritus colleges also offer access to educational resources that can be positive and preventive in mental health terms.

**Involuntary Groups.** Involuntary groups are essentially those in which membership may be unwanted, unplanned, and invoked. In a certain sense, being labeled "old" or a "senior citizen" in our society may be a form of involuntary grouping, verging on what R. Butler has termed *ageism* (Butler 1963; Butler and Lewis 1982). Other illustrations of involuntar[y] include mandatory retirement, patien[t] incarceration, legal guardianship, or [ ] clienthood in its various forms. Involunta[ry] grouping is often resisted and reacted to, largely through feelings of rejection. This may contribute to elders themselves forming groups (for example, the Gray Panthers) to counteract the involuntary groupings of society.

**Natural Groups.** Natural groups are identified through field studies focusing on interactions and interrelationships of elders with their families, kinship groups, the community, and congregate living settings. S. C. Howell (1980) describes the effects of environmental designs upon social interaction among elders, showing spatial determinants of social organization, roles, and relationships. Irving Rosow (1974) and Powell Lawton (1977), among others, have pioneered ecological studies of older adults. These studies examine the behaviors and activities of elders in a variety of natural group or congregate settings. They illustrate the importance of being a careful observer of the milieu and ecology of elders in considering types of groups, group activities, and goals. Caution is needed here, in that establishing or formalizing groups may disrupt natural groupings and the existing social ecology of elders.

There are a variety of natural groups—represented by AARP, the Gray Panthers, Aging Anonymous (Brink 1979), and emerging self-help groups. Groups appear to function best when they are elder-initiated and run, and they often add much to the physical health and well-being, empowerment, and mental health of their older participants. Groups can be established across a wide range of settings, including senior centers, medical centers, and long-term care settings. They are successful if careful attention is paid to establishing the groups, selecting membership, and allowing elders the opportunity to participate in definition of group goals.

## Attitudes

The underlying issue of attitude is very important with respect to group work with elders. Psychologists, mental health profes-

385

public officials, *as* have a major social and develop groups al participation for is prevalent "no toward elders, who used, abused, and ge in the transition ... many elders are prone to live out their proud lives in wretched poverty, isolation, or institutionalization (incarceration). Thus, there is a moral, an ethical, and—increasingly—a legal responsibility to provide opportunities for positive group membership and participation in community and institutional settings (Decker 1980).

It is very important that group leaders define their *own* attitudes with respect to aging and elders when embarking on group work. This is due to the fact that no one is immune to the various social and cultural biases about aging (McTavish 1971–72). S. H. Zarit (1980) notes that despite the presumed value of elder group work, few examples of outpatient groups (versus institutional) are reported. This, in part, may reflect therapist negativism in terms of group treatment and benefit.

Further, leaders' attitudes, shaped by the psychosocial theories noted earlier, may define elder groups. For example, activity theorists might emphasize activity programs, in which elders are kept busy with various projects, while disengagement theorists may focus on role losses and diminished resources in late life.

Successful elder groups may be those that are *member-directed*, where elders themselves define the focus and possibilities for meeting their needs through social interaction. Thus, the role of group leaders' attitudes as group determinants can be minimal, often resulting in leaders' surprise with group activity and outcome.

## Process Variables

There are differences between group work with elders and work with younger adults. For example, A. I. Goldfarb (1975, 124) noted that in working with elders the therapist must often assume a position of authority and responsibility, in effect, serving as a parental surrogate for

those feeling bereft of power and helpless. A. Manaster (1972) notes that elder groups optimally meet frequently and briefly, as opposed to the usual 90-minute sessions or marathons more common with younger adults. Additionally, it has been proposed that a focus on reality, or the here-and-now, is most beneficial to elders regardless of the specific type of group (Brink 1979).

In a variety of elder groups, the notion of the life review and reminiscing become important, since elders may tend to reflect on past experiences in an attempt to provide identity and meaning to themselves in the present and to integrate their lives as they have lived them with their current selves (Butler 1975; Burnside 1976). Group members are also helped with "props," trangible items that elders can see, hear, touch, or perhaps taste and smell (Robb, Boydand, and Pristash 1980). An additional goal for most elder groups is that of remotivation. In a sense, this involves reactivating interests and social responsivity in the presence of others (Brink 1979).

Groups can also provide significant alternatives to traditional mental health services (Glasscoate, Gudeman, and Miles 1977). Neighborhood organizations, informal drop-in settings and services, and a wide variety of day care and day treatment programs fall into this category.

## Membership Variables

**Whole-Person Model.** The whole-person model, as represented here, includes the physical, psychological, social, and philosophical (spiritual) aspects of the individual in the context of his or her environment. This model can be represented diagrammatically as a four-leaf clover (Figure 30–1). It is important to recognize that the multiple, complex, and interactive problems often presented by elders require multiple and often creative solutions. The group leader can be attentive to such physical aspects as ability for sustained attention, sitting, and mobility as well as sensory-perception modalities. Psychological aspects include the individual's ability to relate and communicate with others, appropriateness of behavior, and self-awareness. Social aspects include social

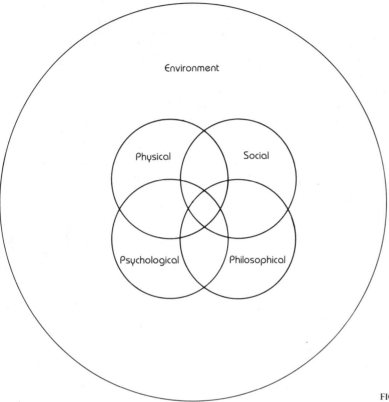

FIGURE 30-1. *Whole-person model.*

learning, history, and interpersonal relation-ships, while spiritual factors may include the more profound later life needs often expressed by elders. All of these aspects can be addressed in a supportive environment that provides opportunities for social interaction.

**Age.** Members of groups for the elderly are often older than the group leaders. There is some difference of opinion in the literature regarding homogeneous as opposed to hetero-geneous groupings of older adults (Rosow 1974). In meeting together, elders can share common backgrounds, historical referents, and cultural differences.

**Membership Selection.** It is important to consider elder group membership selection very carefully. Criteria for screening and assignment to groups have been identified elsewhere in this text. Such considerations include the degree of

impairment, responsivity, ability for both verbal and nonverbal communication, and so forth.

**Member-Directed Groups.** Memberdirected groups have been advocated in the literature. These member-led groups are often very useful and helpful for elders, as they foster in members investment in and responsibility for develop-ing their own sense of group awareness and involvement.

In brief, elder group work includes recogni-tion of various types of groups, sensitivity to attitudinal variables, awareness of differences in terms of process and content, and knowledge of issues affecting membership.

## ELDER GROUP PSYCHOTHERAPY

The following case studies illustrate the posi-tive use of group therapy with elders in several types of settings where it is possible to reengage the elder in meaningful roles through group work. Groups can be supportive of the elder's need, depending on their setting, their characteristics, and the expertise of the leader.

**Case Study 1.** Betty, age 74, is a very proud individual who has helped others virtually all of her life. She was recently confronted with the inability to continue living independently in her own apartment due to health problems. The transition into a retirement center was very traumatic for her, and she engaged in retreat, withdrawal, and avoidance of others. By allowing her time to establish her own personal life space, gradually introducing her to neighbors and staff, and through the use of an activity diary and daily schedule, she was eventually able to engage in the retirement resident's council and involve herself in a variety of leisure and discussion groups available to residents in this setting.

**Case Study 2.** John, age 76, is a perennial chairman of the board, having established and effectively managed his business for some 46 years. Following a stroke and related health problems, he was extremely resistant and reluctant to relinquish his lifelong position of power and influence. A conservatorship was established and a new management committee appointed to operate his business on his behalf; however, John became extremely despondent, feeling relegated to remaining at home and generally feeling useless. He was eventually referred to a local group of retired executives, who volunteer their time and business expertise, and was soon able to reestablish his usual level of activity and participation.

**Case Study 3.** Elsie, age 92, is a resident of a nursing home and she has the diagnosis of dementia. Her behavior is often characterized by meaningless verbalization, wandering, and occasional disruption of others. She was selected for membership in a therapeutic discussion group of five elders; through being directive, the staff was able to involve her in participation. This resulted in increased social awareness, increased concern with her appearance, and a documented decrease in disruptive behavior.

Psychotherapy groups for elders often have as a general objective enhancing adjustment or well-being where the elder's needs and goals are determined *by others*. Detailed aspects of group psychotherapy are reviewed elsewhere (Brink 1979; Brintnell and Mitchell 1981; Zarit 1980). Goals of group psychotherapy with elders include enhancing personal well-being, facilitating social awareness and interaction, and promoting positive adjustment and social behaviors. A review of the literature shows that these principles are applied largely to inpatients (versus community-residing elders) and often have as group themes and structure the following six areas: resocialization, remotivation, reality orientation, reminiscing, rehabilitation, and retraining (Barnes, Sack, and Shore 1973; Eisdorfer and Stotsky 1977; Dye and Erber 1981).

Group psychotherapy with elders can be very useful in structuring and influencing interaction, allowing opportunities for socialization, and preventing or diminishing disruptive behaviors (Hussian 1981). They are time and staff efficient in terms of available mental health personnel and allow group leaders the opportunity to select the group content and focus. Group therapy generally can include change groups or support groups; while education, maintenance, activity, or self-help groups may include some of these variables, they are not often thought of specifically as group psychotherapy and ethically should not be presented or conducted as such (Zarit 1980).

Small groups (three to eight members) can be effectively employed with elders exhibiting signs of disorientation, confusion, depression, isolation, inappropriate social behavior, the need for cognitive retraining, and family conflict. Elder group psychotherapy can be used positively with various transitions in later life, such as widowhood, retirement, marital changes (for example, sexuality, physical decline), disabilities, and institutionalization. In addition, preventive group work for well elders—such as exercise classes, stress and health management instruction, retirement planning, and adding quality to leisure—can be realized.

The assumption is that elders can and do positively change and improve through group psychotherapy (Blum and Tross 1980; Barnes, Sack, and Shore 1973; Brintnell and Mitchell

1981; Gray and Stephenson 1980; Cooper 1981; King 1982; Waters, Fink, and White 1980). It is this author's observation that in long-term care settings, elders are often excluded by staff or activity directors on the apparent basis that elders are unable to participate in groups. However, an argument can be made for attention to developing *pregroup abilities* with the older person, where the goal for the elder initially is simply that of responding to various stimuli and eventually interacting with the respondent and generalizing these behaviors to other residents. Such a process can be started at bedside.

The whole-person model (Figure 30–1) is helpful in considering group psychotherapy principles, and group leaders ideally are aware of the health status and functional limitations of elder participants. Through a survey of elders, observation of the setting, and discussion with staff, the need for and approach to group work can be determined. Attention is paid to the format of the group and to leadership aspects, including co-leadership to provide assistance and coverage if one leader is absent. Groups can be started simply by suggesting to the elder that an activity or opportunity exists to meet and talk with others. Refusal to join, death of a member, and other issues may require special attention as the group proceeds. It is important to acknowledge each member in the group, greeting each member and concluding with acknowledgement and praising participation.

The dynamics of kinship groups and families are discussed elsewhere (Herr and Weakland 1979) and in Chapter 31 of this text, and family involvement has been noted to be of great significance in working with elders (Blum and Tross 1980). By meeting with the family with the elder present or absent, depending on the format, conflicts and needs for information can be met in a preventive fashion (Colquitts 1981). In one interesting study, audiotaped voices of family members were provided to institutionalized elders with positive results (Alvermann 1979).

## ELDER GROUP RESEARCH

Empirical studies of groups are reviewed elsewhere (McGrath and Kravitz 1982). While most of the available literature is positive and supportive of elder groups, there are few actual studies of group process, change, and outcome. In fact, in a recent review of group therapy research, there were no *age* differences discussed where chronological age was a dependent variable (McGrath and Kravitz 1982).

It would seem that research methods (McGrath and Kravitz 1982), group dynamics or variables (Feldman and Wodarski 1975), and formats for evaluating group process (Bales and Cohen 1979) would be useful in studies of elder groups (Zarit 1980). P. Miller and D. A. Russell (1980) showed benefit using interview and life satisfaction forms with elders in nursing homes. Outcome studies of a few elder resident groups are noted in the literature (Gray and Stephenson 1980; Copstead 1980).

Numerous areas remain for empirical investigation—for example, elder group member selection and differences in participation (Trela 1976), such as homogeneous versus heterogeneous membership. Information obtained by direct comparison of group formats (reality orientation versus remotivation) would be useful clinically. Data regarding natural elder groups in the community and how these might be positively influenced would be helpful to mental health specialists, agencies, and program planners (Lawton 1977; Sandall, Hawley, and Gordon 1975). Careful definition of change measures and outcome criteria are needed to support the effectiveness of group work, and direct behavioral analysis may be a useful tool (Linsk, Howe, and Pinkston 1975; Hussian 1981).

In brief, an exciting opportunity exists for gathering more data to explain, analyze, and substantiate experiences in elder group work. Such research is needed in community, clinical, and institutional settings serving elders. Through empirical approaches it seems possible to discover not only differences with respect to elders but also new group therapies and strategies.

## SUMMARY

From the psychological standpoint, groups have a lifelong and lasting influence on all individuals in our society. Further, individual differences *increase* over the life course, resulting in many and varied patterns of social interaction in later life. Thus, as with individual psychotherapy with elders, it is conceivable that group work and group psychotherapy are more, not less, complex in old age. This requires utmost sensitivity and knowledge with respect to such important variables as attitude, types of groups, process variables, settings, ethical issues, purpose, and outcome.

Informed group leaders can facilitate the adjustment and well-being of elders in a wide variety of settings. Opportunities for social interaction and participation should be a basic right of all, while structured group therapies are specially designed and employed. Social policies and programs supportive of such efforts, based on research, are advocated toward establishing a *wellness* versus *illness-oriented* health system.

## EXERCISE 1

Design a format for elder group work that defines who, what, why, when, where, and how. Pay special attention to your own attitudes and needs in analyzing why you developed this format.

## EXERCISE 2

With appropriate permissions, observe social interaction at a senior center or elder facility for several hours. Record your observations of social groups and analyze for frequency and types of group interactions. What do these data mean? How might you influence group process in this setting?

## REFERENCES

Alvermann, M. M. 1979. Toward reducing stress in the institutionalized elderly—Therapeutic tape recordings. *Journal of Gerontological Nursing* 5(12): 21–26 (December).

Atchley, R. C. 1971. Retirement and leisure participation: Continuity or crisis? Part 1. *The Gerontologist* 11(1): 13–17 (Spring).

———. 1980. *The social forces in later life,* 219–26. Belmont, Calif.: Wadsworth.

Bales, R. R., and S. P. Cohen. 1979. *SYMLOG: A system for the multiple level observation of groups.* New York: Free Press.

Baltes, P. B. 1968. Longitudinal and cross-sectional sequences in the study of age and generation effects. *Human Development* 11:145–71.

Baltes, P. B., and K. W. Schaie. 1973. *Life-span development psychology: Personality and socialization.* New York: Academic Press.

Barnes, E. K., A. Sack, and H. Shore. 1973. Guidelines to treatment approaches. *The Gerontologist* 13(4): 513–27 (Winter).

Bengston, V. L., P. L. Kasschaw, and P. K. Ragan. 1977. The impact of social structure on aging individuals. In *The handbook of the psychology of aging,* ed. J. E. Birren and K. W. Schaie, 327–53. New York: Van Nostrand Reinhold.

Birren, J. E. 1968. *The psychology of aging.* Englewood Cliffs, N.J.: Prentice-Hall.

Blum, J. E., and S. Tross. 1980. Psychodynamic treatment of the elderly: A review of issues in theory and practice. In *Annual review of gerontology and geriatrics,* ed. C. Eisdorfer and B. Starr, 204–34. New York: Springer.

Brink, T. L. 1979. Group therapy. In *Geriatric psychotherapy,* 211–32. New York: Human Sciences Press.

Brintnell, J. C., and K. E. Mitchell. 1981. Inpatient group psychotherapy for the elderly. *Journal of*

*Psychosocial Nursing and Mental Health Services* 10 (May): 19–24.

Burnside, I. M. 1976. Overview of group work with the aged. *Journal of Gerontological Nursing* 2(6): 14–17 (November–December).

Butler, R. N. 1963. Ageism: Another form of bigotry. *The Gerontologist* 9(1): 243–46 (Spring).

———. 1975. *Why survive? Being old in America,* 409–22. New York: Harper & Row.

Butler, R. N., and M. I. Lewis. 1982. *Aging and mental health: Positive psychosocial approaches.* 2d ed. St. Louis, Mo.: Mosby.

Colquitts, N. 1981. Preventive group interventions for elderly clients. Are they effective? *Family Community Health* 3(2): 67–85 (February).

Cooper, J. 1981. Patient thinking. *Nursing Mirror,* July: 26–27.

Copstead, L. 1980. Effects of touch on self-appraisal and interaction appraisal for permanently institutionalized older adults. *Journal of Gerontological Nursing* 6(12): 747–51 (December).

Cumming, E., and W. E. Henry. 1961. *Growing old: The process of disengagement.* New York: Basic Books.

Cutler, S. J. 1977. Aging and voluntary association participation. *Journal of Gerontology* 32(4): 470–79 (July).

Decker, D. L. 1980. *Social gerontology: An introduction to the dynamics of aging.* Boston: Little, Brown.

Dye, C. J., and J. T. Erber. 1981. Two group procedures for the treatment of nursing home patients. *The Gerontologist* 21(5): 539–44 (October).

Eisdorfer, C., and B. A. Stotsky. 1977. Intervention, treatment and rehabilitation of psychiatric disorders. In *Handbook of the psychology of aging,* ed. J. E. Birren and K. W. Schaie. New York: Van Nostrand Reinhold.

Feldman, R. A., and J. S. Wodarski. 1975. *Contemporary approaches to group treatment.* San Francisco: Jossey-Bass.

Glasscoate, R., J. E. Gudeman, and D. Miles. 1977. *Creative mental health services for the elderly.* Washington, D.C.: American Psychiatric Association.

Goldfarb, A. I. 1975. Depression in the old and aged. In *The nature and treatment of depression,* ed. F. Flach and S. C. Draghi. New York: Wiley.

Goulet, L. R., and P. B. Baltes. 1970. *Life-span developmental psychology: Research and theory.* New York: Academic Press.

Gray, P., and J. S. Stephenson. 1980. Changes in verbal interaction among members of resocialization groups. *Journal of Gerontological Nursing* 6(3): 121–29 (March).

Havighurst, R. J. 1963. Successful aging. In *Processes of aging,* ed. R. H. Williams, C. Tibbitts, and W. Donahue, 299–320. New York: Atherton Press.

Herr, J. J., and J. H. Weakland. 1979. *Counseling elders and their families.* New York: Springer.

Howell, S. C. 1980. *Designing for aging: Patterns of use.* Cambridge, Mass.: MIT Press.

Hussian, R. A. 1981. Geriatric psychology: A behavioral perspective. New York: Van Nostrand Reinhold.

Kalish, R. A. 1975. Late adulthood: Perspectives on human development. Monterey, Calif.: Brooks/Cole.

King, K. S. 1982. Reminiscing psychotherapy with aging people. *Journal of Psychosocial Nursing and Mental Health Services* 20 (March): 21–25.

Lawton, M. P. 1977. The impact of the environment on aging and behavior. In *Handbook of psychology and aging,* ed. J. E. Birren and K. W. Schaie, 276–301. New York: Van Nostrand Reinhold.

Linsk, N., S. Howe, and E. Pinkston. 1975. Behavioral group work in a home for the aged. *Social Work* 20 (May): 454–63.

McGrath, J. E., and D. A. Kravitz. 1982. Group research. In *Annual review of psychology,* 195–230. New York: Annual Reviews.

McTavish, D. G. 1971–72. Perceptions of old people: A review of research methodologies and findings. *The Gerontologist Third Report,* pp. 90–101.

Manaster, A. 1972. Therapy with the senile geriatric patient. *International Journal of Group Psychotherapy,* 22 (Spring): 250–58.

Miller, P., and D. A. Russell. 1980. Elements promoting life satisfaction as identified by residents in the nursing home. *Journal of Gerontological Nursing* 6(3): 121–29 (March).

Nesselroade, J. R., and H. W. Reese. 1973. *Life-span developmental psychology: Methodological issues.* New York: Academic Press.

Neugarten, B. L. 1968. *Middle age and aging.* Chicago: University of Chicago Press.

———. 1974. Age groups in American society and the rise of the young-old. *Annals of the American Academy of Political and Social Sciences* 415 (Fall): 187–98.

Posner, J. 1974. Notes on the negative implications of being competent in a home for the aged. *Inter-*

national *Journal of Aging and Human Development* 5 (Fall): 357–64.

Riley, M. W. 1971. Social gerontology and the age stratification of society. *The Gerontologist* 11 (Winter): 79–87.

Robb, S., M. Boydand, and C. L. Pristash. 1980. A wine bottle, plant, and puppy: Catalysts for social behavior. *Journal of Gerontological Nursing* 6(12): 721–28 (December).

Rosow, I. 1974. *Socialization to old age.* Berkeley, Calif.: University of California Press.

Sandall, H., T. T. Hawley, and G. C. Gordon. 1975. The St. Louis community homes program: Graduated support for long-term care. *American Journal of Psychiatry* 132(6): 617–22 (June).

Trela, J. E. 1976. Social class and association membership: An analysis of age-graded and non-age-graded voluntary participation. *Journal of Gerontology* 31(2): 198–203 (March).

Ward, R. A. 1979. The meaning of voluntary association to older people. *Journal of Gerontology* 34(3): 438–45 (May).

Waters, E., S. Fink, and B. White. 1980. Peer group counseling for older people. In *Counseling the elderly,* ed. G. Landreth and R. C. Berg, 230–41. Springfield, Ill.: Thomas.

Zarit, S. H. 1980. *Aging and mental disorders.* 322–49. New York: Free Press.

## BIBLIOGRAPHY

Bennett, R. 1980. *Aging, isolation and re-socialization.* New York: Van Nostrand Reinhold.

Devitt, M., and B. Checkoway. 1982. Participation in nursing home resident councils: Promise and practice. *The Gerontologist* 22(1): 49–53 (January–February).

Harbart, A. S., and L. H. Ginsberg. 1979. *Human services for older adults: Concepts and skills.* Belmont, Calif.: Wadsworth.

Merrill, T. 1979. *Activities for the aged and infirm: A handbook for the untrained worker.* Springfield, Ill.: Thomas.

Shaw, M. W. 1981. *Group dynamics: The psychology of small group behavior.* 3d ed. New York: McGraw-Hill.

Sorensen, G. 1981. *Older persons and service providers: An instructor's training guide.* New York: Human Sciences Press.

Wheeler, E. G. 1980. Assertive training groups for the aging. In *Nontraditional therapy and counseling with the aging,* ed. S. S. Sargent, 15–29. New York: Springer.

## RESOURCES

### Videocassettes

*Interviewing the Older Adult Patient* (black-and-white, 30 minutes, 1980). Good Samaritan Hospital, Audio Visual Department, Portland, OR 97210.

# chapter 31

# A Counselor's Perspective

*John H. Herr and John H. Weakland*

*The diagnosis of much of geriatric psychiatric illness is open to question.*

C. EISDORFER AND B. A. STOTSKY
(1977, 725)

## LEARNING OBJECTIVES

- List the reasons why families are important to elders.
- Discuss how to overcome the "disadvantage" of being young or a student when working with elders.
- List the problems associated with arguing with a client in a family.
- Discuss why it is important to determine thoroughly all previous family solutions.
- Describe in detail how you would want your family to care for you should you become confused as an elder.

## KEY WORDS

- Communicating
- Counseling
- Family group
- Participating
- Realistic goals
- Solution
- Techniques
- Understanding

The purpose of this chapter is to sensitize the reader to the possibilities in counseling with the elderly and their families and to discuss the role of counselor with one family. Although relatives from several families could comprise a group, that is not the focus of this discussion.

In terms of service delivery, it is easy to state the importance of working with the family as a group. Practically speaking, the family as a group already exists in one form or another. The idea that most elders are abandoned by their families is a myth (Spark and Brody 1970). Most elders not only have families but they have interested (even if sometimes discouraged) families. Even those elders who do not have blood relatives should not be considered without "family." Some social gerontologists now speak of an extended kin network to describe longstanding social support systems that are

familial in nature (Sussman and Burchinal 1962). Who is more of a family member, a close neighbor known for 20 years or a first cousin whom no one has seen in 20 years? Obviously, in starting a family group, the task is easier and the relationships are more significant if the members are already bound together by some common ties. Counseling family groups is one opportunity to work with a "real" group.

From a practical standpoint, working with families is important because it generally makes the family make final decisions about the future of its elders (Cath 1972). Middle-aged children find their own economic and physical power on the wane as their elder parents experience economic and physical power on the wane. A unified group of such siblings is difficult for a parent to withstand, especially if the children have become convinced that "something has to be done."

It is generally not very useful for a nonfamily member, such as a social worker or a nurse, to engage in a power struggle with the family by unconditionally supporting the elder against the

The authors would like to thank Mary Delehanty and Barbara McLachlan for providing much of the inspiration and support for this chapter. The assistance of Claire Bloom in the preparation of the manuscript is also gratefully acknowledged.

rest of the family. Ordinarily the family will win by attrition. Consequently, any solutions involving elders and their families that are unacceptable to the family—that is, solutions one member cannot live with—are really nonsolutions.

## REVIEW OF THE LITERATURE

From an academic standpoint in gerontology, the influence exerted by the family on the lives of the individual members has been the subject of theoretical and applied examination in the areas of psychoanalysis (Kahana and Levin 1971); rehabilitative medicine (Davies and Hansen 1974; Peck 1974); social work (Bloom and Monro 1972; Brody 1966, 1974); marriage counseling (Peterson 1974); and family therapy for both individual families (Boszormenyi-Nagy and Spark 1973) and groups of members from institutionalized-patient families (Manaster 1967).

Unfortunately, most discussion of family therapy principles in relation to elders has generally been limited to issues of institutionalization (Brody and Spark 1966; Cath 1972; Miller and Harris 1967) and death or loss (Berezin 1970). More recently, other gerontologists (Gurian 1975; Miller, Bernstein, and Sharkey 1975; Savitsky and Sharkey 1972) have elaborated on family systems theory to explain a wide variety of medical and/or psychiatric symptoms that could be triggered or exacerbated by family interactions.

The case for including families of the elderly in the search for solutions to problems of aging is clear. The question is not whether to work with families of the aged, but how? Unfortunately, the relationship between elders and their families is much like the weather—easy to talk about but hard to do something about. Woe is the lot of the helper who encounters a family in distress and who knows something should be done but has no idea of where or how to start! Often the helper resorts to providing external supports that have little lasting effect. This chapter is written to assist readers to help themselves and is offered as a succinct and practical, though necessarily incomplete, approach to problem solving with the aged and their families.

However, before describing the approach we use, it is important to state that in no way should our ideas be considered just our creation. We are heavily indebted to the ideas of others, especially John E. Bell (1961) and Elaine M. Sorensen;* Don D. Jackson (1968a, 1968b); Paul Watzlawick (Watzlawick, Beavin, and Jackson 1967; Watzlawick, Weakland, and Fisch 1974); Richard Fisch; Milton H. Erickson (Haley 1973); and Jay Haley (1963, 1975). If any of the ideas and techniques in this chapter are useful, a major share of the credit goes to them. However, they are not responsible for failures in comprehending, integrating, and/or applying their work in this discussion.

## REALISTIC GOALS IN FAMILY COUNSELING

When working with persons in distress, the question arises of ethics, licensing boards, job descriptions, and so forth. Consequently, it is important to state that the type of counseling described in this chapter is aimed at helping people to resolve situational problems rather than to treat psychopathology. Practically, this means that counselors have to be willing to revise situational problems rather than reform people.

Most people agree that it is better to solve problems by finding the root cause, yet most families do not have the time, money, or interest to pursue such help. In addition are limitations related to the helper's own time and training. It is best to confine one's efforts to the situational problem at hand, and one may find that a vicious cycle in which the family is trapped can be broken.

## COUNSELING TECHNIQUES

### Making the Approach

The difficult part in starting to work with a family is making the initial contact. This may

---

*Dr. Sorensen also created and directed the Family Interaction Center at the Mental Research Institute (MRI) in Palo Alto, California, and provided fundamental practical support. Psychopathology must be left to the psychotherapist. On the other hand, many families find that a little situational relief is better than none at all.

be particularly true in a setting in which "counseling" is not traditionally recognized or written in as part of the job description. Suppose, for example, that a nurse is passing out medications and stumbles into a family crisis between a weeping 80-year-old mother and her red-faced, obviously wracked, 50-year-old daughter. To make certain not to get involved, the nurse can pass by the room (give out the medications later); walk silently into the room without looking anyone in the eye, hand out the medication, and get out; or better still, if mother or daughter say anything to the nurse, mumble something about "running late" and excuse herself. To become involved, be available.

### Reframing the Approach

Sometimes being available is not enough. Some families find it very difficult to share their problems. Reluctance to share feelings may well explain why the family is having a problem in the first place. In such cases it is often possible to get the family to air their problems if you *reframe* the approach situation so that it appears that they will be doing you a favor if they tell you about their problem. This kind of reframing can be easily done by saying something such as, "I'm sorry to intrude, but it's part of my job . . ." or "I really feel awkward, but if I don't find a chance to talk with you folks, I will be in trouble." We find this approach to be particularly effective with elders who would deny help for themselves but are not willing to deny help to a younger person (you). This approach shares more equitably the pleasure of helping between you and the family. Unfortunately, this particular gift is not one that all counselors seem generous enough to bestow.

### FAMILIES DEFINE THE PROBLEMS

In working with families, difficulties are defined in terms of family difficulties rather than in terms of one individual with the problem. Consequently, in family counseling an old man who is wandering around the neighborhood would not be labeled as having the problem; instead, the entire family (including grandfather) would be seen as being affected by grandfather's behavior. Family counselors believe that sometimes family interactions may be responsible for problematic behavior.

### Participation of the Family

Gaining participation of the entire family is more easily said than done. One especially needs to encourage the hesitant. For example, call family members and say, "It would help me in working with your father if you would come in and give me some information." If the family is at war, you might say something like "I know I'm getting only one side of the story now, and I certainly would like to hear your side." For the family members who just cannot get in, you might consider a home visit.

Do not despair if you cannot get full family participation. The most important part of working with families is not having a packed room every session, but rather making sense of an elder's problem as not just an individual problem but a family problem. The concept that the family might be a cause (and is certainly suffering the effects) of the problem is very important.

### Attack by the Family

After the first approach, the counselor may be verbally attacked by one or more family members. Generally, the form of criticism is a direct or indirect challenge to the competence of the counselor. For most people new to working with families, this is an area of great vulnerability, but such a challenge by the family is a good sign. They might be saying, "We won't be treated by just anybody; we're special!" Far better to begin with a family that is trying to take care of themselves than one that will just open a collective mouth and swallow anything offered. As a general rule, when one's competence is attacked, it is best to be as honest and validating as possible. One of the reasons they challenged your competence in the first place might be to test your trustworthiness before they unburden themselves to you. You probably will pass the test if you are frank. If you want to flunk their test, recite your degrees and course work defensively!

## Reaction to Young Counselors

Another question elder members of families often raise to challenge the competence of young workers is "How could anyone your age understand my problems?" It is often helpful to say, "That's a real problem and it often handicaps me. I can't fully understand your problems, so I will really need your help to work with you. Even though I have a few skills, I often find I get more out of working with my older clients than I am able to give, and sometimes I feel guilty about that." *Give the elder a chance to reassure you that you are going to be useful, but also give the elder the opportunity to share the pleasure of helping.*

## Handling Hopelessness

Another challenge to your competence that families may raise is "The situation is hopeless; nobody could possibly help." If you are willing to recognize that people who make such statements have real feelings and that those feelings are facts, then the best way to validate the clients' feelings (and also to show that you are perceptive enough to accept how they feel) is to say something like "You are probably right, and under the circumstances" (recite the problem areas) "I'd probably feel exactly the same way." Then be quiet and see what happens. If you passed the test ("prove to me you really know how desperate I feel"), you can probably expect a flow of information.

## Hindrances to New Counselors

Do not falter unnecessarily. Be aware of stumbling blocks that may hinder new counselors. There will be families you cannot help. However, you can at least increase your chances by avoiding the behaviors that would ensure your not being useful. The first one is the importance of restraining optimism. Unbridled optimism is destructive for several reasons. First, as already stated, when the family members are feeling pessimistic, optimism expressed by the counselor simply invalidates their feelings and demonstrates the counselor's lack of empathy. Second, unrestrained optimism sets the stage for failure. That is, if you are optimistic ("next

week will be much better") and things do not turn out the way you predicted (next week is worse), then either the family loses confidence in you or the family members blame themselves for failing. In either case, the results are destructive for the family. Finally, optimism serves as a crutch for the counselor. It is far better to pay close attention quietly and think about what needs to be done.

## Arguments with Clients

An important rule of thumb is to avoid arguments with clients. Another definition for *argue* is "an insistent attempt to persuade." The most obvious reason one should not get into an argument is that one might be wrong.

One destructive element of arguing is that in arguing one communicates to the clients that one does not know where they are "coming from." Suppose the argument is won; what is gained? Generally when two people in a relationship argue until there is a winner or a loser, the relationship itself suffers. In the counselor-client relationship, as in a husband-wife or brother-sister relationship, the loser either pulls back to lick the wounds or plots a counterattack to even the score.

It is important to recognize when you are talking to the air. If the family members are saying, "Yes, but . . ." then you are not only talking to the air but also not listening. You must learn to communicate with them in a language they can understand.

## Pushing the Family

A paradoxical problem stems from arguing between counselor and family. For example, suppose you are counseling a family in which there is a question of whether to put the elder in a relative's home or a board-and-care facility. The middle-aged daughter and son-in-law have ambivalent feelings about what to do. They do not want their mother in a convalescent hospital, but they are afraid they could not give her proper medical care at home. When family members have ambivalent feelings, if the counselor takes one side the entire family or one or more members will take the other. If you push for a board-and-care facility, they will push for a home placement; you push for home placement, they will push for the board and care. Consequently, if you really feel that an institutional placement is necessary, by arguing vehemently for it you may find that you push the family in just the opposite direction and they opt (because of your pushing) for the home solution.

### Do Not Threaten the Family

Another way to shut down communication with the family is to issue threats ("If you don't do what I say, I'll report you") or make accusations ("You are not taking your share of responsibility for your mother"). It is important to differentiate between talking and communicating. After a threat or accusation by the counselor, talking may continue, but communication will have halted.

### Do Not Speak for Clients

Another pitfall you can avoid by stepping back is speaking for clients. Allow clients to talk for themselves. If you follow this rule, you will often find yourself being surprised by what you hear. By keeping out of the family's way, you allow them to have the satisfaction of arriving at their own solutions. In a sense the obligation of the counselor is to be available as a guide. Often the counselor will perceive the path a family should take. It is helpful to lead the family toward that path, but then step back and let the family discover the path for themselves. If the job is well done, the family will have a valuable sense of their own success.

To allow family members to speak for themselves, you obviously have to be able to sit out some of the silences that will certainly occur. *When in doubt, be quiet.*

### DETERMINE THE PROBLEM

Determine the problem through goal clarification. After one has approached the family, one begins to help the family specify their problems. There are several good reasons for getting down to specifics. The first and most obvious reason is that if a problem has no definition, then it has no solution. Often problems seem insoluble because they have been unmeasurable. Since the family's conception of their problem is so diffuse, they would not know whether they were making progress in solving it. By attempting to get the family to specify their goals for their meetings with the counselor, the problem becomes measurable, hence manageable.

Another excellent reason to pin down the problems is that this process improves communication. By making explicit what has previously been implicit, the air gets cleared. The fear of what someone might say (the implicit) is often greater than what they actually say (the explicit).

Discussing problems and goals can help all the family members to clarify how what is happening in the family affects them personally (problems) and how they would know if the situation were improving (goals). Obviously, it is impossible to negotiate a solution among family members if it is not clear to all involved where everyone is hurting and what everyone wants (or at least can live with).

Early in the first session one might ask, "What seems to be the problem?" or "I wonder what sense you all make of why we're meeting together?" Then be quiet and see how the family reacts. Observe who talks and what they talk about. To make sure that the message the family members are sending to you is the same message you receive (it often is not), echo back what you believe they said. For example, the daughter of an old farmer says, "Our problem is that Dad is always drooling tobacco juice and never zips his fly." The counselor might reply in several different ways—for example, "Let me check this out to see that I've got it right; you are saying that your father has some social habits that leave you feeling embarrassed," or "I think I hear you saying that you are feeling some concern over what you see as some memory problems in your Dad," or "Am I accurate in saying that you are feeling really caught because you're not sure how much longer you want your father to remain living in your home?"

Notice that the content of each of these responses is slightly different. They point out the importance of reflective listening as a method to ensure that the message sent by the client is accurately received by the counselor. Also notice that in each of the examples the "echo" was phrased as a question rather than an interpretation.

Encourage the family to correct you if your perceptions are inaccurate. This process allows the family to use you as a sounding board. Observe, too, that in each example the vague term *our problem,* as said by the daughter, was echoed back in personal terms. *It is important to remember that echoing is not necessarily agreeing with what people say, but making sure that you understand what they mean.*

Although discussion may have fairly free rein during the early part of the session, toward the end it is important to secure some statements of goals and problems from each individual so that the emphasis shifts from "Dad has a problem" to "Because of my perception of Dad's behavior, my life is being affected; therefore, I have an emotional investment in being here." If necessary, ask each family member directly, "How is all of this affecting you personally?" When defining goals, urge families to think small. "What would be the smallest change that would give you a sense of progress?" Do not set families up for certain failure by aiming too high.

### Previous Family Solutions

Determine what the family has been doing about the problem. At this point you want to find out how the family has been trying to solve their problem. Asking also gives each family member the opportunity to prove that he or she has been *trying.* To elicit this information, one might ask directly, "I wonder if you folks could give me some idea of what you have been trying to do about the situation to this point?" Or "What seems to have worked?" Or "What have you tried that hasn't seemed to work?" Often the "what hasn't worked" question can be rephrased to be a very useful question for the family to answer: "I know it's often hard to figure out what you could do that would improve the situation, but I wonder if you could tell me some things that each of you could do that would make sure that things never improved?" Often the family will then list all of the things they are doing now! Gently one can point out, "Well,

I'm not certain what you can do to make things better, but at least you know what you can do that will never result in any change." At this point you may have returned something precious to the family that they thought they had lost: free will. Without confrontation or criticism you have led them to see that destructive, repetitious behavior that is not getting them anywhere is a matter of choice.

### The Family System

Make sense of the family system. After one has approached the family, gained information about the members' problems and goals, and explored what the family has been trying to do to solve their problems up to now, one needs some time to digest what has been learned. We find that it is often helpful to excuse oneself from the room for a few minutes to think in peace. In making sense of what is going on in the family, one needs to ask all of the following questions.

**Facets of the Problem.** Is the problem the problem, or *is the problem the solution?* A classic case of the solution's being the problem is when an elder who is living independently is in the process of being coerced by his or her children to reside with one of them. Not infrequently disaster strikes because the child who emerges to claim the elder finds that the elder does not want to move. Intergenerational friction, as well as resentment between siblings ("You've got to do something"), escalates until a crisis occurs.

**Meaning of Communications.** The next question you have to ask yourself is "What do the family members mean by what they have said?" In other words, communication exists on different levels: The meaning of any communication comes from what is said, how it is said, and in what context it is said. One must be attentive to what is not said by family members. Often what is not said may be the most important clue because it may give you some notion of what topics are taboo or threatening to the family.

**The Family Rules.** It is helpful to ask, "Are there any family rules?" A family rule is an agreement among family members, generally unspoken, about how the family is to function. Family rules may include some of the following: "We never allow ourselves to be emotional" or "Father always has the last word" or "It is important to be logical." Often, when circumstances force the family to abandon the rules (say, the father has had a stroke and can no longer be the final arbitrator and pillar of strength in the family), one family member or another may act in a way to distract the family from dealing with the fact that the rule must now be changed.

**The Identified Patient.** Another question to think about is "Is there an *identified patient* in the family?" An identified patient (IP) is generally the individual the family members initially pinpoint as the one with "the problem." Often the IP will appear to be presenting a combination of physical and psychological symptoms to indicate that, indeed, they do have "the problem." In family work with elders, often the IP is the old person. In fact, elders quite often label themselves as the IP. Occasionally, one family member really does have a discrete problem that has minimal effect on other family members. On the other hand, you need to be aware that an IP can be a handy item for a family system to have. For example, an IP provides a great distraction from the personal or interactional problems of other family members ("If only Mother were better, then I'd be happy"). Often you can get a sense of "why an IP?" if you think, "What would happen in the family if the IP were really cured?" Related to this question is "How would the IP get what he wanted if he had no symptoms?"

**Expressions of Power.** Also consider, "How does each member of this family system express personal power?" Some members may exercise power through the bankbook; others, through psychological intimidation; still others, by acting weak or sick. To make progress in understanding the family system, one needs to have a sense of what family members do to get what they want.

**Perpetuation.** Finally, ask, "How is this problem being perpetuated?" Possibly one or more family members have a stake (perhaps unconsciously) in keeping the fat in the fire. For example, suppose there is a family rule that appears to be "We don't believe in quitting."

It is important to note that information gained in the analysis is not something that is straightforwardly shared with the family. A rule of thumb: Never share your working hypotheses with a family unless they reflect *positively* on the family members.

## EMPATHY AND JUDGMENT

A counselor does not have to resort to telling lies to validate the feelings of clients. It cannot be stressed enough that in every case a counselor can understand (validate) how a client feels without expressing approval or disapproval of what the client is doing. The concepts of understanding (empathy) and approval (judgment) are independent of each other. Do not confuse being honest with being unable to control an impulse to blurt out a value judgment. Conversely, you should not consider yourself dishonest because you can control your impulses and have empathy for clients even when their behavior does not jibe with your own set of values and beliefs. To deny a family or its individual members the sense of being understood because their actions do not meet with your approval could be called empathic malpractice.

## MOBILIZING THE ENERGY OF THE FAMILY

Mobilize the energy of the family to move toward a solution. Is it necessary to go any further with the family? Be willing to consider that you may be dispensable. You have made contact; you have convened interested family members; you have specified the problem and helped the family system to set goals. Is your job over? For most families, the answer is probably "yes."

If the answer is "no," then the task is to lead the family gently around the obstacles that are keeping them stuck. To achieve this task the family must be helped to arrive at a solution to their problem by communicating with them in their own language. In other words, you must speak to the members of the family system in such a way that they can hear you.

In a sense, being willing to alter your own communication style to fit that of your clients demonstrates that you respect your clients' perceptions of the world as being as valid as your own.

Sometimes the family is stuck because they are afraid to do *anything* differently. In such a case it is often more feasible to ease the family's risk in a behavior transition by reframing a suggested change of behavior into an "information-gathering assignment." For example, in a long-term care facility the son of an 85-year-old man hesitatingly asks the counselor to disconnect his father's telephone. The counselor determines that the father is calling his son eight to ten times each day, despite the fact that the son visits him every night. The son confides that it is driving him wild because he feels guilty if he does not take the calls and resentful if he does. In his language the son has revealed guilt and resentment. Frame suggestions to show him how to get off that hook and he will listen.

### WINDING UP

When the original goals have been met, let go. If the job was done well, the family may not have even realized that the counselor did anything. If the family does recognize the importance of the role you played, be modest and let the family take the credit for their own solutions. If you need to boast, then do your boasting to a colleague.

It is useful when winding up with a family that solved its problems to ask something along the lines of "How do you make sense of things being better now?" rather than to tell them why you think things are better.

In winding up it is also important to remember the virtue of restrained optimism. Generally, if the counselor was useful, the family will be feeling highly optimistic for the future. Rather than setting them up for a failure, say something like "Well, things do seem to be better and you all seem to have made a lot of progress. Often, after a lot of forward progress, families

may slip back a bit, so don't be surprised if things become more difficult again for a while."

### SUGGESTIONS

In working with families, you can increase your options by additional reading (Herr and Weakland 1979) and/or by studying audiocassettes and videotapes made by family counselors demonstrating how to work with families. One problem is that not enough proven techniques for working with families of the elderly are available. Therefore, you will probably need to improvise much of your own training. One way to learn is to find local counselors who are working with elders and their families (even though they may not be writing about their clinical practice). Simply observe what they do, how they do it, and when they do it. Ask questions. If you are lucky enough to have such professionals available to you, ask one or more of them to sit in with you when you try working with families. If that sort of arrangement is impossible, consider taping your sessions to play back to "clinical supervisors" later.

If there is no family expert around who is used to dealing with elders, form a peer supervision group of others with whom you share this interest, to discuss cases and the family approach. See whether you can interest a child-oriented or couple-oriented family therapist to sit with your group to review cases and/or tapes with you. Many of the techniques mentioned in this chapter come from family therapy experience based on younger clients. Take advantage of the family therapy expertise in your community.

Finally, and most important, pay attention to the fact that you may get in over your head. You are dealing with people's lives. If things start to get worse for one of your families or if nothing is happening (and it is obvious to you that it is imperative that something does happen), seek professional help. If you are unwilling to admit that you can ever get in over your head or if you believe that anything you can do with a family is better than doing nothing at all, then perhaps consider another field of endeavor.

Plan to be discouraged for at least the first 10 families. They are the toughest. Plan to seek much help when you are working with those first 10 families. The second 10 will be considerably less difficult and might even leave you feeling that you are being genuinely useful.

## SUMMARY

The need for working with families of aged persons is clear, but how does one begin? A family can be considered a group. Multiple families could also comprise a group. This chapter is about counseling a single family through a crisis situation regarding an elderly family member. External supports do not provide lasting effects, and the involvement of a concerned counselor may help a family in distress ride out a stormy period by using the following guidelines:

1. Make the approach.
2. Determine the problem through goal clarification; make sense of the family system to yourself.
3. Determine what the family of the elderly person has been doing about the problem.
4. Ask, "Is the problem the problem, or is the problem the solution?"
5. What do family members mean by what they have said?
6. List the family rules.
7. Mobilize the energy of the family to move toward a solution.
8. Wind up.

The new counselor will need to read extensively and study films made by family counselors. The present lack of successful techniques will hamper the style of the new counselor. You should be prepared to plan and improvise much of your own training.

## EXERCISE 1

Counseling technique with the elderly as applied to one family is described in the following case history. Details have been altered to protect the identity of the clients. Indicate in the margin each step of the counseling technique as described in the chapter.

In a teaching hospital there was a counselor who expressed interest in counseling older people and their families. A medical social worker from a psychiatric self-care ward contacted him about an 83-year-old man. He had been brought to the emergency room by his family after suffering a "seizure," which the elder denied. The family insisted he had. The medical staff accepted the family's word and ordered two weeks of observation and tests for the old man. All they found was a rational, delightful farmer with an abdominal cancer in remission. *No seizures.* When the hospital tried to release him, the family, particularly the elder daughter, refused to take him. Since he had limited funds and since the elder daughter threatened to sue the hospital if he was released, the old man was transferred to a self-care psychiatric ward for further observation. Again he was observed to be an intelligent, witty, delightful old man. Still no seizures. In fact, all the old man wanted was bus fare back to his farm in the Midwest!

The medical social worker was at the end of his rope. The family insisted the man was sick. The daughter was calling the hospital administrator and writing letters to her congressman, senator, and lawyer. The staff became quite attached to the old man and supported his claim that his family was just trying to "dump" him in the hospital. The old man said his children had "kidnapped" him to bring him there and now would not let him go home. The consensus of the staff was that (1) the old man was sane, (2) his elder daughter was very disturbed, and (3) the hospital should do all it could to return him to his farm in the Midwest.

The hospital staff had become surrogate family members locked into a classic *Us* (the people who are logical and sensitive) versus *Them* (the people who are disturbed and unfeeling) struggle. The battle escalated.

It was soon clear to the counselor that the children (daugher, age 55; son, age 50; son, age 48; daughter, age 45) were being led by the elder daughter. She was the first contact; the counselor called her to commiserate about the "appalling treatment" she was getting from the hospital. He told her he didn't blame her at all for writing her congressman. He followed with "Your family's wishes just don't seem to have been taken into account at all. Sometimes it seems like the patients around here are treated as if their families didn't even have feelings. I'd really like to meet with the whole family to see if I could be helpful to you in straightening out this whole mess that the hospital seems to have made. I'd even be willing to set up evening appointments to do it." The counselor was attempting to use what he knew of the family's position to validate the feelings of the daughter and establish his credibility with the family.

Being willing to meet after hours not only set the counselor apart from the rest of the staff but also made the potential "I can't possibly leave work" excuse invalid. An appointment was set for all four children with their spouses, in addition to the mother and father.

When the family arrived, they were greeted, offered coffee and doughnuts, and then led into the conference room. The group was large; spouses were included due to the obvious consequences a placement would have for each couple.

The counselor opened with "Well, now that we're all assembled, I wonder what sense each of you makes as to why we are here?" The first to reply was the older son, with open contempt, "I don't make any sense of it at all. Everyone knows that the lives of all of us, Mommy's and Daddy's included, are in the hands of the Lord. This should be the work of Jesus Christ Almighty. We need less talk and more praying." The counselor did not argue the merits of fundamentalist Christianity. The counselor then asked that son to lead an invocation so that the meeting might be productive. After the invocation, everyone began to spill out thoughts and ideas at one time. The counselor said, "I know that all of you are used to hearing one another's voices, but it's very difficult for me to make sense out of what one of you is saying when others are also talking. I'll have to ask for your patience. Please speak one at a time." Note that the counselor makes the interruptions his problem, not the family's. It is easier to hear and respond to such a statement than to "It's rude to interrupt your brother."

About a year before, the 75-year-old mother had contacted the children in Washington and asked to be moved from the farm into town. She was suffering from a combination of congestive heart failure, arthritis, obesity, and lethargy; she was "confined" to a wheelchair. A few months after they moved, her husband began to tipple a bit to excess and had to be driven home by the sheriff (who fortunately lived on the adjoining farm). The elder daughter had received calls from the sheriff expressing his concern. As a result of the calls the daughter and her husband drove back to the Midwest "to bring Daddy back for an indefinite visit." The point of family conflict was that the children and their spouses all agreed Daddy knew the visit was permanent. Daddy insisted that he was out only for a temporary visit.

Since the mother was temporarily housed in a convalescent hospital, the father had been circulating from child to child until his "seizure." Still, the father refused to admit that he had ever been troubled by "spells" of any sort.

Regarding specific problems, the elder daughter said the whole thing was affecting her work; her husband said it was affecting their relationship. The elder son was losing sleep; his wife felt quite put upon. The younger son complained that his life was disrupted by constant telephone calls over new family crises. The younger daughter complained bitterly that this situation put her in the traditional role of family baby. Her husband said he did not like to come home from work with her feeling the way she was feeling.

It was fairly obvious to the counselor that this present crisis probably would not have occurred had the father (and the mother) been left in their own home.

From the voice tones, expressions of concern, and attendance, it was obvious that the family was close. It was also clear that all the children would have liked to see the parents living in one of the children's homes. Only the younger son offered, with the concurrence of his wife. When the elder daughter bluntly stated that they could not live with her, the old man looked her in the eye and said, "I understand, honey. I love you and Sam [her husband] very much too, but I don't want to live with you either. That's what I've been trying to tell you ever since I came to Washington."

Everyone was relieved. As siblings and spouses spoke, all made statements similar to that of the elder daughter except the younger son and his wife. To each child, the father reaffirmed his love and stated flatly that he was not interested in living with them.

The session lasted an hour and a half. An agreement was made to reconvene in a week. The counselor concluded by saying, "I think it's important not to make any decisions next week but to go slow and just sort of think things out. Things have been moving pretty fast up till now and maybe we need to slow the pace." Note the family rule in operation: "This family sticks together through thick and thin." This rule meant that all family members were going to need to participate in the solution.

The father had been labeled the IP. Since in the past he had been a very powerful figure in the family, the IP label gave the rest of the family, particularly the elder daughter, some maneuvering room in wresting away his absolute power of decision.

How did the family *perpetuate* the problem? By failing to take action. The counselor sought to help the family make (and then act on) a compromise decision that everyone would be able to live with.

The father's power seemed the weakest; if he moved back to the Midwest (his bluff having been called), the family would probably be angry with him; and if he needed their help later, they might fail to respond or they might bring him back to Washington only on terms of unconditional surrender. Therefore, the counselor wanted to help the father settle into local living circumstances while he still had some negotiating power left. Since (1) one child had volunteered his home, (2) the rest said that they would like to see him living with one of them, and (3) the father had not ruled out that possibility, the best solution seemed to be to lead the family to "try out" placing the parents in the younger son's home.

The elder daughter seemed to be the key in the family decision making. It was imperative that she continue to feel as though she were moving the family but that her energy be put to use in a more positive way. She was feeling cornered and tired. The more cornered and tired she felt, the harder she pushed for "the final solution," which in this case was institutionalization of both parents. The counselor needed to make enough space so that she could get out of the corner to take some rest while allowing her still to feel a significant member of the family.

At the next session the counselor began by summing up the last meeting: "I am feeling the need to recall how things seemed to be shaping up at the end of last week's meeting. Be sure to correct me if I misstate something you were saying or feeling. As I recall, all of you children agreed that you'd like to see your folks living together with one of you, but only Ed and Julie [the younger son and his wife] feel that they would really be comfortable with Mr. and Mrs. Smith [the parents] moving in with them. It seemed to me that all of you love your mother and father very much, and Mr. Smith, you seem to care very much for your children. All of you recognize that you can love someone without being able to live with them. I also had the impression that you, Mr. Smith, would prefer to be on your farm, but living with Ed and Julie was a solution that you might be willing to try. [Mr. Smith nodded his head in grudging affirmation.] It seems to me that this is a close, loving family that doesn't want to see some of its members take on more responsibility than they might be able to handle. What might the rest of the family do to make your parents' moving in with Ed and Julie easier? If it turns out that the rest of the family can help sufficiently, then we have an agreeable situation. If, on the other hand, after giving it a try, we fail, then we're back to where we are right now."

The rest of the hour was spent in economic negotiation. The counselor continued to urge everyone to speak honestly, offer only what they were sure they could deliver comfortably, and make clear whether the offer for support was economic (money, furniture, food, and so on) or social (providing rides, visiting, and so on). A tentative agreement and schedule emerged. At that point the counselor asked: "Is this a decision that you can live with?" Each family member affirmed that it was.

Concluding the session, the counselor said, "Well, we seem to have made some progress tonight, but remember, there are no easy solutions. You can probably expect that the next week will be a stormy one. You may have some second thoughts about what you have volunteered to do, and change your minds. That's to be expected. Think about what you've agreed to tonight and decide whether you have enough energy to see this thing through for three months. I'd also like you to anticipate any problems that might come up."

In the last meeting there was a discussion of what might go wrong. The counselor asked, "I wonder if each of you would tell me what you could personally do to make sure things go wrong." The father said, "I don't want things to go wrong." To which the counselor replied, "But if they did, what would you do?" Such a technique makes covert subversion more difficult. It also usefully restrains optimism.

Anticipating problems can be useful in preventing them. The younger son brought up the problem of "Daddy's spells." Now that the father was no longer in danger of being institutionalized for life, he confessed that from time to time (every three or four months) he did in fact have blackouts. The counselor agreed to relay the information to the hospital staff so that they would be supportive instead of antagonistic to the family if the father had another "spell."

The elder daughter and her husband failed to appear for the final session. The rest of the family (now led in discussion by the father) confided to the counselor that she and her husband had been having severe marital difficulties. The rest of the children admitted that while "what to do with Mommy and Daddy" had been pressing on their minds, they also worried about that daughter. The family consensus was that the father and the older son (who at one time had had to deal with his own drinking) should call on her to share the family's concern with her. Since the family chose not to ask the counselor for help with her, the counselor did not offer. The family had been solving its own problems rather successfully until they found themselves stuck with this one sticky situation; now that collective energies were freed, there was no reason to think they would not return to dealing competently with life's problems.

## EXERCISE 2

If you had been counseling the family described in this case study, what would you have done differently? Why?

## EXERCISE 3*

To better understand the family system and the relationships between family members, it is useful for the student to fill in a diagram such as the one in Figure 31–1 to indicate the sex, marital status, occupation, ethnicity, and school year of each family member. Complete a chart for your own family, to increase your understanding of your roots. Use the guidelines below.

*Three-Generation Genogram Guidelines*

1. Divide paper, sideways, into three levels.
2. Begin in the middle, with husband on the left.
3. Males are in squares; females are in circles.
4. Aborted fetuses (too early to determine sex) are triangles.
5. Place birthdates below symbol, prefaced by a "b."
6. Place deathdates below symbol, prefaced by a "d"; mark an X through identity symbol.
7. Place marriage date, preceded by "m," on the paired solid line.
8. Separation is an "s." Divorce is a "d."
9. Place adoption date below symbol, prefaced by an "a." Broken vertical line indicates adoption.
10. Indicate occupation and ethnicity of first generation alongside symbols.
11. Indicate occupation of middle generation.
12. Indicate school year or occupation of third generation (children of major couple).

---

*Adapted from "Genograms: a guide to understanding one's own family system," by P. J. Starkey, *Perspectives in Psychiatric Care,* 1981, *19*(5&6), 164–73. Reprinted by permission.

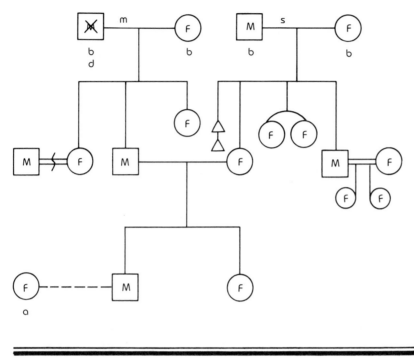

FIGURE 31-1. *Three-generation genogram.*

*SOURCE:* Adapted from "Genograms: a guide to understanding one's own family system," by P. J. Starkey, *Perspectives in Psychiatric Care,* 1981, *19*(5&6), 164–73. Reprinted by permission.

## REFERENCES

Bell, J. E. 1961. *Family group therapy.* Public Health Mongraph no. 64. Washington, D.C.: U.S. Department of Health, Education, and Welfare.

Berezin, M. A. 1970. The psychiatrists and the geriatric patient: Partial grief in family members and others who care for the elderly patient. *Journal of Geriatric Psychiatry* 4(1): 53–64 (Fall).

Bloom, M., and A. Monro. 1972. Social work and the aging family. *Family Coordinator* 21:103–15.

Boszormenyi-Nagy, I., and G. M. Spark. 1973. *Invisible loyalties: Reciprocity in intergenerational family therapy.* New York: Harper & Row.

Brody, E. 1966. The aging family. *The Gerontologist* 6(4): 201–6 (December).

_____. 1974. Aging and family personality: A developmental view. *Family Process* 13(1): 23–28 (March).

Brody, E., and G. M. Spark. 1966. Institutionalization of the elderly: A family crisis. *Family Process* 5(1): 76–90 (March).

Cath, S. H. 1972. The geriatric patient and his family: The institutionalization of a parent—A nadir of life. *Journal of Geriatric Psychiatry* 5(1): 25–46.

Davies, N. H., and E. Hansen. 1974. Family focus: A transitional cottage in an acute care hospital. *Family Process* 13(4): 481–88 (December).

Eisdorfer, C., and B. A. Stotsky. 1977. In *Handbook of the psychology of aging,* ed. J. E. Birren and K. W. Schaie, 725. New York: Van Nostrand.

Gurian, B. S. 1975. Psychogeriatrics and family medicine. *The Gerontologist* 15(4): 308–10 (August).

Haley, J. 1963. *Strategies of psychotherapy.* New York: Grune & Stratton.

_____. 1973. *Uncommon therapy: The psychiatric techniques of Milton H. Erickson, M.D.* New York: Norton.

_____. 1975. *Family therapy.* New York: Aronson.

Herr, J. J., and J. H. Weakland. 1979. *Counseling elders and their families: Practical techniques for applied gerontologists.* New York: Springer.

Jackson, D. D. 1968a. *Communication, family, and marriage.* Palo Alto, Calif.: Science & Behavior Books.

_____. 1968b. *Therapy, communication, and change.* Palo Alto, Calif.: Science & Behavior Books.

Kahana, R. J., and S. Levin. 1971. Aging and the conflict of generations. *Journal of Geriatric Psychiatry* 4(2): 115–35 (Spring).

Manaster, A. 1967. The family group therapy program at Park View home for the aged. *Journal of the American Geriatrics Society* 15(3): 302–6 (March).

Miller, M. B., H. Bernstein, and H. Sharkey. 1975. Family extrusion of the aged patient: Family homeostasis and sexual conflict. *The Gerontologist* 15(4): 291–96 (August).

Miller, M. B., and A. P. Harris. 1967. The chronically ill aged: Paradoxical patient-family behavior. *Journal of the American Geriatrics Society* 15(5): 480–95 (May).

Peck, B. B. 1974. Physical medicine and family dynamics: The dialectics of rehabilitation. *Family Process* 13(4): 469–80 (December).

Peterson, J. A. 1974. Therapeutic interventions in marital and family problems of aging persons. In *Professional obligations and approaches to the aged,* ed. A. N. Schwartz and I. N. Mensh. Springfield, Ill.: Thomas.

Savitsky, E., and H. Sharkey. 1972. The geriatric patient and his family: Study of family interaction in the aged. *Journal of Geriatric Psychiatry* 5(1): 3–24.

Spark, G. M., and E. M. Brody. 1970. The aged are family members. *Family Process* 9(2): 195–210 (June).

Sussman, M., and L. Burchinal. 1962. Kin family network: Unheralded structure in current conceptualizations of family functioning. *Marriage and Family Living* 24:231–40.

Watzlawick, P., J. H. Beavin, and D. D. Jackson. 1967. *Pragmatics of human communication.* New York: Norton.

Watzlawick, P., J. H. Weakland, and R. Fisch. 1974. *Change: Principles of problem formation and problem resolution.* New York: Norton.

## BIBLIOGRAPHY

Aldous, N. R. 1967. The "adult" children of the patient and their involvement in a psychiatric home care program. *Laval Medical* 38(1): 131–36 (January).

Alpaugh, P., and M. Haney. 1978. *Counseling the older adult: A training manual.* Monograph. Los Angeles: University of Southern California Press.

Bell, B. D. 1973. The family life cycle, primary relationships, and social participation patterns. *The Gerontologist* 13(1): 78–81 (Spring).

Bengston, V. L. 1971. Inter-age perceptions and the generation gap. Part 2. *The Gerontologist* 2(4): 85–89 (Winter).

Bild, B., and R. Havighurst. 1976. Family and social support. Part 2. *The Gerontologist* 16(1): 63–69 (February).

Blenkner, M. 1965. Social work and family relationships in later life with some thoughts on filial maturity, in social structure and the family. In *Generational relations,* ed. E. Shanas and G. F. Streib. Englewood Cliffs, N.J.: Prentice-Hall.

Evangelica, Sr. M. 1968. The influence of family relationships on the geriatric patient—The nurse's role. *Nursing Clinics of North America* 3(4): 653–62 (December).

Goodell, G. E. 1975. Rehabilitation: Family involved in patient's care. *Hospitals* 49(6): 96–98 (March).

Hall, J. E., and B. R. Weaver. 1974. *Nursing of families in crisis.* Philadelphia: Lippincott.

Isaacs, B. 1971. Geriatric patients: Do their families care? *British Medical Journal* 4(30): 282–86 (October).

Kaplan, J. 1975. The family in aging. Part 1. *The Gerontologist* 15(5): 385 (October).

Kimmel, D. 1974. *Adulthood and aging.* New York: Wiley.

Krims, M. B. 1972. The geriatric patient and his family . . . General discussion. *Journal of Geriatric Psychiatry* 5(1): 3–24.

Okun, B. F. 1982. *Effective helping.* 2d ed. Belmont, Calif.: Wadsworth.

Peterson, J. A. 1973. Marital and family therapy involving the aged. *The Gerontologist* 13(1): 27–30 (Spring).

Sager, C., and H. Kaplan. 1972. *Progress in group and family therapy.* New York: Brunner/Mazel.

Schmidt, S. A. 1970. Staff helps family help itself. *Modern Nursing Home* 25(2): 35–37 (August).

Simos, B. G. 1973. Adult children and their aging parents. *Social Work* 18(3): 78–85 (May).

Soyer, D. 1972. The geriatric patient and his family: Helping the family to live with itself. *Journal of Geriatric Psychiatry* 5(1): 52–70.

Treas, J. 1975. Aging and the family: Sociological perspectives. In *Aging: Scientific perspectives and social issues,* ed. D. S. Woodruff and J. E. Birren. Princeton, N.J.: Van Nostrand.

## RESOURCES

### Films

*Family Life Education and Human Growth* (color, 13 minutes, 1970). An opinionated, inconsiderate grandfather moves in with his daughter and her family. Conflicts result, and he thinks no one cares about him and asks if he should move out. Sterling Educational Films, 241 East 34th Street, New York, NY 10016.

# chapter 32

# A Bibliotherapist's Perspective

*Lorraine O'Dell*

*The greatest good we can do to others is not to share our riches with them, but to reveal theirs to themselves, by giving them a chance to hear themselves speak.*

L. LAVELLE (MERRILL 1974, 28-29)

## LEARNING OBJECTIVES

- Define **bibliotherapy**.

- Differentiate between bibliotherapy and other adjunctive therapies.

- Discuss techniques for leading bibliotherapy groups.

- List techniques needed by the leader using bibliotheraphy with the elderly.

- State how reminiscing therapy connects with bibliotherapy.

## KEY WORDS

- Clinical bibliotherapy

- Developmental bibliotherapy

- Discussion

- Emotional response

- Intellectual capacity

- Reading material

- Stimulation

- Therapeutic direction

## DEFINITION

The definition of bibliotherapy has changed over the years. Librarians have, probably from the beginning, suggested reading material for people. Readers have at one time or another happened to discover emotional release through identification with historic or fictional persons and the events of their lives. Most librarians are readers themselves, in addition to their professional knowledge of reading materials. Librarians frequently become very familiar with a number of individual readers. The librarian's role has extended to advising readers of selections that perhaps might provide understanding or catharsis to resolve problems; this was perhaps the first understanding of the term *bibliotherapy*. In the field of psychiatry, some patients have been assigned reading about their particular situation; this, too, has been called bibliotherapy.

Bibliotherapy, in its many forms, has existed since people have read and shared their reading with others. There is much discussion over the definition of bibliotherapy, the validity of the term, and the "therapy" in the process.

Most bibliotherapists use some form of definition that has evolved from former practices. In my own career, I observed several practitioners, read program descriptions, and struggled with my own style as a bibliotherapist. I have formed my own definition that bibliotherapy is an active process involving the combination of reading material, emotional response to the material, and intimate discussion with others about those feelings.

## CLINICAL VERSUS DEVELOPMENTAL BIBLIOTHERAPY

There has been a distinction made between clinical bibliotherapy, employed as a part of treatment with mentally disturbed clients, and developmental bibliotherapy, used as a growth process with more healthy individuals.

As a public librarian, I am more familiar with the latter. In developmental bibliotherapy there is no clinical contract and no psychiatric evalua-

I would like to express my appreciation to Barbara Allen, for her support and encouragement and her comments and suggestions for this chapter; the San Rafael Public Library and the California State Library for the opportunity to become involved in bibliotherapy; and Maureen Cannon for her permission to include her poem "Of Poems."

tion or diagnosis. *The focus is on health, strength, and growth.* "The essential difference between bibliotherapy and other therapies as I have seen them emphasized is that bibliotherapy addresses itself directly and consistently to healthy, progressive aspects of the person's character" (Sweeney 1978). While the focus is on health, this does not mean that problematic feelings are disregarded. If they arise, they are acknowledged and discussed; they are just not searched for.

Developmental bibliotherapy groups are usually called something else: poetry groups, reading groups, discussion groups. The group members are not considered "in therapy." One of the advantages of developmental bibliotherapy is that it is removed from the formal medical, mental-health realm and thereby poses less of a threat to many people and meets less resistance.

The goals of bibliotherapy are summarized in the following list:

1. To use *reading materials* as a focus and arena for discussion of personal feelings and experiences.
2. To provide an *enjoyable pastime* that can become an opportunity for intimate discussion.
3. To provide an activity that requires active participation and that *stimulates* thinking and opining.
4. To make possible a pleasant *social* interchange through shared personal interests.
5. To *reveal* to group members their own *strengths, talents,* and *accomplishments* through their responses to identification with the events, objects, people, and feelings in the reading selections.
6. To improve *self-esteem and self-image* by *affirming* those revealed achievements and skills and by calling upon them whenever possible in the group process.
7. To *encourage growth* by applying those assets discovered in group members to problematic feelings and situations, past or present.

These goals are reached by using literature to provide a focus and structure that encourages

reminiscing, which in turn provides information about each participant.

## Therapeutic Model

There is an excellent article by Daniel Sweeney (1978) on "Bibliotherapy and the Elderly" in Rhea Rubin's *Bibliotherapy Sourcebook.* In this article, Sweeney discusses the formulation of the therapeutic model he worked with. He describes very well four goals as the basis for his practice:

1. The restoration of morale.
2. The tapping of the joy of life.
3. The demand to be active.
4. The fostering of competence.

In my experience, bibliotherapy is a client-centered, health-focused process. The bibliotherapist must have the ability to listen empathetically and the attitude of unconditional regard. An understanding of the aging process should bring with it acceptance of group members and their physical and emotional condition. Positive regard includes the restraint of expectations, both negative and positive. We are initially unable to prejudge the capabilities or competency of another.

These attitudes make it possible to listen to and look at each person as unique, with something special to discover and offer; take the lead and tempo from the group as the group develops; set aside our preset ideas about behavior, relationships, and discussion plans; focus on the strengths, talents, and resources of the elderly; accept at face value whatever comes up until evidence shows discrepancy; and appreciate the life that has been lived — the experiences, the feelings.

## BIBLIOTHERAPY WITH THE ELDERLY

Working with any group of people successfully requires that the process taking place conform to the needs and interests of the members of the group.

Bibliotherapy with the elderly requires that the bibliotherapist have some knowledge of the aging process, particularly the psychology of aging. In selecting materials, the bibliotherapist must become familiar with historical events and life-styles that have been of possible significance to the group members. The participants must be able to relate to the subjects of the reading selections.

For elderly participants who are institutionalized, and the best years of their lives are behind them. The present means fewer choices, greater losses, and diminishing capabilities. Because developmental bibliotherapy focuses on the affirmative, it takes place with the elderly most often through reminiscence. Many group members are already occupied with their own private reminiscing. Memories of the past are often clearer than those of more recent events. The confused elderly may utter fragments of memories and tangle them with the present.

Bibliotherapy is initially nonconfrontative, slow, and gentle because there is a reserve among some members that is associated with gentility and propriety. One doesn't discuss one's private life. This can be difficult to work with.

Bibliotherapy works through response to reading. The bibliotherapist can gently lead the discussion from the feelings of the character or writer to similar or differing feelings of the reader. A direct question about family to someone whose family is seldom seen is probably very painful. Response is often evasive or there is none at all. Reading about someone else's family outing, reunion, or Christmas celebration can elicit strong memories, which can be approached by the reader at his or her own pace.

It is important to think about what is known about aging and human needs and to set goals and objectives for carrying out the program. What is bibliotherapy for? What is its direction? Why are you doing bibliotherapy? What help can it give?

In addition to the objectives of carrying out the program, one should formulate several other kinds of goals: for the outcomes of the process itself, for each group if appropriate, and for individuals in each group. Outcomes that one would like to achieve keep one on the track. Setting goals for individuals and striving to facilitate the satisfaction of those goals keeps one aware of each person and of changes that may be taking place. For example:

- *Outcome goal:* I would like to see people in the group talking more with each other.
- *Individual goal:* I would like to see Mrs. A. speak more in the group.

You will perhaps recognize some of the above goals of bibliotherapy as corresponding to some of the developmental problems of the aging outlined by R. N. Butler (1974).

## THE BIBLIOTHERAPY PROCESS

Some selection of reading materials has to take place before meetings can begin. It is not enough to gather material for the first couple of sessions. The need for reading selections is great, but ideas become exhausted quickly. It is advisable to spend some time thinking about the kinds of subjects that may be of interest to the group as a whole and, if you are familiar with the members as individuals, to each member.

Arrangements must be made with administrators and staff:

1. Describe and offer the service.
2. Agree on a regular schedule.
3. Outline criteria for inclusion in the group.
4. Request a consistent contact staff person.
5. Arrange for staff assistance in gathering the group.
6. Request a quiet room for the meetings.

Weekly meetings are desirable in order to overcome as much memory loss as possible. A group of six to ten individuals is preferable.

Once the preliminaries have been taken care of, the first session consists of explaining the process and using reading selections chosen for their ice-breaking potential.

Set the atmosphere. Seating all members facing you, placing a table between, and standing in front of the group is not conducive to bibliotherapy. You will have a "class," most of them asleep. Since many people are in wheelchairs or have walkers, placing members in a circle with no barriers between people, and as close as possible to each other for hearing purposes, is most appropriate for conversation. The idea is for the group eventually to have an identity of its own, and for the bibliotherapist to be just one more member.

Copies of selections *in large print* are provided for each person in the group. The material is usually read once by the bibliotherapist clearly, loudly, and slowly. It may be read several more times by members of the group. Discussion takes place after each reading. During the discussion, personal responses to each reading are solicited, reminiscence is encouraged, and experiences are shared.

### Two Special Aims

Two aims of the bibliotherapy process are important to consider when thinking about forming a group and its development.

*Intimacy* must be developed in the bibliotherapy group. The group leader must have a firm image of each group member. Group members should also have some awareness of each other as unique individuals.

*Stimulation* of mental processes and emotional response are basic goals of bibliotherapy. Reading material, initial motivation, and therapeutic direction come from the group leader. Without the interest and increasing excitement of group members, however, discussion will not happen. It is anticipated, too, that as group identity grows, the group will motivate itself and give direction to the discussion.

Keeping these two objectives, in particular, in mind, it is important when forming a group to consider how large or small it should be and what the structure of the leader/group relationship will be.

### Group Structure

I have worked with groups of from four to fifteen people. The optimum range for a bibliotherapy group is around six to eight people. Larger groups become unwieldy; not everyone gets the attention he or she may desire. In large groups there may be a greater range of capabilities. The needs of the confused and disabled can become a serious distraction for the rest of the group. The facility and increased tempo of the alert can be intimidating for the less able; they are left behind.

The group must, however, be large enough to supply the energy to produce results. A group of four people plus the group leader may never grow. The group leader may remain just that and find the process caught in the pattern of reading and asking and answering questions. Real personal conversation may never take place unless each of those four individuals is dynamic and exceptional. This is rare.

A great deal of work goes into a bibliotherapy session. Count on an average of two hours preparation time per one-hour session. (If a bibliotherapist has several similar groups, the single preparation time may be spread over several sessions.) This does not include the preliminary work of arranging for the service and gathering a beginning collection of materials. A decision must be made, when working with a group, whether the investment in preparation and in managing a group that is too large or too small is paying off for the group and its individual members.

Here are a few ways to solve problems of group size. If a group is too small to really get started, it is possible to encourage group members to bring friends or roommates who might be interested. Generally, the group is formed from individuals recommended by activity directors, who have their own criteria for selecting participants. There may be many others in a convalescent or retirement facility who would benefit from and enjoy the group. It is possible, in most facilities, for the bibliotherapist to seek out new participants by describing the reading discussion group at a large-group activity or by making the rounds of rooms during a library book delivery or with the activity director. A simple request that the activity director bring more people may suffice to maintain a group that is otherwise too small to justify the service expense.

A large group can be restructured if it proves to be unmanageable as it is. A simple solution is to split the group into two separate groups, scheduled separately. This, of course, requires making decisions about who will be in which group. Does the bibliotherapist decide or do the group members? What will be the deciding factors for membership in either group and how will understanding of those affect each individual?

Another method of handling large groups is to use co-leaders. This structure was used for some groups in San Rafael, California (Allen and O'Dell 1981). There are a number of advantages to co-leadership:

- Two can gather a group in facilities where staff is unable or unwilling to assist.

- In high-stress periods the group and the facilitators need the extra support. We experienced this during the sudden closure of a local residential care facility. We were thankful there were two of us to help the group with the feelings that arose.

- The energy of two bibliotherapists can maintain a large group and its varied needs.

- In groups where hearing, sight, and speech disabilities are many, the two facilitators become a communication system.

- When transition from one facilitator to another is necessary, co-leading between the two can soften the impact.

- Having another bibliotherapist to share the process and one's own personal responses to it is a valuable resource for stimulating new ideas and reducing tensions.

## Criteria for Inclusion

The people who have been in my groups have ranged from those who walk in on their own and are avid, educated readers with little obvious disability or illness to people who are wheeled in, others who are nearly deaf and blind, and some with a very tenuous grasp on the present.

There are a number of very small, human steps one can take to deal with the problems that arise with the confused and the disabled; these will be discussed later in the chapter.

If the process is intended to serve those in need, then eligibility criteria should be minimal. I have not yet denied anyone inclusion in any of my groups. I have, in fact, included people who have not been recommended by staff. The chronically disruptive may be impossible to work with, however; I have had none in any of my groups, but this is something that may have to be considered.

## Group Work Phases

In my experience, the effort to work toward set goals with the skills and attitudes requisite to that effort must respond to the stages through which the group appears to move in evolving an identity.

These phases may vary in length depending on the group. Some groups may seem never to move along, yet others seems to fall into place immediately. Phases overlap, repeat, regress.

**Getting-Acquainted Phase.** Some time must be spent getting to know each group member. This takes place in the group with everyone taking part and making discoveries. This is accomplished, in part, through selection of material that will, if one is to respond to it, require some sharing of self. The skill of the bibliotherapist in responding to nonverbal cues and in listening facilitates this process.

For some time now the song "Getting to Know You" has been a theme song for my personal therapeutic model of bibliotherapy. It is important to concentrate on the members as individuals: where are they from, what is their family like, what are their interests, are they from the city or the country, what kinds of work have they done, what hobbies have they had, and so on?

It may be helpful to make up a profile on each person to reinforce what has been learned. These facts about people are the tools of future sessions. See Figure 32-1 for an example of a mid-year group summary, which includes profiles of group members.

**Exploring Phase.** As the group progresses, one hopes that what is discussed in one session will lead to the next session's material and discussion. What interests the group members, what touches them in the material, is the direction to take.

When the bibliotherapist brings the appropriate material and asks the right questions, individual members reveal themselves not only to the bibliotherapist but to everyone else in the group. People are amazed when they learn that someone they have passed in the hall hundreds of times lived in the same city or likes the same

This group has become complacent and nonparticipatory. I really have no idea whether it is just a mood or whether it is a result of my skills inadequacy. I find myself talking more than I would like. I find them reluctant to share reactions or talk at all. When I request suggestions, they do not have any. They are a large, diverse group with differing interests and capabilities that must be addressed.

**B. M.**  Youngest member of the group. Quite sharp. Can handle just about any subject.

**Mrs. A**  Apparently self-taught. Is capable and interested in a more sophisticated, intellectual discussion. Very intelligent but somewhat shy. Has recently become withdrawn. Very soft voice. Incapacity of others bothers her.

**Mrs. B**  Girlish. Has wonderful childhood memories. Very soft voice. Focuses on enjoyment and pleasure. Sometimes becomes emotional, cries.

**Mrs. C**  Somewhat confused. Very hard-of-hearing. Focuses on phrases that touch her. Falls asleep sometimes.

**Mrs. L**  Moderately confused. Not open. Repeats a great deal but will occasionally, suddenly, momentarily offer an open, insightful utterance. Somewhat negative—stereotypically Scotch. Is hung up on Scotland. May be illiterate.

**A. C.**  Very emotional. Often refuses to come. Gets very depressed. Cries easily. A very real, caring person who had a great enjoyment of life. May have been spoiled as a child and is now neglected. Underestimates her capabilities. Her father was editor of a major local newspaper.

**Mrs. C**  Sometimes sits in. Speech problem? Don't know much about her. Seems to like to listen.

**Mrs. K**  Seems to be very disoriented. Can't get her to participate. Falls asleep a lot.

**Mrs. P**  Falls asleep a lot. Very shy. Quiet voice. Appears to be very intelligent. Hesitant to participate.

**Mrs. Y**  Very nice person. Occasionally depressed. Wants to take part, belong.

**Mrs. R**  Very shy and quiet; unassuming.

**Mrs. V**  Never tells you much about herself. Everything is wonderful, beautiful, lovely, cute, nice. Very happy-go-lucky—can't handle deterioration of others. Openly expresses her embarrassment, anger, disgust.

**Mrs. W**  Has sat in sometimes. Aloof from the others. Very angry and bitter. Conscious of status. Likes attention.

**Mrs. O**  Beginning to get confused; repeats. Wants the world to be good. Means well. Annoys some of the others for some reason. Gets lost during a discussion.

**M. L.**  Very down-to-earth person. Her hearing is increasingly deteriorating. Is becoming disoriented and delusion. Is becoming unhappy, depressed, quarrelsome, and emotional.

**Mrs. D**  Appears lucid; then becomes confused. Falls asleep. Cries a great deal. Does not really participate.

**D. P.**  Is not really part of the group but wheels herself in frequently. Has often tried to disrupt the group and a nurse usually takes her out. Have recently made subtle attempts to begin to include her. Can be quite belligerent but I have a feeling that there is little behind it. Get the impression that she is quite lonely but her pride and anger get in the way of making friends. Can be totally in a world of her own and then again totally lucid and intelligent. I began to give her copies of the selections as I left, if she would take them. If she is unpleasant, I give it back to her and she takes it well. She initially refused the offerings. Then she would take them but not without a nasty remark. Finally, she takes them during the group, says "thank you," wheels her chair up to listen to the reading, then wheels away when the discussion starts. I think there is hope if the effort is kept very subtle and tentative. Let her make the decision.

FIGURE 32–1. *Bibliotherapy group mid-year summary.*

kinds of flowers or did the same kind of work as they did. They begin to talk to each other automatically. They begin to feel a sense of camaraderie. They begin to trust.

I think of this stage as the "exploring stage," which actually does not end until the group ends. Group identity grows, emotions are revealed more, strengths are discovered and affirmed, interests are shared, and commonalities are strengthened. More direct questions can be used at this point. Trust has been built and people are more willing to share openly. At this point, too, the resources of group members can be relied on. If a picture of flowers is being passed around the group and someone asks what variety they are, rather than giving the answer yourself, direct the question to the person in the group who is a gardener. Let that person have the spotlight. If someone is remembering a difficult event of the past, acknowledge the feelings; then ask if someone else has had a similar experience and how they handled it.

Exploring, sharing, and affirming is the life of bibliotherapy, and these activities continue throughout the life of the group. There are endless avenues to travel, forward and backward. The pleasure for the bibliotherapist lies in the discoveries made about the people in the group. Selecting material is a challenge. What can I find on that subject? What will get Mrs. C interested? What will help Mr. A to see his own humor? What memories will reveal Mrs. K's accomplishments to her? What materials will stimulate those memories? Where can I find something on the railroad days? Is there something other than reading material that I can bring to the meeting that will have meaning to the members?

**Closure Phase.** There is one last phase in group work, and it is the most difficult to confront. This is closure.

- Closure can occur for positive reasons—because the group has served its purpose and another group has need—or it can occur because of loss of funding or closing of a facility or some other less-than-wished-for circumstances.

- Closure can be an experience that celebrates growth and independence and it can be a time of sad goodbyes.

- Closure is, in any case, a time when full uses of resources is necessary. Co-leading can be helpful if both leaders are familiar to the group. In the closure phase, the attention reverts back to the bibliotherapist, who must reinforce strongly the resources that were discovered during the relationship.

Closure means leaving everyone with the feeling of what they have gained: friendship, self, and independence.

When intimacy has grown and a relationship has value and meaning, it is difficult for both parties to say goodbye. The groups of which I have been a part were ongoing groups meeting every week at the same time for the same activity. That activity is designed to open people to each other. When the time comes to end the group relationship, feelings can be intense and many.

The intensity of feeling and the need for attention to the process of closure is directly related to the degree to which group identity has grown. Groups that are little past a formal discussion are more easily ended than those in which real friendships and mutual support have grown. The loss is felt less in the former.

In bibliotherapy with the elderly, closure is an important issue. Loss is one of the most important aspects of the aging process. Most members of any group have experienced and will continue to experience many endings.

In my view, closure is best seen as a combination of addressing problematic feelings and exploring the positive, growth aspects of endings. The process evolves out of the relationship between the group leader and group members.

### Problems to Anticipate

Bibliotherapy is largely spontaneous and creative. After selecting reading material, the discussion is ultimately the responsibility of the group. Reaching goals can be difficult. Add to this the variety of problems that may arise. In dealing with problems, the key words are "common sense."

**Silence.** Many of us find silence very uncomfortable. We fill it in with chatter. Long silences can be excruciating. As a bibliotherapist, I begin to imagine: "They're bored. I've failed them." It is helpful to remember that, in working with the elderly, the pace is slower. What seems like a very long silence is for most of the group a relatively short time. This can be a time of rest, to think and collect oneself, to remember. Let it be.

I am a talker. I still find silences uncomfortable. I take the lead, fill in the gaps. A friend and colleague once suggested that I try going to a group, reading the selection, and sitting back without another word. I tried it. There was some initial confusion but it was by and large one of the best group meetings I've ever experienced. The group took responsibility and had a wonderful conversation that continued as the session ended.

The group is not there for the bibliotherapist; the bibliotherapist is there for the group. Beware of being on stage, of teaching.

**Emotional and Cognitive Problems.** You may find a variety of emotional and cognitive problems among group members. Strong emotions are often difficult to deal with. In developmental bibliotherapy, the group leader is most likely a librarian without credentials for counseling anyone. Intense outbursts may require the assistance of facility staff. Compassion and honesty are important when emotions arise.

While bibliotherapy is designed to promote enjoyment and celebration of life and relationships, problematic feelings of depression, despair, and anger do come up. They cannot be ignored or brushed aside. To do so is a breach of trust and reduces the practice of bibliotherapy and its goals to nothing more than formal recreational programming.

All emotions are acknowledged and named. Questions are unnecessary. These are the honest feelings of an individual. Like property, they will be shared or not at the discretion of that person. A simple "You seem agitated (or whatever is apparent) today" will suffice. Again, it is not the object of developmental bibliotherapy to probe.

If, however, someone begins to cry, it is important to stop and ask what the problem is. Sometimes the selection touches a sensitive area and can be a purge. Sometimes the outburst has no relationship to the reading or the discussion.

A held hand and an empathetic ear may bring the person slowly back to the group. Occasionally the person wants to be alone and is supported in leaving the group.

Withdrawn members may be consistently shy and reserved. They should be encouraged to participate. Interest in them must be clear. It is not wise, however, to insist. Perhaps they will take part in time. Withdrawal in a normally gregarious person is approached, gently, with concern. Asking shows regard and interest. Again, the individual's privacy is respected.

The group can help with all of this by individually sharing experiences, by comforting, by empathizing, and by showing their presence and support.

**Anger.**  Anger is accepted within limits. It is treated as an honest emotion to be acknowledged. When it becomes disagreeable in the bibliotherapist's estimation, a clear message as to boundaries is given. "Mrs. Y, you may not speak that way to Mr. C in the group meeting. Everyone is treated with respect during the group meeting." When anger becomes uncontrollable or breaks out into blows, the staff is needed. The group will often censor undesirable behavior.

**Illiteracy.**  There is an occasional illiterate person in a group. This is not always made known to you by staff. The signs are refusal to read accompanied by leafing through the material while reading is taking place, giving the material to someone else, complaining of headaches, forgetting to bring glasses (often there are no glasses). If there is a suspicion that someone can't read, ask the staff. Do not confront the person in group or otherwise. Accept the situation and find other skills that the person can contribute.

**Confusion and Repetition.**  Bystanders have been most surprised by the fact that we work with *confused people* and *people who repeat* consistently. The bibliotherapy process, as well as the specific topic for discussion and the physical reading material on paper, can have an effect on confusion and repetition. Allen and O'Dell (1981) note that reading and thinking reawakened the intellectual capacities of group members and that members were supportive of others' efforts, particularly when their own were appreciated by the group. Relying on the resources of the group and on individuals within the group strengthens those called on and creates a general atmosphere and expectation that we are all together for each other and everyone has something to offer.

A specific example of how one case of repetition was handled will show how very simple steps can lead to double benefits.

*Case example 1:* There was a woman in one of my groups who said almost nothing but "I'm from Scotland."* Her limited but continuous repertoire made conversation with her next to impossible. This, in turn, resulted in her exclusion from conversation. When she was brought into the group, given the reading material, and asked questions, the response from the group was: "Oh, don't bother with her. All she can say is 'I'm from Scotland.'" After a period of time, I found myself losing interest in working with her. I had to get her past Scotland to at least one more statement. That was all I felt I could hope for, although I felt that she could do much more.

I decided to plan an entire session around Mrs. L. I found recordings of bagpipe music and Scottish folk songs, collected picture books on Scotland, and compiled a brief outline of the country of the kind one might find in an encyclopedia: history, agriculture, industry, geography, and so on. I knew that information of this sort was of interest to the group from previous sessions on travel, although it is not conducive to personal discussion. I did very little but take the material to the meeting, play the records, and ask a couple of preliminary questions after reading the information about Scotland. Mrs. L immediately began talking in detail about Scotland. The group asked her questions. She was the center of attention. She glowed. And, the rest of the group gained a real sense of the reason she repeated the fact that she was from Scotland so often. In looking at the books, they exclaimed, "Look at that green — no wonder she talks about it so much."

This very simple effort accomplished a great deal: Mrs. L became a part of the group, she was given much-needed attention and appreciation, and she could converse, at least temporarily. While Mrs. L did slip back into her repetition later, she could take part in discussion if she was given the nudge. Her daughter happened to visit during a later session and was amazed to find her responding to a question I had asked about a poem. She said she hadn't known that her mother was able to respond.

**Extraneous Noises and Disruptions.** Noises and disruptions are an inevitable problem in convalescent hospitals. Medication has to be administered on time. Busy staff schedules require showers and elimination reports to be completed when time is available. Every effort should be made to eliminate as many disruptions as possible; but if these unavoidably take place during the group, it's something that must be tolerated.

It is desirable to have a room with a door that you can close, although this is not always possible. Collecting the group in a corner can help. A screen would give privacy. Scheduling a time when vacuums and floor polishers are off is essential. After all efforts have been made, what noise is left has to be tolerated.

I have held groups in corridors with vacuum cleaners running, near doorways with staff going in and out, and where garbage is taken out. I have had relatives visit and take someone out of the group. These are not the best situations but they are livable. One can make efforts to resolve the situation, but for one reason or another it is not always possible to have the best of all possible worlds. Tolerating situations such as these requires an inner remembering of the purpose of the process: "I am here for the group, not for myself." Sometimes the distractions can even be useful in the group as comic relief or as a reminder that circumstances are not always as we wish them but we manage to continue on.

Disruptions within the group must be confronted as they arise. Chronic yellers and hitters cannot be in the group. Sleeping is accepted. Sometimes someone will wake the sleeper; sometimes not.

---

*This behavior is called perseveration and can be frustrating to handle.

One of the biggest fears for the bibliotherapist is that there will be *no discussion*. It does happen. Many groups of elderly people require a great deal of the bibliotherapist initially. Every response has to be pulled out of each person. There is no interaction. This can be draining and disheartening. Keep in mind that many of the participants have not been asked their opinion in some time. They're out of practice. It may take some time. Then again there are those groups that just click and flow very nicely. They balance each other.

## Important Components of Bibliotherapy

**Reading Materials.**   The basis of the process —and that which distinguishes it from other therapies—is the reading material. Selection is of major importance and requires time: initial time before meetings begin to collect a basic store of reading selections and continuous time spent in planning for each subsequent meeting.

Reading selections are chosen to facilitate reaching goals. There are a number of criteria for selecting materials to ensure their appropriateness.

Materials should be *brief*, accommodating the attention span and available energy of the group members. One or two pages are the limit. For this reason poems and very short excerpts from prose works and perhaps one-act plays are most appropriate. A long piece with particular appeal can be broken into sections. Each fragment can then be read and discussed separately.

Wyatt Cooper's *Families: A Memoir and a Celebration* (1975) describes a large family reunion that stirs very pleasant memories. Rose Butter Browne's *Love My Children* (1969) includes lovely, detailed memories of her grandparents' home and the delicious meals served there. I have a favorite subject that I have shared with several groups. I have extracted information on Grandma Moses and examples of her writing from art books (Kallir 1946, 1973). I take with me to the meeting a book with color plates of Grandma Moses' paintings to show to everyone. The material and the prints are magic. The result is a clear demonstration of the contribution and achievement that can be made in late life.

Reading selections should be *simple and understandable*. Clear, everyday language and concrete images are most effective. The purpose of bibliotherapy is to provide literature with which to identify and to which to respond. Literary contrivances and difficult vocabulary can be intimidating and distracting.

The reading matter should be *enjoyable*. Familiar images and events are important. Style and subject matter that are distasteful or offensive to the group members will destroy the possibility of discussion.

Some *emotional content* is necessary. This may be found in a subject or theme, such as family, that is of importance to group members. It may be an actual statement of feeling: "Rain makes me sad." The intent is that at some point discussion of feelings will take place.

The content of the reading selections is very important and can be used to reach goals. An effective way of getting to know people is to find out their feelings and thoughts on particular subjects. Responses to themes—family, home, church, work, first car, marriage—pinpoint interests. Vocations—gardening, childhood games, sewing and needlework, sports, cooking, and so on—are very interesting subjects.

As the group progresses, the content of the reading material can address more specific, issue-oriented themes. Without asking direct questions, a great deal of information can be revealed. The poem "Of Poems" opens the avenue to a discussion on creativity and all of the unique ways people have of contributing to beauty and pleasure in the world.

*Of Poems*
We *all* create. You turn to silk a
Piece of wood whose symmetry enchants
Us. With flour, milk, and love (the
Selfsame love you bring to carpentry),
She molds her cakes, confections,
Each a perfect thing, her own,
Unique. Her sister makes the stranger
Smile with honeycombs of gentle words,
With wisdoms of the heart. There are
As many "poems" as there is love.*
        Maureen Cannon (1980)

---

*This is the poem as I found it published in *Ladies Home Journal*, but after corresponding with Ms. Cannon, I learned that the original includes the following first line: "Beloved, listen, don't you see."

This area of exploration not only makes it possible to focus on each individual's talents but is an opportunity to encourage an openness to all of the many talents and diversity in the group. This particular subject, creativity, can also be a means of introducing new activities in the group, such as writing, drawing, and so forth.

The content of a reading selection can be a stimulus for reminiscence. Remembering a lovely garden once cared for can produce many emotional responses: pride in giving beauty to the world, sadness at the loss, pleasure in recalling the beauty of the flowers. These are acknowledged, accepted, and shared with the group. Allen and O'Dell (1981) note that in selecting the themes of the reading material, they allow room for feelings, rather than dictating them.

Children's literature can be very useful because it fits the above criteria. In addition, it is fresh in outlook and addresses emotional issues with an attitude of discovery and surprise.

Selection of materials can be as exciting and rewarding as the discussion itself. I reached a point with a few of my groups when I wanted to demonstrate to them that each of them had something of value to offer—that they could contribute to another.

During this period, I pulled together the session on Grandma Moses described earlier in this chapter, through which I tried to show that old age does not preclude individual achievement. I collected wonderful recipes from people. I mostly wanted to discover something the members could teach me, a craft that isn't practiced as much today as in the past. The idea of passing on something of value from one generation to another was what I had in mind. *Annie and the Old One* (Miles 1971), a children's book, was the inspiration. I remembered that someone had brought a handmade lavender sachet to Irene Burnside's workshop on Group Work With the Elderly. The sachet was unique to me. It was actually dried stalks of lavender flowers bound by a woven casing of lavender satin ribbons. I began a search for instructions or photographs of similar sachets but found no references to them. I finally wrote a letter to Irene, who remembered the sachet but not the person who had brought it to the workshop. In the meantime, I stumbled on an illustration of the sachet in *Back to Basics* (*Reader's Digest* 1981), a copy of which I sent to Irene. In return

Irene sent me one of the sachets, which she happened to find in a thrift store. It was a wonderful surprise.

I have made similar searches on other subjects. If anyone has photographs, illustrated articles, or prose or poetry selections on country fairs, kewpie dolls, or carnival midways, these are subjects that may become a lifelong research for me. (I would appreciate any materials anyone would like to share with me.)

If a particular reading selection falls flat with one group, it does not necessarily mean that it will not work with another. Before discarding any material as unusable, it is advisable to test it two or three times. Some selections just do not work at all. Perhaps the subject is inappropriate, the language unfamiliar, the point of view foreign. It is important to evaluate material as it is used. The criteria for choosing material will then be continuously refined.

The session report form shown in Figure 32–2 is a useful tool for evaluating the effectiveness of reading selections, as well as for assessing whether progress is being made in meeting the goals of bibliotherapy. It provides room to record choice of materials, reasons for the choice, members' responses, and stage of group process.

*The group is used to quiet the disruptive, to encourage the shy, and to give direction to the discussion.* The desired evolution is that the group will acquire its own identity and will choose its own direction. At this point it becomes clear that group members are competent, cooperative, and independent adults.

## REMINISCENCE AND BIBLIOTHERAPY

Reminiscing is thoroughly covered in Part 5 of this book. The reader is referred to Chapters 22 through 26 for overviews of the literature.

Reminiscence is an important activity in bibliotherapy with the elderly. Many of the group members may already be actively reminiscing. The positive focus of bibliotherapy requires discussion topics that are pleasant and interesting. The lives of the institutionalized elderly are severely limited. Much of the best part of their lives is in the past. In addition, for many older people long-term memory is stronger than more recent memory. Finally, topics about the pres-

**SESSION REPORT**

**Date:**

**Place:**

**Facilitator:**

**Times:** Preparation: (a) review of possibilities _____
                                  (b) immediate preparation: _____

          Travel: _____

          Reporting: _____

**Logistics** (incl. staff cooperation; give examples):

**Attendance:**

**Materials:**

A.   Title, Author, Format, Equipment:

B.   Objective(s) in Choosing:

C.   Evaluation:
     Elicited discussion?
     Met objectives?
     Physical factors (format, length, level, etc.)

**Group Process:**

A.   Discussion (brief outline):

B.   Theme (overall, of session):

C.   Interaction (with facilitator, each other):

D.   Phase or Stage in Group Progress (and any specific objectives as
     they develop):

E.   Individuals (brief capsule, in relation to goals—(enjoyment,
     stimulation, self-expression, morale/self-esteem, socialization):

**Facilitator:**

A.   Own Response:

B.   Skills Issues:

**Ideas for Next Time:**

FIGURE 32–2. *Readers' discussion group report form.*

ent and the future often lead to philosophical discussions. This is not the aim of bibliotherapy. Large subjects—such as politics, economics, the future of civilization as we know it—are irresolvable. The likely outcome of such discussions is a feeling of impotence, just the opposite of the goals of bibliotherapy.

Reminiscence is encouraged in bibliotherapy by selecting reading material that is about past events, childhood activities, former life-styles, and so forth. While many group members are convinced that their memories are failing them, memories slip out unconsciously. When this is pointed out and encouraged, memory sometimes improves. The apparent confusion and fantasizing of some group members can be a path to reminiscence. If attention is given to sometimes almost incoherent utterances, an internal effort often takes place to try harder to remember clearly in order to answer questions.

*Case example 2:* One woman in one of my groups, Mrs. B, was very confused, often began speaking while someone else was speaking, and could barely be understood, except for brief phrases that appeared to have no connection with each other. One day, after reading a poem, I heard her say something about a path and water and flowers. There was in my mind an image she had in mind. I turned my attention to her and asked her questions. What did this place look like? Was it some place she once lived? Did she remember where it was? The group was not at all encouraging. The confused babblings of one can be very frightening for others who fear the same fate. She tried very hard and could answer some of my questions. The effort and difficulty were obvious. She seemed to feel good about the effort and pleased that someone cared to know.

I felt a need to confront those who were uncomfortable with this focus on a confused person's utterances. I am not a confronter normally, but my role as a bibliotherapist is to be there for members as individuals and as a group. If Mrs. B is confused, I have a responsibility to her to see if I can help her find clarity. If Mrs. A is uncomfortable listening to Mrs. B's struggle, I have a responsibility to her to help her resolve her discomfort. If the group is to grow in intimacy, I have a responsibility to facilitate understanding between individuals. In this particular case, I simply turned to the few people who had begun to titter and stated that I felt that if someone was willing to listen to the confusion long enough, perhaps Mrs. B would find her way out of it. I hope that this also assured them that I would be there for them if they needed similar assistance.

Support of the weaker frail members of a group is one responsibility of the leader.

Rediscovering the past is rediscovering oneself. Accomplishments, talents, strengths, and individuality are restored. The uniqueness of each group member is acknowledged, shared, and enjoyed.

### SUMMARY

In this chapter I have attempted to define bibliotherapy; how it differs from other therapeutic activities; the techniques of bibliotherapy, particularly those used in working with the elderly; and how reminiscence and bibliotherapy interrelate. I have presented my style and stressed the importance of listening and flexibility.

Bibliotherapy is a human enterprise that cannot be outlined in a rigid, step-by-step fashion because it grows out of the relationship between the people involved.

### EXERCISE 1

Select a period of time, beginning realistically with half an hour, or a particular situation and focus your attention on your normal pattern of conversation. Where is your attention while you are speaking? While you are listening? Then think about the goals of bibliotherapy, make notes to yourself on improvements you can make in your listening habits in view of those goals, and begin to put those improvements into practice. A hint: Our listening is largely unconscious. To be conscious of your attention while listening, focus a portion of your attention on one part of your body and its sensation: your left foot or your right hand, for example. When you've lost touch with your foot or hand, you've probably also stopped listening.

## EXERCISE 2

For those who feel a lack of confidence as a group leader or who cannot seem to get the feel for the difference between facilitating and leading, try the approach that was suggested to me. Prepare for your group; read the selection aloud in the group; then sit back and wait for the conversation to begin. Make an agreement with yourself that you will speak only if asked a question and that you will keep your answer brief. In most cases, your response can be a question directed back to the person who originally asked you the question. The idea is to move the responsibility and the attention to the group and away from you. The following are examples, but you will need to think of others.

*Group member:* Are you going to say anything?
*Bibliotherapist:* No.

*Group member:* What does he mean here?
*Bibliotherapist:* What do you think he means? [or] What does it mean to you?

*Group member:* Aren't you going to help us?
*Bibliotherapist:* Not right now. If you need it—we'll see.

## REFERENCES

Allen, B., and L. O'Dell. 1981. *Bibliotherapy and the public library: The San Rafael experience.* Sacramento: California State Library.

Browne, R. B. 1969. *Love my children, An autobiography.* New York: Meredith Press.

Butler, R. N. 1974. Successful aging and the role of the life review. *Journal of the American Geriatrics Society* 22(12): 529–35 (December).

Cannon, M. 1980. Of poems. *Ladies Home Journal* 97(8): 62 (August).

Cooper, W. 1975. *Families: A memoir and a celebration.* New York: Harper & Row.

Kallir, O. 1946. *Grandma Moses, American primitive.* New York: Dryden Press.

Miles, M. 1971. *Annie and the old one.* Boston: Little, Brown.

*Reader's Digest.* 1981. *Back to basics.* New York: Norton.

Sweeney, D. 1978. Bibliotherapy and the elderly. In *Bibliotherapy soucebook,* ed. R. Rubin. Phoenix, Ariz.: Oryx Press.

## BIBLIOGRAPHY

Adams, E. B. 1979. *Reminiscence and life review in the aged: A guide for the elderly, their families, friends and service providers.* Denton, Tex.: North Texas State University, Center for Studies in Aging.

Brammer, L. M. 1979. *The helping relationship.* Englewood Cliffs, N.J.: Prentice-Hall.

Cannon, M. 1980. Words and wheelchairs. *American Journal of Care for the Aging* 1(1): 61–63 (May–June).

Kemp, C. G. 1979. *Small groups and self-renewal.* New York: Seabury Press.

Merrill, T. 1974. *Discussion topics for oldsters in nursing homes.* Springfield, Ill.: Thomas.

Our versifying friends. *Modern Maturity.* Publication of the American Association of Retired Persons, Washington, D.C. (Each issue of *Modern Maturity* contains this page of readers' works.)

Rubin, R., ed. 1978. *Bibliotherapy sourcebook.* Phoenix, Ariz.: Oryx Press.

## RESOURCES

### Films

Charatan, F. B. 1979. *Management of confusion in the elderly.* Taped course. New Hyde Park, N.Y.: Jewish Institute for Geriatric Care (January).

### Organizations

*Bibliotherapy Discussion Group.* Publishes a newsletter for members; dues are very reasonable. Address: Bibliotherapy Discussion Group, 8532 State Board Road 302 N.W., Gig Harbor, WA 98335.

*National Council on the Aging.* Provides a variety of materials from which reading selections can be made. Address: Senior Center Humanities Program, National Council on the Aging Inc., 600 Maryland Avenue S.W., West Wing 100, Washington, D.C. 20024.

## chapter 33

# A Music Therapist's Perspective

*E. Catherine Moore*

*Music, by its very nature, draws people together for the purpose of intimate, yet ordered, function. . . . It unifies the group for common action, and it is this setting that elicits or changes many extramusicial behaviors.*

<small>E. THAYER GASTON (1968)</small>

<small>FRANK SITEMAN/STOCK, BOSTON</small>

## LEARNING OBJECTIVES

- Discuss how music can be used to influence behavior.
- Discuss the relationship between socialization and music.
- List four guidelines for selection of music.
- Compare and contrast instruments to use in music groups with the elderly.

## KEY WORDS

- Autoharp
- Baritone ukulele
- Body sounds
- Environmental sounds
- Kazoo
- Mood level
- Music-mood matching
- Psychological well-being
- Sensory overload
- Tempo
- Volume

"Music is a universal language." Music hath charms to soothe the savage beast." These clichés reflect our sense of the multiple values of music and of the possibility that music can be manipulated to realize those values. Both statements suggest two of the cornerstones of modern music therapy: Music can nonverbally communicate many things, and music is a mighty tool of subtle persuasion. Figure 33–1 illustrates the scope of music therapy.

Musicality is not limited to a talented few. Everyone has it simply by virtue of being alive. You have absorbed some of music's language because it has been spoken to you psychologically, sociologically, and physiologically since you were a baby. By becoming more aware of what you already know about music, you can learn to use it as an effective tool in working with elderly groups. Perhaps with a little guidance you can avoid some of the mistakes well-intentioned people (musicians included) have unwittingly made when they have used music in clinical settings.

A great many of these mistakes are related to our incorrectly viewing music as something mystical or as something whose only value is that it mysteriously lifts people out of their present unhappy situations. When thought of in this way, music becomes little more than a pacifier that requires no thought, preparation, or know-how for its "soothing charms" to go to work. I encourage you to explore your natural musicality in your group work, but always be aware that more is called for than the mere inclusion of music.

## USING MUSIC TO INFLUENCE BEHAVIOR

People are complex and music is many-faceted. Therefore, their combination is an extremely volatile one. But if you take neither people nor music for granted, it is possible to combine them in such a way as to obtain a *fairly* predictable result.

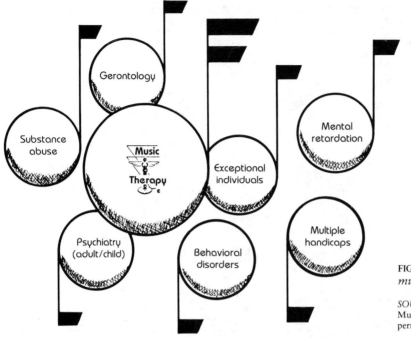

FIGURE 33–1. *The many uses of music therapy.*

SOURCE: National Association for Music Therapy, Inc. Reprinted by permission.

For example, music can be used to affect mood. We instinctively know this and research has documented it (Hevner 1936, 1937). But studies have also revealed that if used improperly, music can have a mood effect opposite to what we would think (more so in a clinical setting than in a normal population). A cheery song with happy lyrics can drive depressed patients deeper into their isolation if it is also fast, loud, brassy, and excessively syncopated. The key to achieving desired mood changes with music is to begin with selections in which the musical elements parallel the patient's psychological level and proceed gradually until the mood is altered (Shatin 1970). This principle of matching music to mood is valid whether you are doing a whole session with music or using it only as an incidental part of your plan, or whether your activity is primarily one of listening or one of active participation in the music.

The reason this principle is so important is that psychological responses to music are closely tied to physiological responses to music. Clinically depressed patients' perceptual sets are such that music in which there is too much going on, too fast, has the effect of triggering a physiological defense reaction, and the result can be a blockage of behavior change. Similarly, music that has too little going on, too slowly, will be out of sync with hyperactive patients. But if we begin where the patients are rather than where we want them to be, we open the communication system between people and music. And it is on the basis of the flow between them that mood—and, consequently, behavior—can be altered.

Tempo is of a paramount importance in selecting music that parallels mood. If the tempo is either too fast or too slow for a patient's needs, the piece is wrong and should be changed. The second-most-critical musical element to consider is rhythm. The rhythmic stimulus value is low when the melody and accompanying lines are simple and smooth. It is high when they are busy and jumpy. Volume (intensity) is also highly important. The lower the mood level or the greater the brain damage, the lower the initial volume should be. Finally, tone quality is one of the more subtle but relevant musical elements to keep in mind. High, shrill, sharp sounds are initially too stimulating for most geriatric patients; low, mellow tones are more appropriate.

You should not regard the manipulation of tempo, rhythm, volume, and tone quality as some kind of magic prescription for curing mental illness. It is not. If it were, life would be simple and neither people nor music would be very interesting. In other words, not even a skilled music clinician can say, "Take two waltzes and call me in the morning." Music is not like a pill that acts on people.

### Increasing Social Skills

People bring to the encounter all their prior experiences with music and the situations and feelings that surrounded those experiences. One of the reasons music is effective therapeutically is that it is the most social of all the arts, and it is precisely the social aspects of life that are the most affected by mental illness and old age (Capurso 1948). Through the use of familiar music, a strange and/or hostile environment can be made to feel safe, with the result that conversation and interaction are less threatening and more easily entered (Dollins 1956). Under the protection of this kind of musical security blanket and with your active intervention as a group leader, interpersonal relationships can be established and fostered. Needless to say, these are of tremendous importance to a group of elderly persons.

In accomplishing increased socialization two factors just mentioned need to be emphasized. First, the use of familiar music is an obvious tactic, but it is seldom fully appreciated. Familiar music has more penetrating power than nonfamiliar music, for the simple but strikingly important reason that people bring more of themselves (psychologically, sociologically, and physiologically) to the encounter. Second, your active involvement in furthering the social process is indispensable in creating a safe environment, aside from the wonders of music. Used properly, familiar music in and of itself can be an effective morale builder, but it becomes a treatment mode only when someone capitalizes on the safety and protection it provides patients.

### Increasing Psychological Well-Being

Music is sound. It is physical vibrations that enter the ear, become electrical energy, and alert the brain. If there is functional hearing present, music cannot be totally shut out. This can be said of all sound, including environmental noise and speech. But music is unique in that it is organized nonverbal sound. The beat and the rhythm of song reach the most primal, basic areas of the brain, energizing the entire nervous system and giving rise to a variety of physiological changes. Consequently, music has the potential to arouse regressed, withdrawn patients who are beyond the reach of verbal communication. It can arouse them whether or not they are consciously listening, but as before, the give-and-take between people and music must be maximized by the use of selections that are familiar to the patients.

The arousal may be strictly physiological, which is therapeutic in itself, but the physiological and sociological may spill over into the psychological, with the result that a disoriented patient is "miraculously" brought into contact with the reality of what is happening in the here-and-now. When this happens, it is the responsibility of the group leader to intervene, making the most of the lucid moment through the use of standard reality orientation methods. We can use music to arouse, but if we give hope to patients and then ignore them as people, we have inadvertently approached the borders of cruelty.

## LISTENING ACTIVITIES

Listening to music is equivalent, physiologically, to being exposed to a great multitude of sensory stimuli (Grunewald 1953). Consequently, with geriatric patients there is a danger of sensory overload. If music is being used as a part of the environment—in a dayroom, for instance—it should be peppered with silences approximately equal to the length of the musical stimulation. This can be done easily and precisely with taped selections; but if a radio is being used (tuned to a good FM station, needless to say), it should be played only intermittently. This also prevents the music from becoming part of the very monotony it was intended to break. Another plan using this principle is to open a session with several recorded selections in order to stimulate a group gradually, progress to some type of active-participation activity, and return to recorded music to taper off the session. Sound and silence can and should also be a part of sessions billed strictly as listening when an alert group leader is active in furthering music's social and psychological stimulation.

On the technical side, strive for the best sound equipment you can manage. Poor-quality sound is an irritant, especially for the aged. If possible, use equipment that allows you to regulate the bass and treble. Keep the bass high, especially for those with hearing losses. Control the volume constantly, keeping it reasonably level. Depressed and brain-damaged patients, even those who are hard-of-hearing, can react very strongly and negatively to increases in intensity. Another tactic to avoid this extreme reaction is to place sensitive patients far from the speakers. Pretaping the material you choose allows you to make advance decisions on volume and bass-treble settings, thereby allowing you greater freedom during the session. Cassette recorders are perfectly good for these purposes, provided they can be hooked up to larger speakers.

### Making Selections

In making selections, be continually aware of the principle of music-mood matching, especially at the beginning of a session. After the group has been warmed up, the stimulus value of the music can be increased to the level of polkas, rinky-tink, piano, and the like.

Vocal music should be selected with care because it may frustrate those who are hard-of-hearing more than instrumental music. However, this is less of a factor with songs that are familiar enough to the patients that they can remember the words automatically without having to rely on their hearing.

Try to honor individual tastes and ethnic backgrounds as much as possible, but enforce the idea that there is no one kind of music that is better than another. Beware lest certain members of the group build barriers with their favorite music, turning the "universal language" into a war cry.

There are no hard-and-fast rules for determining which songs will be familiar to a group because musical exposure and preference are very much an individual matter, not simply a function of age. *However, a general rule to follow is to make selections from the earlier years of a patient's life—that is, the childhood, dating, and young-married years.* But remember that music from a patient's early years has great penetrating power and therefore must be used with great discretion.

Members of your group will identify with music up through the 1920s and possibly early 1930s. However, those who have been actively interested in music may know songs into the 1950s, particularly Broadway material. It is often hard to find the date a song came out. In these cases your group is the best source for the information you need. Use them. It is another way of making listening a participation activity.

In addition to regional, folk, pop, and musical comedy songs, possibilities for selections exist among spirituals, college songs, Army and Navy songs, patriotic songs, the light classics, and some classical material. Strive for variety in a program by using at least several of these different categories of music.

The principle of choosing familiar music does not always have to be interpreted to mean specific songs already known to your patients. Depending on your purposes, it can also mean any music that does not sound dissonant. Within reason, it is possible to challenge your group and build familiarity through repetition. This is especially true for fairly high functioning groups. For example, the sound track from any current, well-known song could be used as background music while you are getting the group assembled. After several weeks they will be familiar with it and will have a link to the present-day world outside. Depending on your group, you may or may not want to spend some time talking about the singing portions of the record. If you do, let the eye help the ear and be sure to have the words printed large so that everyone can read them.

### Finding Records

Most public libraries have a variety of records that can be checked out, and music librarians are usually most helpful. Check with them on whether their pop standards are listed separately by decades. Keep your eye out for sing-along records, but be forewarned that it may take several trips to the library to get them because they are extremely popular. You might also inquire about recordings of flute, recorder, guitar, and French horn materials. The instruments have tone qualities well suited to geriatric problems, and if you choose the selections wisely (keeping the pitch level fairly low), they are good possibilities for building familiarity.

Discount stores and drugstores often carry reprints of old records that you might like to add to your own library in addition to using them with your group. There are also several good collections put out by *Reader's Digest* and similar special offers of old favorites by other companies that you might like to use. Or if you should happen to have friends who teach elementary or junior high school, check with them on what their music departments have. There are several fine record sets compiled for educational use that contain old folk and spiritual material not generally found in recorded form. These educational sets also include some light classics that could be useful because they have often been chosen for the collection specifically for their brevity and sparkle.

Keep all selections reasonably short and listen to them beforehand for the stimulus value of the tempo, rhythm, intensity, and tone qualities. But do not be discouraged if this is not always as simple as it sounds. For example, several times I have carefully weighed stimulus values and chosen songs that I found soothing, only to discover that the group thought them sad. When such things happen, try to analyze as well as you can why they occurred, and chalk it up to experience. It simply attests that the combination of people and music will always be full of surprises, no matter how well we plan.

## PARTICIPATION ACTIVITIES

It is not necessary to have a music degree to lead the music participation activities that follow. What is required is a realization that making music, both vocally and instrumentally, is normal, natural, and fun. E. Thayer Gaston (1968, 7), founder of the National Association for Music Therapy, says, "Music is human behavior." It follows, therefore, that mistakes are part and parcel of the bargain. So just plunge ahead, mistakes or not. It will set a good example for your group and free them to participate and make their own mistakes.

### Singing for Fun and Therapy

One of the many benefits of group singing is that it encourages deeper breathing than normal. In fact, it is a good idea to begin a session with a few relaxation and breathing exercises in order to stress this. They can be picked up from any yoga book and adapted for the group.

Facial muscles both reflect and affect mood. Exercises that relax the eye, neck, and jaw muscles can be introduced into a session under the guise of improving the pronunciation of lyrics and loosening up the vocal mechanism but for the actual purpose of changing mood. Peppering a session with face exercises (such as sticking out the tongue, rolling the eyes, squeezing the face, and flapping the lips (adds levity and variety, embodies the sound-silence principle, and also places singing in a realm totally different from what your group has probably ever experienced in the past. In other words, the more stress placed on matters other than the quality of the singing, the fewer inhibitions your group is likely to have about participating fully.

Regressed patients have special needs that are best met by choosing only those songs that are *most* familiar to them and that have repetitive lines giving them a chance to join in. For example, the lines "doo-dah, doo-dah" in "Camptown Races" are repeated throughout the song. Or you could choose a song with a simple chorus, like "Sweet Betsy from Pikes' " "too-rah-loo, oo-rah-loo, oo-rah-lee-ay." I usually repeat this chorus twice because it is so short that some group members do not get a chance to sing the first time through.

**Easy Accompaniments.** The simpler an accompaniment is, the better it is. Accompaniments that are too fancy can squelch participation because a group will listen rather than sing. Experience has taught me that it is more fun and spontaneous to operate without any instrumental accompaniment whatever, which is about as simple as you can get. A group can get going just by your singing confidently and acting as

ANTHONY J. SKIRLICK

*Music is an important part of the programming at this senior center. Participants with any musical background should be encouraged to express those abilities.*

though you know what you are doing. (Notice I did not say that you had to know what you are doing. Just act like it!) If you get into the fun of singing, the group will follow and no one will notice if you hit a wrong note. On the other hand, a leader who sounds like an opera singer will end up giving a performance to a silent group.

Working without any instrumental accompaniment opens the way to making full use of body and environmental sounds as a kind of informal accompaniment. By body sounds I mean clapping, slapping knees and elbows, stamping the feet, and so on. Environmental sounds include rapping table tops, geriatric chair trays, and other objects around the room that strike you as good sound sources. These sounds are so natural that the group will spontaneously imitate what you do. They fit easily and naturally into fun songs like "Show Me the Way to Go Home" simply by making a sound— any sound—at the ends of the phrases. For example:

Show me the way to go home, ##
'Cause I'm tired and I wanna go to bed, ##
I had a little drink about an hour ago,
And it went right to my head. ##
Wherever I may roam, ##
On land, or sea, or foam, ##
You can always hear me singing this song, #
Show me the way to go home. ##

Vary the sounds as you see fit and in accordance with the physical motions that are easiest and/or most beneficial for the group members. You may have to help some members find ways to make sounds; if two hands do not work, one hand and a table top will do fine.

It may or may not be possible for your group to accompany themselves by clapping a steady beat. Do not stress clapping if it is hard for them, because they can often tell when they are off the beat, and this provides negative feedback. I have found that swaying or nodding to and fro is a good substitute for steady clapping. To and fro seems to work better than left to right, perhaps because people can tell when they are off in a group that is swaying from side to side, but with a forward-back motion there is little in their past experience for them to judge who is "right" and who is "wrong." Consequently, they are freed to feel the rhythm in their own way and not be dominated by the group. This technique is also handy because body sounds do not fit all songs, such as ballads or love songs, but swaying can be done with just about anything.

If you prefer some kind of instrumental accompaniment and are working with a co-leader, one of you can handle the instrument and the other the singing. A guitar is a good possibility because with it you can move about the room encouraging participation. However, if neither of you plays an instrument, one of you might consider taking up the baritone ukulele. It is a good all-around social instrument, has a full sound, is cheaper than a guitar, and has only four strings to master rather than the guitar's six.

Autoharps are even easier to learn how to play. All they involve is pushing a button and strumming; and by putting a guitar strap on the back, you can also have the mobility of a guitar or ukulele. When kept in tune, they have a nice sound and are appropriate for most folk material and hymns or for any song that has no more than three different chords. There are small autoharps and larger ones, with the price varying accordingly. The ones with 12 to 15 buttons are the best for your purposes because they allow you to play in several keys.

The ability to accompany in different keys is important because it enables you to choose the one in which the melody goes neither too high nor too low. Consult a musician friend to decide on the keys in which the vocal range of the songs you choose will not exceed the C above middle C. Our vocal cords lose elasticity with age and breath support weakens with illness, making anything higher than that discouraging for most elderly people.

**Songbooks and Selections.** There are a variety of songbooks available in good music stores. Ask for the ones compiled according to decade or for what are sometimes called community songbooks. You do not need the ones with beautiful piano arrangements and large music manuscript, so generally the cheaper a songbook is, the better it is for your purposes. Keep the materials you work from during a session as simple as possible so that they are easy to use. All you need are the words, the chords, and the decade the song came out. If you are working without accompaniment, you may want to jot down the beginning note in the key you have chosen and then use a pitch pipe for the first couple of sessions you lead. Before long you will have a general feel for the best pitch level and will be able to work without the pitch pipe.

In choosing songs that come from the decades you have decided to emphasize, the date written at the bottom of a page of music may or may not be helpful; if a song's copyright has been renewed, only the later date appears. Also, many times no date is given at all. As is true when choosing records, your group is the best source of the information you need.

You may or may not want to use song sheets, depending on the size and type of group. In general, be sure that you have enough and that they are sturdy and printed in large letters—possibly even in broad, felt-tipped pen for group members with visual difficulties. For a small regressed group, print no more than one song on a page and be sure to collect old song sheets before handing out new ones. Co-leaders come in handy in this regard; otherwise song sheets can seem to be more trouble than they are worth. However, they can be helpful not only in making the lyrics available to everyone but also in giving some patients the security of having something to hold onto. If you should decide to work without song sheets, an old but effective method is simply to call out the lyrics, line by line, as the group sings.

Be aware that some songs, such as folk songs, drinking songs, and hymns, have a greater initial sing-along impact than others because they have been part of group-singing experiences in the past. These songs are especially useful at the beginning of a session when the group is getting used to hearing their own voices. After a bit, the members will join just as easily in pop and musical comedy songs that they probably listened to only when they first came out.

Use humorous songs freely. You will find them in books, in memories of your childhood, and in your group's memories. Some of them may even be a trifle racy. Also, you may want to rewrite the lyrics of an old familiar song to add a bit of humor. Clare Schaeffer,* who is a music and reality therapist at the Handmaker Jewish Nursing Home in Tucson, Arizona, does this so well. My favorite is one she wrote to the tune "You Tell Me Your Dream." Her version pokes fun at the one-upmanship often seen in nursing homes over who is the worst off:

You tell me your pains. I'll tell you mine.
Count all your sicknesses—they don't add up
   to mine.
Arthritis, phlebitis, neuritis, bad eyes and
   heart trouble too.
So stop your belly-aching. 'cause I suffer much
   more than you!

The criteria for choosing sing-along songs are basically the same as those for choosing records. Be alert to the stimulus values of the tempo and rhythm of the song itself. Build up to the highly stimulating songs and then back off. If you are using accompaniment, be sure that it does not obscure the beat, complicate the rhythms, or become too loud or sharp.

### Instrumental Participation

Using instruments to enable geriatric patients to take an active part in music has advantages because it is strictly nonverbal, while group singing may exclude some people. Particularly for aphasic patients, it is useful to combine listening, singing, and instruments, so that they can be included as much as possible.

**Rhythm Instruments.** One of the problems in setting up an instrumental program with geriatric patients is the scarcity of money for instruments. Perhaps this is the reason rhythm bands have been so widely used in nursing homes and on geriatric wards. However, there are many other activities suitable for these settings, activities that are superior to rhythm bands both aesthetically and therapeutically.

*Personal communication, 1976.

On the surface these other activities may appear to be more expensive than rhythm bands because they involve about the same amount of money for fewer instruments, but it is money well spent. One of the principal reasons is that poor-quality sound, which is a main characteristic of rhythm bands, is an irritant to depressed, brain-damaged patients, hindering their relationship with the music and therefore hampering therapy. Another reason not to put money into rhythm bands is that their rhythmic stimulus value is lost in the clatter. True, the main beat can be pounded out by any number of instruments, but its therapeutic value is obscured because there are so many other sounds happening in so many other instruments. Rhythm's strength is that it is organized nonverbal sound; but in a rhythm band the organization is often lost. A third reason money is better spent on a few instruments of decent quality rather than a boxful of rhythm instruments is that clangers, whangers, and bangers (as I call them) are kindergarten instruments, and they convey the message to the patients that that is all people think of them. In the community, rhythm bands, complete with costumes and corn, have a place with children and among the well aged who have the ego strength to make a joke of them. But they do not belong in an institution.

On the other hand, if handled carefully, used one or two at a time, and in moderation, it is possible to capitalize on simple instruments often seen in rhythm bands, such as the kazoo. Kazoos are extremely easy to play; cost about a dollar; are generally regarded as toys; and, like body sounds, are not suitable for serious or sentimental songs, such as "Let Me Call You Sweetheart." But they are great when used while the group sings fun songs like "Hot Time in the Old Town Tonight," "Swanee," or "How Ya Gonna Keep 'Em Down on the Farm."

The sound of a kazoo is created by singing or humming through it, causing a thin paper inside to vibrate. The resulting tone is so raucous and admittedly grating that kazoos should not be used at the beginning of a session, before the group is warmed up and capable of handling such a stimulating sound. If used improperly, they can invite defensive reactions from some patients.

Kazoos are especially good with aphasic patients because they permit full participation in a singing activity. In fact, they not only permit it but reinforce it because with kazoos there is an actual physical sensation tied to the sound. Blowing through a kazoo produces neither sound nor sensation, but humming through it does both. In other words, playing a kazoo does not feel like an extension of the self as other instruments do; with kazoos the players are part of the sound just as singers are their own instruments. Perhaps this sounds obscure but, believe me, it is very reinforcing.

Kazoos are easy to play and generally ensure quick satisfaction. However, even simple instruments should not simply be handed to a patient with the expectation that no groundwork need be laid for a first experience. Beginning material should have uncomplicated melodies and rhythms; that is, choose "Show Me the Way to Go Home" over "K-K-K-Katy" because the first challenge is simply to produce sound. After that, it is easy. The tendency is for people to blow, not hum or sing, through the kazoo, and it may take a little time. Note that some patients may be apprehensive about the new contraption, with the result that some may exhibit oral apraxia and be unable to put the instrument into their mouths. Direct intervention may help, but the best thing is not to rush them and to take the spotlight off them by continuing the group singing.

**Musical Instruments.** Musical instruments, in contrast to rhythm instruments, enable groups to participate in the harmony of music. One of the simplest ways to use musical instruments with your group is to have individual members accompany the group singing with autoharps. It is not as hard as it sounds if you stick to songs with only two chords in them. To use this method simply color-code the two chord buttons that will be used; assign instruments to two individuals; and as the group sings, cue the players with color cards when their chord is to sound. It is as simple as two chords, two colors, two players, and two instruments. The same thing can be done with open-tuned guitars. A friend or a music store clerk can help you with the tuning. Here is a partial list of two-chord songs:

- "Hail, Hail, the Gang's All Here"
- "Long, Long Ago"
- "Hinky Dinky Parlee-Voo"
- "Billy Boy"
- "Shortenin' Bread"
- "Buffalo Gals"
- "Cockles and Mussels"
- "Rig-a-Jig-Jig"
- "O Dear, What Can the Matter Be?"
- "Clementine"
- "The Old Gray Goose"
- "Little Liza Jane"
- "Hush, Little Baby"
- "Shoo Fly"
- "Polly Wolly Doodle"
- "Comin' Thru the Rye"

### REFLECTIONS

As I look back on my volunteer music therapy work in a Phoenix nursing home, two things come to mind. First, I was very fortunate that the activity director suggested I spend a couple of afternoons just going from room to room meeting the people. No contracts were made (in fact, I had not heard of contracts yet), but I got to know the faces and had some names to go with them. If my first day had been a music day and if I had walked into a room filled with 20 or 25 geriatric chairs, wheelchairs, and walkers—well, that is all I would have seen. I would have been so frightened that I would never have seen the people, would never have requested another assignment there, and would never have begun planning a career with the aged. Second, my biggest challenge was to learn about geriatric problems and the group methods developed for them. My experience with and knowledge of music was a help, but I would gladly have traded it for some guidance in group work.

### SUMMARY

The ability to use music in a group is not limited to a few talented leaders. All people absorb some of music's language.

Some consideration about the music to be used is important because music does influence behavior. It is well to remember, for instance, that music can be used to affect mood and therefore should be carefully selected. Music is also a listening activity that can create multiple sensory stimuli. Therefor the music leader should be wary about sensory overload. Another caution is to select the best sound equipment possible.

Music can improve the social interaction of group members, and it can greatly help in the reorientation process of the regressed elderly. However, it is not enough simply to extol the wonders of music and let it go at that. To do so

is to fall prey to the "take two waltzes" syndrome. Whether you are using music as a listening activity, a singing activity, an instrumental activity, or all three, remember to respect both people and music. Facilitate the relationship between them by following the principle of music-mood matching and gradually raise the stimulus value; maximize people's input with the use of familiar selections, especially with the regressed. But do not stop at the morale-building, security-blanket stage. Enter the process yourself. Then and only then can you truly say that you are using music as a tool for growth, not simply treating it as window dressing.

## EXERCISE 1

Join with two of your classmates to be leaders in experimenting with a game of musical bingo.

Musical Bingo Game*

*Materials List:*

  10 songbooks with large print
  10 sturdy (9" × 15") cards†
  35 songs appropriate for players
  35 small pieces of paper

*Method:*

1 . Write the name of each song on a small piece of paper. (See list of suggested songs at end of exercise.)

2. Construct 25 squares on each card (five rows across and five rows down).†

3. Head each vertical column with the letters in the word M, U, S, I, C.

4. Fill the squares with song names from among a list of seven, making sure that no two cards are the same.

5. Follow the same procedure for each vertical column until all the squares are filled. You may leave a free space in the center.

6. Choose players and play the game two to three times.

*Outcome:*

The whole group gets to sing the songs in the winner's line. The person who called the game gets to lead the songs.

*Music Bingo was designed by Siobhan Managhan. The idea came from Catherine Moore's Chapter 33.

†Make cards as easy to read as possible; markers should be easy to handle for arthritic members.

Choose only songs *most* familiar to the patients. Lyrics with repeated lines give patients time to join in. In additon to singing, you can add various combinations of swaying, nodding, clapping, slapping knees and elbows, stamping feet, rapping, and playing rhythm instruments.

*Suggested songs for elderly:*

1. He's Got the Whole world
2. I've Been Working on the Railroad
3. Kum Ba Ya
4. How Great Thou Art
5. Michael, Row the Boat Ashore
6. This Land Is Your Land
7. If I Had a Hammer
8. My Bonnie
9. Lord of the Dance
10. Oh My Darling Clementine
11. Early One Morning
12. Let Me Call You Sweetheart
13. Show Me the Way to Go Home
14. Pack Up Your Troubles
15. Swing Low, Sweet Chariot
16. Home on the Range
17. Flow Gently, Sweet Afton
18. Loch Lomond
19. Auld Lang Syne
20. In the Good Old Summertime

What are some ways to make the cards as visually clear as possible? Other than ordinary bingo markers, what would make good markers for arthritic patients?

## EXERCISE 2

During the sing-along, which songs surprised you because they were unfamiliar to the group? Which songs were familiar to the group but were not very successful as sing-along material? How can you account for these differences?

## REFERENCES

Capurso, A. 1948. Certain considerations of psycho-social music. *Music Teachers' National Association Proceedings* 42:246–59.

Dollins, C. N. 1956. The use of background music in a psychiatric hospital to increase group conversational frequency. *Journal of Music Therapy* 6:229–31.

Gaston, E. T. 1968. Music and man. In *Music in therapy,* ed. E. T. Gaston. New York: Macmillan.

Grunewald, M. 1953. A physiological aspect of experiencing music. *American Journal of Psychotherapy* 7(1): 59–67 (January).

Hevner, K. 1936. Experimental studies of the elements of expression in music. *American Journal of Psychology* 48(2): 246–68 (April).

———. 1937. The affective value of pitch and tempo in music. *American Journal of Psychology* 49(4): 621–30 (October).

Shatin, L. 1970. Alertation of mood via music: A study of the vectoring effect. *Journal of Psychology* 75: 81–89 (May).

## BIBLIOGRAPHY

Alvin, J. 1975. *Music therapy.* New York: Basic Books.

Bright, R. 1979. Report: music therapy study tour to USA, Canada, & UK, *Lamp* 36(11): 43–52 (December).

_____. 1972. *Music in geriatric care.* New York: St. Martin's Press.

Gaston, E. T. 1968. *Music in therapy.* New York: Macmillan.

Gilbert, J. P. 1977. Music therapy perspectives on death and dying. *Journal of Music Therapy* 14 (Winter): 170.

Graham, R. M. 1977. Music therapy: a new song for LP/VN's, *Nursing Care* 10: 18–19 (September).

Kartman, L. 1977. The use of music as a program tool with regressed geriatric patients. *Journal of Gerontological Nursing* 3(4): 38–42 (July–August).

_____. 1980. The power of music with patients in a nursing home. *Activities, Adaptation and Aging* 1(1): 9–17 (Fall).

Orzech, M. J., K. C. Smith, S. Brekhus, and J. Pyrek. 1977. Group sings involving impaired elderly nursing home residents. Paper prepared for Thirtieth annual Scientific Meeting of Gerontological Society, San Francisco, Calif., November 18–22.

Palmer, M. D. 1977. Music therapy in a comprehensive program of treatment and rehabilitation for the geriatric resident. *Journal of Music Therapy* 14:190–97.

_____. 1980. Music therapy and gerontology. *Activities, Adaptation, and Aging* 1(1): 37–40 (Fall).

Parriot, S. 1969. Music as therapy. *American Journal of Nursing* 69(8): 1723–26 (August).

Shapiro, A. 1969. A pilot program in music therapy with residents of a home for the aged. *Gerontology* 9:128–33.

## RESOURCES

### Films

*Antonia: A Portrait of the Woman.* An affectionate portrait of Antonia Brico, the 73-year-old conductor of a community symphony orchestra in Denver, Colorado. Contact: Phoenix Films Inc., 470 Park Avenue South, New York, NY 10016.

*Close Harmony* (16 mm or video, 30 minutes). A film about members of an intergenerational chorus made up of people from 9 to 90. (Award: CINE Golden Eagle.) Contact: Learning Corporation of America, 1350 Avenue of the Americas, New York, NY 10019.

*Sunshine's on the Way* (16 mm or video, 30 minutes). The story of a young girl who works part-time at a nursing home, where she encourages some of the residents to form a jazz group. This is an inspirational film. Contact: Learning Corporation of America, 1350 Avenue of the Americas, New York, NY 10019.

### Cassettes

*Special Music for Special People* (cassette no. 85). By E. C. Lindner, L. Harpaz, and S. Samberg. Contact: Lindner-Harpaz, P.O. Box 993, Woodside, NY 11377.

## APPENDIX
## MUSIC THERAPY DEGREE PROGRAMS

The following colleges and universities offer degree programs approved by the National Association for Music Therapy Inc. as of August 1980.

**Arizona**
Arizona State University, Tempe, AZ 85281
   Betty I. Howery, RMT, Dept. of Music

**Arkansas**
Henderson State University, Arkadelphia, AR 71923
   C. Wayland Lankford, RMT, School of Fine Arts

**California**
California State University, Long Beach, CA 90840
   Kay Roskam, Ph.D., RMT, Dept. of Music
*University of the Pacific, Stockton, CA 95211
   Suzanne B. Hanser, Ed.D., RMT, Dept. of Music Therapy

**Colorado**
Colorado State University, Fort Collins, CO 80523
   Frederick Tims, Ph.D., RMT, Dept. of Music

**District of Columbia**
*Catholic University of America, Washington, DC 20064
   Jo Delle Waller, RMT, School of Music
Howard University, Washington, DC 20056
   Ara Rachal, RMT, Dept. of Music

**Florida**
†Florida State University, Tallahassee, FL 32306
   Jayne M. Alley, Ph.D., RMT, School of Music
†University of Georgia, Athens, GA 30602
   Melvyn D. Arnold, RMT, Dept. of Music Education

_____
*Also award master's degree.
†Also award master's degree and doctoral study.
#Award graduate degrees only.

**Georgia**
Georgia College, Milledgeville, GA 31061
  Carol Prickett Simmons, RMT, Dept. of Music
†University of Kansas, Lawrench, KS 66045
  Richard M. Graham, Ph.D., RMT, Dept. of Music

**Illinois**
DePaul University, 804 W. Belden Ave., Chicago, IL 60614
  Christina Lucia, RMT, School of Music
Illinois State University, Normal, IL 61761
  James F. McQuiston, RMT, Music Dept.
Western Illinois University, Macomb, IL 61455
  Bruce A. Prueter, RMT, Dept. of Music, Browne Hall

**Indiana**
Indiana University–Fort Wayne, Fort Wayne, IN 46815
  Barbara Crowe, RMT, Div. of Music
University of Evansville, Evansville, IN 47702
  Alan L. Solomon, RMT, Music Dept.

**Iowa**
University of Iowa, The, Iowa City, IA 52242
  Erwin Schneider, Ph.D., RMT, Div. of Music Education
Wartburg College, Waverly, IA 50677
  Carol Culton, RMT, Dept. of Music.

**Kansas**
†University of Kansas, Lawrence, KS 66045
  Alicia C. Gibbons, Ph.D., RMT, Dept. of Music Education-Music Therapy

**Louisiana**
*Loyola University, New Orleans, LA 70118
  Charles Braswell, RMT, Dept. of Music Therapy

**Massachusetts**
Anna Maria College, Paxton, MA 01612
  Director of Music Therapy, Dept. of Music

**Michigan**
Eastern Michigan University, Ypsilanti, MI 48197
  Director of Music Therapy, Dept. of Music
†Michigan State University, East Lansing, MI 48824
  Robert F. Unkefer, RMT, Dept. of Music
Wayne State University, Detroit, MI 48202
  Carol Collins, RMT, Dept. of Music
*Western Michigan University, Kalamazoo, MI 49008
  Brian Wilson, RMT, School of Music

**Minnesota**
Augsburg College, Minneapolis, MN 55454
  Roberta Kagin Metzler, RMT, Dept. of Music
College of Saint Teresa, Winona, MN 55987
  Director of Music Therapy, Dept. of Music
*University of Minnesota, Minneapolis, MN 55455
  Judith Jellison, Ph.D., RMT, School of Music, Scott Hall

**Mississippi**
William Carey College, Hattiesburg, MS 39401
  Carylee Hammons, RMT, School of Music

**Missouri**
Maryville College, 13550 Conway Rd., St. Louis, MO 63141
  Clive Muncaster, RMT, Dept. of Music
*University of Missouri-Kansas City, Kansas City, MO 64111
  Wanda Lathom, Ph.D., RMT, Conservatory of Music

**Montana**
Eastern Montana College, Billings, MT 59101
  Mark S. Rider, RMT, Dept. of Music

**New Jersey**
Montclair State College, Upper Montclair, NJ 07043
  Barbara Wheeler, RMT, Dept. of Music

**New Mexico**
Eastern New Mexico University, Portales, NM 88130
  Director of Music Therapy, Dept. of Music

**New York**
Nazareth College of Rochester, 4245 East Ave., Rochester, NY 14610
  Michael G. McGuire, RMT, Music Dept.
State University College-Fredonia, Fredonia, NY 14063
  Constance Willeford, RMT, Dept. of Music
State University College–New Paltz, New Paltz, NY 12561
  Joseph Moreno, RMT, Dept. of Music
#Teachers College, Columbia University, New York, NY 10027
  Laura G. Dorow, Ed.D., RMT, Dept. of Special Education

**North Carolina**
East Carolina University, Greenville, NC 27834
  Ruth Boxberger, Ph.D., RMT, School of Music
Queens College, Charlotte, NC 28274
  Barbara C. Memory, RMT, Dept. of Music

**Ohio**
Cleveland Consortia Schools:
  Baldwin-Wallace College, Berea, OH 44017
  Case Western Reserve University, Cleveland, OH 44106
  Cleveland State University, Euclid at East 24th St., Cleveland, OH 44114
  College of Wooster, The, Wooster, OH 44691
  Oberlin College, Oberlin, OH 44074
  Consortia Director: Susan Kane, RMT, Director of Music Therapy, Merner-Pfeiffer Hall, Conservatory of Music, Baldwin-Wallace College, Berea, OH 44017

College of Mt. St. Joseph on the Ohio, Mt. St. Joseph, OH 45051
    F. D. Patrick III, RMT, Music Dept.
Ohio University, Athens, OH 45701
    Michael Kellogg, RMT, School of Music
University of Dayton, Dayton, OH 45469
    Marilyn Sandness, RMT, Music Div. of Performing & Visual Arts Dept.

**Oklahoma**
Phillips University, Enid, OK 73701
    Betty Shirm, RMT, School of Music

**Oregon**
Willamette University, Salem, OR 97301
    Donna Douglass, RMT, Dept. of Music

**Pennsylvania**
College Misericordia, Dallas, PA 18612
    Rosemary, J. Crock, RMT, Music Dept.
Duquesne University, Pittsburg, PA 15219
    Richard Gray, RMT, School of Music
Elizabethtown College, Elizabethtown, PA 17022
    David A. Barger, RMT, Dept. of Music
#Hahnemann Medical College, 230 N. Broad St., Philadelphia, PA 19102
    Cynthia A. Briggs, RMT, Dept. of Mental Health Science, Creative Arts in Therapy
Mansfield State College, Mansfield, PA 16933
    Elizabeth Eidenier, RMT, Dept. of Music
Marywood College, Scranton, PA 18509
    Sr. Donna Marie Beck, RMT, Dept. of Music
Slippery Rock State College, Slippery Rock, PA 16057
    Sue A. Shuttleworth, RMT, Dept. of Music

**South Carolina**
Baptist College at Charleston, Charleston, SC 29411
    Carolyn Hancock, RMT, Music Dept.

**Tennessee**
Tennessee Technological University, Box 5045, Cookeville, TN 38501
    Nancy H. Howard, RMT, Dept. of Music

**Texas**
*Southern Methodist University, Dallas, TX 75275
    Charles Eagle, Ph.D., RMT, Div. of Music
†Texas Woman's University, Denton, TX 76204
    Donald E. Michel, Ph.D., RMT, Dept. of Music and Drama
West Texas State University, Canyon, TX 79016
    Martha Estes Beard, RMT, Dept. of Music

**Utah**
Utah State University, Logan, UT 84322
    David Wolfe, RMT, Dept. of Music

**Virginia**
Shenandoah College and Conservatory of Music, Winchester, VA 22601
    Marian Sung, RMT, Music Therapy Dept.

**Wisconsin**
Alverno College, Milwaukee, WI 53215
    Sr. Josepha Schorsch, RMT, Dept. of Music
University of Wisconsin–Eau Claire, Eau Claire, WI 54701
    Dale Taylor, RMT, Dept. of Music
*University of Wisconsin–Milwaukee, Milwaukee, WI 53201
    Leo Muskatevc, RMT, Dept. of Music
University of Wisconsin–Oshkosh, Oshkosh, WI 54901
    Nancy M. Lloyd, RMT, Dept. of Music

# chapter 34

# A Volunteer's Perspective

*Linda A. Byrne*

*"It is extraordinary how music sends one back into memories of the past."*

GEORGE SAND (1977)

## LEARNING OBJECTIVES

- List four purposes of volunteers in day care centers for the elderly.

- Describe the rights of volunteers in agencies.

- Describe the responsibilities of volunteers.

- List 11 qualities that are desirable in volunteer group leaders of the elderly.

- Discuss how volunteers can assist in relaying experiences and feelings of both past and present.

- Describe how volunteers can use music to enhance social skills and self-esteem in the elderly.

- Discuss four reasons why music is a valuable adjunct in volunteer group work with elderly and/or disabled individuals.

## KEY WORDS

- Accountability

- Ahistoric

- Cohesion

- Reminiscing therapy

- Rhythm

- Tempo

- Tension

- Volume

There is a sign hanging in the sunny dining room of the day care center where I have conducted groups. It reads, "Volunteers—We couldn't do it without you." What exactly is a volunteer? One author (Howard 1975) defines volunteerism as "the act of free will service to others without monetary remuneration."

## PURPOSES, RIGHTS, AND RESPONSIBILITIES

Volunteers can help with all aspects of running programs in day care centers. They bake desserts, serve coffee, hang up coats, lead all sorts of activities, and plan special activities. Volunteers lead or contribute to such activities as crafts (soapstone, watercolor painting, wood projects) poetry reading, current events, exercise, singing, walking, special musical treats, visits from school kids, choirs, short bus tours, grooming, individual talk sessions, discussion groups, lip reading, and many more. Volunteers perform plays, garden, and brainstorm—often together with participants at day care centers.

According to Rosemary Howard (1975, 25), purposes of the volunteer in institutions for older persons are

1. To bring the warmth of human personality to the elderly.

2. To help to stimulate new experiences to promote the mental, physical, emotional, and social growth of older people.

The author wishes to thank Delia Vicerra, Robert Byrne, Peninsula Volunteers, and the participants at Rosener House for their assistance with this chapter.

3. To assist in retaining and restoring the function of older people to a level at which they can continue their life-styles.

4. To encourage a milieu in which older people feel self-confidence and self-worth.

5. To motivate older people to look forward happily to tomorrow because of today.

6. To strengthen meaning and purpose in the lives of older people.

Why do so many people volunteer at the day care center where I work? The volunteers feel appreciated, respected, and needed. A volunteer has the right to be treated as a co-worker, to be given a suitable assignment, to know as much about the organization as possible, to receive training for the job, to receive continuing education for the job, to have regular evaluation of performance, to be given sound guidance and direction, to be promoted (where applicable) and given a variety of experience, to be heard, to be recognized, and to receive enabling funds when needed. These rights of the volunteer are important.

However, volunteers also have certain responsibilities. Some of them are to be sincere in the offer of service and to believe in the value of the job to be done; to be loyal to the community service with which they work; to maintain the dignity and integrity of the community service with the public; to carry out duties promptly and reliably; to accept the guidance and decisions of the coordinator of volunteers; to be willing to learn and to participate in orientation, training programs, and meetings and to continue to learn on the job; and to understand the function of the paid staff, maintain a smooth working relationship with them, and stay within the bounds of volunteer responsibility (Haines 1977).

Other specific responsibilities of the volunteer, from Howard (1975, 29), are that she or he

1. Follow the philosophy and policies of the home.

2. Be a team player for the benefit of the older person, fellow volunteers, and the staff/board of the institution.

3. Report problems and concerns to director of volunteers so that a solution or understanding can follow.

4. Report any unusual or changed behavior of older person to director of volunteers.

5. Not get geriatric patients out of/into bed.

6. Not move the older person if he/she falls, but immediately push the call button for the nurse.

7. Have a yearly physical and chest X ray.

In this chapter I will share my experience as a volunteer group/music leader at a day care center. I hope the ideas expressed here might encourage and motivate other volunteers to begin such groups. I will describe how I blended reminiscing therapy and music to create a special type of group.

*By carefully planning sessions, the volunteer leader can get the group to respond in a certain way. A sense of joy and hope can be instilled by using certain musical selections.*

## REMINISCING AND MUSIC

Reminiscing is a reminder to the elderly of past achievements and self-worth. There is a great value in this exercise for the person doing it as well as for those who follow him or her. Many people engage in remembering the past because it holds more self-gratification for them than the present does. By knowing the past, people often learn more about themselves. Reminiscing therapy is discussed in depth in Part 5, and the reader should see that section for further information.

Music holds a formidable power to communicate without regard to age, culture, or disability of the listener. The universality of it is a great strength in communication with all types of people. Since music forms a part of every person's life, it should be used to enhance pleasure and enjoyment. See Chapters 17, 18, and 33 of this book for additional information on music therapy groups and the use of music in group work with the elderly.

Since I have been involved in music in one way or another for most of my life and I thoroughly enjoy the elderly, I decided to combine the two areas. Using reminiscences that were instigated by music seemed natural and important to me. By explaining the methods I use with the groups with which I am involved, I hope to demonstrate that volunteers with similar interests can also be successful in combining these two areas and promoting similar groups.

### Group Makeup

Abraham Maslow (1970) has organized human needs according to a hierarchy in which basic physiological needs, such as breathing, eating, sleeping, and other survival needs, are the most elemental and must be satisfied before other levels of needs can be met. After basic survival needs, humans seek to satisfy safety and security needs. With these satisfied, individuals can begin to satisfy love and the desire to belong. Another step up the hierarchy are ego and self-esteem, finally culminating in the highest needs of man, which are self-actualization and cognitive and aesthetic needs.

The satisfying of any need level does not ensure that those needs will remain satisfied forever. The rich man may suffer financial reverses and reexperience the basic physiological need to satisfy hunger. Likewise, the elderly often suffer the loss of self-esteem and self-actualization. They must again meet the earlier needs for security and safety. With the losses they suffer as they age, choices narrow. They may be concerned with the most basic needs of life, such as those discussed above. The group leader should attempt to lessen the narrowing of choices that becomes more and more a part of the lives of the elderly by inviting and interviewing individuals to see whether they choose to join a particular group. Giving them a choice permits them to exercise judgment and preference. The knowledge that they can try the group to see if they enjoy it and are free to leave if they do not show them respect.

Music plays a part in everyone's life, from the first lullaby to skip-rope jingles to love songs and back to lullabyes again. Memories, present emotions, future hopes, and dreams can all be tied to music. Its strength lies in the fact that no language governs its powers of communication. No demands are placed on the listener except his or her presence. The receiver needs no particular physical strength or ability. This is why music fits my particular sort of group work so well.

The day care center where I am a volunteer serves frail, elderly participants who come to the center on a regular basis. The programs prepared for them are varied and stimulating and offer a number of activities.

### Group Members

The members are very diverse: I have wheelchair individuals, stroke victims, people with degenerative diseases, and also those who are healthy but very elderly. The age range is from 53 to 93. I happen to have more male members than female, which is unlike the general elderly population and much different from the nursing home ratio.

The youngest member is Mr. P, who suffers from a degenerative disease and is wheelchair bound. Although he has lost the use of major muscles, he has a quick mind and can express himself very well, even if his speech is halting. He has marvelous spirit and seems to accept his condition. His background is rich in music. He played piano, composed, and presented musicals in his younger days. He now plays scales on the piano but has a very difficult time controlling his fingers. He cannot paint, do many crafts, or model, but he enjoys discussion and music and contributes to the group a real expertise and sensitivity.

Another participant, Mrs. J, is a 93-year-old retired teacher who occasionally takes a turn at the piano playing Welsh folk songs she remembers from her youth. She also accompanies an occasional soloist who entertains at the center. I heard her accompany a marimba musician who entertained recently. She has no impairments, which is rather unusual. While these two participants have quite extensive musical backgrounds, most members of the groups have always enjoyed music rather passively as listeners, rather than as performers.

Mr. and Mrs. S have been members of the group for several months. Mr. S is wheelchair bound; Mrs. S has trouble focusing her mind on anything for a long period of time. Both come to the center everyday by a van equipped with a wheelchair lift. He likes to talk and enjoys group meetings. She takes care of wheeling him into the room. Another member, Mrs. H, is hard-of-hearing but enjoys participating. She often sits close to the piano where she can hear the vibrations better. She, too, is wheelchair bound.

Mr. J. W. is a stroke victim and uses a cane. He is a southern gentleman who ends every statement with the uplifted inflection typical of that region's speech. He shakes his head affirmatively very often and gives a general feeling of joy to the members. He always looks neat and clean and is ready to try many different things.

Mr. H. W. has had several strokes and suffers from a very poor vocal projection, yet he insists on being a part of the group and will attempt to discuss issues even in very short, halting outbursts of voice.

Mrs. E. C. has no use of her voice at all, even though she suffers no known physical problem with it. She uses eye contact and physi-cal touch very meaningfully and so communicates with us in this way.

### Physical Set-Up

When the group first formed, I was a co-leader. The group would open with all of us having coffee, juice, and a snack together around the card table; this was a lovely, intimate way to begin the meeting.

However, I found that in working alone, I had to stop the practice of having a snack together. Gathering the participants, remembering who requested what to drink, and arranging chairs was too much for me. I couldn't remember who wanted which snack and it took entirely too long a time and too much energy to do this myself. Since I stopped this practice, my members now gather with the rest of the day care participants to have their morning coffee. Then when they are through, we gather around our small table and begin our meeting.

The leader of the group must be able to change some physical things that don't add to the purpose of the meeting. If I had had to continue to serve our snack, my interest in the meeting would have been diverted and I would have fallen short of what I could achieve by focusing on what I wanted to do. Also the leader must always allow time for preparation, and I was being cheated of this important time.

Since I work without a co-leader, I must be able to play the selection on the piano and lead the group at the same time. For that reason I place a card table as close to the piano as possible. I arrange several folding chairs on two sides of the table and leave two sides open for my wheelchair participants. The size of the group often grows from the recommended number of 6 to sometimes 10 or 12. I never discourage anyone from attending. We do not feel a lack of intimacy, even though the group is rather large.

Placing the table close to the piano helps me lead as well as play. It also helps hard-of-hearing people keep up with the conversation.

One gentleman in the group, Mr. H. W., insists on having a very large chair, a sort of easy chair, moved near the group for his own use. The chair is cumbersome to move and to place in such a way that he will be a part of us. I almost objected to his being in the group because of the big chair until I realized that he has so few choices left in his life that this is very important to him.

If the leader is using a record player or tape, the group can be located anywhere there is an electrical outlet. A separate small table to hold the recordings would be useful and would give the members a place to lean or place their hands. This is why preparation time is so important. Sometimes something like a small table can be hard to locate.

Before playing the selections, some discussion usually takes place about the purpose of the group. I repeat that we will discuss feelings and events that the music brings to mind. I ask if anyone has heard of the composer or the work to be played. Then I tell them the name of the selection. I may talk about the composer's life and times, when I first heard the selection, or some other information before playing it. After they've heard the title, they close their eyes and ready themselves to listen quietly to the selection. I ask them to concentrate on the feelings the music recalls and what events they think about.

### Examples of Sessions

A composer we have spent a lot of time on is Robert Schumann. In using him as a subject for discussion, I first gave a short sketch of his life. When I told his birth and death dates, 1810 and 1856, I asked the group how old he was at his death. They figured that out and sighed at his youthful death. When I talked about his early life and related that his father had died when Robert was 16, more sympathy was expressed for him. The fact that his mother insisted on sending him to law school when he wanted to become a musician brought lots of discussion about other people making decisions for their children.

We discussed his maiming of his hand in his attempt to strengthen his finger. To illustrate this I had members place their hands on the table and raise both thumbs with the other fingers held down, then both second fingers, both third fingers, both fourth fingers and both little fingers. They discovered that they, too, had a

hard time raising their fourth fingers very far from the table. Mrs. F. P. thought it very sad that Schumann's career as a pianist was so soon ended. Others joined in at this point.

His love-affair with and marriage to Clara Weick brought romantic thoughts to the group. The love songs he composed for her formed the music portion of our meeting. I played several short pieces he had written for her. We discussed the joy he had found in his music and in her. Mrs. C talked about her life as a young bride but Mr. V wanted to discuss the mechanics of the music.

This composer formed our discussions for several meetings. His life is rich in emotional content and the members relate readily to this. His eventual institutionalization was the basis of a long discussion about madness and institutional treatment in the early 1800s. We eventually made a poster to illustrate some of the facts we had gathered about him.

One woman commented that these sessions, coupled with the music, are so interesting to her because we discuss topics that she would otherwise never get to deal with. One man claps at the end of each session.

Often the discussion focuses on past material and reminiscences. However, we also discuss current issues in the members' lives. Sometimes we even discuss how the composer got us to feel the way we do when we hear a selection, through his use of line, tempo, volume, and rhythm.

I've found that short selections are the most effective for this purpose. Two- or three-page tunes that take only a few minutes focus the group more on the discussion that follows rather than on the music played.

Children's songs and easy-to-play classics work very well. For instance, Schumann's "Scenes from Childhood" has given us many interesting opportunities for discussion. Besides the delicate and thought-provoking melodies of these selections, the titles themselves lend great openings to discussions of past experiences. Some titles from this book are "Frightening," "At the Fireside," "Perfectly Contented," and "Important Event." These titles are very conducive to interesting and thoughtful interchange between the members of the group.

When I played "Frightening," our talk centered on what is frightening. Halloween and spooks crept into our discussion. This led Mr. J. W., from Louisiana, to tell us about voodoo practices he had been told about in his childhood. Another member became frightened just with the discussion. She had spent time in a mental hospital and although she has progressed very well, some residual fears still linger. We moved the discussion from imaginative areas to what is fearful in the present. This quieted her. Another member held her hand and smiled at her. This session left us all feeling close, but a little scared. The date was appropriate. It was late October. Fortunately the day was bright and clear, not rainy and dark. The mood conveyed in the music really set the pace for our discussion.

Shortly after New Year's Day it was only natural to listen to "Auld Lang Syne." The discussion focused on new beginnings and resolutions for the New Year. Mrs. H, another wheelchair person, declared that her resolution was to walk into church with her family for the next Christmas Eve service. She fully intends to strengthen herself to be able to do that.

Brahms' "Lullaby" set quite another tone. At this meeting discussion followed about what brings us peace and joy. Babies and the handling of young children entered into it. Mr. W. W., a 91-year-old retired midwestern farmer, then began to give advice on how children should be raised. A spirited discussion followed with the women in the group about his methods and how he exercised his obligations as a father.

When I played "Humoresque" by Dvorak, a playful and silly mood came over the group. Teasing and joking reflected the composer's use of rhythm and quick notes with vivid dynamics.

Seasonal melodies at holiday times lead to pleasant and tender discussions. Mrs. C told us about celebrating the 4th of July in her early years. March rhythms seem to bring automatic patriotic thoughts. One woman told about her father taking her to Golden Gate Park to hear John Philip Sousa.

Song material can sometimes come from the group members. One Russian woman took the time to teach us the words and melody to "Volga Boatmen" and then told us about her early life in Russia.

The activity appeals to different group members for different reasons. The musically astute consider why the composer chose the particular title and what in the selection makes the title appropriate, while less musically educated people consider their own experiences and ties to the subject we discuss. They express enjoyment and anticipation of meeting for this purpose.

While music remembered from their youth plays a big part in the enjoyment and discussion activity of these elders, they have expressed a very open and adventurous spirit in experimenting with new and familiar melodies. Mrs. C says, "I'm game. Let's try it." So I've been thinking of using opera selections and parts of orchestral interludes. The possibilities are limited only by the time and interest of the leader.

At times I have purposefully and very thoughtfully tried to set a particular mood. Following is information that can help other people do the same thing. A particular mood may be called for if you especially want to comfort someone who has had a recent loss, if someone new is going to join the group and you want a quiet session, or if it is a holiday and you want to raise spirits to a gay level.

### Use of Tension in Music

Tensions in music are outward manifestations of what goes on within our bodies (McLaughlin 1970). Walking and heartbeats follow inner rhythms of the nervous system. A comfortable sense of tempo centers around 80 to 90 beats per minute. If the tempo is much faster, a sense of excitement and exhilaration results in the listener—for example, Chopin's Waltz, Op. 64, No. 1 (The Minute Waltz).

If the tempo is much slower, emotions of sadness and resignation may commonly result. These are called incoming emotions.

Because people have an innate sense of order and regularity, regular-time units in rhythm are most compatible with inner rhythms. Any departure from regular beats results in tension. An example of this is "Italian Pipers" by Gounod.

Volume is most comfortable at a moderate level. Again, any rash departure from this level results in tension. Composers use dynamics to take us to very loud and very soft levels. They return to a moderate level because the tension must be relieved and resolved.

Tension, in any of the ways demonstrated, gives variety and interest to music and consequently to the group. The leader may want to discuss why a feeling of excitement takes hold of a person when a specific selection is played. The use of this information in putting a program together can make it entertaining for leader and members alike.

Dramatic tension is broken or resolved by the use of comedy. We see this in plays, but it also occurs in music.

By carefully planning sessions, the leader can get the group to respond in a certain way. A sense of joy and hope can be instilled by using particular music. A sense of quiet and peace can be generated in this way. Likewise, the past can be explored by the use of slow, mellow, and pleasant tunes. The music does not need to be limited to what the group members have heard in the past. Classical selections with a ring of familiarity can be explored.

### Use of Past Material

Reminiscing not only brings back the past but also involves the reliving, reexperiencing, or savoring of past events. It involves an emotional experience in which selective factors, intimately related to the personality, shape the process of reconstructing the past (Pincus 1970).

The value of reliving the past is apparent since one must work through grief, loss, and life review to be able to put the past in its proper perspective. For some people this is particularly painful.

One woman in my original group shied away from any discussion of her past. When I asked her if she wished to share her early life, she said that it was too sad and she didn't want to think or talk about it. I later discovered that she had lost her husband and a close friend within one year and was extremely depressed. However, she enjoyed and seemed to respond to the group whenever the topics were on an optimistic subject area or when we would do small craft projects.

Yalom (1975, 110) discusses this preference for the "here-and-now," or ahistoric, approach:

A here-and-now or an ahistoric approach to therapy focuses on what is happening in the group in the present—at that very moment. There is a decreased emphasis on the patient's historical past or in the details of his current life problems; far more pertinent are the immediate patterns of interpersonal interaction in the group.

. . . interpersonal behavior in the group of each patient is an accurate representation of his interpersonal behavior outside the group. By using this material, which is experienced by all the group members, rather than past material ("there-and-then") or material from the current life of one patient outside the group ("there-and-now"), which may concern only one patient, the leader may more meaningfully involve all the members in the group therapeutic work. By focusing on the here-and-now process, the therapist creates optimal conditions for the operation of the primary curative factors. The group's attention is turned upon itself, and the amount and intensity of the interpersonal interaction is increased, thereby enhancing the development of group cohesiveness and the opportunities for interpersonal learning.

See Chapter 5 for further elaboration on Yalom's work.

Since some goals in using music are to eliminate feelings of isolation and to promote group cohesion, self-understanding, and understanding of others, the focus should not be limited to the past but should be open to what the member is experiencing now. Immediate reactions to music can be used as material in group discussion. They are experienced by all members at the same time, so members can relate feelings about the present or the past as they choose.

While the past is very important to each of us and has formed what we are at present, we must keep the past in perspective and realize that we all have a future. The futures of the group members may have obvious limitations, but by focusing on the head and the heart rather than on physical losses, we try to keep everyone on an even level. Music groups such as I have discussed can be participated in by a great many of the physically impaired.

### Group Cohesion

Slowly, as the group continues to meet and share experiences, cohesion occurs. Isolation diminishes and members begin to feel closer to each other. Sometimes they even refer to themselves as "family," which they really are. As they grow together and learn to understand and respect each other more, they experience a growth in self-esteem and self-respect. They look forward to meeting and being together. They carry this feeling and posture with them throughout the day. The director at the center has commented that members who are involved in growth groups do emerge from their shells and are more vocal and helpful whenever they can be. They also look for each other when the time comes for group. They hold each other accountable for coming and speaking up at discussion time. They even hold the leader accountable.

One time I had to miss a session and did not have the opportunity to tell them about it the week before. When I came the following week, I went from person to person to ask if they would like to be part of the group that day. When I got to Mr. H. W., he said he'd rather not because I hadn't shown up the week before and he was angry with me for letting him down. And that is the man who can barely utter a word!

We made up and I got him to come to the table. I immediately apologized to them, and for the first time I realized how much they depended on me and, furthermore, how much they had come to mean to me.

## Leadership Qualities

The following qualities for successful leadership might be helpful in selecting and screening for volunteers who wish to work with elders. According to Gerald and Marianne Corey (1977), a leader should have certain qualities to be successful in work with the elderly. These are

1. Genuine respect for old people.
2. A history of positive experiences with old people.
3. A deep sense of caring for the elderly.
4. An ability and desire to learn from old people.
5. An understanding of the biological aspects of aging.
6. The conviction that the last years of life can be challenging.

7. Patience, especially with repetition of stories.
8. Knowledge of the special biological, psychological, and social needs of the aged.
9. Sensitivity to the burdens and anxieties of old people.
10. The ability to get old people to challenge many of the myths about old age.
11. A healthy attitude regarding one's own eventual old age.

## The Environment: Recommendations

The setting where the group activities I have described take place has certain distinct advantages over convalescent hospitals. The day care participants are able to be cared for at home during the evenings. Some people live in their own apartments, some in board-and-care homes, and some in senior housing facilities. They come to the center via private cars, public transportation, or vans equipped with wheelchair lifts. Participants come voluntarily and are dressed, fed, and eager to see friends they have made and to participate in activities planned for them and announced in advance on a weekly schedule.

Anticipation of events and interest in each other and the program are enhanced by the environment. The participants should be greeted openly, called by name, and helped into the building. Coats need to be taken. It helps them feel comfortable if snacks are served. Volunteers as well as the staff can play a role in welcoming and serving the participants.

Walls should be decorated with bright paint. Cheerful paintings done by the participants are displayed. Murals could cover some walls. Cleanliness is important. Large windows and comfortable furniture in the sitting room help to make it pleasant. A piano and organ are needed to provide music for and by participants. A separate large room is helpful for crafts and exercise sessions. Films also can be shown there.

There should be no offensive odors and when accidents occur, they must be immediately tended to. An atmosphere of hope and joy is apparent to the participants and any visitors who arrive.

First impressions are often based on what is seen, heard or smelled; they should not be negative.

### Closure of Meeting

When we close a group meeting, we hold hands, lower our eyes, and someone in the group offers a prayer or word of thanks. At one meeting Mr. J. W. said "The Lord's Prayer." At another meeting I played "Reverie" as a closing gesture. The group seemed to be particularly moved by this selection. A spirit of reverence and quiet reflection was present. The group seemed not to want to part. Music in a group setting can set a powerful tone in a very gentle and subtle way.

We concentrate on the present when we close the group. We often give thanks for our present state of health and our being together during this time and express our hope of being together again very soon. This focus on both the present and the future fosters a spirit of hope and anticipation of meeting again, rather than leaving us open for sad thoughts about who is not with us this time. (During my months of volunteer service, two groups members have had to be placed in total care facilities.)

### SUMMARY

Whether played by a musician or on a record player, music is an appropriate vehicle for group discussion. Music is fitting because it requires nothing but listening skill on the part of the receiver. Therefore, no matter what the degree of disability or age, one can participate. Music communicates to us on a level often more meaningful than words. It can draw people together in joy, understanding, and community. Music has played a part in everyone's life, and at many special times in life. Therefore, it can be drawn upon for reminiscence of the past as well as present happenings.

Senior day care centers can utilize volunteers in many specific ways. The diverse skills and interests of volunteers add to the fabric of the programs available for seniors. Volunteers have to have certain qualities and certain attitudes about the elderly in order to be most effective. They also have certain rights and responsibilities, which must be acknowledged by both the center and the volunteer. This chapter is intended to encourage volunteers with musical interests and/or abilities to become part of this special type of group work.

## EXERCISE 1

Decide on an overall emotion you wish to discuss with your group members. Use information about tensions and musical selections given in this chapter or use selections you find on your own. Play music according to the prescribed plan. Ask for discussion about how participants felt while listening and what specific memories arose.

## EXERCISE 2

Select short, positive musical numbers that are each about one minute long. Focus on a past or future holiday—for instance, marches for July 4, Irish melodies for March 17, carols for Christmas. Direct the discussion to childhood observances of the holiday, present feelings, and plans for future observance of the holiday.

## EXERCISE 3

Research facts about the life of a particular composer—for example, Schumann or Chopin. Present these facts to the group members. Are they empathetic? Can they add to the information? After some discussion, play some selections of the composer's work. Can you observe a better understanding of the composer's music when the group members know something about his life and times? Do the group members relate the emotions presented in the musical numbers to events in the composer's life or in their own lives, past or present?

## EXERCISE 4

Select a short composition with an interesting title that reflects a feeling, such as Schumann's "Frightening" or Debussy's "The little shepherd" from a book of children's songs. Discuss the title of the music with the group members. Have them concentrate on it while you play the music. Afterward, direct the discussion to what they thought about during the music. Did thoughts of the past arise? Ask about the circumstances and events that the music brought to mind.

## REFERENCES

Corey, G., and M. S. Corey. 1977. *Groups: Process and practice.* Monterey, Calif.: Brooks/Cole.

Haines, M. 1977. *Volunteers: How to find them, how to keep them: A workbook.* Department of State of Canada and Vancouver Foundation, ZA/RC Publishers.

Howard, R. 1975. In-service education for volunteers working in the field of gerontology. Monograph. San Jose, Calif.: San Jose State University. January. Reprinted by permission.

Maslow, A. 1970. *Motivation and personality.* 2d ed. New York: Harper & Row.

McLaughlin, T. 1970. *Music and communication.* London: Faber & Faber.

Pincus, A. 1970. Reminiscence in aging and its implications for social work practice. *Social Work* 15(3): 47–53 (July).

Sand, George. 1977. *Story of my Life,* Vol. 1, 1856, quoted by Elaine Partnow in *The Quotable Woman,* Los Angeles: Pinnacle Books, p. 20.

Yalom, I. 1975. *Theory and practice of group psychotherapy.* New York: Basic Books.

## BIBLIOGRAPHY

Howard, R. 1974. Development of an adult day care center. Monograph. San Jose, Calif.: San Jose State University. November.

Kane, R. L., R. A. Kane. 1980. Alternatives to institutional care of the elderly. Beyond the dichotomy, *The Gerontologist* 20(3): 249–59.

Rogers, D. 1980. *Issues in adult development.* Monterey, Calif.: Brooks/Cole.

Smith, E. 1983. Nurses in policymaking and volunteerism. *Nursing & Health Care* 4(3): 135–37 (March).

Troll, L. E. 1975. *Early and middle adulthood.* Monterey, Calif.: Brooks/Cole.

## RESOURCES

### Recordings

*Anniversary Songs* (Columbia CL 586). Ken Griffin on organ.

*Fifteen Piano Pieces* of Debussy (Angel Records #35026).

*Grieg: Piano Concerto in A Minor and Norwegian Dances; Lyric Suite* (Seraphim S 60032). Gina Bachauer. The dances and the Lyric Suite are valuable for group work with the elderly.

*Spanish Music* (Columbia M 30057). John Williams on guitar.

*The Sound of Horowitz.* (Columbia ML 5811). This record contains Schumann's "Scenes from Childhood" and some wonderful Scriabin compositions.

*Yankee Organ Music* (Nonesuch Records). Richard Ellsasser.

**Videocassettes**

*Love and Learn* (3/4-inch U-matic cassette, color, 10 minutes). Study guide included. Produced by Adelphi Productions Inc.

*The Nursing Home Volunteer* (16 minutes). This program is directed toward volunteers working in nursing homes and convalescent hospitals. It is divided into four sections: (1) the emotional needs of the patient, (2) the role of the volunteer, (3) the feelings of a new volunteer, and (4) the rewards of the work. Contact: Shirley A. Selby, Mt. Zion Hospital Volunteer, 336 Country Club Drive, San Francisco, CA 94132.

# INSTRUCTION FOR GROUP WORKERS AND EPILOGUE

NATIONAL INSTITUTE OF AGING

Part 7 contains four chapters. Three are written specifically for instructors of group work with the elderly or for in-service educators.

Regarding teaching (or even conducting groups), I am reminded of a poem by Piet Hein*

"The road to wisdom?
  Well, it's plain
  and simple to express,
Err
  and err
  and err again,
  but less
  and less
  and less."

---

*From *Grooks*, by Piet Hein. Copyright © 1969 by Piet Hein. (New York: Doubleday, Inc.)

The importance of preceptorship for a new group leader is described in Chapter 35. Qualified supervisors are often not available for a new leader, who must struggle alone in the group work experience. Classes on group work may not be available, and some existing classes are too short and too intense, presenting only an overview. Such classes do not provide the student with the supervised experience that is so necessary if one is to absorb the components of group work. This chapter should be helpful for both preceptors and students.

Chapter 36 elaborates on the actual teaching and supervision of groups led by students.

Examples of supervising concurrent multiple groups are presented.

Chapter 37, by Bernita Steffl, discusses gerontology curricula and points out the need for clinical practice for students. She offers suggestions based on 14 years of experience supervising students working with the elderly.

Chapter 38, the epilogue, expresses concern over the lack of qualified group leaders and acknowledges that debt many of us owe old people for having taught us so well, a theme and acknowledgment just beginning to appear in the literature.

# chapter 35

# Responsibilities of the Preceptor

*Irene Burnside*

"We want to create an atmosphere in which creation is possible."

MARIE RAMBERT (1973)

HUGH ROGERS/MONKMEYER

## LEARNING OBJECTIVES

- Discuss 10 ways in which group work with elderly persons may differ from that with other age groups.

- List four specific qualities of group work with older people as designated by Corey and Corey.

- Discuss three pitfalls for new group leaders.

- Explain the role of feedback given to students.

- Discuss four ways to increase self-esteem in the learner.

- Analyze one format for teaching group work.

## KEY WORDS

- Directive
- Ego enhancement
- Feedback
- Preceptor
- Responsibility
- Self-esteem
- Supportive
- Understanding

---

Because group work with the elderly is arduous, draining, and sometimes discouraging for the beginning group leader, considerable support is needed from a preceptor or supervisor. This chapter gives students, instructors, health care workers, and volunteers an understanding of the preceptor's responsibilities. Topics include the value of humor and feedback for students, pitfalls for new group leaders to avoid, anxiety and depression in new group leaders, how to increase self-esteem among new leaders, and some suggested formats for teaching group work.

## DIFFERENCES BETWEEN ELDERLY AND OTHER AGE GROUPS

The new leader working with the aged may have conducted other groups but will need help in discovering the ways in which group work with the elderly is different. Some of the differences follow.

1. Elderly people tend to be grateful and to express their appreciation to the leader in a variety of ways.

2. The groups tend to be smaller—for example, four individuals for reality orientation or six members if the group is composed of disabled or regressed individuals. Most leaders recommend six to eight in a group; an exception is remotivation groups, which may have up to fifteen persons.

3. The pace of the group may be slower, and the goals will be more limited than in other groups.

4. Losses of all kinds are a constant theme.

5. The members will have physical, psychological, and socioeconomic problems to juggle.

6. Sensory defects are frequent and sometimes severe.

7. Physical ailments are many; a single member may have several.

8. The physical environment of the meeting place is very important for the aged. Extreme temperatures, glare, noisy intercoms, and so on

are generally poorly tolerated by elderly group members.

9. The leader may have to be very active, especially with groups of long-institutionalized people, and accept increased responsibility for group movement. Older people do not believe that joining a group will have any magical effects, so the leader must be willing to engage in one-to-one relationships within the group to get it off the ground.

10. Although outside-the-group socializing and meetings are generally discouraged in most groups, such activities should be encouraged with the elderly group because they may improve the members' enjoyment of life.

11. Leaders are usually expected to share about themselves.

12. Elderly people tend to conserve energy; therefore, anxiety may be more difficult to assess in groups of elderly persons.

13. Physical dependence needs may be very high because of the frailty of group members or the extreme age of some participants.

14. Transportation to and from the group (whether it is an inpatient or an outpatient group) can create many problems.

15. Evening meetings are generally not acceptable. The institutionalized patient is sent to bed early; the outpatient client is afraid to be out after dark.

16. Groups should be planned around elderly people's maximum-functioning portion of the day. If residents like to nap after lunch, that is not the best time for a group meeting. The rhythmicity of the individual members must be considered.

17. There may be a vast age difference between the leaders and the members.

18. The subject of death and dying will come up frequently; death may occur within the group experience.

19. Because of the poverty of many elderly people, those who could benefit from a group experience may not be able to afford it or have transportation available.

20. Boredom and loneliness may be pervasive themes.

21. Confrontation groups are usually not appropriate for most elderly; they need *ego enhancement*—a term used by James E. Birren (1973)—rather than confrontation.

In sum, group work with older people is (1) more directive, (2) less confrontive, (3) more supportive, and (4) more an ongoing function of teaching members ways of expressing themselves and listening to others (Corey and Corey 1977).

## TASKS OF THE PRECEPTOR

The preceptor has several obligations to a student, the most important of which is to reduce new leaders' anxiety so that they can function reasonably well from the beginning. The preceptor will also need to help new leaders to be cognizant of the differences in group work with the older population and to make the necessary adaptations.

It has been my experience that when a student and I are having difficulties in the instructor-student relationship, the student is also having difficulty in the agency or with the group. Therefore, the supervisor must take the responsibility for improving a stormy relationship with the student and try to work through the difficulties. Doing so frees the student's psychic energies for the group experience.

### Humor and Understanding

The use of humor helps both students doing group work and student-instructor conferences. Often we become so grim and determined in our work with the aged that we fail to see the joy and wit around us. Sometimes it takes an old person to teach the value of joy and humor.

In my first year of teaching I had a maverick student who was going to change nurses, doctors, and agencies. She bulldozed her way along and wondered why there was such chaos in her wake. One day when I was trying to help her realign her ideals with realism, she flared up: "Irene, you sound just like my mother!" Too weary for further explanation, I asked her if she would change it to "grandmother" because at the moment my arthritis was bothering me. She laughed suddenly, and our heretofore stormy relationship seemed to change for the better.

Students often hear their peers comment, "How dull," "How depressing," or "How do you stand it?" It becomes tiring after a while continually to defend one's interest in the aged; until society's attitudes are turned around, these comments will probably persist. But students do need to find some rewards for themselves as they work with the elderly, and preceptors can give feedback to help the student find pleasure in group work.

As students begin to see traits they admire and respect in old people and find that the aged are very human, they begin to appreciate their group work and their relationships with the elderly. Not infrequently, students develop close relationships with aged clients and keep in touch long after studenthood has passed.

On one occasion I attended a student's wedding, which was held in a lovely park. The terrain was a bit rough, so during the reception I said to the 90-year-old grandmother of the bride, "Could I get you another glass of champagne?" She looked me squarely in the eye and said, "What's the matter, don't you think I can get it by myself?" (I did not know she was leaving for Greece the next day.) When students begin to experience similar incidents and see the strengths, flair, and uniqueness of so many of the elderly, they often become staunch advocates of the aged client.

### Identifying Pitfalls for Beginning Group Leaders

Preceptors bear the responsibility of discouraging students without the appropriate background who may take on the role of psychotherapist. The instructor should be alert for such a stance in a student and watch for: (1) too much probing of group members, (2) constant confrontations with members about behavior or statements made in meetings, and (3) a desire to push in especially painful areas—for example, grief, losses, or uncomfortable discussion areas such as sexuality. Although it seems to be true that elderly persons reveal only what they wish to, a new leader may affront them or aggressively challenge them, and the members may subsequently refuse to participate in the group.

The preceptor also has to watch for occasions when new leaders' needs are usurping group needs. For example, a leader's need to help may end in infantilizing elderly people. Other leaders may give free rein to their curiosity and want the older person to reveal all while they sit back and share nothing. In the reverse situation leaders use the group setting to vent their own problems and anxieties.

### Feedback to Students

Feedback is crucial in teaching. One reason the preceptor should give feedback to students is that the instructor becomes a role model for the students, who can then begin to give feedback to the elderly in their care. Many older persons suffer from lack of feedback, especially those who live alone. A second reason is that students do flourish with feedback. Students gain self-confidence with prompt, positive, and constructive feedback from a preceptor. There is no substitute for actual group leading, however, as indicated in Figure 35-1.

Students should receive both positive and negative feedback on their performance with groups. How much of each should be given is up to the supervisor. Some students require a lot of "stroking"; others need to be restrained because they come on too strongly. Skillful observation of each student is required to find out the mode of supervision that will maximize the student's potential. Every effort should be made to prevent failures, which foster discouragement and depression in a student leader. The instructor should bring out the best in each student. Some students have had so much negative feedback that they do not know what their best is.

### Recognizing Anxiety in the New Group Leader

The instructor must also be on the alert for anxiety in a new group leader. As previously stated, the supervisor must help students understand their anxiety. Beginners often fear failure or are not sure what they can accomplish in the group (Burnside 1969). If a student has never been in an extended care facility before and the group meetings are to be held there, the student may have horrified initial reactions to everything from the smell of the place to the behavior of the personnel. When students are indignant and their complaints seem unending, they can often be reminded that they are forgetting the aged persons, that they are spending so much of their time and energy grumbling or coping with the staff that they have little energy left for creative work with the old people. This sort of behavior in a student may be one form of resistance. A student may hold back, as though stalling long enough will prevent having to go through the group experience. Procrastination is a common way for beginning group leaders to handle their anxiety.

Asking students what would help the most in their state of apprehension can bring a variety of requests—for example, just a desire to talk, to go for a cup of coffee, to go for a walk, to cry for a while. The preceptor should try to respond to any such requests; launching a new leader well into group work is important.

### Preventing Depression in the New Leader

Other reactions a preceptor may view in a group leader include depression and low self-esteem. Students beginning group work may become depressed for a variety of reasons. Former students have discussed some of these reasons with me.

1. The student's lack of experience and knowledge may cause depression.
2. The deplorable living conditions of the aged where the student may be placed can be a factor.
3. The attitudes and behavior of staff and doctors toward the patients may depress a student.
4. Similarly, the attitude and behavior of the staff toward the student may cause depression.
5. A visit to parents and/or grandparents can suddenly make students aware of the aging process in their own relatives. As one nurse said, "I get goose bumps when I think of how my mother has aged." Another time I met a colleague in an air terminal; she looked wan and drawn. "I've just returned from seeing my folks in Boston; I can't believe how they have gone downhill," she said sadly, and readily acknowledged her depression.
6. Deaths that occur in the agency (but outside the group) can cause depression and sometimes guilt. For example, one student placed in a senior citizen residence was battling with an older social worker, soon ready to retire, over what seemed like inconsequential issues to me. I asked the student to write process records on her interactions with the social worker. The analysis of her own communication and behavior patterns brought about some change in the student. But the real change occurred when the student discovered that the social worker had terminal cancer and had chosen to work until she could no longer cope physically with the job. The depression and the guilt of the student in this particular case had nothing to do with the older people at the senior center.

7. Young students often get depressed because of slow results or not meeting their goals (which often are too high in the first place). Beginners have to be helped to get a more realistic view of what they and the group can accomplish in the allotted time.
8. Grade-hungry students often get depressed when they do not get the grade they had hoped for in the group work experience.
9. Termination of the group experience and the relationship with the instructor can cause depressed feelings, especially if the student terminates both at the same time. Supervisors must be able to handle their terminations well and to guide students through the group termination experience. Role-modeling behavior is important here; students will model their terminations with the aged after the way that preceptors handle their terminations with the students. Role modeling is still one of the most effective teaching strategies. (Barbara Sene's 1969 article on termination behavior is recommended for the reader.)

### Increasing the Student's Self-Esteem

Guiding new group leaders often requires pumping up deflated egos. Many students have low self-esteem and do not have a realistic idea of their assets and liabilities. If they have never led a group before, it takes a while for them to view themselves in the role of group leader.

Anxiety, lack of experience in group work, and fear of failure blend to make a new leader's trepidation blatant. Positive rewards in the way of immediate feedback (either verbally or on written assignments) on student accomplishments seem to help students quickly.

Availability of the supervisor is also important, especially in the beginning of the group experience. The dependency needs of the new leader usually diminish rapidly if the anxiety, depression, or lack of self-esteem are met with effective interventions by the supervisor and if sincere feedback, both constructive and corrective, is given very soon after each group meeting.

To provide effective interventions and feedback, the supervisor should occasionally attend student-led group meetings as an observer. According to Irvin Yalom (1970, 377):

> Group therapy supervision is generally more taxing than individual therapy supervision. Mastering the cast of characters, a formidable task in itself, is facilitated if the supervisor observes the group periodically or at least once. The student's written or verbal summary of the session often fails to capture the emotional flavor of the group, and ongoing audio or preferably videotapes are invaluable supervision aids.

It has been helpful for me as a preceptor to be an observer once or twice while a student is leading a group. One student leading her first group was having trouble with a man in his seventies who would interject statements with a sexual connotation that always brought the group and the leader to a sudden halt. The leader was so concerned about it that I decided to observe one group meeting. The group was going smoothly; the residents were reminiscing; and the old man blurted out, "No matter how much you shake it, the last drop always ends up in your pants." Everything skidded to a stop, and two of the quiet, genteel ladies in the group stared at him incredulously, as though they were mentally playing the remark through again to make sure they had heard it right. During another meeting, an 80-year-old woman said during a lull, "You know, Irene, no man has a decent orgasm until he is twenty-five years old." She startled me, but all the men in the group became noticeably more alert.

It has been my observation that young students may be comfortable discussing sexuality with their peers and/or the preceptor, but, they can squirm noticeably when the subject of sexuality comes up in their group leadership. Sometimes they have to look at their own behavior. Are they overreacting? Are they unusually curious? Are they showing signs of disgust?

Although the student wanted to change the man's behavior in the group, she failed to realize how much he kept everyone in that group on their toes. If she had gotten him to stop making such remarks, perhaps the listening and alertness of all the group members would have diminished. Students bent on changing behaviors need to understand and discuss thoroughly their rationale for such changes. Moreover,

BERNITA M. STEFL

*Students often need guidance in selecting the type of group and group members they want to lead. In this illustration, an exercise group receives instructions from the leader before attempting the exercise in the group. It is important not to rush participants into exercise; take the time to get everyone into place slowly. The preceptor is observing from the hallway. Observers can change group behavior and may stultify a new leader.*

group members often decide what behaviors they cannot tolerate in one another; that is the ideal way for changes to occur in group work.

## Increasing Knowledge Base

The preceptor must help the student to increase knowledge in two areas: the aging process and group process. An excellent overview by Jean Hayter (1983) about necessary modifications in the environment of older persons is highly recommended for beginning group leaders. The author gives practical suggestions regarding deficits in vision, hearing, taste, smell, and touch. Territoriality is also discussed.

For a student who is weak in group dynamics and process and is in need of remedial reading, I recommend Madelyn Nordmark and Anne W. Rohweder's book (1975, pp. 395–398).

## Stressing Individualization

It goes without saying that individualization is a very important consideration in work with the older adult. Tappen and Touhy (1983) remind us that "flexibility, consideration of individual interests, and a wide range of choices" are needed. It is important for the preceptor to convey this understanding to students. Most of all, the preceptor should individualize the learning techniques with the student and be the role model. One might say that individualization begins at home, because teachers often fail to operationalize with students the content they are endeavoring to teach.

## Assisting Student Analysis

Preceptors play a critical role in assisting students to analyze and evaluate the group process in their practicum experiences. Because many refinements and changes may have to be made due to the age, abilities, disabilities, and losses of the elderly, the student will need to know group dynamics. It is by knowing and understanding the basics of group dynamics and theory that the student can better understand what must be changed and why. The student will also need to know that the outcomes for groups of aged persons might differ from those for groups of other ages. Students who expect

unrealistic outcomes of their groups are bound to be disappointed when they evaluate the accomplishments of their group.

Tappen and Touhy (1983, 38) state that "evaluation of the effectiveness of group work with the older adult is usually based on relevant but global measures of change such as morale, life satisfaction, mental status, or ability to carry out activities of daily living. Communication skills, learning, ability to relate to others, resolution of problems, development of insight, and other more specific outcomes are measured less often. . . . In order to promote positive outcomes, group leaders need to be aware of the way in which their actions affect the group.

Outcomes should also be studied in relationship to the skill, expertise, and education of the leader. The practice continues of allowing untrained personnel to lead a group of frail elderly. These leaders must have some basic communication skills and some understanding of group dynamics. Their own attitudes about aging should also be examined since our attitudes ultimately shape our behaviors toward the older individual."

## SUGGESTED FORMATS FOR TEACHING GROUP WORK

It is useful to have a few structured formats when teaching group work. The following checklist may be helpful for both preceptor and student.

1. Number of individuals in the group.
2. Length of meetings.
3. Number of meetings each week; duration in months.
4. Days of the week meetings will be held.
5. Number of men and women in the group (if group is not mixed, give rationale).
6. Age range.
7. Disabilities that will be accepted.
8. Whether confidentiality will be a ground rule stated by the leader.
9. Whether the group will have a single leader or co-leaders.
10. The theoretical framework(s) to be used.

11. The special problems of the proposed group, to include:

    a. Attention span.
    b. Communication or speech difficulties.
    c. Diet regimens.
    d. Ex-alcoholics.
    e. Ex-drug addicts.
    f. Hearing problems.
    g. Impending death.
    h. Incontinence.
    i. Lack of social graces.
    j. Loss of spouse.
    k. Losses such as economic, home.
    l. Mental health problems, such as withdrawal, loneliness.
    m. Physical health problems.
    n. Vision problems.
    o. Transporation problems.
    p. Whether plans have been made for transportation.

12. Whether support or supervision will be given and by whom.

13. Arrangements for pay (if beginner is not on a volunteer or student basis).

14. Responsibilities for charting and reporting to the staff and doctor.

15. Philosophy and rules of the agency that will influence the group leader and/or the group.

16. Plans for terminating the group.

17. Props, supplies, materials that may be needed for the group.

18. Who will pay for supplies.

19. If plans are made to record sessions on a tape recorder or to take photographs, from whom permission has been obtained. (Administrator's permission is required plus that of the patient or relative or conservator if the patient cannot sign for self.)

20. Plans for individuals who cannot handle group membership.

Preceptors bear the responsibility for double-checking the list to see that the items have been covered. In teaching it is helpful if students give a rationale (and there may be several) for their choices. Giving reasons will help them think through the group experience more carefully.

If the instructor prefers not to use tapes or process records, using the list format in Exercise 2 can expedite reporting for the student and reading by the preceptor.

## SUMMARY

This chapter deals with the delicate, sometimes difficult task of preceptorship. The reader will note that both the reference list and the bibliography are quite short, indicating the need for more literature about the topic.

A preceptor should have a strong background in group work to be able to advise, instruct, and motivate the beginning group worker. Tasks of the supervisor include reducing students' anxiety, preventing depression, and raising their low self-esteem. Another responsibility is helping them distinguish the differences between group work with the elderly and work with other groups. The preceptor should also advise students of the level of group they are qualified to handle and prevent them from assuming the posture of psychotherapists by probing, confronting, or pushing for insight into such areas as grief, losses, and sexuality. The instructor will also have to be alert to the problem of students' needs displacing group needs. In all these tasks humor and prompt

FIGURE 35–1. *Students will gain confidence more quickly from actual group-leading experiences.*

SOURCE: Reprinted with permission of Marsh & McLennan Companies, New York.

feedback to the students are extremely important. For preceptors, group therapy supervision is draining—more so than supervising one-to-one relationships.

This chapter also provides a detailed checklist to help both supervisors and new group leaders handle the group experience. Bernita Steffl (1973) gives recommendations for instructors of gerontological nursing who are supervising clinical experiences. She also discusses professional curricula for group work with the elderly in Chapter 37.

---

## EXERCISE 1

Write a one-page description of the leader's role in a group of older persons. How does the role differ from that of a group leader of persons who are adolescents, young adults, or middle aged?

---

## EXERCISE 2

Collecting accurate, meaningful data is important in analyzing the effectiveness of group work. The following format can be used by either group leaders or observers. If you are an observer, you should keep in mind that your presence will alter the group process. You should also confer with the group leader to determine what the goals for that meeting were before you answer the questions on the list. If you are currently leading a group, thoughtfully analyze what happened. Ask your instructor or supervisor to read your answers and give you feedback. The last step is to analyze the feedback from your instructor or supervisor. Was it helpful? If so, why? If it was not helpful, consider why not.

### Before the Group Meeting

1. List attendance in the group.
2. Draw the seating arrangement of the group members. Describe any noticeable activity such as moving chairs, changing places, leaving the group, sitting on the periphery, and so on.
3. What was the group mood when you walked in? Were there any noticeable feelings in individuals? Were there any unusual events prior to the meeting, such as a death, an accident, a fire, an upset ward routine?

### During the Group Meeting

1. List a few of the outstanding themes of the group meeting. If the mood of the group was related to the themes, explain.
2. Write one-paragraph descriptions of the mood activity of the members and of the leader.
3. Illustrate with:
   a. One intervention that was goal directed. List the goal and your rationale for your intervention and evaluate its success.
   b. One verbal or nonverbal intervention that was unsatisfactory. Explain why you think it was unsatisfactory and why a correction is desirable.

*After the Meeting*

1. Did anything unusual occur immediately following the group meeting?

*Future Meetings*

1. List proposed future interventions and the rationale for each.
2. List questions or problems with which you would like assistance.

## REFERENCES

Birren, J. E. 1973. Panel discussion. Conference entitled Aging: Issues and Concepts, North Hollywood, Calif., January.

Burnside, I. M. 1969. Group work among the aged. *Nursing Outlook* 17 (June): 68–72.

Corey, G. and M. Corey. 1977. Groups with the elderly. In *Groups: Process and practice,* ed. G. Corey and M. Corey. Monterey, Calif.: Brooks/Cole.

Hayter, J. 1983. Modifying the environment to help older persons. *Nursing and Health Care* 4(5): 265–69 (May).

Nordmark, M., A. Rohweder. 1975. "Small Group Behavior" *Scientific Foundations of Nursing,* Philadelphia: J. B. Lippincott Co. (3rd ed.) ff. 395–398.

Rambert, Marie quoted in "Ballet Rambert: The company that changed its mind," John Percivel, *Dance Magazine,* February, 1973, p. 21.

Sene, B. S. 1969. "Termination" in the student-patient relationship. *Perspectives in Psychiatric Care* 71): 39–45.

Steffl, B. M. 1973. Innovative clinical experiences in an elective course in gerontological nursing. Paper presented at Gerontological Society meeting, Miami, Fla., November 5–9.

Tappen, R., and T. Touhy. 1983. Group leader— Are you a controller? *Journal of Gerontological Nursing* 9(1): 34 (January).

Yalom, I. D. 1970. *The theory and practice of group psychotherapy.* New York: Basic Books.

Fisher, A. 1980. *Small group decision making: Communication and the group process.* 2d ed. New York: McGraw-Hill.

Harbert, A., and L. Ginsberg. 1979. *Human services for older adults: Concepts and skills.* Belmont, Calif.: Wadsworth.

Kottler, J. 1983. *Pragmatic group leadership.* Monterey, Calif.: Brooks/Cole.

Lifton, W. 1972. *Groups: Facilitating individual growth and societal change.* New York: Wiley.

Luft, J. 1969. *Of human interaction: The Johari model.* Palo Alto, Calif.: Mayfield.

Panneton, P. E. 1979. Current and future needs in geriatric education. *Public Health Reports* 94 (January/February): 73–79.

Rudestam, K. 1982. *Experiential groups in theory and practice.* Monterey, Calif.: Brooks/Cole.

Sampson, E., and M. Marthas. 1981. *Group process for the health professions.* 2d ed. New York: Wiley.

Sargent, D. 1980. *Nontraditional therapy and counseling with the aging.* New York: Springer.

Shaw, M. E. 1981. *Group dynamics, The psychology of small group behavior.* 3d ed. New York: McGraw-Hill.

Siegel, H. 1979. Baccalaureate education and gerontology. *Journal of Nursing Education* 18 (September): 4–6.

## BIBLIOGRAPHY

Corey, G. 1981. *Theory and practice of group counseling.* Monterey, Calif.: Brooks/Cole.

Corey, G., and M. Corey. 1982. *Groups: Process and practice.* Monterey, Calif.: Brooks/Cole.

## RESOURCES

### Games

*Into Aging* (a simulation game). By T. L. Hoffman and S. D. Reif. This game is described in book format and played with colorful "Life Event" cards. It could be used to help students experience some of the daily struggles of the aged. One game may be played by 5 to 15 players. Publisher: Charles B. Slack Inc., 6900 Grove Road, Thorofare, NJ 08086; phone (800) 257-8290.

# chapter 36

# A Method of Teaching Group Work

*Irene Burnside*

*Eclecticism may prove a burden
for the beginning practitioner
trying to master a solid
theoretical framework.*

L. PHIPPS (1982)

PETER VILMS/JEROBOAM, INC.

## LEARNING OBJECTIVES

- Discuss four factors that must be considered in group work with the elderly.

- Discuss the four stages in the development of a small group, as delineated by B. W. Tuckman.

- Discuss four ways to learn about group leading.

- Describe one method of teaching mutiple group supervision.

- List the life cycle of a group according to Lacoursiere.

- Discuss the four stages of communication in group work with the elderly.

- List 10 guidelines for the beginning leader of groups of elderly.

## KEY WORDS

- Clumping

- Cohesiveness

- Contact

- Contract

- Dissatifaction state

- Multiple groups

- Negative orientation

- Orientation stage

- Production stage

- Resolution stage

- Termination stage

- Theoretical framework

## NEED FOR THEORETICAL FRAMEWORKS

A theoretical framework is important in all group work, and that is true for conducting groups with the elderly. However, since the theoretical frameworks for other age groups are not always applicable in work with the elderly, adaptations must be made. The adaptations are based on gerontological knowledge and research findings about groups of elderly. Therefore the leader must exercise care in selecting frameworks for group work/therapy and must not assume that any group theory or method will be therapeutic or comfortable for the group members. Students will need much assistance from preceptors to analyze the frameworks and select the most appropriate one for the type of group they will be leading. As indicated in the opening quote, the instructor is cautioned not to overload the beginning student with too many frameworks.

Decisions about group work should be based on information gathered regarding the mental and physical health of the elders, and known needs. Theories provide rationale for decisions about and implementations of group work. But because information about group work with the elderly is widely scattered in a variety of journals from many disciplines, it is difficult to chase down articles.

While "theory organizes knowledge into useful information and encourages economy of thought" (King 1978, 16), there is much for the student to synthesize in group work. For example, normal aging, pathology, group dynamics, sensory losses or changes, mobility, translocation trauma, leadership styles, hierarchy of needs, humanism—all must be part of a group worker's armamentarium. So much content can be an overload for an unsophisticated group leader. Abraham Kaplan (1964, 310) states it best, "Theories are not just means to other ends, and certainly not just to ends outside the scientific enterprise, but they may also serve as ends in themselves—to provide understanding which may be prized for its own sake." To use a theory purposefully and to bring about desired outcomes, the professional will have to be able to change some of the variables that are part of the theory (Hardy 1978, 85).

At times this is not only difficult to teach, but may be the difficult part for the student group leader also.

One useful, and often quoted, theoretical approach to small groups is offered by B. W. Tuckman (1965). It is an easy one to remember because of its poetic terseness. However, when contrasted with other theorists' stages of group development, Tuckman has omitted the termination stage of the group.

- *Forming:* The stage of dependency and testing.
- *Storming:* The stage of expressing emotions and existing conflicts.
- *Norming:* The stage of establishing group norms and developing cohesion.
- *Performing:* The stage of accomplishment and relatedness.

Another theorist is recommended: For a more in-depth approach, read R. B. Lacoursiere's (1980) book on the life cycle of groups. He studied group developmental stages (GDS) and defined the terms *developmental stages, phases,* and *trends;* all of these terms have been used by group therapists. "Stages" is used by Tuckman (1965) and Runkel et al. (1971). "Phases" is used by R. F. Bales and F. L. Strodtbeck (1951), L. J. Braaten (1974–75), D. C. Dunphy (1968), and S. R. Kaplan and M. Roman (1963). "Trends" has been used by C. L. Cooper and I. L. Mangham (1971). While all of these authors are describing something generally considered similar, Lacoursiere prefers the term *stages,* considering it the best choice. He delineates five stages in group development:

1. Orientation stage
2. Dissatisfaction stage
3. Resolution stage
4. Production stage
5. Termination stage

## STAGES IN GROUP DEVELOPMENT

Because Lacoursiere has delineated the stages and named them in easily understood terms, his framework is discussed here. While his book is not geared for the aged group in particular, group leaders can decide for themselves whether the stages are applicable to their group.

### Orientation Stage

Lacoursiere (1980, 29) states that in the orientation stage "the participants are mildly to moderately eager. They generally have positive expectations that something good will come from participation in their training or therapy group, class, or job." This may not hold true for all potential group members, as they may lack energy, be depressed, or be guarded and suspicious. They often wonder why they are there, and even after the group's purpose has been explained several times, they may not be sure what it is all about. This is true not only of the confused person; often some very intelligent and savvy people will be unsure what a group is all about. At this stage the members are dependent on the situation and the group leader, as Lacoursiere so aptly points out. For the frail elderly, this point is especially relevant. The group leader's approach and finesse are important. Figure 36-1 likens group work with the elderly—particularly in its early stages—to a wheel.

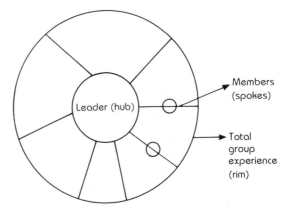

FIGURE 36-1. *The leader of a group of elderly is the hub of the wheel, most especially in the beginning stages.*

### Dissatisfaction Stage

The dissatisfaction stage is one in which the members learn that the group may not bring them what they thought it would. They find that the reality of the group situation does not meet their expectations. The anger sometimes comes out in commenting about the youthfulness of the leader, who cannot teach them anything; snide remarks about the group (inside or outside of the group); and general dissatisfaction among the members. It is a trying time for the leader, who must work hard not to lose the members. I think that a leader of aged members is instrumental in this stage and, in essence, has to say, "Trust me and stay with me and you will pass through this dissatisfied and uneasy stage." It depends a great deal on the leader's sensitivity to the group, their reactions, and their needs.

If a person joins a group reluctantly or under some degree of coercion, as is all too often the case in groups in nursing homes, there may be problems. Lacoursiere calls this the "negative orientation stage." In this stage, the sequence begins with resistance and hostility. Lacoursiere states that the entire first part of the GDS sequence tends to be negative; sometimes a negative orientation stage will be followed by the usual stages, but he states that this does not usually happen.

I recall observing an elderly woman being rapidly pushed in her wheelchair by a nurses' aide. The woman did not understand where she was going or why and kept grabbing at the leaves of the bushes on the edge of the patio to stop the fast flight. She arrived at the group with leaves in her hands, and bewilderment written on her face.

### Resolution Stage

The resolution stage is what Tuckman (1965) describes as the "norming stage." It is at this time that there is some meeting of the expectations of the members and the group purpose and what is happening in the group. If the members can master the situation and develop some new skills, enough positive feelings of increased self-esteem "will help to exceed earlier negative feelings of frustration and anger" (Lacoursiere 1980, 32). One of the new skills

the leader can focus on is improved communication, which gives members a chance to discuss their lives in reminiscing sessions. The new skills may also be simple tasks learned in group, such as how to negotiate with medical personnel, how to sign a name, how to order talking books, and so forth. See Chapters 4 and 22 through 26 for an elaboration of reminiscing by a variety of disciplines.

### Production Stage

The production stage is characterized by the eagerness of the members to be a part of the group experience. At this stage in the life of the group, members should be working together and should have some agreement about the relationships in their group. There should be increased autonomy. This stage may be quite slow in appearing, especially in a group of frail and/or demented elderly persons. The student group leader needs encouragement during this stage, and progress may go unnoticed. The preceptor might be able to point out minute changes, which could be verbal or nonverbal.

### Termination Stage

The termination stage is a difficult one, especially for young and/or new leaders of a group of aged persons. Students are often quite ambivalent about terminating or are relieved to be finished, but they also may feel guilty about this if they have felt truly needed or realize the importance of the group meetings to the members. The preceptor will need to spend adequate time with the students in regard to termination; this phase is difficult for most students.

Old people really do feel a sense of loss and mourn for the leader and for the experience itself. I returned to visit members one year after a group had terminated. Two of the men told me how much they had missed the group and what fine memories they still had about those meetings. Elders may not be able to express how they feel about the group not meeting any more, or they may be very candid and honest. Some will cry. The leader should be sensitive about the feelings and listen for the sadness and the sense of loss. Although the termination stage could occur during the last meeting of the group, it is best to use the last several meetings to prepare groups of elders—that is, if the group has cohesion and has met for a long period of time. Ending the group in the happiest possible way—with a coffee or a special event—is especially important for the elderly, who received much nurturing and support from the group. Emphasize "pleasant sorrow," as Lacoursiere (1980, 276) would say. One group of students in Lubbock, Texas, terminated with a picnic in the park. A local television station filmed the event and subsequently did a five-part series on aging. The termination event was incorporated into the television series.

The theoretical framework just described has been oversimplified and the reader is referred to the book by Lacoursiere (1980). However, it offers a takeoff point and may help beginning group leaders to analyze the dynamics occurring in their groups. G. Stanford and A. E. Roark (1974, 55) also delineate group development stages. The reader may wish to compare and contrast their framework, which follows, with Lacoursiere's.

1. Beginning—basic orientation and getting acquainted.
2. Norm Development—establishing "ground rules" for operation.
3. Conflict Phase—members asserting individual ideas.
4. Transition—replacing initial conflicts with acceptance of others.
5. Production—sharing of tasks, leadership, and trust.
6. Affection—appreciation for the group, and
7. Actualization—flexibility, consensus, decision-making.

## STAGES IN COMMUNICATION DEVELOPMENT

Some of the problems and dynamics of group work with elders have been diagrammed for this chapter. See Figure 36–1 for an analogy representing group work as a wheel. Figures 36–2 through 36–5 illustrate the four stages of communication development that I've found the elderly (especially the frail) to progress through along with the stages of group development.

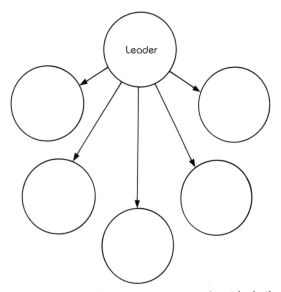

FIGURE 36–2. *In beginning group work with frail and/or confused elderly, the first stage of communication consists of the leader doing one-to-one within a group context.*

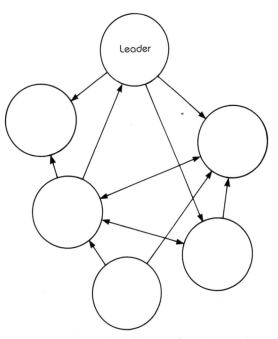

FIGURE 36–3. *In the second stage of communication, the members begin to talk to the leader and to ask questions.*

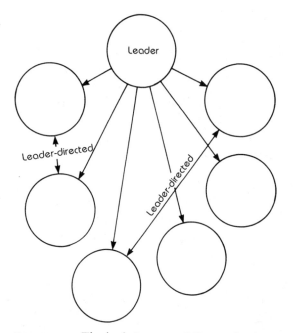

FIGURE 36-4. *The leader's responsibility in the third stage is to encourage interaction among the members.*

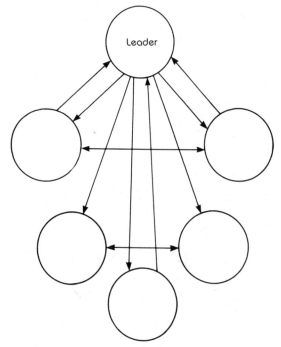

FIGURE 36-5. *In the fourth stage, verbal activity is greatly increased and moves in many directions. The hard-of-hearing and the visually impaired may show less interaction.*

Two common problems that occur in group work with the elderly I call the "satellite member" and the "exiting member." These problems are diagrammed and explained in Figure 36-6 and Figure 36-7, respectively.

The satellite member is reluctant to join the group. Reasons may be lack of knowledge about groups; mistrust, both of the new leader and the members; shyness; low self-esteem, poor body image; and lack of socializing skills. I. D. Yalom (1975) considers social learning, the development of basic social skills, as a curative factor that operates in all therapy groups. I would agree. (See Chapter 5 for other curative factors described by Yalom.)

The leader's gentle encouragement or quiet acceptance of the member who sits close by (but always outside of the circle) will often serve to draw the member into the group. It almost seems that as trust increases, the satellite member moves physically closer to the group circle.

The exiting member leaves the group suddenly. This can occur for a variety of reasons: high anxiety, need to go to the bathroom, fear, short attention span, or a proclivity to wander. A leader's skill and expertise comes sharply into focus when the leader intervenes. Students need help with these types of behaviors. Preceptors should prepare students for such behaviors by role-playing. See Chapter 35 for further discussion of preceptor responsibilities.

Students may learn by observation of groups; by co-leadership of groups with the preceptor, supervisor, or a peer; or by leading a group alone. The last two methods are preferred because they place responsibility for learning and performance on the student.

## STUDENT OBSERVATION OF GROUPS

The student may observe a group leader either by being in the room where the group is being held or by observing the group through a one-way glass. Many leaders are uncomfortable with the observer outside of the group and prefer that the person sit with the group and participate, at least minimally. Some leaders will not permit the observer into the group until the members have decided whether they approve of the outsider joining the group for a temporary

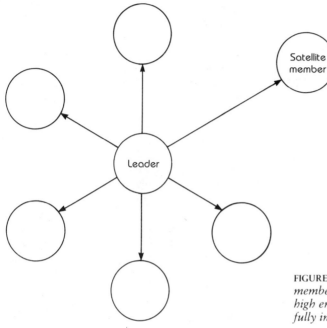

FIGURE 36–6. *Sometimes at the beginning of a group a member will remain on the periphery until trust is high enough to join the circle. The leader must carefully include that "satellite member."*

period of time. It does seem to be important to allow the decision to be a group one. Leaders who lean toward an authoritarian style of leadership may not consider the group's feelings of concerns and may make decisions for them. This can be true in nongroup situations as well; we often rob the elderly of their autonomy.

Another way of observing groups is for the instructor to conduct demonstration groups. I have found this to be a particularly successful way for students to observe group methods and leader techniques when there is a large class or a large audience to teach—for example, in a continuing education program or perhaps a summer class. I have found this method to be successful for a variety of reasons:

- The effect on the group members who participate is consistently ego-enhancing and beneficial, even for the most confused members.
- The effect on the staff members is noticeable. There is a certain pride in having their clients perform well. The staff will also usually make a special effort to have their clients well-groomed, shaven, and their hair styled. The staff's increased interest in the appearance of the old person in turn makes the older person feel better.

- Many old people living in institutions are bored; a venture to a local university or hotel or whatever is most exciting for them. When we took a quite confused lady into a posh hotel in Beverly Hills, she stopped dead in her tracks in the front lobby, looked up at the ceiling, and said to me, "My heavens, did you ever see such a gorgeous chandelier in your whole life?"

Another time in Canada, six old people made the trip from their nursing home to the university in 36-below weather and found it "quite invigorating"! They came down the center aisle of the auditorium using canes and three-pronged walkers; their entrance was quite dramatic and the audience watched them intently (although that was not intended; it was simply the easiest way to get them up front.) Later, as they made their way through the snow to go to the cafeteria for lunch, one was heard to say, "Isn't this exciting? To be able to eat in a university dining room with students?" (Many of today's elderly have had

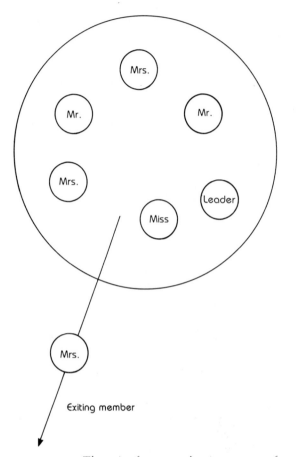

FIGURE 36–7. *The exit of one member in a group of elderly complicates group leadership because it disrupts the circle. The physical arrangements often must be readjusted and members regrouped to place them closer to one another.*

only an eighth-grade education. The university is a revered, mysterious, and hallowed institution to them.)

Still another man in Phoenix was given a ride by the public health nurse from his home to the hotel where the conference was being held. He had a bad case of emphysema and on the way home confided to the nurse that he was in distress. She learned that he was out of oxygen and had no money to order a new tank but had not told her this when she picked him up prior to the conference because, "I was so afraid that you would not let me go to the hotel

to have a beer and lunch with the rest of the group and help teach that class."

- Many staff and instructors think that old people will not be able to handle the stress of a demonstration group; however, they do surprisingly well and sometimes perform better than I do in a group demonstration! On one occasion a very controlling administrator would not let residents from her nursing home attend such an experience because "I cannot stand my people being used as guinea pigs" (an example of authoritarian leadership).

One way an instructor can counteract that is to pay the participants a stipend in cash or a check; no matter how little it may seem to us, to the old person it may be a great deal. One old farmer, who had farmed with one mule in the hills of Arkansas, very carefully placed his bill into a tattered billfold that had not another thing in it. The audience watched him spellbound as he patted the money carefully into place and slipped the billfold into a back pocket. In another instance, in Hawaii, a man who had once worked for $1 a day, seven days a week, in a sugar beet factory said of his $5 payment, which had been placed in a university envelope, "Thank you so much. My first great-grandchild has a birthday soon. Now I have a gift to give him and I have a very nice envelope to use to give it to him. I appreciate that."

### Guidelines for Demonstration Groups

Guidelines to consider in demonstration groups are as follows:

1. Let the aged person decide for himself or herself; do not coerce and do not let staff members use coercion.

2. Do not tell the elders about the group too far in advance. They may back out or spend much time worrying about how well they will perform.

3. The elderly are afraid of not performing well and will often ask after the meeting, "Did I do all right?" One should, there-

fore, praise them often and sincerely and thank them for their assistance.

4. Know the stress tolerance of the members so that there are no "catastrophic reactions." A catastrophic reaction can occur when a client is pushed too long or too hard to perform a task that is difficult for him or her. The phenomenon was first described by Kurt Goldstein (1939). (See Chapters 7 and 10 for further explanation of this phenomenon.)

5. Keep the group very close together so that they can see and hear you and so that they can gain support and strength in front of the audience from the closeness of one another.

6. If there are confused members, hold the microphone for them. One man kept trying to lick the microphone (it was an ice cream cone—shaped mike) when I handed it to him. Another man tried to smell it. Also, even the alert ones need to focus on words and on forming their thoughts; it is helpful to them if you relieve them of the mike. Also keep in mind that sometimes when they get it, they will not want to relinquish it; if you have a monopolizer, it might be difficult to get the mike back.

7. If there are funds, pay members for participating in a group.

8. The impact of group members on universities, hotels, and local people cannot be easily measured. In Edmonton, Canada, the doormen graciously helped six elderly in wheelchairs out of the big bus into the hotel lobby. The waitress who served them cocktails after the group meeting commented, "They surely had a good time. Do you do this very often?"

I have had no experience with observations through a one-way glass so I cannot discuss that, but it certainly is a possibility in facilities that have the design.

## CO-LEADERSHIP WITH THE PRECEPTOR

Perhaps the ideal and most expedient method for teaching group work with the elderly to

beginning students is to have students co-lead a group with an instructor. However, this is usually not feasible either for reasons of time or due to the sheer numbers of students a teacher must instruct. And, it is often difficult to get the student to participate, especially if the student is rather overwhelmed by the setting or by the aged people themselves. The teacher must walk a fine line and not intimidate the student with the knowledge and skills that, in the student's eyes seem to come so easily to the instructor.

It is important to keep the same students in the weekly group. During one semester of teaching, I tried to rotate the students through my group so that all of them would get a chance to co-lead with me. Disaster was the result. When we assembled the group, the students had great difficulty finding the regular members of the group; they often brought people to the meetings who were not in the group. There was no continuity for the students either and they did not have a chance to pick up on the group themes that did develop from week to week (for example, "it's like being in jail here," complaints about the food, or discussions of losses in the members' lives).

## A METHOD OF TEACHING GROUP WORK

As an instructor in a baccalaureate nursing program, I realized that I was teaching group work to students using the same methods by which I had been taught when I was a student. It did seem that there was an easier, more expedient way to teach a number of students about group work and process. Currently, there are many chronically ill aged individuals in institutions and too few group leaders. The experiences are readily available "out there." I have long been concerned about the lack of groups available to older institutionalized individuals, whether they are in nursing homes or in subacute or acute psychiatric facilities. The frail elderly who have mental problems do not fare well in psychiatric settings—they are physically and psychologically run over by the younger patients—yet that is where many frail elderly are placed. Students in the health care field are often shortchanged in their experiences with the elderly, and do need geropsychiatric experiences. I considered concurrent multiple groups, but a literature search revealed absolutely nothing about supervising and observing multiple groups of aged members with student leaders.

Because the neophyte leader of aged persons usually can handle only five or six frail elderly members in group, group work tends to be costly and can be a very time-consuming therapeutic endeavor to implement and to maintain—and, of course, to supervise—on a weekly basis.

The clinical experiences needed by students do give students and instructors freedom to try new ideas—to be creative and innovative. For the most part, in the clinical area we are without the pressures of the workaday world faced by most health care professionals. Most students in the health care field have had group process or dynamics.

Let's move on to operationalizing a teaching method designed to give students maximum group experience in a limited class time period. The method was also planned to encourage student autonomy regarding their groups, yet to provide enough structure to minimize anxiety. This method also allowed for role modeling by the instructor.

Students were anxious because they were new to a locked ward in a 174-bed subacute psychiatric setting, and in some later groups (conducted in an intermediate care facility) they were anxious because of lack of experience in group work and/or care of the elderly.

Students were first taught the importance of planning and organizing their groups. That knowledge can mean the difference between success and failure and rewards and frustrations for the new leader.

### The Planning Phase for Students

In the planning phase students were assigned to:

- Learn the correct definitions for the various group modalities (see Table 36–1*).
- Read charts on all patients who were to be in their group, so that they would know

special diet needs, mobility problems, medication regimen, life-styles, support persons, and so forth.

- Select a list of potential group members.
- Make contact with them even if they are mute and unresponsive.
- Discuss each patient's potential with the primary caregiver (nurse, psychiatrist; also team leaders, counselors).
- Prior to the first group meeting, make a contract (if patient seemed appropriate). See Chapter 9 on contract-making.

Objectives and goals are important components of the planning of group work. Student leader objectives were to:

- Lead a group weekly with a co-leader for 45 minutes to one hour for a period of seven weeks (or whatever the length of the practicum).
- Study the dynamics of group process.
- Analyze the meaning of the group behaviors of individual members and of the group collectively.
- Identify prevalent group themes.
- Identify needs of group members.

Leader expectations of group members were that they

- Identify a new friend (or friends) in the group.
- Attend meetings regularly.
- Stay for the entire meeting.
- Participate in the group by verbally sharing.

System expectations of group leaders were that they

- Provide role models of group leadership with regressed individuals.
- Supplement an existing, rich program in the institution for the motivated patients.
- Provide groups to individuals who were not in weekly psychiatrist-led groups.

### Learning Goals

The students were assigned to a seven-week clinical practicum on a subacute psychiatric setting or an intermediate care facility. As pre-

---

*Reality orientation groups continue to be called reality therapy or reality testing. See Chapters 14 and 15 for further discussion.

TABLE 36-1. Comparison of reality therapy and reality orientation

| Reality therapy | Reality orien... |
|---|---|
| Is a variation of psychotherapy. | Is a communication tool. |
| Focus: morality of *behavior*. | Focus: rehabilitation of person, t... confusion, Actvities of Daily Livin... |
| Treats irresponsible behavior. | Awareness of existing situation. |
| Finds alternative *responsible behavior*. | Teaches organized behavior. |
| Doesn't believe in mental illness—irresponsible behavior due to inability to cope with stress. | Traditional diagnosis of mental disorder. |
| Six principles easily learned—application time varies with ability to establish relationship. | Techniques—easily learned with immediate application. No personal relationship need be established. |
| Therapist—trained, must be *meaningful* to client. | Therapist—any trained person interacting with client. |
| No props used—only verbal and nonverbal communication. | Use of environmental props and verbal communication— orient to time, place, and person. |
| No correction—removed from group with undesirable behavior. | Correction of inappropriate behavior and verbal response. Use of repeated instructions. |
| Communication ability required. | No communication ability required. |
| Mutual contract required. | No contract required. |
| Behavior evaluation by client required. | No evaluation by client required. |
| Personal involvement by therapist necessary. | No personal involvement necessary. |
| Time progression—usually short, may be long. | Time progression—unlimited. |
| No excuses, sympathy, or punishment. | Excuses made by care giver. |
| Only realistic behavior acknowledged. | Emphasizes functioning of ADL. |
| Consistency, firmness, patience, and perseverance are important. | |

SOURCE: B. Barkley, P. Howard, G. Ikeda, K. Mason, and L. Sater. 1981. Lecture entitled Reality Therapy. San Jose State University Department of Nursing, San Jose, Calif.

viously described, I had tried teaching students by conducting two weekly group meetings and rotating the students through the experience with me; I was the group leader. The method was confusing for all, to put it mildly. Students did not really learn the patients very well because of the rotation, and of course, the confused patients did not need the additional confusion produced by the rotation of new leaders into the group. Sometimes the students brought in the wrong patients, who were then reluctant to leave, especially when they saw the coffeepot nearby; they did perceive the ambience.

While I believe the students did learn something, they certainly did not get the maximum-benefit learning experience in the groups. Nor did they carry much responsibility. Since I was the group leader, they often chose to be observers rather than to co-lead actively with me.

When the next group of students arrived, I negotiated with the personnel in the psychiatric facility for a different type of learning experience in group for students. This model could be adapted to other disciplines, of course. Co-leaders were assigned to conduct their own weekly group. Groups were held concurrently in the large, cheerful dining room, five groups at a time. We chose the dining room because it was light, bright, and roomy and had many round tables, which facilitated the various types of group projects. Together we planned a master program with specific timely themes and motifs for each meeting. (See Chapter 7 by Burnside, Baumler, and Weaverdyck; that chapter explains the use of the model for day care centers and covers the importance of planning group meetings and theme selection.) Students were, of course, free to deviate, change, or add according to the particular needs of their group members. Within the general theme, each pair of students was free to carry out the meeting as they wished; however, the structure eem to help them, especially in the beginning when anxiety flourished.

When the students went to collect their patients for the meeting, I stayed in the dining room to be sure that patients did not leave in the early meetings. I helped members find their places at their assigned group table and acted as a "hostess," so to speak. I encouraged each of them to drink a glass of water while they waited, because many of them were on antidepressant or antipsychotic drugs, which cause dry mouths in the user. The elderly person often has dry skin and/or may be dehydrated from forgetting or neglecting to drink adequate fluids daily (Todd 1976; Chapter 7 of this book). At the beginning of the group experience, the patients were quite negative about the water and most of them had to be encouraged to drink it.

The group was planned to be a catalyst for the formation of friendships among group members. I had seen this happen many times in my previous groups of institutionalized aged. The group would also help encourage and promote more appropriate behavior in the members when they were outside of the group. One group member, who had once been in the Seabees, wrote graffiti on the walls, managed to take the sprinkler heads off the sprinklers outside, and in general, continually dismantled parts of the building. Our goal with him was instantly to reward *appropriate nondestructive* behavior observed in the group meetings.

The group members would verbalize or be assisted in verbalizing some of the feelings they were experiencing. For example, one woman who was extremely angry prior to a group meeting (and very paranoid) came to the meeting, where she had a listening audience and received much support. She left the group hugging the nurses and smiling, and the students were surprised to find out how warm and loving this lady could be.

The group members chosen were not active in the interesting daily activities provided for them by the activities department. The pace seemed to be too fast for the older residents. In the very structured and closed group, however, they were able to participate because of the slow pace of the leaders, the steady assistance they received, and the simplicity of the tasks and projects. There were two student-nurse leaders for five or six patients; such a high student-patient ratio also provided an important learning factor for students. This method provided learning about co-therapy principles.

## Problems Anticipated by Students

The students asked me these questions before the meetings began:

1. What do we do if members decide to leave our group?
2. Will members talk to us?
3. Will members be violent or misbehave in the group?
4. What will we do or talk about for half an hour or 45 minutes?

None of the anticipated problems occurred; in fact, the students reported that time went fast in the first meeting. Much to the surprise of the students, the patients did not want to leave. In fact, some stayed on much past the time that had been allowed for the group meeting. One woman who manifested much anxiety in the first group continued to stay after the meetings; she seemed held fast by the attention she had received during the meeting.

After the students had gathered their groups, they told me which patients had refused to come. The challenge was mine! I went to each person to see if they would reconsider. Some did and some did not. It will be no surprise to read that they were usually found lying on their beds. If they had never been in a group before, they were most reluctant. The demented patients vacillated so much from week to week and minute to minute that they often were ready to come to the meetings with me only moments after they had vehemently told the student no. One white-haired lady was best enticed to group with a warm bear hug, which new students, of course, did not know.

When the groups were in place, I moved through the dining room observing students and their techniques. Occasionally I had students move to the opposite side of the table when they were seated incorrectly in their group. New students have a habit of "clumping" when they are a new unit; this phenomenon also occurred in their group leadership. (By clump-ing, I mean that two or more students stay close together, either on the unit or within the group.) One of my roles was to "declump" them so that they could be more effective as leaders. Co-leaders need to be able to see one another to acknowledge each other's verbal messages. Also, by sitting apart, each could place two anxious patients on either side of them, which helps to stabilize a group faster and reduces anxiety. The leader can touch the person, move closer, or hold hands if necessary. The warmth and vitality of the leader is felt from such close-ness, even by the very withdrawn or demented individual.

## GROUP WORK GUIDELINES

In general, the following constitute adapta-tions made to group work.

### An Instructor's Guidelines for Beginning Group Leaders

The general pointers offered here should be useful to beginning group leaders.

- Help each member to feel a part of the group. Control the more vocal. Help members interact with each other.
- Recognize that feelings can't always be accurately read from a person's words; lis-ten with a "third ear."
- Leader needs to hold the group together and direct it. A great deal of the success of group work depends on the leader's ability to recognize and direct.
- Play up the positive; always reward "desired" behavior.
- Praise and reward generously.
- Sit beside nervous or jittery members or the most confused.
- Learn to be an active listener; tune in to the various needs of the members.
- Let the members teach you; they have a need to be needed.
- Be flexible enough to relate to different types of people in a group. Remember that

the group is for the purpose of helping peo-ple do what they *can* do.

- *Each individual has value.* Identify the impairments of each member and note how each has coped or is coping.
- The leader's goal is to bring out the best in the patient and help each other gain confidence.
- Use co-leadership if you feel anxious about group leading.
- Give each member equal time in the group; never neglect to include a member.
- Be careful that you do not put members on the spot; change the subject quickly if you observe this occurring.
- Older folks can provide social stimulation among themselves; a group can help bring out quiet individuals.
- Learn the ability to block out extraneous noises and happenings and focus only on your group.
- Be sure you have adequate space and no background noise; noise is a definite distraction.
- Schedule the group meeting for a time when most of the members are at their optimum performance.
- Always use the names *the members* want you to use.
- Relate to all personnel in the agency as well as the patients.
- Support of the agency is crucial.
- Support of the kitchen personnel is impor-tant if fluids or refreshments are served.
- Space is needed to accommodate enough tables for the groups.
- Lock the area, or other patients will come in and expect to be included.
- Keep a closed group if possible.

### Guidelines for Beginners in Institutions

The following list of guidelines has been developed over the years that I have supervised students from a variety of disciplines.

- Limit group to six to eight members.

- Include women and men (if possible).
- Begin meeting for half an hour; then increase time.
- Use big, easy-to-read name tags for each person at each meeting.
- Sit in a circle; use a round table if possible.
- Always serve fluids (to reduce dehydration, increase "flushing out").
- Serve snacks if at all possible.
- Discuss "easy" topics at first: pets, cars, holidays, and so on.
- Be sure everyone is included in the meeting.
- Welcome everyone with a handshake as soon as he or she arrives.
- Use props: old jewelry, old clocks, old tools, toaster, potato masher, washboard, and so on, to create interest in your reminiscing groups. Pass the props around to be touched and looked at closely.
- Don't let one member be a monopolizer.
- Sit beside the most anxious member of the group.
- If a member leaves, always say, "I hope you'll come back."
- Expect some sad topics; do not discourage them.
- Do not permit aggressive behavior in the group; remove the aggressive person immediately so that other members are not afraid.
- Use songs and music when you can.
- Do simple things with the group: for example, make toast with butter or pop some popcorn.
- Discuss spices, perfume, onions, and other things with pronounced scents, and let them smell the item. (Put cologne on the ladies and shaving lotion on the men that day.)
- Insist on politeness in everyone.
- Keep your promises to the members.
- Go slowly—both in speech and movement.
- Celebrate any type of occasion, but do not assume that everyone wants a birthday cake.

- Make holidays very special.
- Work on social graces; improve eating manners when you can.
- Share a tad about yourself (and/or your family and pets) once in a while.
- Say goodbye and thank each member for coming at each meeting.
- Enjoy your group experience and the members will enjoy you and the group.

It is very important for the instructor to show the students exactly how to work in the group—physical distance, standing behind members, where to touch members, and so on. Group leadership may be so new to students in the beginning that they are not sure how to begin, how close to be to patients, or how to handle aberrant behavior (which sometimes occurs).

### Guidelines for Beginners from Beginners

I asked one group of students* who had been effective as group leaders to offer suggestions for the next class. They gave their advice willingly.

- A group needs some type of facilitator. The leader is a role model and a communicator and can make or break a group.
- Members and leader feel more comfortable with each meeting.
- Be very careful to respect personal spaces; for example, do not assume that it is okay to have a small group meet in someone's room without asking permission.
- Some older people are not accustomed to being in groups; they may feel that their personal space is being invaded and it may be difficult for them to open up at first to strangers.
- Allow silent ones to participate at their own pace; be sure to maintain eye contact.
- Use physical contact—for example, hand touch, leg tap, hug.
- Never treat the elderly as though they were children; they know more than any book

---

*Student group leaders G. Marks, S. Sobel, and M. Cashman offer these guidelines after their first group leadership experience with the elderly.

can ever teach us. Give them a chance to be the leader's teacher.

- Laugh with them; they have a great sense of humor.

- Let them know how interesting their stories about their lives are to listen to.

- Keep your questions short and open-ended — for example, "I can't imagine living without electricity; how did you read at night?" Such a question can lead to many topics you may not have thought of (no books, newspapers, radio; candles, lanterns; "Who had time to read?")

- Learn new ways to encourage everyone in the group to participate.

- Let the group establish goals. (For example, I originally thought I had to have a topic set each week. After the third week I asked how it was going, and if they preferred having a topic set. They said they enjoyed spur-of-the-moment conversations because it made them remember more.)

- Take time to listen — *really* listen — to them.

- Individualize care within the group. (Individualize interactions with members; individualize technique for raising self-esteem).

- Always have other ideas you can talk about in case you need them. Holidays are great starters.

- Share things about yourself; don't expect to *get* if you don't *give.*

- If someone seems uncomfortable with a topic, change it. Let them know you are not there to analyze; you are there to learn

- I found that it is okay to let someone dominate a group as long as it is not the same person every week. Other members often enjoy listening. Do draw out quiet ones in a gentle way, or at least always acknowledge their presence by telling them you appreciate their spending time with you.

- It is difficult to keep the group together; wanderers can create problems.

- Providing snacks does help; they love to have things brought in "special" for them.

- For those who have a hard time remembering, keep a 5-inch by 8-inch card on each patient and write down after each group

what the patient shared; for example, "I have five brothers and two sisters. My mother died when I was three. I lived in Illinois until I was ten."

- Be sure to notice differences — new dress, hair style, nail polish. Little things really count.

- Dress casually but with enough "taste" to show your respect for the members of the group. The message might be, "I think you're important enough to dress up for" (without overdoing it to outshine them).

- Be patient and let ideas that arise in the group lead the discussion.

- Do not push when the group runs out of gas; start to wind things up.

- Always keep several topics in reserve because what you think may be a good idea to discuss sometimes turns into a dead end!

- Make sure everyone in the group is treated the same and is given equal time to speak so that no one in the group feels left out.

- Follow through with anything you promise to do, to prevent disappointment.

- I feel I have increased my creativity.

Another sensitive student* had this to say about her first group leadership experience:

As I got to know each one of the members of the group better, I began to individualize my discussion strategies. By this I mean that each member has specific interests because of past experiences and enjoys reminiscing about specific things they relate to. One member who had never been married who is very well read does not care to talk about flowers, gardening, cooking, or children, but she does love talking politics, history, and current events. After our third group (it took me long enough) I finally became aware that she perked up when we talked about the topics I have just mentioned. I made sure I included a topic of discussion she might like. I have learned to form a close circle; it helps the elderly hear one another better. I have learned not to set a specific amount of time for the group because their attention span is limited. I have also learned not to get insulted when a member drops out (at first, I took it personally). I have adjusted to members leav-

---

*S. Achim, personal communication, 1982.

ing the group early. I have learned that they love to hear about life and what I am doing—it helps them to remember back when they did similar things.

I think the most important thing I have learned is how to actually just sit down and talk with the elderly. I don't have grandparents and I have had little exposure to the elderly, so I've always thought that they would be dull to talk to; on the contrary, I have learned a lot about the past by speaking to these wonderful people.

I forgot to mention one member in the group who I thought was not too excited about me or the group in the beginning. Well, at our last session she gave me a kiss—boy, did that make my day!

## TRAINING PROCEDURES

In an article entitled "Current Practice in the Training of Group Psychotherapists," R. R. Dies (1980) lists effective textbooks and specialized training methods (Table 36–2). Although the reader will find little on group work with the aged in these books, they do provide a broad base on group therapy. (In regard to training, note the importance given to item 3, experiential groups, in Table 36–2).

Dies (1980) also delineates methods for evaluating training experiences:

1. Co-therapy experience with a qualified therapist;
2. Discussion of your own therapy tapes with a supervisor;
3. Supervised experience in individual therapy;
4. Co-therapy experience with a peer, followed by sessions with a supervisor;
5. Attendance at group psychotherapy workshops;
6. Attendance at T-group training workshops;
7. Participation as a patient in a therapy group;
8. Discussion of films or videotapes produced by experts;
9. Careful analysis and discussion of audiotapes produced by experts;
10. Serving as a recorder-observer in a group;

TABLE 36–2.  **Training procedures**

| Recommendation | % Endorsement |
| --- | --- |
| **Readings suggested by 5% or more of the sample** | |
| 1. Yalom (1975), *The Theory and Practice of Group Psychotherapy.* | 76 |
| 2. Bion (1959), *Experiences in Groups.* | 29 |
| 3. *International Journal of Group Psychotherapy.* | 16 |
| 4. Whitaker and Lieberman (1970), *Psychotherapy through the Group Process.* | 14 |
| 5. Lieberman, Yalom, and Miles (1973), *Encounter Groups: First Facts.* | 12 |
| 6. Durkin (1964), *The Group in Depth.* | 11 |
| 7. Kaplan and Sadock (1971). *Comprehensive Group Psychotherapy.* | 10 |
| 8. Sager and Kaplan (1973), *Progress in Group and Family Therapy.* | 10 |
| 9. Mullan and Rosenbaum (1962), *Group Psychotherapy: Theory and Practice.* | 8 |
| 10. Foulkes and Anthony (1965), *Group Psychotherapy: The Psychoanalytic Approach.* | 6 |
| 11. Rosenbaum and Berger (1975), *Group Psychotherapy and Group Function.* | 6 |
| 12. Slavson (1964), *A Textbook in Analytic Group Psychotherapy.* | 6 |
| 13. Parloff (1968), Analytic Group Psychotherapy. | 5 |
| 14. Rioch (1970), The Work of Wilfred Bion on Groups. | 5 |
| | |
| **Specialized training methods** | |
| 1. Didactic Seminars and Readings | 26 |
| 2. Observation | 21 |
| 3. Experiential Groups | |
|   a. Process, therapy, and/or training groups | 47 |
|   b. Workshops or role plays | 43 |
| 4. Supervisory Methods | |
|   a. Dyadic supervision | 28 |
|   b. Group supervision | 20 |
|   c. Co-therapy | 27 |
|   d. Video, audio, or one-way mirrors | 32 |
|   e. Miscellaneous (individual therapy supervision, listen to own tapes, etc. | 10 |

SOURCE: From "Current Practice in the Training of Group Psychotherapists," by R. R. Dies, *International Journal of Group Psychotherapy*, 1980, 30(2), 173. Reprinted by permission.

11. Didactic seminars (theory, research, case study);

12. Learning by doing, self-taught (practice, reading).

For beginning students (not psychotherapists), the most relevant and effective methods on the list are co-therapy experience with a peer; discussion of group experience; and didactic seminars on group theory, research, and case examples.

The intense loneliness and alienation one sees in some of the mentally ill patients—for example, the demented (Alzheimer's type, for one) or the burned out schizophrenic—does spur an instructor on to refine group methods. The challenges to the instructor and to students are tremendous.

## SUMMARY

With the ever-increasing number elderly with mental impairment (as note information on demographic trends in Ch 1 and also described in Chapter 13), educa will have to consider methods to teach clinic skills to increasing numbers of students. We will need to upgrade and improve the psychosocial care of the elderly as we teach, and we will be constant role models. Students who have not been particularly interested in the elderly can be "turned on" by an intense, meaningful group experience in which they assume leadership, just as described by S. Achim. This advice to instructors comes from Lewis Carroll (1975, 75):

> Would you tell me, please which way I ought to go from here?
> That depends a good deal on where you want to get to.

## EXERCISE 1*

Select a group therapy session to observe. Make an appointment with the group leader; request a time to observe a complete group session. After the meeting, complete the following analysis:

1. Describe the type of group you observed (psychotherapy, remotivation, reminiscing, and so forth).
2. What instructions were given to you by the group leader(s)?
3. What was the ratio of staff to patient/client?
4. Was the staff/client ratio workable in your terms? For example, were there too few or too many staff for the size of the patient group?
5. Describe the members in the group.
6. Was this an open or a closed group?
7. What were the qualifications of the group leader(s)?
8. Did you see differences in the level of function of the group leaders? (If so, to what do you attribute this?)
9. What did you like about the group? Were any therapeutic techniques demonstrated that you would like to try the next time you are a group leader of older people?
10. What would you change about the group you observed?
11. What unanswered questions do you have about this group experience (or about groups in general)?

*This exercise is used by my colleague, Mary Jo Gorney Fadiman, in teaching group therapy. She kindly gave permission to reprint it here.

ise to simulate a group experience. For each group ...ould have six to eight members), the instructor ...an envelope and adds enough "member" slips to ...p. For example, for a group of eight, the enve-...r slips and one group leader slip. To determine ...t draws a slip from the envelope.

...s follows: *You are a member of a reminiscing* ...on one topic for this group session. After the ses-...our own reminiscing:

- ...ere you uncomfortable in sharing with the group? If so, why?
- Were your memories sad or happy or both?
- What positive thing happened in the group while you were sharing memories?

The group leader slip should read as follows: *You are the group leader of a reminiscing group. As leader, make sure that everyone gets a chance to speak and to reminisce if they like. You may suggest one of these topics for your reminiscing group:*

- Do you remember your favorite toy?
- Do you remember your first day at school?
- Do you remember a very special occasion from your childhood?
- Do you remember the first wedding you attended?
- Do you remember your first pet?

Start the group off by explaining the purpose and noting the time you will have to reminisce; bring closure to the group by briefly summarizing what each person talked about in the group. Then return to the large group for discussion.

*Note:* The members have the following questions written on their slips. You can use these questions for a summary or a group discussion:

- Were you uncomfortable in sharing with the group? If so, why?
- Were your memories sad or happy or both?
- What positive thing happened in the group while you were sharing memories?

Allow 45 minutes for reminiscing. Then discuss the group experiences.

---

## EXERCISE 3

This is an exercise I began using in 1970. Give each student a blank piece of white 8½- by 11-inch paper and give only the following instruction: "Draw your aged self."* Encourage those who are hesitant by saying that only a simple sketch is expected. Have students share their drawing with a peer. Then lead a class discussion on sensory losses, other losses, positive versus negative drawings, and students' feelings about their own aging as they drew their pictures.

Have them compare their drawings to Figures 36–8a through 36–8n. Do they see similarities?

---

*If you have a class with older students, have them draw themselves as centenarians.

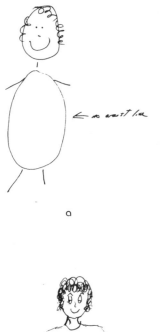

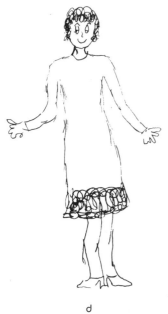

FIGURE 36-8a through 36-8n. *Drawings of aged self.*

Mike @ 100 years of age

h

DISCO

i

At last, time to do what I want (read)
and resources to collect art

j

Me at 100
rocking my
great-great-grandchild

k

l

m

n

## EXERCISE 4

Read the article "A Modified Group Treatment for Elderly Narcissistic Patients," by Brian Levine and Marcia Poston (*International Journal of Group Psychotherapy* 30[2]: 153–67, [April 1980]). Replicate that group experience as closely as you can with a group of frail, narcissistic elderly in any setting. Write a two-page paper on what modifications you made in your group and why they were necessary.

## REFERENCES

Bales, R. F., and F. L. Strodtbeck. 1951. Phases in group problem-solving. *Journal of Abnormal Social Psychology* 46:485–95.

Braaten, L. J. 1974–75. Developmental phases of encounter groups and related intensive groups. *Interpersonal Development* 5:112–29.

Carroll, L. 1975. *Alice's adventures in wonderland.* New York: Viking Press.

Cooper, C. L., and I. L. Mangham. 1971. *T-groups: A survey of research.* New York: Wiley.

Dies, R. R. 1980. Current practice in the training of group psychotherapists. *International Journal of Group Psychotherapy* 30(2): 171 (April).

Dunphy, D. C. 1968. Phases, roles, and myths in self-analytic groups. *Applied Behavioral Science* 4:195–224.

Goldstein, K. 1939. *The organism.* New York: American Book.

Hardy, M. 1978. Evaluation nursing theory. In *Theory development: What, why, how?,* ed. M. Hardy. New York: National League for Nurses.

Janosik, E., and J. Miller. 1982. Group work with the elderly. In *Life cycle group work in nursing,* ed. E. Janosik and L. Phipps. Belmont, Calif.: Wadsworth.

Kaplan, A. 1974. *The conduct of inquiry.* San Francisco, Calif.: Chandler.

Kaplan, S. R., and M. Roman. 1963. Phases of development in an adult therapy group. *International Journal of Group Psychotherapy* 13:10–26.

King, I. 1978. The 'What' of Theory Development. In *Theory development: What, why, how?,* ed. M. Hardy. New York: National League for Nursing.

Lacoursiere, R. B. 1980. *The life cycle of groups: Group developmental stage theory.* New York: Human Sciences Press.

Phipps, L. 1982. *Life cycle group work in nursing,* ed. E. Janosik and L. Phipps. Belmont, Calif.: Wadsworth.

Runkel, P. J., M. Lawrence, S. Oldfield, et al. 1971. Stages of group development: An empirical test of Tuckman's hypothesis. *Journal of Applied Behavioral Science* 7:180–93.

Stanford, G., and A. E. Roark. 1974. *Human interaction in education.* Boston: Allyn & Bacon.

Todd, J. 1976. Water depletion in mentally disturbed patients. *Nursing Mirror* 142(18): 60–61 (April 29).

Tuckman, B. W. 1965. Developmental sequence in small groups. *Psychological Bulletin* 63:384–99.

Yalom, I. 1975. *The theory and practice of group psychotherapy.* New York: Basic Books.

## BIBLIOGRAPHY

Maslow, A. 1970. *Motivation and personality.* 2d ed. New York: Harper & Row.

Nordmark, M., and A. Rohweder. 1975. *Scientific foundations of nursing.* 3d ed., p. 33. Philadelphia: Lippincott.

Pfeiffer, J., and J. Jones. 1981. *A handbook of structured experiences for human relations.* San Diego, Calif.: University Associates.

Reynolds, P. 1971. *Primer in theory construction.* Indianapolis, Ind.: Bobbs-Merrill.

Ross, M. 1963. A review of some recent group psychotherapy methods for elderly psychiatric patients. In *Group psychotherapy and group function,* ed. M. Rosenbaum and M. Berger. New York: Basic Books.

Smith, E. F. 1973. Teaching group therapy in an undergraduate curriculum. *Perspectives on Psychiatric Care* 11:70–74 (April–May–June).

Veninga, R., and D. Fredlund. 1974. Teaching the group approach. *Nursing Outlook* 22(6): 373–76 (June).

## RESOURCES

### Monograph

Specific content on long term care. *Current Gerontology: Long Term Care.* 1982. Sheldon S. Tobin (ed). Gerontology Society of America, 1835 K. Street, N.W., Washington, D.C.

    This is a premiere issue of a monograph series with articles from *The Gerontologist* and *The Journal of Gerontology.*

### Kit

Working with older people: A resource kit. Slide/tape overview (7 min.), 16 mm color/sound film. Linely Productions, Inc. Attn. Nils Lindquist, 4784 No. High Street, Columbus, Ohio 43214.

# chapter 37

# Group Work and Professional Curricula

*Bernita M. Steffl*

*Through group work students develop a profound and sincere respect for old people.*

## LEARNING OBJECTIVES

- Define **preparatory steps** for group work with older individuals.

- Plan and implement a group work experience with an older age group.

- Identify possible pitfalls and barriers to professional group work with the elderly.

## KEY WORDS

- Barriers
- Concept
- Evaluation
- Objectives
- Remotivation
- Rewards
- Settings
- Socialization
- Therapeutic

The increase in the aging population; the explosive escalation of community services and programs for the aging, such as the thousands of nutrition sites; and the growing number of long-term care facilities have created a need and opportunity for group services, treatment, and recreation. The resocialization of elderly individuals who suffer physical and psychosocial losses and relocation provides a fertile setting for development and growth of group work with older individuals.

Since the first edition of this text was published, there has been extensive development of medical, nursing, social work, and multidisciplinary courses in gerontology with clinical components that lend themselves to group work with older age groups (Brower 1981; Ellison 1981; Carter and Galliano 1981). In discussion about courses with faculty around the country and in observing students in various service areas, I have noted a great deal of interest in and activity with groups. I have also had many requests for assistance specifically for group work with well elderly. However, I have also observed situations where I believe specific guidelines for working with the elderly were sorely needed, not available, and not included in the course content. Thus, we have a mandate to provide this. There are specific basic human needs; developmental tasks; special characteristics; and special topics, strategies, and techniques to be considered in curricula for group work with older persons.

Much responsibility for meeting some of these needs falls on the professional schools, especially those of nursing and social work. Gerontology is not given the same time and attention in nursing curricula as child growth and development. The same is true in social work and in medicine (Cassell 1972). Inroads are being made, and now we are clearly identifying gerontological content in the curricula. Basic human needs and developmental tasks of aging are considered from a biopsychosocial aspect, and students are provided practice opportunities to demonstrate application of theory. The developmental model is steadily gaining in curricula content, thanks to E. Erikson (1950), R. N. Butler and M. Lewis (1982), D. C. Kimmel (1974), and J. H. Barrett (1972).

This chapter presents content for preparing students to do group work within the older population.

## STUDENTS AS GROUP WORKERS

The use of groups falls into three main categories: (1) for effect on participants, (2) for collective problem solving, and (3) for change in social situations or conditions outside the groups (Hartford 1972). Groups are also used for research and often as a major part of a clinical learning experience. L. Bellak and T. Karasu (1976) state that group interventions with the elderly are a valuable source of therapeutic help and that they can range from the psychotherapeutic to task-oriented socialization groups (Table 37-1). Butler and Lewis (1982) suggest that group therapy should be widely used in institutions and outpatient seminars for the elderly and that volunteers as well as professionals and paraprofessionals have been "trained" to varying degrees of competence, but nurses probably conduct more group work with older persons than do other professionals.

Rationale for introducing group work with the elderly into curricula is that it provides a contact for students that accomplishes several goals. First, it quickly teaches students whether they are doing what they want to do, or at least provides the practical experience necessary for a realistic career or specialty choice. Second, it gives an invaluable opportunity for students to test what they have been taught against reality. Finally, and equally important, it helps teach the unwritten content of any profession—the ethics and values that determine behavior and underlie responsibility in the profession (Cassell 1972, 255).

Students need assistance to relate group work experience to theoretical concepts. This is particularly true in the planning stages of their group work.

### The Beginning Student

Because of changes in life-style in our culture —for example, movement away from the extended family and longer life—older people have to depend more on groups outside the family for social interaction. Current trends suggest that future cohorts of older persons may belong to and participate more in voluntary associations (Cutler 1976). This is group participation in its broadest sense. A neophyte in group work might first be exposed to old people by visiting an organization such as a senior center. Such an indoctrination provides an opportunity to study well older adults before dealing with the sick or seriously disabled.

### More Advanced Students

Students with more background, sophistication, and preparation in basic social science courses are better able to handle some of the multiple losses of the elderly, grief work, and the increasing physical infirmities of group members. The possibilities and settings for group work increase for these students and

TABLE 37-1.  Categories of group service and intervention

| Type | Example of kind of participant | Goal |
|---|---|---|
| Psychotherapeutically oriented group | Older person who is hurt, frightened, and disappointed by multiple losses. | Stepping stone to resocialization. |
| Task-oriented groups | Elderly psychiatric patient who resists direct psychotherapy. Person who suffers a major permanent loss. | Reexperience pleasure of shared tasks. Regain self-confidence. |
| Socialization groups | Those suffering social isolation or who have a painful social vacuum in their lives. | Transition from structured socialization to state of emotional stability and confidence in seeking involvement. |
| Recreation groups | The handicapped and those with limited transportation. Residents of senior citizen housing. Participants of nutrition programs. | Diversion, entertainment, and stimulation. Socialization. |

SOURCE: Adapted from L. Bellak and T. Karasu. 1976. *Geriatric psychiatry* (New York: Grune & Stratton), 211–12.

could easily range from hospital geriatric wards, extended care facilities, and psychiatric settings to day care centers for the elderly. (See Chapter 10 for a detailed list of possible placements.) A clinical component should be dovetailed with theory and practice, whether the student is in an elective course in gerontology or in a clinically geared course. Essential gerontological content can be applied to clinical practice by nurses, social workers, psychologists, counselors, occupational therapists, physical therapists, ministers, and paraprofessionals at various stages in the educational curriculum and in a variety of settings.

For the past five years I have encouraged an optional experience in gerontology during the senior course in community health nursing. There are four or five students each semester who are interested enough to spend eight weeks in a community setting such as a day care center, a storefront senior center, and centers established primarily for Title III nutrition programs. There is unlimited opportunity for group work in such settings. Most students have been able to try out several levels of group work. They were surprised at the interest and hunger for knowledge about health problems. The old people themselves like to lecture or teach and share when they are given the opportunity. Many have not had much formal education, so positive feedback about their knowledge and skills from professionals is important to them and is also a way to increase sagging self-esteem.

### Two Examples of Student-Led Groups

**Example 1.** A paraprofessional health worker in a day care center attended a continuing educational extension course; her wealth of experience in family life and interest in her job made my teaching a joy. She began a reminiscence group at a day care center. Because it was difficult for her to use the university library, I made an effort to furnish her with literature and share experiences of other students. Within several weeks she developed goals and started a reminiscing group with six Spanish-speaking old people. The entire group work was conducted in Spanish!

The following quote is from the student's report after the second session:

At least no one fell asleep during the sessions, and each contributed something of himself that enabled the others in the group to appreciate their common background of being Mexican, of being able to speak to each other in the language they consider their mother tongue, and of being able to look back on some of the hardships that they had endured and had been able to survive. Just as we left the lounge, Mr. M. quoted an old Mexican proverb that expressed their ideas on living. *"Vivir es triumfar."* "To live is to triumph." Looking back over his 87 years, because he still lives as fully as he is able, for Mr. M., life is a triumph (Montoya 1976, 10).

Several months later the coordinator of the day care center reported that the reminiscing group was going well and that the staff was learning much more about their clients!

**Example 2.** Three students conducted an exercise program for a group of 10 to 15 senior citizens in a low-cost high-rise housing facility. The students rotated the leadership for half-hour sessions. After six weeks the students felt that they had stimulated and motivated several of the members to add more physical activity to their daily routine.

Such an experience offers students a chance to assess older individuals physically as well as psychosocially. For example, the students became aware of the cumulative deficits resulting from a hearing loss. One distinguished man in the group was often criticized by the members. He was willing and able, but he was never in step becuase he could not hear the instructions or the cadence. He was always at ½ when the group was ¾. The women in the group got very angry with him.

The students also had to learn to let old people give. The members took up a collection for the students on the last day of the group meetings. Many professionals have long been taught that it is not professional to accept gifts, but such a philosophy bogs down in work with the aged.

## STEPS IN PREPARING STUDENTS FOR GROUP WORK

### Evaluating Students' Background Knowledge of Group Work

Students are expected to learn principles and techniques of group work, such as: (1) levels of groups, (2) theories of group interaction, (3) group roles, and (4) group rules. They also learn therapeutic communication skills and interviewing techniques. This kind of content is usually taught early in the curriculum, and students are encouraged to analyze and use these skills and techniques in group discussions and group conferences for their own learning. In spite of exposure to theory and experience, however, one cannot assume that the student is ready to lead a group, so assess your students' knowledge and skills in group work and help the student prepare accordingly. Asking the following questions helps students prepare and plan for a positive group experience.

- What are your objectives? Are they client centered?
- Have you assessed the mechanics, such as place, space, equipment, dates, time, accessibility and availability, and so on?
- Have you included agency and clients in your plans?
- Do you plan to do this alone? Will you need help?
- What about continuity after you move on?
- What kind of records or documentation will you keep?

How will you evaluate the effectiveness of your group?

Since a great deal of group work with the elderly involves interviewing, it is necessary to assess students' skills in this area (see Burnside 1980). In any group work or communication with the elderly, one should automatically: (1) assess distance, both physical and psychological; (2) assess hearing—older persons usually hear better from one ear than from the other; and (3) assess comprehension.

Students sometimes need considerable coaching and reinforcement to assess and maintain the above. I find it helpful to role-play with the students and demonstrate distances (by, for example, the placement of chairs), sitting at the same height level, facing the interviewee, eye contact, and speaking slowly and waiting for answers.

### Choosing Type of Group and Group Members

Students generally need help in determining the level of group they want to lead and how to select the members. Students may desire a socializing group that ends up being a therapy session or vice versa. Does it matter if this happens? It is important that students do not get in over their heads. It is also important that student and teacher have well-stated objectives and evaluate according to the objectives. Whether the objectives were met is not as important as knowing if they were achieved and understanding what happened if they were not.

It is also necessary for students to develop well-defined criteria for group member selection. Help will be needed to consider age, sex, ethnicity, educational background, disabilities, diagnoses, and the number of persons to include. For example, a group of four to six persons with physical handicaps may be more realistic than six to eight because of the time involved in seating, the mobility problems, and so forth. (See Chapter 10 on group membership.)

Groups have to have momentum and vitality to maintain continuity and reduce absenteeism and dropouts. Selection of members is critical. Butler and Lewis (1982) argue for heterogeneity. It is also helpful to combine a female-male team as leaders (Linden 1954).

Since many older individuals hunger for knowledge and seek learning opportunities attending discussion groups, faculty and students might consider some specific preparation listed in William Hill's *Learning through Discussion* (1969), such as Fawcett's guide for leaders and members of discussion groups. This guide is more than a "how to" manual; it includes roles, skills, and a list of criteria for learning-through-discussion group.

### Group Setting and Mechanics

Students need continual reminding and assistance to choose an adequate setting in terms of space, light, accessibility, safety of tables and chairs, armrests, and work space. For example, older people often feel more comfortable if they can sit with their legs under a table and have the table top to lean on and put things on. Teenagers or college students may prefer pillows on the floor or a casual living room atmosphere for their group meetings.

## Planning, Announcements, Dates, and Directions

I saw a student completely devastated after six weeks of group work when all the plans for her classes with a group of senior citizens in the community failed because, on the big day for her, the seniors did not show up. She did not follow up the telephone communications with specific written information on date, time, and place. Repetition is important not only because old people forget but because they are busy. Sometimes we forget that they have lived a long time and sat through lots of useless information. They may be pretty choosy about what they want to hear or do. Accurate, written communication should be combined with verbal plans.

## Group Interaction and Response

It is helpful to go over topics and expected responses with students. Doing so offers an excellent opportunity to demonstrate to the student group leader how to learn more about gerontology and relate learning to the literature and research. One way is for the student to make a continuing biopsychosocial assessment during group interaction. For example, the student needs to note the types of losses existing in group members. Do these losses fit with textbook descriptions? Body language and other nonverbal communications are important. Regarding verbal communication, can the student hear what the patient did not say?

Two students planned a series of reminiscing group sessions for eight to ten older persons (late seventies and eighties) in a church-sponsored guest house for the aged. Since this was in Canada in a Scotch-French-Irish community, the group meetings were to begin with afternoon tea. A great deal of planning was done, and the

students were excited and eager to start the first session. It turned out to be a big disappointment. Nothing went well except the tea! The report (Holder and Tilford 1974) went like this:

*Students:* "These people have lived through so much and most are very sharp, but when we started our reminiscing it fell flat. We got no response."
*Instructor:* "How did you begin?"
*Students:* "We asked the group this—'There have been many changes in the past fifty years. What has been most exciting or important to you?'"

The students were then quizzed further about their ideas on why this may have happened, and eventually I suggested that perhaps because they were dealing with thought processes of persons in their eighties (keeping in mind that there is a slowing in registration and retrieval), it may have been quite difficult on the spur of the moment to sift through 50 years! I suggested that they try again—but pose a single question, such as "What do you think about man going to the moon?" or "What do you think about the long hair styles for young men these days?" When they did try again, they had a good response. This is one example of carefully relating theory to practice.

Students will need help in termination and dealing with separation anxiety. Because there is such a need for maintaining socialization among the elderly, instructors should insist on building in plans for the group to carry on for a reasonable length of time.

## Dealing with Problems

Students will need help and feedback in dealing with problems common to all groups, such as handling a manipulator, a distractor, a silent member, a monopolizer, an overly anxious member.

It is also helpful to prepare students for the special problems of the elderly and their behavior in relation to loneliness, depression, and sensory deprivation. Students should be well prepared to deal with tears, withdrawal, anger, and very candid opinions. Old people can afford to be outspoken. They have less to lose.

## Rewards and Evaluation

Together with problems usually come much positive feedback and satisfaction if the student's goals are realistic. The student leader must have clearly stated objectives, and it is up to the instructor to help the student develop realistic ones. Most leaders want to accomplish too much too fast. Even if groups fail, I believe that the process of trying provides activity for the client and usually an unforgettable learning experience for the student. However, this viewpoint may need to be pointed out to the student.

## Instructor Guidelines

No matter where in the curriculum, at what level or in what kind of course, elective or required, the following reminders usually work well:

1. Be flexible about the setting.
2. Be flexible about the type of clinical experience you will accept for student experience.
3. Encourage creativity and remember to reinforce positively when you observe it.
4. Allow the "right to fail" by giving support and constructive criticism if something does not work.
5. Foster independent behavior and study, but be available for frequent individual conferences and for giving guidance and suggestions.
6. Encourage unique and different activities, but expect students to share with the class and validate what they do.
7. Insist on documented theory.
8. Examine your own attitudes and values regarding the aged and your knowledge level in gerontology.
9. Examine your own commitment and willingness to invest in planning, arranging, and evaluating the clinical aspects of the group experience (Steffl 1973).

Richard Grant, who has for several years used group work with older adults as a clinical experience for students in psychiatric nursing, states: "Above all, the students develop a profound and sincere respect for old people. Kids get in touch with their own heritage. A typical remark from a student is, 'I talk to my grandmother different now' " (Grant 1982).

## Experiential Teaching and Learning in Groups

Experiential exercises are especially useful in helping students understand and develop empathy—that is, getting oneself under the skin and into the feelings of the client. (It is important always to help students differentiate between empathy and sympathy. Sympathy is "feeling sorry for" and empathy is "feeling with.") Experiential exercises can be individually and creatively designed to fit the setting, situation, and group using art, music, dance, or exercises. Impact and/or success is directly dependent upon the preparation, skill, and comfort of the teacher or leader. Since experiential work deals with affect and exposure of self, it is imperative that the participants be prepared in a supportive manner for cohesiveness and self-actualization.

Students and participants should always be allowed the option of not participating. Those who resist or seem uncomfortable may try the exercise themselves later when they have grown and/or are in different circumstances.

## RESEARCH

Group work and group therapy are more widely used in community and institutional settings for older adults than is generally realized or reflected in professional and scientific literature.

H. Dennis (1976) used group work to examine the effects of remotivation therapy on acute and chronic hospitalized psychiatric patients. D. Voelkel (1978) reported a comparative study that demonstrated greater improvement among moderately to severely mentally impaired residents of a nursing home who experienced a resocialization group than among those in reality orientation groups. J. Maney and M. A. Edinberg (1976) explored the potential of using social competency groups in senior citizen centers where the participant can improve self-maintenance skills.

An unpublished study by F. F. Roberts (1981) attempted to demonstrate a positive effect of group reminiscing upon morale in the aged. No definite conclusions were possible.

One reason for the wide use of groups is necessity: It is economical and therapists (and other professionals) are not very interested in working with older individuals (Butler and Lewis 1982). A problem that tends to exist when working with students is maintaining continuity of a group(s) over a long period of time for evaluation and research.

## EDUCATIONAL BARRIERS TO PROVIDING CLINICAL PRACTICE

In addition to the scramble for time in the overloaded curriculum of most professional programs, negative attitudes toward old people still prevail among faculty. The problems of when, where, and how to place this content in the curriculum has been compounded by the many transitions in education for the helping professions, such as:

1. It is a problem to mold separate courses into the integrated curriculum where there is insufficient time for everything.
2. There are not enough educators with a broad background in gerontology.
3. Gerontology is not a pure science. It is a body of knowledge that cuts across and draws from many disciplines; therefore, disciplines need to communicate and work together. This is not easy when everyone guards his or her own turf.
4. Developmental tasks of aging are only recently being defined and added to theoretical content in human development.

Instructors become discouraged and impatient when they visualize experience for students in agencies or institutions and then discover the limitations around which they must plan and negotiate—for example, (1) limited number of students to be accommodated at one time, (2) times of day and days available in the agency, (3) amount of reporting and recording required, (4) cumbersome policies and procedures to reach the patient or client, (5) amount of time for instructor and student orientation, (6) limited assistance from staff due to staffing or financial problems, and (7) traveling time and expense to supervise students.

## SUMMARY

Group work with the elderly provides a valuable way for students to meet a variety of educational objectives at all learning levels. There is opportunity to (1) gain knowledge, (2) test skills, (3) test and practice observational skills, (4) evaluate assessment skills, (5) analyze and relate theory to practice and synthesize theory and practice with research, (6) learn about oneself, (7) develop a relationship with a preceptor, and (8) develop a leadership and co-leadership role. Clinical practice involving groups of clients and staff fosters empirical research.

In the past few years educators' interest in gerontology has grown considerably. Presently there are interesting and creative experiences for students to be developed, tried, and evaluated. As Brearly (1975, 79) says, "One positive thing that can be said about the use of group situations with elderly clients is that there is considerable scope for experiment." A cadre of gerontologists from both education and service fields are visible at national meetings; professional publications are increasing. Publications are also emerging from the ranks of students who have had opportunities for independent and creative experiences in group work with older individuals.

## EXERCISE 1

If a video camera and viewing material are available, videotape a short session with several older persons and evaluate your interviewing techniques in terms of

Irene Burnside's "Interviewing the Aged" (1980). If no vide〔
select a partner, and write an evaluation of each other's intervi〔

## EXERCISE 2

Select a current newspaper article appropriate for one mode of gr〔
the elderly, such as a reality orientation, remotivation, discussion, 〔
group. List:

1. Four objectives that are teacher centered.
2. Four objectives that are participant centered.
3. Rationale for selection of the article.
4. Preparations you would have to make before the meeting, such 〔 ...cm-
   bering to bring a magnifying glass, and things you would do during the
   meeting to accomplish your objectives.
5. Criteria for evaluating your group leading.
6. What you learned by doing this exercise. (If you can, carry out an actual
   experience.)

## EXERCISE 3: The Life Review*

Methods: 1) Write it—autobiography, diary or journal.
           2) Tell it—tape recorder, interview.
           3) Draw it—below is a line, divided into time-segments, which you
              are asked to consider as representing your life.

| Birth | 10 | 15 | 20 | 25 | 30 | 35 | 40 | 45 | 50 | 55 | 60 | 70 | 80 |
|-------|----|----|----|----|----|----|----|----|----|----|----|----|----|

Here are some questions that may help your meditation:

- What moments on the Life line stand out in sharpest detail to your memory?
- What faces from your past can you see most clearly?
- Whose voices can you hear most vividly? (from among your family, class-mates, playmates, colleagues, lovers, idols, rivals)
- Which of these did you trust the most?
- Which of these did you want to be most like?
- Which were the events which moved you the most deeply?
- What were the experiences which molded or affected you the most?
- What were the scenes of your greatest sadnesses?
- What were the scenes of your deepest joys?
- What helped to preserve Constancy in your life? (people [who], for example, lack of geographical movement, few deaths, crises, religion, etc.)

*SOURCE: From *The Three Boxes of Life* by Richard Nelson Bolles.
Copyright 1981. Used with permission. Available from Ten Speed
Press, Box 7123, Berkeley, CA 94707.

to preserve Change in your life? (need for adventure, risk-
graphical movement, societal change, divorce, marriage, chang-
s, deaths, aging, or what?)
at decision that you made do you regret the most?
What decision that you made do you feel happiest about?
Did this review help you better to get a handle on how effective you feel your life
has been?

## REFERENCES

Barrett, J. H. 1972. *Gerontological psychology.* Springfield, Ill.: Thomas.

Bellak, L., and T. Karasu. 1976. *Geriatric psychiatry.* New York: Grune & Stratton.

Brearly, C. P. 1975. *Social Work, Ageing and Society.* London: Routledge & Kegan Paul. p. 79.

Brower, H. T. 1981. Groups and student teaching: Putting health education into practice. *Journal of Gerontological Nursing* 7(8): 483–88 (August).

Burnside, I. M. 1980. Interviewing the aged. In *Psychosocial nursing care of the aged.* 2d ed., ed. I. M. Burnside. New York: McGraw-Hill.

Butler, R. N., and M. Lewis. 1982. *Aging and mental health.* 3d ed. St. Louis, Mo.: Mosby.

Carter, C., and D. Galliano. 1981. Fear of loss and attachment. *Journal of Gerontological Nursing* 7(6): 342–49 (June).

Cassell, E. J. 1972. On educational changes for the field of aging. Part 1. *The Gerontologist* 12(3): 251–56 (Autumn).

Cutler, S. J. 1976. Age profiles of membership in sixteen types of voluntary organizations. *Journal of Gerontology* 31(3): 462–70 (July).

Dennis, H. 1976. Remotivation therapy for the elderly. *Journal of Gerontological Nursing* 2(6): 28–30 (November–December).

Ellison, K. B. 1981. Working with the elderly in a life review group. *Journal of Gerontological Nursing* 7(9): 537–41 (September).

Erikson, E. 1950. *Childhood and society.* 2d ed. New York: Norton.

Grant, R. 1982. Assistant professor of psychiatric nursing, College of Nursing, Arizona State University, Tempe. Personal communication (May 15).

Hartford, M. E. 1972. *Groups in social work: Application of small group theory and research to social work practice.* New York: Columbia University Press.

Hill, W. F. 1969. *Learning through discussion.* Beverly Hills, Calif.: Sage.

Holder, M., and L. Tilford. 1974. Student reports on group work. School of Nursing. St. Francis Xavier University, Antigonish, Nova Scotia, Canada (July).

Kimmel, D. C. 1974. *Adulthood and aging.* New York: Wiley.

Linden, M. E. 1954. The significance of dual leadership in gerontologic group psychotherapy. *International Journal of Group Psychotherapy* 4:262–327.

Maney, J., and M. A. Edinberg. 1976. Social competency groups: A training and treatment modality for the gerontological nurse practitioners. *Journal of Gerontological Nursing* 2(6): 31–33 (November–December).

Montoya, D. 1976. Student report on group work in a day care center for the elderly. Arizona State University, Tempe (June).

Roberts, F. F. 1981. The effect of group reminiscing upon morale of the aged. Unpublished master's thesis, Hayden Library, Arizona State University, Tempe.

Steffl, B. 1973. Clinical experiences for nursing students. Paper presented at National Gerontology Society meeting, Miami, Fla. (November).

Voelkel, D. 1978. A study of reality orientation and resocialization groups with confused elderly. *Journal of Gerontological Nursing* 4(3): 13–18 (May–June).

## BIBLIOGRAPHY

*Developing curricula in aging: Proceedings of an international workshop for educators, practition-*

*ers, and consumers in the field of aging,* April 1973. (Available from David Beattie, Ph.D., School of Social Work, University of Washington, Seattle.

Havighurst, R. J. 1965. *Developmental tasks and education.* New York: McKay.

Hyman, R. T. 1974. *Ways of teaching.* Philadelphia: Lippincott.

Krathwohl, D. R., B. S. Bloom, and B. B. Masiz. 1964. *Taxonomy of educational objectives: Handbook II—Affective domain.* New York: McKay.

Maddox, G. L. 1971. *The future of aging and the aged.* Atlanta, Ga.: Southern Newspaper Publishers Association Foundation.

Margolis, F. H. 1970. *Training by objectives: A participant-oriented approach.* Cambridge, Mass.: McBert Co., Sterling Institute.

U.S. Senate. Special Committee on Aging. 1971. *Research and training in aging.* Working paper.

Washington, D.C.: U.S. Government Printing Office.

## RESOURCES

### Module

*Modular Gerontology Curriculum for Health Professionals.* 1981. I. Parham, J. Teitelman, D. Yancy. Gerontology Program, Medical College of Virginia/Virginia Commonwealth University, Richmond, Virginia.

This book of modules would be helpful to a new instructor. The modules could easily be used independently of each other. Audiovisual aids, classroom activities, test questions and annotated bibliographies are well-done. There is no specific module on group work however. The modules are suggested only to assist the instructor to present basic knowledge about aging.

# chapter 38

# Epilogue

*Irene Burnside*

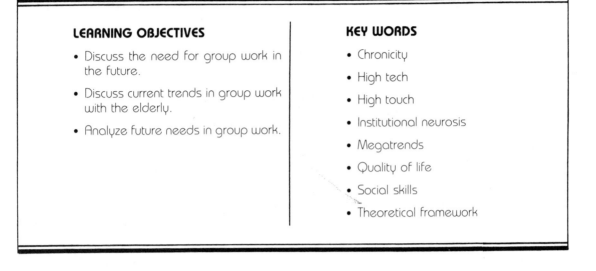

**LEARNING OBJECTIVES**

- Discuss the need for group work in the future.
- Discuss current trends in group work with the elderly.
- Analyze future needs in group work.

**KEY WORDS**

- Chronicity
- High tech
- High touch
- Institutional neurosis
- Megatrends
- Quality of life
- Social skills
- Theoretical framework

The increase in general interest in group work over the past years is heartening, but papers presented at both the yearly gerontology conferences and the international conferences (held every four years) still indicate a lack of reporting on group work by all professionals. (See Chapter 2 for a review of the few abstracts of papers presented at recent international meetings.) The lack of reporting cannot be assumed to be a lack of interest, however, since many group workers do not write about their experiences.

The *International Journal of Group Psychotherapy* carried an overview of all the group psychotherapy literature for the year 1980 (Lieberman and Gourash 1979). There was one article in 1980 on group psychotherapy with the elderly—*one* out of 536 articles reviewed. That figure does say something about the art of group psychotherapy and the aged.

## NEED FOR HEALTH CARE PERSONNEL

The tremendous need for more health care personnel who work with the aged, especially sophisticated practitioners, will continue to increase. If we look at data gathered by the U.S. Department of Health, Education, and Welfare,

we can predict that educational institutions will have to make some tremendous strides and continue to increase gerontological curricula at all levels if the growing needs of present-day and future aged persons are to be met (Figure 38–1). Figure 38–1 also shows that we must take a close look at group work with elderly women in the future. I am reminded of U. LeGuin (1976, 110): "Let women die old, white-crowned with human hearts."

The number of the elderly in the country will double by 2030—from the present level of 11 to 20 percent of the population. The group over 75, a very frail and extremely vulnerable group will increase at an even faster rate. The projection is that 1,500 academic geriatricians in academia and 47,000 additional staff for training, consultation and primary care will be needed. About 8,000 persons specializing in geriatrics will be needed in the next decade alone. (Kane, Solomon, Beck, Keeler, Kane, 1981).

The rewards of caring for the chronically ill are insufficient for some professionals. The changes are always less dramatic (Gadow 1979; Dans and Kerr 1979). The long-term involvement and personal commitment required to conduct groups with the elderly are not accepted by many health professionals.

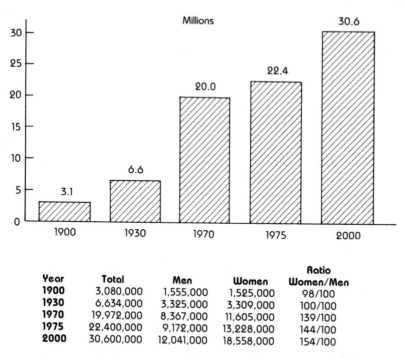

| Year | Total | Men | Women | Ratio Women/Men |
|------|-------|-----|-------|-----------------|
| **1900** | 3,080,000 | 1,555,000 | 1,525,000 | 98/100 |
| **1930** | 6,634,000 | 3,325,000 | 3,309,000 | 100/100 |
| **1970** | 19,972,000 | 8,367,000 | 11,605,000 | 139/100 |
| **1975** | 22,400,000 | 9,172,000 | 13,228,000 | 144/100 |
| **2000** | 30,600,000 | 12,041,000 | 18,558,000 | 154/100 |

**FIGURE 38–1.** *The older population in the twentieth century.*

*SOURCE:* U.S. Department of Health, Education, and Welfare. 1976. *Facts about older Americans.* DHEW Publication no. (OHD) 77-20006 (Washington, D.C.: U.S. Government Printing Office).

The chronic shortage of health care personnel makes group work even more attractive. Eric Pfeiffer (1975) discussed the advantages of group therapy at a conference focusing on successful treatment of the elderly mentally ill:

It is possible to treat anywhere from six to twelve older persons at the same time, resulting in a savings of scarce treatment personnel. . . . More important is the fact that older patients oftentimes learn as much or more from older persons in the group than they do from the group leader; and it is amazing how not only the person who learns something, but the person from whom he learns, benefits. He benefits because he has been able to be useful to someone else—and that helps. In a group, also, the older person learns that other people, too, have problems like his own. He is not the only one having a hard time. Finally—and perhaps most important of all—group therapy provides an older person with membership in a real social group. . . . Many older persons have become socially isolated, and have lost membership in groups. In group therapy, not only do they become members of a social group again, but the social skills they develop oftentimes allow them to re-establish membership in social groups outside of therapy—in other words, in the real world.

S. I. Finkel and G. Cohen (1982) state that

. . . research and research training emphasize prevention, treatment and improvement of mental health in later life through: (a) Research aimed at improving the capacity to prevent psychiatric illness secondary to physical health problems; (b) Research aimed at preventing psychiatric illness secondary to severe psychosocial stress and loss; (c) Research aimed at improving the capacity of families and social support systems to be more effective in preventing inappropriate institutionalization; (d) Research aimed at finding optimal forms of social involvement for different groups of older persons with a goal of maintaining high morale and mental health; (e) Research aimed at better understanding the etiology, diagnosis, course treatment, prognosis, and prevention of mental illness in the elderly, research that would be especially timely given dramatic new developments in the neurosciences, in biobehavioral studies, and in psychopharmacologic investigations, (f) Research focused on improved designs of services and service term treatment programs, in both community based and institutional settings for care.

## Need for Research

In a brochure published by the Gerontological Society of America, (n.d.) there is a section entitled, "The future is now." These questions are asked:

- How can these later years be enhanced?
- How can health and productivity be further increased?
- How will a prolonged older work force affect the labor market?
- What types of services will be needed?
- How can we tap the skills and experience of older Americans?

## NEW GROUP WORK APPROACHES

The responsiveness of the elderly to group methods should be encouraging to administrators, activity directors, nurses, instructors, physicians, psychologists, students, health personnel, and family members. The economic aspect of group work cannot be overlooked; here is one treatment mode by which health care personnel can improve the quality of life for some aged persons. We need to tap new ways to provide groups to the elderly.

I have been impressed with the use of conference calls in the business world. Several persons can talk during a phone hook-up. Since transportation is such a major barrier to health care for the elderly, new uses for the telephone could offer major advantages. Could "conference calls" be used for elderly groups? R. Evans and B. Jaureguy (1981) report that telephone-mediated group therapy was successful in alleviating loneliness, increasing social activities, and encouraging accomplishment of household tasks. Michael Storrie* used weekly telephone calls to include members in a support group. One member felt included even though she lived several hundred miles from the support group members.

Besides developing a variety of groups, we will need to tap the wisdom and ideas of the aged. We often fail to do that.

Peer Counselling is one form of using the skills and experiences. One group of researchers

demonstrated the impact of 38 undergraduate students who were assigned as Friendly Visitors. (Reinke, Holme, Denny, 1981). Shulameth Weisman (1981) writes about nursing home residents using computers for games, but no commercially available games. There's a new market! Naisbitt (1982) discusses in his fascinating book, *Megatrends* (important changes or trends seen across the United States), "High tech" vs. "High touch." The high touch is the counterbalancing response so we do not reject the new technologies.

## COLLABORATIVE DECISION MAKING

In an experimental study of nursing home residents, E. Langer and J. Rodin (1976) state that one group of elderly residents who were given the freedom to make choices, assume responsibilities, and be self-directed showed a greater degree of alertness, active involvement, and in general a sense of well-being. H. Kim (1983) states that application of this knowledge is beginning to emerge in the field of health care. Collaborative decision making is still one of our weakest areas in group work with the elderly.

## GROUP WORK—SOME FINAL THOUGHTS

A variety of group approaches in different disciplines were presented in this book. It is possible for a student to begin at one level of group work and move through a variety of group work experiences to become a more sophisticated practitioner. A learner might also become interested in just one type of group and work intensively in that type, as Mary Jane Hennessey and Catherine Moore have done in music therapy or as Heather Booth has in movement therapy.

Resident floor groups, new-resident orientation groups, and discharge planning groups are increasingly seen in long-term care facilities and can counteract the ill effects of institutionalization, often called institutional neurosis.

While I have endeavored to provide a variety of group methods in this second edition, the reader will note that a chapter on art therapy is missing. Unfortunately, the intended contribu-

*Personal communication, 1977.

tor was unable to sign the contract and her material could not be used. However, the reader is referred to a publication entitled *Art with Elders in Long-Term Care* (Merker-Benton 1983). See resources.

One thrust of this book is the need for theoretical frameworks for group leaders of the aged. The need for research and for more stringent evaluation of groups is also important. The qualities of the leader and their impact on the group are stressed, and some ideas about the quality of group work in and of itself are provided. A constant endeavor has been to make the teacher and learner roles creative and interesting.

Group work with the aged is not for the willy-nilly, the fainthearted, or those who tire easily. Group work with the aged is demanding and exhausting, and it requires meticulous, thoughtful planning and organization. The group leader of the aged must be able to tolerate dependency, chronicity, and also death of group members. Perhaps these are the reasons there seem to be so few in the health care field who undertake group leadership. But not all are ill and the reader is reminded of Erik Erikson's (1983, 22) words, "So our large groups of well-preserved old people leads us to speak now of 'elderlies'. The existence of this group means that we need to rethink the role of old age."

Describing the state-of-the-art of group work for so many disciplines has been a major task. I hope that all of us who have written about group work have been general enough to appeal to a wide audience of readers and caregivers, yet specific enough to be helpful. Our own honesty and sharing of our experiences might give courage to the hesitant or wary student or reader. Our own aging makes some of us pensive and concerned about all elderly. Carl Eisdorfer said it so well, "We have met the aging and they are us."[*]

In a thought-provoking article, he wrote about the narrow models of care that have existed in the care of the elderly. He states we are now participants in the second phase of a revolution (the first revolution being the seven-fold increase in the number of persons over 65). The second phase is the over 75 growth rate. He reminds us that "narrow conceptual turf reflects the training of most mental health professionals." And suggests that, "Our challenge is to generalize data and integrate the broadest range of ideas to find the best approach to appropriate care for those in need."

We must not forget how much the elderly can teach us. Judah Folkman (1975, 41), in a commencement address to medical students, spoke specifically about surgeons, but his words are relevant for those working with the aged: "We are in a position to learn from our mistakes and, most important, to appreciate the debt we owe our patients for our education." Group workers with older persons realize that they have learned from their mistakes (some of which are shared in this book) and do indeed owe a debt of gratitude to the elderly group members who taught them so well.

---

## EXERCISE 1

As a new group leader you will need to learn the importance of taking care of yourself. This exercise is designed to help you consider how you do (or do not) take care of yourself. (This exercise can also be modified for use in group meetings.)

Energy is needed to lead a group. Anticipation and learning a new skill frequently arouse anxiety, which depletes energy. Health professionals often give and give until there is little energy left. This can cause resentment and loss of

---

[*]Personal communication, 1983.

interest in one's job and result in poor care. How do you expand your energy and plan alternative ways of coping?

Pair off with a classmate. Discuss ways in which you take care of yourself when you feel especially drained.

## EXERCISE 2

Match the individual to the needs you think he or she will have, and then pick the appropriate group. There is *only one answer* from columns B and C to match column A. Check yourself by comparing your answers with those listed below.*

| Column A<br>*Patient or client* | Column B<br>*Need of elderly person* | Column C<br>Group experience<br>*recommended* |
|---|---|---|
| 1. Alert man, 92, recently admitted to a skilled nursing facility (SNF). | A. To replace friendships and to decrease loneliness. | a. Group psychotherapy |
| 2. Male, 60, recently suffered a stroke and is convalescing in a nursing home. Is severely depressed (his business manager is concerned about his future as an employee). Has a plan for suicide. | B. To understand better a physical condition and how to live with it. | b. No group—one-to-one treatment method |
| 3. Female, 70, shy and lonely; worried about her diabetic condition and failing eyesight due to retinopathy. Poor foot care. | C. To reduce confusion and disorientation. | c. Reality orientation |
| 4. Female, 75, chronic brain syndrome; spent 15 years in back ward of state hospital; very regressed. | D. To learn more adaptive ways of responding to stress and interpersonal relationships. To become more self-sufficient. | d. Reminiscing group |
| 5. Male alcoholic, 65, living in community, fired recently; is in the throes of fourth divorce. | E. To share day-to-day experiences in a structured environment. | e. Health-oriented group |
| 6. Female, 82, former school teacher, bored and complaining. Once had Guggenheim Fellowship and studied abroad. | F. To learn the written and unwritten rules and the layout of a facility and to become acquainted with other residents. | f. Discussion group |
| 7. Female, 70, in wheelchair and too weak to push herself; will talk if encouraged. | G. To adjust to change in body image and to accept role change. | g. Remotivation group |
| 8. Widow, 100, frail, losing sight. No relatives or visitors. | H. To be intellectually stimulated. | h. New-admission group |

*Answers: 1. Fh; 2. Gb; 3. Be; 4. Cc; 5. Da; 6. Hf; 7. Eg; 8. Ib; 9. Ai.

| Column A Patient or client | Column B Need of elderly person | Column C Group experience recommended |
|---|---|---|
| 9. Alert man, 82, whose wife died a month ago; admitted to skilled nursing facility because he cannot handle housework. | I. To maintain present functioning ability, prevent loneliness and hallucinations, and improve communications. | i. Group for grieving persons |

## REFERENCES

Dans, P., and M. Kerr. 1979. Gerontology and geriatrics in medical education. *New England Journal of Medicine* 300:228–32.

Erikson, E. 1983. A conversation with Erik Erikson. *Psychology Today* 17(6): 22–30, June, 1983.

Evans, R., and B. Jaureguy. 1981. Group therapy by phone: A cognitive behavioral program for visually impaired elderly. *Social Work in Health Care* 7(2): 79–90 (Winter).

Finkel, S. I., and G. Cohen. 1982. The mental health of the aging. Guest editorial. *The Gerontologist* 22(3): 227–28 (June).

Folkman, J. M. 1975. Don't practice on me. *Harvard Medical School Alumni Bulletin* 49(6): 39–41 (July–August).

Gadow, S. 1979. Advocacy nursing and new meanings of aging. *Nursing Clinics of North America* 14:81–91.

Gerontology Society of America. n.d. "Research in Action," Washington, D.C. Brochure.

Jack, R. 1983. Out of the geriatric ghetto. *Social Work Today* 14(20): 7–10 (January).

Kane, R. L., D. Solomon, J. Beck, E. Keeler, R. A. Kane, 1981. *Geriatrics in the United States: Manpower Projections and Training Considerations.* Lexington, D.C. Heath & Co.

Kim, H. 1983. Collaborative decision making. Chapter 16 in *Advances in nursing theory development,* ed. P. L. Chinn, 271–83. Rockville, Md.: Aspen Systems.

Langer, E., and J. Rodin. 1976. The effects of choice and enhanced personal responsibility for the aged: A field experiment in an institutional setting. *Journal of Personality and Social Psychology* 34: 191–98.

LeGuin, U. 1976. The space crone. *The Co-evolution Quarterly,* Summer: 110.

Lieberman, M., and N. Gourash. 1979. Evaluating the effects of change groups on the elderly. *International Journal of Group Psychotherapy* 29(3): 283–85 (July).

Marsh, L. C. 1935. Group therapy and the psychiatric clinic. *Journal New. Ment. Dis* 32:381–92.

Merker-Benton, M. 1983. *Art with elders in long-term care.* Berkeley, Calif.: Vista College, Peralta Community College District.

Naisbitt, J. 1982. *Megatrends.* New York: Warner Books, pp. 39–53.

Pfeiffer, E. 1975. Successful treatment of the mentally ill. Cassette tape of conference at Duke University, Chapel Hill, N.C., May. New York: Wyeth Laboratories.

Reinke, B., D. Holmes, N. Denny. 1981. "Influence of a Friendly Visitors program or cognitive functioning and morale of elderly. *American Journal of Community Psychology* 9(4): 491–504.

Weisman, S. 1982. Nursing Home residents savor a new kind of "apple." *Aging.* Nos. 333–334. Nov. Dec. pp. 28–29.

## BIBLIOGRAPHY

Anderson, S., and E. Bauwens. 1981. *Chronic health problems.* St. Louis, Mo.: Mosby.

Atchley, R. 1980. *The social forces in later life.* 2d ed. Belmont, Calif.: Wadsworth.

Butler, R. 1975. *Why survive? Growing old in America.* New York: Harper & Row.

Butler, R., and M. Lewis. 1982. *Aging and mental health.* 3d ed. St. Louis, Mo.: Mosby.

Cahill, J. B., and D. Smith. 1975. Considerate care of the elderly. *Nursing '75* 10 (September): 38, 39.

Cantor, M. 1983. Social care for the aged in the United States: Issues and challenges. In *Group work with the frail elderly.* New York: Haworth Press.

Decker, D. 1980. *Social gerontology*. Boston: Little, Brown.

Finkel, S., and W. Fillmore. 1971. Experiences with an older adult group at a private psychiatric hospital. *Journal of Geriatric Psychiatry* 4(2): 188–99 (Spring).

Harbert, A., and L. Ginsberg. 1979. *Human services for older adults*. Belmont, Calif.: Wadsworth.

Hendricks, J., and C. Hendricks. 1981. *Aging in mass society*. Cambridge, Mass.: Winthrop.

Hess, B. 1976. *Growing old in America*. New Brunswick, N.J.: Transaction Books.

Hickey, T. 1980. *Health and aging*. Monterey, Calif.: Brooks/Cole.

Hultsch, D., and F. Deutsch. 1981. *Adult development and aging*. New York: McGraw-Hill.

Hurlock, E. 1980. *Developmental psychology: A life span approach*. New York: McGraw-Hill.

Huyck, M., and W. Hoyer. 1982. *Adult development and aging*. Belmont, Calif.: Wadsworth.

Jonas, S. 1981. *Health Care Delivery in the United States* 2d ed. New York: Springer.

Kalish, R. 1975. *Late adulthood: Perspectives on human development*. Monterey, Calif.: Brooks/Cole.

————. 1977. *The later years: Social applications of gerontology*. Belmont, Calif.: Wadsworth.

Landgarten, H. 1981. *Clinical art therapy: A comprehensive guide*. New York: Brunner/Mazel.

Lonergan, E. 1980. Humanizing the hospital experience: Report of a group program for medical patients. *Health and Social Work* 5(4): 53–63 (November).

Lyell, R. 1980. *Middle age, Old age*. New York: Harcourt Brace Jovanovich.

Magnuson, E., H. Gorney. 1983. "Spokesman for the Elderly: Congressman Claude Pepper." *Time* 121(17): 3t, April 25, 1983.

Nelson, G. 1982. Support for the aged: public and private responsibility. *Social Work* 27(2): 137–143.

Place, L., L. Parker, and F. Berghorn. 1981. *Aging and aged, An annotated bibliography*. Boulder, Colo.: Westview Press.

Spicker, S., K. Woodward, and D. Van Tassel. 1978. *Aging in the elderly: Humanistic perspectives in gerontology*. Cleveland, Ohio: Case Western Reserve University.

Troll, L. 1975. *Early and middle adulthood*. Monterey, Calif.: Brooks/Cole.

U.S. Department of Health, Education, and Welfare. 1979. *Healthy people*. Washington, D.C.

Watson, W. 1982. *Aging and social behavior*. Belmont, Calif.: Wadsworth.

Weisman, A. 1974. Does old age make sense? Decisions and destiny in growing older. *Journal of Geriatric Psychiatry* 7(1): 93.

Willer, B., and G. Miller. 1976. Client involvement in goal setting and its relationship to therapeutic outcome. *Journal of Clinical Psychology* 32:687–90.

Wondolowski, M. 1978. Interpersonal problem-solving training groups for hospitalized aged psychiatric patients. Doctoral dissertation, Temple University, Philadelphia, Pa. (*Dissertation Abstracts International* 39, 1975B; University Microfilms no. 7817359.)

Zarit, S. 1980. *Aging and mental disorder*. New York: Free Press.

## RESOURCES

### Videotapes and/or Slides

*Art with Elders in Long-Term Care*. Contact Mary Ann Merker-Benton, 2020 Milvia Street, Berkeley, CA 94704; phone (415) 841-8431.

### Film (commercial)

Ballad of Narayama, Best film, 1983 Cannes Film Festival, Director, Shohei Imamura. A story of life and death in an isolated Japanese mountain village. The hero, a 69 year old peasant, must die at age 70 — according to village tradition — to leave scarce food and other resources to the young.

### Peer Counselor Program

Project PACE (Psychological Alternative Counseling for Elders). Christopher Hayes, P.O. Box 3372, Santa Ana, CA 92703 (714) 667-6026.

### Program Directory

Gerontology Graduate Program Directory 1984. 1725 Race Drive, Decatur, IL 38521 (217) 422-9200. Comprehensive guide with program descriptions, names and addresses of institutions of gerontology programs.

# Author Index

# Subject Index